Strategic Innovation

In today's fast-changing business environment, those firms that want to remain competitive must also be innovative. Innovation is not simply developing new technologies into new products or services, but in many cases finding new models for doing business in the face of change. It often entails changing the rules of the game.

From the late 1990s to today, the dominant themes in the strategy literature have been strategic innovation, the impact of information and communications technologies on commerce, and globalization. The primary issues have been and continue to be how to gain a competitive advantage through strategic innovation using new game strategies, and how to compete in a world with rapid technological change and increasing globalization. *Strategic Innovation* demonstrates to students how to create and appropriate value using these "new game" strategies. Beginning with a summary of the major strategic frameworks showing the origins of strategic innovation, Afuah gives a thorough examination of contemporary strategy from an innovation standpoint with several key advantages:

- Focus on developing strategy in the face of change.
- A wealth of quantitative examples of successful strategies, as well as descriptive cases.
- Emphasis on the analysis of strategy, not just descriptions of strategies.
- A detailed, change-inclusive framework for assessing the profitability potential of a strategy or product, the AVAC (activities, value, appropriability, and change) model.
- Emphasis on the aspects of strategy that can be linked to the determinants of profitability.
- Consideration of how both for-profit and non-profit organizations can benefit from new game strategies.

Allan Afuah is Associate Professor of Strategy and International Business at the Stephen M. Ross School of Business, University of Michigan.

Strategic Innovation

New Game Strategies for Competitive Advantage

Allan Afuah

Stephen M. Ross School of Business
University of Michigan

 Routledge
Taylor & Francis Group

NEW YORK AND LONDON

First published 2009
by Routledge
270 Madison Ave, New York, NY 10016

Simultaneously published in the UK
by Routledge
2 Park Square, Milton Park, Abingdon, Oxon OX14 4RN

*Routledge is an imprint of the Taylor & Francis Group,
an informa business*

Typeset in Sabon by RefineCatch Limited, Bungay, Suffolk
Printed and bound in the United States of America on acid-free
paper by Edwards Brothers, Inc.

Library of Congress Cataloging-in-Publication Data
Afuah, Allan.
Strategic innovation: new game strategies for competitive
advantage / by Allan Afuah.
    p. cm.
Includes index.
1. Strategic planning. 2. Originality. 3. Resourcefulness.
4. Technological innovations. 5. Competition. I. Title.
HD30.28.A3473 2009
658.4′063—dc22
2008034812

ISBN10: 0–415–99781–X (hbk)
ISBN10: 0–415–99782–8 (pbk)
ISBN10: 0–203–88324–1 (ebk)

ISBN13: 978–0–415–99781–2 (hbk)
ISBN13: 978–0–415–99782–9 (pbk)
ISBN13: 978–0–203–88324–2 (ebk)

To my grandmother, Veronica Masang-Namang Nkweta, and the Bamboutos highlands which she tilled to feed me.

To every family that has been kind enough to welcome a foreign student to its home.

Contents

Figures

Tables

Exhibits for Cases

Preface

The first question that potential readers might be tempted to ask is, why another book on strategy? *Strategic Innovation: New Game Strategies for Competitive Advantage* has many of the same features that existing textbooks have. It draws on the latest research in strategic management and innovation, it is peppered with the latest examples from key business cases, it is easy to read, and so on. However, it has six distinctive features that give it a unique position vis-à-vis existing strategy and innovation books.

Distinctive Features

First, *Strategic Innovation: New Game Strategies for Competitive Advantage* is about change. While existing textbooks acknowledge the importance of change, especially in an ever-changing world, they devote very little or no attention to the subject of change. All the chapters in *New Game Strategies* are about change and strategic management—about how to create and appropriate value in the face of new games. Second, existing strategic management texts tend to have very few or no numerical examples. This lack of numerical examples does little to reinforce the growing consensus that strategy is about winning but rather, it might be promoting the "anything goes in strategy" attitude that is not uncommon to students who are new to the field of strategic management. Nine of the thirteen chapters in the book have numerical examples that link elements of the balance sheet to components of the income statement. Of course, the book is also full of case examples. Third, while other texts are more descriptive than analytical, this book is more analytical than descriptive. It is largely about the *why* and *how* of things, and less about the *what* of things. Fourth, the book includes a detailed framework for assessing the profitability potential of a strategy, resource, business unit, brand, product, etc. Called the AVAC (activities, value, appropriability, and change), the framework is distinctive in that it includes not only both firm-specific and industry-specific factors that impact firm profitability, but also a change component. Fifth, the book's emphasis is on those activities that can be linked to the determinants of profitability; that is, the book focuses on those aspects of strategy that can be logically linked to elements of the balance sheet and income statement. Sixth, the book summarizes the major strategic management frameworks that are otherwise scattered in other texts. This is a useful one-stop reference for many students.

The Dawn of Strategic Innovation

To understand why a book with these six features is needed today in the field of strategic management, it is important to take a quick look at the evolution of the field. In the 1960s, the dominant theme in the field of strategic management was corporate planning and managers were largely concerned with planning for the growth that had been spurred by reconstruction of Europe and Japan, and the Cold War, following World War II. The SWOT (Strength, Weaknesses, Opportunities, and Threats) framework became popular as the tool of choice for identifying and analyzing those internal and external factors that were favorable or unfavorable to achieving firm objectives. In the late 1960s and early 1970s, the primary theme had shifted to corporate strategy and the issues of the day were dominated by diversification and portfolio planning. Tools such as BCG's Growth/Share matrix, and the McKinsey/GE matrix enjoyed a lot of popularity as analysis tools. In the late 1970s and early 1980s, the theme shifted to industry and competitive analysis, and the primary issues became the choice of which industries, markets, and market segments in which to compete, and where within each industry or market to position oneself. Porter's Five Forces and business system (value chain) were the analytical tools of the day. In the late 1980s and early 1990s, the theme had evolved into the pursuit of competitive advantage and its sources within a firm. Professors C.K. Prahalad and Gary Hamel's core competence of the firm and the resource-based view of the firm emerged as the dominant themes.

From the late 1990s to today, the dominant themes have been strategic innovation, globalization, and the impact of information and communications technologies on value-adding activities. The primary issues have been and continue to be how to gain a competitive advantage through strategic innovation using new game strategies, and how to compete in a world with rapid technological change and increasing globalization. A strategic innovation is a game-changing innovation in products/services, business models, business processes, and/or positioning vis-à-vis coopetitors to improve performance. A firm's new game strategy is what enables it to perform well or not so well in the face of a strategic innovation. Thus, to perform better than its competitors in the face of a new game, a firm needs to have the right new game strategies. This book is about the new game strategies that firms use to exploit strategic innovations. It is about change. It is about how to create and appropriate value using new game strategies. These new game strategies can be revolutionary or incremental, or somewhere in-between. This book is not only about a firm using new game activities to offer customers new value (from new products/services) that they prefer to that from competitors, but also about how the firm can better position itself to appropriate the value created in the face of change or no change, and to translate the value and position to money. It is also about some of the more recent issues about the digital economy such as the Long Tail, and the not-so-recent issues such as disruptive technologies. Firms that initiate new games, and are therefore first movers, can make a lot of money; but so can firms that follow the first movers. It all depends on the new game strategy that each firm pursues.

Some Strategic Innovation Questions

New game strategies often overturn the way value is created and appropriated. They can create new markets and industries, destroy or reinforce existing product-market positions, and most important of all, they can be very profitable for some firms. This raises some very interesting questions. What exactly are new game strategies? What do we mean by creation and appropriation of value? Which new game strategies are likely to be most profitable for a firm—to give a firm a competitive advantage? If resources are really the cornerstones of competitive advantage, what is the role of resources during new games? Since, in playing new games, firms often move first, what really are first-mover advantages and *dis*advantages, and how can one take advantage of them? What are competitor's handicaps and how can a first mover take advantage of them? How can the profitability potential of a strategy—new game or non-new game—be analyzed? Is entering a new business using new game strategies any better than entering using non-new game strategies? Does game theory have anything to do with new game strategies? What is likely to be the reaction of competitors when a firm pursues a new game strategy? Given competitors' likely reaction, what should a firm do in pursuing new game strategies? Does implementing new game strategies require more precaution than implementing any other strategy? What are the sources of new game strategies? What is the role of globalization and a firm's macroenvironment in its ability to create and appropriate value using new game strategies? Are some environments more conducive to new game strategies than others? What is the role of government in new games? How many of the new game concepts and tools detailed for for-profit firms applicable to nonprofit organizations?

This book explores these questions, or provides the concepts and tools to explore them. The book takes the perspective of a general manager who has overall responsibility for the performance of his or her firm, for a business unit within the firm, or for any organization for which performance is important. Such a manager needs to understand the basis for the firm's performance in the face of change. The manager needs to know what determines the performance, what other change might erode that performance, and when and what the firm could do to gain and maintain a competitive advantage. The manager must then use the firm's resources to formulate and implement a strategy that will give it a competitive advantage. Thus, the book should be useful in courses whose goal is to challenge students to *think strategically* when confronting day-to-day activities. It should also be useful to managers who want to challenge themselves to think strategically, irrespective of their functional role within their organization.

The seeds of the book were sowed in the period from 1997 to 2006 when I taught the Strategy Core Course at the Stephen M. Ross School of Business at the University of Michigan. During that time, I also taught an elective in Innovation Management. In 2003/2004 when I was on academic sabbatical leave from Michigan, I also taught the core course in strategy at The Wharton School of the University of Pennsylvania in the USA, and at INSEAD, in Fontainebleau, France. The ideas that most of my students in these schools found fascinating had a common theme—changing the rules of the game. Students could not have enough of the concepts and cases about strategic innovation, and the associated new game strategies for a competitive advantage.

Intended Audience

The book is written for courses in strategic management, entrepreneurship, or marketing that emphasize *strategic innovation* or *change* in a graduate or undergraduate curriculum. It should also be useful to managers who want to challenge themselves to think strategically, irrespective of their functional role within their organization. Managers and scholars who are interested in exploring any of the questions raised above would also find the book useful; so should those managers who are in positions that have a direct impact on firm profitability, or who are in consulting, entrepreneurship, or venture capital. It should also be of interest to those functional specialists (finance, marketing, HRM, engineering) who must participate in game-changing activities.

Acknowledgments

I continue to owe a huge debt of gratitude to my Professors and mentors at the Massachusetts Institute of Technology (MIT); in particular, Professors Rebecca Henderson, James M. Utterback, and Thomas Allen. They introduced me to the subject of strategic innovation, and to the virtues of patience and tolerance. When I arrived at the University of Michigan from MIT, I was lucky that the Dean of the Business School at the time, B. Joseph White (now the President of the University of Illinois) had created an environment in which we could thrive as researchers and teachers. That meant a lot to me and I am forever grateful! I would also like to thank three anonymous reviewers for their suggestions and help in reshaping this book. Some of my students at the Stephen M. Ross School of Business at the University of Michigan gave me very useful feedback when I pre-tested the concepts of the book, at the formative stage. Some of the cases in Part V of the book were written by some of these students under my supervision. I am grateful to all of them. I would also like to thank Joseph Lui, who read through some of the chapters and gave me useful feedback. Katie Chang provided me with dependable research assistance. Finally, I would like to thank Michael and Mary Kay Hallman for the funding that enabled me to explore the topic of strategic innovation with a little more freedom.

I would like to thank Nancy Hale, Routledge editor for business books, whose professionalism convinced me to work with Routledge.

Allan Afuah
Ann Arbor, Michigan
July 29, 2008

Part I

Introduction

Chapter 1

Introduction and Overview

Reading this chapter should provide you with the conceptual and analytical tools to:

- Define strategy, new games, *new game strategies*, value creation and *value appropriation*, and *strategic innovation*.
- Understand the characteristics of new games and how a firm can exploit them to gain and prolong a *competitive advantage*.
- Begin to understand how to use an AVAC analysis to evaluate the profitability potential of a new game strategy.
- Describe types of new game (regular, resource-building, position-building, and revolutionary).

Introduction

Consider the following business performances:

With a market value of over $160 billion for most of 2008, Google was one of the most valuable companies in the world. Its net income in 2007 was $4.2 billion on sales of $16.6 billion, giving it a net profit margin of 25.4%, one of the highest of any company of its size. This was a remarkable performance for a company that only four years earlier, in 2002, had revenues of $439 million and a net income of $99 million in a struggling dotcom industry.

In 2006, Threadless, an online T-shirt company founded in 2000, had profits of $6 million on revenues of $18 million, from T-shirts that had been designed, marketed, and bought by members of the public.[1] This made the firm one of the most profitable in the clothing retail business.

In 2007, Pfizer's Lipitor was the world's best-selling drug with sales of $12.7 billion, more than twice its nearest competitor's sales (Plavix, with $5.9 billion). This was the third year in a row that Lipitor had topped the best-seller list. One of the most remarkable things about Lipitor is that it was the fifth cholesterol drug in its category (statins) in a pharmaceuticals industry where the third or fourth product in a category usually has little chance of surviving, let alone of becoming the best seller in the industry.

During the 2007 Christmas season, demand for the Nintendo Wii was so strong that Nintendo was forced to issue rain checks to customers. On eBay, bids for the $249 machine were in the thousands of dollars. What was even more remarkable was that each Wii console was sold at a profit, unlike competing consoles from Microsoft and Sony that were being sold at a loss.

Goldcorp, a Canadian gold mining company, offered prizes totalling $575,000 to anyone who would analyze its banks of geological survey data and suggest where, in its Red Lake, Canada, property gold could be found.[2] Fractal Graphics, an Australian company, won the top prize of $105,000. More importantly, the contest yielded targets that were so productive that Goldcorp was said to have mined eight million ounces of gold worth more than $3 billion in the six years following the launch.[3]

Between 1994 and 1998, Dell's sales increased by five times, its profits increased by ten times, its stock shot up by 5,600%, its revenue growth was twice as fast as that of its rivals while its operating earnings were greater than the combined operating earnings of all of its major rivals.[4]

From 2000 to 2005, Ryanair posted after-tax profit margins of 20–28% in an airline industry where most firms were losing hundreds of millions of dollars. These record high after-tax profit margins made Ryanair not only the most profitable major airline company in the world over that period, but also one of the most profitable *European* companies!

Definitions

New Game Strategies

At the core of each of these remarkable performances are strategic innovations, and new game strategies. A *strategic innovation* is a game-changing innovation in products/services, business models, business processes, and/or positioning vis-à-vis *coopetitors* to improve performance. A *new game strategy* is a set of *activities* that creates and/or appropriates *value* in new ways.[5] It is what determines a firm's performance in the face of a strategic innovation. It entails performing new value chain activities or existing ones differently from the way they have been performed in the past, to create value and/or position a firm to appropriate (capture) value.[6] It is about not only creating value in different ways, but also about putting a firm in a position to profit from the value created. It is often about rewriting the rules of the game, overturning existing ways of creating and appropriating value. For example, rather than keep its databanks of geological survey data on its Red Lake, Ontario property secret, and struggle to find where gold might be located, Goldcorp made the data available to the public and challenged it to locate the gold. Goldcorp was looking to the public, rather than to its employees or a contractor, to solve its problem. Only the winners, those who produced desirable results, would be paid. Contrast this with employees who would be paid whether or not they succeeded in locating gold. Rather than design and market its own T-shirts, Threadless had members of its registered users design and submit designs to the firm each week. Members of the community then voted for the best design, and winners were awarded prizes. The winning design was then produced and sold to members of the community. Effectively, the firm did not perform many of the activities that T-shirt companies traditionally performed, or did so differently.

The winner of a new game can be a first mover or follower; that is, the winner of a new game can be the firm that moved first to *change* the rules of the game, or a firm that came in later and played the game better. The important thing is that a firm pursues the right new game strategy to create and capture value. Google was not the first to introduce search engines but it played the new game very well—it was better at monetizing search engines. Its new game strategy in the early 2000s included undertaking paid listings rather than pop-ups or banner advertising for monetizing searches, developing those algorithms that delivered more relevant searches to its customers than competitors' search engines, and placing the paid-listing ads on its website as well as on third-party sites.

New games are not always about product innovation. In fact, some of the more interesting cases of new games have nothing to do with new products or services. Rather, they have been about changing the rules of the game in getting an existing product to customers *or* in positioning a firm to appropriate existing value better. Take the case of Dell. It introduced direct sales to end-customers, bypassing distributors. It also established build-to-order manufacturing and business processes in which each customer's computer was built to the customer's specification and only after the customer had ordered and paid for the computer. Both activities gave Dell some advantages over its competitors. By bypassing distributors, for example, it was moving away from having to confront the more concentrated and powerful distributors to dealing directly with the more fragmented end-customers where it could build switching costs, brand identity, and identify other sources of revenue such as services.

New games do not always have to be about leapfrogging competitors with products that have better product characteristics than competitors'. In fact, some of the more interesting new game strategies are those in which firms cut back some product/service characteristics that had come to be considered sacred cows, but at the same time, they add a few new features. For example, when Nintendo offered its Wii, it deliberately used much cheaper three-year-old microprocessor and graphics technologies, rather than trying to outmuscle Microsoft and Sony, which used the latest and fastest but much more expensive technologies which many avid gamers had come to expect in each new generation of game consoles. The Wii had other features that appealed more to nonavid gamers, such as the ability to play games that enabled people also to get some physical exercise.

Both first movers and followers can also make money during new games. For example, Merck revolutionized the cholesterol-lowering drug market when it pioneered the statin cholesterol drug category, and made lots of money. Warner Lambert, which came into the new game late when it introduced Lipitor (a statin), was able to make even more money using its own new game strategies. It entered an alliance with Pfizer to gain access to Pfizer's large sales force and marketing might, to sell the drug to doctors and conduct direct-to-consumer (DTC) marketing.

Finally, what is a new game in one industry or country, may not be a new game in another. Take the case of Ryanair. In addition to performing some of the activities that had set Southwest Airlines apart from its US competitors—such as flying only one type of airplane model (Boeing 737s for Southwest and A320s for Ryanair) and operating largely out of secondary airports—Ryanair went further. It sold snacks, advertised inside as well as on its planes, and collected commissions on the proceeds made from hotel and car rental sales made through its website. It also forged lucrative relationships with local authorities of the secondary airports where it established operations.

Usually, a new game strategy entails some type of commitment that is made by the firm pursuing the *strategy*.[7] It also involves tradeoffs.[8] For example, Google invested a lot of money in research and development (R&D) to keep improving the relevance of its searches; and by committing to paid listing ads, it was foregoing banner and pop-up ads and associated benefits and costs.

Value Creation and Appropriation

Since we have defined a new game strategy as the set of activities that creates and/or captures value in new ways, it is only appropriate that we define *value creation* and value appropriation. A firm *creates value* when it offers customers products or services whose perceived benefits to customers exceed the cost of providing the benefits.[9] A firm *appropriates* (captures) value when it profits from it. For example, if a musician writes, composes, and produces a song that customers want, the musician has created value, provided that the cost of offering the music does not exceed the benefits perceived by customers. The profits that the musician receives from his or her music are the value that he or she captures. As the case of many a musician would suggest, value captured is not always equal to the value created. Before the Internet, recording studio managers and distribution channels usually had the bargaining power over musicians and therefore captured more value from each record sold than they created. Musicians usually appropriated less value than they created, ten cents of every dollar.

Cooperating to Create Value and Competing to Appropriate it

When a customer buys a product, the value that it perceives in the product is not only a function of the value created by the maker of the product, it is also a function of the components that go into the product, the complements that work with the product, and of what the customer puts into using the product. Effectively, the value that a customer perceives in a product is a function of the contribution of coopetitors—of the suppliers, customers, rivals, complementors, and other actors with whom a firm cooperates and competes to create and appropriate value. For example, the value that a customer perceives in an iPhone is not only a function of what Apple puts into designing and getting the product produced, but also a function of the contribution of the suppliers of the chips, LCDs, and other components that go into the product. It is also a function of the quality and availability of the type of phone service on it, of the music and other content that can be played on the machine, and of how well the user can use the product.

Thus, firms cooperate with suppliers, customers, complementors, and sometimes rivals to create value and compete with them to capture the value. *Cooperation* can be direct as is the case with strategic alliances, joint ventures, and long-term contracts; but often, "cooperation" is indirect as in suppliers contracting with firms to supply products to a firm's specifications. "Competition" exists not only when a firm has to select a supplier and bargain with the supplier but also when the firm has to bargain with buyers over the price of its products. More importantly, competition also exists in an indirect way during direct cooperation. When firms are in an alliance or joint venture to cooperatively create value, they also have to compete to determine who incurs what costs and who will capture what fraction of the value created. Thus, where there is cooperation to create value, there is nearly always competition to appropriate the value; and where there is competition to capture value, there is probably some cooperation to create the value. Even competition among rivals often has elements that could benefit from cooperation. For example, rivals stand to benefit when their market grows and therefore can cooperate to grow the market where such cooperation is legal. They also stand to profit when they do not get into unnecessary price wars, or get entangled in government overregulation or taxation.

New Games

New Game Activities

Recall that a new game strategy is the *set* of activities that creates and/or captures value in new ways. The cornerstones of this set are new game activities. A *new game activity* is an activity that is performed *differently* from the way existing industry value chain activities have been performed to create or capture value.[10] The activity can be completely new or it can be an existing activity that is being performed differently. The important thing is that, (1) the way the activity is performed is *different* from the way existing value chain activities have been performed, and (2) the activity contributes to creating or capturing value. For example, recall that Google's new game strategy in the early 2000s included undertaking paid listings rather than pop-ups or banner advertising for monetizing searches, developing those algorithms that delivered more relevant searches to its customers, and placing the paid-listing ads on its website as well as on third-party sites. Undertaking paid listings was a new game activity to firms in the search engine industry. So was developing the algorithms to deliver more relevant searches to customers; and so was placing paid listing adds on third-party sites. Because a set can have only one member, there will be times when a firm's new game strategy consists of one new game activity, thereby making the activity a strategy. In fact, very often people refer to a new game activity as a new game strategy. Finally, strategic innovations are new games.

Value Systems and Options for New Game Strategies— Which, Where, When, What, and How?

To understand the options that each firm has for pursuing new game strategies, consider the business system (value chain) of Figure 1.1. At each stage of the chain, a firm has many options for performing the activities needed to add value at that stage to create and deliver products to end-customers.[11] For example, at the technology stage, a firm has many options for sourcing the technology. It can develop the technology internally using its own R&D resources, license the technology from another firm, form a strategic alliance with partners to develop

Technology	Product design	Manufacturing	Marketing	Distribution	Service
• Patents • Product/process choices • Sophistication • Sources	• Aesthetics • Function • Physical characteristics • Quality	• Assembly • Capacity • Integration • Location • Parts production • Procurement • Raw materials	• Advertising/ promotion • Brand • Packaging • Prices • Sales force	• Channels • Integration • Inventory • Transportation • Warehousing	• Captive/ independent • Prices • Speed • Warranty

Figure 1.1 Business System and Options for New Games.

the technology, or decide to wait for the next-generation technology. If it decides to develop the technology, the firm can patent aggressively to protect its technology, or give away the technology. Suppose firms in an industry develop their technologies internally and keep them proprietary; then a firm that gives away its own technology to anyone who wants it is pursuing a new game strategy. That is what Sun Microsystems did when it gave away its SPARC workstation computer technology in the early 1990s. Of course, a firm is also pursuing a new game strategy if it decides to use a radically different technology.

At the distribution level, a firm also has many choices. It can use all the channels available to it for distribution, or use only a few. It can also decide to sell directly to customers or depend completely on distributors. It can decide to build products and warehouse lots of finished goods inventory, or have a build-to-order system with little or no finished goods inventory. Again, suppose firms in a market all depend on distributors to deliver products to end-customers. A firm that decides to sell directly to end-customers is effectively performing a new game activity. This is what Dell did when it decided to start selling directly to end-customers. At the manufacturing level, a firm can be vertically integrated into producing its components or buy the components; it can produce the components at home or in foreign countries; it can locate all its plants in one country or in different countries; it can perform its own purchasing or have an agent do it, etc.

Effectively, since there are many options for performing value chain activities at every stage of the value chain, there also exist options for performing new game activities at all stages of a value chain. Thus, the opportunity to gain a strategic advantage is not limited to product innovation (new game strategies at the technology and product design stages). Opportunities for a strategic advantage through new game strategies exist at all the stages of a value chain—manufacturing, marketing, distribution, and service included. They also exist in vertically integrating backwards to supply one's inputs, integrating vertically forwards to dispose of one's outputs, and integrating horizontally into complements or other related segments.

Moreover, options also exist as to *which* activities to perform, *when* to perform them, *how* to perform them, *where* to perform them, and *what* to expect as the output. At the R&D stage, for example, a firm may decide to perform basic R&D and not applied R&D while its competitors perform both. It might decide to perform that R&D in the USA, China, and South Africa while its competitors do so only in Europe. It might decide to be the first mover rather than a follower in the R&D activities that it performs. It might also decide to patent religiously while its competitors depend on trade secrets.

In any case, new game activities can create new customer value for existing or new customers, address newer and more valuable market segments, better position a firm to capture value created in its value system, or generate new revenues from existing or new revenue sources. They constitute the cornerstones of new game strategies.

Finally, note that although new game activities are the cornerstones of new game strategies, the latter often contain some non-new game activities. For example, not all the activities that Google performed to be profitable were new game; but the cornerstones of its new game strategy are new game activities.

From Activities to Profits

How do activities become profits? When a firm performs business systems activities, (1) it produces a product with benefits that customers value, (2) it better positions itself vis-à-vis its coopetitors, or (3) it does both. The product, or the position attained then has to be converted to profits. Although each category of activities sometimes takes a different path to profits, activities often complement each other. Let us examine both.

Product with Benefits that Customers Value

Many firms perform activities to offer products that customers want. R&D, product development, purchasing, and manufacturing are examples of activities that are designed largely to add value along a value chain so as to offer customers products that they value. If a firm's product offers benefits that customers perceive as unique—e.g. low-cost or differentiated products—customers are more likely to gravitate towards the firm rather than its competitors. Offering customers low-cost or differentiated products is just one step, albeit a very important one, for a firm to profit from performing value-adding activities. The firm must also price the product well since too high a price drives away some customers while too low a price leaves money on the table. It must seek out as many customers as possible, since customers usually do not come knocking at a firm's door. It could also seek different profitable sources of revenue that exploit the product. For example, many US car dealers make more money from servicing cars than from selling new ones. A firm could also locate its product in a market with few or no competitors such as a new market segment, a different region of a country, or another country.

Effectively, when value-adding activities produce low-cost or differentiated products, the products must still be translated into money—they still have to be priced well, the number of customers that perceive value in the products increased, profitable sources of revenues sought, and the product also positioned in the right market spaces to profit more fully from it.

Better Positioning vis-à-vis Coopetitors

A firm can also perform activities to position itself better vis-à-vis its coopetitors in order to profit from the value that the firm or its coopetitors have created. A firm has a *superior position* vis-à-vis a coopetitor if the coopetitor needs the firm more than the firm needs the coopetitor. For example, when a firm purchases its rivals, it increases its power over customers since there are now fewer firms (competitors) for a customer to play against each other. Buyers now need the firm more than they did before the firm purchased its rivals. Such a firm can use its increased power to raise its prices, or extract other concessions from customers. This is a practice that Tyco International pursued profitably for many years. If a firm integrates vertically forwards to sell directly to consumers, it is bypassing the more concentrated distributors to deal directly with the more fragmented consumers. In addition to saving on the sales commissions that are usually paid to distributors, such a firm can also build switching costs at customers (see Chapters 4 and 6) and seek other sources of revenues. It also has the freedom and flexibility to introduce more innovative products to customers. If a firm instead integrates vertically backwards to produce its own critical inputs, it increases its bargaining power over suppliers. The firm can use such power to encourage suppliers to provide second sources for its inputs. Doing so can allow a firm to extract concessions from suppliers, including lower prices and higher quality, both of which can increase the firm's profits.

Value Creation and Better Positioning

Some activities result in value creation and better positioning vis-à-vis coopetitors. For example, by offering a differentiated product, a firm is not only creating value but also positioning better itself vis-à-vis customers, rivals, and potential new entrants since differentiation reduces rivalry, power of suppliers, and the threat of new entry.[12] By marketing a product in a location with no competition, one is introducing value to customers in the location. At the same time, since there are no competitors, the firm has a monopolistic position in the space and is therefore well-positioned vis-à-vis some coopetitors.

In any case, when a firm performs a value-adding activity, the activity contributes to value creation and capture in one or more of the following ways. The activity:

a Lowers the cost of, or adds to the differentiation of a product—it contributes to value creation, and customer benefits.
b Positions the firm better vis-à-vis its coopetitors.
c Transforms the value created into profits.
d Exploits the *position vis-à-vis coopetitors* to profit from the value created by the firm and that created by its coopetitors.

Characteristics of New Games

When firms perform new value chain activities, or existing ones differently, they are playing *new games*. (Each firm's strategy is then the set of activities, including non-new game activities, that it pursues to create and appropriate value in the face of the new game.) Since the activities that underpin new games are new or existing ones that are performed differently, new games create new value or generate new ways of capturing value; and since performing activities requires resources/capabilities, performing new game activities may require new resources/capabilities that build on a firm's existing resources/capabilities or require very different ones. Because, in pursuing a new game, a firm may be moving first, such a firm has an opportunity to build and take advantage of first-mover advantages. Moreover, when a firm pursues a new game strategy, its competitors are likely to react to the strategy. Therefore a firm is better off anticipating and taking into consideration the likely reaction of competitors when it pursues a new game strategy; and since firms usually pursue new game strategies within the context of their industry, macro, or global environments, a firm is also better off identifying and responding to the opportunities and threats of these environments. Effectively, new games exhibit several character-istics of which firms can take advantage. New games:

1 Generate *new* ways of creating and appropriating new value.
2 Offer opportunity to build new resources/capabilities or translate existing ones in new ways into value.
3 Create the potential to build and exploit *first-mover advantages and* dis*advantages*.
4 Attract *reactions* from new and existing competitors.
5 Have their roots in the *opportunities* and *threats* of the firm's environments.

The first three characteristics are about a firm's internal environment—the activities, resources, and capabilities that it can use to exploit the opportunities and threats of its external environment. The fourth and fifth characteristics are about the external threats and opportunities. We explore each of these charac-teristics of new games.

Generate New Ways of Creating and Appropriating Value

As we have seen above, a firm creates value when it offers customers benefits that they perceive as being valuable to them and the firm's cost of providing the benefits does not exceed the benefits. Innovation (product or business process) is a good example of value creation by new games, since it entails doing things differently and results in differentiated and/or low-cost new products.

New games give a firm an opportunity to create unique benefits for a valuable set of customers, and/or uniquely position the firm vis-à-vis its coopetitors to appropriate the value created. In choosing which new game strategy to pursue, a firm can opt for those activities that enable it to offer unique benefits that meet the needs of customers with a high willingness to pay. In so doing, the firm is avoiding head-on competition, thereby keeping down the profit-sapping effects of rivalry. For example, when Ryanair decided to expand its activities into southern Europe, it did not try to fight established airlines head-on at larger congested airports and try to outdo them at what they had been doing for decades. Rather, it went for the less congested secondary airports where it did not have to compete head-on with incumbent big airlines. Because the value is unique, a firm also has more power over its customers than it would have if the benefits were not unique; and if customers have a high willingness to pay, a firm can afford to set its prices closer to customers' reservation prices without driving the customers away, since the customers need the unique benefits from the firm's products. (A customer's reservation price for a product is the highest price that the customer is willing to pay for the product.) A firm can offer unique benefits to such valuable customers by working with them to help them discover their latent needs for a new product that it has invented or discovered, leapfrogging existing needs through innovation, reaching out for a market segment that had never been served with the benefits in question, or following so-called *reverse positioning* in which the firm strips some of the benefits that some customers have come to expect but which other customers have no need for while adding some new ones.[13]

Offering a select group of customers unique benefits can dampen the power of the customers and the effects of rivalry as well as the threat of substitutes and potential new entries, but it may not do much about suppliers and some complementors. Thus, beyond pursuing activities that offer unique customer benefits, a firm may also want to pursue the kinds of activity that dampen or reverse the power of its suppliers. For example, by making sure that there are second sources for all its key components, a firm can considerably dampen the power of suppliers for the particular component. Cooperation with other coopetitors, not just suppliers, can also dampen their power vis-à-vis a firm. Effectively, a new game offers a firm an opportunity to build a system of activities that is difficult to imitate and that enables the firm to create unique benefits for valuable customers and uniquely position it vis-à-vis its coopetitors to appropriate the value.[14]

The *change* element side of new game activities suggests that the new ways of creating and capturing value can render existing ways obsolete or can build on them. It also suggests that the value created or the new position attained can be so superior to existing ones that the products that embody them render existing products noncompetitive or can be moderate enough to allow existing products to remain in the market. For example, the activities that are performed to create and appropriate value in online auctions are so different from those for offline auctions that the latter are largely obsolete as far as online auctions are concerned. The value created is also so superior that for most items, offline auctions have been completely displaced by online auctions.

The change element also suggests that new games may result in an industry that is more or less attractive than before the games. An industry is more attractive after change if the competitive forces that impinge on industry firms are more friendly than before—that is, if rivalry, the bargaining power of suppliers, the bargaining power of customers, the threat of potential new entry and of substitutes are low. If the industry is more attractive, industry firms are, on average, more profitable. As we will see when we explore disruptive technologies, many new games increase the competitive forces on incumbents as barriers to entry drop, and rivalry increases.

Offer Opportunity to Build New Resources/Capabilities or Translate Existing Ones in New Ways

New games also offer a firm an opportunity to build scarce distinctive resources/capabilities for use in creating and appropriating value, or to use existing resources/capabilities in new ways to create and appropriate value. To perform the activities that enable a firm to create and/or appropriate value, a firm needs resources (assets). These can be tangible (physical assets such as plants, equipment, patents, and cash), intangible (the nonphysical ones such as brand-name reputation, technological know-how, and client relations), or organizational (routines, processes, structure, systems, and culture).[15] A firm's capabilities or competences are its ability to integrate resources and/or translate them into products.[16] New game strategies can be used to build resources/capabilities and/or translate existing ones into value that customers want. The case of eBay serves as a good example. By taking a series of measures to make its online auction market feel safe, building a brand, and increasing the number of members in its community of registered users, eBay was able to build a large and safe community—a critical resource—that attracted even more members every year. It was then able to use this large base of buyers and sellers to move from an auctions format into a multiformat that included fixed pricing and auction formats, and from collectibles to many other categories.

Again, the *change* side of new games suggests that the resources/capabilities that are needed to perform new game activities can build on existing resources/ capabilities or be so different that existing resources/capabilities are rendered obsolete. For example, the resources/capabilities needed by eBay are so different from those needed for an offline auction that offline resources such as offline physical locations, bidding systems, etc., are obsolete as far as online auctions are concerned. This has strategic implications that we will explore in later chapters.

Create the Potential to Build and Exploit First-mover Advantages and Disadvantages

A first-mover advantage is an advantage that a firm gains by being the first to carry out a value creation and/or value appropriation activity or strategy.[17] Since, in pursuing a new game, a firm may be effectively moving first, such a firm has an opportunity to *earn* first-mover advantages. If a firm performs the right activities to enable it to attain first-mover advantages, it can take advantage of them to build or consolidate its competitive advantage. For example, when a firm introduces a new product, moves into a new market, or performs any other new game activity that can allow it to create or appropriate value in new ways, the firm has an opportunity to build and exploit first-mover advantages. For example, a firm that introduces a new product first can build switching costs or establish a large installed customer base before its competitors introduce competing products. In such a case, the switching costs or installed base is said to be the firm's first-mover advantage. Perhaps one of the most popular examples of a firm that built and exploited first-mover advantages is Wal-Mart. When it first started building its stores in the Southwestern USA, large powerful suppliers refused to give it goods on consignment. Wal-Mart turned things around in its favor when it grew big by pursuing the right activities: it saturated contiguous towns with stores and built associated distribution centers, logistics, information technology infrastructure, and relevant "Wal-Mart culture." By scaling up its efficient activities, Wal-Mart became very large and effectively reversed the direction of power between it and its supplier—with Wal-Mart now having the power over suppliers. Effectively, a firm that uses new games to offer unique value to customers and uniquely position itself to appropriate the value, can use first-mover advantages to solidify its advantage in value creation and appropriation.

The more counterintuitive a new game strategy, the more opportunities that the first-mover has to build advantages before followers move in. As we will argue in Chapter 6, first-mover advantages are usually not automatically endowed on whoever moves first. They have to be earned. Of course, wherever there are first-mover advantages, there are usually also first-mover *dis*advantages that can give followers an advantage. Competitors that follow, rather than move first, can take advantage of first-mover *dis*advantages (also called follower's advantages). For example, when a firm is the first to pursue a new game, it is likely to incur the cost of resolving technological and marketing uncertainties such as proving that the product works and that there is a market for it. Followers can free-ride on first movers' investments to resolve these uncertainties and be spared these extra expenses. If the technology and market are changing, the first mover may make commitments in the early stages of the technology and market that reduce its flexibility in some later decisions. This again opens up opportunities for followers. We will also explore first-mover *dis*advantages in more detail in Chapter 6.

Attract Reactions from New and Existing Competitors

If a firm pursues a new game first, the chances are that competitors are not likely to sit by and watch the firm make money alone. They are likely to react to the firm's actions. Thus, it is important to try to anticipate competitors' likely reactions to one's actions. In fact, business history suggests that many firms that ultimately made the most money from innovations were not the first to introduce the innovations. So-called followers, not first movers, won. One reason is because followers often can exploit first-mover's disadvantages (also called followers' advantages). However, a first mover can have three things going for it. First, it can build and exploit first-mover advantages. Second, it can take advantage of the fact that new games are often counterintuitive, making it difficult for followers to understand the rationale behind the utility of the new games. The more that the idea behind a new game strategy is counter to the prevailing dominant industry logic about how to perform activities to make money in the industry, the more that a first mover will not be followed immediately by potential competitors; and if a firm follows a first mover, its dominant logic may handicap it from effectively replicating the first mover's activities. While potential followers are still getting over their industry's dominant logic to understand the potential of the new game, a first mover can preemptively accumulate valuable important resources/capabilities that are needed to profit from the activities.

Third, a firm that pursues a new game strategy can take advantage of the fact that when a pioneer pursues a new game strategy, some of its competitors may have prior commitments or other inseparabilities that handicap them when they try to react to the pioneer's actions. The role of prior commitments is best illustrated by the case of Compaq when it tried to react to Dell's direct sales and build-to-order new game strategy. Compaq decided to incorporate the same two activities into its business model. Citing previous contracts, Compaq's distributors refused Compaq from selling directly to end-customers and the firm had to abandon its proposed new business model. Some firms may decide not to follow a first mover for fear of cannibalizing their existing products. In some cases, the inertia of large firms may prevent them from moving to compete with first movers.

In any case, an important part of profiting from a new game is in anticipating and proactively trying to respond to the likely reaction of competitors. This entails asking questions such as: if I offer that new product, raise my prices, invest more in R&D, adopt that new technology, advertise more, launch that product promotion, form the strategic alliance, etc., what is likely to be the reaction of my competitors? This also entails obtaining competitive intelligence not only on competitors' *handicaps* but also on their goals, resources/capabilities and past behavior to help in making judgments about competitors' likely reactions. With such information, a firm can better anticipate competitors' likely reactions and incorporate counter-measures in formulating and executing new game strategies. Of course, the likely reaction of suppliers, complementors, and customers should also be taken into consideration.

Have their Roots in the Opportunities and Threats of a Firm's Environments

Firms that pursue new games do not do so in a vacuum. They operate in their industry, macro, and global environments. In fact, many of the new game activities that are performed to create value or improve a firm's ability to appropriate value are triggered by opportunities or threats from both their industry, macro, and global environments. An industry environment consists of the actors and activities such as supply and demand that take place among suppliers, rivals, complementors, substitutes, and buyers. A firm may offer a new product because it wants to occupy some white space that it has identified in the markets that it serves. Airbus' offering of the A380 super jumbo plane falls in this category. Sometimes, new games can be a result of a hostile competitive environment. Dell's decision to sell directly to customers rather than pass through distributors was actually because the distributors would not carry its products at the time. It was a fledgling startup and many distributors were busy selling products for the IBMs and the Compaqs. The macroenvironment is made up of the political-legal, economic, socio-cultural, technological, and natural environments (PESTN) in which firms and industries operate. A firm may enter a market because it fears that a disruptive technology will erode its competitive advantage. Another may use the same disruptive technology to attack incumbents that have been successful at using an existing technology. Yet another firm may be responding to opportunities in its political-legal environment. For example, Ryanair's expansion into secondary airports in the European Union followed the union's deregulation of the airline industry. The drop in its profits in 2008 was largely attributable to the sharp rise in the cost of oil to more than three times what it had been paying for in earlier years.

The global environment consists of a world in which countries and their industries and firms are increasingly interconnected, interdependent, and more integrated, thereby moving towards having similar political-legal, economic, socio-cultural, technological, and natural environments (PESTN). The opportunities and threats of the global environment are exhibited through globalization. **Globalization** is the interdependence and integration of people, firms, and governments to produce and exchange products and services.[18] Globalization creates opportunities for some firms and individuals but creates threats for others. There are opportunities to market products to, outsource work to export to, or import from foreign countries in new ways.

In any case, external environments differ from one industry to the other, and from one country or region to another. In the carbonated soft drinks industry, for example, regular and diet colas have been the major sellers for decades. In fact, when coke tried to change the formula for its regular coke, customers did not like it and the company had to revert to the old product. Other industries are relatively less stable. Rapid technological change, globalization, changing customer tastes, and more availability of skilled human resources in different countries make some industries very turbulent. In such industries, firms often have to cannibalize their own products before someone else does. Effectively, how firms need to interact with or react to environments can differ considerably from one industry to the other, or from one country to the other, and can constitute opportunities and threats that firms can exploit through new games.

Concern for the natural environment also creates many opportunities to use innovation to build better cars, build better power plants, better dispose of waste, and reduce carbon emissions. Understanding these opportunities and threats not only helps a firm to make better choices about which activities to perform, but when to perform them and how to perform them.

Multigames and Dynamics

A new game usually does not take place in isolation. It usually takes place in the context of other games and is usually preceded by, followed by, or played in parallel with other games. When a firm introduces a new game, it often does so in response to another game. For example, when Dell decided to sell its built-to-order PCs directly to businesses and consumers, it did so in the context of a larger new game—the introduction of PCs that were disrupting minicomputers. When Google developed its search engine and pursued paid listings to monetize the engine, it was doing so in the context of the Internet, a much larger new game. When Wal-Mart initially located its stores in small towns in parts of the Southwestern USA, it was doing so in the context of the larger game of discount retailing that was challenging the standard department store. Each firm usually plays multigames over a period. For example, Wal-Mart started out selling only goods at discount prices in its discount stores but in 1988, it introduced its version of superstores, selling both food and goods in its Wal-Mart Supercenters. This multigame and dynamic nature of new games has implications that we will encounter when we explore first-mover advantages and disadvantages, and competitors' handicaps in Chapter 6.

Competitive Advantage from New Games

Many firms pursue new game strategies in search of a competitive advantage, or just to make money. A firm's **competitive advantage** is its ability to earn a higher rate of profits than the average rate of profits of the market in which it competes. Since revenues come from customers, any firm that wants to make money must offer customers benefits that they perceive as valuable compared to what competitors offer. Thus, an important step in gaining a competitive advantage is to create unique benefits for customers without exceeding the cost of the benefits—creating unique **value**; but to create value, a firm has to perform the relevant value-adding **activities**; and for a firm to perform value-adding activities effectively, it needs to have the relevant resources and capabilities. Since, as we saw earlier, not even unique value can guarantee that one will profit from it, the activities that a firm performs should also position it to **appropriate** the value created. If the activities are a new game, then there is a **change** element in the creation and appropriation of value since new games generate new ways of creating and appropriating value, offer opportunities to build new resources or translate existing ones in new ways, create the potential to build and exploit first-mover advantages, attract reactions from coopetitors, or identify and respond to the opportunities and threats of the environment. Effectively, competitive advantage is about creating and appropriating value better than competitors; but creating and appropriating value requires the right activities and the underpinning of resources and capabilities. Moreover, there is always the element of change from the new game component of activities—either from a firm or from the actors in its external environment.

Components of a New Game Strategy

In effect, when a firm pursues a new game strategy, the extent to which the strategy can give the firm a competitive advantage is a function of the activities that the firm performs, the value that it creates, how much value it captures, and how much it is able to take advantage of change. It is a function of the four components: Activities, Value, Appropriability, and Change (AVAC) (Figure 1.2). Thus, one can estimate the extent to which a new game strategy stands to give a firm a competitive advantage by answering the following four questions:

1 Activities: is the firm performing the right activities? Does it have what it takes to perform them?
2 Value: do customers perceive the value created by the strategy as unique?
3 Appropriability: does the firm make money from the value created?
4 Change: does the strategy take advantage of change (present or future) to create unique value and/or position itself to appropriate the value?

Answering these four questions constitutes an AVAC analysis. The AVAC analysis can be used to estimate the profitability potential of a strategy or the extent to which a strategy is likely to give a firm a competitive advantage. The more that the answers to these question are Yes rather than No, the more that the strategy is likely to give the firm a competitive advantage. Although a detailed

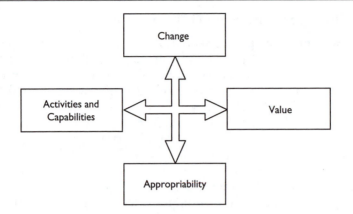

Figure 1.2 Components of a New Game Strategy.

exploration of the AVAC analysis is postponed until Chapter 2, the analysis is simple and fundamental enough for us to start using it below.

Competitive Consequences of Strategies

Each strategy—new game or otherwise—has competitive consequences. Depending on the strategy that a firm pursues, the firm may have a sustainable competitive advantage, temporary competitive advantage, competitive parity, or competitive disadvantage (Table 1.1). An AVAC analysis enables a firm to identify and rank strategies by their competitive consequences. Table 1.1 shows six different strategies and the competitive consequence for each. In Strategy 1, the set of activities that the firm performs creates value that customers perceive as unique and the firm is able to appropriate the value so created. The firm also has the resources and capabilities needed to perform the activities. Moreover, the strategy takes advantage of change (present or future) to create and/or appropriate value better. All the answers to the questions are Yes, and the firm is thus said to have a sustainable competitive advantage.

In many industries, however, the more common cases are Strategy 2 and Strategy 3, which give a firm a temporary competitive advantage. In Strategy 2, the firm has a set of activities that enables it to create value that customers perceive as unique, and put it in a position to appropriate the value. It also has what it takes to perform the activities; but the strategy is such that the firm cannot take advantage of change. During the period before the change, the firm has a temporary competitive advantage. In Strategy 3, the set of activities that the firm performs enables it to create value and take advantage of change, but can appropriate the value created only for the short period that it takes competitors to imitate it. It has the resources and capabilities to perform the value-creating activities. Thus, the firm also has a temporary competitive advantage. In pharmaceuticals, for example, strategies are often anchored on patents which usually give their owners a competitive advantage for the duration of the patent. When a patent expires, however, many imitators produce generic versions of the drug, eroding the advantage of the original patent owners. In Strategy 4, the firm can neither appropriate the value created nor take advantage of change, even though it creates value and has what it takes to perform the

Table 1.1 Competitive Consequences of New Game Strategy

First-mover advantage	Activities: Is the firm performing the right activities? Does it have what it takes (resources and capabilities) to perform the activities?	Value: Is the value created by the strategy unique, as perceived by customers, compared to that from competitors?	Appropriability: Does the firm make money from the value created?	Change: Does the strategy take advantage of change (present or future) to create unique value and/or position itself to appropriate the value?	Competitive consequence
Strategy 1	Yes	Yes	Yes	Yes	Sustainable competitive advantage
Strategy 2	Yes	Yes	Yes	No	Temporary competitive advantage
Strategy 3	Yes	Yes	Yes/No	Yes	Temporary competitive advantage
Strategy 4	Yes	Yes	No	No	Competitive parity
Strategy 5	No/Yes	No	Yes	No	Competitive parity
Strategy 6	No	No	No	No	Competitive disadvantage
Strategic action	What can a firm do to reinforce the Yesses and reverse or dampen the Noes, and what is the impact of doing so?				

activities. Such a strategy is also said to give the firm competitive parity. Most producers of commodity products have comparative parity. In Strategy 5, the firm has what it takes to perform some activities but not others. It can appropriate some of the value created, even though the value is not unique. It is vulnerable to change. A firm that pursues such a strategy also has competitive parity with competitors. In Strategy 6, the set of activities that a firm performs neither creates unique value nor puts the firm in a position to appropriate value created by others; nor does the firm have what it takes to perform the activities. The firm is said to have a competitive *dis*advantage.

Thus, the more that the answers to these question are Yes rather than No, the more that the strategy is likely to give the firm a competitive advantage. What should a firm do if an AVAC analysis shows that it has a temporary competitive advantage, competitive parity, or a competitive disadvantage? Such a firm can decide whether to perform the types of activity that will enable it to turn the Noes to Yesses or at least dampen them, thereby giving it a more sustainable competitive advantage or something closer to it. It may also decide to abandon the strategy.

Illustrative Example

We illustrate the significance of a good new game strategy using the example of Nintendo's introduction of its Wii video game console.

Estimating the Value of a New Game Strategy: The Case of Video Consoles

Nintendo introduced its Wii video console in the Americas on November 19, 2006, only about a week after Sony had introduced its PS3 console on November 11. Microsoft's Xbox had been available for purchase about a year earlier on November 22, 2005. Game developers, such as Electronic Arts, developed the video games that customers bought to play on their consoles. For every video game that a game developer sold to be played on a particular console, the game developer paid the console-maker a royalty. This aspect of the game console business model differed from the PC business model where software developers did not pay any royalties to PC makers. Console-makers also developed some games in-house. Each console-maker, on average, collected 0.415 of every game sold.[19] The average wholesale price of Xbox 360/PS3-generation games was about $43.[20]

The Xbox 360 and the PS3 used ever more powerful computing and graphics chips to offer customers more lifelike images than those from their predecessors. They also focused on advanced and experienced gamers, neglecting novices and casual games, many of whom were scared by the complexity of the games, some of which took hours or days to play.[21] These faster chips and more lifelike images enabled game developers to develop even more complex games for avid gamers. The Nintendo Wii differed from the PS3 and the Xbox 360 in several ways. It went after the less experienced, new, or lapsed potential gamers that Sony and Microsoft had neglected. The Wii used less complex and cheaper components than the PS3 and Xbox. The games were simpler to play and could last a few minutes rather than the dozens of hours or days that it took to play some Xbox 360/PS3 games. Rather than use the complicated joypad of the PS3 and Xbox that was full of buttons, the Nintendo Wii had simpler controls that were easier to use and a wandlike controller that looked more like a simplified TV remote-control.[22] When connected to the Internet, the Wii could display weather and news.

The estimated costs, wholesale prices, and suggested retail prices for the three products are shown in Table 1.2, while the forecasted number of units are shown in Table 1.3.

Question: What is the financial impact of the difference between the Nintendo Wii business model and the PS3 and Xbox 360 business models?

Answer: The calculations that are summarized in Table 1.4 demonstrate how much a good new game strategy can contribute to the bottom line of a company. The forecasted profits from each product are also shown in Table 1.4. Over the three-year period from 2007 to 2009:

- The Xbox 360 was projected to bring in profits of $105 + 105 + 53 = $263 million.

Table 1.2 Costs, Retail, and Wholesale Prices

Product	Year introduced	First year			After first year		
		Cost ($)	Suggested retail price ($)	Wholesale price ($)	Cost	Suggested retail price ($)	Wholesale price ($)
Xbox 360	2005	525	399	280	323	399	280
Sony PS3	2006	806	499	349	496	399	280
Nintendo Wii	Late 2006	158.30	249	199	126	200	150

Sources: Company and analysts' forecasts. Author's estimates.

Table 1.3 Forecasted Console and Games Sales

	2005	2006	2007	2008	2009	2010
Console						
Xbox 360	1.5	8.5	10	10	5	
Sony PS3		2	11	13	13	7
Nintendo Wii			5.8	14.5	17.4	18.3
Games						
Xbox 360	4.5	25.5	30	30	15	
Sony PS3		6	33	39	39	21
Nintendo Wii			28.8	66.5	114.3	128.8

Sources: Company and analysts' reports. Author's estimates.

- The PS3 was projected (not) to bring in – $478 – 565 – 565 = – 1,608 million = $(1,608 million).
- The Wii was projected to pull in profits of $749 + 1,535 + 2,457 = $4,741 million.

Effectively, Nintendo's new game strategy for its Wii enabled it to expect profits of $4.741 million over the three-year period while Microsoft could only expect profits of $0.263 million from its Xbox 360 while Sony stood to lose large amounts, to the tune of $1.608 million. Why? The primary reason was that Nintendo's reverse-positioning strategy enabled it not only to attract more customers but also to keep its cost so low that it could sell each of its consoles at a profit, while Microsoft and Sony sold their consoles at a loss, hoping to make up the losses by selling more games.

Types of New Game

Not all new games exhibit the same degree of new gameness. For example, the change from horse-driven carts to the internal combustion engine automobile was a new game; but so was the decision of Japanese automobile makers Honda, Nissan, and Toyota to offer the luxury brands Acura, Infiniti, and Lexus, respectively. So was Dell's decision to sell directly to end-customers. This raises an interesting question: how new game is a new game? What is the new gameness of a new game? In this section, we explore this question.

Table 1.4 Estimates of the Profitability of Three Different Strategies

Microsoft			2005	2006	2007	2008	2009	2010
Xbox 360 units (million units)	A		1.5	8.5	10	10	5	
Wholesale price	B		399	280	280	280	280	
Console production costs	C		525	323	323	323	323	
Profits from Console ($ million)	D	A*(B – C)	(189)	(366)	(430)	(430)	(215)	
Software units (using attach rate of 3.0) (million)	E	3*A	4.5	25.5	30	30	15	
Profits from games ($ million)	F	0.415*43*E	80	455	535	535	268	
Total profits ($ million)	G	D + F	(109)	90	**105**	**105**	**53**	

Sony			2005	2006	2007	2008	2009	2010
Console sales (million units)	H			2	11	13	13	7
Wholesale price	I			499	399	399	399	399
Console production costs	J			806	496	496	496	496
Profits from Console ($ million)	K	H*(I – J)		(614)	(1,067)	(1,261)	(1,261)	(679)
Software units (using attach rate of 3.0) (million)	L	3*H		6	33	39	39	21
Profits from games ($ million)	M	0.415*43*L		107	589	696	696	375
Total profits ($ million)	N	K + M		(507)	**(478)**	**(565)**	**(565)**	(304)

Nintendo Wii			2005	2006	2007	2008	2009	2010
Console sales (million units)	O				6	14.5	17.4	18.3
Wholesale price	P				199	150	150	150
Console production costs	Q				158	126	126	126
Profits from Console ($ million)	R	O*(P – Q)			246	348	418	439
Software units (games) (million)	S				28.2	66.5	114.3	128.8
Profits from games ($ million)	T	0.415*43*S			503	1,187	2,040	2,298
Total profits ($ million)	U	R + T			**749**	**1,535**	**2,457**	2,738

The Classification

How new game is a new game? We start answering this question by classifying new games as a function of their new gameness. Since the ultimate goal of many firms is to gain a sustainable competitive advantage, one way to classify new games is by how much they impact a firm's (1) product space, and (2) resources/capabilities. Why these two variables? Because they are key determinants of competitive advantage. According to the *product-market-position (PMP)* view of strategic management, the extent to which a firm can earn a higher rate of returns than its rivals is a function of the benefits (low cost or differentiated products, or both) that the firm offers its customers, and its position vis-à-vis coopetitors (bargaining power over suppliers and customers, power of substitutes, threat of potential new entry, rivalry) that help the firm capture the value that customers see in the benefits.[23] The more that customers perceive the benefits from a firm as unique and superior to those from competitors, the better the chances of the firm capturing the value from the benefits and having a higher rate of return. The better a firm's position vis-à-vis its coopetitors—that is, the more that the firm has bargaining power over its suppliers and customers, and the more that rivalry, the threat of substitutes, and of new entry are low—the better the firm's chances of having a higher rate of return. For want of a better phrase, we will call the product (with associated benefits) that a firm offers customers, and its position vis-à-vis coopetitors the firm's *product position*.

According to the *resource-based view (RBV),* a firm that has valuable, scarce, and difficult-to-imitate-or-substitute resources/capabilities is more likely to create and offer unique benefits to customers and/or to position itself to capture the value created than its competitors.[24] A firm's resources/capabilities are valuable if they can be translated into benefits that customers like. They are scarce if the firm is the only one that owns them or if its level of the resources is superior to that of competitors. They are difficult-to-imitate if there is something about the resources that makes it difficult for competitors to replicate or leapfrog them.

From these two views of strategic management, a firm's product position and its resources are key determinants of its competitive advantage. Thus, in the two-by-two matrix of Figure 1.3, we can classify new games along these two variables. The vertical dimension captures a new game's impact on a firm's *product position*. In particular, it captures the extent to which a game is so new game as to render existing products and/or positions vis-à-vis coopetitors noncompetitive. The horizontal axis captures a new game's impact on resources/capabilities. It captures the extent to which the resources/capabilities needed to play the new game are so different from existing ones that the latter are rendered obsolete. These are the resources/capabilities that go into offering a product to customers—resources/capabilities such as the equipment, locations, skills, knowledge, intellectual property, relationships with coopetitors, and know-how that underpin value chain activities such as R&D, design, manufacturing, operations, marketing, sales, distribution, human resources/capabilities, purchasing, and logistics. The resulting four quadrants of the two-by-two matrix represent different types of new games (Figure 1.3). New gameness increases as one moves from the origin of the matrix of Figure 1.3 to the top right corner, with the *regular new game* being the least new game while the

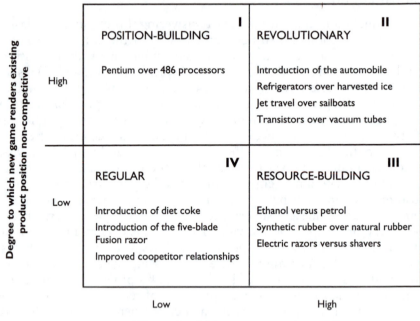

Figure 1.3 Types of New Game.

revolutionary game is the most new game. We now explore each of the four types of new games.[25]

Regular

In a *regular* new game, a firm uses existing value chain resources/capabilities or builds on them to (1) offer a new product that customers value but the new product is such that existing products in the market are still very competitive, and/or (2) improve its position vis-à-vis coopetitors but the new position does not render existing ones noncompetitive.

New Product

If a regular new game offers a new product, the product may take some market share from existing products, but the latter remain profitable enough to be a competitive force in the market. The new games pursued by Coke and Pepsi in introducing products such as diet or caffeine-free colas were regular new games. Both firms did some things differently but the resources/capabilities that they used built on existing ones and the resulting products allowed their regular colas to remain competitive. Gillette also played a regular new game when it introduced most of its razors. For example, the Mach3 razor with three blades, introduced in 1998, allowed the twin-blade Sensor and competing products to remain in the market.[26] The five-blade Fusion, introduced in 2006, allowed the three-blade razor to remain competitive. All razors used different extensions of Gillette's mechanical blade technology to offer each new product, and each product, despite being well received by customers, allowed previous products to remain a competitive force in the market. Marketing was also designed to make improvements to the firm's positioning vis-à-vis its coopetitors. Effectively, in a regular new game, a firm builds on existing resources/capabilities to deliver new products that are valued by customers but the new products are positioned so that existing products remain competitive forces in the market.

Rather than introduce a brand new product, a regular new game can instead make refinements to an existing product and/or to the firm's position vis-à-vis its coopetitors through extensions of its resources/capabilities. The offering of many so-called new car models that are introduced every year are a good example. When this year's model car is introduced, last year's model is still a competitive force to be aware of. Effectively, in a regular new game, what is different about the activities being performed and therefore what qualifies them as new game is the fact that some of them are performed differently to improve products and the underpinning skills, knowledge, and know-how, or to position a firm better vis-à-vis coopetitors. Offering a diet drink, for example, requires keeping sugar out, adding an artificial sweetener, and convincing people that the new drink tastes good and is good for them.

Position vis-à-vis Coopetitors

A regular new game can also better position a firm vis-à-vis coopetitors. For example, if a firm successfully convinces its suppliers to create a second source for the components that it buys from the suppliers, it is effectively improving its position vis-à-vis suppliers using its existing resources/capabilities and without rendering existing positions noncompetitive.

A firm with an attractive PMP or valuable distinctive difficult-to-imitate-or-substitute resources/capabilities is the most likely to profit from a regular new game. So-called strategic moves such as product preannouncement or how much to spend on R&D may be able to give a firm a temporary advantage; but long-term competitive advantage depends on the existing resources/capabilities and product-market position.

Resource-building

In a *resource-building new game*, the resources/capabilities that are needed to make the new product are so different from those that are used to make existing products that these existing resources/capabilities are largely useless for performing the new activities; that is, the degree to which existing resources are rendered obsolete is high (Figure 1.3). However, the resulting (1) new product is such that existing products remain largely competitive in the market, and/or (2) new position vis-à-vis coopetitors is such that existing positions remain largely competitive. Changes in the rules of the game are largely resource/capabilities-related.

New Product

The pursuit of ethanol as a fuel for cars is a good example of a resource-building new game. Making ethanol—especially from cane sugar, sugar beat, corn, or sweet potatoes—requires very different capabilities from those used to drill, pump out, transport, and refine petrol to get gasoline for use in cars; but both fuels coexist in the market. The strategies for pursuing the electric razor were also resource-building but position-reinforcing. The electric razor uses a radic-ally different technology (combination of battery, electric motor, and moving parts) from the mechanical razor, which has only mechanical parts. Thus, the engineering capabilities needed for one can be very different from those needed for the other. However, the electric razor and the manual mechanical razor coexist in the market for shavers. Another example is the use of synthetic rub-ber (made from oil) and natural rubber from trees to make tires and other rubber products. Making synthetic rubber from petroleum is very different from tapping sap from trees and turning it into rubber, but the rubber from both sources remains competitive.

Position vis-à-vis Coopetitors

From a positioning vis-à-vis the coopetitor's point of view, a new game is resource-building if the resulting new position allows existing positions to remain competitive but the resources/capabilities needed are radically different from existing resources/capabilities. A good example is Dell's direct sales, which improved its power vis-à-vis buyers by bypassing the more powerful distributors to deal directly with the more fragmented end-customers. Distribu-tors still remained a viable sales avenue for Dell's competitors. Dell needed very different manufacturing, business processes, and relationships to support the new game.

Position-building

In a *position-building new game*, the resulting new PMP is so superior to existing PMPs that (1) new products introduced render existing ones largely noncompetitive, and/or (2) the new positions, vis-à-vis coopetitors, render existing ones primarily noncompetitive; that is, the degree to which the new game renders existing products and/or positions vis-à-vis coopetitors noncom-petitive is high (Figure 1.3). However, the resources/capabilities needed to make new products are the same as existing resources/capabilities or build on them. Changes in the rules of the game are largely PMP-related.

New Product

The new games pursued by Intel over the years in introducing different gener-ations of its microprocessors fall into this category. The P6 (Pentium Pro intro-duced in 1995 and Pentium II introduced in 1997) replaced the P5 (Pentium), which had been introduced in 1993. The Pentium replaced the 486 which replaced the 386 which had replaced the 286. Each new product met the new needs of customers. Throughout, Intel built on its core X86 processor and semiconductor technologies as well as on its distribution capabilities to introduce each new product. This is not to say that the semiconductor technology was not advancing. It did advance at tremendous rates, especially if measured by the benefits perceived by customers; but each generation of the technology built on the previous generation while introducing things that were new and different. Existing core capabilities were not rendered obsolete.

Some of the new games used to exploit disruptive technologies fall into this category. For example, the strategies pursued by the firms that used the PC to displace minicomputers were position-building, since PC technology built on minicomputer technology but minicomputers were rendered noncompetitive by PCs. Other examples include the strategies for the mini-mills used to make steel versus integrated steel mills.

Position vis-à-vis Coopetitors

There are also position-building strategies that have little to do with offering a new product. For example, software firms can sell their software directly to customers who can download the software directly from the firms' sites. By dealing directly with the more fragmented end-customer rather than the more concentrated distributors, software firms are effectively better positioned vis-à-vis their customers than before the days of the Internet. Another example of a position-building new game would be to eliminate competitors, where legal, to a point where one becomes a monopoly and the resources/capabilities needed to exploit the monopoly position build on existing resources/capabilities. This can be done through acquisition of competitors or predatory activities such as pricing, where legal.

Revolutionary

In a *revolutionary new game*, the organizational resources/capabilities needed to build new products are so different from those used to make existing products that these existing resources/capabilities are largely useless for performing the new activities. At the same time, the new PMP is so different from existing ones that (1) new products render existing ones largely noncompetitive, and/or (2) any new positions vis-à-vis coopetitors created render existing ones noncompetitive. A revolutionary new game redefines what creating and capturing value is all about while overturning the way value chain activities have been performed before. The rules of the game are changed both resource/capabilities-wise and PMP-wise. It is the most new game of all the new games. Examples, from a new products point of view, include the new games pursued by makers of refrigerators which replaced harvested ice as a cooling device, automobiles which displaced horse-driven carts, online auctions which replaced offline auctions, electronic point of sales registers that replaced mechanical cash registers, and iPods which have displaced Walkmans. In each case, the technological resources/capabilities needed to offer the new product were radically different from those that underpinned the displaced product. Moreover, the new product displaced existing products from the market. The new games played in the face of most disruptive technologies also fall into this category.

What is Strategy?

In defining a *new game strategy* as a set of activities that creates and/or appropriates value in *new* ways, we are implying that a firm's strategy is the set of activities that the firm performs to create and appropriate value. The question is, how does this definition of strategy compare to other definitions in the strategic management literature? The problem with this question is that strategy has too many definitions. One reason for the multitude of definitions is that strategy is about winning, and since what it takes to win in business has evolved over the years, the definition of strategy has also evolved. For example, in the 1960s, when most reconstruction, following World War II, had already taken place and there was a lot of demand for goods in the growing economies of the capitalist world, the biggest challenge for managers was to plan for this growth and keep up with demand. Thus, the dominant theme in the field of strategic management at the time was corporate planning, and managers were largely concerned with planning growth—how to allocate resources/capabilities to meet demand. The following two definitions of strategy fit the context at the time:

> the determination of the basic long-term goals and objectives of an enterprise, and the adoption of courses of action and the allocation of resources necessary for carrying out these goals.
>
> (Alfred Chandler in 1962)[27]

> the pattern of objectives, purposes, or goals and major policies and plans for achieving these goals, stated in such a way as to define what business the company is in or is to be in and the kind of company it is or is to be.
>
> (Kenneth Andrews in 1971)[28]

In the late 1970s and early 1980s, emphasis moved to strategy as position, in a large measure because of Professor Michael Porter's influential work.[29] In the late 1980s and early 1990s, emphasis changed to include resources, capabilities, and core competences, following Professors C.K. Prahalad's and Gary Hamel's influential work on the core competence of the firm and the increasing popularity of the resource-based view of the firm.[30] These changes would lead to definitions such as:

> Strategy is the creation of a unique and valuable position, involving a different set of activities.
>
> (Michael Porter in 1996)[31]

> A strategy is a commitment to undertake one set of actions rather than another and this commitment necessarily describes allocation of resources.
>
> (Sharon Oster in 1999)[32]

> Strategy is an overall plan for deploying resources to establish a favorable position vis-à-vis competitors.
>
> (Robert Grant in 2002)[33]

A strategy is an integrated and coordinated set of commitments and actions designed to exploit core competences and gain a competitive advantage.

(Hitt, Ireland and Hoskisson, 2007)[34]

Mintzberg's classification of strategies using his 5Ps captured this diversity of definitions. He argued that strategy can be a:

Plan—"some sort of *consciously intended* course of action, a guideline (or set of guidelines) to deal with a situation."[35]

Ploy—"specific 'maneuver' intended to outwit an opponent or competitor."[36]

Pattern—"specifically, a pattern in a stream of actions . . . consistency in behavior, *whether or not* intended."[37]

Position—"a means of locating an organization in its 'environment' . . . usually identified with competitors."[38]

Perspective—"the ingrained way of perceiving the world."[39]

More lately, Professors Hambrick and Frederickson have argued that a firm's mission drives its objectives, which drive its strategy.[40] This strategy has five elements:

Arenas: Where will the firm be active?

Vehicles: How will the firm get there?

Staging: What will be the firm's speed and sequence of the moves to get there?

Differentiators: How will the firm set itself apart so as to win?

Economic logic: How will the firm generate returns on its investment?

Whatever the definition of strategy, the bottom line is that firms have to make money if they are going to stay in business for long—they have to create economic value; and revenues come from customers who pay for what they perceive as valuable to them. If these customers are to keep going to a firm rather than to its competitors, the firm must offer these customers unique benefits that competitors do not. The firm has to create unique value for these customers—value that is difficult for competitors to replicate, leapfrog, or substitute. However, creating value—even unique value—does not always mean that one can appropriate it. Thus, a firm should also be well positioned—vis-à-vis its coopetitors—to appropriate the value that it creates. Effectively, then, winning or making money in business is about creating and appropriating value; and since strategy is about winning, we can define business strategy as the set of activities that a firm performs to create and appropriate value.

Flow of the Book

This book is about value creation and appropriation, and the underpinning activities and resources/capabilities in the face of new games. It is about strategic innovation. Thus all the chapters of the book are about some element of activities, value, appropriation, and change. The book is divided into four parts (Figure 1.4). Part I is made up of Chapters 1, 2, and 3. Chapter 1 is the

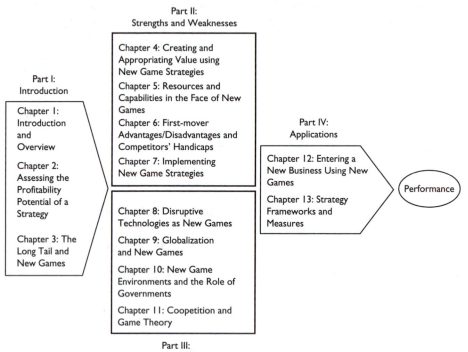

Figure 1.4 Flow of the Book.

introduction to new game strategies and an overview of the book. Chapter 2 explores the AVAC framework for analyzing the profitability potential of not only strategies but also of brands, technologies, business units, etc. Only such a detailed analysis can help managers understand why their firms are not performing well and what they could do to improve that performance. Chapter 3 is about the long-tail phenomenon—an example of the sources and opportunities for new game strategies.

Part II is about a firm's strengths and weaknesses in the face of a new game—about a firm's activities and underpinning resources/capabilities as well as the value that it creates and appropriates. It follows from the first three characteristics of new games. It is about the concepts, frameworks, and analytics that underpin the exploitation of the characteristics of new games to gain and/or prolong a competitive advantage. Recall that, in the face of a new game, a firm can take advantage of the characteristics of new games. It can:

- Take advantage of the new ways of creating and capturing new value generated by a new game.
- Take advantage of the opportunities to build new resources/capabilities and/or translate existing ones in new ways into value generated by new game.
- Take advantage of the potential to build and exploit first-mover advantages.
- Anticipate and respond to the likely reactions of coopetitors.

- Identify and exploit the opportunities and threats from the industry, macro, or global environment.

Since strategy is about creating and appropriating value, taking advantage of the new ways of creating and capturing value generated by a new game is critical to profiting from a new game. Thus, Chapter 4 is about value creation and appropriation in the face of new games; and since resources/capabilities are a cornerstone of value creation and appropriation, taking advantage of the opportunity to build new resources/capabilities and/or translate existing ones in new ways into value can play a significant role during new games. Thus, in Chapter 5, we explore the role of resources and capabilities in the face of new game strategies. Since a firm can build and exploit first-mover advantages to attain or solidify its competitive advantage, we explore first-mover advantages and *dis*advantages as well as competitors' handicaps in Chapter 6. Since a strategy is often only as good as its implementation, we dedicate Chapter 7 to the implementation of new game strategies; we explore more about resources/capabilities, this time focusing on implementation resources/capabilities—those resources and capabilities that are used to execute a strategy.

Part III is about the opportunities and threats that a firm faces when it pursues a new game strategy, and follows from the last two characteristics of new games—the fact that (1) new games attract reactions from new and existing competitors, and (2) have their roots in the opportunities and threats of a firm's environments. Disruptive technologies are a very good example of opportunities or threats from new games. Thus, we start Part III with an exposition of disruptive technologies in Chapter 8. In particular, we explore how one can use the concept of disruptive technologies to detect opportunities and threats from new games. This is followed by an exploration of globalization through new games and value appropriation by global players in Chapter 9. In Chapter 10, we briefly explore the environments in which new games take place. In particular, we explore which environments are conducive to new game activities and the role that governments can play in shaping such environments. We conclude Part III by exploring how and why a firm should take the likely reaction of coopetitors into consideration when it takes a decision. Although game theory is not the theory of strategy, it can be very useful in exploring how a firm can take the likely reaction of its coopetitors into consideration when making its decisions. In Chapter 11, we summarize the relevant cooperative and non-cooperative game theory, and start applying it to coopetition and competition in the face of new games.

In Part IV, we explore the application of the concepts and tools of Parts II and III to strategy and business model questions. Chapter 12 is about entering a new business using new games. For entrepreneurs or any new entrant, the chapter suggests that a firm is much better off entering a new business using new games rather than trying to beat incumbents at their game. Although strategy literature usually does not encourage entering unrelated businesses, using new games to enter new businesses can reduce some of the pitfalls of entering unrelated businesses. Chapter 13 presents a summary of key strategy frameworks. This is a good and popular reference for students, professors, and managers alike.

Part V consists of twelve cases of firms and products in game-changing situations. These include New World wine makers, Sephora, Netflix, Threadless,

Pixar, Lipitor, New Belgium Brewery, Botox, IKEA, Esperion, Xbox 360, and the Nintendo Wii. These cases are meant to illustrate the concepts of the book.

More chapters, cases, and potential additions to the book can be found at acateh.com:

Key Takeaways

- Strategy is about winning. It is about creating value and putting a firm in a position to appropriate the value. It is about not only creating benefits for customers but also putting a firm in a position, vis-à-vis coopetitors, to profit from the value created.
- A *new game strategy* is a set of activities that creates and/or captures value in new ways. New game strategies often overturn the way value has been created and/or appropriated—they often redefine the rules of the game. New game strategies are an excellent way to create and appropriate value. They can be very profitable if well pursued.
- A firm *creates value* when it offers customers something that they perceive as valuable (beneficial) to them and the benefits that these customers perceive exceed the cost of providing them. The *value appropriated* (captured) is the profit that a firm receives from the value it created.
- New games go beyond product innovation; they are often about delivering existing products to customers in new ways, *or* better positioning a firm to capture existing value.
- First movers, in defining new rules of the game, often make money; but so do followers. The important thing is to pursue the right new game strategy.
- Firms often must cooperate to create value and compete to appropriate it.
- The cornerstones of new game strategies are new game *activities*. A *new game activity* is a *new* value chain activity or an existing activity that is performed *differently* from the way existing industry value chain activities have been performed to create and/or appropriate value. Because a set can have only one member, a new game *activity* can be a new game *strategy*.
- New game activities are of interest not only because they are the cornerstones of new game strategies, but also because many strategy decisions are taken one action at a time.
- When a firm performs activities, it can (1) produce a product with benefits that customers value, (2) better position itself vis-à-vis its coopetitors, or (3) do both.
- To profit fully from the product, the firm must price it well, seek relevant sources of revenue, seek out customers for the product, and position it in product spaces with little competition.
- To profit from the better position vis-à-vis coopetitors, a firm must exploit the position to capture the value that it has created, or capture the value that its coopetitors have created.
- When firms perform new value chain activities or perform existing activities differently, they are effectively playing *new games*. New games posses the following characteristics. They:

○ Generate new ways of creating and capturing new value.
○ Offer opportunities to build new resources/capabilities and/or translate existing ones in new ways into value.
○ Create the potential to build and exploit first-mover advantages and *dis*advantages.
○ Potentially attract reactions from new and existing competitors.
○ Often have their roots in the opportunities and threats of a firm's environments.

- A firm that uses new games to offer unique value to customers and uniquely position itself to appropriate the value, can use first-mover advantages to solidify its advantage in value creation and appropriation. The firm can further solidify the advantage by anticipating and responding appropriately to coopetitors' likely reactions, and identifying and taking advantage of the opportunities and threats of its environment.
- A new game usually does not take place in isolation. It is usually preceded, followed or played in parallel with other games.
- Strategic management has been evolving. And so has the definition of strategy from one that had more to do with long-term plans, objectives, and allocation of resources to one that is now more about creating and appropriating value.
- New games can be grouped by their new gameness. In particular, they can be grouped by the extent to which they impact two determinants of competitive advantage: (1) *product-market position (PMP)* and (2) *distinctive difficult-to-imitate resources/capabilities*. Such a grouping results in four types of new games—*regular, resource-building, position-building*, and *revolutionary*—with the *regular* new game being the least new game, and *revolutionary* being the most new game.
- Regular new games are about making improvements and refinements to both existing resources/capabilities and product-market positions. They are the least new game of the four types. Capabilities needed are the same as existing ones or build on them. The resulting product or position allows existing products to still be competitive in the market.
- In resource-building games existing products or positions remain competitive but the resources/capabilities needed are radically different from existing ones. Changes in the rules of the game are largely resource/capabilities-related.
- In position-building games, the resources/capabilities needed are existing ones or build on them but the new product-market positions are radically different. Changes in the rules of the game are largely PMP-related.
- In revolutionary games, the resources/capabilities needed and the product-market-positions pursued are radically different from existing ones. They are the most new game of the four new game strategies. Changes in the rules of the game are both PMP and resource/capabilities-related.

Key Terms

Activities
Appropriability

Change
Competitive advantage
Coopetitors
Handicaps
New game activities
New game strategies
Position vis-à-vis coopetitors
Position-building new game
Regular new game
Resource-building new game
Revolutionary new game
Strategic innovation
Strategy
Value
Value appropriation
Value creation

Chapter 2

Assessing the Profitability Potential of a Strategy

Reading this chapter should provide you with the conceptual and analytical tools to:

- Go beneath a firm's financial performance to understand the profitability potential of the firm's strategy.
- Use the Activities, Value, Appropriability, and Change (AVAC) framework to explore the profitability potential of products, resources, brands, business units, etc.
- Question the use of P/E financial ratios to determine whether or not a stock is overvalued.

Introduction

How can a firm or an investor tell if one strategy is better than others? Since business strategies are usually about performance, a trivial answer to this question is to compare the profitability of each business and the one with the highest profitability is judged to have the best strategy. But suppose one of the businesses is a startup that is not yet profitable but has the potential to be profitable in the future. Better still, suppose one wants to find out what can be done to improve the profitability of a strategy. Only a detailed analysis of the underpinnings of profitability can unearth any hidden potential or faults that a strategy might have. Even better still, if an investor wants to invest in a startup that does not have a long history of steady earnings, profitability numbers are not likely to tell a good enough story. Existing frameworks such as the Balanced Scorecard, Porter's Five Forces, Growth/Share matrix, SWOT analysis, the 7Cs, and other frameworks are useful in exploring different aspects of firm profitability. However, they are not integrative enough and therefore leave out important determinants of profitability potential.

In this chapter we explore a framework for assessing not only why a firm is performing well or not so well, but also for assessing the profitability potential of a strategy or business model, and strategic actions. Called the AVAC framework, it is predicated on the argument that strategy is about value creation and appropriation.[1] A related framework, called the 7Cs, also adequately explores why a firm is performing well or not so well but the AVAC is better for exploring new game strategies. The AVAC framework is about understanding how a firm creates value and positions itself to appropriate the value, and about what else it could do to perform even better. It can therefore be used not only to analyze the profitability potential of a firm's strategy but also to analyze the profitability potential of business models, business units, products, technologies, brands, market segments, acquisitions, investment opportunities, partnerships such as alliances, different departments such as an R&D group, and corporate strategies, and make recommendations as to what needs to be done to improve the profitability potential of the target. We start the chapter by briefly exploring two financial measures that are sometimes used to estimate the profitability potential of strategies. We will then lay out the key elements of the AVAC framework, and follow that with an example to illustrate the use of the model.

Financial Measures

Financial measures are sometimes used to measure the extent to which one strategy is better than another. We consider two of them: historical earnings and market value.

Historical Earnings

A firm's historical earnings are sometimes used to measure the profitability potential of the firm's strategy. Actual earnings-before-interest-depreciation-and-tax (EBIDT), net income, income per sales, etc. over a period are used to predict future earnings and therefore the effectiveness of a strategy. These estimates provide some idea of how profitable a firm's strategy has been and might be in the future. This approach has many shortcomings. First, it assumes that historical earnings are a predictor of future earnings. Such an assumption undermines the fact that a firm's strategy might change, competitors might change their own strategies, or the environment in which the firm operates might change. Earnings are not always a good predictor of future earnings, let alone a good indicator of the profitability potential of a strategy. Second, earnings say nothing about the scale, difficulty, and shortcomings of activities that were performed to earn the profits and that might have to be performed to earn future income. They say nothing about what is being done in the trenches to create and appropriate value; that is, there is little about the cornerstones of profits—the resources and activities that go into creating and appropriating value.

Market Value

Another measure of a firm's strategy's profitability potential is the firm's market value. Recall that the value of a stock or business is determined by the cash inflows and outflows—discounted at the appropriate interest rate—that can be expected to accrue from the stock or business. Thus, since strategy drives profits and cash flows, a firm's market value can be used to estimate the profitability potential of the underpinning strategy. The value of a business or firm is the present value of its future free cash flows discounted at its cost of capital, and is given by:[2]

$$V = C_0 + \frac{C_1}{(1 + r_k)} + \frac{C_2}{(1 + r_k)^2} + \frac{C_3}{(1 + r_k)^3} + \cdots \frac{C_n}{(1 + r_k)^n}$$

$$= \sum_{t=0}^{t=n} \frac{C_t}{(1 + r_k)^t} \tag{1}$$

where C_t is the **free cash** flow at time t. This is the cash from operations that is available for distribution to claimholders—equity investors and debtors—who provide capital. It is the difference between cash earnings and cash investments; r_k is the firm's *discount rate*.

An important assumption in using a firm's market value as a measure of its strategy's profitability potential is that the future cash flows from the strategy can be forecasted. The problem with this assumption is that forecasting future cash flows accurately is extremely difficult. To determine the market value at time t, for example, we need to estimate the cash flows for all the years beyond t (see equation (1)). This can be difficult when $t > 5$. However, equation (1) can be further simplified by assuming that the free cash flows generated by the firm being valued will reach a constant amount (an annuity) of C_f, after n years. Doing so, equation (1) reduces to:

$$V = \frac{C_f}{r_k (1 + r_k)^n} \tag{2}$$

If we further assume that the constant free cash flows start in the present year, then $n = 0$, and equation (2) reduces to:

$$V = \frac{C_f}{r_k} \tag{3}$$

Another way to simplify equation (1) is to assume that today's free cash flows, C_0, which we know, will grow at a constant rate g forever. If we do so, equation (1) reduces to:

$$V = \frac{C_0}{r_k - g} \tag{4}$$

Equations (2), (3), and (4) have an advantage over equation (1) in that only one cash flow value has to be estimated rather than many difficult-to-forecast values. However, there may be more room to make mistakes when one depends on only one value.

Example

On March 15, 2000, Cisco's market valuation was $453.88 billion. Its profits in 1999 were $2.10 billion.[3] Was Cisco overvalued? We can explore this question using equations (2), (3), or (4). From equation (3):

$$453.88 = \frac{C_f}{r_k}$$

From whence, $C_f = \$453.88 \times r_k$ billion; that is, the free cash flows that Cisco would have to generate every year, forever, to justify its $453.88 billion valuation are $C_f = \$453.88 \times r_k$ billion. If we assume a discount rate of 15%, then Cisco would have to generate $68.8 (that is, $453.88 × 15) billion in free cash flows every year to infinity. Since free cash flows are usually less than profits after tax, Cisco would have to make annual *profits* of more than $68 billion to justify this valuation. Its profits in 1999 were $2 billion. How can any company generate after-tax profits of more than $68 billion a year, forever? In particular, what is it about Cisco's business model, its industry and competitors that would make one believe that the company could quickly ramp its profits from $2 billion to more than $68 billion and maintain that advantage forever? Only a detailed analysis of the company's underpinning strategy can help us understand what it is about a company such as Cisco that would make it possible for the firm to earn this much cash.

Beneath the Numbers

The AVAC analysis goes beyond profitability or market value numbers and digs deeper into what drives the numbers; so do some previous strategy frameworks; but, as we will see later, AVAC does more. A. Porter's Five Forces framework, for example, was designed to analyze the average profitability of industries but has been used to evaluate the extent to which a firm's strategy dampens or reinforces the competitive forces that impinge on a firm and its profitability. However, the Five Forces framework leaves out important aspects of value creation and appropriation that can be critical to the profitability of a strategy. It neglects the role of (1) change (the new game factor), (2) resources/capabilities/competences (including complementary assets), (3) industry value drivers, (4) pricing, (5) the number and quality of customers, and (6) market segments and sources of revenue. In the Balanced Scorecard, a firm is viewed from four perspectives in developing metrics, collecting and analyzing data: learning and growth, internal business processes, customer, and financial.[4] The Scorecard incorporates some aspects of value creation such as learning but falls short of incorporating appropriation activities. It also has little or nothing about the macro and competitive forces that impact a firm as it creates value and positions itself to appropriate value. The 7Cs framework goes beneath profitability numbers and explores why some strategies are more profitable than others.[5] However, it does not adequately get into what can be done to improve the profitability of a new game strategy. The player-type framework that we will see in Chapter 6 is good when a top-level manager wants to cut through lots of detailed information and get a feel for where his or her firm stands as far as being a superstar, adventurer, exploiter, or me-too; but it does not dig deep into the activities that a firm performs to create and appropriate value. Popular strategy frameworks such as the Growth/Share matrix and SWOT analysis do not explicitly evaluate the profitability of a strategy. The AVAC framework overcomes these shortcomings.

The AVAC Framework

The AVAC framework gets its name from the first letter of each of its four components (Activities, Value, Appropriability, and Change). These components are displayed in Figure 2.1.[6]

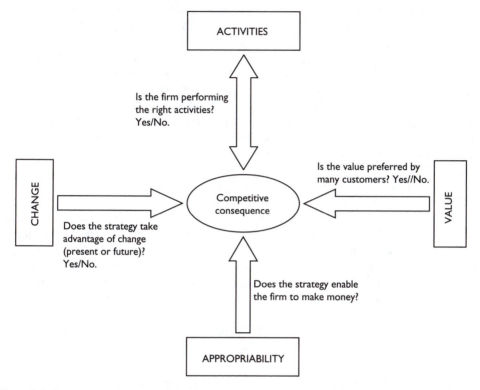

Figure 2.1 Components of an AVAC Analysis.

Brief Logic of the Framework

Before describing the components of the framework in detail, let us briefly explore the rationale behind them. The framework has its roots in the definition of strategy. Since we have defined a firm's strategy as the set of activities that it performs to create and appropriate value, we can assess a strategy by examining how and the extent to which these activities contribute to value creation and appropriation. Since not all activities contribute equally to value creation, the types of activity *which* a firm chooses to perform, *when* it chooses to perform them, *where* it performs them, and *how* it performs them are important—that is, a firm has to choose the right set of activities to perform to increase its chances of creating the most value possible and capturing as much value from its value system as possible. Thus, the **Activities** component of the AVAC framework is about determining whether the right set of activities has been chosen. For a firm to keep making money from the *value* that it has created, there must be something about the value that makes customers prefer to buy from the firm rather than from its competitors—the value should be unique.

Hence the *Value* component, which is about whether the activities, collectively, contribute enough to value creation for customers to prefer the perceived benefits in the value as better than those from competitors. Since not even unique value can always guarantee profits, it is also important that the firm translates the value into money—that the firm finds a way to appropriate the value. The firm should be positioned well enough vis-à-vis its coopetitors to make sure that the coopetitors do not capture the value that it has created. In fact, if it positions itself well, it can capture not only the value that it has created but also the value created by its coopetitors. Hence the *Appropriability* component, which is about whether the activities performed are such that the firm makes money. Finally, a firm will continue to create and capture value using the same activities and underpinning resources only if there is no major change, or when there is change, the change reinforces what the firm is doing, or the firm can react well to it. Hence the *Change* component that is behind the question: does or will the firm take advantage of change in value creation and appropriation?

Effectively, the activities component of the analysis tells us which activities make up the strategy, what and how each activity contributes to value creation and appropriation, and where or when the contribution is made. The value component explores the extent to which the contributions made by the activities are unique enough for customers to prefer the firm's products to competitors' products. The appropriability component explores whether the contributions made by the activities are large enough to put the firm in a superior position vis-à-vis its coopetitors and for the firm to profit from the position and the value created. The change component is about whether the firm is doing what it can to exploit existing change or future change. We now explore each of these components in detail (Figure 2.2).

Activities (Is the Firm Performing the Right Activities?)

The activities *which* a firm performs, *when* it performs them, *where* it performs them, and *how* it performs them determine the extent to which the firm creates and appropriates value and the level of competitive advantage that it can have. Therefore the central question for this component is whether the firm is performing the activities which it should be performing, when it should be performing, where it should be performing, and how it should be performing them to give it a competitive advantage? We answer this question indirectly by exploring whether or not *each activity contributes* to value creation and appropriation. In Chapter 1, we saw that when a firm performs an activity, the activity can contribute to lowering the cost of its products, differentiating the product, moving its price towards the reservation price of customers, increasing the number of customers, or finding profitable sources of revenue. We also saw that an activity can also contribute to improving the firm's position vis-à-vis its coopetitors by, for example, dampening or reversing repressive competitive forces while reinforcing favorable ones, or improving relationships from adversarial to friendly. Thus, two questions that can give us a good idea of whether a firm is performing the right activity are, if the activity contributes, (1) to low cost, differentiation, better pricing, reaching more customers, and better sources of revenues, and

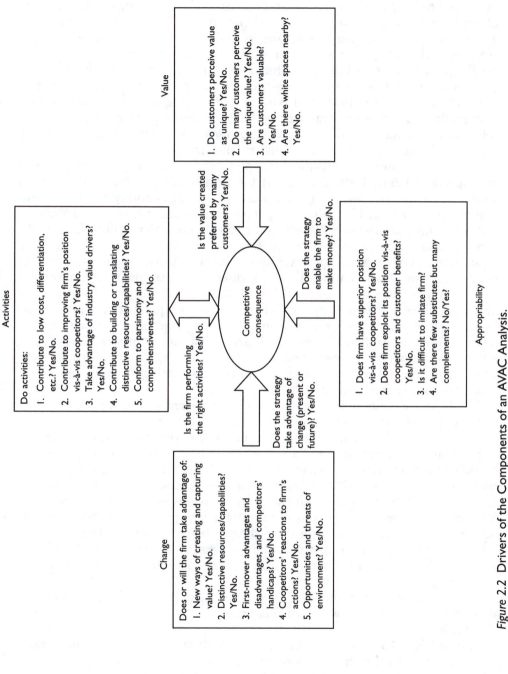

Activities

Do activities:

1. Contribute to low cost, differentiation, etc.? Yes/No.
2. Contribute to improving firm's position vis-à-vis coopetitors? Yes/No.
3. Take advantage of industry value drivers? Yes/No.
4. Contribute to building or translating distinctive resources/capabilities? Yes/No.
5. Conform to parsimony and comprehensiveness? Yes/No.

Value

1. Do customers perceive value as unique? Yes/No.
2. Do many customers perceive the unique value? Yes/No.
3. Are customers valuable? Yes/No.
4. Are there white spaces nearby? Yes/No.

Is the firm performing the right activities? Yes/No.

Is the value created preferred by many customers? Yes/No.

Competitive consequence

Does the strategy take advantage of change (present or future)? Yes/No.

Does the strategy enable the firm to make money? Yes/No.

Change

Does or will the firm take advantage of:

1. New ways of creating and capturing value? Yes/No.
2. Distinctive resources/capabilities? Yes/No.
3. First-mover advantages and disadvantages, and competitors' handicaps? Yes/No.
4. Coopetitors' reactions to firm's actions? Yes/No.
5. Opportunities and threats of environment? Yes/No.

Appropriability

1. Does firm have superior position vis-à-vis coopetitors? Yes/No.
2. Does firm exploit its position vis-à-vis coopetitors and customer benefits? Yes/No.
3. Is it difficult to imitate firm?
4. Are there few substitutes but many complements? No/Yes?

Figure 2.2 Drivers of the Components of an AVAC Analysis.

(2) to improving the firm's position vis-à-vis coopetitors—for example, dampening repressive competitive and macroenvironmental forces while reinforcing friendly ones.

However, in each industry, there are usually some industry-specific factors that stand to have a substantial impact on cost, differentiation, or other drivers of profitability such as the number of customers. Thus, activities that take advantage of these *industry value drivers* make a larger contribution to value creation and appropriation than those that do not. For example, in offline retailing, location is an industry value driver since it determines the type and number of customers who can shop there, the cost of operations, the cost of retail space, and the number and types of competitor, and so on. A firm that chooses the right location is taking advantage of industry value drivers. Thus, a third important question that helps us determine if an activity is the right one is if the activity takes advantage of industry value drivers.

Moreover, resources and capabilities play two crucial roles in creating and appropriating value. First, they are at the root of all activities and can be a source of competitive advantage. For example, Toyota's ability to develop and manufacture dependable cars, using its lean manufacturing processes, is a scarce resource/capability that enables it to create value that is difficult to replicate. Second, resources act as differentiators. For example, a firm's brand or reputation can be the reason why customers buy the firm's products rather than competitors' products. Thus, a firm's activities can contribute to value creation and appropriation when they contribute either to building valuable resources and capabilities, or to translating existing ones into unique customer benefits, to better position a firm vis-à-vis its coopetitors, or to translate customer benefits and position into profits. Therefore, a fourth question the answer to which can tell us if an activity is the right one is—does the activity contribute to building new distinctive resources/capabilities, or to translating existing ones into unique positions and profits?

Finally, in choosing how many activities to perform, a firm is guided by two rather opposing forces. On the one hand, a firm does not want to leave out some activity that could have made a significant contribution to value creation and appropriation. It wants its set of activities to be as *comprehensive* as possible—to include as many relevant activities as possible. On the other hand, having too many activities, especially low value-adding activities, can be costly. A firm wants to be *parsimonious*—perform as few activities as possible without leaving out key activities. Thus, a firm not only has to perform the right *types* of activities, it also has to perform the right *number* of activities. Therefore, the final question that a firm ought to ask in assessing its strategy is—is it performing superfluous activities, or are there some activities that it should be performing?

Effectively, analyzing the Activities component of an AVAC consists of determining the extent to which *each activity*:[7]

1 Contributes to low cost, differentiation, better pricing, reaching more customers, and better sources of revenues.
2 Contributes to improving its position vis-à-vis coopetitors.
3 Takes advantage of industry value drivers.
4 Contributes to building new distinctive resources/capabilities or translating

existing ones into unique positions and profits (including complementary assets).

5 Fits the comprehensiveness and parsimony criteria.

We now explore all five questions.

Contribute to Low Cost, Differentiation, or other Drivers of Profitability?

The idea is to determine whether each activity *which* a firm performs, *when* it performs it, *how* it performs it, and *where* it performs it contributes towards lowering its cost, differentiating its products, increasing the number of its customers, improving its pricing, or better identifying and serving profitable sources of revenues. If the activity does, the answer to the question is Yes. If it does not, the answer is No. For example, when a luxury goods maker advertises to the affluent, the activity may be contributing to differentiating its products, and therefore contributing to value creation. Thus the answer to this question would be Yes. If a firm obtains a second source for a critical input, it may be able to extract lower prices from its suppliers, thereby lowering its cost, and contributing to the value that it creates and appropriates. Activities that contribute to increasing the number of customers that buy a product, getting the price right, and pursuing the right sources of revenue also make a contribution to the revenue earned.

Contribute to Improving a Firm's Position vis-à-vis Coopetitors?

An activity contributes to improving a firm's position vis-à-vis its coopetitors if it improves the extent to which coopetitors need the firm more than it needs them. For example, if a firm convinces its suppliers of a key component to have second sources for the component, the firm now needs the supplier less and this increases the firm's position vis-à-vis the supplier. A classic example of a firm improving its position vis-à-vis coopetitors is that of Wal-Mart. When the company started out, it had very little influence over major suppliers such as Procter & Gamble, who dictated the terms of exchange. As Wal-Mart scaled up its activities by saturating contiguous small towns with discount stores and building appropriate distribution centers, using information technology extensively, and establishing the Wal-Mart culture, it chipped away at the balance of who needed whom more. The firm would grow to become the world's largest retailer at some point. Many of Wal-Mart's activities were new game activities in the retail industry at the time and helped the company to reverse the balance of who needed whom more in Wal-Mart's favor.

When we talk of improving a firm's position, it does not necessarily mean that the firm is starting from a bad situation. A firm can already be in a good position and perform an activity that improves the situation, putting it in an even better position vis-à-vis its coopetitors. For example, if industry firms are in a superior position vis-à-vis buyers and one of the firms buys some of its competitors, it improves its position vis-à-vis buyers since there are now fewer firms. This is likely to increase the amount of value that the firm appropriates.

Take Advantage of Industry Value Drivers?

The next question is, whether, in performing an activity, a firm has taken advantage of industry value drivers. A firm takes advantage of industry value drivers if the activity exploits an industry-specific factor to reduce cost, further differentiate its products, or improve other profit drivers such as the number of its customers. Answering this question entails listing the industry value drivers in the industry and identifying which activities take advantage of them. The answer to the question is Yes, if the firm's activities take advantage of the industry value drivers identified.

Contribute to Building New Distinctive Resources/Capabilities or Translating Existing Ones into Unique Value?

Each activity that a firm performs exploits some of its resources and capabilities, or contributes to building new resources/capabilities. Thus, one of the questions that a firm should ask about each activity that it performs is whether the activity contributes to exploiting its existing resources/capabilities better, or to building distinctive resources/capabilities (new or old). By identifying the resources/capabilities that are valuable to a firm, one can determine which of them are being exploited by existing activities or are being built by these activities.

Are Comprehensive and Parsimonious?

Whereas the other questions are about each individual activity, the comprehensiveness and parsimony question is about the whole set of activities that constitutes the firm's strategy. After laying out the set of activities, a firm should carefully explore what other activities it should be performing, that it is not presently performing. It should also think about dropping some of the activities that make the least contribution towards value creation and appropriation. If there are no activities that it should be performing, or that it should drop, the answer is Yes, since the strategy is comprehensive and parsimonious.

Effectively, the Activities component of the AVAC analysis starts out by identifying all the key activities that make up the strategy. Then, for each question, see if any of the identified activities make the contribution called for in the question. If the answer to a question is a No, the firm may need to take another look at the particular factor and find ways to reverse things. When the answer is a Yes, there is still always room for improvement. For example, if the answer is Yes, the firm still has to think of ways to reinforce the Yes. Note that where there are multiple answers to a question, it only takes one positive for the question to get a Yes. Take Question 1, for example. If an activity contributes to low costs but does not contribute to differentiation, etc., Question 1 still gets a Yes. However, the analyst now knows that something could be done to improve differentiation, increase number of customers, etc. One of the most useful applications of an AVAC analysis is in identifying possible areas for improvement; and these areas of improvement come out clearly when a question scores a No.

Value (Is the Value Created by the Strategy Preferred by Many Customers? Yes/No)

The *Activities* component tells us whether or not each activity contributes to value creation, but it does not tell us whether the contributions are enough to make a difference with customers. It does not tell us if the contributions of all the activities, when added together, are unique enough to make customers prefer the firm's products to competitors' products. The *Values* component allows one to explore whether the set of activities that is a firm's strategy creates value that is unique enough for customers to prefer it to competing value. If customers are going to keep buying from a firm, its strategy needs to create benefits that they perceive as being unique compared to competitors' offerings. Thus, the first question in the Value component is whether the value created is unique enough, as perceived by customers, for them to prefer it to competing value. Since the number of customers that perceive value as unique is also important, the next question is, do many customers perceive the value as unique? The more customers that perceive the benefits created, the higher the revenue potential is likely to be and the better the chances of having economies of scale and of reducing the per unit costs; also, the more valuable a customer, the better the profitability potential of the firm is likely to be in selling to the customer. A customer is valuable if it has a high willingness to pay, represents a decent share of revenues, and does not cost much (relative to the revenues from the customer) to acquire and maintain. Finally, nearby white spaces into which a firm can easily move, can also increase the profitability potential of a firm. A white space is a market segment that is not being served—it has potential customers.

Effectively, an analysis of the Value component is about determining the extent to which a firm's strategy results in differentiated or low-cost products that are targeted at many valuable customers. Such an analysis is done by answering the following simple questions with a Yes or No (Figure 2.2):

1 Do customers perceive the value created by the strategy as unique?
2 Do many customers perceive this value?
3 Are these customers valuable?
4 Are there any nearby white spaces?

If the answer to the first three questions is Yes, the strategy is OK as far as the Value component is concerned. The firm can then work on reinforcing the Yesses. If any of the answers are No, the firm may need to take another look at its strategy by asking the following questions: how can the value be improved? How can the firm gain new valuable customers or enter new market segments? If the answer to the fourth question is Yes, the firm may want to explore the possibilities of getting into the white space. Finally, any opportunities and threats to value, such as shifts in customer tastes or demographics, or a technological change that can influence expected customer benefits, are also examined.

Appropriability

The *Activities* component tells us whether the activities which a firm performs contribute to better positioning it vis-à-vis its coopetitors, but it does not tell us if the contributions are enough to put the firm in a superior position relative to its coopetitors. Neither does it tell us if a firm that has a superior position vis-à-vis coopetitors exploits that position by, for example, setting its prices as close as possible to the reservation prices of customers, or obtaining other concessions from customers. The *Apropriability* component tells us whether a firm has a superior position vis-à-vis coopetitors, and whether the firm translates the customer benefits created and its position vis-à-vis coopetitors into money. The analysis consists of asking whether:

1 The firm has a superior position vis-à-vis its coopetitors.
2 The firm exploits its position vis-à-vis its coopetitors and customer benefits.
3 It is difficult to imitate the firm.
4 There are few viable substitutes but many complements.

Does the Firm Have a Superior Position vis-à-vis Coopetitors?

A firm has a superior position vis-à-vis its coopetitors if it needs the coopetitors less than they need it. Two factors determine whether a firm needs a coopetitor more, or vice versa: industry factors, and firm-specific factors. Take a firm and its suppliers, for example. Suppliers need a firm more than the firm needs them, if there are more suppliers than there are firms; that is because there are more suppliers competing for the firm's business. Effectively, the concentration of both the coopetitor's and firm's industries matter. Firm-specific factors are those things about firms that differ from one firm to the other, even within the same industry, and that often distinguish one firm from others. A firm's valuable, scarce, difficult-to-imitate resources, such as its brand, are firm-specific factors. Such distinctive factors increase the likelihood of a firm being better positioned vis-à-vis coopetitors. For example, Coke's brand pulls customers into stores and that pull makes even large firms such as Wal-Mart carry Coke drinks even though there are many competing drinks. Coke's brand makes Wal-Mart need Coke more than they would have without the brand.

Effectively, one can determine if a firm has a superior position vis-à-vis its coopetitors by determining if the firm needs the coopetitor more, or the other way around. The firm has a superior position vis-à-vis its coopetitors if the firm needs them less.

Does the Firm Exploit its Position vis-à-vis Coopetitors, and Profit from Customer Benefits?

The next question is whether a firm exploits its position vis-à-vis coopetitors and whether it profits from the benefits that customers perceive in the firm's products. The value that a firm captures is a function of how well it exploits its position. For example, if a firm has a superior position vis-à-vis its suppliers, it can extract lower input prices from them, thereby lowering its costs and increasing the value that it captures. (Recall that value captured equals price paid by customers less the cost of providing the customer with the product.) If a firm has a superior position vis-à-vis its complementors, it can more easily convince them to sell complements at lower prices, which will increase its own sales. It effectively captures some of the value created by complementors. For example,

Microsoft is very powerful in the PC world and therefore, compared to PC makers, appropriates a lot of the value created. A firm's appropriation of value created also depends on its position vis-à-vis coopetitors' customers. If customers have a superior position, they are likely to extract low prices from the firm, diminishing its share of the pie (share of the value created that it appropriates).

The value that a firm captures is also a very strong function of the firm's pricing strategy. Developing low-cost or differentiated products is great; but the products must be priced carefully so as not to drive customers away or leave money on the table. The closer that a firm can set its prices to each customer's reservation price without driving customers away, the more money that a firm is likely to make. Recall that a customer's reservation price for a product is the maximum price that the customer is willing to pay for the product. If the price is higher than the reservation price, the customer may be lost. If the price is below the customer's reservation price, the customer pockets the difference as consumer surplus. Back to the question, does the firm exploit its position vis-à-vis coopetitors, and profit from customer benefits? The answer is Yes, if either the firm sets its prices as close as possible to the reservation prices of customers, or if it exercises its superior position in some other way.

Is it Difficult to Imitate the Firm?

If the value that a firm creates can be easily imitated, it will be difficult for the firm to make money. Thus, an important question for a firm that creates value is whether it is easy for existing rivals and potential competitors to imitate or leapfrog the firm's set of activities. Two factors determine the extent to which a firm's activities can be imitated. First, it depends on the firm and its set of activities. A firm can reduce imitability of its activities or resources/capabilities, for example, by acquiring and defending any intellectual property that underpins such activities or resources. It can also establish a history of retaliating against any firms that attempt to imitate its activities by seeking legal action, lowering its prices, introducing competitive products, or making early product announcements. The complexity of the system of activities that a firm performs can also prevent competitors from imitating its set of activities. Imitating one activity may be easy; but imitating a system of activities is a lot more difficult since one has to imitate not only the many activities that form the system but also the interactions among the components. Resources and capabilities can also be difficult to imitate when they are protected by law, are rooted in a history that cannot be re-enacted, are scarce and cannot be recreated, or require a critical mass to be effective.

Second, whether a firm's set of activities can be imitated is also a function of the potential imitators. Sometimes, potential imitators are unable to imitate a firm not so much because of the firm and its system of activities and resources but because of the potential competitors' prior commitments and lack of what it takes to imitate. Prior commitments include union contracts, and agreements with suppliers, distributors, governments, shareholders, employers, or other stakeholders. When Ryanair started moving into secondary airports in Europe, it was difficult for established airlines such as Air France to abandon the major airports such as General de Gaulle in Paris for secondary airports if they wanted to replicate Ryanair's strategy. Performing activities requires resources and when such resources are scarce, a potential imitator might not be able to find the resources that it needs to compete. For example, a firm may want to start producing new cars but may not have what it takes to do so. Thus, in exploring appropriability, it is important to ask the following two questions: is there something about the firm and its set of activities and resources that makes it difficult for competitors to imitate its strategy? Is there something about competitors that impedes them from imitating the firm?

Are There Few Substitutes but Many Complements?

If a firm offers rare value that is difficult to imitate, it may still not be able to profit enough from the value if there are products that can act as substitutes for the value that customers derive from the firm's products. Thus, a firm may be better off understanding the extent to which substitutes can take away the firm's customers. Complements have the opposite effect (compared to substitutes) on a firm's products. Availability of complements tends to boost a product's sales. Thus, customers would perceive a firm's products as being more valuable if such a product required complements and there were many such complements available at good prices. For example, availability of software at low prices boosted the sale of PCs. Two important questions for a firm, then, are: is the value that it creates nonsubstitutable? Do complements (if relevant) play a good enough role to boost the benefits that customers perceive from the firm?

Change: The New Game Factor

Change can have a profound effect on a firm's ability to create and appropriate value. Change can originate from a firm's environment, or from its new game strategies. It can come from a firm's industry or macroenvironment. For example, government laws can raise or lower barriers to entry or exit, introduce price limits, put limitations on the type of cooperation that firms can have, or impose import quotas or tariffs, forcing them to change. Consumer tastes can change, and changes in demographics can alter the willingness to pay of a market segment. Technological change can result in new markets or industries, the disruption of existing ways of doing things, and the erosion of existing industries and competitive advantages. Witness the case of the Internet. In responding to these changes from their environments, firms often introduce change in the way they create and appropriate value.

Change is often initiated by entrepreneurs or firms, through new game activities. Firms invent new products that create new markets or new industries, and/or overturn the way value is created and appropriated in existing industries. Witness Intel's invention of the microprocessor and its revolution of computing, or Wal-Mart's reinnovation of discount retailing. Firms can also introduce change when they move into a new market or business, reposition themselves vis-à-vis coopetitors, develop a new product, or restructure their internal activities.

In any case, a firm has to deal with existing change and potential future changes. It has to create and appropriate value in the face of existing change but

must also anticipate and prepare for future changes. Without constantly anticipating and preparing for future change, a firm's existing competitive advantage
can easily be undermined by events such as disruptive technologies.

   The role of change and the extent to which a firm can take advantage of it are
analyzed in two parts: determination of strengths and handicaps, and the
exploration of some key change questions.

Determination of Strengths and Handicaps

As we will detail in Chapter 5, when a firm faces a new game, some of its pre-
new game strengths remain strengths while others become handicaps. These
strengths and handicaps play a key role in determining the extent to which the
firm can perform value chain activities to create and appropriate value, in the
face of the change. Strengths and handicaps can be resources (distribution
channels, shelf space, plants, equipment, manufacturing know-how, marketing
know-how, R&D skills, patents, cash, brand-name reputations, technological
know-how, client or supplier relationships, dominant managerial logic, routines, processes, culture, and so on), or product positions (low-cost, differentiation, or positioning vis-à-vis coopetitors). A classic example of a strength that
became a handicap is that of Compaq, which wanted to participate in the new
game created by Dell when the latter introduced the direct-sales and build-to-
order business model. Prior to this new game, Compaq's relationships with
distributors were a strength; but when the company decided to sell directly to
end-customers, bypassing distributors, the distributors would not let Compaq
dump them that easily. Compaq had to abandon its new business model. Effectively, Compaq's pre-new game strength had become a handicap in the face of
the new game. Of course, many pregame strengths, such as brands, usually
remain strengths in the face of a new game. Thus, the first step in a Change
analysis is to determine which of a firm's prechange strengths remain strengths
and which ones become handicaps in the face of the change. (In Chapter 5, we
will see how a firm can determine its strengths and handicaps in the face of a
new game.)

The Questions

Having determined a firm's strengths and handicaps, the next step is to determine how the firm can take or is taking advantage of the change by asking the
following questions: Given its strengths and handicaps in creating and
appropriating value in the face of the change, does or will the firm take advantage of:

1 The new ways of creating and capturing new value generated by the
   change?
2 The opportunities generated by change to build new resources or translate
   existing ones in new ways?
3 First mover's advantages and disadvantages, and competitors' handicaps
   that result from change?
4 Coopetitors' potential reactions to its actions?
5 Opportunities and threats of environment? Are there no better alternatives?

These factors are a direct outcome of the characteristics of new games that we explored in Chapter 1. Effectively, the change component is about the new game factors of activities.

Does the Firm Take Advantage of the New Ways of Creating and Capturing Value Generated by Change?

A firm takes advantage of new ways of creating and appropriating value generated by a change if, given the change and the firm's associated strengths and handicaps, it can still offer customers the benefits that they prefer, position itself well vis-à-vis coopetitors, and profit from the benefits and position. Identifying the new ways of creating and capturing value generated by change consists of picking those activities that are being performed differently—or should be performed differently—in the face of the change, and verifying that these new game activities have made (or will make) a significant contribution towards value creation and appropriation. The activities make a significant contribution if customers prefer the value from them, or the firm profits from them. Thus, the question here is, do the new game activities (1) create value that customers prefer over value from competitors, and (2) enable the firm to make money? If the answer to any of these questions is Yes, the answer to the question, does the firm take advantage of the new ways of creating and capturing value generated by change? is Yes.

Does the Firm Take Advantage of Opportunities Generated by Change to Build New Resources, or Translate Existing Ones in New Ways?

In the face of change, firms usually require both new and old resources to perform the new game activities. The first step towards seeing whether a firm has taken advantage of these resources, is to identify them. To identify them, construct the value chain, and pinpoint the activities that are being performed differently or should be performed differently as a result of the change. The relevant resources are those that are needed to perform the new activities. The next step is to answer the question, do the identified resources make a significant contribution towards (1) creating value that customers prefer over value from competitors, (2) enabling the firm to make money? If the answer to either question is Yes, then the firm takes advantage of the opportunities generated by change to build new resources, or translate existing ones in new ways.

Does the Firm Take Advantage of First-mover's Advantages and Disadvantages, and Competitors' Handicaps?

If a firm initiates change, or is the first to take advantage of change, it has an opportunity to build and take advantage of first-mover advantages. A first-mover advantage is a resource, capability, or product position that (1) a firm acquires by being the first to carry out an activity, and (2) gives the firm an advantage in creating and appropriating value. These include preemption of scarce resources such as gates and landing slots at an airport such as Heathrow's London Airport. The first step towards seeing whether a firm has taken advantage of first-mover advantages is to identify them. Chapter 6 contains a complete list of first-mover advantages. The next step is to establish whether the advantages make a significant contribution to the benefits that customers perceive, or to the profits that the firm makes.

First-mover *disadvantages* are those shortcomings that a firm has by being the first to pursue a particular activity. For example, a firm that moves first into a virgin market spends a great deal to establish the market. Followers that move into the established market are effectively free-riding on the investments that the first mover made to establish the market. A first mover would rather the follower did not get so much free. Interestingly, the cure to first-mover *dis*advantages can be better first-mover advantages. For example, by seeking intellectual property protection, a first mover can reduce the extent to which followers free-ride on its investments. Of course, if a firm is a following, it can take advantage of first-mover *dis*advantages. A firm can also take advantage of competitor's handicaps. Thus, the answer to this question is Yes, if a firm takes advantage of first-mover advantages and *dis*advantages, OR of competitors' handicaps in performing its activities.

Does the Firm Anticipate and Respond to Coopetitors' Reactions to its Actions?

A firm is better able to perform the activities that allow it to create and appropriate value in the face of change if the firm anticipates and responds to its coopetitor's actions and reactions to the change. To determine if a firm's strategy anticipates and responds to coopetitors' reactions, we list the activities that the firm performs as a result of the change and ask whether, for each of the key activities, the firm took the actions and reactions of the relevant coopetitor into consideration.

Identify and Take Advantage of Opportunities and Threats from the Macroenvironment? Are there no Better Alternatives?

In taking advantage of change, it is critical for a firm to identify and take advantage of opportunities and threats, beyond the change, from its environment. For example, most new pharmaceutical products in the USA need approval from the Food and Drug Administration (FDA) and therefore firms that pursue new game activities in pharmaceuticals are better off exploring how they can take advantage of the FDA's approval processes. For example, in developing Lipitor, Warner Lambert took advantage of an FDA law that gives fast-track reviews to drugs that treat special conditions. Doing so shortened the FDA approval of Lipitor by six months, saving the firm billions of dollars in revenues. Sometimes, the opportunities are complementary technologies that enhance the effectiveness of the new game. For example, Dell's direct sales and build-to-order model were more effective because Dell used the available technologies to reach customers directly. It started out using telephone banks to reach customers and when the Internet emerged, Dell used it.

The benefits of changes are often ended by other changes. For example, many innovations are usually displaced by so-called disruptive technologies. Thus, paying attention to one's environment can enable a firm to be better prepared for disruption. Sometimes, by looking into its environment, a firm may find better alternatives to its new game. After developing its search engine, Google found an alternative monetization model in paid listings that was much better than pop-up ads.

Applications of the AVAC Framework

What Can be Analyzed Using the AVAC?

Since the AVAC can be used to analyze the profitability potential of a firm's strategy, it can also be used to analyze the profitability potential of most things whose profitability rests on performing a set of activities. (Recall that we defined a strategy as a set of activities for creating and appropriating value.) Thus, the AVAC can be used to analyze business models, business units, products, technologies, brands, market segments, acquisitions, investment opportunities, partnerships such as alliances, an R&D group, corporate strategies, and so on. The different main questions that a firm may want to ask in an analysis are shown in Table 2.1 below. The subquestions remain primarily the

Table 2.1 Applications of AVAC Analysis

	Activities	Value	Appropriability	Change (new game factor)
Acquisition	In making and exploiting the acquisition, is the firm performing the right set of activities?	Do customers prefer the value from the acquisition, compared to that from competitors?	Does the firm profit from the activities?	Does the set of activities take advantage of change (present or future) to create and appropriate value?
Brand	Does the firm perform the right activities, in building and exploiting the brand?	Do customers prefer the value from the brand, compared to that from competitors?	Ditto	Ditto
Business model	Does the firm perform the right business model activities?	Do customers prefer the value from the business model activities, compared to that from competitors?	Ditto	Ditto
Business unit	Does the firm perform the right business unit activities?	Do customers prefer the value from the business unit, compared to that from competitors?	Ditto	Ditto
Corporate strategy	Does the firm perform the right corporate level activities?	Do customers prefer the value from the corporate-level activities, compared to that from competitors?	Ditto	Ditto

Market segment	Does the firm perform the right market segment activities?	Do customers prefer the value from the market segment, compared to that from competitors?	Ditto	Ditto
Partnership	Does the firm perform the right activities to support and exploit the partnership?	Do customers prefer the value from the partnership, compared to that from competitors?	Ditto	Ditto
Product	Does the firm perform the right activities to offer the product?	Do customers prefer the value from the product, compared to that from competitors?	Ditto	Ditto
R&D group	Does the group perform the right R&D activities?	Do customers prefer the value from the R&D, compared to that from competitors?	Ditto	Ditto
Technology	Does the firm perform the right activities, as far as the technology is concerned?	Do customers prefer the value from the technology, compared to that from competitors?	Ditto	Ditto

same as those explored above. Take brand, for example. The first question is, does the firm perform the right activities for building and exploiting the brand? Is the value created using the brand preferred by customers compared to the value from competitors. Does the firm make money from the brand? And finally, in building and exploiting the brand, does the firm take advantage of change or expect to take advantage of it?

When Should Such an Analysis be Undertaken?

The question is, when would one want to analyze the profitability potential of a business unit, brand, product, etc. and therefore need to use the AVAC?

Compare Outcomes

AVAC can be used to compare the profitability potential of different business strategies, business units, brands, products, corporate strategies, technologies, R&G strategies, partnerships, acquisitions, market segments, etc. The AVAC analysis is particularly suitable for such comparisons because it pinpoints the likely weaknesses and strengths of each activity and shows (via the associated questions) what questions need to be asked to remedy the weaknesses and reinforce the strengths.

Organizing Platform for Data

Like most frameworks, from the Growth/Share matrix to a Porter's Five Forces, AVAC can be an excellent organizing stage for displaying data in some meaningful way for discussions before a decision is taken. For example, before taking a major strategic decision, managers may want to discuss the profitability of the firm before the decision and compare it to the projected profitability after the decision. An AVAC enables managers to see the before and potential after. It provides a common platform and language to start off discussions.

Strategic Planning

Strategic planning builds on strategic analysis; that is, before performing strategic planning, a firm needs first to understand its existing strategy and profitability potential. Strategic planning then follows. This process consists of pinpointing a firm's strengths and weaknesses as well as the opportunities and threats that the firm faces as far as each component of AVAC is concerned.

Example 2.1: AVAC Analysis of a Strategy

To illustrate the AVAC analysis, we now analyze Ryanair's strategy.

Ryanair 2008

To customers, a visit to Ryanair's website (www.ryanair.com) in 2008 showed some remarkable things: one could fly from a number of airports in the United Kingdom (UK) to towns in southern Europe for as little as £10, make hotel reservations, find apartments, rent a car, or find out about important events going on in many cities in Europe.[8] There were even buttons for "Ryanair Casino," "Airport transfers," "Money" and "Ski." To investors, Ryanair's financial performance was remarkable: from 2000 to 2007, the company's *after-tax* profit margins were some of the highest of any company in Europe, ranging from 20–26%, slowing down to 18% because of higher per barrel oil prices. In 2007, Ryanair's Chief Executive Officer (CEO), Mr Michael O'Leary, was estimated to be worth over US$ 800 million.[9]

Ryanair was founded in Ireland in 1985 by Tom Ryan, made its first profits in 1991, and by 2000 had become one of the most profitable airlines in the world (Tables 2.2 to 2.4).[10] After almost going bankrupt in 1990, O'Leary had visited Southwest Airlines in the USA to see why the latter had been profitable since incorporation, compared to other US airlines.[11] Deregulation of the airline industry by the European Union (EU) in 1997 allowed any airline from any EU

Table 2.2 Selected Financials

Year ended	2000	2001	2002	2003	2004	2005	2006	2007
Passengers flown (million)	6.1	8.1	11.1	15.7	23.1	27.6	34.8	42.5
Load factor (%)				85	81	84	83	82
Revenues (in € million)	370.1	487.4	624.1	842.5	1,074	1,337	1,693	2,237
Profit after Tax (in € million)	72.5	104.5	150.4	239.4	227	269	302	401
Net margin (%)	20	21	24	28	21	20	18	18
EBITFAR (%)	36	37	36	41	36	34	31	30
Cash earnings (%)	31	34	34	38	30	27	25	26

Sources: Ryanair's investor relationships. Retrieved August 27, 2007, from http://www.ryanair.com/site/about/invest/docs/present/quarter4_2007.pdf

Table 2.3 Customer Service for Year Ending March 2005

	% on time	Lost bags per 1,000 passengers
Ryanair	89.4	0.6
Alitalia	82.5	12.9
Air France	80.5	14.9
Iberia	80.3	11.5
SAS	79.6	11.3
Austrian	79.4	18.8
Lufthansa	79.3	18.6
easyJet	78.3	RTP
British Airways	74.2	18.3

Sources: Ryanair's investor relationships. Retrieved August 27, 2007, from http://www.ryanair.com/site/about/invest/docs/present/quarter4_2007.pdf

Table 2.4 Industry Leading Margins for Year Ending March 2005

	Revenues per passenger (€)	Cost per passenger (€)	Net profit margin (%)
Ryanair	48	39	20.10
Southwest Airlines	72	69	4.80
British Airways	268	257	4.10
Iberia	178	171	3.90
easyJet	66	63	3.80
JetBlue	84	81	3.70
Air France	298	292	1.80
Lufthansa	333	328	1.60
Alitalia	184	204	−11.30

Sources: Ryanair's investor relationships. Retrieved August 27, 2007, from http://www.ryanair.com/site/about/invest/docs/present/quarter4_2007.pdf

country to operate scheduled flights to any other EU country. This was a great opportunity that Ryanair seized. It also went public that same year.

In January of 2000, the company launched Europe's largest booking website (*www.ryanair.com*) and within three months, the site was taking over 50,000 bookings a week. By 2004, 96% of its tickets were sold online.[12] Thus, it was able to avoid the $2 per reservation fee that booking a seat via the Sabre or Apollo reservation systems cost. A customer could also book hotels, rent cars, or apartments using the site. Agreements with hotels, transportation companies, casinos, financial institutions, and car rental agencies allowed Ryanair to "handover" customers to each.

In the financial year ending March 2007, the company carried 42.5 million passengers. At the check-in desk, customers received a boarding pass but with no seat assignment. Unlike other carriers, however, passengers were not allowed to check baggage through to connecting flights on other airlines. It charged for baggage in excess of 10 kg (22 lbs) so that some passengers could end up paying as much as $200 for extra baggage. At most airports, Ryanair negotiated with private companies or airport authorities to handle check-in, baggage handling, and aircraft servicing. Its targeted turnaround time at these secondary airports was 25 minutes, half the turnaround time of competitors at major airports.[13]

In 1994, the company had decided to fly only Boeing 737 aircraft, taking delivery of its first eight Boeing 737s that year to replace its fleet of BAC 1–11 jets. By 2007, the fleet had grown to over 120 737–800s, giving Ryanair the youngest fleet of any airline. The list price of a 737 in 2007 ranged from $50–85 million depending on the options, with each plane estimated to have a lifespan of over 20 years. In 2004, a typical Ryanair flight lasted over an hour (1.2 h) and covered about 491 miles. By 2005, partly because of the frequent flights and short distances flown, more passengers flew on Ryanair per year than on any other European airline. In-flight, three or four flight attendants sold drinks, snacks, and other merchandise that together accounted for 5–7% of Ryanair's revenues.

Whenever possible, it served only secondary airports such as Beauvais in the Paris region and Charleroi near Brussels. When it sought airports in cities that had been declining, it usually received concessions and cash in exchange for promotion and injection of "life" into the area. Passenger traffic on a route usually skyrocketed after Ryanair initiated service on the route, leading to what has come to be called the "Ryanair effect" in Europe. At these secondary airports, gate fees per passenger could be as low as $3 below rates at the more prestigious but more congested airports.

The spaces behind seat-back trays and on headrests were sold to advertisers. For a fee of €150,000–200,000 per year, an advertiser could splash the exterior of a Ryanair plane with its logo. In-flight magazines were made up entirely of advertising so that while other in-flight magazines struggled to break even, Ryanair's were profitable. The company also collected fees from car rental and hotel referrals. All ancillary services accounted for 13.9% of operating revenues in 2004.

Employees were paid according to their productivity. For example, flight attendants received a fixed salary, a payment based on how many sectors or flights they flew, and a commission on in-flight sales. On average, Ryanair flight attendants earned more money than their counterparts at other airlines. Their pilots earned a fixed salary and a payment per sector flown. These pilots earned 10% more than the typical pilot in the industry and flew 50% more sectors. Unlike other European airlines, Ryanair did not pay employees based on the length of their tenure with the airline. Only engineers and maintenance personal were paid on the basis of their qualifications. For the year ended March 31, 2004, Ryanair's average pay of €50,582 looked good compared to €42,077 for Iberia, €41,384 for easyJet, €41,377 for Lufthansa, €38,329 for Aer Lingus, and €37,602 for British Airways.[14]

Ryanair also had its share of criticism ranging from false advertising to anti-unionism to not treating customers well.

An AVAC Analysis of Ryanair's Strategy in 2007

We explore each of the components of the AVAC analysis separately.

Activities

The question here is, is Ryanair performing the right activities? There are two parts to this component. In the first part, we answer the questions: what is the **set of activities** that constitutes the firm's **strategy**? Does Ryanair have the resources and capabilities to perform the activities? Here is Ryanair's set of activities. The firm:

1 Operated largely out of secondary airports, preemptively acquiring as many gates and landing slots as possible at each airport.
2 Operated only Boeing 737s.
3 Instituted onboard sales and advertising.
4 Built and tried to maintain a low-cost culture.
5 Established relationships and links with local airport authorities, hotels, transportation, and events.

Do the Activities Contribute to Low Cost, Differentiation, etc?

By operating largely out of secondary airports, Ryanair reduced takeoff and landing delays, thereby reducing its turnaround time (and increasing aircraft utilization). It was also keeping its landing and gate fees low, accessing a low-cost labor force for its operations, and had an opportunity preemptively to acquire gates, landing slots, and other access rights when it moved into these airports and had little or no competition. It also had an opportunity to expand its activities to increase the number of passengers that it carried. Because some of these airports were in economically depressed zones, local officials were eager to work with Ryanair to bring in business in an effort to jumpstart their local economies. Effectively, moving into secondary airports was consistent with keeping its costs low so that it could pass on costs savings to customers in the form of low prices. It was also consistent with offering frequent flights, and attracting and keeping many valuable customers—differentiation.

By advertising to its passengers, its cost of advertising was lower than those of media such as TV and newspapers, which had to pay for programming or news to attract eyeballs. Ryanair did not have to pay for its eyeballs—that is, the number of people that were likely to see an advertisement; the eyeballs paid Ryanair. Thus, Ryanair could pass on some of its costs savings to advertisers in the form of lower advertising prices. It could also pass on some of the costs savings from advertising to passengers in the form of lower ticket prices. Like Southwest Airlines, whose business model Ryanair had copied, Ryanair did not offer free meals on its flights; but Ryanair went even further: it sold the snacks that Southwest Airlines gave away. It also sold duty-free goods. By selling its own tickets using its own website, the airline avoided the fees charged by travel agents and reservation systems. Direct contact with customers also helped the company build relationships with customers that could not be built through travel agents. Moreover, Ryanair was effectively doing what travel agents would do by providing links to hotels, car rental, and local events. By flying only Boeing 737s, the company potentially kept its maintenance costs low and reduced downtime since any mechanic could repair any plane and Ryanair did not have to track many different types of spare part for different planes. This also meant that any of the company's 737-certified pilots could fly any of its planes, and any plane could pull up to any gate. Effectively, flying only 737s not only reduced costs but also reduced turnaround time, thereby increasing the utilization of planes. These activities were consistent with attracting and keeping many valuable customers. By offering no baggage transfers, the firm kept its turnaround time low since its planes could take off without waiting for luggage from other planes.

Table 2.5 shows some estimates of the contribution of some activities to cost reductions, and revenues. For example, the company's activities saved at least $193.5 + 85 + 212.5 + 127.5 + 87.75+ 209 million = $915.25 million, plus $34,000 per pilot. It also had extra revenues of $352 million from non-airline operations.

Table 2.5 Back-of-the-envelope Estimates of the Contribution of Some Activities to Low Cost and Revenues

Activity	Cost savings or extra revenues in 2007	Source of data used in estimate, and assumptions made
Used its own booking-website for its reservations	Cost savings of 96% × $2.24B × 9% = $193.5M	Did 96% of own booking, agents charged 9% of ticket sales. In 2007 revenues were $2.24B
Did not use Sabre and Apollo reservation systems	Cost savings of 42.5M × $2 = $85M	Saved on $2 per passenger reservation fee. In 2007, there were 42.5 million passengers
Offered no free meals	Cost savings of 42.5M × $5 = $212.5M	There were 42.5 million passengers in 2007. Assume that each meal cost airline $5
Operated out of secondary airports	Cost savings of 42.5M × $3 = $127.5M	Gate fees were $3 per passenger lower at secondary airports than at primary airports
Kept turnaround time low (from operating out of secondary airports, using only one type of airplane, having Ryanair culture, etc., etc.)	Ryanair's planes were utilized 122/97 = 1.26 as much as the average competitor's planes. Thus, Ryanair needed 26 fewer planes than the average competitor. Cost savings = $67.5M × 26/20 = $87.75M	Turnaround time was 25 minutes, half the average turn time of competitors. Average Ryanair flight lasted 1.2 hours. Therefore flight time for average competitor was 72 + 50 = 122 while for Ryanair, the number was 72 + 25 = 97. Planes cost $50–$85M and lasted 20 years
Had pilots working 50% more but earning only 10% more	Costs savings of 50/(100*1.1)*$0.075 =$0.034M per pilot	Assume that an average pilot's salary was $75,000 in 2007
Splashed advertiser's logo on plane	Extra revenues of $175,000 × 120 = $21M	€150,000–200,000 per year to advertise on the outside of a plane. 120 planes in 2007
Offered ancillary goods and services	Extra revenues of $2.24B × 0.139 = $311.4M	All ancillary services accounted for 13.9% of operating revenues in 2004. Assume that same percentage held for 2007
No baggage transfers to or from other airlines, more dedicated employees, etc. resulting in the least number of bags lost	Cost savings from not losing bags 200*(25.19–0.6)*42.5M/1,000 = $209M	Assume that, in 2007, each piece of baggage lost cost an airline $200. Average number of bags lost by other airlines =15.19 bags per 1,000 passengers. But Ryanair lost only 0.6

Do Activities Contribute to Improving Its Position vis-à-vis its Coopetitors?

By flying only 737s and ramping up its activities to a point where it bought very many of these planes, Ryanair was increasing its bargaining power over Boeing. It was also making itself more dependent on just one aircraft maker, setting itself up for opportunistic behavior from the maker. It often cooperated with local authorities in order to start up operations in a secondary airport. Local authorities in southern Europe wanted tourists and jobs for their towns while Ryanair wanted the airports to bring in the tourists. Both parties worked to start operations at these local airports. Contrast this with starting operations at the larger and busier airports where local authorities were not as hungry for more traffic. Ryanair also worked with local hotels and transporters to provide them with tourists.

Do Activities Take Advantage of Industry Value Drivers?

Recall that industry value drivers are those characteristics of an industry that stand to have the most impact on cost, differentiation, and other drivers of profits such as the number of customers. Thus, a firm that takes advantage of these factors in formulating and executing its strategy stands to have the most impact on customer value and the profits that the firm can make. In the airline industry, utilization of airplanes is an industry value driver. Utilization here includes two things: (1) higher load factor (filling up planes with passengers) so that planes do not fly around empty, and (2) reducing the turnaround time of the plane so that planes are busy flying people to their destinations instead of sitting around at terminals or under repair. The idea here is that airplanes make money when flying full, not while sitting on the ground or flying empty. Many of the activities that Ryanair performed increased utilization. For example, as we pointed out earlier, operating out of secondary airports reduced the turnaround time since planes did not have to queue for takeoff or landing.

The firm's other source of revenues was advertising; and in advertising a critical industry value driver was the number of eyeballs. Firms with advertising business models spent lots of money generating eyeballs. For example, TV stations spent money on programming while online advertisers such as Google spent on expensive R&D to develop search engines and other software to attract viewers. An airline had a captive audience in passengers and it cost the airline relatively little or nothing to advertise to them. By advertising to its passengers, Ryanair was taking advantage of the eyeballs that it already had. Because it did not have to spend on acquiring these eyeballs, Ryanair could charge less for some of its tickets than competing airlines that did not advertise. Of course, there was the chance that the airline lost some passengers who did not like advertising.

Finally, the cost of labor in an airline constituted a high percentage of its overall cost. By building a workforce that worked 150% more hours for only 110% more in pay, Ryanair was taking advantage of this driver of costs to keep its overall costs low.

Do Activities Build or Translate Distinctive Resources/Capabilities into Unique Positions?

A key distinctive resource for Ryanair was its network of secondary airports and the associated gates, landing slots, and contracts with local authorities, hotels, and transportation providers. By moving into these airports (sometimes being the first), securing the gates and agreements, and ramping up its activities there, Ryanair was able to build its network system. Each time that it occupied one airport, it used it as a starting point to move to adjoining locations, offering low-cost frequent flights; and each time it took up gates and landing slots, or built relationships with local authorities, it was preempting some potential new entrants to these airports. Its low-cost culture, airplanes, relationships with local authorities, and its brand also contributed to keeping its costs low or differentiated it. These are important resources/capabilities.

Are the Activities Comprehensive and Parsimonious?

One signal that Ryanair's activities were parsimonious was the fact that its employees worked 150% more for only 110% the pay of the average European airline.

Value

Ryanair had many types of customers. These included flying passengers, advertisers, hotels, car rental companies, and local authorities of the secondary airports in which the company operated. To passengers, the company offered low-cost, frequent flights, access to hotels, cars, apartments, and other components of a vacation package. To what extent was the value that Ryanair offered its customers unique compared to that offered by its competitors? It offered very low prices compared to other European airlines. It also offered advertising, onboard sales, links to hotels, apartments and ground transportation that most of its competitors did not. Passengers were valuable in that, in addition to paying for the flight, they also constituted "eyeballs" that the firm could use as "value" to advertisers. (We cannot tell from the case whether or not they had a high willingness to pay.) The eyeballs came cheap compared to what TV and other media had to spend for eyeballs. In fact, most of Ryanair's eyeballs paid to be on the plane. In the year 2008, Ryanair flew over 42 million passengers, all of them potential eyeballs for advertising revenues. In addition to paying for seats and providing eyeballs, passengers also provided another source of revenues: they purchased snacks and duty-free goods. To advertisers, the company offered eyeballs not only to its own passengers but potentially those of its competitors, who could see the advertisements on the outside of Ryanair's airplanes. To hotels, car rental companies, and local authorities of the secondary airports, Ryanair provided traffic. As far as white spaces were concerned, there were many other cities in Europe and the rest of the world with secondary airports into which Ryanair could fly. There could also be white spaces in what it could advertise or sell to passengers.

Appropriability

Did Ryanair make money from the value that it created? Yes. From 2000–8, the company recorded after-tax profit margins of 18–28%, making Ryanair one of the most profitable companies in Europe.

Does Ryanair Have a Superior Position vis-à-vis Coopetitors?

European airlines did not have a superior position vis-à-vis suppliers and customers but, as we saw above, Ryanair managed to position itself well relative to its suppliers and customers than its rivals. Moreover, switching costs were low for customers. Ryanair may have extracted low prices for the airplanes that it bought from Boeing, given the relatively large number of 737s that it purchased, but we are not told whether this is the case. Because Ryanair's costs were very low compared to those of its rivals, and it also offered advertising and sales, the effects of rivalry and substitutes on it was not as large as it was on competitors.

Did Ryanair Exploit its Position vis-à-vis Coopetitors?

Like many airlines, Ryanair practiced price discrimination, charging different prices for different types of customer. This got the company closer to the average reservation price of each group of customers. Additionally, Ryanair also charged for extra baggage. Some of the company's very low prices were meant to attract passengers who would otherwise not travel but who then contributed to the number of eyeballs, buying products in the plane, staying in hotels, renting cars, or attending local events, thereby contributing to its revenues.

Did Ryanair Have the Right Resources/Capabilities, Including Complementary Assets?

Ryanair had the resources, including its brand, low-cost culture, and the network of secondary airports that it built (see below). It also had the complementary assets to profit from its advertising and on-board sales activities, both of them new game activities since they had not been offered in the European airline industry before. It had the eyeballs and passengers to whom sales could be made.

Imitability

Although it was easy for some airlines to imitate some of what Ryanair did, it was difficult to imitate the whole system of activities that it performed. Its system of activities—operating out of a network of secondary airports, advertising, onboard sales, offering no meals, a culture that made people work 50% more than their competitors while paid only 10% more, operating only Boeing 737s, offering no baggage transfers, with their own website for ticketing and hotel and car rental booking—was difficult to replicate. Existing rivals or potential new entrants might have been able to replicate some of these activities but replicating the whole system was difficult. Moreover, Ryanair was up the learning curve for most of these activities and was already carrying many passengers. Moreover, resources such as the network of secondary airports with associated landing slots and gates were scarce valuable resources and once taken by an airline such as Ryanair, were gone.

Existing rivals such as Air France or Lufthansa may also have been handicapped by prior commitments. For example, switching to operate only out of secondary airports would have meant having to give up their existing space, landing slots, and gates at existing primary airports. Doing so may have meant reneging on existing contracts with the local municipalities that owned or operated the airports, unions, and some employees. Switching to flying only one type of plane such as the Boeing 737 or the Airbus 320 may have meant having to get rid of all the Boeing 777s, 757s, 767s, 747s, A330s, A300s, A340s, and other airplanes that the airline had been flying for decades. Contracts with suppliers, pilots, and unions may have made such a switch difficult. Getting employees to work 50% more than they had in the past and for only 10% more would be very difficult in some European countries. Of course, imitability was difficult but not impossible. One thing that a firm such as Ryanair, which did more than one thing, had to watch out for was so-called category killers. For example, some airlines may have decided to take the advertising on airplanes even further, stealing customers from Ryanair.

Substitutability and Complementarity

Cars and trains were good substitutes for those travelers who had time as far as air transportation was concerned. The lower that Ryanair's prices were, the less of a problem that these substitutes may have been. Advertisers could also advertise elsewhere other than on airplanes; but the more eyeballs and the more effective the advertising was with Ryanair, the more that advertisers were likely to stay with Ryanair rather than seek substitutes. Passengers could buy snacks and goods elsewhere. Important complements in air travel included security and air traffic control over which Ryanair had little control. Business was affected by government security-related decisions. For example, security concerns often cut into turnaround time.

By having a low-cost structure that allowed it to keep its prices low, offering frequent flights, and providing connections to hotels, cars, and local events, Ryanair was effectively reducing the power of substitutes, since travelers were more likely to find it more convenient and inexpensive flying Ryanair than driving or taking a train.

Change: The New Game Factors

We first explore the change with which the firm was dealing. Change came from two major sources: from its environment and from its new game activities. The EU deregulated the airline industry in Europe, and Ryanair took advantage of the changes to pursue new game activities that allowed it to create and appropriate value. When the EU deregulated air travel Ryanair already had the beginnings of a low-cost culture in place as well as an operating base in Dublin. These were strengths that would continue to be strengths in the new game. It was not bound by major contracts that could have become handicaps.

In 2008, the biggest threat that Ryanair faced was the rapidly increasing price of oil.

Take Advantage of the New Ways of Creating and Capturing New Value Generated by Change?

Yes. In deregulating the airline industry in Europe, the EU created an opportunity for Ryanair to keep offering low-cost service to customers in more of Europe. The company took advantage of the deregulation to extend its activities to a lot more of the EU. The firm was able to build on its low-cost culture and extend its network of secondary airports beyond the UK and Ireland. Its low-cost system of activities resulted in a low-cost structure that allowed the firm to pass on some of its costs savings to customers in the form of low prices. Many of the firm's new activities to exploit these changes built on its prechange system of activities and product-market position. Deregulation of the industry increased the competitive forces in it; but Ryanair's system of activities allowed it to dampen the repressive forces and reinforce the favorable ones. Effectively, Ryanair took advantage of the new ways of creating and appropriating value created by deregulation and Ryanair's new game activities. Its new game activities enabled Ryanair better to create value and position itself rather than its rivals to appropriate it.

The other change with which Ryanair had to deal was the Internet. It too reinforced Ryanair's position vis-à-vis customers. Ryanair had performed most of its own bookings rather than go through travel agents. The advent of the Internet enabled the firm to create a website that allowed customers to book their own flights, finalizing the bypassing of travel agents.

Take Advantage of Opportunities Generated by Change to Build New Resources or Translate Existing Ones in New Ways?

Yes. Ryanair took advantage of opportunities generated by change to build new resources and translate new ones into unique value. It was fast to take up space at airports in southern Europe. Its resulting network of secondary airports and low-cost cultures built on its prechange culture and hubs in Ireland and England. It also built valuable relationships with authorities at airports. More importantly, the Internet allowed the firm to build its brand with customers via its website.

Does the Firm Take Advantage of First-mover's Advantages and Disadvantages, and Competitors' Handicaps?

Ryanair took advantage of first-mover advantages by quickly ramping up its activities at secondary airports and taking up gates and landing slots at the airports. It quickly built up a network of secondary airports in each of which it had a large number of gates, landing slots, and relationships with local officials. By preemptively taking up these resources, Ryanair was also raising barriers to entry for potential new entrants into its secondary airports. By establishing good relationships with authorities at secondary airports, it was preemptively acquiring a valuable scarce resource. By quickly setting up a website to reach its customers, it was preemptively taking up customer perceptual space. In the process, it built a reputation and brand as a low-cost carrier. By being the first to accumulate scarce resources such as gates and landing slots at the secondary airports that it used, to build relationships with local officials, and to establish a brand name reputation as the low-cost airline for its routes, Ryanair was effectively taking advantage of first-mover advantages.

Does the Firm Anticipate and Respond to Coopetitors' Reactions to its Actions?

One can argue that, in preemptively taking up gates and landing slots at airports, Ryanair was anticipating its competitors' likely reaction. Competitors would like to get into the same airports from which it was operating but Ryanair responded to this anticipated entry by preemptively capturing many of the valuable scarce resources that were critical to operating profitably out of the secondary airports.

Identify and Take Advantage of Opportunities and Threats of Environment? Are There no Better Alternatives?

The firm took advantage of opportunities from its environment when it expanded its activities following EU deregulation of the airline industry. It was also one of the first to take advantage of the Internet to build a website to enhance its decision to undertake its own reservations. Opportunities also existed for low-cost transatlantic flights and short-hall flights in the former eastern European economies.

The firm had alternative airline market segments, but these were not very attractive ones for Ryanair. It could have tried to compete head-on with the major European airlines such as Air France—a mistake. It could have also invested its money in other firms, diversified into other businesses; but the fact that it had one of the highest profit rates of any major European company suggested that it was not likely to have done much better investing in these other companies that were not as profitable as Ryanair.

In 2008, the price of oil hit many airlines hard. Traditionally, the cost of fuel was second only to employee wages in the hierarchy of airline costs; but in 2008, the price of oil had become the biggest cost item for many airlines. The price of oil was one of those macroeconomic threats over which airlines had little control. Although many airlines stood to lose money as a result of the high oil prices, those with good strategies stood to lose less money than those without good strategies. The case says very little about other future changes. It was not clear what the EU was likely to do about air traffic in the future; nor is it clear about what Ryanair's next steps or its competitors' moves might be.

Key Takeaways

- Although profitability numbers can tell us something about the success of an underpinning strategy, they say very little about what drives the numbers. They say little about the value creation and appropriation that underpin the numbers. Without an understanding of the underpinning strategy and its profitability potential, it is difficult for managers to know how to improve or maintain present performance. Strategy frameworks can be used to analyze firm strategies and understand their profitability potential.

- The AVAC framework can be used not only to explore the profitability potential of a firm's *strategy* and make recommendations on what the firm could do to improve the strategy and its performance, but also to explore the profitability potential of business models, business units, products, technologies, brands, market segments, acquisitions, investment opportunities, partnerships such as alliances, an R&D group, corporate strategies, and more (Table 2.1).
- Each of the four components explores critical questions that are meant to bring out the extent to which the profitability potential of a strategy has been reached and what can be done to improve or sustain profitability.
- **Activities.** The main question here is whether a firm is performing the right activities—activities that contribute to value creation and appropriation. This larger question is explored via the following subquestions. Do the activities:

   - Contribute to low cost, differentiation, number and type of customers, better pricing, better sources of revenues?
   - Contribute to improving a firm's position vis-à-vis coopetitors?
   - Take advantage of industry value drivers?
   - Contribute to building new distinctive resources/capabilities or translate existing ones into unique value and positions?
   - Conform to parsimony and comprehensiveness criteria?

- **Value.** The primary question here is whether the value created is preferred by customers over competitor's offerings: how unique is the value created, as perceived by customers, compared to that from competitors? This question is explored via the following subquestions:

   - Do customers perceive the value created by the strategy as unique?
   - Do many customers perceive this value?
   - Are these customers precious (valuable)? What are the market segments and sources of revenues?
   - Are there any white spaces nearby?

- **Appropriability.** The primary question here is whether the firm makes money from the value created? (How much money and why?) This question is answered using the following more detailed questions:

   - Does the firm have a superior position vis-à-vis its coopetitors (buyers, suppliers, rivals, partners, etc.)?
   - Does the firm profit from customer benefits and its position vis-à-vis coopetitors?
   - Is there something about the firm and its set of activities and resources that makes it difficult for competitors to imitate its strategy? Is there something about competitors that impedes them from imitating the firm?
   - Is the value nonsubstitutable? If there are complements, are they being strategically used?

- **Change.** The overarching question here is whether the strategy takes advantage of change (present or future). This larger question is explored via the following questions: does or will the firm take advantage of:

  ○ The new ways of creating and appropriating value generated by change?
  ○ New ways of building new distinctive resources or translating existing ones into unique value?
  ○ First-mover's advantages and disadvantages, and competitors' handicaps?
  ○ Coopetitors' reactions to its actions?
  ○ Opportunities and threats of environment? Are there no better alternatives?

- The AVAC framework is more comprehensive than existing models. Compared to Porter's Five Forces, for example, it includes the role of (1) change (the new game factor), (2) resources/capabilities/competences (including complementary assets), (3) industry value drivers, (4) pricing, (5) the number and quality of customers, and (6) market segments and sources of revenue.

- AVAC Applications. It:

  ○ Serves as an organizing platform for displaying information and data in a common business language that managers can use as a starting point for exploring strategic management questions.
  ○ Can be used to compare different strategy outcomes.
  ○ Constitutes a parsimonious and comprehensive checklist.
  ○ Can be used as a platform for business model or strategy planning.

- More than anything else, the AVAC is an organizing framework for displaying information in a common business language that managers can use as a starting point for exploring strategic management questions to help them take decisions.

Chapter 3

The Long Tail and New Games

Reading this chapter should provide you with the conceptual and analytical tools to:

- Understand the *long tail* concept.
- Understand that the long tail is not limited to the Internet and products.
- Explore how a firm can make money from a long tail.
- Begin to understand how all members of the value system—aggregators, producers; and suppliers—can benefit from the long tail.
- Begin to understand the strategic impact of the long tail.

Introduction

Every year, hundreds of movies are released, but only a few of them become box office hits or blockbusters. Each of the hits accounts for hundreds of millions of dollars in revenues while many of the nonhits each account for a lot less. Every year, hundreds of thousands of books are published, but only a select few make the best-seller list. In the music industry, only a few songs go on to become hits. In all three cases, a few "blockbuster" products or best-sellers are each responsible for millions of dollars in sales while the great majority of the products each account for only thousands or fewer dollars. This behavior can be captured by the graph of Figure 3.1 in which the vertical axis represents the sales while the horizontal axis captures the products (movies, books, songs) that bring in the revenues. As one progresses along the horizontal axis away from the origin to the right, sales start out high but tail off as one moves further away from the origin. Effectively, the graph has a *long tail* to the right and a *short head* to the left. This phenomenon in which a few get most of the action while many get very little is not limited to product sales. In the Internet, a few blogs each get thousands of visitors while thousands of other blogs get a few hits each. In a book such as this one, a few words like "the" are used frequently while many others such as "consequently" are used less frequently. In some countries, 80% of the wealth is owned by less than 10% of the population.

Although the long tail phenomenon has been described by statisticians using the graph of Figure 3.1 and given names such as Pareto Law, Pareto Principle, 80/20 rule, heavy tail, power-law tail, Pareto tails, and so on, it was Chris Anderson, Editor-in-Chief of *Wired* magazine and former correspondent for *The Economist*, who used the term *long tail* specifically to refer to this often-neglected group of products and developed the argument for why, in the face of

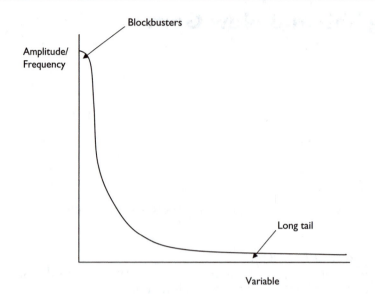

Figure 3.1 A Long Tail Distribution.

the Internet, firms can make money by selling products that had languished in the long tail.[1] He argued that if a store or distribution channel is large enough, the many products in the long tail can jointly make up a market share that is as high as, if not higher than, that of the relatively fewer hits and block-busters in the short head.[2] Thus, by focusing on the long tail of the distribution where there are many products, each of which sells a few units, one can bring in as much in revenues (if not more) as a firm that focuses on a few blockbuster products, by taking advantage of the Internet's properties such as its near infinite shelf space. eBay's business model was originally based largely on products that are in the long tail—that is, many one-of-a-kind products such as antiques and collectibles, few units of which are sold; but by selling very many such articles, the firm was able to bring in lots of revenues. Although Amazon sells many best-seller books, it also carries very many titles each of which sells a few units. Since there are many such books (from the long tail), the total revenues from selling the many books can be large enough to parallel the revenues from the best-sellers. Many of Google's advertisers are very small firms that ordinarily would not advertise in an offline world. By aggregating the revenues from these small but many customers, the company can make as much money as, if not more than, it would make from a few big customers. To understand why and when the long tail may offer an opportunity for profitable new game business models, let us explore the rationale behind blockbuster products, the so-called hits that form the short head, and the laggards that form the tail of the long-tail distribution.

The Phenomenon

Rationale for the Long Tail of Products

The question is, why do some products become hits, bestsellers, or blockbusters while others end up languishing in the long tail? How do we explain the shape of the long tail distribution for products of Figure 3.1? There are three reasons why a few products usually do very well, forming the short head of a distribution, while many products can languish in the long tail:

1 The high cost and scarcity of distribution channels and shelf space.
2 Customers' cognitive limitations and difficulties in making choices.
3 Customer heterogeneity, and the high cost of and difficulties in meeting the individual unique needs of all customers.

High Cost and Scarcity of Distribution Channels and Shelf Space

First, shelf space and distribution channels for many products are limited, especially in the offline world; that is, the cost of providing the space to display products in an offline world is very high, and so are the inventory carrying costs for distributors who decide to carry too many products. Thus, even if a producer were to try to offer products that satisfy the unique needs of everyone, there would not be enough space on shelves to display all such products at low cost. There just isn't enough room in stores or in distribution channels to hold everything for everyone at affordable costs. Moreover, without access to everyone, most producers would not be able to reach every customer to find out what their needs are so as to incorporate them in each customer's product. Effectively, shelf space and distribution channels are a scarce resource and a barrier to entry for many products. The few products that have access to these scarce resources have a good chance of becoming best-sellers or hits. Those products that do not have access to the scarce sources are more likely to end up in the long tail.

Customers' Cognitive Limitations and Difficulties in Making Choices

Even if there were enough shelf space to carry all the products that satisfy all individual needs, most customers would have a difficult time choosing from the huge variety. Given human cognitive limitations, it can be a frustrating experience choosing between five similar products, let alone hundreds or thousands. Think about how difficult it can be choosing between the cars that you can afford. Because of this cognitive limitation of many customers, some of them end up buying the mass-produced and mass-marketed products that may not be what they really need.

Customer Heterogeneity, and the Difficulties and High Cost of Meeting Individual Unique Needs

No two people have identical tastes (with the exception of some identical twins). Thus, it would be nice if each product were custom-made to meet the unique needs of each individual; but doing so would be exorbitantly expensive for some products. Imagine how much it would cost if a pharmaceutical company had to develop and produce a drug for each patient since each patient's physiology differs from that of other patients. Thus, most firms would rather mass-produce one product and mass-market it to as many customers as possible. Doing so enables them to enjoy the benefits of economies of scale that usually come from specialization in designing, producing, marketing, promoting, and selling one product for many customers. If the one product that is mass-produced and marketed wins, it can become a hit.

For these three reasons, a limited number of products are produced and mass marketed, and some go on to occupy the limited shelf space and distribution channels. Some of these products gain wide acceptance and end up in the short head of the distribution while others are relegated to the long tail.

Then Comes the Internet

Information technology (IT) innovations have changed some of the reasons why products in the short head do so much better than those in the long tail. This change potentially alters the long tail distribution. How? Because of the tremendous amount of improvements in the cost-performance of computer hardware, software, and the Internet, websites can represent shelf space for many products. Thus, a bookstore or any other retailer can have millions of items on display on its website rather than the thousands that are possible in an offline world. Digital products such as music and movies can also be distributed electronically. Additionally, search engines, online reviews, online community chats, software that makes suggestions using buyers' past purchases, and blogs can help consumers choose from the many available choices. Moreover, because IT gives more producers and customers more low-cost access to each other, producers have an opportunity to find out more about customers and work with them to offer products that more closely match individual needs. Because of the low cost of interactions, firms can afford to sell to very small customers to whom they would ordinarily not pay attention. That is why, for example, Google could afford to sell advertising to many small advertisers. It developed software that many of these advertisers could use to "interact" with the company. Firms and their customers also have more tools that they can use for lower-cost customization of products.

Effectively, the Internet's and other IT innovation's properties—low-cost shelf space and distribution channel, tools for making better purchase choices, and a lower-cost tool for producers better to meet customer needs—have mitigated some of the reasons why some products were relegated to the long tail. Products that may never have found themselves on offline shelves can now find their way onto electronic shelves. For example, rare books that were not in demand enough to be put on shelf space can now be listed on an online shop. Available software also helps consumers choose products that better meet their individual tastes from the many available products. Thus, products that would ordinarily have languished in the long tail may find their way to people with diverse tastes who want them. The Internet not only extends the tail, it thickens it (Figure 3.2).[3]

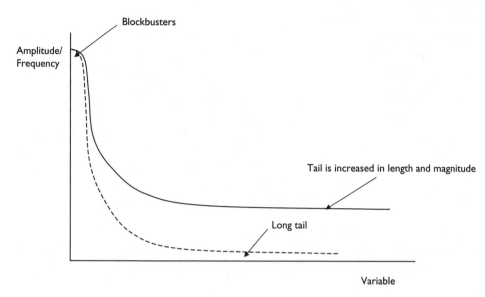

Figure 3.2 Impact of the Internet on a Long Tail Distribution.

Who Profits from the Long Tail?

The phenomenon of the long tail tells us that money can be made from the long tail. However, it does not say who is more likely to make that money and why. After all, not all the firms that can aggregate old books or movies and sell can make money or have a competitive advantage in doing so. A firm's ability to profit from the long tail depends on (1) the industry in which it competes (industry factors), and (2) the firm's ability to create and appropriate value in the markets in which it competes in the industry (firm-specific factors).

Industry Factors

A firm's ability to profit from the long tail is a function of its industry—of the competitive forces that impinge on industry firms and determine average profitability for industry firms. These forces depend on, among other factors, the location of the industry along the value system for the products or services in the long tail (Figure 3.2). There are at least three categories of firms in this value system that can take advantage of the long tail: distributors or so-called aggregators, the producers of the products, and the suppliers to producers (Figure 3.3).

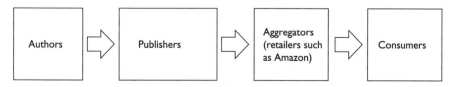

Figure 3.3 Value System of Long Tail Potential Coopetitors.

Distributors and Aggregators

Firms such as Amazon.com and Wal-Mart that buy books, movies, DVDs, etc. and sell them over the Internet stand to benefit from the long tail since they can reach out to the long tail of nonbest-seller books, nonhit music DVDs, and nonblockbuster movies, and sell them to their customers by taking advantage of the low-cost almost-limitless shelf space of the Internet, better interaction with customers, and lower-cost information technologies for consumers to make better choices. For example, when Blockbuster Inc. first started renting movies in its brick-and-mortar stores, 90% of the movies rented from them were new releases;[4] but when Netflix first started using the Internet to rent out movies, 70% were new releases while 30% were back catalog. According to Chris Anderson, 25% of Amazon's book sales are from outside its website's top 100,000 best-sellers, about 3.6 million of them.[5]

However, as we will see below, the same technologies that create these opportunities for aggregators also create a threat of forward vertical integration from producers (book publishers, record labels, movie firms, etc.). Moreover, depending on the power of producers, they can also capture most of the value created by aggregators.

Producers (Manufacturers)

Although the literature on the long tail so far has focused largely on how aggregators can make money reselling what they bought from producers, producers also stand to make money from the long tail if they are well-positioned visa-vis their coopetitors and have the right strategies to boot. Every old book that Amazon sells means some money for its publisher and author. Every classic movie that Netflix can rent means a royalty for its producers. Moreover, makers of products or content can also use the Internet to sell their products directly to end-customers or find out what their customers want in the products. Dell used the Internet to sell more varieties (as perceived by customers) of its build-to-order PCs directly to end-customers than it would have been able to sell through distributors. If a product is digital, producers can deliver it directly to consumers using the Internet. For example, consumers can download movies directly from the movie maker's site, bypassing aggregators such as Blockbuster and Netflix. Customers can buy books directly from the publisher's site. Effectively, makers of content and other products can also profit from the long tail.

However, the competitive advantage of some producers may be eroded. If sales of products from the long tail are at the expense of blockbusters from the short head, the makers of these blockbusters may lose sales. If content providers and other producers bypass publishers and aggregators, the latter may lose some of their competitive advantage.

Suppliers

If suppliers are well-positioned vis-à-vis producers, they can capture more of the value that producers create in exploiting the long tail than they did prior to the technological change. Suppliers, such as authors and musicians, who usually depend on publishers and record labels, respectively, can produce and sell their products directly to customers, bypassing producers and aggregators.

Firm-specific Factors: Ability to Create and Appropriate Value

How well a firm performs in its industry, relative to its competitors, is a function of firm-specific factors. It is a function of how well the firm is able to create value and appropriate value. And as we saw in Chapter 2, it is a function of:

1 Whether the firm is performing the right set of activities—activities that contribute to creating value, better positioning the firm vis-à-vis coopetitors, and to the firm's exploitation of the value and position.
2 The extent to which the value created is preferred by customers over value from competitors.
3 The extent to which the firm makes money from the value created and its position vis-à-vis coopetitors.
4 The extent to which the firm can take advantage of the innovation that is changing the status quo of the long tail, and any future change.

Effectively, a firm's ability to create and appropriate value in a long tail can be explored using the AVAC analysis. We will return to this shortly with an example.

Beyond the Internet: Some Long Tail Cases

Although we have limited our discussion of the long tail phenomenon to the context of the Internet, the phenomenon exists in many other contexts. As the following cases illustrate, there is an opportunity to take advantage of the long tail in the face of many innovations—technological and nontechnological.

Botox and Cosmetic Surgery

Cosmetic surgery is the use of surgical or medical procedures to enhance the appearance of a person. Until the introduction of Botox, cosmetic procedures were performed by surgeons. In the USA, the best surgeons performed the most surgeries and made the most money while the not-so-good surgeons and generalist doctors made very little money from surgery. Thus, great surgeons were in the short head while not-so-good surgeons and general practitioners were in the long tail of the cosmetic surgery Pareto distribution. The FDA approval of Botox in April 2002 for use in cosmetic procedures promised to change all of that.[6] A Botox procedure involved injecting the substance into the wrinkle, frowning line, or targeted area using a fine gauge needle. The procedure lasted a few minutes, there was no surgery or anesthesia needed, and the patient could return to work the same day. More importantly, any doctor could apply it— that is, the procedure was not limited to surgeons. Thus, the not-so-good surgeons and general practitioners who were in the long tail of the cosmetic surgery distribution could now earn more money from the cosmetic procedures using Botox than they did before Botox.

Cell Phones in Developing Countries

Before wireless cell phones, most villages and small towns in developing countries had little or no phone services. Only fixed-line telephones were available and because it was very costly to lay the wires (cabling) and exchanges to low population centers, it was very uneconomical to offer phone services to rural areas. (Government-mandated monopoly phone companies were also very inefficient.) Thus, many communities had no phone service. If a person in one of these underserved areas wanted to make a phone call, he or she would go to a small town and make the phone call there. Thus, the number of phone calls made by people in cities was very large relative to that made by people from villages or small towns. Effectively phone service for villagers was in the long tail of each country's phone system. Cell phone service changed all of that. Because wireless phone services did not require wires, the cost of cabling was no longer a large constraint. Moreover, government monopolies were eliminated and competition was introduced in many countries. Suddenly, not only did phone service in rural areas increase considerably, but that in cities also increased. Thus, both the short head and long tail phone service increased.

Discount Retailing in Rural Areas

Before Wal-Mart moved into rural areas of the Southwestern USA, sales of most products in rural areas were at the long tail of discount retailing. Most discount retailing sales were at large discount stores built in large cities. Occasionally, people from the rural areas would drive the long distance to cities to buy some of what they needed or use catalogs from the likes of Sears to order products. Wal-Mart's strategy was to saturate contiguous small towns with small stores. Thus, by aggregating the sales in many small stores, Wal-Mart was able to generate the volumes that its competitors generated by building large stores in big cities, and more. It also adopted the latest in information technology at the time, built a first-class logistics system, established the Wal-Mart low-cost culture, grew in size, and so on. Wal-Mart performed the right set of activities to create value in rural areas and appropriate much of the value created.

Internet and Political Contributions in the USA

Prior to the Internet, most political contributions, especially those to presidential candidates, were made by a few influential donors who made large contributions at fundraising dinners, dances, or other gatherings. Organizations such as unions could also raise money for candidates using their mailing lists or meetings. Many small donors who could have contributed were largely in the long tail of donations since each of them donated little or nothing. The advent of the Internet not only increased the amplitude of the tail but extended it, since many more small donors made more contributions. By appealing to these small donors, candidates such as would-be President Barack Obama, were able to raise huge amounts of donations from ordinary Americans.

Internet and User Innovation

For years now, Professor Eric von Hippel of the Massachusetts Institute of Technology (MIT) has argued that users and suppliers can be as good a source of product innovations as manufacturers of products. Each user, for example, can make improvements to a product that other users and the manufacturer have not or cannot. Technologies such as the Internet enable manufacturers to aggregate these innovations and come up with a greatly improved product.

Microfinancing

In many developing countries, a few rich people or businesses get most of the loans from banks, credit unions, and other major lenders. The large majority has no access to financing and when it does, interest rates are extremely high. This large majority can be said to be in the long tail of loans. Very small potential lenders can also be said to be in the long tail of lenders too, since they do not have enough money to lend to large borrowers. Microfinancing is an innovation that tackles these two long tails. It makes small loans available to poor people in developing countries at reasonable interest rates in an attempt to enable them to dig themselves out of poverty. When aggregated, these microloans can be large enough for big lenders to enter the business. Also, small lenders can also get into the business of lending since they are people who want small loans. Effectively, we get more borrowers and more lenders borrowing and lending more money.

Organic Foods at the Long Tail of Foods

For a long time in developed countries, conventional foods (crops and animals) have been at the short head of foods while organic foods have been at the long tail. Organic crops are grown without using artificial fertilizers, conventional pesticides, human waste, or sewage sludge, while organic animals are grown without the use of growth hormones and routine use of antibiotics. Neither food is processed with ionizing radiation or food additives, and in some countries, they cannot be genetically altered. Producers of organic foods emphasize the conservation of soil and water as well as the use of renewable resources. Because conventional foods did not have these constraints, and the benefits of organic foods were not widely understood, most of the foods grown were conventional. Availability of organic foods tended to be limited to what local farmers could grow and sell in their local farmers' market or cooperative. They did not enjoy the economies of scale of conventional foods.

In 1978, Whole Foods Markets was founded to sell organic foods. It took advantage of the growing awareness of the health and environmental benefits of organic foods, and built many organic and natural foods stores in the USA. Whole Foods and its competitors increased the share of organic foods in the communities in which they built stores. Effectively, they increased the sales of organic foods—the products that had languished in the long tail of groceries.

Printing and the Written Word

Before printing, all works were handwritten and duplicating such works was manual and therefore very expensive and time-consuming. Thus, only a select few rich people or religious figures such as kings, monks, and priests had access to written information. Ordinary people were in the long tail of the written word since they had little or no access to it. The library helped people to the written word; but it was the invention of the printing press that changed all that. It made a lot of the written word available to the masses. Thus the amount of learning from books by ordinary people, when added, may have rivaled or surpassed that by kings, priests, and other well-placed people.

Radio and TV Broadcasting

Before radio and TV, news reception was available largely to people in cities who were close enough to each other to spread it by word of mouth, or get it from city theatres. Some of the news also spread via newspapers. Many villages and small cities were in the long tail of news. TV and radio changed all that, since people in these small villages and towns with TV could now have access to news before it had become history.

Video Tape Recorders and Blockbuster

Although Netflix's use of the Internet to erode Blockbuster Inc.'s competitive advantage is a classic example of a firm exploiting the long tail to displace an incumbent, Blockbuster actually attained its own competitive advantage by taking advantage of a new technology to exploit the long tail. The new technology at the time was the home videotape recorder. Before home videotape recorders, people had go to theatres to see movies or hope that the movie would appear on TV some day. (A select few people had their own projectors at home.) Moreover, when a movie was released, it had a few days to prove itself. After a few weeks in theatres, movies would be relegated to storage, unless a TV station came calling.

Sony introduced the home videotape recorder (Betamax format) in 1975 and in 1977 George Atkinson launched the first video rental store called Video Station, in Los Angeles.[7] Blockbuster Video was founded in 1985 to also rent out videocassettes for people to play in the comfort of their own homes. Suddenly each person with a videotape recorder who lived near a video rental store could turn his or her house into a theatre. The choices for each customer increased considerably from the ten or so movies that were available in one's local theatre, to the thousands of movies that were available in a rental store. The result was that sales of both the hits in the short head and the nonhits in the long tail increased. How? First, people who wanted to watch hits after they were out of theatres could now watch them again, at home, thereby increasing the sales of hits. Second, nonhits that did not do well in theatres or never even entered theatres could also be watched at home. This increased sales of the long tail. Third, some movies, such as adult entertainment movies, that would never have been allowed in some theatres, could now be played at home. This also increased sales of stuff from the long tail. There were also some changes in the vertical chain. First, some moviemakers bypassed the theatres and went straight to the video store or to end-customers. Many makers of adult movies could now sell their movies directly to consumers with video recorders. At a later time, DVDs, the Internet, and movies on demand also offered opportunities to exploit long tail effects.

Effectively, for a firm to exploit the long tail effect, an innovation with one or more of the following properties should impact the relevant value system. The innovation should:

1 Reduce the high cost and scarcity of distribution channels and shelf space.
2 Help cognitively limited customers better make product choices.
3 Help firms better to meet the individual needs of heterogeneous customers—lower cost of product being one of them.

Take the case of movies. Videotape recorders, DVDs, and computers became individual screening theatres for movies, giving moviemakers the option to bypass theatres. Consumers did not have to go to theaters to see a movie. Effectively, the cost of distribution per movie seen by consumers dropped. Movie-rental stores could help customers with some of their movie choices. Moreover, customers could now watch movies that were not allowed in local theatres. Thus, all three conditions were met. In the case of organic foods, Whole Foods brought different organic foods to populations, thereby decreasing the cost that each grower would have to bear if he or she had to take his or her own produce to each individual market and sell it. By aggregating the different products and providing information on them, Whole Foods also helped consumers better to make their choices of organic products to buy. Whole Foods was also meeting the individual needs of people who believed in organic foods but could not find enough of them in their local grocery stores. The case of Wal-Mart in rural areas is similar to that of Whole Foods in organic foods. In the case of cell phones in developing countries, the cost of distributing phone services to villages using cell phones was a lot lower than that of distributing fixed-line phone services. Elimination of monopolies gave consumers choices that they never had before; but not too many choices. Cell phones also satisfied the needs of people who were on the move, people who did not want to wait at a particular place to receive a phone call, or go there to make one. Because Botox could be administered by any doctor, compared to cosmetic surgery that could be performed only by surgeons, Botox-based cosmetic procedures were available to more people in more places. This effectively reduced distribution costs of cosmetic procedures. Moreover, cosmetic procedures were now available to people who hated going under the knife, being put under anesthetic, or missing work for days. The product also created an opportunity for general practitioners who wanted to be in the cosmetic medicine business but could not become good surgeons.

Implications for Managers

So what does all of this mean to a manager? Before answering this question, let us recap the short version of the long tail story so far. In many games, there are likely to be a few hits, blockbusters, high frequency, or high amplitude occurrences that occupy the short head of a distribution—the so-called 20% that get 80% of the action of the Pareto 20/80 rule. The nonhits, nonblock-buster, low-amplitude, or low frequency occurrences occupy the long tail—the so-called 80% that see only 20% of the action. Innovations usually shake up the distribution, enabling more of the 20% to see more action. Thus, a firm that exploits such an innovation, in creating and appropriating value, increases its chances of profiting from the long tail. The question is, how can you, as a manager, help your firm exploit the long tail effect? You can improve your firm's chances by going through the following four steps:

1 Identify the long tail distributions in your markets or any markets that you might like to attack, and their drivers.
2 Identify those new game ideas or innovations that can eliminate or take advantage of those conditions that make some products languish in each long tail.
3 Perform an AVAC analysis to determine which activities stand to give your firm a competitive advantage as it uses new games to create and appropriate value in the long tail.
4 Decide on which activities to focus, and how to execute the strategy.

Identify the Long Tail Distributions in your Markets and their Drivers

As a manager, the first thing to do is identify the long tails (niches) in the industries in which your firm competes or would like to compete. For each of these niches, determine which of the three factors that drive long tail distribu-tions are responsible for the long tails that you would like to exploit; that is, determine the extent to which the high cost and scarcity of distribution channels, difficulties in customers making product choices, and difficulties in producers meeting the unique needs of heterogeneous customers are responsible for products/services languishing in the long tail rather than thriving in the short head.

Identify New Game Ideas or Innovations that Eliminate or Take Advantage of Long Tail Factors

Next, scan within your firm and its environment for those new game ideas or innovations that the firm can use to exploit the identified long tail. That is, search for those new game ideas or innovations that can overcome those factors that have been identified as being responsible for relegating products/services to the long tail. The environment can be internal to the firm or external. Scanning the internal environment involves combing through a firm's resources/capabil-ities to see if any of them can be used to pursue the sort of new game that can overcome or take advantage of those factors that relegate products to the long tail. Scanning the external environment entails searching for those new game ideas, knowledge, and capabilities from coopetitors, other industries, and other countries that can be used to exploit the long tail. Note that the new game ideas and innovations can be technological or nontechnological.

Perform an AVAC Analysis to Determine How Best to Exploit Tail

Having determined what new game ideas or innovations can be used to exploit the long tail, the next step is to perform a detailed AVAC analysis to understand those activities that must be performed to create and appropriate value in exploiting the long tail in such a way that your firm has a competitive advantage. There are two kinds of analysis that can be performed here. If the firm already offers some of the products in the long tail, the analysis is very similar to the one that we perform next for iTunes Music Store, except that the *change* component will be about the new game or innovation that was identified in Step 2 above as the key to overcoming or taking advantage of the factors that relegated products to the long tail. If a firm does not offer any products in the long tail, the analysis starts with the type of value that the firm would like to offer and how much of the value the firm would like to appropriate, given the new game. From there, the firm can work backwards to the types of activities that it needs to perform to create and appropriate the value needed to have a competitive advantage in exploiting the long tail. Note that when a firm chooses which activities to perform, it is also choosing the industry in the value system in which it wants to locate.

Decide Which Activities to Focus on and How to Execute the Strategy

From the AVAC analysis, the firm can zoom in on those activities that must be reinforced or reversed to enable it to have a competitive advantage. It must then hire the right people and build the right organizational structure and systems to execute the strategy, given its environment.

Effectively, the long tail concept offers managers one way to identify white space. You would recall that when a firm introduces a new product or service, it usually chooses between entering a battlefield with many existing competitors, or pursuing white space where there is little or no existing competition. The long tail concept offers one method for locating such white space. The short head has the established providers of the hits who are likely to be strong competitors. The long tail is where there is more room to enter, using the innovation. Thus, by identifying the reasons why a long tail exists, one can innovate around these reasons and improve one's chances of having a competitive advantage. Many disruptive technologies actually start by addressing long tail needs before moving on to attack the hits of the short head.

Example 3.1

When a firm takes advantage of the Internet's properties—low-cost shelf space and distribution channel, a tool for making better purchase choices, and a lower-cost tool for producers to meet customer needs better—to pursue a strategy to profit from a long tail, the firm is playing a new game. It must cooperate with its coopetitors to create value and compete with them to appropriate the value in the face of the changes brought about by the Internet. As we detailed in Chapter 2, an AVAC analysis can be used to not only explore the profitability potential of a strategy but also to develop a business plan or strategic plan. We use the case of the iTunes Music Store (iTMS) to illustrate how the AVAC can be used to explore what a firm is doing or should be doing to exploit a long tail.

The Case of iTunes Music Store in 2007

iTunes Music Store was launched on the Mac on April 28, 2003, and in seven days, customers bought one million songs. In October 2003, a Windows version of the software was launched and in just three and a half days, over one million copies of it were downloaded and over one million songs purchased through the store.[8] Later that year, *Time* Magazine declared iTunes Music Store "the coolest invention of 2003."[9] Music from the store could be played without difficulty only in iTunes or on Apple's iPods. However the songs could be burnt onto a CD and then played on another digital audio player. Apple also developed its FairPlay digital rights management (DRM) system that protected songs from piracy. When protected songs were purchased from the iTunes Store, they were encoded with Fairplay which digitally prevented users from playing the files on unauthorized computers. By December 2005, more than one billion songs had been sold through iTunes Music Store. In 2007, iTunes had two primary functions: It was used for organizing and playing music and video files, for interfacing with the iTunes Music Store (iTMS) to purchase digital music and movie files, and for interfacing with the iPod to record and play music and video.[10] Effectively, iTunes, in conjuction with iPod and iTunes Music Stores enabled users to access millions of songs, make a choice of what to purchase, backup songs onto DVDs and CDs, copy files to a digital audio player, download and play podcasts, organize music into playlists, and so on.

Customers paid $0.99 for each song purchased in the iTunes store, of which $0.65 went to the record label while distribution collected $0.25.[11] Apple was therefore left with about 10 cents. Question: to what extent was Apple exploiting the long tail effect?

An Analysis of Apple's Exploitation of the Long Tail Effect Using iTunes: The AVAC Analysis

The products in the case were songs, some of which were hits at one time or the other but most of which were nonhits or old hits (oldies) that languished in the long tail. The combination of the Internet, MP3 technology, and other information technologies constituted the innovation that made exploitation of the long tail possible. The combination (1) made more shelf space and distribution channels available for music at much lower costs, (2) enabled more low-cost and effective access between producers and customers since offline record stores could be bypassed, and (3) offered customers better ways of choosing between the many songs available. For Apple to have a competitive advantage in exploiting the long tail, it had to create and appropriate value better than its competitors. We use an AVAC analysis to examine the extent to which Apple was able to take advantage of the changes introduced by the Internet and other technologies to exploit the long tail.

Activities

Recall that the *Activities* component of an AVAC framework is about exploring the extent to which the firm is performing the right set of activities—activities that contribute to creating value, better positioning the firm vis-à-vis coopetitors, and to the firm's exploitation of the value and position. The AVAC questions that are explored to understand the role of activities are shown in Table 3.1:

Table 3.1 The **Activities** Component of an iTunes AVAC Analysis

Questions	Answers
A. Was Apple performing the right activities? What was the **set of activities** (and associated resources) that constituted Apple's **strategy for iTunes**? Did the activities and/or resources/capabilities: 1. contribute to low cost, differentiation, and other drivers of profitability? 2. contribute to better position Apple vis-à-vis coopetitors? 3. take advantage of industry value drivers? 4. build new distinctive resources/ capabilities or translate existing ones into unique positions? 5. maintain parsimony and comprehensiveness?	A: *What* • Introduced iTunes on both the Mac and Windows platforms • Offered a complementary product, iPod, to match • Developed the FairPlay digital rights management (DRM) system • Entered into agreements with content providers to provide music • Priced the music at 99 cents a song B: *How* 1. YES. NO. Availability of iTunes on both the Mac and PC, together with the Apple brand, DRM and iPod contributed to differentiation. Two sources of revenue: songs and iPod. Not clear if customers stayed. 2. YES. NO. DRM better positioned Apple vis-à-vis content suppliers. 3. YES. Took advantage of two key industry value drivers: intellectual property protection of songs, and network externalities effects of Windows and Mac installed base. 4. YES. Built iPod brand, installed base in Windows, relationships with coopetitors, and DRM system. Exploited the Apple brand. 5. NO. No mention of superfluous activities being performed by Apple; but it appears there are other activities that it could perform to create and appropriate value better.

Apple performed the following iTunes-associated activities. It:

• Introduced iTunes on both the Mac and Windows platforms.
• Offered a complementary product, iPod, to match.
• Developed the FairPlay digital rights management (DRM) system.
• Entered into agreements with content providers to provide music.
• Priced the music at 99 cents a song.

In performing these activities, the firm contributed to differentiating Apple's offerings in several ways. By offering iTunes on both the Mac and Windows computers, Apple made it accessible not only to its Mac users but also to the much larger installed base of Windows users and machines. This was the first product that Apple had offered on both its Mac and the competing Windows platforms. By making sure that music from the store could be played without difficulty only in iTunes or on iPods, Apple may have been slowing access to its music store but limiting the competition faced by its iPod—a much higher margin product for Apple than songs. By developing the FairPlay digital rights management (DRM) system that protected songs from piracy, Apple reduced the fear of piracy by record labels and musicians. Thus, Apple could enter agreements with these record companies, giving it the right to sell their songs online. By demonstrating to the recording companies that it could protect their intellectual property from online piracy and cooperating with them, Apple was also effectively dampening their bargaining power. The agreements also reduced the amount of rivalry that Apple ordinarily faced. By developing Fair-Play, Apple was also taking advantage of a key industry value driver in the music industry: intellectual property protection. By porting its iTunes software to the Windows camp, continuing to build the iPod brand, and offering attractive iPod models, Apple was able to build a loyal audience within the Windows camp. This Windows-installed base was a valuable resource. The Apple brand and Steve Jobs were also valuable resources. None of the activities that Apple is performing appear to be superfluous. There is limited information in the case, but it would appear that there is more that Apple can perform to improve value creation and appropriation.

Value

The *Activities* component above tells us *how* the activities *contributed* to the value created and appropriated. The *Value* component is about the *uniqueness* of the value created and who perceived it—whether the contributions made to value creation were enough. The questions for exploring the Value component are shown in Table 3.2.

Music customers perceived the value from iTunes Music Store as being

Table 3.2 The **Value** Component of an iTunes AVAC Analysis

Questions	Answers
How unique was the value created by Apple's strategy for iTunes, as perceived by customers, compared to that from competitors?	When iTunes, the music store, and associated DRM were introduced, they were the only ones on both the Mac and Windows.
1. Did customers perceive value created by Apple as unique relative to what competitors offered?	1. YES. Features of iTunes, the Apple brand, and iTunes availability on Macs and PCs were perceived as unique.
2. Did many customers perceive this value?	2. YES. Millions of customers downloaded the software and a billion songs were bought in a very short time.
3. Were these customers precious (valuable)? What are the market segments and sources of revenue?	3. YES. NO. There were some valuable customers in the large base of Mac and Windows users but it was difficult to tell which ones were valuable.
4. Were there any white spaces nearby?	4. There were white spaces in phones, and other handhelds. Apple offered an iPhone.

unique. Through the store and associated information technologies, customers had access to millions of songs. They also had the means to choose from the millions of songs. Customers did not have to buy an album because of one good song on it. They could also see the rating of the popularity of a song to help them make their choices. They could shop 24 hours a day, seven days a week, from anywhere in the world, and could test-play portions of any song on iTunes. Because Apple made iTunes available on Windows, it had a lot more valuable customers than it may have had, had it limited iTunes to the Mac platform. As of 2007, customers with the Apple or Microsoft operating systems on their computers and access to the Internet could shop at the music store. However, computers with the Linux operating system could not. Many customers with PCs and access to the Internet were probably more willing to pay the $0.99 per song that they liked than the average music offline customer. As far as white spaces were concerned, there were lots of handheld devices, outside of MP3 devices, that did not have access to iTunes when Apple introduced iTunes on Windows. One of these white spaces was the phone, which Apple would later occupy by introducing the iPhone.

Appropriability

The *Activities* component tells us how a firm's activities contribute to value appropriation but does not tell us the *extent* to which the activities actually result in value appropriation. The *Appropriability* component tells us the extent to which value was appropriated by the activities performed by Apple. The questions for exploring the appropriability component are shown in Table 3.3.

Table 3.3 The **Appropriability** Component of an iTunes AVAC Analysis

Questions	Answers
Did Apple's strategy for iTunes (set of activities) enable the firm to make money from the value created? (How much money?)	Apple did not make much money directly from songs. It made money indirectly from iPods and iPhones.
1. Did Apple have a superior position vis-à-vis its coopetitors?	1. NO. Although its activities improved its position vis-à-vis coopetitors, Apple still did not have a superior position vis-à-vis its suppliers and customers.
2. Did Apple exploit its position vis-à-vis coopetitors and take advantage of the value perceived by customers?	2. YES. NO. Was able to get content providers to agree on something. Possible that by fixing its price at $0.99 per song, Apple's price for songs was not close enough to customers' reservation prices.
3. Was Apple's iTunes strategy difficult to imitate? (a) Was there something about Apple and its set of activities and resources that made it difficult for competitors to imitate its strategy? (b) Was there something about competitors that impeded them from imitating Apple?	3. YES. NO. Apple's brand, DRM, and system of activities were not easy to imitate; but there was nothing about competitors that prevented them from offering similar products or performing similar activities.
4. (a) Was the value non-substitutable? (b) Were complements being strategically well used?	4. NO. YES. In 2007, offline music stores were still viable substitutes. Apple used the iPod and iPhones strategically. These were priced to give Apple better margins than songs.

Although Apple did not make much money directly from sales of songs in the iTunes digital music store, it may have been making money from sales of its iPods and iPhones. Content providers still had lots of bargaining power over Apple since other channels for selling their content to end-customers existed. Thus, Apple made only 10 cents out of every 99 cents collected for each song sold, while the record labels made 65 cents and distribution the remaining 24%. This constituted a very low profit margin for Apple, but the margins on iPods were a lot larger; and without the iTunes music store, the iPod would not have had access to many songs, reducing its value to customers. Having access to both Windows and Mac users gave access to many valuable customers; but with a fixed price of $0.99 per song, there was little attempt to get closer to customers' reservation prices. Apple's brand and the iPod constituted important complementary assets. There was little about Apple and its competitors to show that iTunes would not be imitated. In fact, because iTunes worked only with iPods, many competitors who wanted a piece of the action were more likely to try to build their own online music stores. Substitutes for iTunes were the other channels that artists and record labels could use to sell their music. Complements were all compatible MP3 players.

Change: New Game

The primary change in this case was the Internet—the innovation that created the opportunity to exploit the long tail of music. When a firm took advantage of the Internet's properties—low-cost shelf space and distribution channel, a tool for making better purchase choices, and a lower-cost tool for producers to meet customer needs better—the firm was playing a new game. Apple was taking advantage of the change brought about by the Internet to exploit the long tail of music, and we can explore the extent to which Apple succeeded in doing so using the questions of Table 3.4.

Apple's primary strength in the pre-iTunes era was its brand name reputation as well as its installed base of Mac users. These strengths continued to be strengths in the iTunes era. Its biggest weakness in the pre-iTunes era had been its rather small installed base of Macs (4%) compared to the much larger (94%) installed base of Windows. In making software available on both the Mac and Windows, Apple has eliminated this weakness. In offering iTunes, Apple took advantage of the Internet in several ways. It utilized the Internet's huge low-cost virtual shelf space to offer millions of song titles to customers who could access the store from anywhere in the world with a Mac or a PC. Complemented by the FairPlay DRM system that protected songs from piracy, iTunes was unique on the web when it was introduced. Effectively, Apple was offering unique value. By offering the iPod and later, the iPhone, Apple was making sure that customers not only had access to songs, but that they also had access to more platforms to play them. Apple used iTunes and iPod not only to reinforce its brand name reputation but also to establish new Internet-based brands in iPod and iTunes. We now have podcast as a verb, thanks to Apple and its iPod/iTunes.

Apple took advantage of some opportunities for first-mover advantages. By being the first with a system that could protect songs from piracy—its FairPlay DRM system—Apple demonstrated to record labels and musicians that their

Table 3.4 The **Change** Component of an iTunes AVAC Analysis

Change

Did the strategy take advantage of change (present or future) to create unique value and/or position Apple to appropriate the value? In creating and appropriating value in the face of the change, given its strengths and handicaps, did the firm: 1. Take advantage of the new ways of creating and capturing new value generated by change? 2. Take advantage of opportunities generated by change to build new resources or translate existing ones in new ways? 3. Take advantage of first-mover's advantages and *disadvantages*, and competitors' handicaps that result from change? 4. Anticipate and respond to coopetitors' reactions to its actions? 5. Identify and take advantage of the opportunities and threats of the environment? Were there no better alternatives?	The strategy took advantage of change. Apple's brand was a strength. 1. YES. Apple took advantage of the new ways of creating and capturing value created by the Internet. It offered unique value in iTunes, iPod and its brand. 2. YES. It built new resources: Windows installed base, iPod/iTunes brand, and relationships with record labels. 3. YES. Apple built and took advantage of some first-mover advantages. Its DRM system allowed it to convince record labels that their music would not be pirated. It also moved on to build an Internet music brand. It took advantage of an established market and technology for MP3 players. 4. YES. In porting iTunes to Windows, Apple was anticipating the likely reaction of Windows-based competitors such as mighty Microsoft. It was expected that many competitors would still enter. 5. YES. NO. In creating and appropriating value the way it did, Apple was taking advantage of opportunities and threats of environment. Musicians, record labels, and competitors could also build their own online music stores, thanks to change (the Internet).

songs would not be pirated away. The timing was right given the amount of music piracy that was taking place on the Internet. This enabled the firm to establish relationships with content providers. It was not the first to offer an MP3 player, and therefore took advantage of MP3 first-mover disadvantages—the fact that the technology and market for MP3s had already been established by first movers—when Apple offered its own MP3—the iPod.

One can argue that, in porting iTunes to Windows, Apple was anticipating the likely reaction of Windows-based competitors who could have offered an iTunes equivalent for Windows. By offering iTunes on Windows first, Apple was effectively preempting potential competitors. By the time other firms offered competing online music stores on Windows, Apple had built switching costs and other first-mover advantages at many customers.

The Internet offered both opportunities and threats. The same properties of the Internet that Apple took advantage of could also be threats to it later since competitors could take advantage of them to attack Apple.

Strategic Consequence of the iTunes AVAC Analysis

Apple's strategy for iTunes in 2007 is compared to alternate strategies in Table 3.5. The strategy compares well vis-à-vis alternatives. The competitive parity designation reflects the fact that Apple did not make much money directly from iTunes. The record labels make most of the money. However Apple makes money indirectly from its iPods and iPhones. It also reflects the fact that although Apple took advantage of the Internet, it was not clear that it would be able to take advantage of future change.

As we saw in Chapter 2, the most important thing about an AVAC analysis may not be so much that we can classify a strategy as having a sustainable competitive advantage, temporary competitive advantage, competitive parity, or competitive disadvantage. The important thing is what the firm can do to reverse the Noes or reinforce the Yesses and in the process, get ever so closer to having a sustainable competitive advantage. The question for Apple was, what could it do to have a competitive advantage rather than competitive parity? Apple was taking some steps in the right direction. Introduction of the iPhone, patenting its DRM, etc. were all good steps.

Table 3.5 Strategic Consequences of an AVAC analysis of Apple's iTunes Activities

	Activities: Is Apple performing the right activities?	Value: Is the value created by Apple's iTunes strategy unique, as perceived by customers, compared to that from competitors?	Appropriability: Does Apple make money from the value created?	Change: Does the strategy take advantage of change (present or future) to create unique value and/or position itself to appropriate the value?	Strategic consequence
Strategy 1	Yes	Yes	Yes	Yes	Sustainable competitive advantage
Strategy 2	Yes	Yes	Yes	No	Temporary competitive advantage
Apple's iTunes strategy in 2007	Yes	**Yes**	**No/Yes**	**Yes/No**	**Competitive parity**
Strategy 4	Yes	Yes	No	No	Competitive parity
Strategy 5	No	No	No	No	Competitive disadvantage
Strategic action		What can Apple do to reinforce the YESes and reverse or dampen the NOes			

AVAC for Record Labels and Musicians

Note that the analysis that we have just completed is for an aggregator, Apple, which exploited the long tail by aggregating songs from different record labels and musicians and selling them; but as we saw earlier, aggregators were not the only ones that could exploit the long tail. Record labels (producers), and musicians (suppliers) could also exploit the long tail effect. Thus, an AVAC analysis could be conducted for each of them to explore the extent to which each takes advantage of the characteristics of the Internet to make money from the long tail.

Key Takeaways

- In many markets, there are likely to be a few hit or blockbuster products/ services, and many nonhits. The hits occupy the so-called short head while the nonhits occupy the long tail of a distribution that has been called names such as Pareto Law, Pareto Principle, 80/20 rule, heavy tail, power-law tail, Pareto tails, and long tail.
- Chris Anderson was the first to use the name *long tail* to describe the non-hits that end up in the long tail (niches) of each distribution. He argued that in the face of the internet, the combined sales of the many products in the long tail can be equal to, if not more than, sales of the relatively fewer hits in the short head. Thus, by aggregating these nonhits, a firm may be able to make as much money from them as it could from hits.
- In general, distributions in which there are a few product hits and many nonhits are a result of:
  1. The high cost and scarcity of distribution channels and shelf space.
  2. Customers' cognitive limitations and difficulties in making product/service choices.
  3. Customer heterogeneity and the high cost of and difficulties in meeting individual unique needs of all customers.

- Any new games or innovations that alleviate the above three factors can alter the shape of the long tail distribution.
- The Internet, for example, drastically reduces the cost of distribution and shelf space for some products, facilitates consumer choices, and makes it possible to better meet more varied kinds of consumer taste. Thus, firms can use the Internet to improve sales of products that once languished in the long tail. The question is, which firm is likely to have a competitive advantage in exploiting the long tail?
- The Internet is not the only innovation that drives or drove the long tail phenomenon. Many others did and continue to do so:
  - Botox and cosmetic surgery
  - Cell phones
  - Discount retailing in rural areas
  - Internet and political contributions
  - Internet and user innovations
  - Microfinancing
  - Organic food stores

  ○ Printing press
  ○ Radio and TV broadcasting
  ○ Video tape recorders.

- To have a competitive advantage in exploiting the long tail, a firm has to create and appropriate value in the face of the innovation that makes exploitation of the long tail possible.
- An AVAC analysis is a good tool for exploring which activities are best for creating and appropriating value in a long tail.
- To take advantage of what we know about the long tail, you, as a manager, should:

  1 Identify the long tail distributions in your markets, or the markets that you want to attack, and their drivers.
  2 Identify those new game ideas or innovations that can eliminate or take advantage of those conditions that make some products languish in each long tail.
  3 Perform an AVAC analysis to determine which activities stand to give a firm a competitive advantage as it uses new games to create and appropriate value in the long tail.
  4 Decide which activities to focus on, and how to execute the strategy.

Key Terms

Long tail
Short head

Part II

Strengths and Weaknesses

Chapter 4

Creating and Appropriating Value Using New Game Strategies

Reading this chapter should provide you with the conceptual and analytical tools to:

- Increase your understanding of the determinants of value creation and appropriation.
- Analyze how much value each member of a value system captures and why.
- Understand the contribution of new game and *value chain factors* to a firm's competitive advantage.
- Strengthen your ability to think strategically.

Introduction

Do you own a PC, iPhone, car, airplane, shoes, or a watch? How much of what you value in each of these products do you think was created by the "maker" of the product? How much of the value does the "maker" appropriate? What is its strategy for creating and appropriating value? How many countries contribute to the benefits that you value in the product? Consider one of these products, the iPhone: Each owner of an iPhone perceives value in the device when he or she navigates through the device by touching the screen, makes or receives phone calls, surfs the Web, sends or receives e-mail, takes or views pictures, and so on. Apple conceived of and designed the iPhone but did not manufacture the product when it introduced it in 2007. The hundreds of components that went into the product came from numerous suppliers from the USA, Europe, and Asia, and were shipped to an Asian manufacturer who assembled and shipped them to the USA for distribution. Many of the critical components, especially the microchips, were themselves systems that were designed and either manufactured by the suppliers, or manufactured by their subcontractors before being shipped to Apple's own subcontractors for assembly. (Microchips, with their rapidly increasing functionality but dropping prices, are what have made innovations such as the iPhone possible.) Infenion AG, a German company, supplied the digital baseband, radio-frequency transceiver, and power-management devices.[1] Samsung, a Korean company, made the video processor chip, while Sharp and Sanyo, Japanese firms, supplied the LCD display. The touch-sensitive modules that were overlaid unto the phone's LCD screen to make the multitouch control possible were designed by Balda AG, a German company and produced in its factories in China. Marvel Semiconductor of the US provided the WiFi chips. The Camera Lens was supplied by Largan

Precision of Taiwan while the camera module was supplied by three Taiwanese companies: Altus-Tech, Primax, and Lite On. Delta Electronics supplied the battery charger. Various other firms supplied other components. Apple also supplied the operating system and other software that manages the device.

The question is, how much value does Apple create and appropriate in offering the iPhone? How much value is created and/or appropriated by each supplier? How much value is created by which country? We will return to these questions later in this chapter. We start the chapter with a very important discussion of what creating and appropriating value is all about. We then explore the impact of new game activities on the creation and appropriation of value. In particular, we argue that the contribution of a set of new game activities to value creation and appropriation has two components: a component that is due to the fact that the activities are *value chain* activities and another that is due to the fact that they are *new game*. We conclude with the reminder that value creation can be as important as value appropriation and focusing only on one and not the other can make for bad strategy. One need only recall the example of musicians, who create lots of value but often do not appropriate all of it, to be reminded of the significance of value appropriation.

Creating and Appropriating Value

The concepts of creating and appropriating value are central to strategy and one way to understand them is through the illustration of Figure 4.1. Recall that business strategy is about making money and that revenues come from customers who buy products or services from firms. A customer buys a product from a firm because it perceives the product as providing it (the customer) with benefits, B; but to provide the benefits, B, a firm has to perform value-adding activities such as R&D, purchasing of equipment, components and materials, transformation of these components and materials into products or services, marketing these products and services to customers, and distributing the products to customers. These activities cost C. The economic *value created*, V,

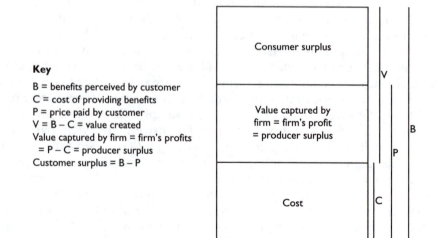

Key

B = benefits perceived by customer
C = cost of providing benefits
P = price paid by customer
V = B – C = value created
Value captured by firm = firm's profits
    = P – C = producer surplus
Customer surplus = B – P

Figure 4.1 Value Creation and Appropriation.

by the firm is the difference between the benefits, B, that a customer perceives to be in the product and how much it costs the firm to provide the benefits;[2] that is, V = B – C. The customer pays a price P for the benefits that it receives. This gives the firm a profit of P – C, and the customer gets to keep B – P; that is, the *value captured (value appropriated)* by the firm is the profit, P – C, from the value created. In economics, this profit is sometimes called the producer's surplus while what the customer gets to keep, B – P, is called the consumer's surplus. As an example, consider the value created when a firm builds and sells a car. Suppose a carmaker develops and markets a new car that customers love so much that they would be willing to pay $30,000 for the benefits that they perceive in owning the car. Also suppose that it costs the firm $15,000 to produce the car (including R&D, marketing and manufacturing costs) whose price the firm sets at $20,000. From Figure 4.1, the value created is $15,000 (30,000 – 15,000), the carmaker's profit is $5,000 (20,000 – 15,000). The customer's consumer surplus is $10,000 (30,000 – 20,000).

Note that although the value created by the firm is B – C, the firm only captures a fraction of it in the form of profits (P – C). In other words, it only *appropriates* part of the value that is created, P – C. The other part of the value created is captured by the customer in the form of consumer surplus. In other words, making money involves both creating value and appropriating the value created. We now discuss both value creation and appropriation in detail.

Value Creation

Recall that the value created is the difference between the benefits that customers perceive and the cost of providing the benefits. Effectively, value creation is about performing value chain activities so as to offer customers something that they perceive as beneficial to them, and insuring that the cost of offering the benefits does not exceed the benefits—it is about benefits and costs. The benefits that customers derive from a product can be from the product's features (performance, quality, aesthetics, durability, ease of use), the product's or firm's brand, location of the product, network effects associated with the product, or the service that comes with the product. Thus, designing a product, manufacturing and testing it all add value since they all contribute to the product's features. Advertising a product also adds value when it improves customers' perception of the product. Distributing a product adds value when it brings the product closer to customers who would otherwise not have access to it. For products which exhibit network effects, performing activities that add more customers constitutes value creation because the more people that use the product, the more valuable that it becomes to each user.

There are numerous things that a firm can do to keep its costs down while creating benefits for customers. It can innovate by using new knowledge or a combination of existing knowledge to drastically improve existing ways of performing activities, thereby drastically lowering its costs. It can take advantage of economies of scale, if its products are such that the higher its output, the lower the per unit costs of its products. It can take advantage of economies of scope, if the different products that it sells are such that the per unit costs of producing these products together is less than the per unit cost of producing each product alone. It can lower its costs by taking advantage of what it has learnt from its experiences in moving up different learning curves. It can also take advantage of any unique location that it may have such as being close to a cheap source of labor. A firm can also take advantage of industry or macro-related factors. For example, if a firm has bargaining power over its suppliers, it can negotiate to pay lower prices for its inputs, thereby keeping its costs lower. It can also use that power to work more closely with suppliers to keep component costs lower so that the supplier can pass on some of the costs savings to the firm in the form of lower input costs. Finally, a firm can keep its costs low by putting in place the right incentives and monitoring systems to reduce agency costs. Recall that agency costs are the costs that firms incur because employees or other agents are not doing what they are supposed to be doing. Effectively, firms can create value by offering more benefits and keeping down the costs of providing the benefits. We will revisit some of these factors when we explore the role of new game activities.

Value Appropriation

Value appropriation is about who gets to profit from the value created. It is about what slice of the pie one ends up getting. Referring to Figure 4.1, again, the producer firm only keeps a fraction of the value created (firm's profit) while the customer or supplier keeps the rest (consumer profit). There are five reasons why a firm that creates new value using new game activities may not be able to appropriate all of the value created:

1 The firm may not have the complementary assets needed.
2 The firm may not be well-positioned vis-à-vis its coopetitors.
3 The firm may not have the right pricing strategy.
4 The value that the firm offers may be easy to imitate or substitute.
5 The firm may not have enough valuable customers that want the benefits that it offers.

Complementary Assets

If the product that encapsulates the value created requires scarce and important complementary assets to profit from it, the owner of the complementary assets may be the one that captures the value and not the firm that created the value. This is particularly true if the product is easy to imitate. Complementary assets are all the other resources, beyond those that underpin the new game, that a firm needs to create and capture value. They include brands, distribution channels, shelf space, manufacturing, relationships with coopetitors, complementary technologies, access to complementary products, installed base, relationships with governments, and so on. Therefore a firm that invents or discovers something (through its new game activities) may need to use other new game activities to establish prior positions in complementary assets so as to profit from the invention. In the music industry case, recording companies and agents have complementary assets such as contacts, brands, and distribution channels. We will explore complementary assets in much more detail in Chapter 5.

Relationships with Coopetitors

Another reason why a firm that creates value may not be able to capture all of it is that the party with the most bargaining power is not always the one that created the value or that makes the largest contribution towards value co-creation. (In fact, the one with the most power might contribute the least to value creation.) In the **coopetition** between Intel, Microsoft, and PC makers that delivers value to PC users, Microsoft is the most profitable but it is doubtful that it creates the most value in that value system. (Creating value is synonymous with working together to make a pie while appropriating value is equivalent to dividing the pie.) The position vis-à-vis coopetitors determines the share of the pie that each firm receives. If a firm's suppliers or buyers have bargaining power over the firm, it may have difficulties capturing the value that it has created. For example, if a firm has only one supplier of a critical component, the supplier can charge so much for the component that the firm's profit margins will be reduced to zero—the supplier effectively captures most of the value that the firm has created. Buyers with power can also extract low prices out of the firm, reducing the amount of value that it can capture. Thus, pursuing new game activities that increase a firm's bargaining power can better position the firm to appropriate the value created. A classic example is that of Dell which we saw in Chapter 1. By bypassing distributors to sell directly to businesses and consumers, it was moving away from having to confront the more concentrated and powerful distributors to dealing directly with the more fragmented end-customers who had less power than distributors.

Good relationships with coopetitors can also help a firm to appropriate value better. For example, as we saw earlier, if a firm works more closely with its customers to help them discover their latent needs for its products, the willingness to pay of these customers may go up, thereby increasing the firm's chances of appropriating more of the value it creates.

Pricing Strategy and Sources of Revenue

The third reason why a firm which creates new value may not be able to capture all of it has to do with pricing and sources of revenue. The closer that a firm sets its price to each **customer's reservation price**, the more of the value created that the firm gets to keep, if the higher price does not drive the customer to competitors. Recall that a customer's reservation price for a product is the maximum price that it is willing to pay for the product. The higher a customer's reservation price, the higher the chances that the price demanded will fall enough below the customer's reservation price to leave it some consumer surplus. Also, the higher a customer's reservation price, the better the chances that the price demanded by the firm will not drive the customer away. The price demanded, in turn, is a function of the relationship between the firm and the customer, especially the bargaining power of one over the other, and the firm's pricing strategy. The higher a firm's bargaining power over its customer, the more that it can extract higher prices from the customer, thereby raising the fraction of the value that it keeps (profits). Also, a firm that has good relationships with its customers can better work with such customers to discover and meet their needs, thereby increasing the customer's reservation price and lowering costs, all of which increase the value created and appropriated.

Effectively, if a customer has a high reservation price but a firm sets its price below the reservation price, the customer keeps the difference and walks away with a higher consumer surplus while the firm leaves with a lower profit. Pricing above customers' reservation prices drives them away. Thus, a firm is better off pursuing a pricing strategy that gets it as close as possible to a customer's reservation price, without driving customers to competitors. A firm's *sources of revenue* also determine the amount of revenues that it collects and in a way, the value that it captures. New game activities that create new sources of revenue can increase the value that a firm can capture. Take the case of Ryanair. In addition to the revenues that it collects from airline tickets, it also receives revenues from advertising, sales of snacks and duty free goods, and commissions on hotel accommodation and car rental reservations made through its website. Effectively, the primary value that Ryanair offers its passengers is flying them from one place to the other. These other sources of revenue help it appropriate more of the value that it creates in an indirect way.

Imitability and Substitutability

Imitability and substitutability can also curb the extent to which a firm can appropriate all the value that it creates. If competitors are able to imitate the value that a firm creates, its prices and the quantity that it sells are likely to drop. If other firms can offer viable substitute products, customers can switch to these substitutes if a firm's prices are higher than they would like. This reduces the value that the firm can appropriate.

Number of Valuable Customers

The number of valuable customers that a firm can attract with the value that it offers also contributes towards how much value is captured. This depends on the ratio of fixed costs relative to variable costs. The lower the variable costs relative to fixed costs, the more that each extra unit sold is likely to bring in more profits than earlier units. By definition, valuable customers have a high willingness to pay and therefore are likely to have higher reservation prices and be more likely to buy more than one unit. Effectively, the number of customers also matters; and so does the market or market segment that a firm targets, since not all customers have the same willingness to pay for a given set of benefits or cost the same to acquire and keep. Moreover, customers have to have enough information about the products that firms offer to be able to choose which benefits they want. Thus, it is also important to perform activities that identify and target the right customers and that increase the number of customers who like the benefits offered. One reason offered for Dell's success in the mid to late 1990s was the fact that over 70% of the firm's customers were businesses with PC purchases of over $1 million. Such customers not only have higher reservation prices; they may also make for better targets for building switching costs. Moreover, they are likely to cost less (per unit sold) to maintain than smaller less dependable ones.

Coopetition and Value Creation

Since value created is the difference between the benefits that a customer perceives and the costs to a firm of providing these benefits, value creation can be as much a function of what the firm does as it is a function of what its coopetitors—the customers, complementors, rivals, and suppliers with whom a firm cooperates to create value and competes to capture it—do.[3] The quality of the inputs from a firm's suppliers impacts the quality of the benefits that the firm can offer customers. For example, the benefits that a customer enjoys in a PC are as much a function of how the PC maker designs, manufactures, and markets the product as they are a function of the quality of the microprocessor (from suppliers Intel or AMD), and of the software from complementors (Microsoft and others) as well as of how the customer uses the PC. The cost to a firm of providing benefits to its customers is also a function of its suppliers and the relationship between the firm and these suppliers. Additionally, the extent to which a customer perceives a product as meeting his or her needs is a function of the customer's unique characteristics, including what the customer wants the product for. Moreover, the price that a customer gets to pay a firm is a function of the relationship between the customer and the firm. In fact, sometimes value is often created by coopetitors who cooperate through alliances, informal understandings, joint ventures, venture capital investments, etc. Effectively, *a firm usually has to cooperate to create value and compete to appropriate the value.* In a fair world, each firm would capture value equivalent to how much it created. (Your slice of the pie would be equivalent to your contribution.) But often, firms with power in their value system capture more of the value created in the system than their contribution would merit. Effectively, a very important part of strategy is positioning oneself to capture as much value in one's value system as possible.

Example 4.1: Who Appropriates What in a Book Value System

In 2000, it was estimated that for each dollar a customer paid for a book, the author received 10 cents, the publisher of the book got 32 cents, the printer received 8 cents, while the distributor and retailer received 20 cents and 30 cents respectively.[4] Profit margins for authors, publishers, printers, distributors, and retailers were −3.2%, 13.1%, 6.0%, 6.8%, and 17.3%, respectively.[5] How much value did each player in the value chain appropriate? Are the players who capture the most value really the ones that create the most value?

Solution to Example 4.1

Consider publishers. They received 32 cents of each dollar of sales and had profit margins of 13.1%. The value appropriated by publishers is the profit that they make from the value created. Therefore:

$$\text{Profit margin} = \frac{\text{Profit}}{\text{Sales}} = \frac{\text{Profit}}{\$0.32} = 0.131 = 13.1\%$$

Thus, Profit $= \$0.32 \times 0.131 = \$0.042$. This is the value appropriated by publishers. Publishers' costs are $\$0.32 - 0.042 = 0.278$.

Similarly, we can calculate the amounts appropriated by each player and its cost. These numbers are shown in Figure 4.2. Also shown in the figure is the percentage of value that each player appropriated. Retailers appropriated 47.6% of the value created, the most of any player. Why did retailers appropriate so much value compared to other players? First, retailers controlled the shelf space in the *offline world* and therefore had bargaining power over their suppliers and buyers. They typically paid publishers only 50% of the suggested retail price.[6] At some locations, such as universities and retail malls, book retailers constituted local monopolies. Effectively, retailers have complementary assets and power over coopetitors, and good locations differentiate them from rivals. Second, many retailers could resale old books, making good profits without lifting a finger. Publishers appropriated 38.5% of the value created, second only to retailers. They had a great deal of power over the average author, although famous authors commanded a lot of power over publishers because of the pull that famous-author names establish with consumers.

Distributors (including wholesalers) were next with 12.5% of the value appropriated. They transported the books and often stored them in warehouses until retailers needed them. The least value was appropriated by printers and authors with 4.4% and −2.9% respectively. Printers were highly fragmented with little or no power over their suppliers or buyers. Authors were also highly fragmented and therefore had little power over publishers (except famous authors). Although famous authors commanded lots of money, the average author lost money. He or she appropriated no value; rather, he or she had to "pay" other members of the value system to take the book from him or her. He or she "paid" the equivalent of 2.9% of the price of a book. Effectively, the average author makes little or no money directly from books. Since most people who buy books buy them for their content, it is doubtful that 47.6% of what readers get out of a book comes from retailers. Effectively, some players captured more value than they created.

	Author	Publisher	Printer	Distributor	Retailer	Total
Revenues ($)	0.100	0.320	0.080	0.200	0.300	1.000
Profit margins (%)	−3.2	13.1	6.0	6.8	17.3	10.9
Costs ($)	0.103	0.278	0.075	0.186	0.248	0.891
Value captured ($)	−0.003	0.042	0.005	0.014	0.052	0.109
Value captured (%)	−2.9	38.5	4.4	12.5	47.6	100

Figure 4.2 A Book Value Chain.

Example 4.2: Who Creates and Appropriates What Value in an iPhone

In 2007 when Apple shipped the first iPhones, some financial analysts estimated that the cost of the components and final manufacturing for the phone were $234.83 and $258.83 for the 4 GB and 8 GB versions, respectively (Table 4.1).[7] The recommended retail prices for both versions (4 GB and 8 GB) were $499 and $599. The wholesale discount for electronic products was estimated to be 25%. The question is, how much of the value that customers saw in the iPhone

Table 4.1 Some Estimated Costs for the iPhone in 2007

Component	Supplier	Cost for 4GB iPhone (US$)		Cost for 8GB iPhone (US$)	
		US$	%	US$	%
ARM RISC application processor	Samsung, Korea	14.25	6.07	14.25	5.51
NAND flash memory	Samsung, Korea	24	10.22	48	18.54
SDRAM (1GB)	Samsung, Korea	14	5.96	14	5.41
3 chips: digital base band LSI, transceiver LSI, and power management unit	Infineon Technologies AG, Germany	15.25	6.49	15.25	5.89
Touch screen module	Balda AG, German, and Tpk Solutions, Taiwan	27	11.50	27	10.43
LCD module	Epson Imaging Devices Corp., Sharp Corp. and Toshiba Matsushita Display Technology Co.	24.5	10.43	24.5	9.47
Bluetooth chip	CSR plc of the UK	1.9	0.81	1.9	0.73
Wi-Fi base band chip	Marvel Semiconductor Inc, USA	6	2.56	6	2.32
802.11b/q		15.35	6.54	15.35	5.93
Accessories/packaging etc.		8.5	3.62	8.5	3.28
Final manufacturing	Various contractors?	15.5	6.60	15.5	5.99
Royalties for EDGE		4.61	1.96	4.61	1.78
Operating system (OS X)	Apple	7	2.98	7	2.70
Voice processing software		3	1.28	3	1.16
Camera module	Altus-Tech, Primax, and Lite on.	11	4.68	11	4.25
Battery		5.2	2.21	5.2	2.01
Mechanical components/enclosure		12	5.11	12	4.64
Other hardware/software components		25.77	10.97	25.77	9.96
Total cost of inputs		234.83	100.00	258.83	100.00

Source: iSuppli Corporation: Applied Market Intelligence. Author's estimates.

did Apple and each of its suppliers capture? How much value was created by each actor? How much of it was created in the US?

Solution to Example 4.2

Value Captured

Recall that value captured = price – cost of providing benefits. The retail price for the 4GB iPhone was $499. Therefore, the wholesale price = (1 – 0.25) × $499 = 374.25. (Distributors and retailers received $124.75 of the $499—i.e. 25% of the retail price). The cost of inputs for the 4 GB is $234.83 (from Table 4.1). Therefore, the estimated value captured by Apple = Price – Cost = $374.25 – 234.83 = 139.42.

How much value was captured by Apple's suppliers? Consider Samsung which supplied at least three components. The problem here is that although we know the prices of each component, we do not know Samsung's cost for each component. Firms do not release details of individual product costs. However, they provide gross profit margins in their financial statements, which we will use for our estimates. Samsung's gross profit margin in 2006 was 18.6; that is:

$$\frac{P - C}{P} = 18.6\%$$

Therefore P – C = P × 0.186 = value added.

For NAND Flash memory (Table 4.1), the value captured by Samsung = $24 × 0.186 = $4.46.

If the LCD module were provided by Sharp, we could also calculate the value captured by Sharp using its 2006 gross profit margin of 22.6%. This value was $24.5 × 0.226 = 5.54. If we assume that the firms that did the final manufacturing (assembly) for Apple had profit margins of 15%, then each received $15.5 × 0.15 = 2.33 for every 4 GB iPhone that it manufactured.

Effectively, for each $499 that a customer paid for a 4GB iPhone, retailers and distributors took $124.75, Apple captured $139.42, Samsung captured $4.60 for the NAND flash memory alone, Sharp captured $5.54 for the LCD module when it was bought from Sharp, each final "manufacturer" (assembler) received $2.33, and so on. The value captured by any of the other suppliers can be similarly calculated.

Value Added

Recall that

> Value created = benefits perceived by customers—cost of providing the benefits;
> = customer's willingness to pay—cost of providing the benefits;
> = customer's reservation price—cost of providing the benefits.

One problem here is that it is not always easy to determine a customer's reservation price or willingness to pay. In the case of Apple, for example, we know that many of the customers who bought the iPhone could have paid a lot more than the listed retail price; that is, their reservation prices for the product were higher than the retail prices. However, we do not know exactly how much more each one would have paid. What we can say is that the average reservation price of customers was higher than the retail price that they ended up paying. Neither do we know what Apple's reservation prices for each of the components were. The important thing for a strategist to remember is always to look for ways to get as close as possible to each customer's reservation price so as to extract as much of the value created as possible, without driving the customer to competitors. At the same time, a firm also tries to do the best to extract a price from its suppliers that is below its reservation price, without adversely affecting the ability of the supplier to keep supplying high quality components.

International Component to Value Creation and Appropriation

One interesting thing to observe in the example above is that although each contract manufacturer that assembled the iPhone for Apple only captured $2.33 of every $499 that each customer paid for a 4GB iPhone, the manufacturer's home country was credited with exports of $234.83, the factor cost of the product assembled in the country. This is unfortunate because even though the manufacturing country captured very little value, it was still seen as the largest benefactor of the exports.

Consider the opposite example, where a large US exporter may be getting more credit for exports than the value-added approach would suggest. In the 1980s, 1990s, and 2000s, Boeing Corporation was one of America's largest exporters. How much of the value that airlines saw in a Boeing 787 in 2007, for example, was created in the USA? Boeing designed the aircraft and performed the R&D and rigorous testing that are critical to aircraft success. The aircraft was being assembled in Everett, Washington, USA. However, almost all of the major components (subassemblies) that were put together in Everett—all of them systems in themselves—were manufactured and tested in other countries before being shipped to Everett for assembly.[8] For example, the wings, center wing box, main landing gear wheel well, and forward fuselage were manufactured by Mitsubishi and Kawasaki Heavy Industries in Nagoya, Japan. The other forward fuselage was produced in the US by Vought in South Carolina, the center fuselage in Italy by Alenia, while the aft fuselage was produced in Wichita, Kansas, US, by Spirit AeroSystems.[9] The horizontal stabilizers were manufactured in Italy by Alenia Aeronautica. Passenger doors were made in France by Latecoere while the cargo doors, access doors, and crew escape door were made in Sweden by Saab. The ailerons and flaps were manufactured in Australia by Boeing Australia, while the fairings were produced in Canada by Boeing Canada Technology. Finally, the 787 would be powered by the General Electric (USA) GEnx and Rolls-Royce (UK) Trent 1000 engines.

Thus, although Boeing added value to the 787 by conceiving of and designing the plane, integrating all the components, coordinating all the suppliers, and assembling the subassemblies, the critical components of the airplane—such as the engines, fuselage, landing gear systems, wings, tail, etc.—were designed, developed, tested and assembled by its suppliers. These firms added a huge amount of the value that airlines and passengers saw in a 787. Moreover, in designing the plane, Boeing also worked very closely with its customers—the airlines that would buy the planes. Also, many of these coopetitors were outside the USA. However, if a Japanese airline were to buy a 787, the full cost of the plane would be credited to US exports to Japan. We might have a better picture of what is going on when we think in terms of value created and appropriated rather than products exported or imported.

New Game Activities for Creating and Appropriating Value

New Game Activities and Value Creation

Recall that new game activities are activities that are performed *differently* from the way existing industry value chain activities have been performed to create or capture value. Also recall that value creation is about providing unique benefits to customers while keeping the cost of providing the benefits low. Therefore, value creation using new game activities is about performing value chain, value network, or value shop activities *differently* to offer customers something new that they perceive as beneficial to them, and insuring that the cost of offering the benefits does not exceed the benefits. The activities can be *different* with respect to *which* activities are performed, *when* they are performed, *where*, or *how*? (Note that *where* here can mean where along the value chain, where in geography, where in a product space, where in the resource space, and so on.) The new benefits can be new product features, a new brand image, better product location, a larger network for products that exhibit network externalities, or better product service. Such benefits can come from innovations in product design, R&D, manufacturing, advertising, and distribution that improve the benefits perceived by customers. A firm can also offer new benefits by being the first in an industry to move to a particular market. This was the case with Wal-Mart when it moved into small towns in the Southwestern USA that other discount retailers had neglected. It was also the case when Ryanair moved into secondary airports in European cities to which major airlines had paid no attention. New game activities can also create value by only reducing costs. For example, a firm can drastically reduce its costs by reorganizing its business processes so as to perform tasks more efficiently. In some ways, this is what business process re-engineering has been all about—firms re-organizing their business processes to perform tasks more efficiently. Firms can also find new ways to learn from their past experiences or other firms and apply the new knowledge to existing tasks to lower costs.

New game advertising activities can reveal the benefits of a product to more customers in new ways, or change customers' perception of the benefits from a firm's products. In either case, such activities are likely to increase customers' willingness to pay for a product and the number of such customers, thereby increasing the total value created. Pfizer was one of the first in the cholesterol drug market to conduct so-called direct-to-consumer (DTC) marketing of its Lipitor cholesterol drug by advertising directly to patients, instead of to doctors. This not only increased the number of people who knew something about cholesterol and the benefits of cholesterol drugs; it may have also changed Pfizer's drug's image and customers' willingness to pay for it.

Reverse Positioning: More Is Not Always Better

In using new game activities to create value for customers, a firm does not always have to offer products with better attributes than those of competing products. A firm can strip off some of the attributes that have come to be considered as sacred cows by customers. In *reverse positioning*, a firm strips off some of a product's major attributes but at the same time, adds new attributes that may not have been expected.[10] For example, in offering its Wii, Nintendo did not try to outdo Microsoft's Xbox 360 and Sony's PS3 by offering a video game console with the more computing power, graphical detail, and complicated controls that avid gamers had come to consider as sacred cows. Rather, Nintendo offered a product with less computing power, less graphical detail, and easy-to-use controls. However, the Wii had "channels" on which news and weather information could be displayed. In reverse positioning, some of the customers who cannot do without the sacred cows that have been stripped are likely to stay away from the new product; but the new product, if well conceived, is likely to attract its own customers. There is self-selection in which some customers gravitate towards the new product, despite the fact that it does not have some of the sacred cows that some customers have come to expect. For example, although many avid gamers did not care much for the Nintendo Wii, many beginners, lapsed and casual gamers loved the machine. Effectively, more is not always better. One does not have to outdo existing competitors on their performance curve.

New Game Activities and Value Appropriation

Recall that value appropriation is about how much a firm profits from the value that has been created, and that how much a firm appropriates is a function of five factors: availability and importance of complementary assets, the relationship between a firm and its coopetitors, pricing strategy, imitability and substitutability, and the number of valuable customers. Thus, any new game activities that influence any of these factors can have an impact on appropriability. Take technological innovation activities, for example. A pharmaceutical firm that pursues and obtains protection (patents, copyrights, or trade secrets) for the intellectual property that underpins its products may be effectively increasing barriers to entry into its market space, reducing rivalry, and increasing switching costs for customers. Increased barriers-to-entry and reduced rivalry mean that the firm can keep its prices high, since there is less threat of potential new entry and less threat of price wars from rivals. Increasing switching costs for customers also means less bargaining power for customers, and some chance of the firm extracting higher prices from the customer. Defendable patents for many pharmaceutical products are partly responsible for the ability of pharmaceutical firms to appropriate much of the value that they create.

eBay's activities in online auctions also offer another example of how a firm can use new game activities to create and appropriate value. The firm built a large and relatively safe community of registered users, and implemented auction pricing. The larger the size of such a safe community for online auctions, the more valuable it is for each user, since each seller is more likely to find a buyer and each buyer is more likely to find a seller in a larger network than in a smaller one. Thus, users are less likely to switch to a smaller or less safe network, thereby giving eBay some bargaining power. When it uses an auction format, eBay gets closer to each buyer's reservation price than it would if rivals had networks with similar attributes or when it uses a fixed-pricing format.

New Game Activities, Value Creation, and Appropriation

Although we have described value creation and value appropriation separately, new game activities can and often result in both value creation *and* appropriation. For example, when a pharmaceutical company develops a new effective drug and obtains enforceable patents for it, the firm has effectively created value and put itself in a position to appropriate the value. If the drug is very good at curing the ailment for which it is earmarked, patients would prefer the drug over less effective ones, and the firm has bargaining power over patients and can obtain high prices where government regulations permit. Moreover, substitutes have less of an effect because of the drug's effectiveness, and the threat of potential new entry and of rivalry have less of an effect on the firm because of the enforceable patents.

Shifts in the Locus of Value Creation and Appropriation

So far, we have focused on how and why value is created and appropriated during new games; but new games can also shift the locus of value creation and appropriation along a value system. For example, in the mainframe and mini-computer era, most of the value in the computer industry was created and appropriated by vertically integrated computer firms such as IBM and DEC that produced the microchips and software critical to their products. In the new game ushered in by the PC, much of the value in the industry was appropriated by Microsoft, a complementor and supplier, and Intel, a supplier. Effectively, value creation and appropriation shifted from computer makers to their suppliers and complementors. One of the more interesting examples of a shift in value creation and appropriation during new games is that of Botox. Before Botox, cosmetic procedures were performed primarily by surgeons who charged high specialist fees for the procedure and their suppliers obtained little or nothing per procedure. Surgery could last hours and patients were put under anesthetic and after the surgery, it took weeks for the patient to recover fully. After the FDA approval of Botox in 2002, many cosmetic procedures could be performed by any doctor using Botox. A vial of Botox cost its maker, Allergan, $40 and it sold it to doctors for $400, who marked it up to about $2,800.[11] Each vial could be used to treat three to four patients. The Botox procedure lasted a few minutes and the patient could return to work or other normal activity the same day. Effectively, the introduction of Botox substituted some of a cosmetic surgeon's skills with a product and shifted some of the value creation and appropriation from cosmetic surgeons to Allergan, their supplier.

Latent Link Between Cooperation and Competition

On the one hand, most strategy frameworks are either all about competition or all about cooperation. Porter's Five Forces, for example, is all about competitive forces impinging on industry firms. Even the versions of the Five Forces that incorporate complementors say little or nothing about the cooperation that may exist between industry firms and suppliers, buyers, rivals, and potential new entrants. On the other hand, models of cooperation between firms say very little or nothing about the underlying implicit competition that exists between the cooperating firms. As we argued earlier, where there is cooperation there is likely to be competition, and where there is competition, there are probably opportunities for cooperation. For two reasons, these two statements are even more apropos in the face of new game activities. First, new game activities, especially those that underpin revolutionary new games, usually have more uncertainties to be resolved than non-new game activities. Such uncertainties, especially when they are technological, are best resolved through some sort of cooperation.[12] Thus, for example, a firm that is developing a new product whose components are also innovations is better off cooperating with suppliers of such components to resolve product development uncertainties that they face rather than seeing each supplier only as an adversary over whom the firm wants to have bargaining power.[13] Moreover, competitors in a relatively young market have an incentive to cooperate to grow in the market. Second, as we saw earlier in this chapter, profiting from new game activities often requires complementary assets, many of which are often obtained through some form of cooperation; and where there is cooperation to create value, there is also competition, even if only implicit, to share costs and the value created.

The Missed Opportunities During Cooperation and Competition

Effectively then, each time firms miss out on an opportunity to cooperate during competition, they may be missing out on making a larger pie; and each time a firm forgets about the implicit competition that is taking place during cooperation, it may be reducing its share of the pie. For example, rather than use its bargaining power over suppliers and force them to take low prices, a firm can work with the suppliers to reduce their costs and improve the functionality and quality of the components. In so doing, the firm may end up with better components that cost less than the previous inferior ones and a supplier that is even more profitable and happier than before.

The Whole Grape or a Slice of the Watermelon

One mistake that is easy for coopetitors to make in the face of the competition that often takes place during cooperation is to forget to think of one's alternatives. In particular, before dumping your partner because your percentage of the pie is small relative to your partner's share and your contribution, think very carefully about who else is out there with whom you can create a pie. Will the value that you create with this new partner be as large as the one that you can create with your existing partner? In leaving your existing partner for an outsider, you may be leaving 10% of a watermelon for 90% of a grape.[14]

Value Creation Using the Internet: *Crowdsourcing*

An innovating firm usually has to interact or collaborate with outside firms to be successful. This process of interaction and collaboration is vastly facilitated by the use of the Internet and its game-changing value-creation possibilities. We explore another example of how firms can take advantage of the game-changing nature of the Internet to create value. We start with the captivating case of Goldcorp Inc.

The Case of Goldcorp Inc.

Don Tapscott and Anthony Williams,[15] and Linda Tischler[16] offer a fascinating account of how a firm can take advantage of a technological innovation such as the Internet to pursue a revolutionary new game strategy. In 1999, things were not going very well at Goldcorp Inc., a Toronto-based miner. Rob McEwen, the firm's CEO, believed that the high-grade gold ore that ran through neighboring mines had to run through his firm's 55,000-acre Red Lake stake. However, Goldcorp's geologists had difficulties providing an accurate estimate of the value and location of the gold. McEwen took time out from work, and while at a seminar for young presidents at the Massachusetts Institute of Technology (MIT) in 1999, he stumbled on a session about the story of Linux and the open-source phenomenon. He listened absorbedly to how Linus Torvalds and a group of volunteers had built the Linux operating system over the Internet, revealing the software's code to the world and therefore allowing thousands of anonymous programmers to make valuable contributions to building and improving the operating system. It suddenly dawned on McEwen what his firm ought to do. "I said, 'Open-source code! That's what I want!'," McEwen would later recall.[17] He wanted to open up the exploration process to the world the way the open-source team had opened up the operating system development process.

McEwen rushed back to Toronto and told his chief geologists his plan—to put all of their geological data, going back to 1948, on a databank and share it with the world, and then ask the world to tell them where to find the gold. The idea of putting their ultra-secret geological data out there, for the public to mess with, appalled the geologists whose mental logic was deeply rooted in the super secrecy of this conservative industry. McEwen went ahead anyway and in 2000 launched the "Goldcorp Challenge" with $575,000 in prize money for anyone out there who could come up with the best estimates and methods for striking the gold at Goldcorp's Red Lake property. All 400 megabytes of the firm's geological data were put on its website.

The response was instantaneous and impressive. More than 1,400 engineers, geologists, mathematicians, consultants, military officers, and scientists downloaded the data and went to work. Yes, it wasn't just select geologists. As McEwen would later recall, "We had applied math, advanced physics, intelligent systems, computer graphics, and organic solutions to inorganic problems. There were capabilities I had never seen before in the industry."[18]

The five-judge panel was impressed by the ingenuity of the submissions. The

Top winner was a collaborative team of two groups from Australia: Fractal Graphics of West Perth, and Taylor Wall & Associates of Queensland. They had developed an impressive three-dimensional graphical model of the mine. "When I saw the computer graphics, I almost fell out of my chair," McEwen would later recall.[19] The contestants identified 110 targets, of which 50% had not been previously identified. Substantial quantities of gold were found in over 80% of the new targets that had been identified. What is more, McEwen estimated that using the crowd to solve the problem had taken two to three years off the their normal exploration time, with substantial cost savings to boot.

The gold that Goldcorp had struck, together with its upgraded mines, now enabled the firm to perform up to the potential for which McEwen had hoped when he bought a majority share in the mine in 1989. By 2001, the Red Lake mine was producing 504,000 ounces of gold per year, at a cost of $59 per ounce.[20] Contrast that with a pre-"Gold Challenge" 1996 annual rate of 53,000 ounces at a cost of $360.

Looking to the future, McEwen saw more. "But what's really important is that from a remote site, the winners were able to analyze a database and generate targets without ever visiting the property. It's clear that this is part of the future,"[21] he would say.

Crowdsourcing, Wikinomics, Mass Collaboration?

Goldcorp's outsourcing of the task of analyzing data to estimate the value and location of gold on its site is a classic example of crowdsourcing. A firm is said to be *crowdsourcing* if it outsources a task to the general public in the form of an open call to anyone who can perform the task, rather than outsourcing it to a specific firm, group, or individual. The task can be anywhere along any value chain—from design to refining algorithms to marketing. Crowdsourcing has also been called wikinomics, mass collaboration, and open innovation. It was first coined by Jeff Howe and Mark Robinson of *Wired* magazine.[22] In 2008, there was still some disagreement as to what name to give to this phenomenon in which tasks are outsourced via open calls to anyone in the public who can perform the tasks. The important thing is that the phenomenon is real and can be expected to become more and more the center of new games. There are numerous other examples. Threadless, founded in 2000, depends on the public to design, select designs, market, and buy its T-shirts. InnoCentive, founded in 2002, acts as a B2B firm that outsources R&D for biomedical and pharmaceutical companies to other firms in other industries and other countries. Examples of crowdsourcing are not limited to for-profit activities. Wikipedia, the free online encyclopedia, lets anyone provide input. In June 2008, Encyclopedia Britannica also decided to have the public edit its pages. The open source project in which Linux was developed also falls into this category. Crowdsourcing has several advantages:

Public May Be Better

If the best solution to the problem whose solution is being sought requires radically different ways of doing things, there is a good chance that the public may hold a better solution than the firm seeking the solution. Why? The public is not handicapped by prior commitments, mental frames, and the not-invented-here syndrome of the outsourcing firm that might prevent it from taking the radical approach. The public is comprised of lots of people with different backgrounds, mental models, and disciplines, and one of whom may be the right one for the radical approach needed.

Solution May Already Exist

In some cases, the solution to a problem may already exist outside there, or someone is already very close to solving the problem. Thus, going outside not only saves time and money, it can save the firm from reinventing the wheel.

Breadth and Depth of Talent

Depending on the task and industry, the breadth and depth of talent out there in the public may be better than what is available within the outsourcing organization or within a specific entity chosen by a firm to solve the problem. Even the best firms cannot hire everyone that they need. Some of the best talent may prefer to live in another country, state, or city. Some people may thrive among a different set of people than that available at the firm. Some may prefer to work only when there is a challenging and interesting problem to solve, and therefore find the confines of the outsourcing firm inhospitable.

Better Incentive for Competitors

Someone or group in the public may have a better incentive than the firm to solve the problem. Some people may thrive only when there is the possibly of showing off their skills in a contest. They want to be able to say, "I was the best in the world."

Cheaper and Faster

The firm gets to pay only for the best solutions. It is effectively paying only for results. It does not have to pay for any deadwood. For this reason and the others outlined above, the firm's cost of crowdsourcing is likely to be lower than that of internal development or cooperation with a specific firm or individual. The solution is also likely to be arrived at in a much shorter time.

Signaling

By outsourcing a task to the public, a firm is signaling to its coopetitors that it is going to engage in some activities. For example, if a firm's competitor introduces a new product and the firm wants its competitors to know that it has a similar product on its way, it can crowdsource some of the activities or components that go into the upcoming product. In so doing, the firm is telling its loyal customers not to switch to its competitors, since it has a newer and better product around the corner.

Disadvantages of Crowdsourcing

Crowdsourcing also has disadvantages. First, it is more difficult to protect one's intellectual property when one opens up to the public as much as one has to when crowdsourcing. There are no written contracts or nondisclosure agreements. Second, crowdsourcing may not be suitable for tasks that require tacit knowledge since such knowledge cannot be encoded and sent over the Internet. Tacit knowledge is best transferred in-person through learning-by-doing. Crowdsourcing may not be ideal for long and complex tasks such as designing and building an airplane. Such tasks require monitoring, continuous motivation, and other long-term commitments. Third, it may be difficult to integrate the outsourced solution into an organization that suffers from not-invented-here syndrome. Fourth, opportunistic competitors can target your calls with malicious solutions that they know will not work, hoping that you will not be able to catch them. These disadvantages can be mitigated through the right management.

New Game Strategies for Profitability

Having explored value creation and appropriation, the question now is: in pursuing a new game strategy, is there anything that a firm can do to increase its chances of contributing the most to value creation and appropriation and therefore its profitability? After all, not all firms that pursue new game strategies do well. Yes, it depends on (1) the firm's strengths and handicaps, and (2) how it performs its new value chain activities while taking advantage of the new game's characteristics (Figure 4.3).

Strengths and Handicaps

When a firm faces a new game, some of its pre-new game strengths remain strengths while others become handicaps. These strengths and handicaps then determine the extent to which the firm can perform value chain activities to create and appropriate value, taking advantage of the characteristics of the new game (Figure 4.3). Strengths and handicaps can be resources (distribution channels, shelf space, plants, equipment, manufacturing know-how, marketing know-how, R&D skills, patents, cash, brand-name reputations, technological know-how, client or supplier relationships, dominant managerial logic, routines, processes, culture and so on), or product-market positions (low-cost, differentiation, or positioning vis-à-vis coopetitors). A firm's strengths and weaknesses in the face of a new game can determine its failure or success. For example, even in the face of revolutionary technologies, some brands, distribution channels, and relationships with customers often continue to be strengths for a firm.[23] (In Chapter 5, we will see how a firm can determine its strengths and handicaps in the face of a new game.)

Value Chain and New Game Factors

Given a firm's strengths and handicaps, the question becomes, how can the firm create and appropriate the most value? To answer this question, recall from

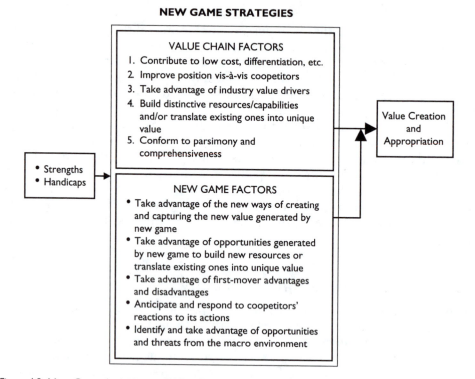

Figure 4.3 New Game Activities and Value Creation and Capture.

Chapter 2 that the extent to which activities—any value chain activities—are likely to contribute optimally to value creation and appropriation is a function of the extent to which the activities contribute to low cost, differentiation, more customers, and other drivers of profits; contribute to better position the firm vis-à-vis its coopetitors; take advantage of *industry value drivers*; build or translate distinctive resources/capabilities into new value; are parsimonious and comprehensive. Let us call these factors on which value creation and appropriation depends *value chain factors*, given that they are about value chain activities. Since the new game activities that are the cornerstones of any new game strategy are also value chain activities, their contribution to optimal value creation and appropriation is also a function of these value chain factors. Additionally, however, the contribution of new game strategies to value creation and appropriation is also a function of *new game factors*—a function of the fact that, as we saw in Chapter 1, new games generate new ways of creating and appropriating new value; offer an opportunity to build new resources/capabilities or translate existing ones in new ways into value; create the potential to build and exploit first-mover advantages; attract reactions from new and existing competitors; and have their roots in the opportunities and threats of an industry or macroenvironment.

The contributions of a new game strategy's value chain and new game factors to value creation and appropriation are shown in Figure 4.3. The value chain factor makes a direct contribution. However, the new game factor contributes to value creation and appropriation only indirectly—it contributes by moderating the contribution of the value chain component. A moderating variable plays the role that stirring tea plays. Stirring tea without sugar does not make the tea sweet. But stirring plays a critical role in the sweetness of the tea when there is sugar present. Effectively, whether the effect of value chain factors on value creation and appropriation is large or small is a function of the new game factors. We now explore how each value chain factor, moderated by new game factors, impacts value creation and appropriation (Figure 4.3).

Contribute to Low Cost, Differentiation, More Customers, Better Pricing, and Sources of Revenues

A firm can use new game activities, just as it can use any other value chain activities, to contribute to low cost, differentiation, attracting more customers, pricing better, and identifying or pursuing the right sources of revenues. However, since new games generate new ways of creating and/or capturing new value, a firm can take advantage of these new ways by, for example, choosing those activities that enable it to offer unique value to customers, or to position itself better vis-à-vis its coopetitors. Doing so is tantamount to occupying a unique product space or so-called "sweet spot" or "white space" in which there is little or no head-on competition and therefore less rivalry. This creates an opportunity for firms to better attract the right customers with the right value and pursue the right pricing strategies and sources of revenue. Also, since new games create opportunities for a firm to build and exploit first-mover advantages, a firm can build switching costs at customers if it is the first to move to the white space. For example, when Dell targeted volume-buying business customers as the primary focus for its direct-sales/build-to-order business model, it built its brand at these customers and performed extra customization tasks for such firms—including the loading of firm-specific software—efforts that may have built some switching costs at these customers. Switching costs decrease the effect of rivalry, the power of buyers, and the threat of potential new entry and substitutes. They can also increase a customer's willingness to pay. Thus, building switching costs as a result of moving first strengthens a firm's position, thereby improving its ability to create and appropriate value. Switching costs are easier to build if the firm has strengths such as prior relationships with such customers or a well-established brand.

In pursuing the right pricing strategy, a firm can also take advantage of first-mover advantages. For example, in pharmaceuticals, firms that are the first to discover a new drug in a therapeutic category usually set the price of the drug very high since there is no similar drug in the market and there is usually a high willingness to pay in countries where pharmaceutical prices are not regulated. This practice is called *skimming* and is meant to allow a firm to collect as much cash as possible before competitors move in with close substitutes. Effectively, in attracting the right customers using the right benefits and pursuing the right pricing strategies and sources of revenue, a firm can build first-mover advantages that will help to amplify its ability to create and appropriate value.

Improve its Position vis-à-vis Coopetitors

If a firm uses new game strategies to offer its customers unique benefits, for example, it improves its position vis-à-vis coopetitors. Additionally, because the activities are new game, there is the potential to take advantage of first-mover advantages to further improve the position. For example, a firm can obtain protection for its intellectual property (patents, copyrights, trade secrets). Such protection raises barriers to entry into the firm's product-market-space. Also, because a firm's strategy is new game, coopetitors are likely to react to it by following or leapfrogging the firm, or pursuing any other activities that can enable them to outperform the firm. If, in performing new game activities, a firm anticipates and takes into consideration the likely reaction of coopetitors, the firm is more likely to cooperate better or compete with coopetitors. In pursuing its regular new game strategies, Coke often anticipates what Pepsi's reaction is likely to be, and vice versa. In pursuing their regular, position-building and resource-building new game strategies, Boeing and Airbus often take each other's likely reaction into consideration.

As we saw in Chapter 1, prior commitments that competitors make can prevent them from performing new game activities. Thus, in creating and appropriating value using new game activities, a firm can take advantage of its competitors' handicaps. For example, if the new game activity is counterintuitive and competitors are prevented by their dominant managerial logic from understanding the rational behind the activity, a firm may want to concentrate on convincing customers, not competitors, that the idea works. If competitors are prevented by laws or regulation from performing any activities that would allow them to catch up with a first mover, the first mover may want to ensure that such laws or regulations are enforced.

We will have more to say about anticipating and responding to competitors' likely reactions in Chapter 11 when we explore game theory, coopetition, and competition.

Take Advantage of Industry Value Drivers

If a firm uses new game activities to take advantage of industry value drivers, the new game factor can also amplify the impact of taking advantage of value drivers on value creation and appropriation. For example, network size is an important industry value driver in markets for products/services that exhibit network externalities. A firm that pursues the right new game activities can earn a large network size by virtue of value chain factors. But because the activities are new game, the firm can take advantage of the opportunity to build new resources, or build and exploit first-mover advantages. The case of eBay is a good example. It established a large community of registered users, giving it a large network size; and because it was the first in the online auctions business, it was easier to build a brand that reinforced its large network size, making the effects of its large network size even more valuable in creating and appropriating value.

A firm's strengths in the face of a new game can also facilitate its ability to take advantage of industry value drivers. For example, when IBM entered the PC market, its PC standard quickly became the industry standard, laying the foundation for what would become the Wintel network. One reason why IBM won the standard (creating a lot of value for the Wintel network) was because it brought in some important strengths: its brand name reputation and relationships with customers and software developers. The fear of cannibalizing its mainframe and minicomputer businesses may have negatively impacted IBM's ability to appropriate the value created in PCs.

Build and/or Translate Distinctive Resources/Capabilities into Unique Value

Some of the best new game strategies have been those that were used to build scarce resources for later use, taking advantage of the new gameness of the strategies. For example, when Ryanair moved into secondary airports, it could take advantage of the fact that the operating costs at these airports were low relative to those at their primary counterparts; but because it was the first to ramp up its activities at many of these airports, Ryanair was able to take up most of the gates and landing slots at the airports, thereby preemptively locking up important resources that would anchor its operations. Once the firm had a network of such airports, it became difficult for its competitors to replicate the network. Because it was the first to pursue digital animation technology, Pixar had a chance to cooperate with Disney and take advantage of its storytelling capabilities and distribution channels to complement its digital animation technology so as to create the likes of *Toy Story* and *Finding Nemo*.

Are Parsimonious and Comprehensive

It costs money to pursue a new game—to effect change. Therefore a firm should perform only the activities that are necessary—the activities that contribute enough towards value creation and appropriation, given their costs; that is, the activities that a firm performs should be parsimonious. For example, Airbus's decision to build the A380 was to occupy the white space for long-range planes that carry 500–800 passengers and operate at lower costs than existing planes (20% less cost per passenger). This was a good new game strategy. However, the company ended up performing some activities in a way that it should not have performed them and that cost it dearly. For example, the firm ended up with two incompatible computer-aided design (CAD) systems, one German and the other French, that led to mistakes in the design of the A380's wiring harnesses.[24] This necessitated redoing the CAD systems with their associated delays and extra costs. Because of such activities, the firm was two years late in delivering the first plane and racked up large cost overruns. Moreover, when word of the mistake came out, the parent company's stock (EADS' stock) dropped by 26%.[25]

A firm must also make sure that it is performing the activities that it ought to be performing. To determine which activities it ought to be performing, the firm can perform an AVAC analysis and from it, perform the activities that reverse the Noes into Yesses, and reinforce the Yesses.

To summarize, a firm's ability to create and appropriate value in the face of a new game depends on, (1) value chain factors that arise by virtue of the fact that new game activities are value chain activities, and (2) new game factors that arise by virtue of the fact that new game activities have a new game component. Value chain factors contribute directly to value creation and appropriation while new game factors moderate this contribution. Both components rest on a firm's pre-new game strengths that remain strengths or become handicaps in the face of the new game.

Key Takeaways

- Strategy is about creating and appropriating value.
- A firm creates value when it offers customers something that they perceive as valuable (beneficial) to them and the cost of offering the benefits does not exceed them. The value appropriated (captured) is the profit that a firm receives from the value it created.
- As the case of many authors and musicians suggests, many firms or individuals that create lots of value get to appropriate only a small fraction of it. A firm may not be able to appropriate all the value that it creates because: it lacks complementary assets, does not have bargaining power over its coopetitors, the value is easy to imitate, it has the wrong pricing strategy, or it does not have enough valuable customers that want the benefits it offers.
- Value creation is often undertaken by coopetitors, not one firm. Thus, firms often have to cooperate to create value and compete to appropriate it. Where there is cooperation, there is likely to be competition; and where there is competition, there are opportunities to cooperate.
- The value added by many exporting countries is often a lot less or more than the export value attributed to them.
- In the face of new game activities, there are likely to be opportunities for cooperation during competition; and during cooperation, there is always implied competition.
- In the competition to appropriate value that takes place during cooperation, it is important not to forget to think of what one's alternatives are; that is, before dumping your partner because your percentage of the pie is small, think very carefully about who else is out there that you can create a pie with. How much more pie will cooperation with your new partner create and how much of it will you get? In leaving your existing partner for an outsider, you may be leaving 10% of a watermelon for 90% of a grape.
- A new game can shift value creation and appropriability along a value system.
- Firms usually have pre-new game strengths that can remain strengths or become handicaps in the face of a new game.
- Creating new value does not always mean outdoing competitors with products that have superior attributes. A firm can also locate in a unique market position through reverse positioning. In *reverse positioning*, a firm strips off some of a product's major attributes but at the same time, adds new attributes that may not have been expected.
- The contribution of new game activities to a firm's value creation and appropriation depends on its strengths and handicaps in the new game, and both the *value chain factors* and the *new game factors* of the new game activities. The effect of the new game factor is a moderating one.
- By virtue of being *value chain* activities, new game activities can:

1 Contribute to low cost, differentiation, and other drivers of profitability.
2 Improve position vis-à-vis coopetitors.
3 Take advantage of industry value drivers.
4 Build and translate distinctive resources/capabilities into new value.
5 Be parsimonious and comprehensive.

- The impact of each value chain factor on value creation and appropriation is moderated by each new game factor. That is, the magnitude and direction of the impact of each value chain factor on a firm's ability to create and appropriate value is a function of whether the firm:

  o Takes advantage of the new ways of creating and capturing new value generated by change.
  o Takes advantage of opportunities generated by change to build new resources or translates existing ones in new ways.
  o Takes advantage of first-mover's advantages and disadvantages, and competitors' handicaps that result from change.
  o Anticipates and responds to coopetitors' reactions to its actions.
  o Identifies and takes advantage of opportunities and threats from competitive, macro and global environments.

Key Terms

Coopetition
Crowdsourcing
Customer's reservation price
Industry value driver
New game factors
Reverse positioning
Skimming
Value appropriated
Value chain factors
Value created

Questions

1 Table 4.2 overleaf shows the eight most expensive components/inputs of the 30 GB Video iPod that Apple introduced in October of 2005. According to Portelligent Inc, the product had 451 components, with a total cost of $144.40.[26] The iPod retailed for $299. Assuming a wholesale discount of 25%, what is the value appropriated by Apple and each of the suppliers. How much value is captured by each country? How much of that value is added by each actor?
2 How can a firm take advantage of first-mover disadvantages?

Table 4.2 October 2005 Top 8 Most Expensive Components/Inputs of a 30GB iPod

Component/Input	Supplier	Firm's country HQ	Manufacturing location	Price (US$)
Hard drive	Toshiba	Japan	China	73.39
Display module	Toshiba-Matsushita	Japan	Japan	20.39
Video/multimedia processor	Broadcom	USA	Taiwan or Singapore	8.36
Portal player CPU	PortalPlayer	USA	US or Taiwan	4.94
Insertion, test, and assembly	Inventec	Taiwan	China	3.70
Battery pack	Unknown			2.89
Display driver	Renesas	Japan	Japan	2.88
Mobile SDRAM 32 MB memory	Samsung	Korea	Korea	2.37

Source: Linden, G., Kraemer, K.L., & Dedrick, J. (2007). Who captures value in a global innovation system? The case of Apple's iPod. Retrieved July 10, 2007, from http://www.teardown.com/AllReports/product.aspx?reportid=8.

Resources and Capabilities in the Face of New Games

Reading this chapter should provide you with the conceptual and analytical tools to:

- Define tangible, intangible, and organizational resources as well as capabilities and *core competences*.
- Begin to understand the strategic significance of *network externalities*.
- Understand the significance of complementary assets in the face of new games.
- Use the AVAC (Activities, Value, Appropriability, and Change) framework for exploring the profitability potential of resources/*capabilities*.
- Understand how to narrow down the list of *complementary assets*, capabilities, core competences, or any other resource to important ones.
- Understand the basic role of resources as a cornerstone of competitive advantage.

Introduction

To create value and position itself to appropriate the value, a firm needs *resources*. For example, behind the Google search engines that some surfers perceive as giving them more relevant search results than competitors' engines are skills and know-how in software and computer engineering, patents, trademarks, trade secrets, banks of servers, the Google brand, equipment, and other resources without which the relevant searches and the firm's ability to monetize the searches would not be possible. To operate out of secondary uncongested airports in the European Union (EU), Ryanair had to acquire the gates and landing rights at these airports, build relationships with local officials, obtain the airplanes, and build the right low-cost culture. A pharmaceutical company such as Merck or Elli Lilly needs well-equipped R&D laboratories, scientists, and patents to be able to produce blockbuster drugs such as Zocor or Prozac that customers find valuable. To make its cola drinks readily available to customers whenever they want them, Coca Cola needs shelf space at its distributors and contracts with its bottlers. However, resources in and of themselves do not customer benefits and profits make. Firms must also have the capabilities or ability to turn resources into customer value and profits. For ExxonMobil to make money, it needs resources such as exploration rights, sophisticated exploration equipment, geologists as well as an ability to find oil and turn it into something that its customers want. In the face of new games, firms have an opportunity to build new valuable resources or translate existing ones in new ways into new unique value.

In this chapter, we explore the critical role that resources and capabilities can play in a firm's value creation and appropriation. In particular, we explore the role of resources in the face of new games. We start the chapter by defining resources and capabilities, and by exploring what makes one resource more profitable than others. We then examine the role of resources in the face of new games. In particular, we explore the role of complementary assets as a driver of profitability during new games.

Resources and Capabilities

Resources

Creating and appropriating value requires resources (or assets) such as plants, equipment, patents, skilled scientists, brand name reputation, supplier relations, geographic location, client relations, distribution channels, trade secrets, and so on. Resources can be classified as tangible, intangible, or organizational.[1] *Tangible resources* are the resources that are usually identified and accounted for in financial statements under the category "assets." They can be physical, such as plants and equipment or financial such as cash. *Intangible resources* are the nonphysical and nonfinancial assets such as patents, copyrights, brand name reputation, trade secrets, research findings, relationships with customers, shelf space, and relationships with vendors that are not accounted for in financial statements and cannot be physically touched.[2] Intangible resources are usually not identified in financial statements but can be excellent sources of profits. For example, a patent or trade secret that enables a firm to occupy a unique product space and therefore earn monopoly rents is not listed as an asset in financial statements. That is usually the case with important drug discoveries in pharmaceuticals in the USA where patented drugs enjoy intellectual property protection and can earn companies billions of dollars. Intangible resources are also referred to as *intangible assets* or just *intangibles*. *Organizational* resources consist of the know-how and knowledge embodied in employees as well as the routines, processes, and culture that are embedded in the organization.

Capabilities

Although resources are critical to value creation and appropriation, resources in and of themselves are not enough to make money. A firm also needs to have the ability to transform resources into customer benefits. Customers are not likely to scramble to a firm's doors because the firm has modern plants, geniuses, and patents. The firm has to use the plants, geniuses, and the knowledge and protections embodied in its patents to offer customers something that they value. Patients do not buy patents or skilled scientists from pharmaceutical companies; they buy medicines that have been developed by skilled scientists using knowledge embodied in patents and the patents help to give firms monopoly rights over the patent life of the drug. Effectively, resources usually have to be converted into benefits that customers want. A firm's ability to transform its resources into customer benefits and profits is usually called a *capability*. For example, a pharmaceutical company's ability to turn patents and relationships with doctors into blockbuster drugs and profits is a capability. Capabilities often involve the use or integration of more than one resource.[3] In the literature in strategic management, there is some disagreement as to how to define resources, capabilities, and competences.[4] Some scholars define them the way we have here. Others argue that resources include assets, capabilities, and competences. The central theme remains the same: that performing activities to create value and position a firm to appropriate the value requires resources and some ability to translate them into customer benefits. The names given to the resources and their transformation should not matter that much.

Core Competences

The phrase *"core competence"* was coined by Professors C.K. Prahalad of the University of Michigan and Gary Hamel of Strategos and the London Business School to designate a resource or capability that meets the following three criteria.[5] The resource or capability:

1 Makes a significant contribution to the benefits that customers perceive in a product or service.
2 Is difficult for competitors to imitate.
3 Is extendable to other products in different markets.

Core competences include technological know-how, relationships with coopetitors, and an ability to integrate different activities or translate resources into products. A popular example of core competence is Honda's ability to build dependable smooth-running internal combustion engines. It meets all three criteria. First, each Honda engine makes a significant contribution to the benefits that customers perceive in the Honda product. Second, although other firms have internal combustion engine capabilities, it is difficult to replicate the level of Honda's engine capabilities. Third, Honda has been able to use its engine capabilities to offer motorcycles, cars, lawnmowers, marine vehicles, electrical generators, and small jets. The phrase "core competence" is often used by individuals and firms to refer to what one does very well. One implication of the concept of core competence is that competition is not only important in the product market that a firm occupies but also in the factor markets for competences that a firm can build and leverage in many markets.

Network Externalities Effects

With the growing importance of technologies such as the Internet, computers, cell phones, video games, and so on, resources that are associated with network externalities effects have become increasingly important. In this section, we explore network externalities.

Definition and Role of Size

The value of a product to customers usually depends on the attributes of the product in question.[6] However, for some products, customer value depends not only on product attributes but also on the network of consumers that use the product or a compatible one; that is, a technology or product exhibits *network externalities effects* if the more people that use it, the more valuable it becomes to each user.[7] Telephones exhibit network externalities since their value to each user increases with the number of people that are on the network. Applications software products such as Adobe's Acrobat (for creating and reading pdf files) exhibit network externalities because the more people that own the software that can read pdf files, the more useful is each user's software for creating and mailing pdf files. In an auction network, the more sellers that are in the network, the more valuable that the network is to each buyer. Such network externalities effects are called *direct* effects because the benefits that each user of a product derives from the network of other users come directly from the network—from interacting (economically or socially) with other actors within the network.

Products that need complements also exhibit network externalities. Take computers, for example. The more people that own computers of a particular standard such as the Wintel standard, the more software that is likely to be developed for them, since developers want to sell to the large number of users; and the more software that is available for a computer standard, the more valuable the computers are to users, since software is critical to computers. Such externalities are called *indirect* externalities because the increased value experienced by each user is indirect, through increased availability of complements.

How valuable is size to a network? Theoretical estimates of the value of network size have been as high as N^2 and N^N (where N is the number of users in the network).[8] However, a larger network size does not always mean more value for customers. For example, a network in which there is only one seller and the rest are buyers (e.g. Amazon books) is not as valuable to each user as one in which there are many sellers and many buyers (e.g. eBay). The value of a network to each member may actually decrease with increasing size if each new member is dishonest. In general, the structure and nature of a network may be just as important as its size.[9]

Structure

The *structure of a network* is the pattern of relationships between the players in the network. In a consumer-to-consumer (C2C) auction network, any consumer can be a seller or buyer. This structure contrasts with that of a business-to-consumer (B2C) online retail network in which one seller sells to many buyers. Thus, while both types of network are valuable to customers, the C2C network is more valuable to each buyer than the B2C one, since buyers in the latter network only have one seller from whom to buy while those in the former have many sellers from whom to choose. A network with both sellers and buyers belongs to a group of networks called *two-sided networks*. A two-sided network has two distinct user groups that provide each other with benefits.[10] There are numerous other examples of two-sided networks. A credit card network has two groups: cardholders and merchants. A video game network has two groups: gamers and game developers. Users of pdf files consist of creators of pdf files and readers of pdf files. In a *single-sided network*, there is only one type of user. Examples include telephone networks, e-mail, and Faxes.

Nature of Network

The value of a network also depends on the conduct of the players within the network. For example, the reputation of a network also matters. Although the size of eBay's network is large, one reason why some customers may find the network more valuable than another network of equal size is its reputation for safety and its brand as the place for auctions. The company built the reputation partly by rating sellers and buyers, a practice that may have selectively kept out some potential opportunistic members and discouraged some members from behaving opportunistically.

Exploiting Network Externalities

What if a technology or product exhibits network externalities? Although the value of a network to users increases with the number of other users, it is usually the provider of the network that makes most of the money from the network. Google is the provider of its two-sided network of surfers who use its search engine and advertisers who value the surfers' eyeballs. Banks profit from their networks of borrowers and depositors. The question is: what can a *provider* of the network infrastructure and service do to have a network that increases its chances of profiting from the network? Firms can (1) exploit *direct* network effects by building an early lead in network size and reputation, (2) price strategically, and (3) take advantage of *indirect* network effects by boosting complements.

Exploit Direct Network Effects by Building an Early Lead in Size and Reputation

The idea here is simple. Since an early lead in a network market share can escalate into a dominant market position, a firm may want to pursue the kinds of actions that would give its products/service a critical market share or installed base lead. One such action is to team up with other firms to flood the market with one's version of the product/technology. A classic example is that of Matsushita, which freely licensed its VHS video cassette recording technology, while competitor Sony kept its Beta technology proprietary. Effectively, Matsushita flooded the market with VHS sets and may have tipped the scales away from Sony's Betamax, in favor of VHS.[11] Another tactic is to build an early reputation as the safe place to sell or buy as eBay did.

Price Strategically

A firm's pricing strategy can also play an important role in increasing the size of its network. In one-sided networks, a supplying firm (provider of network) can pursue penetration pricing in which it initially sells its network product/services at very low prices and makes money by raising prices later or offering related products for which customers have a higher willingness to pay. In two-sided networks, the platform provider can set the price of the service/product low for the group with a lower willingness to pay but with the potential to increase the number of users on the other side. It can then charge the side with a higher willingness to pay.[12] For example, surfers who conduct Web searches on Google have a lower willingness to pay for the searches than advertisers' willingness to pay for searchers' "eye balls." Thus, searches on Google are free but advertisers are charged. Adobe gave away its reader software to anyone who wanted to be able to read pdf files, but charged anyone who wanted to create pdf files.

Exploit Indirect Network Effects by Boosting Complements

Since, early in the life of a network technology, there potentially exists a chicken-and-egg cycle in which complementors prefer to develop complements for the product with many users, and users want the product with many complements, the cycle can be jumpstarted by boosting the number of complements. Thus, for example, a supplier of the network product might produce some of the complements itself, help the complementor distribute complements, co-develop complements with complementors, or finance the activities of startup complementors.

Example: Social Networking Websites

A social network is made up of individuals or organizations that are linked by one or more factors such as values, types of economic exchange, friendship, political orientation, social views, profession, likes and dislikes, and so on. In 2008, there were numerous social networking websites: Myspace, Facebook, classmates.com, broadcaster.com, Mixi, Cyworld, Reunion, Tagged.com, and Orkut, to name a few. One of the questions asked in 2008 was, how valuable were these networks to users and to the owners of the websites?

Answer to Social Network Question

The size of each social network is important to each member. The question is, how much? Each of these websites enables different groups of people within the network to have their own subnetworks within the larger network. Each subnetwork can be made up of college friends, members of a certain church, people living in the same area, etc. Once a subnetwork is formed, additional members to the larger network do not necessarily increase the value of the network to every subnetwork member. For example, a new member who joins the network because of religious interests may not necessarily add value to members whose primary affiliation is the college they attended. Contrast that with a C2C network where the addition of each new member increases the value to each member.

However, for several reasons, a social network may be very valuable to advertisers and therefore to the owner of the website. First, because a subnetwork within a social network is usually made up of members with the same values, interests, etc., they are likely to be a better subgrouping for marketers than age groups. For example, there are likely to be more similarities among doctors to whom one wants to market a health product than among the much-coveted 18–34-year age group. Second, although members of a social network may not be willing to watch ads, the effect of marketing on them can still be high. Why? People are more likely to believe product recommendations from friends, colleagues, and other people whom they trust and respect than they are to believe advertisements. This is particularly true for *experience goods*—goods whose characteristics are ascertained only after consumption since it is difficult to observe their characteristics in advance. Thus, all that it takes is an ad that will convince a few members of the subnetwork and the members can spread the idea themselves. For example, doctors often depend more on opinion leaders for prescription information than they do on direct advertising to them.[13] Thus, in marketing to a social network of physicians, one can focus on the opinion leaders and they can recommend the product to the rest of their network.

Effectively, since people are more likely to believe someone whom they trust and respect than an ad from a firm, well-targeted social networks can be much better places to pitch an idea than nonsocial networks. If someone who knows your interests and whom you trust recommends a product to you, you are more likely to believe the person than an advertiser. Third, each member of a social network provides information about his/her interests and so on. This is information that firms usually spend lots of money trying to collect. Thus, rather than pay for keywords associated with *products*, as is the case with paid-listings, an advertiser may be able to pay for key words related to *customers' interests* and the characteristics of its subnetwork.

Role of Resources in the Face of New Games

Having defined resources and capabilities, we now turn to a basic question: What is the role of resources and capabilities during value creation and appropriation in the face of new games? Recall that new games are about performing new value chain activities, or performing existing value chain activities differently. We can group the resources that a firm needs to pursue a new game strategy into two categories: (1) The first category is made up of the resources that underpin the new activities or the ability to perform existing activities differently. Since performing new activities or existing ones differently usually results in an invention or discovery, or something new, we will call the resources that underpin such activities *invention resources*. The resources that Google used to develop the search engines that deliver more relevant searches than competitors' search engines fall into this invention resources category. (2) The second category consists of *complementary assets*—all the other resources, beyond invention resources, that a firm needs to create value and position itself to appropriate the value in the face of the new game. Complementary assets include brands, distribution channels, shelf space, manufacturing, relationships with coopetitors, complementary technologies, installed base, relationships with governments, and so on. Effectively, both invention resources and complementary assets play important roles in a firm's ability to profit from an invention.

Complementary Assets

Professor David Teece of the University of California at Berkeley was one of the first business scholars to explore the role of complementary assets in profiting from inventions or discoveries.[14] He was puzzled as to why EMI invented the CAT scan—an invention that was so important that Sir Godfrey Hounsfield won the 1979 Nobel Prize in Medicine for its invention—and yet, GE and Siemens, not EMI, the inventor, made most of the profits from the invention. He was also puzzled as to why R.C. Cola had invented diet and caffeine-free colas, and yet Coke and Pepsi made most of the profits from the two inventions. Professor Teece argued that to make money from an invention or discovery, two factors are important: complementary assets and imitability. Complementary assets, as defined above, are all the other resources, beyond those that underpin the invention or discovery, that a firm needs to create value and position itself to appropriate the value in the face of the new game. For example, in pursuing its direct-sales and build-to-order new game activities, Dell needed manufacturing processes that would enable it to manufacture a customer's computer in less than two hours once the order had been received. It also needed good relationships with suppliers who supplied components just-on-time, for example, delivering monitors directly to customers. Later, Dell also needed a brand. In pursuing DTC marketing for its Lipitor, Pfizer also needed a sales force to call on doctors, and manufacturing to produce the drug once doctors started prescribing it. Dell's manufacturing processes, brand, and its supplier relationships are complementary assets. So are Pfizer's manufacturing capabilities and sales force. *Imitability* comes into the profitability picture for the following reason. If the invention or discovery from a firm's new game activities can be imitated by competitors, customers may go to competitors rather than the firm, thereby reducing the ability of the firm to appropriate the value that it creates. These two variables—complementary assets and imitability—form the basis for the *Teece Model*, which we now explore.

The Teece Model: The Role of Complementary Assets and Imitability[15]

The elements of the Teece Model are shown in Figure 5.1. The vertical axis captures the extent to which an invention or discovery can be imitated while the horizontal axis captures the extent to which complementary assets are scarce and important. When imitability of an invention or discovery is high and complementary assets are easily available or unimportant, it is difficult for the inventor (first mover) to make money for a long time (Cell I in Figure 5.1). That is because any potential competitors that want to offer the same customer benefits that the firm offers can easily imitate the invention and find the complementary assets needed. A new style of jeans for sale on the Internet is a good example. It is easy to imitate new jeans styles and selling them on the Internet is not unique or distinctive to any one firm. Thus, it is difficult to make money for a long time selling a particular style of jeans on the Internet. Effectively, it is difficult to make money in situations such as Cell I.

If, as in Cell II, the invention is easy to imitate but complementary assets are scarce and important, the owner of the complementary assets makes money.

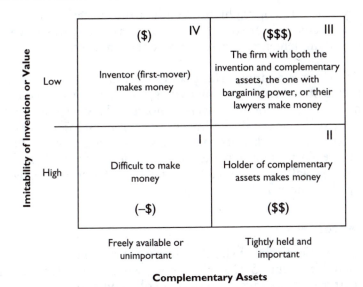

Figure 5.1 The Role of Complementary Assets.

That is because even though competitors can imitate the invention, they cannot easily replicate the complementary assets. More importantly, the owner of the important complementary assets can easily imitate the invention but its complementary assets are difficult to imitate. The invention of CAT scans by EMI falls into this category. The invention was easy to imitate but complementary assets such as relationships with hospitals, sales forces, brands, and manufacturing were scarce and important to selling the machines to hospitals. The inventions of diet and caffeine-free colas by R.C. Cola also fall into this category. Both inventions required brand name reputations, shelf space, marketing, and distribution channels which are important to making money from soft drinks but are tightly held by Coca-Cola and Pepsi. Thus, Coke and Pepsi have profited the most from diet and caffeine-free colas. Light beer offers another good example. The Miller Brewing Company and Budweiser did not invent light beer even though they make the most money from it. It was invented by Dr Joseph Owades at Rheingold Breweries. But because Miller and Budweiser had the complementary assets, they ended up making more money from it than Rheingold.

If imitability of an invention is low and complementary assets are important and scarce, one of two things could happen (Cell III). If the inventor also has the complementary assets, then it stands to make lots of money from its invention. Patented pharmaceutical products in the USA are a good example because their intellectual property protection keeps imitability low, and good sales forces, ability to run clinical tests, and other complementary assets are important to delivering value to customers are scarce. If the firm that has the scarce complementary assets is different from the inventor, both firms will make money if they cooperate. If they do not cooperate, their lawyers could make all the money.

Finally, as in Cell IV, if imitability of the invention is low but complementary assets are freely available or unimportant, the inventor stands to make money (Cell IV). Popular copyrighted software that is offered over the Internet would fall into this category since its copyright protects it from imitation and the Internet, as a distribution channel for software, is readily available to software developers and other complementary assets are either not scarce or are unimportant.

Effectively, firms with scarce and important complementary assets are often the ones that profit the most from new game activities, whether they moved first in performing the new game activities or were followers. Having important scarce complementary assets is one of the hallmarks of exploiters. Microsoft did not invent word processing, spreadsheets, presentation software, windowing operating systems, etc., even though it makes a lot of money from them. Its complementary assets, especially its installed base of compatible software, have been a primary driver of its success.

Strategic Consequences

An important strategy question is, what should a firm do if it found itself in one of the situations depicted in Figure 5.1. For example, what should R.C. Cola have done to profit better from its invention of diet cola, given that the invention was easy to imitate and complementary assets were scarce and important? In that case (Figure 5.2, quadrant II), the firm may have been better off teaming up with a partner that had the complementary assets. Teaming up can be through a joint venture, strategic alliance, or a merger through acquisition. If an inventor decides to team up, it may want to do so early before the potential partner with complementary assets has had a chance to imitate the invention or come up with something even better. The question is, why would a firm with complementary assets want to team up with an inventor if it knows that it can imitate the invention later? The inventor has to show the owner of the complementary assets why it is in their joint interest to team up. For example, R.C. Cola could have gone to Pepsi and explained that teaming up with it (R.C.

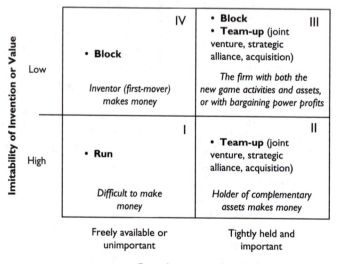

Figure 5.2 Strategies for Exploiting Complementary Assets.

Cola) would allow Pepsi to have a first-mover advantage in diet drinks before Coke and therefore give Pepsi a chance at beating Coke.

Effectively, in Cell II where an invention (from new game activities) is easy to imitate and complementary assets are important and scarce, the inventor is better off teaming up with the owner of complementary assets through strategic alliances, joint ventures, acquisitions, or other teaming-up mechanisms (Figure 5.2).

If an invention is difficult to imitate and complementary assets are scarce but important (Cell III of Figure 5.2), the inventor can pursue one of two strategies: block or team-up. If the inventor also owns the scarce complementary assets, it can block rivals and potential new entrants from having access to either. In a *block* strategy, a firm defends its turf by taking actions to preserve the inimitability of its invention or valuable resources. If another firm (other than the inventor) has the complementary assets, both firms can team up using strategic alliances, joint ventures, acquisitions, or other teaming-up mechanisms. In the pharmaceutical industry, for example, many biotechnology startups usually develop new drugs whose patents limit imitability. However, many of these startups do not have complementary assets such as sales/marketing, and the resources needed to carry out the clinical testing that is critical to getting a new drug approved for marketing in the USA. Consequently, there is a considerable amount of teaming up between biotech startups and the established large pharmaceutical firms that have the complementary assets. Many startups offer themselves to be bought. If the inventor of a difficult-to-imitate invention and the owner of scarce and important complementary assets decide not to cooperate and instead fight, there is a good chance that they will make their lawyers rich—they dissipate rather than create value.

If an invention is difficult to imitate but complementary assets are abundant or unimportant (Cell IV), a firm may be better off pursuing a block strategy in which it tries to prevent potential competitors from imitating its invention or strategy. If the invention is easy to imitate and complementary assets are abundant or unimportant (Cell 1), a firm can pursue a so-called run strategy. In a *run* strategy, the inventor or first mover constantly innovates and moves on to the next invention or new game activity before competitors imitate its existing invention or new game activity.

Dynamics

There are two things to note about the strategies of Figure 5.2. First, in practice, many firms pursue at least two of these strategies at any one time. For example, many firms pursue both *block* and *run* strategies at any one time—they defend their intellectual property for an existing product while forging ahead with the next invention to replace the existing product being protected. Second, a firm can sometimes go contrary to what Figure 5.2 suggests to lay a foundation for future gains. For example, an inventor may decide to team-up in Cell IV, rather than block as suggested by the framework, so as to win a standard and block after winning the standard. Intel's case offers a good example of both instances. In the late 1970s and early 1980s, it encouraged other microprocessor makers to copy its microprocessor architecture. When its architecture emerged as the standard, Intel started blocking—it decided not to let anyone imitate its technology again and sued anyone who tried to.[16] It also practiced the run strategy by introducing a new microprocessor generation before unit sales of an existing generation peaked. Effectively, Intel teamed up early in the life of its microprocessor to win a standard. After winning the standard, it started blocking and running.

Limitations of the Teece Model

It is important to note that although the Complementary Assets/Imitability model can be very useful, it has limitations. Like any model, it makes some simplifying assumptions that may not apply to all contexts all the time. For example, it assumes that the only two variables that underpin appropriability are complementary assets and imitability. It leaves out the other determinants of appropriability that we explored in Chapter 4 such as a firm's position vis-à-vis coopetitors, pricing strategy, and the activities to increase the number of customers that buy a particular product. It is true that an inimitable product and scarce important complementary assets can give their owner some bargaining power over customers; but they may not give the firm bargaining power over suppliers, complementors, or customers with monopoly power in their industry. Moreover, even where a firm has unchallenged power over its coopetitors, it may still leave money on the table if it has the wrong pricing strategy.

Profitability Potential of Resources and Capabilities

From what we have seen so far, resources and capabilities—be they invention resources or complementary assets—are critical to creating and appropriating value in the face of new games; but if you were to ask a firm to give you a list of its resources, you would probably be handed a very long list. Thus, an important question is, how can a firm narrow down the list of resources to those that have the most potential for profitability? How can a firm narrow its catalog of competences to only those that are truly core? We need some way to narrow down the list of potentially profitable resources/capabilities. The AVAC framework that we saw in Chapter 2 can be used to rank-order resources/capabilities as a function of their potential to contribute to value creation and appropriation. The idea is to evaluate the potential of each resource to contribute to a firm's competitive advantage and rank it accordingly. Each resource is ranked by answering the following questions and determining the strategic consequence of having the resource (Table 5.1):

a Activities: does the firm have what it takes to efficiently perform the activities for building and/or translating the resource/capabilities into customer benefits and/or positioning the firm to appropriate value? Is the firm performing the right activities?

b Value: does the resource/capability make a significant contribution towards the benefits that customers perceive as valuable to them?

c Appropriability: does the firm make money from the value that customers perceive in the benefits from the resource?

d Change: do the activities for building and exploiting the resource take advantage of change (present or future) to create and appropriate value?

Table 5.1 Rank Ordering Resources/Capabilities by Competitive Consequence

Resource/ Capability	Activities: Does the firm have what it takes to efficiently perform the activities for building and/or translating its search engine capabilities into customer benefits and/or positioning the firm to appropriate value?	Value: Does the resource make a significant contribution towards the benefits that customers perceive as valuable to them?	Appropriability: Does the firm make money from the value that customers perceive in the benefits from the resource?	Change: Do the activities for building and exploiting the resource take advantage of change to create and appropriate value?	Strategic consequence
Resource/cap-ability 1	Yes	Yes	Yes	Yes	Sustainable competitive advantage
Resource/cap-ability 2	Yes	Yes	Yes	No	Temporary competitive advantage
Resource/cap-ability 3	Yes	Yes	No	Yes	Competitive parity
Resource/cap-ability 4	Yes	Yes	No	No	Competitive parity
Resource/cap-ability 5	No/Yes	No	Yes	No	Competitive parity
Resource/cap-ability 6	No	No	No	No	Competitive disadvantage
Strategic action	What can a firm do to reinforce the Yesses and reverse or dampen the Noes, and what is the impact of doing so?				

Activities

In assessing the *profitability potential of a resource/capability*, the first question is, does the firm have what it takes to efficiently perform the activities for building and/or translating the resource/capabilities into customer benefits and/or positioning the firm to appropriate value; that is, is the firm performing the right activities? The idea here is (1) to identify the activities that the firm uses to build or translate the resource into customer benefits and/or better position the firm to appropriate value, and (2) to examine the firm's ability to perform these activities by determining the extent to which *each activity*:

- Contributes to low cost, differentiation, better pricing, reaching more customers, and better sources of revenue.
- Contributes to improving its position vis-à-vis coopetitors.
- Takes advantage of industry value drivers.
- Contributes to building new distinctive resources/capabilities or translating existing ones into unique positions and profits (including complementary assets).
- Fits the comprehensiveness and parsimony criteria.

These are the Activities questions of an AVAC analysis.

Value

The next question is, does the resource make a significant contribution towards the benefits that customers perceive as valuable to them, relative to value from competitors? This question is answered by exploring the Value component of the AVAC framework. This means exploring the following questions:

- Do customers perceive the value created by the strategy as unique?
- Do many customers perceive this value?
- Are these customers valuable?
- Are there any nearby white spaces?

Appropriability

The next question is, does the firm make money from the value that customers perceive in the benefits from the resource? Making a significant contribution to the value that customers perceive, relative to the value from competitors, is a necessary condition for a resource to earn its owner profits; but it is not a sufficient condition for making money. From the Appropriability component of an AVAC framework, a firm will appropriate value if:

- The firm has superior position vis-à-vis its coopetitors.
- The firm exploits its position vis-à-vis its coopetitors and customer benefits.
- It is difficult to imitate the firm.
- There are few viable substitutes but many complements.

Change

The question here is, do the activities for building and exploiting the resource take advantage of change to create and appropriate value? This question is answered by exploring the following questions from the AVAC framework. Do the activities for building and exploiting the resource:

- Take advantage of new ways of creating and capturing new value?
- Take advantage of opportunities to build new resources/capabilities and/or translate existing ones in new ways into value?
- Take advantage of the potential to build and exploit first-mover advantages?
- Anticipate and respond to potential reactions from new and existing competitors?
- Take advantage of the opportunities and threats of an industry or macroenvironment?

Competitive Consequence

An AVAC analysis enables a firm to identify and rank its resources by their competitive consequences—by the extent to which each resource stands to give the firm a competitive advantage. (To avoid repetition, we use the word resource to mean resource/capability.) Table 5.1 shows six different resources and the competitive consequence for a firm using each. Resource 1 is valuable to customers, and the firm can appropriate the value from it. Moreover, the firm has what it takes to perform the activities to build and exploit the resource efficiently. The resource can also be used to take advantage of change (present or future) to better create and/or appropriate value. The resource is thus said to give the firm a sustainable competitive advantage. The more common case is that of Resources 2, which gives a firm a temporary competitive advantage. The resource is valuable to customers, and the firm has what it takes to efficiently perform the activities to build and exploit the resource; but the resource is vulnerable to change. During the period before the change, the firm has a temporary competitive advantage.

Resource 3 is valuable to customers, the firm has what it takes to perform efficiently the activities to build and exploit the resource, and it can take advantage of change. The only problem with the resource is that there are other things that make it difficult to appropriate the value from it. For example, the firm using the resource may not have bargaining power over its suppliers and buyers, or the firm's pricing strategy may be leaving money on the table or driving customers away. Therefore the firm cannot appropriate all the value that it creates using the resource. The firm has competitive parity using the resource. Resource 4 is valuable to customers, but the value is difficult to appropriate and the resource is vulnerable to change. Thus, the best that Resource 4 can do for its owner is to give it competitive parity. Resource 5 is neither valuable, nor appropriable, nor can it withstand change. Moreover, the firm does not have the ability to perform efficiently the activities for building and exploiting the resource. Such a resource puts its owner at a competitive disadvantage since its competitors can do better.

Strategic Action

The next step after an AVAC analysis is to identify what it is that a firm can do to reinforce the Yesses and either dampen or reverse the Noes. The goal is to move things towards a sustainable competitive advantage. For example, if a firm finds out that it cannot appropriate most of the value that it creates because it has a bad pricing strategy, it can change the strategy. If a resource puts a firm at a competitive disadvantage and the firm cannot reverse or dampen the Noes, it may be better off getting rid of the resource. Effectively, an AVAC analysis should help a firm decide which Yesses to reinforce, which Noes to dampen or reverse, and which resources to dump so as to improve its ability to create and appropriate value.

Example 5.1: Google's Search Engine Capabilities in 2007

To illustrate the use of an AVAC analysis to assess the profitability potential of a resource, we go through an example using Google's search engine capabilities.

Activities

Does Google Have What it Takes to Perform Efficiently the Activities for Building and/or Translating the Resource/capabilities into Customer Benefits and/or Positioning the Firm to Appropriate Value?

Google performed the following activities in building and translating its search capabilities into unique value. It developed and incorporated its PageRank algorithm into its search engine and continued to improve the algorithm. It built a brand from its relevant searches. It emphasized innovative management of technology concepts such as encouraging its engineers to use 20% of their time to work on projects of their own choosing (why not marketing?). It introduced AdWords paid listings to monetize search engines. It teamed up with network affiliates and provided them with search-engine technology in return for share of profits from advertising on the sites. These activities differentiated Google from its competitors. For example, Google's brand and customers' perception that its searches were more relevant than competitors' searches differentiated the value from its search engine. This differentiation also improved Google's position vis-à-vis some coopetitors. For example, some customers might believe that switching to competitors would not give them the benefits that they perceived as coming only from Google. The differentiation also reduced the potential threat of substitutes and made it even more difficult for any potential new entrants who had dreams of entering the market and taking Google head on.

The industry value drivers for the search engine market are: the speed, relevance, and comprehensiveness of searches as well as the R&D that goes into them. By developing its PageRank algorithm that produced most relevant searches, Google took advantage of the "search relevance" industry value driver. Because of its brand, some customers perceived data from its engines as being the most reliable. In addition to the intellectual property (patents, copyrights, and trade secrets) that underpinned its search engines, the firm also cultivated one of the most recognizable brands in the world, earning it a verb in some dictionaries—to google.

Google also did some cool things to keep the cost of its activities low. It used Intel microprocessor-based commodity servers rather than the much more expensive proprietary servers from IBM, Sun Microsystems, and others. Since these servers consumed lots of electricity and generated a lot of heat, it also located them near cheap sources of electricity in cold places. The firm is therefore able to deliver searches at lower cost that it would have been able to.

Value

Does the Resource Make a Significant Contribution Towards the Benefits that Customers Perceive as Valuable to Them?

Google had two sets of customers: Internet users who performed searches, and advertisers who advertised online. Users (surfers) valued the speed, relevance, and comprehensiveness of searches made using Google's search engine. In February 2007, for example, 48.1% of the 6.9 billion monthly online searches conducted by surfers used Google's search engine, compared to 28.1% for

Yahoo, 10.5% for Microsoft, 5.0% for Ask.com and 4.9% for Time Warner.[17] Advertisers valued the billions of eyeballs that Google's website received every month. This amounted to many users to whom these advertisers could advertise. While other factors such as Google's brand may have had an effect on the number of visitors to its search site, its search engine, especially its ability to deliver relevant searches appears to have played a major role. Since Google's users cut across all demographics, it was difficult to say how valuable the users were. However, its advertisers included very small firms who would ordinarily not advertise in the offline world but who could advertise on Google's sites or third-party affiliates because of the low cost of servicing such small customers. Potentially, there was some white space for search engines that answered questions rather than use key words to perform searches—something with more intelligence.

Appropriability

Does the Firm Make Money from the Value that Customers Perceive in the Benefits from the Resource?

Yes. Google's search engine capabilities and associated complementary assets made lots of money for Google in 2007. Google was one of the most profitable and most valuable (from a market capital point of view) companies in the world. Things were not always that way. Even after its search engine became the most popular, it still was not very profitable. It was after it introduced paid listings, an idea pioneered by Overture.com, that Google started to make money. In paid listings, advertisers' links are displayed above or alongside search results.

There are several reasons why Google was able to appropriate the value created by its search engine capabilities. First, Google had the complementary assets to help it appropriate the value created by its search engine capabilities. However, it is difficult to say exactly how much of that money came from its search engine capabilities and how much from complementary assets such as its brand, paid listings technology, relationships with affiliates, etc.

Second, although it was easy to develop a search engine that was comparable to Google's in performance, replicating the combination of the search engine, the Google brand, video, images, and news services that it offered made it difficult for rivals to duplicate all of what Google offered. As the Internet evolves, the possibility that some firm can leapfrog Google is always going to be there. It had no established record of retaliating against competitors although some may view its introduction of free word-processing software as retaliating against Microsoft for offering search engine services. Competitors did not have any clear handicaps such as prior commitments or dominant managerial logic to handicap their efforts to imitate Google. In the late 1990s, when the Web was not overcrowded, companies could catalog and compile Web content without the aid of search engines. With the proliferation of Web content, it was very difficult to find stuff on the Internet without a search engine in 2007. Hence, there were no substitutes for search engines. Complements were things such as computers and handheld devices that enabled individuals to search the Web.

Third, the relevance of searches from its search engine, coupled with Google's brand and other activities, also gave the firm power over many of its coopetitors. For example, its brand and relevant searches attract surfers, whose large numbers attract many advertisers. This gives Google more power over its advertisers than would be expected in a market with four other competitors.

Fourth, in its paid listings business model, Google had customers (advertisers) bid for key words in an auction. Since auction pricing is one of the best ways to get as close as possible to customers' reservation prices, Google was probably getting very close to customers' reservation prices. The firm also had a lot of information about its customers and could therefore price discriminate using the information if it wanted to.

Change

Do the Activities for Building and Exploiting the Resource Take Advantage of Change (Present or Future) to Create and Appropriate Value?

Existing Change came from the Internet and Google's actions to take advantage of the new technology.

The Internet and the growing Web traffic on it made it increasingly difficult to find things on it, thereby creating an opportunity to develop dependable search engines that provided users with relevant search results. Google provided such an engine. So did its competitors, resulting in a relatively unattractive market (using Porter's Five Forces analysis) in 2007. However, Google found a way to make the market more attractive for itself and was therefore better able to create and capture more value than its competitors. It monetized the engine using paid listings and other complementary assets such as its brand.

Google was not the first to develop search engines. It took advantage of reduced marketing and technological uncertainty to, for example, use paid listings to monetize its search engine. The intellectual property (patents, copyrights, and trade secrets) that Google built in developing its search engine, and the preemption of perceptual space at the many surfers who preferred to use Google's search engine could be regarded as first-mover advantages for the activities that it was the first to perform. So were the relationships that it built at the affiliates whose sites used the Google search engine.

In offering complementary products, such as Gmail and GoogleMap, Google may be anticipating the likely reaction of its competitors. Looking to the future, as the Web evolves, there are likely to be many changes. For example, Google's advantage could be eroded by so-called specialist or vertical search engines. Vertical engines address the specialized needs of niches or professionals rather than the general broad-based needs of consumers as do the generalist engines from Google and Yahoo do. For example, GlobalSpec.com is a profitable specialist engine for engineers. A specialized engine for the pharmaceuticals industry could target pharmaceutical advertising.[18] Table 5.2 provides a summary of the strategic consequence of Google's search engines capabilities.

Table 5.2 Strategic Consequence for Google's Search Engine Capabilities

	Activities: Does Google have what it takes to efficiently perform the activities for building and/or translating the resource/ capabilities into customer benefits and/or positioning the firm to appropriate value?	Value: Does Google's search engine capability make a significant contribution towards the benefits that customers perceive as valuable to them?	Appropriability: Does Google make money from the value that customers perceive in the benefits from its search engine capabilities?	Change: Do the activities for building and exploiting search engine capabilities take advantage of change (present or future) to create and appropriate value?	Competitive consequence
Search engine capabilities	Yes	Yes	Yes	Yes/No	Sustainable/ temporary competitive advantage
Strategic action	In the 2000s Google took advantage of the changes from the evolving Internet. It could: 1. do more to monetize searches on "partner" websites; 2. pay more attention to category killers; 3. do more to exploit the exploding Web traffic, especially from video images which take up lots of bandwidth.				

Identifying the Right Complementary Assets

Since we have defined complementary assets as all other resources apart from an invention or discovery that a firm needs to create and appropriate value, the list of potential complementary assets for any particular invention or discovery can be huge. Thus, we need some way to narrow down the list of potential complementary assets. An AVAC analysis can also be used to rank order complementary assets by their potential to contribute to value creation and appropriation. The idea is to evaluate the potential of each complementary asset to contribute to a firm's competitive advantage and rank it accordingly. As shown in Table 5.3, each complementary asset is ranked by answering the following questions and determining the competitive consequence of having the asset:

1 Activities: does the firm have what it takes to efficiently perform the activities for building and/or translating the complementary asset into customer benefits and/or positioning the firm to appropriate value? What are the activities?
2 Value: does the complementary asset make a significant contribution towards the benefits that customers perceive as valuable to them?
3 Appropriability: does the firm make money from the value that customers perceive in the benefits from the complementary asset?
4 Change: do the activities for building and exploiting the complementary asset take advantage of change (present or future) to create and appropriate value?

Table 5.3 Rank Ordering Complementary Assets

Complementary asset	Activities: Does the firm have what it takes to efficiently perform the activities for building and/or translating the complementary asset into customer benefits and/or positioning the firm to appropriate value?	Value: Does the comple- mentary asset make a significant contribution towards the benefits that customers perceive as valuable to them?	Appropriability: Does the firm make money from the value that customers perceive in the benefits from the complementary asset?	Change: Do the activities for building and exploiting the comple- mentary asset take advantage of change (present or future) to create and appropriate value?	Competitive consequence
Complementary assets 1	Yes	Yes	Yes	Yes	Sustainable competitive advantage
Complementary assets 2	Yes	Yes	Yes	No	Temporary competitive advantage
Complementary assets 3	Yes	Yes	No	Yes	Competitive parity
Complementary assets 4	Yes	Yes	No	No	Competitive parity
Complementary assets 5	No/Yes	No	Yes	No	Competitive parity
Complementary assets 6	No	No	No	No	Competitive disadvantage
Strategic action	What can firm do to reinforce the Yesses and reverse or dampen the effect of the Noes				

Each complementary asset is classified by the potential competitive consequence of building and exploiting the asset, from "sustainable competitive advantage" down to "competitive *dis*advantage." The more that the strategic consequence from a complementary asset is a sustainable strategic advantage rather than a strategic disadvantage, the more that a firm may want to pursue the complementary asset. In addition to telling a firm which complementary assets to pursue, the analysis can also point out which Noes could be reversed to Yesses or dampened, and which Yesses could be reinforced.

Strengths and Handicaps in the Face of New Games

Every firm brings to a new game some resources from its pre-new game activities. Some of these resources, including complementary assets, continue to be useful during the new game but others may not only be useless, they can become handicaps. Identifying which resources might become handicaps can, depending on the type of new game, be critical to winning. Identifying which scarce valuable resource is likely still to remain valuable for the firm and which one is likely to become a handicap consists of answering the two simple questions shown in Table 5.4:

1 Is the resource vital in the new game?
2 Is separability possible?

There are two primary determinants of which resource becomes a handicap or strength: whether the resource is *vital* to the new game, and whether the resource is separable. A resource is vital to a new game if it contributes significantly to value creation and appropriability. It is *separable* if the firm has no problems taking the resource away from the old game for use in the new game, or leaving the resource behind when it is more likely to hurt in the new game than help. A firm may be prevented from using a resource in a new game because of prior commitments, contracts, agreements, understandings, emotional attachments, or simply because the resource/asset cannot be moved from the location of the old game to the location of the new one. In that case the resource is inseparable from the old context. A firm may also want to separate itself from a resource from its past, so as to move on but cannot because the resource is inseparable.

To understand these arguments better, consider Resource 1 in Table 5.4. It is vital in the new game and the firm can use it in the new game because there are no prior contracts, agreements, understandings, or anything else that prevents the firm from using the important resource in the new game. Thus the resource is a strength for the firm. Most brands, advertising skills, and shelf space continue to be strengths for many firms even in the face of revolutionary new games in which technologically radical new products are introduced. In pharmaceuticals, for example, a firm's drug approval capabilities, sales force, and brand usually continue to be strengths from one revolutionary drug to another.

Resource 4 is the exact opposite of Resource 1. The resource is useless to the firm in pursuing the new game but unfortunately for the firm, it cannot separate itself from the resource and move on. Resource 4 is therefore a handicap. The Compaq example which we saw earlier in this book illustrates instances of both Resources 1 and 4. Compaq wanted to participate in the new game created by Dell when the latter introduced the direct sales and build-to-order business model, bypassing distributors. Compaq's brand name reputation was a strength in the new game since it could still be used in direct sales. The skills used to

Table 5.4 Is a Strength from a Previous Game a Strength or Handicap in a New Game?

Resource	Is the resource vital in the new game?	Is separability possible?	In the new game, the resource is a:
Resource 1	Y	Y	strength
Resource 2	Y	N	potential strength
Resource 3	N	Y	question mark
Resource 4	N	N	handicap

interact with distributors and old agreements with distributors were no longer needed in the new game. However, Compaq could not get out of the agreements with distributors. The agreements with distributors effectively became a handicap to the firm's efforts to follow Dell and sell directly to end-customers.

A firm's dominant managerial logic is another example. It is usually a good thing since dominant managerial logic makes what managers are supposed to do become second nature to them; but in the face of some types of change, it can become a problem. Take discount retailing, for example. Part of the dominant managerial logic in the USA in the 1970s and early 1980s was that firms made money in discount retailing by building large stores in big cities, so when Wal-Mart was building small stores in rural areas of the Southwestern USA, K-Mart and other competitors did not think much about Wal-Mart and continued to believe in making money by building large stores in large cities. Wal-Mart would go on to become the world's largest company while K-Mart had to file for bankruptcy. Another example is that of the French wine industry that dominated the world market for centuries with wines that were made using no new technologies and no sugar, and were classified and named by French locations such as Bordeaux, Champagne, Cote du Rhone, etc.[19] New entrants from South Africa, Australia, and the USA entered some wine markets with wines that were made using new technologies such as drip irrigation, reverse osmosis, computerized aging, and oak chip flavoring, and classified their wines using grape type such as merlot or chardonnay rather than location. The dominant thinking in the French wine industry still continues to be that fine wines are made the old-fashioned French way using no new technologies, even as French wine continues to lose market share in some markets to South African, Australian, and US wine sellers. Another way to think of how inseparability can lead to handicaps is to think of personal relationships. When a person moves from an important relationship to another, there may be things about the old relationship that he or she would rather leave behind but that just hang around. That might not help the new relationship.

There are two other cases in Table 5.4. Resource 2 is important in the new game but because of prior commitments, agreements, or other inseparability, the firm cannot use it in the new game. The resource is then a potential strength since, with work, it could become separable. For example, a noncompete clause in an important employee's contract with a previous employer may prevent a firm from using the employee on some projects for some time. Resource 3 is not important in the new game and the firm can get away from it. It is therefore, neither a strength nor a handicap. It is a question mark.

A similar analysis can be performed for the product-market position (PMP) that a firm brings to a new game. Here, the question is whether strengths in a firm's previous product (low-cost, differentiated products, or both), and the firm's position vis-à-vis its coopetitors—that a firm brings to a new game—remain strengths or become handicaps. A firm's PMP from a previous game becomes a handicap in a new game if products from the new game potentially can cannibalize the firm's existing products from the previous game. If that is the case, the firm may not invest in the new game for fear of cannibalizing its existing products. A previous PMP can also become a handicap if the new game is about luxury products while the previous PMP was about low-cost products, since customers' perception of the old product may negatively bias their perception of the new one. On the other hand, the seller of a luxury product that decides to sell a low-cost version in a new game may find its old position a strength in selling the new product. Since a firm's position vis-à-vis coopetitors is partially determined by its resources/capabilities, the analyses above for resources can be used to analyze whether such positions become handicaps or remain strengths.

Valuing Intangible Resources/Capabilities from New Games

Suppose a firm builds new resources in the face of a new game and wants quantitatively to estimate their value; how should the firm go about it? A detailed AVAC analysis can tell a firm a lot about the profitability potential of its resources but it does not quantify intangible resources (assets). Financial statements only state the value of tangible assets such as plants, equipment, cash, marketable securities, and inventories but say nothing about intangible assets such as brands, patents, copyrights, trade secrets, installed base, client relations, government relations, and so on. We explore two methods for getting a quick feel for the value of such intangibles.

Assigning Numbers to Intangibles

Consider the simple but important balance sheet relationship of equation (1).

Assets = liabilities + shareholder equity   (1)

An elementary manipulation of equation (1) gives

Assets − liabilities = shareholder equity   (2)

The relationship shown in equation (2) suggests that at any one time, the market value of a firm (shares outstanding multiplied by share price) should be equal to the firm's assets minus its liabilities (equation (2)). The quantity "Assets − Liabilities" is also called the **book value** of the firm. Book value is what would be left over for shareholders if a firm were to sell its assets and pay its creditors. Therefore, according to equation (1), at any one time, a firm's book value should be equal to its shareholder equity or market value. As Table 5.5 shows, that is not always the case. Differences between book value and market value range from Comcast's $9.18 billion to ExxonMobil's $354.65 billion. The difference between book value and market value for each firm suggests two things: (1) that there is something else about the firm, something other than the assets on its books, that makes investors believe that the firm will keep generating free cash flows or earnings; and (2) that the stock market overvalues the firm's stock. If we assume that the market does not overvalue the firm's stock, the difference between book value and market value is a measure of intangible assets, since they are not captured in the book value relationship. The ratio of market value to book value is also a measure of intangibles. In the examples of Table 5.5, Microsoft's intangibles in August of 2007 were a lot more valuable than General Motors' intangibles, since Microsoft's market value to book value was 8.5 while General Motors' was −5.1.

Table 5.5 Sample Values of Intangible Resources (all numbers, except rations, in $ billion)

Company	S Market value on August 22, 2007	T Assets	W Liabilities	X Book value = T − W (Assets liabilities)	Y S − X = Market value − book value	Z Market value − Book value
Intel	141.00	50.29	10.60	39.70	101.30	3.6
Microsoft	263.00	63.17	32.07	31.10	231.90	8.5
General Electric (GE)	397.00	738.53	621.51	117.02	279.98	3.4
Google	157.00	21.42	1.76	19.66	137.34	8.0
Wal-Mart	180.00	155.42	95.51	59.91	120.09	3.0
Pfizer	167.00	110.40	42.31	68.09	98.91	2.5
General Motors (GM)	18.00	186.53	190.09	−3.56	21.56	−5.1
JP Morgan Chase	153.00	1,458.04	1,338.83	119.21	33.79	1.3
Cisco	182.00	53.34	21.86	31.48	150.52	5.8
ExxonMobil	462.00	228.32	111.97	116.35	345.65	4.0
Citicorp	237.00	2,220.87	2,093.11	127.75	109.25	1.9
Merck	109.00	44.18	24.71	19.47	89.53	5.6
Comcast	51.00	110.76	68.93	41.83	9.18	1.2

Using the difference between book value and market value to measure intellectual capital has several shortcomings. First, firms that have not gone public and business units cannot use the measure, since they have no market value. Second, it is an aggregate measure since it estimates a value for all of a firm's intangible resources. While it highlights the extent to which a firm's value depends on its intangible resources, it does not tell us much about the different components of the capital and their relative contribution to the value. Thus, while the measure can tell us whether Pfizer depends more on intangible assets than its competitors, it does not tell us how much of Pfizer's value is from its cholesterol or hypertension technologies.

Numerical Example: Leveraging Effect of Intangible Resources

We explore one more way of indirectly *valuing intangible resources* by considering a numerical example from personal computers.

Example 5.2

At an estimated development cost of $1 billion, Microsoft's Windows XP operating system was released on October 25, 2001 and earned Microsoft an estimated $55 to $60 per copy sold.[20] An operating system is a computer software program that manages the activities of different components (software and hardware) of a computer. From 1996 to 2001, Apple's market share dropped from 5.2% to 3.0%.[21] In 2001, 133.5 million desktops, notebooks, and PC-based servers were shipped worldwide.[22] One estimate in 2007 had Apple's installed base of Macs at 4.5% of total PC-installed base.[23] For many businesses, the active PC life cycle was three years. Given this information, what is the value of installed base to Microsoft and Apple? (Installed base is an intangible resource.)

Answer: One way to get a feel for the value of installed base for each firm is to perform a breakeven analysis. Let us start by making the calculations for Microsoft.

Microsoft

Contribution margin per unit = $P - V_c$ = ($57.50) (average of $55 and $60)

$$\text{Breakeven quantity} = \frac{\text{Fixed Cost}}{\text{Contribution Margin}} = \frac{\$1B}{\$57.5} = 17.39 \text{ million units (3)}$$

Of the 133.5 million PCs that were sold in 2001, 3% or 4 million were Apple machines. The remaining 97% or 129.5 million (10.8 million per month) were Windows machines that use the Microsoft operating system; that is, 10.8 million units of Microsoft's operating system were sold each month for the remaining two months of 2001 and beyond if we assume that sales of PCs remained at about their 2001 levels for the coming years. Since Microsoft needed to sell 17.39 million units of the operating system to break even and it sold 10.8 million units a month, it would have taken the company $\frac{17.39M}{10.8M}$ months = 1.6 months to break even; that is, it would have taken Microsoft 1.6 months to recover the $1 billion that it spent on R&D to develop the operating system. After the 1.6 months, the money coming in was largely profits. Note that equation (4) could be used to calculate the breakeven time where breakeven quantity is 17.39 million while the sales rate is 10.8 million per month.

$$\text{Breakeven time} = \frac{\text{Breakeven Quantity}}{\text{Sales Rate}} \qquad (4)$$

Apple

Suppose Apple developed an operating system at the same cost as Microsoft and sold it at the same price. It too (Apple) would need to sell 17.39 million units to break even. However, because Apple sold only 4 million units a year or 0.333 million per month, its breakeven time would be $\frac{17.39M}{0.333M}$ months = 52.22 months. If Apple wanted to breakeven in the same 1.6 months as Microsoft, it would have to sell each copy of its operating system at $1,856.76 or $\frac{52.22}{1.6}$($57.25).

The Microsoft advantage is largely because of its installed base—that is, the millions of Windows PCs and their owners (businesses and consumers) who have learned how to use the Microsoft operating system, bought software that runs on it, are comfortable with the operating system and applications, and prefer to stay with the Windows PCs rather than change to Apple. For similar reasons, many Apple users do not want to switch from Apple to the Windows camp either. Thus, after the PC active life of three years, many customers who had Windows PCs buy new Windows PCs while many customers who had Apple machines buy new Apple machines. Each new Windows machine means a sale of a Windows operating system for Microsoft. Effectively, the installed base of Windows machines is an intangible asset for Microsoft that is a key driver of how many copies of its operating system it can sell, while the installed base of Apple machines is an asset for Apple and a major driver of how many Macs Apple can sell.

The importance of intangibles is also seen in Apple's iTunes for iPod. Apple launched a Windows version of its iTunes in October 2003. In just three and a half days, over one million copies of the iTunes software for Windows had been downloaded, and over one million songs purchased using the software.[24] In April 2003, it had taken seven days for Apple to sell one million songs when it launched iTunes on Apple machines. Effectively, even Apple stood to benefit from the Windows installed base.

Key Takeaways

- Resources play a critical role in the creation and appropriation of value. There are three types of resource: tangible, intangible, and human. *Tangible resources* are the resources that are usually identified and accounted for in financial statements under the category, "assets." *Intangible resources* are the nonphysical and nonfinancial assets such as patents, copyrights, brand name reputation, trade secrets, research findings, relationships with customers, shelf space, and relationships with vendors that cannot be touched and are usually not accounted for in financial statements. *Organizational* resources consist of the know-how and knowledge embodied in employees as well as the routines, processes, and culture that are embedded in the organization. A firm's capabilities are its ability to turn resources into customer benefits and profits.
- A core competence is a resource or capability that:
  - Makes a significant contribution to the benefits that customers perceive in a product or service.
  - Is difficult for competitors to imitate.
  - Is extendable to other products in different markets.

- A technology or product exhibits *network externalities* if the more people that use it, the more valuable it becomes to each user. Network externalities effects can be direct or indirect.
- Although the size of a network is important, size is not everything. The structure of a network and the conduct of firms within the network also contribute to the value that each user enjoys in a network.
- Complementary assets can be critical to creating and appropriating value using new game activities. *Complementary assets* are all the other resources, beyond those that underpin a new game (an invention or discovery), that a firm needs to create value and position itself to appropriate the value.
- The Teece model helps us to understand better why it is that many inventors do not profit from their inventions. In the model, appropriating value from

an invention depends on (1) the extent to which the value can be imitated, and (2) the extent to which complementary assets are important and scarce. Inventors whose inventions are easy to imitate and require important and scarce complementary assets do not make money from the inventions. Rather, the owners of the complementary assets make the money. Depending on the level of imitability and the need and importance of complementary assets, a firm can use a *run, block*, and *team up* strategy to help its efforts to profit from a new game. This model, while very useful, has some limitations. For example, it leaves out the other factors that impact appropriability: position vis-à-vis coopetitors, pricing strategy, number of customers, etc.

- Since each new game usually requires many complementary assets, it is important to narrow down the list of the assets to those that are critical to a firm's value creation and appropriation activities. An AVAC analysis can be used for the narrowing-down exercise.
- Intangible resources are usually not quantified in financial statements. One way to get a feel for the value of a firm's intangible resources is to estimate the difference between the firm's market capitalization and book value. Another way is to zoom down on intangible resources that can be measured and try to estimate their significance to a firm.
- An AVAC analysis can be used to assess the profitability potential of resources. This analysis consists of answering the following questions:

  o Activities: Does the firm have what it takes to perform efficiently the activities for building and/or translating the resource/capabilities into customer benefits and/or positioning the firm to appropriate value?
  o Value: Does the resource make a significant contribution towards the benefits that customers perceive as valuable to them?
  o Appropriability: Does the firm make money from the value that customers perceive in the benefits from the resource?
  o Change: Do the activities for building and exploiting the resource take advantage of change (present or future) to create and appropriate value?

- An AVAC analysis enables a firm to identify and rank its resources by their competitive consequences—by the extent to which each resource stands to give the firm a competitive advantage. A resource can give a firm a sustainable competitive advantage, temporary competitive advantage, competitive parity, or competitive disadvantage.
- An AVAC analysis helps a firm decide what to do to reinforce a sustainable advantage, turn a temporary advantage into a sustainable advantage or turn competitive parity into competitive advantage.

Key Terms

Capabilities
Complementary assets
Core competences
Intangible resources
Network externalities
Profitability potential of resources/capabilities

Resources
Single-sided networks
Structure of a network
Tangible resources
Teece Model
Two-sided network
Valuing intangible resources

Chapter 6

First-mover Advantages/ Disadvantages and Competitors' Handicaps

Reading this chapter should provide you with the information to:

- Explain the advantages and disadvantages of moving first.
- Understand how to narrow down the list of potential first-mover advantages.
- Understand that first-mover advantages are usually not endowed on everyone who moves first; rather, they have to be earned.
- Understand competitors' potential handicaps.
- Understand why first movers sometimes win and why, sometimes, followers win.
- Understand the roles player by *explorers, superstars*, exploiters, and metoos in the face of new games.

Introduction

Consider the following. eBay was the first online auction firm and went on to dominate its industry. However, Google was not the first search engine company but went on also to dominate its own industry. Coca Cola invented the classic coke and went on to dominate the market for colas, with some help and challenges from Pepsi. However, neither Coke nor Pepsi invented diet cola, even though they dominate that market. Apple did not invent the MP3 player and yet its iPod went on to dominate the market for MP3 players. The question is, why is it that sometimes first movers go on to dominate their markets but at other times, followers (second movers) are the ones that go on to dominate their markets? As we indicated in Chapter 1, whether a first mover or follower wins is also a function of whether it has the right strategy. In Chapters 4 and 5, we started to explore what the right strategy is and is not, and will continue to do so throughout this book. In this chapter, we look deeper into the advantages and disadvantages of moving first. We start the chapter by exploring what *first-mover advantages* are all about. Next, we explore first-mover *dis*advantage— also known as followers' or *second-mover advantages*. In doing so, we are reminded that first-mover advantages and disadvantages are not automatically bestowed on any first mover. Rather, first-mover advantages have to be earned and disadvantages can be minimized. We conclude the chapter by exploring why it is that sometimes first movers win and sometimes, followers win.

First-mover Advantages

A **first-mover advantage** is a resource, capability, or product-market position that (1) a firm acquires by being the first to carry out an activity, and (2) gives the firm an advantage in creating and appropriating value. A firm has an opportunity to acquire first-mover advantages when it is the first to introduce a new product in an existing market, create a new market, invest in an activity first, or perform any other value chain, value network, or value shop activity first, such as bypassing distributors and selling directly to end-customers.[1] First-mover advantages come from six major sources (Table 6.1):

1 Total available market preemption.
2 Lead in technology, innovation, and business processes.
3 Preemption of scarce resources.
4 First-at-buyers.
5 First to establish a system of activities.
6 First to make irreversible commitments.

Total Available Market Preemption

If, in moving first, a firm introduces a new product, it has a chance to do the right things and capture as much of the total available market as possible before followers start to move in. Since such a firm is the only one in the market, it has a 100% share of the new product, no matter how many units it sells. Thus, the emphasis here is in capturing as much of the *total available* market as possible and selling as many units as possible before followers move in—that is,

Table 6.1 First-mover Advantages (FMAs)

Source of first-mover advantage	FMA mechanism
Total available market preemption	Economies of scale Size (beyond economies of scale) Economic rents and equity Network externalities Relationships with coopetitors
Lead in technology, innovation, and business processes	Intellectual property (patents, copyrights, trade secrets) Learning Organizational culture
Preemption of scarce resources	Complementary assets Location Input factors Plant and equipment
First-at-buyers	Buyer switching cost Buyer choice under uncertainty Brand (preemption of consumer perceptual space or mindshare)
First to establish a system of activities	Difficult-to-imitate system of activities
First to make irreversible commitments	Reputation and signals

emphasis is on preemption of total available market. Having captured as much of the total available market as possible, the firm potentially enjoys five advantages: scale economies, size effects (beyond economies of scale), economic rents and equity, network effects, and relations with coopetitors.

Scale Economies

There are economies of scale in production if the more of a product that is produced, the lower the *per unit* cost of production. There can also be economies of scale in R&D, advertising, distribution, marketing, sales, and service if the more units that are sold, the less the *per unit* cost of each activity. This advantage derives largely from the fact that the (total) fixed cost of each activity can be spread over the larger number of units. For example, an ad slot on TV costs the same for Coca Cola's diet cola as it does for Shasta's diet cola. Since Coca Cola sells hundreds of millions of cans of its diet cola compared to a few million cans for Shasta, Coke has lower per unit advertising costs compared to Shasta. If a firm moves first and performs the right activities, it can pre-preemptively capture as much of the total available market as possible; and if the firm's industry and market are such that there are economies of scale, its per unit cost of R&D, advertising, distribution, marketing, sales, service, etc. can be lower. This lower per unit cost from economies of scale has several implications for the different components of its ability to create and appropriate value.

If a firm that moved first has captured as much of the total available market as possible, and enjoys scale economies, rational potential new entrants know that if they were to enter the market to compete head-on with the first mover, they would have to capture the same market share (as the first mover) so as to attain the same per unit costs as the first mover. However, to do so would mean to bring in the same capacity as the first mover to the same market, thereby doubling the capacity. This might result in a price war that lowers profits for the new entrant. Thus, rational potential new entrants might refrain from entering. Effectively, if a first mover can capture as much of the total available market as possible, it can attain scale economies thereby creating barriers to entry for some potential followers. These barriers to entry are more difficult to surmount if the minimum efficient scale is large relative to the total available market and if the first mover has a system of activities or distinctive resources and capabilities that are difficult to imitate. When we say that a first movers' preemption of total available market raises barriers to entry, we do not mean that it is impossible for new entrants to enter. New entrants do enter sometimes but pursue niche markets. They would have a much more difficult time competing head-on with a first mover that has captured most of the total available market where economies of scale exist. Another exception is when a firm pursues a revolutionary strategy and takes advantage of a technological innovation to move in, leap-frogging the first mover.

Size Effects Beyond Economies of Scale

A first mover that pursues the right strategies and captures as much of the total available market as possible has another advantage beyond economies of scale—size. A large firm buys more from its suppliers than its competitors and in some cases, can command considerable bargaining power over its suppliers. For example, Wal-Mart's size gave it a tremendous amount of power over its suppliers in the mid-2000s.[2] Power play or none, it is also easier for suppliers to cooperate with larger firms. For example, to have suppliers locate near a firm, the firm needs to buy large enough output from the supplier to make it worth the supplier's investment in plants, equipment, and people to serve a customer at a particular location. A large firm can also afford to undertake more innovation projects, since it can spread its risk over more stable and less risky projects. Such innovations can allow a first mover to keep any lead that it may have attained.

Economic Rents and Equity

Before competitors move in, a first mover is effectively a monopolist and can collect economic rents if it formulates and executes a profitable business model. If it captures most of the total available market and keeps growing fast, that first mover's market valuation (capitalization) may go up as investors anticipate positive future cash flows from economic rents. Such money can serve the first mover well, especially in cases where capital markets are not efficient enough and therefore financing is not readily available to anyone who needs it. The first mover can use the money to buy fledgling new entrants, make venture capital investments, invest in more R&D, or acquire important complementary assets. If a first mover accumulates cash, a small new entrant is less likely to be tempted to start a price war, since the first mover has more cash to sustain losses.

The other side to a first mover earning economic rents is that these rents are likely to attract potential new entrants who want a share of these profits. If the first mover has accumulated enough cash or has enough equity, it can establish a reputation for fighting or can take other measures such as forming alliances, joint ventures, and so on, to fend off attacks.

Network Externalities

As we saw in Chapter 5, a product (or technology) exhibits network externalities if the more people that use the product or a compatible one, the more useful the product becomes to users. An example is an auction network such as eBay's. The more registered users that eBay has in its community of registered users, the more valuable that the network becomes to each user. That is because, for example, the larger the network, the more that a potential buyer of an antique is likely to find the antique in the network, and the more that the seller of an antique is likely to find a buyer in the network. More people would therefore tend to gravitate towards larger networks rather than smaller ones. Therefore, if a first mover has preemptively captured much of the available market for a product or technology that exhibits network externalities, customers are likely to gravitate towards its network or products, further increasing the number of users of its network or products. Thus a first mover that has an initial lead can see that lead grow to an even larger lead. Products that require complements such as computers also exhibit network externalities effects. That is because the more users who own a particular computer or compatible one, the more software that will be developed for it. The more software that there is for the particular computer or compatible one, the more users who will want the computer. Thus, a first mover that has a large installed base of products that require complements is likely to see more users gravitate towards its products, further increasing its installed base and attracting yet more customers.

A large network size or installed base has several implications for the different components of a firm's business model. First, since the larger a network, the more valuable it is to customers, a large proprietary network can be a differentiating factor for first movers. Second, rational potential new entrants know that if they were to enter, they would need a network as large as the first mover's if they wanted to offer the same value to customers as the first mover. However, new customers tend to gravitate towards the larger network. Thus, a large proprietary network acts as a barrier to entry for some potential new entrants. Again, this does not mean that no firms enter the industry. Some usually enter but compete in niche markets or use technological changes and innovation to compete against the first mover with the large network.[3] Also, a large network acts as a barrier to entry only when it is proprietary. If it is open, as was the case with Wintel PC, barriers to entry are lower. Third, since, all else equal, customers would prefer a large network over a smaller one, customers within a first mover's network would prefer to stay within the larger network than move. Effectively, a large network constitutes *switching costs* for customers. Thus, a first mover can dampen customer bargaining power by building in switching costs for customers in the form of a large proprietary network. Fourth, a large proprietary network also reduces rivalry between the owner of the network and those of smaller networks. That is because its larger network differentiates it from the smaller rivals. As we will see later in this book, other factors beyond size sometimes also impact the value that customers perceive in a network.

Relationships with Coopetitors

In our discussion about first-mover advantages so far, we have treated suppliers, customers, buyers, rivals, and potential new entrants as competitors whose goal is to sap profits out of the first mover. Often, as we saw in Chapter 4, these actors are more than just competitors. They are coopetitors—the firms with which one has to cooperate to create value and compete to appropriate it—and relationships with them can be critical. A first mover has an opportunity to build relationships not only with coopetitors but also with institutions such as government agencies or universities. Such relations can, among other things, help the collaborators to win a standard or dominant design.

Lead in Technology, Innovation, and Business Processes

A first mover often has an opportunity to establish leadership positions in business processes, technology, and organizational innovation. These leadership positions can be manifested in the quality and levels of intellectual property, learning and culture that firms can integrate into their business models.

Intellectual Property

Innovations in business processes, technology and organizational processes can be a source of advantage to firms and consequently, some firms try to protect them using patents, copyrights, trademarks, or trade secrets. For many products, patents do not offer their owners enough protection from imitation, since they can be circumvented. Copyrights and trademarks are not protected by the laws of many countries and when they are protected by law, there is often little monitoring and enforcement of the law. Trade secrets often are revealed through employees who move to other firms or through reverse engineering of products. Despite these often-cited shortcomings of intellectual property protection, intellectual property often serves a useful purpose in the profitability of a first mover's business model. First, in some industries and countries, patents and copyrights give their owners reasonable protection for a period of time during which they can collect monopoly rents from their invention or discovery. For example, one reason why many so-called blockbuster pharmaceutical drugs such as Lipitor bring in such high amounts of revenues is because they enjoy patent protection during their patent lives. Once a drug's patent protection runs out and generics can be introduced, revenues from such drugs can drop by as much as 86%.

Second, although many patents, copyrights, trademarks, and trade secrets may not prevent entry, they can slow it down. Circumventing a patent, though less costly than developing an original patent, can still be costly to get it right, if one ever does. Third, even when intellectual property protection does not prevent entry or slow it down, it can still be the source of revenues and profits. The case of Google and Overture is very illustrative of how intellectual property can be used. Google developed a search engine that, using its PageRank algorithm, delivered some of the most relevant search results. To more optimally make money from its search capabilities, the company needed a better advertising revenue model than pop-up ads. Overture, formerly known as Goto.com, had invented and in July 2001, received a patent for a bid-for-placement mechanism—an ad-placement mechanism that allows advertisers to bid for the placement of ads next to or above search results.[4] In August of 2004, Google and Yahoo (which had bought Overture in July of 2003) settled the lawsuit for 2.7 million shares of Google class A common shares.[5] On June 28, 2006 the 2.7 million shares were worth just over one billion dollars. Qualcomm's case offers another example. Most of the company's profits come from the royalties on its patents. Effectively, first movers can make money from their intellectual properties even when followers enter their market spaces. Third, a first mover can use its intellectual property as bargaining chips for other important resources that it may need to profit from its inventions or discoveries. For example, a startup that invents a new product needs marketing, manufacturing, distribution, shelf space, and other complementary assets so as to profit from the invention. It can use its intellectual property as a bargaining chip to gain access to such complementary assets. That is just what many biotech firms do.

Learning

In performing R&D, manufacturing, marketing, and other value-adding activities, a first mover accumulates know-how and other knowledge. Although some of this knowledge can spill over to potential competitors through employee mobility, informal know-how trading, reverse engineering, plant tours, and research publication, first movers still do benefit from their accumulated learning in several ways. First, as suggested by the standard learning or experience curve model, a firm's production cost for a particular product drops as a function of the cumulative number of units that the firm has produced since it started producing the product. Thus, to the extent that the knowledge is difficult to diffuse or the firm can keep it proprietary, the firm can have a cost advantage over followers. This can reduce potential new entries since any new entrant would have to accumulate as much knowledge in order to bring its costs down to those of the first mover. A firm can also use its accumulated knowledge as a bargaining chip for complementary assets. The case of Pixar and Disney illustrates this. Pixar was the first to move into the digital animation movie technology and used its know-how to gain access to Disney's brand name reputation in animation, storytelling, merchandising might, and its distribution channels through an alliance that was beneficial to both firms.

Organizational Culture

An organization's culture is the set of values, beliefs, and norms that are shared by employees.[6] Since a culture is embedded in a firm's routines, actions, and history, it is often difficult to imitate and takes time to cultivate. Moving first can give a firm the valuable time that it needs to build the culture. Where culture is valuable, difficult to imitate, and rare, it can be a source of competitive advantage.[7] It can lower costs or allow a firm to be more innovative than its competitors, thereby differentiating its products. Southwest Airline's culture was often associated with its being the most profitable airline in the USA in the 1990s and well into the 2000s. The company's employees cared about each other, were flexible in the types of job that they were willing to perform, and were happy to work harder for longer hours than employees at competing airlines.

Preemption of Scarce Resources

A first mover often has the opportunity to acquire important scarce resources, thereby preempting rivals.

Complementary Assets

For many firms, moving first usually means the invention of a new product or the introduction of a new technology. To profit from such an invention or new technology, a firm usually also needs complementary assets—all other assets, apart from those that underpin the invention or discovery, that the firm needs to offer customers superior value and be in a position to appropriate the value.[8] Recall that complementary assets include brand name reputation, distribution channels, shelf space, manufacturing, marketing, relationships with coopetitors, complementary technologies, and so on. Thus, a firm that moves first has the opportunity to preempt rivals and acquire complementary assets. Once such critical resources are gone, there is not much that potential new entrants can do. For example, first movers Coke and Pepsi preempted most potential new entrants in the soda business by taking up most of the shelf space in stores for sodas. Preemption of complementary assets can constitute an important barrier to entry. Since complementary assets are critical to profiting from inventions and new technologies, rational potential new entrants who know that they cannot obtain the necessary complementary assets are less likely to enter, or when they enter, they are likely to seek alliances with those that have the assets. Complementary assets such as brands can also differentiate a first mover's products from those of followers.

Location

In many arenas, there is only so much room for so many competitors. Thus a first mover that pursues the right strategies can preempt rivals by leaving little room for followers. Take geographic space, for example. At airports, there is usually a limited number of gates and landing slots. An airline that moves into an airport early and introduces many flights can take up most of the gates and landing slots, leaving followers to the airport with few gates and landing slots. When Wal-Mart entered the market in the Southwestern USA, it saturated contiguous towns with stores, leaving followers with very little space to build similar stores.[9] Effectively, it erected a barrier to entry since any potential new entrant who expected to enjoy the same costs benefits from economies of scale as Wal-Mart would have to build as many stores and distribution centers; but doing so would result in overcapacity and the threat of a price war. Such a potential threat of price wars would prevent rational potential new entrants from entering. Establishing positions in geographic space does not have to be through saturation of contiguous locations, as Wal-Mart did. The first mover can establish the positions in such a way that occupying the interstices will be unprofitable for a follower.[10] For example, good market research might allow the first mover to pick out the more lucrative locations to occupy, leaving out the less profitable ones for followers.

Location preemption can also take place in product space. First movers can introduce many products with enough variation in attributes to cover the potentially profitable product-attribute spaces, leaving very little or no so-called "white space"—potentially lucrative product space that others can occupy. Such a lack of white space can deter entry.

Input Factors

In some industries, first movers may be able to attract talented employees and with the right incentives, retain them when followers enter. In some situations, moving first and performing the right research can provide superior information about resource needs and availability. Such information can enable a first mover to purchase assets at market prices below those that will prevail as followers move in. (Note that the first mover can also profit from such superior information by buying options for the assets where such markets exist.) For example, a mineral or oil company that goes to a developing country and explores for mineral or oil deposits has superior information about the potential of the country, compared to local officials or competitors that have not yet ventured into the country. Such a firm can secure access to such deposits by signing contracts with local officials. Access to superior information can also help firms in structuring contracts with employees.

Plant and Equipment

If a firm builds a plant to produce a particular product and the plant cannot be profitably used for any other purpose, the firm is said to have made an *irreversible investment* in the plant. First movers who make irreversible investments in equipment, plants, or any other major asset, signal to potential followers that they are committed to maintaining higher output levels following entry by followers. That is because their plants and equipment cannot be profitably used elsewhere and therefore managers are likely to keep producing so long as the prices that they charge are high enough to cover their variable costs. If followers were to enter, such first movers could engage in price wars so long as their prices are high enough to cover their variable costs. Effectively, irreversible investments in plants and equipment can deter entry and can be a first-mover advantage.

First-at-customers

Customers play a critical role in the profitability of a business model and being the first to reach customers can give a firm opportunities to attain first-mover advantages. We explore three such potential advantages:

Switching Cost

A buyer's *switching costs* are the costs that it incurs when it switches from one supplier (firm) to another. These include the costs of training employees to deal with the new supplier; the time and resources for locating, screening, and qualifying new suppliers; and the cost of new equipment such as software to comply with the supplier. Switching costs can also arise from incompatibility of a buyer's assets with the new supplier. For example, frequent flyer miles accumulated on one airline may not work on some other airlines. If buyers' switching costs for a firm's products are high, the buyers are less likely to switch to another firm's products. Potential new entrants who know that buyers will not switch are less likely to try to enter. Rivals who know that buyers are less likely to switch are less likely to try to win customers using lower prices. Thus, if a first mover can build switching costs at buyers before followers move in, it can have an advantage. It is important to note that while switching costs can prevent existing customers from switching to new firms, they usually have little effect on new customers who have no switching costs to worry about. Thus, in a growing market, followers can focus on new customers to increase their market share.

Buyer Choice Under Uncertainty

The information that customers have about the benefits from some products is imperfect. Buyers of such products may therefore stay with the first brand that meets their needs satisfactorily.[11] This is particularly true for *experience goods*—products or services whose characteristics are ascertained only after consumption, since it is difficult to observe the characteristics in advance. For example, because a drug's efficacy and side effects can vary from patient to patient and cannot be determined in advance, doctors tend to stick with the first drug that works for their patients and will not change to a follower's drugs unless there are compelling reasons. Such *brand loyalty* can be particularly strong for low-cost convenience goods, where the search costs of finding another product that meets a customer's taste often exceed the benefits of changing brands. (Convenience goods are products such as soaps and pasta that one purchases frequently and with minimum effort.) The effect is less strong for *search goods*—products or services such as airplanes whose characteristics are easy to evaluate objectively before purchase.

Brand Mindshare: Preemption of Consumer Perceptual Space

Research also suggests that pioneering brands can have a strong influence on consumer preferences.[12] In some cases, the first product introduced may actually receive disproportionate attention in the press and in consumer's minds. A case in question is Viagra, which received lots of free press from unlikely sources such as TV comedians. A follower must have a superior product or have to spend a lot more on building its brand to dislodge the first product.

First To Establish a System of Activities

One of the more durable first-mover advantages that a firm can have is a difficult-to-replicate system of activities. Why is a system of activities difficult to imitate? Although imitating some individual activities in such a system of activities may be easy, imitating a whole system can be difficult, since it entails imitating not only the components of the system but the interactions between the components. The extent to which it can be difficult to imitate a system of new game activities is illustrated by the now familiar Dell example. Dell was the first major PC maker to pursue direct sales and build-to-order. It established a system of activities to support this strategy that followers found difficult to imitate. In 1999, its CEO at the time, Kevin Rollins, was asked, "What is it about the direct sales model and mass customization that has been difficult for competitors to replicate?"[13] His response was:

> It's not as simple as having a direct sales force. It's not as simple as just having mass customization in plant or manufacturing methodology. It's a whole series of things in the value chain from the way we procure, the way we develop product, the way we order and have inventory levels, and manufacturer and service support. The entire value chain has to work together to make it efficient and effective.

Those complex systems of activities can pose problems for potential imitators. As Rollins pointed out,

> What is the competition looking at? So many of our competitors are really looking at our business and saying, "Oh, it's the asset management model— seven days of inventory. That's what we're going to do," rather than looking at every one of 10 things and replicating them.

And we may add that replicating the interactions between the ten things can also be difficult to replicate.

First to Make Irreversible Commitments

First-mover advantages can change not only the likely expectations of followers, they can also change their behavior. One goal of making irreversible investments is to deter or slow down followers; but to have such an effect, there must be something about the first mover that suggests that it is committed to that particular first-mover advantage. For example, a first mover can establish a reputation for retaliating against any firm that infringes on its intellectual property by suing anyone who attempts to violate its patents or copyrights. For a commitment to be effective in deterring or slowing down competitors, it must be credible, visible to competitors, and understandable.[14] A commitment is *credible* if there is something about it that makes competitors believe in it and the options that it creates or limits. The primary drivers of credibility are reputation and irreversibility of the commitment. If a firm has a reputation for fighting the first set of followers that ventures into its product market space, it is likely to do so with the next set. Such a reputation for retaliation can deter likely entrants. A commitment is *irreversible* if it is costly or difficult to walk away from or undo. That would be the case, for example, if the assets that underpin the commitment cannot be profitably redeployed elsewhere. The idea here is that if a first mover's commitment is irreversible, it is more likely to stay and fight followers rather than accommodate them or exit. Commitments such as physical plants are visible to many people but others such as commitment to a culture are more difficult to observe. When commitments are not very visible, signals can be used to indicate their presence. Signals can also be used to help competitors understand the nature of a firm's commitments. Effectively, a firm that moves first has the opportunity to make commitments that are credible, visible, and understandable. Doing so can deter or slow down followers.

It is important to emphasize the fact that first-mover advantages are not automatically endowed on firms that move first. First-mover advantages are not the birthright of firms that move first. They have to be earned.

Earning and Maintaining First-mover Advantages

Earning First-mover Advantages

A firm that performs an activity first is not automatically bestowed with first-mover advantages just because it was the first to perform the activity. Firms usually have to *earn* first-mover advantages. In other words, the fact that a firm is the first to introduce a new product does not mean that, for example, it *automatically* captures most of the total available market thereby enabling it to benefit from economies of scale, get large enough to take advantage of its size, earn profits from its pioneering activities, build and exploit a large installed base, or cultivate important and useful relationships with coopetitors. Neither does moving first mean that a firm automatically preempts the right resources/ capabilities and builds switching costs at customers. Attaining these advantages entails performing the value chain activities with the effectiveness and efficiency that it takes to increase one's chances of creating and capturing the most value. A firm also has to focus on the first-mover advantages that it wants, anticipate and respond to the reaction of followers, and pay attention to any opportunities and threats of its environment. In other words, attaining first-mover advantages requires good strategies. It may be easier to perform some of these activities because one has moved first, but one still has to perform them well.

Total Available Market Preemption

When a firm moves into a market first, the chances are that not all potential customers are going to flock to its doors asking for its products. If the firm wants to capture as much of the total available market as possible, it has to perform the types of activities that locate as many customers as possible that have a high willingness to pay, and whose acquisition and maintenance costs are low, and provide these customers with the types of benefits that they want. If customers do not get the benefits that they want, they may decide to wait for followers or integrate vertically backward to provide their own needs. A first mover will maintain its market lead only if it has built a system of activities to create and capture value, that is difficult to imitate, or has built valuable scarce difficult-to-imitate resources/capabilities that followers cannot replicate.

Lead in Technology and Innovation.

Being the first to introduce a new technology does not automatically endow a firm with intellectual property rights, stocks of knowledge, and the right organizational culture. These advantages have to be pursued correctly. A firm that wants the advantages of intellectual property protection has not only actively to pursue the intellectual property first, but also actively defend its property rights when attempts are made to violate them. One reason why it took AMD a long time to catch up with Intel was because Intel was also good at defending the copyrights for the microcode of its microprocessors.[15] Learning is not automatic either. A firm has to have the right structure, incentive systems, and processes to learn well. Building a culture that is conducive to innovation also takes meticulous work that is not guaranteed just because one moved first.

Preemption of Scarce Resources

First movers are not automatically endowed with scarce resources. Wal-Mart was able to preempt much of the discount retail space in the Southwestern USA because of all the activities that it performed. If it had not saturated contiguous small towns with discount stores, built matching distribution centers, and established a Wal-Mart culture, it may have been easier for competitors to move in. If Ryanair had not ramped up flights to each of the secondary airports into which it moved, established good relationships with local officials, and obtained as many gates and landing slots as possible, it might have been easier for other airlines to move into the same airports that it flew into. To preempt scarce resources, a firm has to pursue them diligently.

First-at-Customers

The fact that a firm was the first to introduce a product does not mean that the firm will reach all the right customers and build all the switching costs possible. The right customers have to be pursued with the right switching costs. Firms have to pursue the right branding messages and so on.

First to Establish a System of Activities

The fact that a firm is first to perform a series of activities does not mean that the firm will automatically be endowed with a system of activities that is difficult-to-imitate and that gives it a competitive advantage. The activities in the system have to be consistent with the positions that they underpin.[16] For example, if a firm is a low-cost competitor, it cannot pursue the type of high-cost activities that are usually pursued by firms that offer luxury goods. The activities should also reinforce rather than neutralize each other's effect. For example, if a firm tries to build a luxury brand through advertising but offers products that do not match the image that it is trying to create, it has a problem. The activities should be consistent with the firm's existing distinctive resources or those that it wants to build. It would not make sense for Toyota to try to produce a new car that does not use its lean manufacturing practices, unless it were experimenting with newer and better processes. Finally, establishing the right system of activities may also require that one takes advantage of industry value drivers. Recall that industry value drivers are those industry factors that stand to have a substantial impact on the benefits (low-cost or differentiation) that customers want, and the quality and number of such customers.

Which First-mover Advantages Should One Pursue?

The list of first-mover advantages that we have outlined is rather long. The question is, which of them should a firm pursue? After all, not all first-mover advantages are important to every firm. One way to narrow down the list to those that make a significant contribution to value creation and appropriation is to use an AVAC analysis to rank order the advantages by the extent to which they contribute to value creation and appropriation. As shown in Table 6.2, each advantage is classified by answering the following questions:

1 Activities: Does the firm have what it takes to perform the activities to build and exploit the first-mover advantage? What are these activities and how do they contribute to value creation and capture?
2 Value: Does the first-mover advantage make a significant contribution

Table 6.2 Rank Ordering First-mover Advantages

First-mover advantage	Activities: Does the firm have what it takes to perform the activities to build and exploit the first-mover advantage?	Value: Does the first-mover advantage make a significant contribution towards the value that customers perceive as unique compared to what competitors offer?	Appropriability: Does the first-mover advantage make a significant contribution to profits?	Change: Does the first-mover advantage take advantage of change to create and appropriate value?	Strategic consequence
Advantage 1	Yes	Yes	Yes	Yes	Sustainable competitive advantage
Advantage 2	Yes	Yes	Yes	No	Temporary competitive advantage
Advantage 3	Yes	Yes	No	Yes	Temporary competitive advantage
Advantage 4	Yes	Yes	No	No	Competitive parity
Advantage 5	No/Yes	No	Yes	No	Competitive parity
Advantage 6	No	No	No	No	Competitive disadvantage
Strategic action	What can a firm do to reinforce the Yesses and reverse or dampen the Noes, and what is the impact of doing so?				

towards the value that customers perceive as unique compared to what competitors offer?

3 Appropriability: Does the first-mover advantage make a significant contribution to profits?

4 Change: Does the first mover advantage take advantage of change to create and appropriate value?

As shown in Table 6.2, each first-mover advantage is classified by the potential competitive consequence of pursuing the particular first-mover advantage, from "sustainable competitive advantage" down to "competitive *dis*advantage." The more that the strategic consequence from a first-mover advantage is a sustainable strategic advantage rather than a strategic *dis*advantage, the more that a firm may want to pursue the first-mover advantage. In addition to telling a firm which first-mover advantage to pursue, the analysis can also point out which Noes could be reversed to Yesses or dampened, and which Yesses should be strengthened.

First-mover *Dis*advantages

There are also *dis*advantages to moving first. These *first-mover disadvantages* are also called *follower advantages*.[17] Followers sometimes stand to benefit from free-riding on the spillovers from first movers' investments, resolution of technological and marketing uncertainty, changes in technology or customer needs, and first-mover inertia.

Free-riding on First-mover's Investments

First movers, especially those that pioneer new products, sometimes have to invest heavily in R&D to develop the new product, in training employees for whom the technology and market are new, in helping suppliers better understand what they should be supplying, in developing distribution channels, and in working with customers to help them discover their latent needs. Followers can take advantage of the now available knowledge from first movers' R&D, hire away some of the employees that the first mover trained, buy from suppliers who have a better idea about what it is that they should be supplying, use proven distribution channels and go after customers who may be willing to switch or new ones who are waiting for a different version of the pioneer's product. Effectively, a follower's costs can be considerably lower than those of the first mover on whose investments the follower free rides. The fact that these free-riding opportunities exist does not mean that every follower can take advantage of them. Whether a follower is able to take advantage of these opportunities is a function of the imitability of the first mover's product and the extent to which the follower has the complementary assets for the product.[18] It is also a function of the business models that the first mover and follower pursue.

Resolution of Technological and Marketing Uncertainty

In some cases, first movers face lots of technological and marketing uncertainty that must be resolved. This uncertainty is gradually resolved as the first mover works with suppliers, customers, and complementors to better deliver what customers want. For example, the emergence of a standard or dominant design can drastically reduce the amount of uncertainty since firms do not have to make major costly design changes and suppliers know better what to supply. Followers who enter after the emergence of a standard or dominant design, for example, do not have to worry as much about what design to pursue or whether a market exists or not, as the pioneer did. Many PC makers such as Dell moved into the PC business only after it had been proven that the technology and market were viable. Thus, when Dell entered the PC market, it had already been proven that there was a market for business customers. All Dell had to do was decide to focus on the business customers. Whether followers can erode a first mover's competitive advantage depends on what the pioneer did when it moved first. A first mover that pursues the right strategies can win the standard or dominant design, and therefore have a say as to the extent to which followers can profit from the standard or dominant design.

Changes in Technology or Customer Needs and First-mover Inertia

Technological change or a shift in customer needs that requires a first mover to change can give a follower an opening if the first mover's inertia prevents it from changing. For example, if a technological change makes it possible to introduce a new product that potentially replaces a first mover's product, the first mover is not likely to be in a rush to introduce the new product for fear of cannibalizing its existing product.

Competitors' Handicaps

When a firm moves *first* and enjoys first mover advantages, it is because its competitors (present and potential) decided not to move first or to follow immediately. The question is, what is it about some firms that would make them not move first or not move at all despite the potential first-mover advantages? Put differently, if there are so many advantages to moving first, the questions is, what is it about a first mover's competitors that prevents them from moving first? We explore five factors that can prevent competitors from moving first or following: competitors' *dominant logic*, lack of strategic fit, prior commitments, resources and capabilities (or lack of them) (strengths and weaknesses), and the fear of cannibalization.

Dominant logic

Every manager has a set of beliefs, biases, and assumptions about the structure and conduct of the industry in which his or her firm operates, what markets her firm should focus on, what the firm's business model should be, whom to hire, who the firm's competitors are, what technologies are best for the firm, and so on.[19] This set of beliefs, biases, and assumptions is a manager's **managerial logic** and defines the frame within which a manager is likely to approach management decisions. Managerial logic is at the core of a manager's ability to search, filter, collect, evaluate, assimilate new information, and take decisions using the newly acquired information.[20] Depending on organizational values, norms, culture, structure, systems, processes, business model, environment (industry and macro), and how successful the firm has been, there usually emerges a **dominant managerial logic**—a common way of viewing how best to do business in the firm. Also called mental map, managerial frame, genetic code, corporate genetics, and corporate mindset, dominant logic is very good for a firm that has been performing well so long as there are no major changes; that is, dominant managerial logic is usually a strength. In the face of an opportunity to take advantage of new information by pursuing a new game activity and thereby moving first to, say, offer a new product, a firm is likely to pass over such an opportunity if it lies outside its managers' dominant logic—outside manager's beliefs, biases, and assumptions about how best to do business. Thus, competitors' dominant logic may be one reason why a first mover and not its competitors is the one that moves first. Competitors' logic may prevent them from seeing the first-mover advantages and moving effectively to exploit them.

Strategic Fit

Competitors' dominant logic may be such that they can understand the benefits of moving first but management might still decide not to move first. That would be the case, for example, if moving first does not fit the firm's strategy. *Exploit-*

ers with valuable scarce complementary assets often pursue a so-called *follower strategy* and wait for others to introduce a new product first. They then quickly imitate the product and use their scarce complementary assets to overcome the first mover and profit from the first mover's inventions. IBM pursued such a follower strategy in the 1970s, 1980s, and 1990s. It did not invent the personal computer but used its brand name reputation and installed base of customers and software developers to gain temporarily about 60% of the PC market share before seeing that share drop dramatically and eventually getting out of the market. It also waited until Apollo Computers and Sun Microsystems had developed the computer workstation business before it entered and used its installed base of customers and brand to quickly attain an important market share. As we saw in Chapter 5, the British music record company invented CAT scans but GE and Siemens used their complementary assets to make most of the profits from the invention.

Prior Commitments

Even if it is in the interest of a competitor to move first in performing the new game activity or follow a first mover, the competitor may still be prevented from taking action because of prior commitments that it made in its earlier activities. We examine two types of commitment: relationship-related and sunk cost-related.

Relationship-related Commitments

Relationship-related commitments are commitments such as contracts, network relationships, alliances, joint ventures, agreements, understandings within political coalitions, and venture capital investments that involve more than one party. Sometimes, performing a new game activity requires a firm to get out of or modify the terms of prior relationship-related commitments. If the new game is not in the interest of the other party, the party might refuse to cooperate. Compaq's case offers an interesting example. To follow Dell's direct sales and build-to-order new game strategy, Compaq wanted to adopt a build-to-order model and sell directly to customers, bypassing distributors. Citing previous agreements, distributors refused to cooperate and Compaq had drastically to modify its proposed new business model.

Sunk Cost-related Commitments

In sunk cost-related commitments, a firm makes irreversible investments in plants, equipment, capacity, or other resources, sometimes to signal its commitment to stay in a market or a particular business. *Irreversible investments* are those investments whose costs are sunk, that is, investments whose costs have already been incurred and cannot be recovered.[21] If performing a new game activity requires resources that are different from a firm's irreversible investments but existing PMPs remain competitive, staying with one's irreversible investments, rather than investing in the new game activities, may appear to be the profitable thing to do. Why? For the incumbent, investing in the new game activity requires new investments and this money must come from somewhere else, since the firm's existing investments are sunk and therefore their costs cannot be recovered and reinvested in the new game activity. Thus, if the firm pursues the new game activity, it must incur all the new costs. If it stays with its existing activities, it does not have to spend any new money, since its products from the sunk investments are still competitive. If products from the new game activities improve at a faster rate than those from existing activities, there may come a time when customers start migrating to new game products and the firm that stuck with the sunk investments will see its market share eroded.

Resources and Capabilities

In some industries, performing a new game activity often requires distinctive resources that competitors may not have. Developing a new microprocessor or operating system can require billions of dollars and many very skilled engineers. These are scarce resources and capabilities that few firms have. Thus, competitors may not be able to compete with a first mover because they do not have the resources or capabilities needed to compete. For example, many countries cannot afford a car industry because they do not have what it takes to build and run one profitably. This is the old barriers to entry story.

Fear of Cannibalization

Firms are not likely to pursue a new game activity if to do so cannibalizes their existing products, especially if the new products have to be priced lower than the ones that they are cannibalizing. For a while, Sun Microsystems was not eager to introduce Linux Intel-based servers, since the latter costs less to buy, use, and service than Sun's UNIX-based servers. Intel-based servers eventually won the battle.

Multigames

As we first suggested in Chapter 1, a new game does not take place in isolation. Rather, each new game is usually preceded by, followed by, or is concurrent with another game. Thus, a firm that wants to play a current game well may have to take into consideration the likely reaction of firms from the preceding, following, and concurrent games. Depending on the differences between the current and preceding games, firms from a preceding game may find out that some of their strengths in the preceding game have become handicaps in the current game. Firms that were not in the preceding game can take advantage of such handicaps. However, many strengths from preceding games often remain strengths. This is the case with many complementary assets. Firms that move first in the current game can build and take advantage of first-mover advantages. At the same time, these firms have to be aware of the fact that in the following game some of their first-mover advantages as well as disadvantages may become handicaps. Thus, these firms may be better off anticipating the likely reaction of players in the following game and responding accordingly to them.

Types of Player: A Framework

Not all the firms that pursue new games in any particular market move at the same time. Nor do all players pursue the right new game strategies. Thus, we can categorize players as a function of when they pursue new game strategies and the extent to which they pursue the right strategies. Such a classification can help a firm understand where it stands strategically, relative to its competitors in the face of a new game, as a first step towards understanding what it needs to do next. It can help an entrepreneur understand what strategic spaces might be good ones to pursue. The classification results in four types of player: explorers, superstars, exploiters, and me-toos (Figure 6.1).

Explorers

An **explorer** is a firm that moves first in performing a set of new game activities but does so largely for the fun of it. It is more of an explorer than an exploiter. Its activities are driven, not so much by a clear strategy for creating and appropriating value, but by what it just happens to find itself doing or enjoys doing. Explorers may pursue the activities more to make a difference than to make money. They may also pursue the activity for knowledge's own sake. They often create value or establish a foundation for creating value but do not appropriate it. They help reduce technological and market uncertainty and pave the way for exploiters (see below) to come in and take advantage of the foundation for value creation and make money. Many inventors (firms and individuals) fall into this category. AT&T which invented the transistor and inventors such as Tesla, are good examples. Another example is Xerox, which, through its Xerox Palo Alto Research Center, invented, among other things,

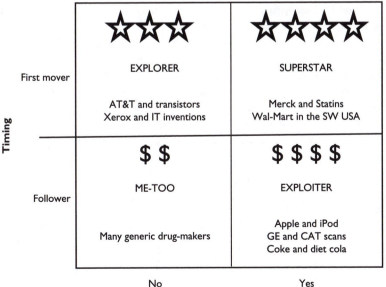

Figure 6.1 Types of Player.

laser printing, Ethernet, the personal computer graphical user interface (GUI) paradigm (or windows), and object-oriented programming, but never made much money from them. This is not to say that some explorers do not appropriate the value that they have created. Some do make money but the money does not come through a deliberate attempt to create and appropriate value.

Superstars

A **superstar** is a firm that moves first in pursuing a new game strategy and diligently performs those activities that substantially improve its chances of building and exploiting first-mover advantages, countering first-mover disadvantages, and taking advantage of competitors' handicaps. Usually, a superstar has a clear strategy for how to create and appropriate value when it moves first. Like explorers, a superstar is interested in exploring new ways of creating value; but unlike explorers, superstars are also genuinely and purposefully interested in exploitation—in creating and appropriating value. A superstar works hard at performing new game activities and taking advantage of both the value chain and new game factors of its new game activities. It does the right things and does them right. With some luck, such a firm can not only gain a competitive advantage, it can also change the structure of its industry to its advantage. It can become the superstar of its industry. Largely because the superstar has built the right first-mover advantages and is taking advantage of them, followers usually have a difficult time catching up with or leapfrogging the superstar. Moreover, a superstar may also have countered potential first-mover disadvantages, and taken advantage of potential competitors' handicaps. This does not mean that a superstar's competitive advantage is forever. Merck was a superstar when it performed the relevant R&D to discover and exploit Mevacor, the first cholesterol drug from the group of cholesterol drugs called statins that would revolutionize cholesterol therapy. Wal-Mart was a superstar when it established its discount retailing operations in rural southwestern USA. Dell was a superstar when it established direct sales and build-to-order in the PC market. Ryanair was a superstar when it established its low-cost airline activities in the EU. Superstars usually make money, but not necessarily all the time. Their deliberate pursuit of value creation and appropriation increases their chances compared to those of an explorer. However, because superstars often face the huge technological and marketing uncertainties associated with moving first, they are not always likely to appropriate most of the value that they have created.

Exploiters

An **exploiter** is a follower that waits for explorers and superstars to move first and reduce technological and market uncertainty, and then enters. An exploiter usually has or can quickly develop the ability to take advantage of first-mover disadvantages better to create and/or appropriate value than first movers. Exploiters usually do not invent or discover anything but can make most of the money from inventions or discoveries. They usually have complementary assets—all the other assets, apart from those that underpin the inventions or discoveries, that firms need to create and appropriate value. Examples of exploiters abound. General Electric and Siemens did not invent the CAT scan but made most of the money from it. Coke and Pepsi did not invent diet or caffeine-free cola but made most of the money from them. Microsoft did not invent many of the products from which it makes money. iPod was not the first MP3 player but dominated the market in 2007. Like superstars, exploiters have clear strategies for creating and appropriating value. In doing so, however, they take advantage of their complementary assets and ability to exploit first-mover *dis*advantages. They usually know when to enter and what to do when they enter. Some entrepreneurs see exploiters as an important part of their exit strategies, since they can sell themselves (and their technologies and ideas) to the exploiters for good money. Others see exploiters more as piranha.

Me-too

Me-too players are followers who have no clear strategy for taking advantage of first-mover *dis*advantages better to create and appropriate value than first movers. Many of them are incumbents who are forced to defend their competitive advantages from attacking first movers or exploiters but do not quite know how. Some are firms that take advantage of first-mover disadvantages to create or enter niche markets. In that case, they may have clear strategies for attacking the niche in question but not for toppling first movers or exploiters. Many suppliers of generic pharmaceuticals are me-too players.

Competition and Coopetition

It is important to note that the success of each player type depends on the competition that it faces. Superstars are less likely to shine brightly if they start executing their strategies at about the same time that other firms with more valuable and scarce complementary assets enter the market. They are also less likely to do well if exploiters enter the market before the superstars have had a chance to build first-mover advantages. If explorers are never challenged by exploiters or superstars, they may make money simply because they do not have strong competitors. Exploiters are less likely to make money if they enter the market at about the same time that other exploiters enter or enter after superstars have had a chance to build first-mover advantages. Me-toos can do well if they enter niche markets and neither superstars nor exploiters bother to challenge them. Effectively, the competition that a player faces plays an important role in the extent to which the player can make money.

A player's performance may also depend on the extent to which it is better able to cooperate with other players in creating and appropriating value. An explorer that is more capable of invention may team up with an exploiter that has complementary assets in order to form a team with a better chance of winning than either player alone. Exploiters and superstars can also team up to exploit their complementary assets, especially if each player comes from a different country that has something unique to offer.

Applications of the player-type framework

Although the player-type framework is very simple, it has some potentially powerful applications. It is versatile, and can be used to provide an elementary but useful look at a firm's new game strategies (1) for different products, (2) in different countries, and (3) over a time period.

Explore Different New Game Product Strategies

It is not unusual that, at any one time, one firm can be an exploiter for one product, an explorer for another product, and a superstar or me-too for yet another. Managers can use the player-type framework to explore the different strategies that underpin each of these products and make some decisions on what to improve. Figure 6.2 offers an example of how the framework can be applied to a computer maker. In the year 2000, the company offered three products: Laptops, servers, and MP3 players. Each circle in Figure 6.2 is proportional to sales revenues or profits at 2000 prices. The earlier a firm introduced a product before its next major competitor, the higher the circle. The more that the firm was seen as having gotten the new game strategy for the product right, the more the circle would lie to the right. Thus, in both 2000 and 2007, the firm was an explorer when it came to strategies for its laptops; but in 2007, it behaved a little more like a superstar, since the laptop circle moved to the right, (the firm was still an explorer). The strategy also appears to have paid off since its 2007 revenues were higher than 2000 revenues. As far as servers were concerned, the firm behaved as a superstar. Its revenues increased from 2000 to 2007 as the firm appeared to have fine-tuned its strategy. Finally, the firm appeared to have improved its strategy for MP3s from 2000 to 2007 as an exploiter but its revenues dropped. Why the drop? It is possible that competition increased even as the firm improved its strategy. While very simple, this analysis is still a good starting point for a management discussion about whether to continue offering all three products, focus on one or two, and if so, whether to still do so as a superstar, exploiter, or explorer, or maybe even as a me-too.

Performance of Different New Game Strategies in Different Countries

The framework can also be used to examine a multiproduct/service firm's strategies in different countries or regions. Consider a firm that pursues different strategies in the EU, China, and the USA (Figure 6.3). Again, the area of the circle is proportional to the revenues or profits that the firm earns in each region in the period being explored. In the EU, the firm does well as an explorer and an exploiter, somewhat well as a me-too, but not so well as a superstar. Such a firm could be a fast-food company such as McDonald's or Kentucky Fried Chicken that operates as an explorer in some countries where it is usually the first fast-food company in each of the locations where it opens its stores, an exploiter in others, and so on. In China, the company acts as a superstar, exploiter, and me-too. It is more successful as an exploiter and me-too than as a superstar (each has a larger circle area than the me-too). The firm could also be a fast-food company or a retailer that has different strategies for different regions of China.

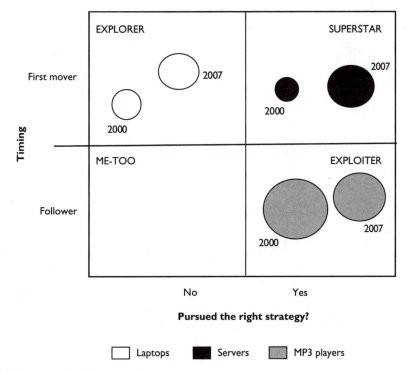

Figure 6.2 Different New Game Product Strategies.

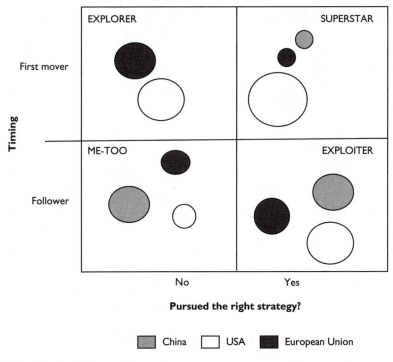

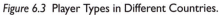

Figure 6.3 Player Types in Different Countries.

In the USA, the firm offers four different products, with each one reflecting a different player type. The firm does best as a superstar, followed by being an exploiter and then an explorer. Being me-too works the least. Such an analysis can be a good starting point for whether to continue trying to be all things to each country/region or focus on only being a superstar, explorer, exploiter, or me-too.

History of Firm's New Game Strategies

In the third example, a firm can use the framework to explore where it has been and how well it has performed as a superstar, explorer, exploiter, and me-too (Figure 6.4). Such a firm could be a pharmaceutical company that introduced different drugs using different strategies. In the example, the firm started out in the 1980s as an explorer and offered two products that did relatively well; but the product for which the firm had more of a strategy than the other (the one to the right in the explorer quadrant) had more revenues. In the 1990s, the firm decided to try being a superstar and me-too in addition to being an explorer. Its revenues as a superstar were much higher than those as an explorer and me-too. In the 2000s, the firm had become an exploiter and was doing very well. This analysis is also a good starting point for managers to discuss what next for the company. It suggests, for example, that the firm might want to continue being an exploiter, assuming that everything else—e.g. competition—remains the same. One other thing that the results suggest is that the firm may have been riding a technology life cycle. At the onset of such a cycle, the

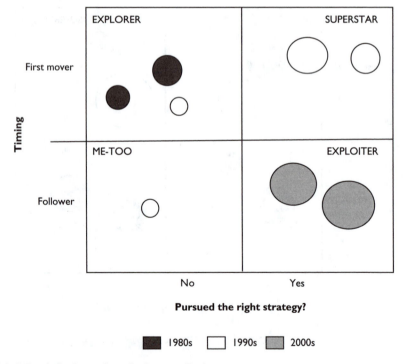

Figure 6.4 A Firm's Evolution from Explorer to Exploiter.

environment is usually more conducive to explorers and superstars. As uncertainty unravels, exploiters and me-toos move in. We will have more to say about technology life cycles in a later chapter when we explore disruptive technologies.

First Movers Versus Followers: Some Conclusions

To conclude this chapter, we return to the question that was posed at the beginning of the chapter: why is it that first movers sometimes go on to dominate their markets and at other times, followers are the ones that go on to dominate their markets? The answer to this question is a combination of the following five reasons:

1   First-mover advantages have to be earned and exploited diligently.
2   The owner of scarce important complementary assets usually has an edge.
3   First-mover *dis*advantages can be minimized.
4   Competitive, macro, and global environments.
5   Type of player and its business strategy.

First-mover Advantages have to be Earned and Exploited Diligently

As we saw earlier, first-mover advantages are not automatically bestowed on whoever moves first. They have not only to be built by pursuing the right new game activities, they also have to be exploited by pursuing the right activities. If first movers do not diligently pursue and exploit first mover advantages, they leave room for followers, especially exploiters, to come in and possibly dominate. For example, if a pharmaceutical company wants the benefits of patent protection, it has to pursue the types of activity that will not only allow it to discover something worth patenting but also to apply for and obtain the patent in the right countries. Moreover, the firm also has to turn its patents into medicine that patients can take, since patents do not cure illnesses. Perhaps more importantly, to perform these activities effectively and efficiently often requires distinctive resource/capabilities that not all first movers have. For example, not all pharmaceutical companies have the R&D skills, knowledge base, and know-how to discover the types of compound that can be patented.

Effectively, if a first mover cannot earn and exploit first-mover advantages—either because it did not know which activities to pursue or did not have or could not build the necessary distinctive resources/capabilities—there is room for followers to come in and do well, especially followers that already have the right complementary assets or can build them quickly.

Owner of Scarce Important Complementary Assets has an Edge

To profit from a new game, a firm usually needs complementary assets. Thus, if a firm moves first to invent or discover something, other firms that enter the market later can make most of the profits from the invention or discovery if they have scarce important complementary assets that the first mover does not have. Effectively, whoever has scarce important complementary assets, be it a first mover or follower, has a better chance of being the one to profit from a new game.

Can Minimize or Exploit First-mover Disadvantages

If a first mover is able to minimize the effects of first-mover *dis*advantages, it has a better chance of doing well. If it does not, it leaves room for followers to take advantage of them. Take, for example, the fact that followers often can free ride on the first mover's investments by taking advantage of the R&D knowledge generated by the first mover, hiring from the first mover, going after its customers, and so on. The first mover can reduce these negative effects by better protection of its intellectual property or by entering into the right agreements with employees or customers. Such measures, coupled with first-mover advantages, may be able to give the first mover a better chance. If this is not possible, a follower can take advantage of first mover disadvantages. A follower can not only free ride on first movers' R&D, it can also take advantage of the reduced technological and marketing uncertainty as well as any changes in technological change or customer needs that may have occurred since the first mover made commitments as to which activities to perform.

The Competitive, Macro, and Global Environments

Whether the firm that goes on to dominate a market is a first mover or follower is also a function of its competitive environment—of its rivals, suppliers, customers, potential new entrants, and substitutes. For example, if the first mover is a new entrant that uses a disruptive technology to attack incumbents, there is a good chance that it will defeat incumbents. If the industry has plenty of white space in the market, first movers have more opportunities to create unique value for customers and build first-mover advantages than if they were in a more crowded market space. A dominant buyer can force a firm to find second sources for the products that the buyer buys, effectively neutralizing some of the firm's first-mover advantages. For example, in the 1970s and 1980s, IBM usually required that chipmakers who supplied it with chips had to cooperate with at least one other chipmaker to help it also supply the same chips.

The extent to which some first-mover advantages amount to something depends on the macroenvironment—on the political, economic, technological, social, and natural environments. For example, if the political/legal environment in a country is such that there is no respect for intellectual property protections, a first mover cannot rely on patents or copyrights as a first-mover advantage. This increases the chances that a follower can free ride on first movers' investments in R&D, manufacturing, and marketing. If the rate of technological change is high, first movers' commitments are more likely to make it difficult for them to adjust to technological changes, allowing followers to have a better chance. In some countries, there are restrictions on how many firms can enter some industries. First movers in such industries are therefore more likely to do well than very late followers.

Type of Player and Business Strategy

Whether a first mover or follower wins in the face of a new game is also a function of whether the firm is pursuing the game as an explorer, superstar, exploiter, or me-too. Many *exploiters* prefer to wait until some other firms have moved first and both technological and marketing uncertainties have been drastically reduced before they enter. Recall that an exploiter is a follower that waits for first movers to reduce technological and market uncertainty, and then enters. Even if exploiters accidentally discover or invent something, they usually still wait until someone else has developed the invention further and tried to commercialize it, thereby proving that there is a market for it. IBM and Microsoft are good examples. Such firms usually have the right distinctive difficult-to-imitate complementary assets. They usually also develop the skills and know-how to quickly develop and commercialize a product once they decide that technological and market uncertainty have dropped enough for them to enter. And after pursuing such strategies for a long time, they may develop competences in excelling as followers. Thus, when exploiters face *explorers,* especially in the face of changing technologies or consumer tastes, the former are more likely to win than the first movers.

Similarly, *superstars* are usually at the forefront of inventions and pursuing the right strategies to allow them to create and appropriate value. Recall that a superstar is a firm that moves first in pursuing a new game and diligently performs those activities that substantially improve its chances of building and exploiting first-mover advantages, countering first-mover disadvantages, and taking advantage of competitors' handicaps. Superstars usually develop competences for moving first and pursing the types of strategy that give them a good chance of doing well. Intel was a superstar when it invented the microprocessor, the EPROM memory device, and advanced its microprocessor technology at a pioneering rate by introducing a newer generation of its microprocessors before unit sales of an older one had peaked. Superstars are particularly likely to do well if they face only explorers or me-toos. One of the biggest problems for superstars is that they usually face huge technological and marketing uncertainty alone, while exploiters are waiting in the wings.

Explorers are also likely to have developed competences for creating value (e.g. inventing or discovering things) but not for appropriating it. Recall that an explorer is a firm that moves first in performing a set of new game activities but does so largely for the fun of it, or because that's what it just happens to be doing. It is more of an explorer than an exploiter and therefore has no purposeful plan for building and exploiting first-mover advantages. That is not to say that explorers do not have first-mover advantages. They sometimes stumble on first-mover advantages but miss out on many others that they could have built and exploited. If there are many exploiters or superstars around, then an explorer's chances of doing well are decreased. *Me-toos* develop competences for pursuing niches and can do well if exploiters and superstars decide to leave such niches alone.

Effectively, if a firm's strategy is predicated on its moving first and it has developed underpinning resources/capabilities to back it, it is likely to move first and go on to dominate its market. If its strategy is to be a follower and it has the resources/capabilities to back it, it is likely to do well as a follower.

What Does this Mean for Managers?

In the face of a new game, a firm that moves first may want to:

1 Go through the list of first-mover advantages and *dis*advantages that were summarized in Table 6.1, and note (catalog) the ones that are relevant for the industry and markets in which the firm competes or intends to compete.
2 Screen the advantages to those that make (1) a significant contribution to value creation and appropriation, and (2) the firm is capable of efficiently performing the activities to build and exploit the advantage. An AVAC analysis can be used for this step.
3 Build and exploit the chosen first-mover advantages while anticipating and countering any first-mover *dis*advantages.

A follower may want to:

1 Catalog the first-mover *dis*advantages and determine the extent to which it has what it takes to exploit them.
2 Find out where the first mover was not able to build first-mover advantages and take advantage of the holes left.
3 Look for where first-mover advantages may have become handicaps and exploit that. For example, a first mover may have made commitments to coopetitors that it cannot get away from. Recall the case of Compaq and Dell. Compaq was one of the first to preemptively take up positions with PC distributors. When Dell (a follower) came along, distributors did not have any more capacity to take on another PC maker. When Dell went direct, and Compaq wanted to follow suit, distributors would not let the latter get off that easily.

Example 6.1: The Value of Efficient Exploitation of First-mover Advantages

In 1997, the cholesterol drug Lipitor was granted FDA approval. This was one year earlier than expected, because of several measures that Warner Lambert, its inventor, had taken. Table 6.3 shows a forecast of sales up to the expiration of the patent life of the drug in 2011. When a drug's patent expires, the price of the drug can drop by as much as 86% as a result of the introduction of generic versions. The number in parentheses in 2010 is the projected sales if the patent did not expire. How much money did the firm save by obtaining FDA approval one year earlier?

Solution to Example:

When a US firm obtains a patent for a drug, it is gaining a first-mover advantage, since the patent gives it intellectual property protection. However, the clock for the patent life starts running from the time the firm files for the patent. Thus, if a firm does not pursue the right activities for turning the discovery (for which the patent is granted) into an approved drug that customers want, the patent life could expire without it making money. The more quickly a firm can

Table 6.3 Lipitor's Projected Sales

Year	1997	1998	1999	2000	2001	2002	2003	2004	2005	2006	2007	2008	2009	2010
Revenues ($B) (1997 FDA)	0.9	2.2	3.4	4.6	5.6	6.7	7.7	8.7	9.7	10.7	11.7	12.7	13.7	2.06 (14.7)

Table 6.4 NPVs for the Different Revenue Flows

Year	1997	1998	1999	2000	2001	2002	2003	2004	2005	2006	2007	2008	2009	2010
Revenues (1997 FDA)	0.9	2.2	3.4	4.6	5.6	6.7	7.7	8.7	9.7	10.7	11.7	12.7	13.7	2.06 (14.7)
Revenues (1998 FDA)		0.9	2.2	3.4	4.6	5.6	6.7	7.7	8.7	9.7	10.7	11.7	12.7	1.92 (13.7)

NPV Revenues (1997 FDA) = $44.5 billion
NPV Revenues (1998 FDA) = $36.86

get the drug approved and to doctors and patients, the more time that it has to exercise its monopoly power before the patent life expires and generics move in. This example illustrates how much money can be at stake. In Table 6.4, two sets of sales numbers have been shown: sales generated when FDA approval was granted in 1997 and those generated if FDA approval had been one year later in 1998.

The NPV of revenues in 1997, given that FDA approval was in 1997 is $44.5 billion (Table 6.4). The NPV of revenues in 1997 dollars if the drug had been approved one year later is $36.86 (Table 6.4). Therefore, extra revenues earned as a result of getting FDA approval one year earlier (in 1997 dollars) are $44.50 billion − $36.86 billion = $7.64 billion. Thus, by performing the type of activities that allowed Lipitor to be approved one year earlier, Warner Lambert stood to make an extra $7.64 billion, in 1997 dollars, over the life of its patent. Effectively, Warner Lambert was better able to exploit its first-mover advantages as far as Lipitor was concerned.

Key Takeaways

- A **first-mover advantage** is a resource, capability, or product-market position that (1) a firm acquires by being the first to carry out an activity, and (2) gives the firm an advantage in creating and appropriating value. In moving first to pursue a new game strategy, a firm usually has an opportunity to build and take advantage of first-mover advantages.

First-mover Advantages include:

- Total available market preemption:
    - Economies of scale
    - Size (beyond economies of scale) advantages
    - Economic rents and equity
    - Network externalities (installed base)
    - Relationships with coopetitors

- Lead in technology and innovation
    - Intellectual property (patents, copyrights, trade secrets)
    - Learning
    - Organizational culture

- Preemption of scarce resources
    - Complementary assets
    - Location
    - Input factors
    - Plant and equipment

- First-at-Buyers
    - Buyer switching cost
    - Buyer choice under uncertainty
    - Brand (preemption of consumer perceptual space)

- First to establish system of activities
  - Difficult-to-imitate or substitute system of activities
- First-to make irreversible commitments

Earning First-mover Advantages

- First-mover advantages are not automatically endowed on whoever moves first. They have to be earned, often by performing value creation and appropriation activities effectively and efficiently.
- Can use an AVAC analysis to narrow down the number of first-mover advantages to the few that stand to make a significant contribution to the firm's competitive advantage.
- Moreover, first-mover advantages also have to be exploited to be meaningful.

First-mover *Dis*advantages (followers' advantages) include:

- Followers can free ride on first-mover's investments.
- Followers enter a market when technological and marketing uncertainties have been considerably resolved.
- Followers can also take advantage of changes in technology or customer needs that have occurred since first movers moved. First movers may also face inertia.

Competitors' Handicaps include:

- Competitors may have developed dominant managerial logics in the old game.
- The new game may not fit a competitor's strategy.
- It may be difficult for competitors to get away from prior commitments made in the old game.
- Competitors may not have the types of resources that are needed to play the new game.
- The fear of cannibalizing their existing products may prevent some firms from moving first or from following a first mover.

Why is it that First Movers Sometimes Go On to Dominate their Markets and at Other Times, Followers are the Ones that Go On to Dominate their Markets? Because of one or more of the following reasons:

- First-mover advantages have to be earned and exploited well. Thus, when first movers (superstars and explorers) do not perform the types of activity that will enable them to earn and exploit first-mover advantages, followers (exploiters and me-toos) have a chance to move in and do well.
- Followers may have critical complementary assets that first movers do not.
- First-mover *dis*advantages can be minimized. Therefore, when first movers (superstars and explorers) do not minimize first-mover *dis*advantages, followers have a chance to exploit them.

- Industry factors, such as the number of competitors in a market, may favor one type of firm over another. Whoever is favored—first mover or follower—is likely to win.
- Macroenvironmental and global factors such as government regulations may favor first movers over followers, or followers over first movers.
- The type of player and business strategy of the player can also determine whether a first mover or follower wins. In industries with very good exploiters, first movers' chances are usually considerably reduced.

What Does All This Mean to Managers?

- In the face of a new game, a firm that moves first may want to:
  - Catalog potential first-mover advantages and *dis*advantages, and note the ones that are relevant for the industry and markets in which the firm competes or intends to compete.
  - Screen the advantages to those that make (1) a significant contribution to value creation and appropriation, and (2) the firm is capable of efficiently performing the activities to build and exploit the advantage. An AVAC analysis can be used for this step.
  - Build and exploit the chosen first-mover advantages while anticipating and countering any first-mover *dis*advantages.
- A follower may want to:
  - Catalog the first-mover *dis*advantages and determine the extent to which it has what it takes to exploit them.
  - Find out where the first mover was not able to build first-mover advantages and take advantage of the holes left. Use AVAC.
  - Look for where first-mover advantages may have become handicaps and exploit them.

Explorers, Superstars, Exploiters, and Me-toos

- Firms can be grouped as a function of when they pursue new game strategies and whether they pursue the right strategy or not:
  - Explorers: move first but have no clear strategy for creating and appropriating value, for building and taking advantage of first-mover advantages and disadvantages, and for exploiting competitors' handicaps.
  - Superstars: move first and have a clear strategy for creating and appropriating value, for building and taking advantage of first-mover advantages and disadvantages, and for exploiting competitors' handicaps.
  - Exploiters: followers that use their complementary assets and other resources/capabilities to take advantage of first movers' disadvantages and other opportunities to better create and appropriate value than first movers.
  - Me-Toos: followers that, unlike exploiters, have no clear strategy for beating first movers at their game. Are sometimes niche players.

Key Terms

Competitors' handicaps
Dominant logic
Exploiters
Explorers
First-mover advantages
First-mover disadvantages
Follower's advantage
Irreversible commitments
Me-toos
Second-mover advantages
Superstars
Switching costs

Chapter 7

Implementing New Game Strategies

Reading this chapter should provide you with the conceptual and analytical tools to:

- Understand the significance of new game strategy implementation.
- Get introduced to the relationship between strategy, structure, systems, people and environment (S^{3}PE).
- Understand some of the different roles that individuals can play during new games.
- Recall the definitions of functional, matrix, network and M-Form organizational structures.
- Explore what structure, systems and people a firm may need in the face of a regular, position-building, resource-building or revolutionary strategy.

Introduction

Every new game strategy has to be executed well if its full potential is going to be realized. Executing a new game strategy involves organizing people to carry out the set of new game activities—it is about who works for whom, how to measure and reward performance, how information should flow in the organization, who to hire, what culture one would like to see develop and so on. For example, when Dell decided to pursue a build-to-order and direct sales strategy, it had to structure its organization to fit the new strategy, put in the right systems to measure and reward performance, hire the right people, and try to build the right culture. To perform all the activities that enabled it to provide relevant searches, and monetize them using a paid-listing revenue model, Google used an organizational structure that fit its informal tech culture, developed its own incentive systems, and hired the right type of technical and other personnel. Effectively, to execute its new game strategy successfully, a firm needs an organizational structure, systems, and people that reflect not only the strategy but also the environment in which it is being pursued. Strategy implementation is about the relationships among the strategy, the structure of the organization that must execute the strategy, the systems and processes that complement the structure, and the people that must carry out the tasks in the given environment. We explore some of these relationships using a strategy, structure, systems, people, and environment (S^{3}PE) framework (Figure 7.1).[1]

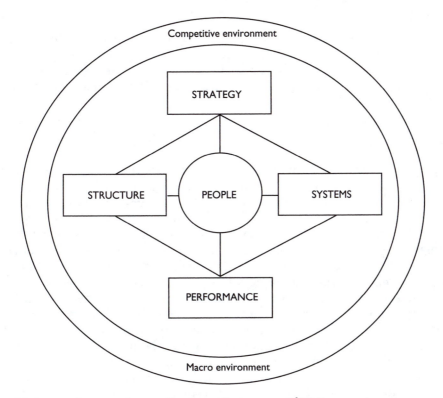

Figure 7.1 Strategy, Structure, Systems, People, and Environment (S³PE) Framework.

The S³PE Framework

The idea behind the *S³PE framework* is simple. Strategies are formulated and carried out by people; and people do differ. Moreover, the tasks that people must perform to execute a new game strategy vary from strategy to strategy. Therefore, not only do individuals need to perform different roles in the face of a new game strategy; what they need to motivate them to be effective at performing the tasks differs from task to task, from individual to individual, industry to industry, and country to country. Therefore, the type of people that a firm hires, who reports to whom, how performance is measured and rewarded, and information systems needed, depend on the type of new game strategy and environment in which the firm operates.[2] Effectively, some organizational structures, systems/processes and people would be more suitable for some strategies than others, given the environments in which the strategies must be executed. The objective, in executing a new game strategy in a given environment, is therefore to find those structures, systems, and people that best fit the set of activities that a firm chooses to perform, how, where, and when it performs them. We quickly explore each component of the S³PE framework before turning to the impact of new games on them.

Strategy

Recall that a firm's strategy is the set of activities that it performs to create and appropriate value. A firm's structure, systems and people usually follow its strategy, although there may be cases where structure, systems and people drive strategy; that is, the structure, systems, and people (S^2P) part of a firm are usually dictated by the firm's strategy.

Structure

While a firm's strategy is about the set of activities that the firm performs to create and appropriate value, a firm's structure tells us who reports to whom and who is responsible for which activities.[3] An organizational structure has three primary goals. First, the structure of an organization should facilitate timely information flows to the right people for decision-making while preventing the wrong people from getting the information. Second, an effective structure requires the ability to be able to joggle *differentiation (in the organizational structure sense)* and integration. A firm's manufacturing and marketing units are maintained as separate functions because each one necessarily has to specialize in what it does in order to be both efficient and effective in carrying out its activities. Giving each unit the opportunity to specialize in what it does so as to be the best at it, is what differentiation is about. However, to efficiently and effectively develop and offer customers unique benefits, a firm's different functions often have to interact across functions; that is, the value creation and appropriation activities of a firm's different functions must be **integrated** if it is going to perform well.[4] Third, a final goal of an organizational structure is to coordinate interactions between units to effect integration. A new product launch would be more effective if the product development and marketing groups coordinated their activities—telling each other what they are doing, when and using information from each other as inputs.

Firms use variants of the following four organizational structures to effect differentiation, integration, and *coordination*: functional, multidivisional (M-form), matrix, and networked.

Functional Structure

In a *functional structure*, employees are organized by the function that they perform in the organization, with employees in marketing or sales reporting to supervisors or managers who are also in marketing or sales functions, employees in engineering and manufacturing reporting to supervisors or managers who are also in engineering and manufacturing, and so on. Formal reporting and communications is primarily within each functional unit, usually up and down the organizational hierarchy. Each functional unit gets its directions from corporate headquarters via the functional head. The functional organization has several advantages. First, since employees are organized by function, there is de facto division of labor that enables employees to acquire in-depth function-specific knowledge, skills, and know-how—to specialize in the functional tasks that differentiate the group from other functions. Second, since each functional unit has people with similar knowledge and know-how that are grouped together and may be located in the same physical location, they can communicate more often and are therefore more likely to develop in-depth knowledge of their functional area. The functional structure also has some disadvantages. First, when tasks entail considerable coordination with other functional units, a functional unit is likely to have subpar performance because of its limited knowledge of and lack of direct communication lines with other units. Second, the more specialized each functional unit, the more difficult it becomes for headquarter's management to know what is going on within each function. This is compounded by the fact that the different functional units do not communicate directly with each other. Third, because of the differences in their skills, experiences, and capabilities, functional departments may have goals that are not consistent with cooperating with other functions.

M-form or Divisional Structure

In an **M-form** or **multidivisional structure**, employees are organized by divisions or business units rather than by function, as is the case with the functional structure.[5] The divisions can be organized by the type of product that each division offers (product line), by the type of customer, by the geographic scope that the firm covers, or by the brand name that the firm offers. Authority in the **M-form structure** is decentralized to the divisions in contrast to the functional structure where authority is centralized at corporate headquarters. Each unit usually has profit-and-loss responsibility. The multidivisional structure has two major advantages. First, since each division has profit-and-loss responsibility, there is better accountability for the firm's performance. Second, since management responsibility is not as centralized as in the functional structure, managers in the M-form only need focus their attention on their division. This is a more manageable task since each manager is more likely to have the type of in-depth knowledge of his/her product line, brand, customer, or geographic scope that they need to manage the business better. The major disadvantage of the divisional structure is that firms may not be able to build as much in-depth knowledge of functional areas such as R&D as they would in a functional structure.

Matrix Structure

The goal of a **matrix structure** is to capture some of the benefits of both the functional and divisional structure. It is a type of hybrid structure between function and divisional, and therefore comes in many different forms. In one form, individuals from different functional areas are assigned to a project, but rather than report only to a project or functional manager, each employee reports to both a functional *and* a project manager. The idea is to (1) have cross-functional coordination that is needed to carry out projects that require skills and knowledge from different functional areas, (2) maintain some performance accountability at the project level, and (3) allow project members to keep in close touch with their functional areas so as to benefit from intra-functional learning, especially in industries where deep functional knowledge is important. The matrix structure has three major advantages. First, the structure captures some of the benefits of both the functional and divisional structures. Second, since employees have one foot in their functional areas and the other in their project group, they can bring the latest thinking from their functional areas to the project and vice versa. Third, since the rate of change of technological or market knowledge is likely to vary from one function to another, employees can spend time on project management commensurate with the rate of change of the knowledge in their functional area. This can lead to more efficient use of personnel. Fourth, some employees may be able to work on more than one project, thereby helping cross-pollinate not only functional knowledge but also project knowledge. The matrix structure has some disadvantages. First, since physical colocation with fellow project members can be critical to project performance, and physical colocation with functional colleagues can also be critical to functional learning, employees in a matrix structure may have to physically colocate in both their project and functional areas. This can be costly and inefficient, since an employee cannot be physically present in two different places at the same time. Second, since project members in the matrix organization have to report to both a functional and project manager, they may have to manage two bosses at the same time. When there is a conflict, employees may have difficulties deciding where their allegiance falls—whether to the project manager or functional manager. Third, the matrix structure can be more costly than the functional one since the structure requires some duplication of effort. For example, having both a functional and a project manager means one too many managers. Finally, the matrix structure is still much less accountable than the divisional organization.

Network or Virtual Structure

In the **network** or **virtual** structure, firms outsource all the major value-adding activities of their value chains and coordinate the activities of their contractors.[6] The emergence of this organizational form has been facilitated by advances in technological innovation such as the Internet. In such a structure, the coordinating firm contracts a market research firm to perform market research for a particular product or idea, finds a design firm to design the product, buys the components from suppliers, and finds another firm to manufacture the product. The **network structure** has several advantages. First, a firm can avoid making major investments in assets, since it outsources all the major value-adding activities of its value chain. Second, in industries with a high rate of technological change that often renders existing capabilities obsolete, having a virtual structure means that a firm does not have to worry about important assets being rendered obsolete since it has not invested in any.[7] Such a firm has the flexibility to switch suppliers, or manufacturers, or distributors whenever it finds one that can exploit the new technology better. The network structure has two major disadvantages. First, it is difficult to have a competitive advantage when one does not perform major value-adding activities. However, whether this is a disadvantage depends on the firm's core competence. If a firm has a strong brand or architectural capabilities that are valuable, scarce, and difficult to imitate, the firm may still be able to make money since it can offer customers something that competitors cannot. Second, contracting out all major activities deprives a firm of the ability to learn more about creating value along the value chain.

Systems

Organizational structures are about who reports to whom and what activities they perform, but say very little about how to keep employees motivated as they carry out their assigned tasks and responsibilities in executing a strategy.[8] *Systems* are about the incentives, performance requirements and measures, and information flow and accountability mechanisms that facilitate the efficient and effective execution of strategies. We can group systems into two: organizational systems/processes and information systems.

Organizational Systems/Processes

Organizational systems are about how the performance of individuals, groups, functional units, divisions, and organizations is sought, monitored, measured, and compensated. They include financial measures such as profits, market share, cash flows, gross profit margins, stock market price, return on investment, earnings per share, return on equity, and economic value added (EVA). Organizational systems also include reward systems such as pay scales, profit-sharing, employee stock option plans (EOPs), bonuses, and nonfinancial rewards such as recognition with certificates or having one's name engraved somewhere on a product that one helped develop. Systems also include so-called processes. A firm's *processes* are the "patterns of interaction, coordination, communication, and decision making [that] employees use to transform resources into products and services of greater worth."[9] These patterns of communication, interaction, coordination, and decision-making are a function of the type of strategy, organizational structure, and incentive system in place. For example, in a process it called chemicalization, Sharp Corporation compulsorily transferred the top 3% of the scientists from each of its divisional R&D groups between laboratories every three years. This process forced top scientists to interact with scientists in other laboratories, exchanging knowledge that may not be easily transferred through memos or scientific publications. Even if the information could be transferred through journals, it may get to other Sharp scientists too late to give the company a competitive advantage. Being transferred was also a signal that a scientist was good—an important reward in some scientists' books. Moreover, visiting other laboratories gave the Sharp scientists an opportunity to build social networks that could come in handy later. Another example is "Google's 20% rule," the fact that at Google, employees were encouraged to spend 20% of their time on innovative projects that had very little or nothing to do with their officially assigned projects. Benchmarking, total quality control (TQM), re-engineering, and x-engineering are also processes that firms have used to implement a new game strategy more effectively and efficiently.

Information Systems

Although a good organizational structure, coupled with the right organizational systems, can result in a reasonable amount of internal information flow, information systems can also be used to facilitate the efficient flow of information to the right targets at the right times for decision-making. For discussion purposes, we can group information flow systems into two: (1) the information and communication technologies that allow electronic information to be exchanged and (2) the physical building layouts that facilitate in-person, sometimes unplanned, interaction. Digital networks such as the Internet make it possible for anyone anywhere in an organization anywhere in the world to have access to some types of information anywhere within the organization.[10] For example, during product development, information on the status of products, ideas for better products, and so on, are available to anyone anywhere in the world with permission and access to the company's Intranet. Information systems can be used to supplement or complement information flows that take place by virtue of the structure of the organization.

Although a great deal of information can be exchanged electronically over the Internet, some types of information still need in-person, face-to-face interaction. For example, it is difficult to feel the aura and smell of a new car or painting via the Internet. Moreover, chanced physical encounters can lead to ideas that planned electronic encounters might not. Professor Tom Allen's research suggests that the physical layout of buildings can play a significant role in the amount of communication that takes place between people and therefore can have a significant impact on innovation.[11] Buildings that are designed to facilitate physical in-person interaction can facilitate the flow of new ideas. If different organizational units of a firm—e.g. marketing, R&D, and operations—are located in the same physical space, eat in the same cafeteria, share the same bathrooms, and bump into each other often, they are more likely to exchange new ideas than if they were located in different buildings or regions. Effectively, the way a building is designed can facilitate or augment the integration of different units and ideas that a good organizational structure is supposed to.

People

People are central to any strategy since they conceive of, formulate, and execute strategies. The extent to which a firm's employees can thrive within its organizational structure, are motivated by the performance and reward systems that it has put in place, or effectively use the information systems that it established, is a function of the firm's organizational culture, resources and capabilities, and the types of employee.

Culture

What is culture? Uttal and Fierman defined organizational culture as:

> "a system of shared values (what is important) and beliefs (how things work) that interact with the organization's people, organizational structures, and systems to produce behavioral norms (the way we do things around here)."[12]

Professor Schein of MIT also defined culture as:

> "the pattern of basic assumptions that a given group has invented, dis-

covered, or developed in learning to cope with its problems of external adaptation and internal integration, and that have worked well enough to be considered valid, and, therefore, to be taught to new members as the correct way to perceive, think, and feel in relation to these problems."[13]

A firm's culture is critical to its ability to create and appropriate value.[14] Basically, people within an organizational structure and associated systems, develop shared values (what is important) and beliefs (how things work). These shared values and beliefs then influence who else is hired or stays in the organization, how it is reorganized and how the systems change or do not change. The results of these interactions are behavioral norms (the way we do things) which then determine how well a strategy is implemented or formulated. If the structure, systems, and people are just right, the norms can lead to a system of activities that is difficult to imitate. One reason why Ryanair's employees work 50% more than employees at other airlines for only 10% more pay and still like working there may be because of its culture. If it is not right, culture can be a competitive disadvantage.

Resources and Capabilities

In Chapter 5, we argued that a portion of a firm's resources and capabilities resides in the people within the firm and those with whom it has to interact. Thus an important part of the "people" component of the S^2P E are the resources and capabilities that are embodied in people.

Types of People

Quite simply, not everyone is meant for every job. Nor is every reward system going to motivate every employee. Thus, in executing a strategy, it is important to get the right people to perform the right tasks. In the mid-2000s, Google's advertisements for new hires reflected its overt focus on hiring largely the mathematically and intellectually gifted.[15] However, when Southwest Airlines hired people, it was more interested in their attitude than in their skills.

Environment

For two reasons, a firm's structure, systems, and people (S^2P) are also a function of its competitive and macroenvironments. First, as we have seen on several occasions, a firm's strategy is a function of the competitive forces that impinge on it as well as of the macroenvironment in which it creates and appropriates value; and since structure, systems, and people (S^2P) follow strategy, it must be the case that a firm's S^2P also depend on its competitive and macroenvironments. Second, each of structure, systems and people depends on the environment in its own right. For example, in fast-paced industries where technologies and markets change rapidly, a firm needs to be able to maintain deep knowledge of the technologies that underpin its products and of the markets that it must serve. One good choice of structure in such fast-paced environments is a matrix structure, since it allows employees who are working on a project to have one foot in the project group and another in their functional groups. In countries where people's identities are closely tied to the firms that employ them, employees may be more willing to do whatever it takes for their company to win. Countries with well-educated workforces offer firms more opportunities to hire the types of employee that they need for high value-adding jobs.

S³PE in the Face of New Games

New games have an impact on structure, systems, and people. We explore this impact and what a firm can do to improve its chances of doing well in the face of the impact.

Impact on Structure, Systems, and People (S²P)

The impact of a new game on a firm's structure, systems, and people (S²P) is a function of the type of new game—of whether the new game is regular, position-building, resource-building, or revolutionary (Figure 7.2).

Regular New Game

In a regular new game, only incremental changes are made to existing resources/capabilities and product-market positions (PMPs). Moreover, these incremental changes in resources and positions build on existing ones. Therefore, in the face of a regular game, any changes that incumbents have to make to their pregame resources and positions in a regular game are incremental. Since structure, systems, and people follow strategy, any changes that need to be made to an

	Low	High
High Degree to which new game renders existing product position noncompetitive	**Position-building** Market-oriented project unit Champions, sponsors, gatekeepers, project managers, boundary spanners	**Revolutionary** Autonomous unit Champions, sponsors, gatekeepers
Low	**Regular** Use or build on pregame structure, systems, and people Project managers	**Resource-building** Product-oriented project unit Champions, sponsors, gatekeepers, project managers, boundary spanners

**Degree to which new game renders existing
resources/capabilities obsolete**

Figure 7.2 What Should a Firm Do?

incumbent's structure, systems, and people (S^{2}P) are also incremental. Take culture, for example. Those incumbent values (what is important) and beliefs (how things work) and behavioral norms (the way we do things around here) that worked prior to the new game still work during the game. Incumbents' "patterns of interaction, coordination, communication, and decision making" are likely to still work. The introduction of diet cola was a regular new game and both Coke's and Pepsi's S^{2}P did not change when they introduced the product.

Revolutionary New Game

A revolutionary new game is the exact opposite of a regular new game. The resources needed and the resulting PMPs are radically different from what incumbents had prior to the game. Thus, the strategies that firms pursue in the face of the new game are likely to be radically different from those that incumbents pursued prior to the new game. Since structure, systems, and people (S^{2}P) follow strategy, we can expect to see some big changes in S^{2}P. For example, because the changes are radical, a firm with a functional structure (with its vertical flow of information) may have to migrate to a matrix or network organization to accommodate the large intra- and interorganizational horizontal information flows that take place in the face of a radical innovation. Incumbent values (what is important), beliefs (how things work), and behavioral norms (the way we do things around here) that worked prior to the new game are not likely to work during the new game. In fact, as we show later, these values, beliefs, and norms may become handicaps. Pregame processes—"patterns of interaction, coordination, communication, and decision making"—are also likely to be rendered useless and may become handicaps. Consider the case of online auctions, a revolutionary new game compared to offline auctions. Offline auctions take place at a particular place and time, for a certain duration, and the number of items and of attendees are usually limited. The number of people that attend the auction is important and location is king. Those who attend can usually touch and feel the product being auctioned. Online auctions go on 24-hours a day and anyone from anywhere in the world can bid for objects which can be delivered after the sale is made. The size and character of the network of sellers and buyers are king. An organizational structure for running an offline auction company that operates various sites in a country is likely to have elements of the M-form structure with units that focus on one or more locations where auctions take place. By contrast, location is not central to an online auction. Thus, an online auction firm may use the M-form organization but with each unit focusing on a product or service category such as collectibles, antiques, and automobiles, rather than location. It may also use a network organization.

What is important to an offline auction firm revolves around the location where the auctions take place while for an online auction firm, what is important revolves around the number of users that can visit a website to buy or sell, and a reduction in the level of fraud. The norms (the way we do things around here) that arise from interactions in an offline firm are likely to be very different from those at its online counterpart; so are the processes—"patterns of interaction, coordination, communication, and decision making." Effectively, pregame S²Ps that are often rendered obsolete can become handicaps in the face of some revolutionary games.

Position-building New Game

In a position-building new game, the new product replaces existing products and/or the firm's position vis-à-vis coopetitors is radically different from the pregame position. If the market addressed by the new game is the same as the pregame market, an incumbent's S²P may not have to change that much. For example, when Intel introduced the Pentium that replaced the 486, it did not have to restructure its organization to better address the PC market in which the Pentium was replacing the 486s. However, if the market is different, some important elements of S²P may have to change. The PC used the same technology as minicomputers but in addition to addressing the minicomputer market, it also addressed the home computer market. The market for consumers was very different from the business market that minicomputers had addressed before the PC. Clearly, selling to this new market required something different from incumbents' sales norms. IBM created a separate unit to develop and sell the PC.

Resource-building New Game

In a resource-building new game, the resources/capabilities that a player needs to play the game are radically different from pregame resources/capabilities but existing products can still compete in the new game. Thus, as far as the activities for building products are concerned, S²P requirements should be similar to those for revolutionary games—they are likely to require changes in structure, systems, and people. Take the example of an electric razor, which requires a radically different technology from that for mechanical razors. A firm that has been supplying mechanical razors but wants to enter the electric razor market may need a unit or units that reflect the fact that the design, development, and manufacturing for electric razors are very different from those for their mechanical counterparts.

Roles that People Play During Innovation

Given the impact of new games on a firm's structure, systems, and people (S²P), the question becomes, what should a firm do in the face of new games as far as structures, systems, and people are concerned? Before we explore this question, it is important to describe quickly what the literature on innovation says about the roles that people can play in the face of an innovation to better exploit it.

Top Management Team and Dominant Managerial Logic

Each manager brings to every new game a set of beliefs, biases, and assumptions about the new game, the market that his/her firm serves, whom to hire, what technologies the game needs, who the other players in the game are, and what it takes to create and appropriate value in the game.[16] These beliefs, assumptions, and biases are a manager's **managerial logic**. They define the mental frame or model within which a manager is likely to approach decision-making.[17] Depending on the new game, a firm's strategy, structure, systems, processes, values, norms, and how successful it has been, there usually emerges a **dominant managerial logic**, a common way of viewing how best to create and appropriate value in the firm.[18] Dominant managerial logic is usually good for a firm that has the right strategy and has taken the right measures to implement it. However, during new games in which a new strategy, structure, systems, processes, values, or norms are needed, pregame dominant managerial logic that had worked so well can become a handicap. Managers may be stuck in the old values (what was important), and old beliefs (how things worked), and behavioral norms (the way we did things around here), and not be able to move into the new values (what is important in the new game), new beliefs (how things should work in the new game), and behavioral norms (the way we should be doing things around here now).

Champions

Formulating and implementing a strategy to win in a new game usually requires a champion. A **champion** for a new game strategy is someone who articulates a vision of what the strategy is all about, and what's in it for the firm and employees who are engaged in formulating and implementing the strategy.[19] By evangelically articulating a captivating vision of the potential of the strategy to the different players, a champion can help other employees to understand the rationale behind the strategy, especially how value will be created and appropriated, thereby motivating and inspiring the same employees who will implement the strategy. A firm often has also to champion the strategy to its coopetitors—the other players in the new game. In fact, in many revolutionary and position-building games, a firm has to articulate a vision of a new product to customers and help them discover their latent need for the product. Steve Jobs is usually a great champion for Apple's products.

Sponsors

A **sponsor** of a new game strategy or innovation is a senior-level manager who provides behind-the-scenes support for it.[20] This senior-level manager is like the godfather who protects the new product or new game strategy from political enemies. By acting as a sponsor, the top manager is also sending a signal to political foes of the new game strategy or product, that they would face the wrath of a senior manager and sponsor. In so doing, a sponsor is also sending a message to the champion and other key individuals who are working on the strategy that they have the support of a senior manager. In some cases, the champion is also the sponsor. Steve Jobs plays both the role of champion and sponsor for some key products.

Gatekeeper and Boundary Spanners

In many firms, especially those with functional organizational structures, each employee is likely to have deep knowledge of his/her unit and little or no knowledge of the other units. Moreover, each unit may have its own culture, language, needs, and history that have an effect on the information that the unit can or cannot share. For example, an R&D department may have its own acronyms, scientific jargon, and culture that marketing and manufacturing do not understand. Marketing and manufacturing may see R&D scientists as snobs that live in an ivory tower. **Boundary spanners** are individuals that span the "hole" between two units within a firm, acting as a transducer for information between units. They take information from one department and translate it into what people in another department can understand.[21] They understand the idiosyncrasies of their units and those of other units and can take unit-specific questions, translate them into a language that other departments can understand, obtain answers, and translate them into something that their home units can understand. While boundary spanners span the holes between units within the same firm, **gatekeepers** span the holes between different companies.

Project Manager

If a new game strategy entails developing a new product, **project managers** can play important roles. Project managers are responsible for plotting out who should do what and when so as to complete a project that meets or exceeds requirements. A project manager is to meeting schedules what a champion is to articulating a vision of the potential of a strategy. He or she is the central nervous system of information that has to do with who is supposed to do what and when and what has been done so far, its cost, and so on. Project managers have been classified as heavyweight or lightweight based on the managers' span of control.[22] A **heavyweight project manager** is one with extensive authority and responsibility for the project from concept creation through design to manufacturing to marketing and making money, including the project's budget.[23] A lightweight project manager's authority and responsibilities are not as extensive as those of the heavyweight project manager—his or her authority is usually limited largely to engineering functions with no authority or responsibility over concept creation and other market-related aspects of the product such as budgeting. Professors Kim Clark and Takahira Fujimoto found that the use of heavyweight project managers helped to reduce product development lead times, total engineering hours (and therefore cost), and improved design quality for Japanese automobile companies.[24]

What Should Firms Do About Their Structures, Systems, and People?

Now we can return to our question: given the impact of new games on a firm's structure, systems, and people (S²P), what should a firm do in the face of new games as far as structures, systems, and people are concerned? What a firm does depends on (1) which of the components of its pregame S²P are strengths or handicaps in the face of the new game, (2) the type of new game—whether the new game is regular, position-building, resource-building, or revolutionary.

Which PreGame S²P Components are Strengths or Handicaps?

Every player in a new game brings to the game some components of its S²P—values, beliefs, norms, information systems, performance measures, patterns of interaction, communications and coordination, and reward systems, and functional, matrix, network, or M-Form structure—from its pregame era that can be strengths or handicaps in the new game. For example, a firm's culture (values, beliefs, and norms) can be strengths in the face of certain new games but become a handicap in the face of other games. To determine which components of a firm's S²P become a handicap and which ones remain or become strengths, we use the same framework that we used in Chapter 5 to determine which of a firm's pregame strengths become handicaps or remain strengths (Table 7.1). Whether a component of an S²P is a strength or handicap in a new game depends on whether the component is vital to the new game, and whether the component is separable (Table 7.1). A component is vital to a new game if it contributes significantly to value creation and appropriation. It is *separable* if the firm has no problems taking the component away from the old game for use in the new game, sharing the component, or leaving the component behind when it is more likely to hurt in the new game than help.

Consider Component 1 in Table 7.1. It is vital in the new game and the firm can use it in the new game because nothing from its past prevents it from doing so. Thus the component is a strength for the firm in the face of the new game. For example, if a firm's pregame norms (they way we did things around here) are the same kinds of norms that the new game requires, the norms are a strength. The way makers of diet cola advertised the drink when it was first introduced was very similar to the way regular cola had been advertised. Thus, when Coke introduced its diet cola, the advertising norms needed effectively to advertise the drink used the same norms as before the introduction. Thus its pregame strengths constituted a new game strength for the firm.

Component 4 is the exact opposite of Component 1. The component is useless to the firm in pursuing the new game but unfortunately for the firm, it cannot separate itself from the resource and move on. Component 4 is therefore a handicap. Again, take the example of a norm. If the new game calls for doing things differently, but a firm is still stuck in its old norms (the way we used to do things) and cannot move on to the new way of doing things, the old norms are likely to become handicaps, since it is difficult for a firm *quickly* to get rid of its norms and acquire new ones. Handicaps can not only prevent a firm from

Table 7.1 Is an S²P Component from a Previous Game a Strength or Handicap in a New Game?

S²P component	Is the resource vital in the new game?	Is separability possible?	In the new game, the component is a:
Component 1	Y	Y	strength
Component 2	Y	N	potential strength
Component 3	N	Y	question mark
Component 4	N	N	handicap

playing a new game well, they can prevent a firm from entering the game. As we argued in Chapter 6, a firm's dominant managerial logic is a good example. In the face of some types of change, a firm's dominant managerial logic can become a handicap. For example, some executives who had been hired from old media such as TV and magazines to help with advertising on websites may have been prevented from understanding new business models, such as paid listings, because they were blinded by the old media logic of capturing the attention of viewers and retaining it long enough to advertise to them. Such a logic would not work when the activity being monetized is conducting a search on the Internet. Surfers usually want to perform a search quickly and move on. Paid listings work very well for such surfers since they can quickly perform the search and move on, for example, to make purchases or do something that might interest advertisers. The belief that to advertise, one's audience must be able to spend lots of time on one's medium may have prevented some old media executives from inventing paid listings.

Component 2 is important in the new game but because of prior commitments, agreements, or other inseparability, the firm cannot use it in the new game. The component is therefore a potential strength since, with work, it could become separable. For example, a firm may have the right systems and processes to get a new product designed, built, and manufactured but the fear of cannibalizing existing products may prevent the firm from using the systems and processes. Component 3 is not important in the new game and the firm can get away from it. It is therefore neither a strength nor a handicap. It is a question mark.

Type of New Game

What a firm does in the face of a new game, as far as its S^2P is concerned, also depends on the type of new game—it depends on whether the new game is regular, position-building, resource-building, or revolutionary (Figure 7.2). Since any changes that need to be made to an incumbent's S^2P in the face of a regular new game are incremental, incumbent firms can keep their pregame S^2P or build on them. Effectively, pregame S^2Ps are strengths in the face of a regular new game. If the new game is revolutionary, a firm may want to use an autonomous unit that has its own structure, systems, and people. Why an autonomous unit? As we saw above, pregame values (what was important before the new game), beliefs (how things worked), and behavioral norms (the way we did things around here) are not likely to work in the face of a revolutionary new game; and since it takes time to change values, beliefs, and behavioral norms, if they can be changed at all, maintaining the same S^2P is not likely to help. An autonomous unit with its own structure, systems, and people can more quickly build the types of values, beliefs, and norms that are needed to successfully create and appropriate value in the face of a revolutionary game. Moreover, having an autonomous unit prevents elements of the pregame S^2P from handicapping the efforts of the unit. Effectively, pregame S^2Ps can be handicaps in the face of revolutionary new games and should be avoided using an autonomous unit. In addition to creating an autonomous unit, a firm that is playing a revolutionary game may also want to use champions, sponsors, and gatekeepers. The existence of a sponsor reminds upper level management that the autonomous unit is important and no one should think of messing with it. Since things are usually in a state of flux early in the life of a revolutionary game, a champion can help articulate a vision of what the game is all about and what needs to be done to win. Gatekeepers act as transducers between the autonomous unit and the rest of the firm as well as outside organizations.

If the new game is a position-building game, a firm can use a market-targeting project unit whose primary responsibility is to make sure that the needs of the market are incorporated into the new product on time. Such a focus on the market is particularly important if the market for the product is new. Why not use an autonomous unit? Since the product in the new game must still be built using pregame technological resources/capabilities, using an autonomous unit would mean moving the resources//capabilities to the new unit or duplicating them, either one of which can be very costly. In other words, in the face of a position-building new game, resource-related S²Ps are strengths that could be useful in the new game and forgoing such strengths can be costly. The case of IBM and the PC illustrates this. When IBM decided to enter the PC market, it formed an autonomous group to design, manufacture, and market the product. Because the PC group was autonomous, it decided to use an Intel microprocessor and a Microsoft operating system when other units at IBM could have used their existing computer resources to quickly build the two components. Effectively, IBM missed out on the two components of the Wintel world that appropriate the most value created. However, by not using an autonomous unit, a firm runs the risk of being handicapped by old market-targeting values, beliefs, and norms. These handicaps can be identified as we showed above, and avoided. To complement the project unit, a firm also needs sponsors, champions, and boundary spanners. A sponsor would signal to all units that the program is important and therefore the project unit can get the support that it needs. A champion would articulate the benefits of the project for the different units that must corporate with the project group. Boundary spanners would span the hole between the project unit and other units.

If the new game is a resource-building game, a firm can use a product-targeting project unit whose activities are geared towards building the new resources/capabilities and using them to build the new product. As is the case with position-building games, there are advantages and disadvantages to using a project unit rather than an autonomous unit. By using a project unit, a firm can more easily take advantage of marketing and other buyer-focused capabilities than using an autonomous unit since in a resource-building game, the PMP does not change much. At the same time, by not using an autonomous unit, a firm risks being handicapped by the values, beliefs, and norms from the resources that are being displaced. These handicaps can also be identified. The task could also be crowdsourced.

Key Takeaways

- A new game strategy is not likely to attain its full potential unless it is well implemented. Implementing a new game strategy is about getting the relationships among strategy, structure, systems, people, and environment right. To execute its new game strategy successfully, a firm needs an organizational structure, systems, and people (S²P) that reflect not only the strategy but also the environment in which the strategy is being pursued.

- An organizational structure is about who reports to whom and performs what activities when. It has three primary goals:

  - An organizational structure should facilitate timely information flows to the right people for decision-making while preventing the wrong people from getting the information.
  - An effective structure requires the ability to be able to joggle differentiation (in the organizational structure sense) and integration.
  - An effective organization should help coordinate interactions between units to effect integration.

- Firms use variants of the following four organizational structures to effect differentiation, integration, and coordination: functional, multidivisional (M-form), matrix, and networked structures.
- Systems are about the incentives, performance requirements and measures, and information flow and accountability mechanisms that facilitate the efficient and effective execution of strategies. They are about what it takes to motivate employees.
- The extent to which a firm's employees thrive within its organizational structure, is motivated by the performance and reward systems that it has put in place, or effectively used the information systems that it established is a function of the firm's organizational culture, and the types of employee.
- Culture is "a system of shared values (what is important) and beliefs (how things work) that interact with the organization's people, organizational structures, and systems to produce behavioral norms (the way we do things around here)."[25]
- Since structure, systems, and people follow strategy, and strategy is a function of the environment, it must be the case that structure, systems, and people are a function of the environment.
- The impact of a new game on a structure, systems, and people (S²P) is a function of the type of new game—it is a function of whether the new game is regular, position-building, resource-building, or revolutionary

  - If the new game is regular, the S²P needed is about the same as the one before the game, or an enhanced version of it.
  - If the new game is revolutionary, the S²P required is likely to be radically different from existing ones.
  - If the new game is position-building, the market-targeting S²P of the new game is likely to be radically different from the pregame one.
  - If the new game is resource-building, the product-targeting S²P of the new game is likely to be radically different from the pregame one.

- During innovation or a new game, people play different important roles.

  - Top management plays the leadership role but the dominant management logic that is a strength when there is no major change can become a handicap in the face of revolutionary, position-building, or resource-building new game.
  - A champion for a new game strategy is someone who articulates a

vision of what the strategy is all about, what's in it for the firm and employees who are engaged in formulating and implementing the strategy.

- o A sponsor of a new game strategy or innovation is a senior-level manager or godfather who provides behind-the-scenes support for it.
- o Boundary spanners are individuals who span the "hole" between two units within a firm, acting as a transducer for information between units.
- o Gatekeepers span the holes between different companies.
- o Project managers are responsible for plotting out who should do what and when so as to complete a project that meets or exceeds requirements.

- What a firm does in the face of a new game as far as its structure, systems and people (S^2P) are concerned depends on (1) whether the firm's pregame S^2P is a strength or handicap in the face of the new game, (2) the type of new game being pursued:

  - o In the face of a regular new game, an incumbent is better off keeping its pregame S^2P.
  - o In the face of a revolutionary new game, a firm may be better off creating an autonomous unit to be used to pursue the new game.
  - o If the new game is position-building, a firm may want to create a market-targeting project unit.
  - o If the new game is resource-building, the firm may be better off creating a product-targeting project unit.

Key Terms

Champions
Coordination
Culture
Differentiation (in the organizational structure sense)
Dominant managerial logic
Functional structure
Matrix structure
M-form structure
Multidivisional structure
Network structure
Organizational systems
Processes
Project managers
S^3PE framework
Sponsors

Part III

Opportunities and Threats

Chapter 8

Disruptive Technologies as New Games

Reading this chapter should provide you with the conceptual and analytical tools to:

- Explain what disruptive technologies are all about.
- Understand what makes some technologies more disruptive than others and why that matters.
- Explain how incumbents can tell when to expect new technologies to erode their competitive advantages.
- Explain why incumbents, even very successful ones, often lose out to attackers that use disruptive technologies.
- Offer incumbents and new entrants advice on what to do in the face of disruptive technologies.

Introduction

In 2008, millions of people could make *free* high-quality international phone calls, something that had been unheard of only a decade earlier. One major reason for these free calls was voice over Internet protocol (VOIP) technology—a technology for routing phone calls over free Internet networks. VOIP threatened the very future of the telephone business as the traditional phone companies had come to know it. To many of these traditional phone companies, VOIP represented a threat. To new startups such as Skype, VOIP was a great opportunity. This phenomenon in which existing business models are threatened and often rendered obsolete by a new technology is nothing new. Electric refrigerators replaced kerosene refrigerators which had replaced hauled ice as a means of keeping foods and medicines cold. PCs replaced mainframe and minicomputers. Internal combustion engine automobiles replaced horse-driven carts. iPods and other MP3 players replaced Walkmans, flat-panel displays displaced cathode ray tube (CRT) displays, and online auctions replaced offline auctions. In some instances, such as the case of contact lenses and eye glasses, the displacements were only partial. As the partial listing of Table 8.1 suggests, the list of such displacements is long.

Effectively, almost every product we use today is the result of technological innovation, and each innovation has created opportunities for some companies and threats for others. One of the first things that business scholars observed about these technological changes in which new technologies displaced established ones was that many incumbent firms were displaced by new entrants.

Table 8.1 The New Replacing the Old: A Partial List

Today's technology	Ancestral technologies
Airplanes	Sail boats, steam boats, trains
Automobiles	Horse-driven carts
Computers	Spike abacus, slide rules
Contact lenses	Eye glasses
Cotton, silk, polyester, nylon	Grass, bark, animal hides
Digital audio player (MP3)	Record player, eight track, cassette tape, compact disc
Digital photography	Artists, film-based photography
Discount brokers	Traditional brokers
Digital video disk (DVD)	Veneer records, magnetic tapes, compact discs
Electric and gas stoves	Firewood cooking spaces
Electricity	Whale oil (for lighting), wood, coal, gas
Electronic banking	Brick-and-mortar-based banking
Flat panel displays	Cathode ray tube (CRT) for computer screens, TVs, etc.
Genetically engineered insulin	Pig pancreas-derived insulin
Indoor plumbing	Outdoor services
International ATMs	Traveler's checks
Internet radio TV	Radio, TV
iPod	Walkman
Jet engines	Propeller engine
Mechanical cash registers	Electronic point of sale registers
Money and financial services	Barter system
PCs	Minicomputers
Refrigeration	Hauled ice
Small Japanese cars	Large American cars
Steel	Brick and stone
Telephone	Smoke signals, drums, people, telex
Electronic watches	Mechanical watches

(Incumbents in the face of a technological change are firms that offered products using the established technology before the new technology was introduced.) For example, the major players in personal computers (PCs) today were neither major players in mainframes nor in minicomputers. This observation by business scholars raised some interesting questions:

1 How can incumbents tell when to expect innovations that stand to erode their competitive advantages? Knowing when to expect these innovations would help firms to strategize better.
2 Why is it that incumbents (some of them very successful) often lose out during these technological changes? Just what types of change are these?
3 What can these incumbents do to profit better from such changes?

4 What should new entrants do to be successful? (After all, not all new entrants are successful.)

In this chapter, we explore these questions. In particular, we explore Foster's *S-curve* and Christensen's disruptive technologies models. We then integrate the results from these models with the concepts of new game strategies that we have seen so far to present more complete answers to the four questions raised above. Throughout this chapter, we will use the words "product" and "technology" interchangeably, although they are not always the same. For example, we will talk of the PC as being a *disruptive technology* when we really mean the technologies that go into making a PC.

Foster's S-curve

Managers were interested in the first question—how can incumbents tell when to expect innovations that stand to erode their competitive advantages—for obvious reasons. If they could tell, ex ante, when to expect these disruptive technologies, managers would be better prepared for them and might even prevent new entrants from eroding their firm's competitive advantages. One of the first business scholars to explore this question was Dr Richard Foster of McKinsey.[1] He argued that a firm can predict when it has reached the limit of its technology life cycle (and therefore can expect a radical technological change) using knowledge of the technology's physical limits.[2] Effectively, by observing the evolution of an established technology, a firm can tell when a new radical technology is around the corner about to displace the established technology. One way to model this evolution is through what would later be known as *Foster's S-curve*. In this S-curve, the vertical axis represents the rate of advance of a technology while the horizontal axis captures the amount of effort put into developing the technology (Figure 8.1). Technological progress starts off slowly, then increases very rapidly and then diminishes as the physical limits of

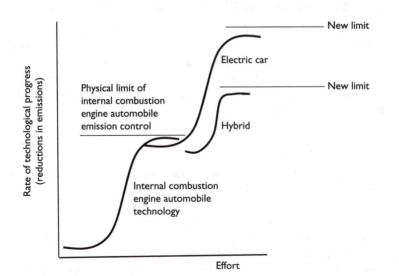

Figure 8.1 S-curves Showing Physical Limits of Technologies.

the technology are approached. Eventually, diminishing returns set in as the return on efforts becomes extremely small. A new technology whose underlying physical properties allow it to overcome the physical limit of the established technology must be used if one is to keep meeting the needs of customers. Effectively, when the returns on efforts become very small, that is a signal that a new technology is around the corner. This is especially the case when the rate of progress is not keeping up with demand. Consider, for example, the emission control technology in automobiles. Early in the life of pollution control technologies, the reductions in emissions were substantial; but as time went on, the increases in improvement relative to the amount of effort put into development became smaller. According to Foster's S-curve model of predicting the arrival of new technologies, this low rate of increase in reductions in emission is a signal that other technologies, such as hybrid or electric car technologies, are around the corner as potential replacements for existing internal combustion engine technologies whose physical limits are being reached (Figure 8.1). By the way, a technology S-curve is usually not the same thing as a product S-curve. The vertical axis of the product S-curve is sales while the horizontal axis is time. Moreover, a technology S-curve usually has many product life cycles within it.

As a predictor of when to expect a radical innovation, the S-curve has some limitations. It is difficult to tell exactly when to invest in the new technology and when to drop the established one. It is also difficult to tell just how much better the new technology will be. Moreover, the model does not say much about what managers should do to be able to exploit the new technology when they eventually face it. More importantly, the focus of Foster's curve was on "more is better" in which firms pursued technologies to outdo existing product performance characteristics. However, many potentially advantage-eroding technologies are not necessarily those that begin by outdoing existing product performance characteristics. The disruptive technologies model and the concepts of this book address these shortcomings.

Disruptive Technologies: The Phenomenon

The disruptive technologies framework, developed by Professor Clayton Christensen of the Harvard Business School, offered some answers to the first three questions: how can incumbents tell when to expect technologies that stand to erode their competitive advantages? Why is it that incumbents often lose out during these technological changes? What can these incumbents do to profit better from such changes?

Characteristics of Disruptive Technologies

Professor Christensen introduced the phrase **disruptive technologies**. These are technologies that exhibit the following three properties.[3]

1 They create new markets by introducing a new kind of product or service. (The dimensions of merit for products in the new market usually are different from those in the established market.)
2 The new product or service costs less than existing products or services, and therefore is priced less.

3 Initially, the new product performs worse than existing products when judged by the performance metrics that mainstream existing customers value. Eventually, however, the performance catches up and addresses the needs of mainstream customers.

Characteristics of Potentially Displaceable Established Technology

In addition to these characteristics of the disruptive technology, the established technology that potentially could be disrupted also has two important properties:

1 The performance of established product overshoots demand in established market. Product may have too many bells and whistles that customers do not need but are being forced to pay high prices for.
2 The cost of switching from the old product to the new one is low.

Rationale for Disruption

Why would a technology that exhibits the properties of disruptive technologies outlined above offer an opportunity for new entrants to attack and replace incumbents who have been exploiting an established technology? First, because the technology creates a new market, incumbents who serve the old (mainstream) market are likely to pay attention to meeting the needs of their existing customers (in the old market) and therefore not give the new technology the attention that it deserves. After all, these mainstream customers are the source of the firm's revenues and deserve attention. Moreover, because the performance of products from the new technology is initially inferior to that of existing products and does not meet the needs of customers in the old market, incumbents are even less likely to pay attention to the new technology. When dimensions of merit in the new market are different from those in the old market, it is even more difficult to give the new technology the attention that it deserves. Sometimes, the "new market" means the least demanding customers of the existing market who are only too happy to use the low-cost product that meets their needs but is perceived as inferior by the high-end segment. Second, because products from the new technology cost less than established ones and are priced accordingly, incumbents are less likely to pursue the new technology for fear of taking the hit in reduced revenues. It is one thing to cannibalize one's existing products with new ones that bring in about the same revenues, but it is quite another to cannibalize them with products that are priced a lot less. Financial markets do not like drops in revenues.

Third, because the performance of the new products keeps improving, there reaches a time when the new product has improved enough to start meeting the needs of the mainstream customers that incumbents had been serving all along. Some of these customers—especially those that are paying too much for bells and whistles or over-performance that they do not need—switch to the new lower-priced products made by the new entrants who have been serving the new market. Many incumbents who now want to start making the new product find out that new entrants are further up the learning curve and perhaps enjoying other first-mover advantages associated with offering the disruptive technology first. Moreover, incumbents' dominant managerial logic in serving the old market, together with the old structures and systems that had been put in place to serve customers in the old market, can become a handicap. These factors increase a new entrant's chances of exploiting the disruptive technology better than an incumbent.

To illustrate these points, consider the invasion of mainframe computers and minicomputers by PCs in the 1980s and 1990s (Figure 8.2). Mainframes and minicomputers were in the market long before PCs and satisfied the needs of many business customers as far as speed, software, and memory capacity were concerned (Figure 8.2). When PCs started out, they were used largely by computer enthusiasts and hobbyists, a new market compared to the business markets served by mainframes and minicomputers. PCs also cost much less than mainframes and minicomputers. PCs' performance was also initially inferior to that of mainframes and minicomputers but often more than met the needs of many computer enthusiasts and hobbyists. As the performance of PCs improved, minicomputer makers kept listening to their customers and offering them the types of minicomputer that they wanted, and not paying enough attention to PCs. Eventually, PC performance improved to a point where it started to meet the needs of some minicomputer customers, and at a much lower price. Understandably, many minicomputer customers switched to PCs. Some minicomputer makers who tried to enter the PC market were handicapped by their dominant managerial logic and the prospects of losing their high-margin, high-revenue minicomputers. Moreover, some PC makers had acquired PC brands and other first-mover advantages and were in a better position to profit from PCs than old minicomputer makers. The result was that as PCs displaced minicomputers in most applications, new PC makers such as Apple and Dell displaced many of the minicomputer and mainframe makers.

Effectively, in the Professor Christensen version of disruptive technology, incumbents are so busy listening to their customers that they do not pay enough

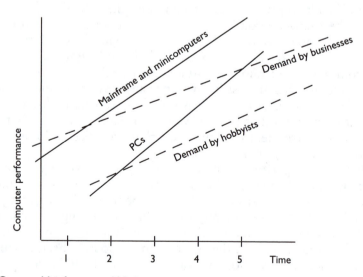

Figure 8.2 PC versus Mainframes and Minicomputers.

attention to the disruptive technology, which starts out serving the less-demanding needs of a new market. Moreover, since the new technology costs less than the established technology, incumbents may be reluctant to suffer the revenue drop that might come with switching to the lower-cost and lower-priced product. Even if incumbents want to switch to the new technology, their established processes, dominant managerial logic, relationships with old mainstream customers and routines may make the transition difficult. Moreover, the new entrants who adopted the technology first may have established first-mover advantages. Table 8.2 provides a list of many technologies that fit the Christensen model of disruptive technologies.

Table 8.2 The Disrupted and Disruptors?

Disruptor	Disrupted
Compact disc	Cassettes and records
Desktop publishing	Traditional publishing
Digital photography	Chemical film-based photography
Distribution of software by Internet	Distribution through distributors
e-mail	Snail mail
High-speed CMOS video sensors	Photographic film
Hydraulic excavators	Cable-operated excavators
Internet	Electronic data interchange (EDI)
Large-scale integration (LSI)	Small-scale integration
Minicomputers	Mainframes
Mini-mills for steel	Integrated steel mills
Online auctions	Offline auctions
PCs	Minicomputers
PowerPoint-type software	Drafting software
Small-scale integration	Discrete components
Steam engine, electric motor, and internal-combustion engine automobiles	Horse-driven cart
Steamships	Sailing ships
Table-top copiers	Large Xerox-type copiers
Telephone (originally worked for only 3 miles, limited to local phone calls)	Telegraph (Western Union) long distance
Transistor radios	Vacuum tube radio sets
Transistors	Vacuum tubes
Wal-Mart's discount stores in small rural southwestern towns	Discount retailing in cities
Wireless phone service	Fixed-wire phone service

Sustaining Technologies

A *sustaining technology* has the opposite effect on incumbents compared to a disruptive technology in that, rather than displace established products, a sustaining technology is an incremental improvement in established products that helps them get even more entrenched. Sustaining technologies are usually initiated and pursued by incumbents who use them to reinforce their competitive advantages.

Usefulness of Disruptive Technologies Framework for Creating and Appropriating Value

The question is, of what use is the disruptive technologies model in creating and appropriating value? As we pointed out earlier, the model provides answers to three of the questions that we stated at the beginning of this chapter, namely: (1) How can incumbents tell when to expect such innovations that stand to erode their competitive advantages? (2) Why is it that incumbents often lose out during these technological changes? (3) What can these incumbents do to better profit from such changes? Answering these questions exposes the role of disruptive technologies in creating and appropriating value.

How Can Incumbents Tell When to Expect Such Innovations that Stand to Erode their Competitive Advantages?

The first thing about taking advantage of the opportunities and threats of an environment is to identify them. Because the disruptive technologies model lays out the characteristics of the type of technology that is likely to be disruptive to incumbents down the line, and which established technologies risk being displaced by firms can use these characteristics to identify disruptive technologies, *ex ante*; that is, firms can use these characteristics to identify disruptive technologies *before* disruption has taken place. In so doing, incumbents can carefully screen the different innovations that potentially represent a threat or opportunity to their core businesses. New entrants can identify which technologies they can use to invade established or new markets. This can be done by asking the simple questions shown in Table 8.3.

If the answer to all five questions is YES, then the technology is potentially disruptive to incumbents of the established market and these incumbents are better off watching out for attackers. For attackers, it means that there is a good chance for them to not only dominate the new market but to move into the old market and erode the competitive advantages of incumbents there. To illustrate these two points, consider the example of VOIP, which we will call Internet telephony, versus fixed line and wireless telephony. The technology was originally used by computer enthusiasts and college students who wanted to make cheap or free phone calls and did not mind the poor quality of the call. By 2007, the quality of Internet telephony calls had increased to a point where it was difficult to tell the difference between an Internet phone call and a wireless or fixed line call. As the quality of calls improved, the service moved to many other markets, well beyond college students and enthusiasts. The cost of switching from the traditional phone to VOIP service was very low for customers. Thus,

Table 8.3 To What Extent is Technological Change Disruptive to an Established Technology?

Question	Answer	Example: VOIP versus old telephone service
Potentially disruptive technology		
1. Does the innovation create a new market whose performance requirements are not as demanding as those of the old market?	Yes/No	Yes
2. Does the innovation cost less than existing products?	Yes/No	Yes
3. Is the innovation inferior in performance but keeps improving enough to be able to meet performance criteria of the old market?	Yes/No	Yes
Established technology		
1. Does the established technology's performance overshoot demand, or are there too many bells and whistles for which customers are being forced to pay?	Yes/No	Yes
2. Are there little or no switching costs to switching from an established technology to a disruptive one?	Yes/No	Yes

the answer to all five questions in Table 8.3 is Yes. In the USA, new entrants such as Vonage and Skype were going after both markets. Incumbent telephone companies were at first not very receptive to Internet telephony.

Why is it that Incumbents Often Lose out in the Face of these Technological Changes?

Professor Christensen argued that two contributors to why incumbents often lose out to new entrants, in the face of a disruptive technology, are old *values* and *processes*. In exploiting an established technology, incumbents usually build resources, processes and values. Processes are the "the patterns of inter-actions, coordination, communication, decision making employees use to trans-form resources into products and services of greater worth"[4] while values are "the standards by which employees set priorities that enable them to judge whether an order is attractive or unattractive, whether a customer is more important or less important, whether an idea for a new product is attractive or marginal and so on."[5] Over time, especially if a firm has been successful, these values and processes become embedded in the firm's routines. Managers also develop a dominant logic.[6] These values, processes and dominant logic are strengths when it comes to exploiting established or sustaining technologies, but in the face of some new games such as disruptive technologies, they can become handicaps.

When a disruptive change or any other new game comes along and requires different values or processes, the tendency is for the employees to stick with the old routines that have worked before because routines, processes, and values are difficult to change quickly. For example, if employees of an incumbent firm have focused their attention on their existing customers so as better to provide these customers' needs, their values and processes are likely to dictate that they keep their attention on these customers, the sources of their revenues. In so doing, they may miss out on the new market in which the disruptive technology started out; and while the technology is gradually improving, employees in the old market are still paying attention to their dominant customers. By the time that these employees realize that the disruptive technology is now invading their own market, it may be too late to quickly build the new values and processes that are required to exploit the disruptive technology. Effectively, the old values and processes have become handicaps for incumbents. Thus, new entrants, without these old values, processes, and dominant managerial logic to handicap them, have a better chance of exploiting the disruptive technology.

What Can these Incumbents do to Profit Better from Such Changes?

What should firms do in the face of disruptive innovations? It depends on whether the firm is an incumbent or a new entrant. Professor Christensen suggests several things that incumbents can do to improve their chances.[7]

First, incumbents should convince upper-level management to see the disruptive innovation as a threat to existing core businesses. In so doing, management can commit the types of resources that are needed to tackle the innovation. Since management's instincts are to protect the core businesses that bring in revenues, management is more likely to pay attention to the disruptive innovation when it understands the enormity of the threat that the disruptive innovation poses to an existing core business.

Second, when funds have been allocated to the innovation, and development of products or services is ready to begin, the incumbent should turn over responsibility to an autonomous unit within the firm that can frame the innovation as an opportunity and pursue it as such. By using an autonomous unit, the incumbent can (1) prevent the old processes and values from handicapping the building of the new processes and values that are needed to exploit the innovation, and (2) avoid the dominant managerial logic of the old business, if the autonomous group is staffed with new employees who do not have the old logic. It is also more difficult for political foes to disrupt the activities of the autonomous unit.

Third, when a product is not yet good enough, the activities to develop the product should be internal and proprietary. When a product becomes good enough and commoditization starts, the incumbent should outsource it.

Fourth, firms should organize their business units as a function of the problems that customers want to solve (and associated solutions), rather than by how easy it is to collect data for the company. Paying attention to customers' problems, solutions, and contexts, rather than to the customers themselves, enables a firm to see other customer's needs better and to provide them.

The third and fourth items suggested for incumbents also apply to new entrants. In addition, new entrants should first go after markets that have been ignored by incumbents, and then methodically work their way to incumbents' existing markets.

Shortcomings of Disruptive Technologies Model

Like any framework, Christensen's disruptive technologies model has its short-comings. We explore three of them here: limited coverage, lack of strategy focus, and not enough about profitability.

Limited Coverage

The characteristics of disruptive innovations are important because understanding them enables firms to identify them and pay attention to the threats and opportunities of potential disruptors. However, some innovations that do not meet all the three characteristics of disruptive innovations still displace existing products—that is, some innovations that are disruptive in outcome do not meet all the characteristics of disruptive technologies spelled out above. Consider the second property: innovation (new product) costs less than existing products. Some innovations that start out costing more than existing products displace the latter. New pharmaceutical drugs that displace existing ones are a case in point—their initial costs are often higher than those of existing therapies. Next, consider the third property: innovation starts out with inferior quality (compared to existing products) but keeps improving enough eventually to meet the needs of customers in the old market. Many innovations that start out with superior performance, relative to existing products, still displace the existing products. For example, many medications that initially outperform existing ones, displace their predecessors. Electronic point of sale registers, which displaced mechanical cash registers, were superior in performance to the latter when they started out. Effectively, disruptive innovations, as defined by Christensen's three characteristics, are but a subset of innovations that can be disruptive. They are an even smaller subset of new games; but the Christensen definition has the advantage that managers can use it to, *ex ante*, tell which innovation will be disruptive and to try to do something about it.

Lack of Focus on Strategy: Prescriptions for Managers Are Only about Implementation

The other shortcoming of the disruptive technologies model is that the prescriptions for managers are largely about implementation issues and say very little about the strategy that is being implemented. Recall that, according to Christensen, an incumbent that has a good chance of doing well in the face of a disruptive technology is one that convinces upper-level management to see disruptive technology as a problem, creates an autonomous unit to pursue disruptive technology, develops the product internally when it is still highly differentiated but outsources it when it becomes a commodity, and organizes business units as a function of the problems/solutions that customers want and not as a function of how data is collected. These prescriptions are largely about the organizational structure, systems, and people—the cornerstones of strategy *implementation*. There is very little about the set of activities of the value chain, value network, or value shop that needs to be performed to create and appropriate value, and when and how these activities should be performed. The prescriptions are also designed largely for incumbent firms, with very little about what a new entrant could do to have a competitive advantage. After all, not all attackers win.

Not Enough about Profitability

The primary emphasis of the disruptive technology model is on using the technology to develop products that customers find valuable. Emphasis is on creating value and very little on appropriating the value; but as we saw in Chapter 4, appropriating value often takes more than getting the technology right. Not only are complementary assets often critical to profiting from a new technology, a firm's position vis-à-vis its coopetitors, its pricing strategy, the extent to which the technology can be imitated, the number and quality of customers, and the sources of revenue can also be critical. These shortcomings can be eliminated by looking at disruptive technologies as the subset of the new games that they are.

Disruptive Technologies as New Games

What have disruptive technologies to do with new game strategies? Everything! Disruptive technologies are often new games or the source of new games and vice versa. On the one hand, for example, PC technology gave birth to all the new game strategies that both new entrants and incumbents in the computer industry pursued when they entered the PC submarket. The Internet is a disruptive technology that has been the source of many new game strategies such as those pursued by Google, eBay, Amazon, to name a few. On the other hand, for example, the many firms whose R&D labs toil every day to invent radically innovative products or processes often produce inventions that go on to become disruptive technologies. For example, the microchip that would go on to replace discrete transistor technology and make it possible to make everything from the PC to the iPhone, was invented by Robert Noyce of Intel Corporation and Jack Kilby of Texas Instruments.

Profiting from Disruptive Technologies: The New Game Strategies Approach

A firm's ability to profit from a disruptive technology starts with the firm's strengths and handicaps when it confronts the technology (Figure 8.3). These strengths and handicaps influence how well the firm is able to take advantage of the value chain and new game factors associated with the disruptive technology to create and appropriate value (Figure 8.3).

Strengths and Handicaps in the Face of a Disruptive Technology

As we saw in Chapter 5, every player in a new game brings some strengths from its past resources/capabilities or product-market position (PMP) that can continue to be strengths or become handicaps in the new game. Since disruptive technologies are new games, we can expect that both new entrants and incumbents bring some strengths from their pasts that can continue to be strengths or become handicaps. Determining which former strengths can still be strengths

NEW GAME STRATEGIES

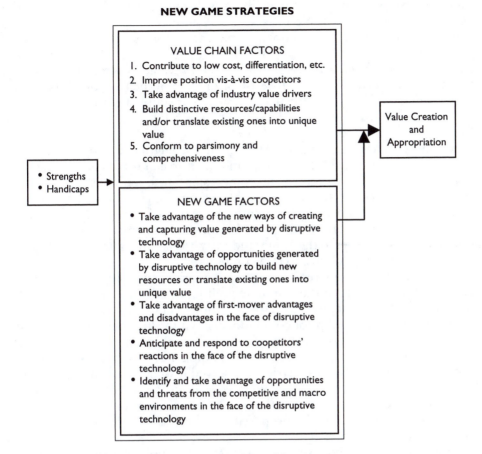

Figure 8.3 Disruptive Technologies and Value Creation and Appropriation.

and which ones have become handicaps can be crucial in profiting from a disruptive technology. Table 8.4 can be used to help make such a determination. As we saw in Chapter 5, there are two primary determinants of which resource becomes a handicap or strength: whether the resource is vital to exploiting the disruptive technology, and whether the resource is separable. A resource is vital

Table 8.4 Are Previous Strengths Still Strengths or Have they Become Handicaps in the Face of a Disruptive Technology?

Resource	Is the resource/capability vital to the disruptive technology?	Is separability costless?	In exploiting the disruptive technology, the resource is a:
Resource 1	Y	Y	strength
Resource 2	Y	N	potential strength
Resource 3	N	Y	question mark
Resource 4	N	N	handicap

to a disruptive technology if it contributes substantially to value creation and appropriability. It is separable if the firm has no problems taking the resource away from a predisruptive technology application for use in a disruptive technology, or leaving the resource behind when it is more likely to hurt in the disruptive technology than help. A firm may be prevented from using a resource in a disruptive technology because of prior commitments, contracts, agreements, understandings, emotional attachments, or simply because the resource/asset cannot be moved from the predisruptive technology game to the location of the disruptive technology.

A resource such as Resource 1 (Table 8.4) is a strength because it is important in exploiting the disruptive technology and the firm can use it because there are no prior commitments, agreements, understandings, or anything else that prevents it from doing so. Many complementary assets such as brands and distribution channels are usually strengths in the face of disruptive technologies. IBM used its brand, relationships with businesses, and software developers to dominate the PC market in the 1980s and early 1990s. (Recall that the PC was a disruptive technology relative to minicomputers.)

A resource that was a strength in a predisruptive technology era becomes a handicap if it is useless to the firm in exploiting the disruptive technology but the firm cannot separate itself from the resource and move on. Separation may not be possible because of prior commitments that the firm made in a predisruptive technology period, or because of a lack of strategic fit between the firm's corporate strategy and the disruptive technology. As we saw in Chapter 5, Compaq's relationships with distributors served it well for a while; but when it decided to sell directly to end-customers, distributors prevented it from doing so. Effectively, Compaq could not shake itself free of its prior commitments and therefore could not pursue the proposed new business model. Often, a firm is stuck with resources that it does not need even as it pursues the disruptive technology. For example, since a disruptive technology usually starts out addressing the needs of a new market with very low prices, incumbents may have to adopt a low cost mentality to be competitive in the new market. Such a mentality may be difficult to adopt successfully, especially if the firm's products in the old market are differentiated and it has a high cost-structure. It is difficult to transform employees, with a high-cost culture born out of the high-cost structure usually associated with a differentiation strategy, into a low-cost one.

Professor Christensen provided another good example. He argued that since disruptive technologies usually first address the needs of a new market, incumbents that were used to addressing the needs of the old market keep listening to their customers—the primary source of their revenues—rather than customers in the new market. Effectively, relationships with customers that were critical to getting customers what they wanted prior to the disruptive change, now handicap the firm's efforts to listen to and address the needs of the new market. As another example, take VOIP telephony. The old telephone company's dominant logic about how to make money carried over to the late 2000s for many old telephone companies who could not understand how any firm would allow people to make free intercontinental phone calls and still make money.

There are also cases where a resource is vital to a firm's success in the face of a disruptive technology but the firm cannot use the resource because of prior agreements that prevent it from doing so (Resource 2, Table 8.4). As we saw in

Chapter 5, a noncompete clause in an important employee's contract with a previous employer can prevent the present employer from using the employee effectively in exploiting a disruptive technology. Resource 3 is not important in the new game and therefore of no significance, since the firm can get away from it.

From a PMP point of view, the question is whether strengths in a firm's previous PMP—the product and the firm's position vis-à-vis its coopetitors—that a firm brings to the disruptive technology remain strengths or become handicaps. Because the product starts out addressing the needs of a smaller market whose performance requirements are initially inferior to those of the existing market, the old market is a handicap. Why? The prices and possibly profit margins in the old market are higher than those in the new market. Not many incumbents are likely to want to cannibalize their existing products, especially with new products whose prices are so low that they will suffer revenue drops and possibly profit drops. It may also be difficult to change an organization that has been built around a high-price high-cost structure and business logic, to a low-price low-cost one.

Value Chain Activities in the Face of Disruptive Technologies

To offer products/services in the face of a disruptive technology, firms—incumbents and entrants alike—have to perform value chain activities. As we argued in Chapter 4, to increase their chances of making the most contribution towards value creation and appropriation, firms take advantage of so-called *value chain factors*. They pursue the types of activities that:

1 Contribute to low cost, differentiation, number of customers and other drivers of profitability.
2 Contribute to position the firm better vis-à-vis its coopetitors.
3 Take advantage of industry value drivers.
4 Build distinctive resources/capabilities and/or translate existing ones into unique value.
5 Are comprehensive and parsimonious.

However, because disruptive technologies are new games, each firm can also take advantage of *new game factors*—of the fact that disruptive technologies generate new ways of creating and appropriating new value; offer opportunities to build new resources/capabilities and/or translate existing ones in new ways into value; create the potential to build and exploit first-mover advantages; attract reactions from new and existing competitors; and have their roots in the opportunities and threats of an industry or macroenvironment. As we argued in Chapter 4, value chain factors have a direct impact on value creation and appropriation while new game factors have an indirect moderating effect. As shown in Figure 8.3, the extent to which each value chain factor impacts value creation and appropriation is moderated (pushed up or down in magnitude and direction) by new game factors. Both factors rest on the strengths and handicaps that the firm has when it faces the disruptive technology. We now explore how.

Contribute to Low Cost, Differentiation, Number of Customers, and Other Drivers of Profitability

Any firm that wants to make money from a disruptive technology has to offer customers benefits that they perceive as more valuable to them than anything that competitors can offer them; that is, irrespective of whether a firm is a new entrant or an incumbent, it has to offer customers something unique if the firm hopes to keep attracting customers. The firm also has to price the product well and pursue the right sources of revenue. To offer distinctive customer benefits, price them well, and pursue the right sources of revenue, a firm must perform the appropriate value chain activities. Because a disruptive technology is a new game, the firm can take advantage of new game factors. For example, since disruptive technologies usually initially address a new market, they offer opportunities to work with so-called lead users—customers who face needs that other customers will encounter later but face them months or years before the bulk of that marketplace does.[8] Because of their knowledge of what customers want in the new product and their willingness to work with firms, lead users can be very helpful in a firm's efforts to offer distinctive value to its customers. The new gameness of disruptive technologies also offers firms the opportunity to move first to build and exploit first-mover advantages. For example, a firm can build switching costs at customers, increasing the uniqueness of its PMP.

However, offering customers something that they value implies that a firm has gotten the technology or aspects of it right. One way to do this is, as suggested by Christensen, to convince upper-level management to see disruptive technology as a problem, create an autonomous unit to pursue disruptive technology, develop a product internally when it is still highly differentiated but outsource it when commoditized, and organize business units as a function of the problems/solutions that customers want. Getting the technology right is not always a guarantee to make money, since coopetitors with power can extract most of the value. Moreover, the technology can be imitated by a firm that has difficult-to-imitate but important complementary assets. Such an imitator will make the money even though the firm being imitated got the technology right— hence, the need to look at other value chain factors apart from getting the disruptive technology right and offering customers the right product features.

Improve the Position of a Firm vis-à-vis Coopetitors

Disruptive technologies also have an impact on industry factors and therefore an impact on a firm's position vis-à-vis its coopetitors. Rivalry increases since both new entrant attackers and incumbents are competing to exploit the new technology, often in both the new and old markets. Growth lessens the intensity of rivalry somewhat. The number of firms increases, thereby increasing the bargaining power of buyers. New entry is high as entrepreneurs enter to exploit the new technology. Suppliers have more firms to sell to than before the disruptive technology. Effectively, the industry is not as attractive as it was before the disruptive change, and appropriating value created depends on how firms take advantage of these forces that are reducing the attractiveness of the markets in performing their activities.

A firm can take advantage of new game factors by improving its position vis-à-vis coopetitors and in the process, dampen some of these repressive forces. First, if a firm bypasses powerful distributors and sells directly to more fragmented end-customers, the firm is effectively increasing its bargaining power vis-à-vis buyers, and increasing its chances of working more closely with lead users to get the technology right. Second, by integrating vertically backwards, early in the life of a disruptive technology, a firm may be able to improve its position vis-à-vis suppliers. It can use this improved position to, for example, convince sole suppliers of important components to find second sources for these components, further improving its position vis-à-vis the suppliers. Finally, working cooperatively with coopetitors, rather than seeing them as antagonists over whom one has to have power, often dampens competitive forces.

Take Advantage of Industry Value Drivers

Recall that industry value drivers are those industry factors that stand to have a substantial impact on the benefits (low cost or differentiation) that customers want, the quality and number of such customers, or any other driver of profitability. Disruptive technologies often change industry value drivers. For example, in offline auctions, the location of the auction was a critical industry value driver since it determined who would attend the auction and the more people at the auction, the better for sellers. In online auctions, the location is no longer a value driver. Now it is the number of registered members that belong to a particular community or website. Consequently, emphasis in the face of the Internet is not on having the best location but on having the largest number of registered users. eBay seems to have understood this well. Another example is Nintendo's introduction of the Wii. One reason why Nintendo was able to make money on each console sold while Sony and Microsoft lost money on their consoles (PS3 and Xbox 360, respectively) was because the video game console industry was an industry in which the prices of the microchips used in consoles dropped rapidly as older chips quickly became obsolete. Since Nintendo was pursuing a reverse positioning strategy, it used these old chips that cost a lot less than the cutting-edge chips used by its competitors. Effectively, Nintendo was able to take advantage of the rapidly falling prices of chips and keep its costs very low.

Build Distinctive Resources/Capabilities and/or Translate Existing Ones into Unique Value

The resources that a firm needs in the face of a disruptive technology can be grouped into two: technology resources and complementary assets. Technology resources are the resources that a firm needs to get the technology right. Complementary assets here are all the other resources, beyond those that underpin the disruptive technology, that a firm needs to offer customers value and position itself to appropriate the value. They include distribution channels, brand name reputation, installed base, shelf space, and so on, and are often critical to profiting from a disruptive technology. Although new technology resources are often needed in the face of a disruptive technology, scarce important complementary assets that were important in profiting from the established technology usually remain useful and important. Firms with such complementary assets often stand to do well. Because disruptive technologies initially address new markets, firms may have to build the complementary assets required to focus on these new markets from scratch and new entrants may have an advantage building the complementary assets for these new markets. Incumbents usually have the complementary asset for the older market and these complementary assets can help them fend off attacks by new entrants. Often, new entrants with the technology resources team up with incumbents that have the complementary assets.

Because a disruptive technology costs less than the older one and is initially inferior in performance, incumbents and new entrants alike often need new technological resources to get the new technology right. By convincing upper-level management to see the disruptive technology as a problem, creating an autonomous unit to pursue the disruptive technology, and so on, an incumbent can mitigate some of the problems of dominant managerial logic to build the types of resource that will enable it to get the new technology right. By moving first, the firm can also build and exploit first-mover advantages.

Conform to Parsimony and Comprehensiveness

In performing the activities that will enable it to create and capture value in the face of a disruptive technology, a firm has to be careful not to perform unnecessary activities or leave out important activities. An AVAC analysis can help a firm sort out which activities contribute to value creation and capture, and which do not.

Implementation of New Game Strategies

As we saw in Chapter 7, the strategy that a firm pursues also has to be implemented well if its full potential is to be realized. A structure, systems/processes, and people that fit the strategy has to be pursued if a firm is going to realize the full potential of its new game strategy. Having the right values and processes are part of the implementation. The four measures advocated by Professor Christensen—convincing upper-level management to see the disruptive technology as a problem, creating an autonomous unit to pursue disruptive technology, developing product internally when it is still highly differentiated but outsource it when commoditized, organizing business units as a function of the problems/solutions that customers want—are a subset of implementing a new game strategy.

Revisiting the Questions

One way to summarize what we have explored in this chapter is to revisit the questions that we raised at the beginning of the chapter.

How Can Incumbents Tell When to Expect Innovations that Stand to Erode their Competitive Advantages?

As part of monitoring the opportunities and threats of its political, economic, social, technological, and natural (PESTN) environments via, for example, a

PESTN analysis, a firm should perform the five-part test of Table 8.3 to determine the extent to which the new technology stands to become disruptive to an established technology. A new technology is potentially disruptive to an established technology if the answers to the questions of Table 8.3 are largely Yes. Moreover, by anticipating the likely actions and reactions of coopetitors, a firm may be able to respond better to disruptive technologies since it is monitoring not only the technology but also the actions of firms. A firm is better prepared to cooperate and compete in the face of a disruptive technology if it knows not only about the technology but also about the coopetitors trying to exploit the technology.

Why Is it that Incumbents (Some of them very Successful) Often Lose Out in the Face of Disruptive Technologies?

Recall that proponents of the disruptive technologies model argue that incumbents fail because, in trying to get the new technology right, the processes and values that they developed in exploiting the established technology handicap their efforts. The primary goal of actors, according to the model, is in getting the technology right—in developing the type of product that customers, in the new and old markets, want. The new game strategies model maintains that there is more to making money from a new technology than getting the technology right. Thus, incumbents can also fail to profit from a disruptive technology if they do not have the right complementary assets, position themselves well vis-à-vis coopetitors, have the wrong pricing strategy, or do not pursue the right sources of revenue in creating and appropriating value. Additionally, a firm may be handicapped by resources/capabilities and PMPs that were strengths in the predisruptive technology era but that have become handicaps. For example, predisruptive technology era strengths such as resources, prior commitments, dominant logic, corporate strategy, existing products, and position vis-à-vis coopetitors can become handicaps.

What Can Incumbents Do to Profit Better from Disruptive Technologies?

The disruptive technologies model argues that an incumbent can improve its performance in exploiting a disruptive technology if it convinces upper-level management to see the technology as a problem, creates an autonomous unit to pursue disruptive technology, develops the product internally when it is still highly differentiated but outsources it when it becomes a commodity, and organizes business units as a function of the problems/solutions that customers want and not as a function of how data is collected. These prescriptions are meant largely to overcome the problems that incumbents face, in trying to get the technology right; but since there is a lot more to profiting from a new technology than getting it right, an incumbent not only has to reduce the effects of its handicaps on its ability to get the technology right but also obtain complementary assets, position itself advantageously vis-à-vis its coopetitors, and perform any other activity that will enable it to create and appropriate value. It has to take advantage of both value chain and new game factors. Note also that incumbents often have at least one advantage over new entrants in the face of a disruptive technology—they usually have complementary assets such as distribution channels, and brands that can be used in exploiting the disruptive technology, especially in the established market. These complementary assets can be used to, among other things, convince a new entrant that has the technology but no complementary assets to team up with the incumbent.

What Should New Entrants Do?

The disruptive technology model suggests that new entrants should start out by attacking the new market first, reserving entry into the old market for later. Given their strengths and handicaps, new entrants should take advantage of both value chain and new game factors to create and appropriate value. Additionally, they can also exploit the fact that incumbents have handicaps that they do not.

Disruptiveness of New Games

In the disruptive technologies framework that we have explored, there are two types of technology: disruptive and sustaining. One implicit assumption is that within each of these groups, there is homogeneity—that is, all disruptive technologies have the same level of disruptiveness while all sustainable technologies have the same level of sustainability. However, since not all technologies have the same characteristics, we can expect disruptive technologies to differ in their level of disruptiveness. Thus, an interesting question is, how disruptive is a disruptive technology? Since disruptive technologies are a subset of new games, we can understand the extent to which some disruptive technologies are more disruptive than others by exploring the new gameness (disruptiveness) of new games. In Chapter 1, we started exploring the new gameness of new games using the framework that has been summarized in Figure 8.4. In the framework, the vertical axis captures the impact of a new game on the competitiveness of existing products—that is, it captures the extent to which a new game renders existing products noncompetitive. The horizontal axis captures the impact of the new game on existing resources/capabilities (technological and marketing)—that is, it captures the extent to which the technological and marketing resources/capabilities that are required to pursue the new game build on existing resources/capabilities or render them obsolete.[9] In the framework, there are four types of new games: regular, position-building, resource-building, and revolutionary.[10] New gameness and disruptiveness increase as one moves from the origin of the matrix to the top right corner, with the regular new game being the least disruptive while the revolutionary new game is the most disruptive.

By definition, disruptive technologies drastically reduce the competitiveness of existing products. Thus, we can expect disruptive technologies to be located in the upper half of the matrix of Figure 8.5. Take PCs, for example. The technology and other resources needed to make PCs built on the existing resources needed to build minicomputers and PCs eventually rendered minicomputers noncompetitive. Thus, in the matrix of Figure 8.5, PCs would be located in the upper-left quadrant. Other examples that fall into this quadrant include mini-mills and different generations of disk drives. However, digital

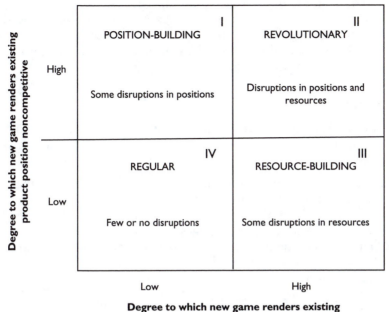

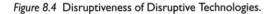

Figure 8.4 Disruptiveness of Disruptive Technologies.

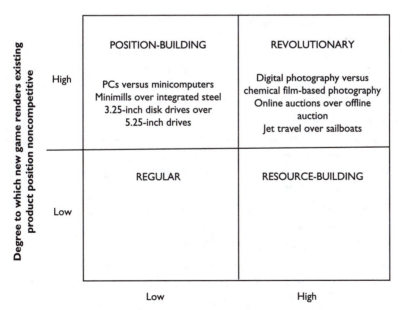

Figure 8.5 Examples of Degrees of Disruptiveness.

photography falls in the upper-right quadrant because the technology is radically different from chemical film-based photography technology. And the quality of digital technology has improved to a point where chemical film-based technology is being phased out. Like PCs, it is a disruptive technology but a revolutionary new game rather than a position-building new game.

Key Takeaways

- Over the years, many new technologies have replaced older ones and in the process, incumbent firms have been replaced. This has raised four questions:

  1 How can incumbents tell when to expect such innovations that stand to erode their competitive advantages?
  2 Why is it that incumbents (some of them very successful) often lose out during these technological changes?
  3 What can these incumbents do to profit better from such changes?
  4 What should new entrants do to be successful? After all, not all new entrants do well.

- Foster's S-curve was one of the first models to explore the first question. He argued that a firm can tell that a new technology is about to displace an existing one when the physical limits of the existing technology have been reached—when the returns on efforts become very small.
- According to Professor Clayton Christensen, disruptive technologies exhibit the following three characteristics:

  1 They create new markets by introducing a new kind of product or service.
  2 The new product or service costs less than existing products or services, and therefore is priced less.
  3 Initially, the new product performs worse than existing products when judged by the performance metrics that mainstream existing customers value. Eventually, however, the performance catches up and addresses the needs of mainstream customers.

- Contrast this with a sustaining technology which is an incremental improvement in established products and is often used by incumbents to reinforce their competitive advantages.
- Meanwhile, those established technologies that are prime candidates for disruption usually have products:

  1 Whose performance overshoots demand, with too many bells and whistles for which customers are being forced to pay.
  2 With little or no switching costs for customers.

- The disruptive technologies model was developed by Professor Christensen and provides some answers to three of the four questions raised:

  1 *How can incumbents tell when to expect innovations that stand to erode their competitive advantages?* Using the following checklist, a firm can determine, *ex ante*, which technology potentially is likely to disruptive its business models:

- Does the new technology create a new market whose performance requirements are not as demanding as those of the old market?
- Does the new technology cost less than existing products?
- Is the new technology inferior in performance (compared to that of established technology) but keeps improving enough to be able to meet performance criteria of the old market?
- Does the performance of the established technology overshoot demand?
- Are the costs of switching from the established technology to the new one low?

2 *Why is it that incumbents (some of them very successful) often lose out in the face of a disruptive technology?* Incumbents fail to exploit disruptive technologies because they are handicapped by:

- Processes developed in exploiting established technology.
- Values developed in exploiting established technology.

3 *What can incumbents do to profit better from disruptive technologies?* Incumbents can overcome these handicaps by:

- Convincing upper-level management to see disruptive technology as a problem.
- Creating an autonomous unit to pursue disruptive technology.
- Developing a product internally when it is still highly differentiated but outsourcing it when it is commoditized.
- Organizing business units as a function of the problems/solutions that customers want.

- The new game strategies framework encompasses the disruptive technologies model, since disruptive technologies are new games. It answers all four questions:

1 *How can incumbents tell when to expect innovations that stand to erode their competitive advantages?*

- When a PEST analysis suggests that the political, economic, social, or technological components of the environment are a threat or an opportunity. This includes the five-question test of disruptive technologies.
- When, by monitoring the likely reaction of coopetitors, incumbents find that coopetitors are likely to adopt the new technology.

2 *Why is it that incumbents (some of them very successful) often lose out in the face of disruptive technologies?* In creating and appropriating value, incumbents are handicapped by:

- Strengths from predisruptive technology era that have become handicaps: resources, prior commitments, dominant managerial logic, corporate strategy, existing products, position vis-à-vis coopetitors, values, systems, and processes.
- Not enough strengths or ability to build them, to exploit value chain and new game factors.

3 *What can incumbents do to profit better from disruptive technologies?*

o Not only reduce the effects of handicaps, but also take advantage of strengths (e.g. complementary assets), in creating and appropriating value. This includes not only getting the technology right, but also doing other things to create value and better position the firm to appropriate the value. It entails taking advantage of both value chain and new game factors. Given its strengths and handicaps, the firm should perform activities that:

□ Contribute to low cost, differentiation, or other drivers of profitability.
□ Contribute to position the firm better vis-à-vis its coopetitors.
□ Take advantage of industry value drivers.
□ Build and translate distinctive resources/capabilities.
□ Are parsimonious and comprehensive.

o While:

□ Taking advantage of the new ways of creating and capturing the new value generated by the new game.
□ Taking advantage of opportunities generated by the new game to build new resources or translating existing ones into unique value.
□ Taking advantage of first-mover advantages and disadvantages.
□ Anticipating and responding to coopetitors' reactions to its actions.
□ Identifying and taking advantage of opportunities and threats from the macroenvironment.

o The strategy must then be properly implemented by:

□ Convincing upper-level management to see disruptive technology as a problem.
□ Creating autonomous unit to pursue disruptive technology.
□ Developing product internally when it is still highly differentiated but outsourcing it when commoditized.
□ Organizing business units as a function of the problems/solutions that customers want.

4 What should new entrants do to be successful?

o The same things that incumbents do but without the handicaps and strengths of incumbents.

• Some disruptive technologies are more disruptive than others. Revolutionary disruptive technologies are the most disruptive.

Key Terms

Disruptive technology
Foster's S-curve
S-curve
Sustaining technology

Chapter 9

Globalization and New Games

Reading this chapter should provide you with the conceptual and analytical tools to:

- Define globalization, and the different strategies that firms can pursue in going international.
- Analyze who appropriates how much value from products that are developed and sold globally.
- Be introduced to the strategies that firms pursue when going global.
- Understand the drivers of globalization and why firms go international.
- Begin to understand the critical role that governments can play in value appropriation.

Introduction

Oil is arguably the most global of all global products. It is explored and extracted from countries in all six continents, by people and equipment from all over the world. It is refined, transported, sold, and used in all corners of the earth. All countries need it and depend on each other for it, and for the technologies that go into finding, transporting, and processing it. The list of products that are produced using oil is endless. Towards the middle of 2008, the price of a liter of gasoline at the pump reached record highs in many countries even as the price of oil futures flirted with the $150 per barrel record price. Oil companies recorded very high profits and some analysts wondered what the high prices would do to the world economy.[1] Some consumers wondered if the oil companies deserved the high profits. Using our terminology, people wondered if the oil companies created all the value that they were appropriating. If that were not the case, who was creating the value that the oil companies were capturing? If they deserved the high profits, who was capturing most of the value perceived by customers? How about the oil-exporting or importing countries? How much of what consumers paid for oil from each of these countries actually went to the countries? We will explore these questions in this chapter. We start the chapter with an example on how to calculate the value that is appropriated by different players along an international oil value chain. We then briefly discuss globalization and its drivers. This is followed by a discussion of new game strategies that firms use when they go global.

Introductory Example: Appropriating Value in Globalization

Suppose a firm pursues the right global new game strategy (given its strengths and handicaps) to create value; how much of the value can it appropriate? It depends on how much of the value created the other players in the international value system, especially governments, appropriate. Governments have infinite power and can use it to appropriate most of the value created in a value chain, leaving the creators of such value with very little to show for their efforts. To illustrate what can happen in a value chain, let us explore a very short minicase. We use the oil industry because it is one of the most global industries in the world. Directly or indirectly, oil touches almost every life on earth. Firms and governments benefit from oil.

Example 9.1. Minicase: Who Creates and Who Appropriates Value in the Oil Industry?

In the 2000s, Nigeria was Africa's largest exporter of oil and exported some of its oil to many countries including the USA, India, France, Italy, Spain, Canada, and the Netherlands.[2] Finding costs for Africa had jumped from $7.55 per barrel in 2002–3 to $15.25 in 2003–5.[3] In 2003, lifting costs and production taxes were $3.57 and $1.00 per barrel respectively. Table 9.1 shows the June 2007 gasoline prices, taxes, cost per barrel of oil, and currency exchange rates for the Organization for Economic Cooperation and Development (OECD) countries as reported by the International Energy Agency (*Agence Internationale de L'energie*), an OECD agency.[4] There are 158.98 liters to the barrel. The joint ventures that produced oil in Nigeria are shown in Table 9.2.[5] The price that consumers paid for gasoline reflected the cost of crude oil to refiners, refinery processing costs, marketing and distribution costs, the retail station costs, and taxes. Crude oil costs, in turn, included the cost of exploring and finding oil, drilling for it, pumping it out, transporting it to refiners, and export taxes paid to the exporting country.

Question 1: How much of the value in a liter of gasoline using crude from Nigeria was captured (1) by each OECD country, (2) by the oil companies, and (3) by Nigeria? How much of the value was created by governments?

Question 2: Can you explain the difference between the amount appropriated by Nigeria and that appropriated by each OECD country?

Answer

We perform the calculations for France first, and simply state the results for the other countries. All calculations are in US dollars and liters.

Of the $1.771 paid by customers in France for a liter of gasoline (Table 9.1), France captured $1.101 (62.17%). Therefore, the amount left to be shared by other players in the value chain is $0.670 ($1.771 – 1.101); that is, $0.670 of the $1.771 has to be shared by (a) the oil companies that explore for crude oil, drill, pump, and transport it to refineries; (b) the refiners (often oil companies)

Table 9.1 June 2007 OECD Gasoline Prices and Taxes

Country	Price (in country's currency)	Tax (in country's currency)	Exchange rate for a dollar	Price (US$)	Tax (US$)	April crude oil prices (US$/ barrel)
France (€)	1.316	0.818	0.743	1.771	1.101	65.72
Germany (€)	1.393	0.877	0.743	1.875	1.180	65.67
Italy (€)	1.348	0.789	0.743	1.815	1.063	64.51
Spain (€)	1.079	0.545	0.743	1.452	0.733	63.73
UK (£)	0.966	0.628	0.504	1.917	1.246	67.73
Japan (Yen)	139.000	60.400	121.610	1.143	0.497	62.38
Canada (C$)	1.066	0.312	1.061	1.005	0.294	65.96
USA (US$)	0.808	0.105	1.000	0.808	0.105	59.64

Source: International Energy Agency (*Agence Internationale de l'Energie*), OECD/IEA (2007). End-user petroleum product prices and average crude oil import costs. Retrieved August 9, 2007, from http://www.iea.org/Textbase/stats/surveys/mps.pdf.

Table 9.2 Oil Joint Ventures in Nigeria

Joint venture operated by:	Estimated production in 2003 (barrels per day)	% of Nigerian production in 2003	Partners in joint venture (share in partnership)
Shell Petroleum Development Company of Nigeria Limited (SPDC) operated by Royal Dutch Shell, a British/Dutch company	950,000	42.51	NNPC (55%) Shell (30%) TotalFinaElf (10%) Agip (5%)
Chevron/Texaco Nigeria Limited (CNL), operated by Chevron/Texaco of USA	485,000	21.70	NNPC (60%) Chevron (40%)
Mobil Producing Nigeria Unlimited (MPNU), operated by Exxon-Mobil of USA	500,000	22.37	NNPC (60%) Exxon-Mobil (40%)
Nigerian Agip Oil Company Limited (NAOC), operated by Agip of Italy	150,000	6.71	NNPC (60%) Agip (20%) ConocoPhillips (20%)
Total Petroleum Nigeria Limited (TPNL), operated by Total of France	150,000	6.71	NNPC (60%) Elf (now Total) (40%)

Source: Energy Information Administration of the US Department of Energy (2003), Nigeria. Retrieved July 30, 2007, from http://www.eia.doe.gov/emeu/cabs/ngia_jv.html.

who refine, market, and transport to gas stations for sale to customers, and the gas station's take; and (c) the exporting country, Nigeria in our case.

We are told that the average crude price in France in April 2007 was $65.72/barrel = ($65.72/158.98) per liter = $0.4134/liter. Therefore distribution and marketing, and refining and profits account for $0.2566 ($0.670 – $0.4134) or

14.49% of the $1.771. The crude price of $0.4134/liter includes finding costs, lifting costs, production taxes, and "profits" for exporting country and oil company partners.

The question now is, what fraction of the $0.4134/liter goes to Nigeria. To estimate Nigeria's share, we first estimate the finding and lifting costs, and production taxes as follows:

the cost of oil extraction is $19.83 ($15.25 finding costs + $3.57 lifting costs + $1.00 production taxes) per barrel = ($19.83/158.97) per liter = $0.1247 per liter.

Thus, finding costs, lifting costs, and production taxes account for $0.1247 or 7.04% of the $1.771 price per liter. Therefore Nigeria and its venture partners (Shell, Chevron/Texaco, Agip, Total, Mobil) are left with $0.2887 ($0.4134 – 0.1247) to share. To estimate Nigeria's share of the oil ventures, we first estimate what share of the oil shipped belongs to it. The weighted average of Nigeria's share is 57.87% (from Table 9.2, the sum of Nigeria's percent ownership in each venture multiplied by the number of barrels produced per day by the venture, all divided by the total number of barrels per day from all ventures). Therefore, of the $0.2887 amount, Nigeria appropriates $0.1671 (0.5787 × 0.2887) or 9.43% of the $1.771 that the customer pays per liter while its partners appropriate the remaining $0.1216 ($0.2887 – 0.1671) or 6.87% of the $1.771. The results are summarized in Table 9.3.

This calculation can be repeated for each OECD country. The results from these calculations are summarized in Table 9.4, and displayed in Figure 9.1. France appropriates more than six times the value that Nigeria appropriates from Nigerian oil and more than eight times the value that Nigeria's oil company partners appropriate. By oil companies, we mean the companies that explore for and find oil, drill for it, lift it (pump it into tankers), transport it to refineries, refine it, distribute it, and sell it—the companies that create most of the value that customers pay for. Germany appropriates a little more than France while Italy and Spain appropriate slightly less than France but still a lot

Table 9.3　What Each Player Gets

Player(s)	Amount appropriated per liter ($)	Percentage appropriated	Comment
The French Government	1.1010	62.17	
Distribution and marketing, and Refining and profits	0.2566	14.49	
Crude oil			
Finding costs, lifting costs and production taxes	0.1247	7.04	
Nigeria	0.1671	9.43	$0.4134 (23.34%)
Venture partners (Shell, Chevron/Texaco, etc) combined	0.1216	6.87	
Total (per liter French price)	1.7710	100.00	

Table 9.4 How Much Does each OECD Member Appropriate from a Gallon of Gasoline?

Country	Value appropriated by country		Distribution, marketing, refining, and profits		Finding costs, lifting costs, production taxes		Value appropriated by Nigeria		Value appropriated by venture partners	
	US$	%	US$	%	US$	%	US$	%	US$	%
France	1.101	62.2	0.2566	14.5	0.1247	7.0	0.1671	9.4	0.1216	6.9
Germany	1.180	62.9	0.2819	15.0	0.1247	6.7	0.1669	8.9	0.1215	6.5
Italy	1.063	58.6	0.3462	19.1	0.1247	6.9	0.1627	9.0	0.1184	6.5
Spain	0.733	50.5	0.3181	21.9	0.1247	8.6	0.1598	11.0	0.1164	8.0
UK (£)	1.246	65.0	0.2449	12.8	0.1247	6.5	0.1744	9.1	0.1270	6.6
Japan (Yen)	0.497	43.5	0.2536	22.2	0.1247	10.9	0.1549	13.6	0.1128	9.9
Canada (C$)	0.294	29.3	0.2961	29.5	0.1247	12.4	0.1680	16.7	0.1223	12.2
USA (US$)	0.105	13.0	0.3278	40.6	0.1247	15.4	0.1449	17.9	0.1055	13.1

| Nigeria | Oil companies' costs & profits | France (62.2%) |

| Nigeria | Oil companies' costs & profits | Germany (62.9%) |

| Nigeria | Oil companies' costs & profits | Italy (58.6%) |

| Nigeria | Oil companies' costs & profits | Spain (50.5%) |

| Nigeria | Oil companies' costs & profits | Japan (43.5%) |

| Nigeria | Oil companies' costs & profits | Canada (29.30%) |

| Nigeria | Oil companies' costs & profits | USA (13.0%) |

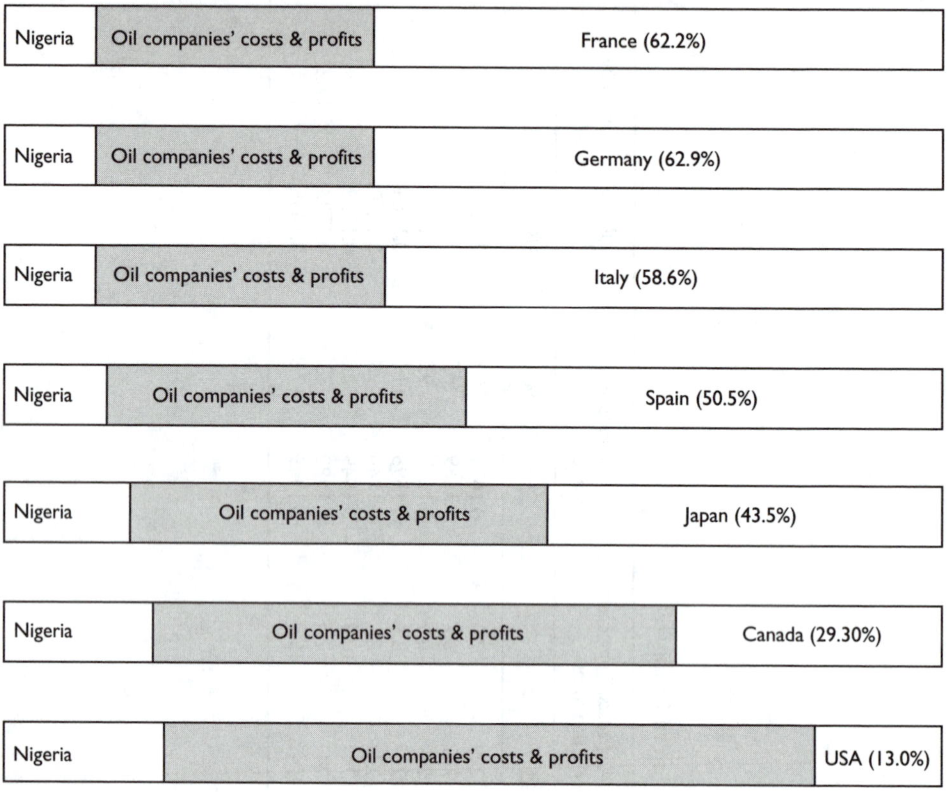

Figure 9.1 Who Appropriates How Much from Nigerian Oil?

more than Nigeria, the oil exporting country. It should be noted that only US federal taxes are included. Including US State taxes could alter the numbers for the USA.

Implications of Government's Insertion into a Value Chain

By imposing a tax on an import or a subsidy on an export, a government is inserting itself into the product's international value chain and influencing the way value is created and appropriated by each player. This can have huge consequences on globalization. We consider the effects of taxes and subsidies separately.

Effect of Import Duties and Taxes

By appropriating 62% of the value in a liter of gasoline, the French government is extracting some consumer surplus from customers as well as some supplier surplus from the oil companies and exporting countries such as Nigeria. (Consumer surplus is the benefit perceived by customers minus the price paid by customers.) How much of the value extracted is supplier surplus and how much is consumer surplus depends on the price elasticity of demand for oil. The *price elasticity of demand* of a product is the change in quantity demanded that results from a change in the product's price. The more elastic the demand, the more that oil suppliers and exporters suffer, since the large taxes reduce the quantity that customers buy. The more inelastic the demand, the more customers suffer, since they still buy a lot of the product, despite higher prices from the high taxes. To illustrate the effect of taxes and value appropriation along an international value chain, let us use the simple but informative illustration of Figure 9.2.[6] If there were no taxes, suppliers would supply the equilibrium quantity Q_E at the equilibrium price P_E. With a tax T, not only does the quantity that is demanded fall from Q_E to Q_T, the price that these suppliers obtain also drops from P_E to P_S. This double whammy of a drop in quantity and price results in a drop in revenues from OP_ERQ_E to OP_SMQ_T. The more elastic the price elasticity of demand, the larger would be the drop in revenues. The drop also means that firms that would have been profitable at prices between P_E and P_S are no longer profitable and likely to go out of business. On their part, the customers who can still afford the high prices get to pay P_C rather than P_E, foregoing P_EP_CNR in consumer surplus that they could have pocketed. Whether the overall effect of taxes on consumers is good or not, depends on what the government does with the money. The effect on suppliers and the supplying country is not good. They lose a supplier surplus of P_EP_SMR.

The demand for the product in Figure 9.2 is elastic, since, for example, the ratio Q_TQ_E/P_CP_E is greater than one, assuming that $OP_E=OQ_E$. If the demand were inelastic, the drop in suppliers' revenues and resulting negative effect on the exporting country would still be there but not as high while the overall effect on consumers would be worse. Returning to the petroleum example, there is some evidence that demand for oil is inelastic in the short run but elastic in the long run. In other words, if the price of gasoline went up today, most people would not, for example, go out and buy a new fuel-efficient car right away, unless they had been planning to buy a car. Rather, they are more likely to keep driving their existing cars but when it is time to buy the next car, they may buy one that is more fuel-efficient. It is also true that some people would forgo that family vacation because of the cost of gas.

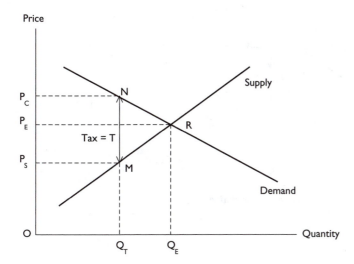

Figure 9.2 Effect of Taxes on Value Appropriation.

Effect of Export Subsidies

A government can also influence globalization activities in an industry by subsidizing exports. An export **subsidy** is an amount that each supplier (exporter) is paid for a certain quantity that it exports. The subsidy can be in the form of a cash payment, a tax break, or the free use of government assets such as land. Subsidies are usually good for the exporters but not for the competitors that the subsidized firms face in the global market. To understand what the impact of export subsidies can be on competitors and the importing country, consider Figure 9.3.[7] Without subsidies, all exporters can sell a quantity Q_E at a price P_E. Suppose a government decides to subsidize its exporters with a subsidy d. With the subsidy, suppliers who would have exported their products at a loss because of their high cost structures can remain in the market because they are now, given the subsidies, getting an effective price of P_S instead of P_E. Because of the subsidy, the price that subsidized exporters charge customers is actually P_C. The overall effect is that more of the product is sold at lower prices than before the subsidy. Customers get lower prices, thanks to the subsidies. However, for suppliers that do not have the subsidies and whose costs are higher than the new subsidized price, subsidies can spell disaster. An example that has been used to illustrate the bad effects of subsidies is that of cotton farmers in Niger and Mali.[8] Many farmers in these countries, most of whom lived on less than a dollar a day, took loans from the World Bank to grow cotton. Because US cotton farmers were subsidized by the US government, they were able to sell cotton in the world market at prices that were well below those of the unsubsidized farmers in Niger and Mali, for example. The result was that farmers from Niger and Mali sold their cotton at a loss and many of them went out of business.

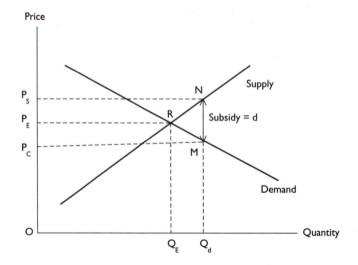

Figure 9.3 Effect of Subsidies on Value Appropriation.

Classifying Value Creators and Appropriators

We can classify members of a value chain as a function of whether they capture more value than they create or create more value than they capture. This classification is shown in Figure 9.4. The vertical axis of the figure captures the extent to which a firm's contribution to value creation is high or low, while the horizontal axis captures the extent to which a firm's value appropriation is low or high. We use animals and insects to represent the different types of player.

Bees

In every value chain, there are usually some firms or individuals who create lots of value but do not get to appropriate a lot of it. Like *bees*, these firms or individuals work very hard all the time to create value but other players capture more it than they deserve, leaving these bees with less than they created (other players take away their honey). From our example above, the companies that find, drill, and pump oil would fall into this category. They capture value, all right; but not as much as they create compared to the exporting and importing governments. As we saw in Chapter 4, there are several reasons why a firm may not be able to capture all the value that it creates. One of these reasons is that the player with more power may capture more value than it creates. In the oil industry case, governments have more power than the oil companies and can therefore appropriate more value than the creators of the value. In countries where governments regulate drug prices, it is possible that pharmaceutical companies appropriate less value than they create when they sell drugs at lower prices than patients or insurance companies and governments may be willing to pay. Where drug prices are not regulated, it is also possible that firms extract

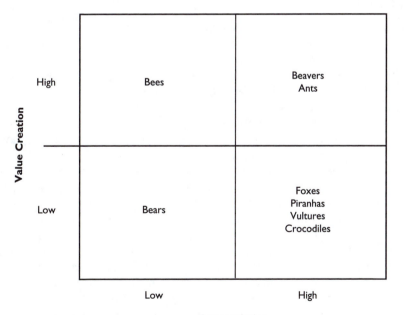

Figure 9.4 Who Appropriates More Value than It Creates?

more from desperate patients than the drugs are worth. It is possible that coffee growers capture very little of the value that coffee drinkers perceive in a cup of coffee. It is also possible that cocoa growers capture only a very small fraction of the value that chocolate lovers perceive in a bar of chocolate.

Beavers (Ants)

In some value chains, the firms that work hard to create value get to appropriate all of it. We liken such firms to *beavers* who work very hard to create value and often derive lots of benefits from their hard work.

Foxes (Piranha, Vulture, Crocodile)

As we saw in the oil industry example, some firms or governments appropriate a lot more value than they create. In some cases, they do not even create value but get to appropriate a lot of it. They reap a lot more than they sowed. Such players are more like *foxes* since they do very little but capture a lot of value. They have been called piranhas, and vultures.

Bears

In their value chains, some firms play niche roles in which they do not care much about having a competitive advantage. They do enough just to get by. They are the opposite of beavers who work all the time. They are more like *bears*. They create very little value and do not appropriate much of it either.

Globalization

Globalization is the interdependence and integration of people, firms, and governments to produce and exchange products and services.[9] It creates opportunities for new jobs, learning, new and improved products/services, increased trade, financial flows, and enhanced standards of living. However, globalization also poses a threat to some businesses, jobs, and ways of living. That is particularly true when globalization is not pursued correctly. If pursued well, globalization can result in improvements in the standard of living of participants—it can be a positive-sum game, that is, if globalization is pursued well, everyone should be better off. If not pursued well, it becomes a zero-sum or even a negative-sum game. That may be one reason why to some people, globalization means the dominance of the rest of the world by a few countries and powerful firms at the expense of local jobs and cultures. And to others, it means exploitation of the poor in developing countries, the destruction of the environment, and the violation of human rights. To advocates of globalization, however, it is a powerful tool for reducing poverty as the world's economies and societies get more and more integrated. Each player has a better chance of creating or adding value to something that someone somewhere in the world values. Each player also has a better chance of finding something that he or she likes.

For a firm, globalization is about asking and answering questions such as: what is the right product space and system of activities—what set of activities meets the need for local responsiveness and exploits the benefits of global integration? How does a firm build the right resources/capabilities from the right countries? How does a firm deal with each country's macroenvironment, especially with the different governments? For an oil firm, for example, deciding which country to explore for oil, working with government officials of the country, investing in the oil fields, locating the right people and equipment, finding the oil, pumping it out, transporting it, dealing with governments of importing countries, and refining and distributing the oil are all globalization issues with which it has to deal.

The Multinational Corporation

A major player in globalization is the multinational corporation. A *multinational* corporation (MNC) is a firm that has market positions and/or resources/capabilities in at least two countries. (From now on, we will use the word "resources" when we really mean "resources/capabilities." We will also use "products" when we really mean "products and services.") MNCs increasingly depend on sales and resources from outside of their home countries. They can be grouped as a function of where they choose to sell their products, and of the resources that they need. This classification is shown in Figure 9.5. In the figure, the vertical axis captures the effect of a firm's market-position. In particular, it captures whether a firm's products and services are sold domestically only or in other countries as well. The horizontal axis captures the extent to which the valuable resources/capabilities that a firm needs to make (conceive, design, develop, and manufacture) the product are domestic only or are also

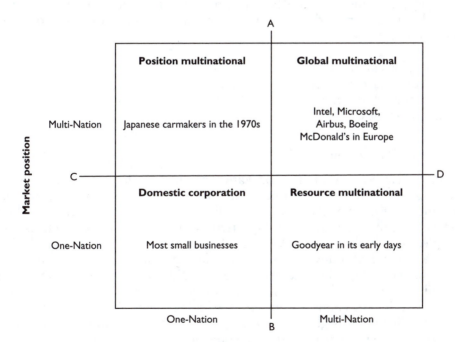

Figure 9.5 Types of Multinational.

foreign. If the resources that a firm needs to make its products are all from its home country and the firm sells all its products within its home country, we call it a *domestic corporation* (Figure 9.5). Many small businesses fall into this category. If a firm designs, develops, and produces its products at home, but sells them in two or more countries, we say the firm is a *position multinational* since it has product-market positions in countries other than its home country. Japanese car companies in the 1960s and 1970s were largely position multinationals. All their cars were designed, developed, and manufactured in Japan and shipped to the US and other countries for sale. When a firm's design, development, and production of a product is done in many countries but the product is sold in only one country, the firm is said to be a *resource multinational* since it depends on more than the home country for its capabilities. Early in the life of US tire companies, they established rubber plantations in different developing countries and shipped the rubber to the USA to be used to make tires that were sold only to domestic car companies. If a firm sells its products in two or more countries and the resources that it needs come from two or more countries, the firm is classified as a *global multinational*. Most of today's major companies fall into this category. Intel's microprocessors are sold all over the world and the company has design centers and microchip fabrication and assembly plants in many countries.

Drivers of Globalization

What makes globalization more likely to take place than not? What drives more cross-border utilization of labor and know-how, exchange of knowledge, movement of capital, trade, human migration, and integration of financial markets and other activities? Four factors influence the process of globalization:

1 Technological innovation
2 Consumer tastes
3 Government policies
4 Firm strategies.

Technological Innovation

One of the largest drivers of globalization has been technological innovation. First, technological innovation has made it possible to develop products that more and more people all over the world like, thereby facilitating trade in these products and the integration of the activities that underpin the products. For example, the cell phone—a technological innovation that is itself a product of many technological innovations—is a product that most people in the world want. The microchips, LCD screen, battery and many components that go into a cell phone are complex systems that require different skills and know-how that many different countries possess. Designing, developing, marketing, selling, and delivering this global product requires the integration of ideas, skills, products, and people from different countries. The same can be said of jet engines, the Internet, jet planes, computers, drugs such as Viagra, Prozac, and Lipitor, and so on.

Second, technological innovation has facilitated communications, capital flows, exchange of know-how, interaction between people and firms, and reduced transportation time and costs. Because of the Internet, designers for a major company in Japan can work on a design, hand it over to fellow designers in Europe before leaving for the day. Before the engineers in Europe go home for the day, they can also hand over the design to engineers in California, who hand over to their Japanese counterparts before going home for the day. The engineers in each of these countries can be of different nationalities who just happen to want to live in the countries. Financial institutions use the Internet and other communications and computer systems to route funds all over the world. These funds can finance international projects from major chip fabrication plants in Silicon Valley or Asia to micro-projects in southern Africa. Availability of the Internet also means that people can compare prices of products and labor from all over the world, often instantaneously. Worldwide telecommunications systems also mean that firms can advertise better and try to harmonize consumer tastes. Lower communications and transportation costs mean that consumers are more exposed to lower-cost products that they may like.

Some of the first innovations to have a huge impact on globalization were in transportation. Motorized ships that ran across the Atlantic Ocean played a major role in the transatlantic migration and trade that were critical to building the American economy. Later, the jet airplane would change world travel not only by transporting people worldwide but also by transporting important business documents in much shorter times. More importantly, ocean transportation has become so cost-effective that steel, as heavy as it is, can be made in Korea and still be cost-competitive in California. Effectively, technological progress moves the vertical line AB in Figure 9.5 leftwards, increasing the zone in which global and resource multinational activities can take place. It also moves the line CD downwards, thereby increasing the zone in which position and global multinational activities can take place.

Consumer Tastes and Needs

Consumer tastes and needs have always been a major driver of globalization. Europeans' taste for spices, for example, was an important reason for their trading with India and why Columbia ended up in the Americas. Diseases in many countries can be cured by medications developed in others. Some of these tastes or needs are dormant until awakened by firms through advertising or the introduction of a new product. Very few people in the world knew that they needed the Internet or cell phones until the products were introduced. Lower communications and transportation costs often mean more availability of low-cost products that can influence consumers' taste. Consumers' tastes can also be influenced by the experiences that they had as a result of innovations in communications and transportation that made it possible for them to travel to other lands, or find out about them via, for example, the Internet.

Government Policies

Government policies play one of the most significant roles of all the drivers of globalization. Governments can use quotas, tariffs, taxes, subsidies, and import duties to stifle or greatly facilitate imports or production. In addition to having an influence on what gets imported, governments can have great influence over what is produced and exported. In some sectors such as healthcare, some governments control prices, and what can or cannot be sold. Governments also influence the other drivers of globalization such as technological innovations in transportation and communications. A country can decide to enforce or not enforce intellectual property protection laws. Governments control the flow of currency and therefore investment capital. A country's ability to protect foreign investments from vandalism or nationalistic activities also plays a role in who invests in the country.

Multinationals' Strategies

Globalization is also driven by the extent to which firms want to take advantage of the other drivers of globalization to create and appropriate value. For example, if a firm's strategy rests on extending its existing core competences to many markets, using worldwide labor, taking advantage of economies of scale, or learning from abroad, the firm may decide to push for globalization. As part of its strategy, a firm may advertise to influence consumer tastes in different countries, or work with policy makers in different countries to obtain legislation that favors globalization. Many multinational corporations have larger budgets than most poor countries and can be very influential when it comes to globalization legislation. They can also innovate to offer the kinds of product that will help consumers discover their latent needs. They can not only influence the flow of capital to their worldwide investment sites but also help bring down trade barriers by influencing policy makers.

Why Firms Go International (Global)

The question is, why would any firm want to enter global markets or expand its existing global activities rather than focus on its home market? Why would any domestic company want to become a multinational? There are several reasons for going global, or expanding globally:

- Search for growth
- Opportunity to stabilize earnings
- High cost of production at home
- Following a buyer
- Offensive move
- Opportunity to take advantage of scale economies
- Easier regulations overseas
- Larger market abroad
- Chance to learn from abroad.

In Search of Growth

If a firm's domestic market is stagnant, declining, too competitive, mature, or not growing fast enough, the firm may see foreign markets as places where it could find the growth that it does not have at home. This is particularly true if the firm's market valuation has factored in growth, and capital markets expect the firm to continue to grow at a rate that the home market cannot support. One of many alternatives is for the firm to diversify into other markets within its home country, unless there are other compelling reasons to go global.

Opportunity to Stabilize Earnings

Since a firm's profits often depend on domestic economic factors, its profits are likely to rise and fall with domestic economic cycles. By going international, a firm may be able to reduce this cyclicality if it can successfully enter a country with the right cyclicality.

High Cost of Production at Home

One of the most common reasons for firms to go international is the high domestic cost of factors of production. For example, the cost of labor for low-tech manufacturing in many western countries and Japan has become so high that many firms in the West move some of their manufacturing activities to China, Taiwan, Korea or India.

Firm May Be Following Buyer

Very often, a firm goes international because its key buyer is going international. Some Japanese auto suppliers moved with the automobile makers when the latter decided to start assembling cars in the USA. When McDonald's entered the Russian market, the J.R. Simplot Company went along to produce potatoes for McDonald's french fries.

Offensive Move

A firm can also start operating in a foreign country to preempt competitors that it believes are likely to enter the foreign country. This is particularly true if there are first-mover advantages to be had in the foreign country.

Economies of Scale and Extension of Capabilities

When a firm offers a product with very high fixed (upfront) costs and very little or no variable costs, every unit sold after the breakeven volume is profit. Going global increases a firm's chances of selling even more units and making even more money. This is particularly true for products such as software that do not need major modifications to suit local tastes and therefore can be sold anywhere in the world at little extra cost. This is also particularly true if the home market is very small relative to the minimum efficient scale of the firm's technology. One reason why many Swiss firms such as Nestlé went international very early was because their home market was too small for the kinds of volume that they needed in order to compete with foreign firms that had larger home markets.

Regulations Overseas May be Easier than at Home

It is not unusual for developing economies to have little or no regulations on safety and environmental pollution, and no anticompetition laws. Some firms may move to these countries to take advantage of these laws.

Larger Market and Free Market Principles

Some markets are simply larger and more free market than others. Thus, firms may enter such markets to take advantage of the large size and free-market atmosphere. The USA is one such country.

Learn from Abroad (Market Idea, Acquire New Skills, etc.)

Although it has traditionally been thought that knowledge flow is one way—from the home country to the host country into which the firm is moving—there is growing recognition that firms can also learn from their host countries and take the knowledge home or to other markets.

Globalization for a Competitive Advantage

Suppose a firm wants to sell its products to a foreign country or take advantage of the resources in the foreign country to produce new products. Is there anything that it can do to increase its chances of having a competitive advantage as a result of the move? A framework for exploring this question is shown in Figure 9.6. As we saw in Chapter 1, a firm's profitability in a market is a function of its PMP and the resources that underpin the position. Recall that a firm's product-market position consists of the benefits (low-cost or differentiated products) that the firm offers and its position vis-à-vis coopetitors. To occupy such a position and perform the relevant activities, a firm needs resources. Thus, we can explore the profitability of a firm's entry into a foreign country as a function of its PMP in the new country and the resources that it uses to create and/or appropriate value in the country (Figure 9.6).

Unique Product-Market Position (PMP)

The vertical axis captures the PMP that the firm occupies—whether the position is unique (white space, sweet spot) or a battlefield. Occupying a *unique* PMP means that a firm (1) offers a product with benefits that no one else in the market segment or country does, and/or (2) performs a distinctive system of activities that underpins the benefits. The benefits can be product features, location, lower cost, or better bang for the buck. The PMP can be unique because of the perceived uniqueness of product features. It can also be unique because of the location or region of the country that the firm serves. The unique position can be in one country or in many countries. Since the benefits that the firm offers its customers are unique, the effect of rivalry on the firm is low, the threat

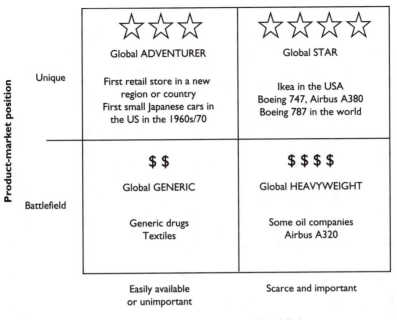

Figure 9.6 Different Global Strategies.

of substitutes is low, and the firm has more power over buyers than it would have if it were in a battlefield. The fact that a firm moves into a unique position does not tell us much about barriers to entry or its position vis-à-vis suppliers but there are things that the firm can do to raise barriers to entry into its unique space and increase its power over coopetitors. For example, it can pursue first-mover advantages such as building switching costs at customers. Building a brand that is associated with the unique space can also raise barriers to entry.

A *battlefield* is a product-market space that already has players. Such players have usually been in the market long enough to have developed rivalries, understandings, cooperative relationships and other capabilities to create and appropriate value in the market. Why would anyone enter a battlefield? Although battlefields can be rife with competition, they have some advantages. Technological and marketing uncertainties are usually reduced and a new entrant with important complementary assets may be able to do well. A firm may also enter because it has distinctive resources that it uses to give it an advantage in the foreign country. Many firms do enter battlefields. Some do so because they believe that there is something distinctive about them that will allow them to win when they come in. Others do so because of other strategic reasons. In any case, a firm is usually better off pursuing a unique PMP.

Valuable Global Resources/Capabilities

The horizontal axis of Figure 9.6 captures the type of major global resources/capabilities that a firm utilizes to conceive of, design, manufacture, market the product, and position itself to make money—whether the resources are scarce and important, or easily available or unimportant. Resources are *scarce and important* if they are difficult to imitate or substitute, and make a significant contribution towards value creation or appropriation. These resources can be in a firm's home country, in the foreign country that the firm is entering, or worldwide. Examples of scarce and important resources include exclusive rights to explore oil in oil-producing countries, relationships with government officials in foreign countries, patents in pharmaceuticals, shelf space in offline stores, some major brands, a large network in an industry that exhibits network externalities, etc. Such resources therefore stand to give a firm a competitive advantage. If the resources are important but easy to imitate, their owners quickly lose any advantage that they may have had as competitors swoop in, making it difficult to appropriate any value that a firm may have created using the important resources. An example of resources that are important but easy to imitate is low-tech manufacturing capabilities. They are important but because they are usually easy to imitate and therefore easily available, we classify them as "easily available or unimportant" in Figure 9.6.

Global Strategy Types

Depending on whether a firm decides to pursue a unique PMP or enter a battle-field, has scarce difficult-to-imitate resources or can build them, a firm's strategy falls into one of the following four categories: *global adventurer, global star, global heavyweight*, and *global generic* (Figure 9.6).

Global Adventurer

In a *global adventurer* strategy, a firm enters a country or countries by occupy-ing a unique PMP, but the major resources/capabilities that it uses to create and appropriate value are easily available or unimportant. The product that embodies the unique value can target one country or many countries. The product can be made in the foreign country or in the home country and exported to the foreign country. Many exports that target an unmet need in a country fall into this category. Japanese automobile makers were utilizing a global adventurer strategy when they exported fuel-efficient dependable cars to the USA during the 1970s when US automakers GM, Ford, American Motors, and Chrysler focused on making larger and less fuel-efficient cars. All the major resources for the cars were Japanese and although it may not feel that way today, selling small Japanese cars in the USA in the late 1960s through the 1970s was an adventure.

A retailer that builds the first retail store in a region of a foreign country is pursuing an adventurer strategy. Whether the global adventurer strategy works for a firm is a function of the drivers of globalization—a function of techno-logical developments, consumer tastes, government policies, firm's corporate strategy, and the type of product in question. Take the example of Japanese cars in the USA in the 1970s. Shipping technology had improved to a point where cars could be shipped cost-efficiently from Japan to California, 5,500 miles away. Because of the oil crises in the USA in the 1970s, some consumers were interested in looking at fuel-efficient dependable cars. US government policies were less protective at the time, compared to those of the governments of other rich countries; that is, until the US government imposed a quota on Japanese cars. There had also been attempts by Japan's powerful Ministry of International Trade and Industry (MITI) to prevent Honda from entering the car production business at home. An important part of Honda's strategy was to expand abroad and the large US market, where it had been selling motorcycles, presented some good opportunities. Its chances of growing profitably were better in the USA than in Japan.

A unique PMP gives a global adventurer some opportunities to take advantage of the new gameness of the position, including first-mover advantages. Honda went on to build a brand that associated the company with zippy engines and dependable reliable low-cost cars. It then, together with Toyota and Nissan, introduced luxury cars to compete with BMW, Mercedes, and other luxury imports to the USA. Honda introduced the Acura, Nissan the Infiniti, and Toyota the Lexus.

The primary advantage to the global adventurer strategy is the fact that it identifies and focuses on a unique PMP with its associated benefits and shortcomings. There is one major drawback to the strategy. Since the resources that a global adventurer uses are easily available or unimportant, the unique PMP can be easily imitated unless the firm takes steps to build first-mover advantages that raise barriers to entry.

Global Star

In a *global star* strategy, a firm enters a country or countries by occupying a unique product-market space, and the global resources/capabilities that it uses to create and appropriate value are scarce and important. Thus, pursuing a star strategy gives a firm both the advantages of having a unique PMP and scarce important resources. Ikea's strategy for entering the US market in the 2000s is an example. It occupied a unique position, relative to its competitors (fun shopping experience, low-cost but fashionable furniture, no delivery, little in-store service, and furniture that was not guaranteed to last forever), and had a scarce and important worldwide network of experienced designers, and an ability to coordinate and integrate the activities of its suppliers of materials and manufacturers worldwide.[10] Strategies for both the Airbus A380 and the Boeing 787 also fall into this category. Each occupies a unique spot on the PMP maps for airplanes and the resources needed to offer the plans are scarce and important. Often, one of the important capabilities of a global star is its ability to coordinate and integrate resources and know-how from different countries and differing cultures. Making both the A380 and Boeing 787 required coordination of many different resources and capabilities from different countries. This coordination and integration is facilitated by technological innovation.

Global Heavyweight

In a *global heavyweight* strategy, a firm enters a country or countries by confronting existing competitors, but has scarce and important resources/capabilities that it uses to create and appropriate value. The resources can be from one country or many countries. Such a firm is effectively in a battlefield where it confronts existing industry firms in creating and appropriating value, using its scarce resources. When an oil company goes into a country where other companies are already exploiting for oil and obtains exploration rights to find and sell oil to the world, it is employing a global heavyweight strategy. Airbus pursued a global heavyweight strategy when it introduced its A320 airplanes. The plane was designed to compete directly with the Boeing 737 and the McDonnell Douglas DC 9 and MD-80. While some of the technological know-how to build the plane may have been easily available, the A320 fly-by-wire technology was the first in the category of planes. Moreover, coordinating the activities of the makers of major airplane components from French, German, and British companies was no easy task. Many of the ideas utilized in McDonald's restaurants in each European country came not only from the country and the USA, but also from other European countries.[11]

Global Generic

In a *global generic* strategy, a firm enters a country or countries by confronting existing competitors, and the major resources/capabilities that it uses are easily available or unimportant. Firms that produce commodity products in low-cost labor nations and export them to other countries to compete with other commodity products from other countries are pursuing this strategy. Many producers of generic drugs for export usually have generic strategies; so do makers of textiles. Many products are usually introduced to a foreign country through exports that were designed, developed, and produced at the home country and exported to the foreign country. As the product gains acceptance, local resources are built to respond better to local differences.

Using New Games to Gain a Competitive Advantage

If a firm's chances of having a sustainable competitive advantage are best when it pursues a global star strategy rather than the other three strategies, why can't all firms pursue the same global star strategy? One reason is that not every firm has the two drivers of success in pursuing each of these strategies: (1) the firm's strengths and handicaps in the face of the new game, (2) its ability to take advantage of the characteristics of new games to create and appropriate value.

Strengths and Handicaps

Recall from Chapter 5 that when a firm faces a new game, it usually has prenew game strengths that can continue to be strengths in the face of the new game or become handicaps. For a domestic company that is going multinational by offering the same products that it offered at home to other countries, two obvious strengths are the firm's domestic PMP and resources. If a firm offers a low-cost product domestically, it can usually take the resources that enabled it to produce the low-cost products to the foreign country or sell a version of the low cost product in the foreign country. Effectively, if a firm's domestic resources are scarce and important in the foreign market, they can become the bases for the firm to pursue a global star or heavyweight strategy. If the domestic PMP is the basis for occupying a unique market segment or position in the foreign country, the firm can pursue a global adventurer or star strategy.

When Toyota and Honda decided to enter the US automobile market, they used both their domestic resources and products to enter. When McDonald's entered foreign countries, many potential customers in the foreign countries had already visited the firm's stores in the USA or were Americans visiting the foreign country or moving there to work. Intel's domestic capabilities in microprocessors and worldwide acceptance of its PC enabled it to establish chip design centers, fabrication and assembly in countries outside the USA to make and sell its products to anyone anywhere in the world. Effectively, if a domestic company has distinctive domestic products and resources, it can build on them to become a multinational.

A firm's strengths at home can also turn out to be handicaps in foreign countries. McDonald's all-American image, which is a strength in the USA, did not play well at first in France.[12]

Ability to Take Advantage of New Game Characteristics

The extent to which a firm can gain a competitive advantage in going international is also a function of the extent to which it takes advantage of the new game characteristics of going international. Recall that new games present a firm with an opportunity to:

- Take advantage of the new ways of creating and capturing new value generated by the new game.
- Take advantage of opportunities generated by the new game to build new resources or translate existing ones in new ways.
- Take advantage of first-mover's advantages and disadvantages, and competitors' handicaps that result from the new game.
- Anticipate and respond to coopetitors' reactions to its actions.
- Identify and take advantage of opportunities and threats from the macroenvironment.

Take Advantage of the New Ways of Creating and Capturing New Value

When a firm decides to go international, it has to locate customers, offer them benefits, and position itself to appropriate the value so created. In doing so, it has the option to occupy a unique product-market space or challenge existing competitors in the country. As we saw above, a unique PMP has the advantage that it is, on average, more attractive than a battlefield—the competitive forces in a unique position are more friendly compared to those in a battlefield with seasoned competitors. However, a firm with distinctive domestic resources that can be transferred to the foreign country to address the needs of customers in the battlefield may be able to enter the battlefield and do well. For example, up to the late 1980s, the US luxury car market had been dominated by BMW, Mercedes, Audi, and Cadillac. Toyota, Nissan, and Honda challenged these incumbents using capabilities that they had built serving the low-end market. Toyota introduced its Lexus line of products in 1989 and using its design, lean manufacturing know-how, relationships with suppliers, and marketing, it won many awards. A firm may also choose to enter a battlefield by using technological innovations that render existing products in the market noncompetitive, or render existing resources obsolete. For example, cell phone technology allowed many firms all over the world to compete successfully head-on with incumbent fixed-line telephone companies and win.

Take Advantage of Opportunities to Build New Resources or Translate Existing Ones in New Ways

Different countries are endowed with different resources or levels of resources. Some countries have oil, others have gold, some have low-cost labor, others high-tech know-how, and so on. The level of the resource varies from one country to the other. For example, the level of high-tech know-how varies even within the group of so-called high-tech countries. Thus, when a firm goes international, it has an opportunity to acquire new resources in the foreign country or bring in resources from its home country. Sometimes, these new resources are distinctive, and a firm can use them to produce and market its products in many countries. For example, oil companies can acquire the rights to explore for oil in different oilfields in different countries. If they are successful, these oil companies own the wells (often in partnership with local governments) and can refine, distribute, and sell the oil from the wells in any country. In going international, a firm can also build strong relationships with government officials to influence legislation and public opinion about its products or presence in the country.

When a firm goes international, it can also use some of its domestic resources to create and appropriate value in the foreign country. Such a firm is effectively translating its resources in new ways.

Take Advantage of First-mover's Advantages and Disadvantages, and Competitors' Handicaps that Result from New Game

If a firm is the first to offer a particular product in a country, it has the opportunity to build and take advantage of first-mover advantages. Such first-mover advantages are particularly important when a finite resource is involved. For example, if a firm is the first to go to a foreign country and discover oil or any other precious material, it has the opportunity preemptively to secure rights to the oil well and exploration rights to nearby properties. Such fields are usually limited and once they have been taken, there may be few or none left. The firm also has an opportunity to form partnerships with government-owned companies such as the "national oil companies" of oil-exporting countries. Moreover, a firm that discovers minerals in a country first and forms partnerships with the government is ahead of the learning curve for exploration in the particular geology and in working with local officials. The firm also has an opportunity to shape regulation, and even the educational system as far as the particular industry is concerned.

In industries where network effects are important, a first mover into a country has an opportunity to build a large network with the right properties, and use the network to its advantage. In online auctions, for example, the more people that belong to an online auction community such as eBay's, the more valuable it is to each member and the more that new potential members are likely to gravitate towards the community. In the countries where eBay was the first to establish an online auction community, it did very well. In the one country where it was not the first—Japan—it did not do as well. Yahoo was the first to move to Japan in the auctions category and did very well.

In retail, for example, when a firm is the first to enter a country or region, it has an opportunity preemptively to take up the good retail locations. If the first mover builds the right number of stores and provides the right service, rational potential second movers would think twice before trying to build in these locations, if to do so would result in price wars and unhealthy rivalry. In some cases, the opposite may happen. Burger King usually locates near McDonalds.

Finally, if a firm moves into a country first, it has an opportunity to hire the best employees first and work with them to build the type of culture that will keep them at the firm, depriving followers of one of the cornerstones of the success of any company.

Anticipate and Respond to Coopetitors' Reactions to its Actions

In going international, it is also important for a firm to anticipate the likely reaction of competitors. If the firm chooses to enter a unique PMP, it is important to think of what competitors are likely to do when they find out that the firm is making money in the unique space. If competing oil companies find out that an oil company has found oil somewhere, they are likely to want to come in. Anticipation of such reactions by competitors is one reason why a firm may want to intensify its efforts to build and take advantage of first-mover advantages since they increase barriers to entry. McDonalds should know that Burger King will be coming and should prepare accordingly.

If a firm chooses to enter a battlefield, incumbents in the field will either fight the entry, forget about it, or cooperate. If the firm believes that incumbents will fight its entry, it can pursue one of several options. First, it can enter and fight if it has the scarce resources that will give it an advantage over incumbents. It can also enter and fight if it is using a disruptive technology or any other innovation that stands to render incumbents' existing products noncompetitive or their resources obsolete. Second, the firm can decide to move into a unique space rather than take on the fight. If the firm believes that incumbents will leave it alone when it enters, it may want to enter but only after assuring itself that the market will be large enough to support its entry and that incumbents might not change their minds and become hostile. If incumbents want to cooperate, the firm may want to enter. The question is, why would incumbents want to cooperate? They may be forced by government regulations to allow entry. In that case, the firm can enter but understand that the competitive forces from rivalry, potential new entry, etc. may still be higher than being in a unique product space. Firms in a market may also welcome entry if they are forced by a powerful buyer to have second sources.

Identify and Take Advantage of Opportunities and Threats of MacroEnvironment

When going international, a firm is moving from one country's political, economic, social, and technological system to another. Differences between home country macroenvironment and foreign macroenvironments can be considerable. In some countries, governments can shut down businesses or nationalize them for no good reason and the businesses have no legal recourse, while in other countries government actions against businesses have to have a legal basis and the firms have the right to challenge the government in a fair court system. In some countries, copyrights, patents, trademarks, and other intellectual property are respected and their protection monitored and enforced by the government. In other countries there is very little or no intellectual property protection. In some countries, governments have extra entry and exit barriers beyond those dictated by the type of industry. In many countries, governments play some role in the merger and acquisition of firms but in others, some governments may take a more nationalistic than economic approach.[13] Some governments pay attention to the natural environment and corporate social responsibility while others do not. The list of differences goes on and on. In any case, a firm that is going international may want to pay attention to the political, economic, social, and technological environment of the foreign country into which it is moving for any opportunities and threats of which it may want to take advantage. For example, if a firm depends on its intellectual property protection to give it a sustainable competitive advantage at home where violation of such protections are prosecuted, the firm may have to find another cornerstone for its competitive advantage or lobby the foreign government for changes in its laws. The other side of the coin is that a firm that always wanted to enter an industry but could not because of intellectual property protection at home can move to a country where such protections are less restrictive. Some generic manufacturers of pharmaceuticals locate where patent protection for some drugs is, for national security and other reasons, not as strong as in the USA.

Privatization and deregulation in foreign countries, and technological change in general often pose opportunities and threats for a firm that is going international. In privatization, businesses that were owned by a government are sold to the private sector (individuals or businesses). Privatization presents an opportunity for a firm to enter a country and take over existing assets and products. Because government-owned businesses are often state monopolies, buying them gives a firm a chance to operate as a near monopoly or as part of a duopoly. The disadvantage is that the culture at government-owned firms may not be conducive to competing for profits, and changing such a culture can be very difficult. In deregulation, governments simplify, reduce, or eliminate restrictions on the way firms conduct business to increase efficiency and to lower prices for consumers. The easing or elimination of restrictions can create an opportunity for a firm to move into the deregulating country in a profitable way. For example, as we saw in Chapter 2, Ryanair took advantage of European Union deregulation of the airline industry in the Union to build a profitable business. Technological innovation also presents opportunities for firms that are going international. The case of cell phones in countries where fixed-line telephones, run by government monopolies, had failed illustrates how the combination of privatization, deregulation, and technological innovation can make a big difference in a foreign country. For example, in Nigeria, Gabon, Kenya, and Cameroon where governments deregulated and privatized tele-coms, foreign companies entered with cell phone businesses in each country and did very well.

Key Takeaways

- At the international level, governments can capture a lot of the value that firms create.
- Actors (firms and governments) can be classified as a function of whether they create the value that they capture: bees create lots of value but others capture most of what they create. Beavers create lots of value and capture most of it. Foxes create little or no value but capture a lot of the value created by others. Bears create little value and capture little too.
- Government-imposed taxes and subsidies can result in value destruction.
- **Globalization** is the interdependence and integration of people, firms, and governments to produce and exchange products and services.
- A key character in globalization is the MNC. This is a firm that has established PMPs and/or resources/capabilities in at least two countries. A firm is a *position multinational* if it designs, develops, and produces its products at home, but sells them in two or more countries. If a firm's design, development, and production of a product is done in many countries but the product is sold in only one country, the firm is said to be a *resource multinational*. If a firm has market positions in two or more companies and the resources that it needs come from two or more countries, the firm is classified as a *global multinational*.
- The extent to which globalization takes place in an industry is a function of:
  - Technological innovation
  - Consumer tastes and needs
  - Government policies
  - Multinationals' strategies.
- Some reasons for firms going global or expanding globally include:
  - The search for growth
  - Opportunity to stabilize earnings
  - High cost of production at home
  - Following a buyer
  - Offensive move
  - Opportunity to take advantage of scale economies
  - Easier regulations overseas
  - Larger market abroad
  - Chance to learn from abroad.
- In using new games to go international, a firm can locate in a unique product-market space where it offers unique value to customers and has few competitors, or can enter a battlefield where there are already competitors. The resources that a firm uses to create and appropriate value in a unique

product space or battlefield can be either scarce and important resources, or easily available or unimportant. In going international, four strategies are possible:

- In a *global adventurer* strategy, a firm enters a country or countries by occupying a unique product-market space, but the major resources/capabilities that it uses to create and appropriate value are easily available or unimportant.
- In a *global star* strategy, a firm enters a country or countries by occupying a unique product-market space, and the global resources/capabilities that it uses to create and appropriate value are scarce and important.
- In a *global heavyweight* strategy, a firm enters a country or countries by confronting existing competitors, but has scarce and important resources/ capabilities that it uses to create and appropriate value.
- In a *global generic* strategy, a firm enters a country or countries by confronting existing competitors, and the major resources/capabilities that it uses are easily available or unimportant.

- If a firm's chances of having a sustainable competitive advantage are best when it pursues a global star strategy rather than the other three strategies, why can't all firms pursue the same global star strategy? One reason is that not every firm has the two drivers of success in pursuing these new game strategies:

  1 A firm may not have the right strengths and handicaps—from its existing PMP and resources/capabilities—in the face of the new game.
  2 A firm may not have the ability to take advantage of the characteristics of new games to create and appropriate value. It may not be able to:

     - Take advantage of the new ways of creating and capturing new value generated by the new game.
     - Take advantage of opportunities generated by the new game to build new resources or translate existing ones in new ways.
     - Take advantage of first-mover's advantages and disadvantages, and competitors' handicaps that result from the new game.
     - Anticipate and respond to coopetitors' reactions to its actions.
     - Identify and take advantage of opportunities and threats from the macroenvironment.

Key Terms

Bears
Beavers
Bees
Drivers of globalization
Foxes
Global adventurer
Global generic
Global heavyweight
Global multinational

Global star
Multinational
Position multinational
Resource multinational

Appendix: Value Appropriation of Oil by the UK

Suppose you did not have the OECD data and wanted to calculate how much the UK appropriated from each liter of gasoline bought there. The UK had a value added tax (VAT) of 17.5% on all imported oil. It also had a tax (duty) of 47.1 pence (US$0.942) per liter of gasoline (petrol) that went in force in October 2003 and was expected to go up.[14] In June 2007, the price of a liter of gasoline in the UK averaged 96.38 pence (US$1.9276).[15] A 2006 US Department of Energy report had shown that distribution and marketing accounted for 9% of the $2.27/gallon gasoline in the USA in 2005, state and federal taxes for 19%, crude oil for 53%, while refining costs and profits accounted for 19%.[16]

(Additional data: in June 2007, the British pound was worth $2 and there are 0.2642 US gallons to the liter. There are 158.97 liters to the barrel or 42 US gallons to the barrel.)

Question

How much of the value in a liter of petrol (gasoline) sold in the UK was captured (1) by the UK Government, (2) by the oil companies.

Solution

An oil value chain consists of four major stages: exploration (and associated finding costs), extraction and shipping (and associated lifting costs, production taxes, and transportation costs), refining (refining costs), and marketing and distribution (marketing and distribution costs, taxes).

For simplicity, we perform all the calculations in US dollars.

In 2007 customers in the UK paid $1.9276 for a liter of gasoline. The UK government's share of the $1.9276 per liter was:

1 US$0.942 duty tax (from UK tax of 47.1 pence per liter ($0.942 per liter, since £1 = $2)).
2 $0.287089 VAT (from 1.9276 − (1.9276/1.175)). This reflects the fact that the $1.9276 price of a gallon is 117.5%, not 100%, since VAT is 17.5%.
3 Therefore, for each US$1.9276 liter of gasoline sold in the UK in 2007, the UK government appropriated 0.942 + 0.287089 = $1.229089.
4 Percentage of value appropriated by UK government = (1.229089/1.9276) = 63.76%.

The remaining $0.698511 per liter ($1.9276 − $1.229089) or 36% has to be shared by (a) the oil companies that explore for crude oil, drill, pump and transport it to refineries (b) the refiners (often oil companies) where it is refined, marketed, and transported to gas stations for sale to customers, and the gas station's take, and (c) the exporting country. Since there is no UK data on what fraction of the remaining 36% (after UK Taxes) goes for crude, refining, exporting country taxes, etc., we will use the US fractions. From the 2006 US data provided, distribution and marketing accounted for 9% of the cost of gasoline, state and federal taxes for 19%, crude oil for 53%, while refining costs and profits accounted for 19%. What we need here to help us with our estimates for the UK, are the ratios of distribution and marketing crude oil, and refining costs and profits without US state and federal taxes. Without taxes, these three are 81% of the cost of gasoline. There:

1   Distribution and marketing represent 11.11% (0.09/0.81).
2   Crude oil represents 65.43% (0.53/0.81).
3   Refining costs and profits represents 23.46% (0.19/0.81).

Recall that $0.698511 per liter ($1.9276 – $1.229089) or 36% represents distribution and marketing (including gas station costs and profits), crude oil costs, and refining and profits. Of the $0.698511 per liter,

a   Distribution and marketing = $0.0776 ($0.698511 × 0.1111) which is 4.03% of the $1.9276 per liter cost (0.0776/1.9276).
b   Crude oil = $0.4571 ($0.698511 × 0.6543) which is 23.71% of the $1.9276 per liter cost (0.4571/1.9276).
c   Refining costs and profits = $0.1638 ($0.698511 × 0.2346) which is 8.50% of the $1.9276 per liter cost (0.1638/1.9276).

In other words, of the $1.9276 that customers in the UK paid for a liter of gasoline in 2007, the government appropriated $1.229089 (63.76%), distribution and marketing captured $0.0776 (4.03%), crude oil took $0.4571 (23.71%), and refining and profits were $0.1638 (8.50%).

Now that we know what fraction of the $1.9276 per liter goes to crude production and transportation, we can determine the exporting country's share.

Per barrel calculations:

Cost of oil extraction = $19.83 ($15.25 finding costs + $3.57 lifting costs + $1.00 production taxes) per barrel = ($19.83/158.97) per liter = $0.1247 per liter.

The amount left for oil companies for their profits, other costs, and royalties for the UK government is $0.4571 – $0.1247 = $0.3323 per liter. These numbers are summarized in Table 9.5.

Table 9.5 What Each Player Appropriates

Player(s)	Amount appropriated per liter ($)	Percentage appropriated	Comment
The UK Government (Duty and VAT)	1.229089	63.76	
Distribution and marketing	0.077600	4.03	
Refining and profits	0.163800	8.50	
Crude oil			
Finding costs, lifting costs, and production taxes	0.124700	6.47	
Oil company profits, UK royalties, other costs	0.332400	17.24	$0.4571 (23.71%)
Total (per liter UK price)	1.927600	100.00	

Chapter 10

New Game Environments and the Role of Governments

Reading this chapter should provide you with the conceptual and analytical tools to:

- Understand how macroenvironments can be the source of opportunities and threats for new games.
- Understand what makes some environments more conducive to innovation and wealth creation than others.
- Understand why governments have a role to play in business and what that role is.
- Appreciate the role that governments must play in creating new-game friendly environments.

Introduction

Firms and the industries in which they create and appropriate value do not function in a vacuum. They are influenced by their macroenvironments—the technological, political-legal, demographic, sociocultural, economic, and natural environments (PESTN) in which firms and industries operate (Figure 10.1). Macroenvironments are often the source of opportunities and threats to firms and their industries. For example, regulation and deregulation both increase or decrease barriers to entry and therefore influence industry dynamics and opportunities to make money. Witness deregulation of the airline industry in the European Union which gave rise to many low-cost startup airlines. Also witness the deregulation and privatization of phone services in developing countries such as Cameroon and Kenya that have allowed wireless phone service businesses to thrive in these countries. National and international economic factors such as interest rates, exchange rates, employment, income, and productivity also impact industry competitiveness and therefore the types of new game activities that can be performed. For example, income growth may increase some customers' willingness to pay for certain products, making these customers more precious to firms that are able to offer them the type of value that they want. As globalization increases, the opportunities to pursue new game strategies and the threat to existing business models increase. In this chapter, we explore the role of macroenvironments as sources of opportunity and threats for new games, and examine the role that governments can play to help firms create and appropriate value. We start the chapter with a description of macroenvironments and their role as a source of opportunities and threats to

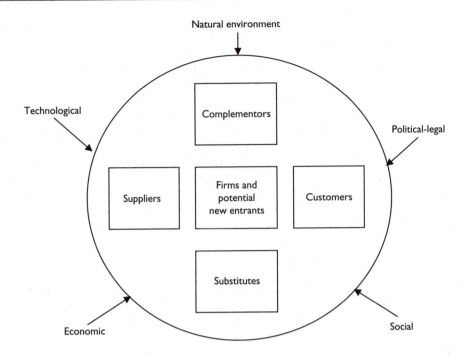

Figure 10.1 The Macroenvironment.

new games. We then explore those characteristics of some environments that make them more conducive to innovation than others. Next, we explore the rationale for why governments have a role to play, and examine what that role is in the face of new games.

Macroenvironments as Sources of Opportunity and Threat

The macroenvironment—made up of the technological, political-legal, socio-demographic, economic, and natural environments—is a source of opportunities and threats that firms can exploit using new game activities.

Technological Environment

Some of the best opportunities to perform new game activities have been driven by technological change. The change from mainframe computers to personal computers gave many firms the opportunity to overturn the way value had been created and appropriated in the computer industry. For example, startup software developers such as Microsoft pursued new business models in which they focused on software alone rather than software and hardware, as had been the practice in the computer industry. Hardware and software makers also sold their products rather than lease them as had been practiced by many firms. The discovery of DNA laid the foundation for the creation of many biotech firms and is fundamentally changing many activities, from the way pharmaceutical firms pursue cures for different ailments to how crimes are solved. The invention of the Internet spurred the creation of many firms, changed the way many so-called offline firms perform their activities, and had a big influence on the lifestyles of many consumers.

The invention of railways, steamships, airplanes, steel, cement, transistors, microchips, alternating current, and numerous other inventions also presented opportunities for new firms to be created and for new ways of creating and appropriating value. At the same time, however, these opportunities were threats to existing technologies and the incumbent firms whose competitive advantages were rooted in the older technologies. Railroads were a threat to the horse-driven carts, the transistor was a threat to the vacuum tube and associated businesses, the Internet is a threat to some bricks-and-mortar businesses, and so on. In many cases, the technological change was at the periphery of value creation but played a role in positioning a firm. For example, one reason for the success of Dell's build-to-order business model was the Internet.

Political-legal Environment

The political-legal environment includes antitrust regulation, tax laws, foreign trade regulation, and employee protection laws. The political-legal environment can have tremendous influence on the way new value is created. Consider the case of the Bayh–Dole Act in the USA. Before 1980, the intellectual property rights to any discoveries or inventions that universities and other nonprofit organizations made while performing federally-sponsored research belonged to the US Federal government. The government effectively appropriated most of the value created. On December 12, 1980, the Bayh–Dole Act or Patent and Trademark Law Amendments Act, sponsored by Senators Birch Bayh of Indiana and Robert Dole of Kansas was passed.[1] Among other things, the Bayh–Dole act, which was amended in 1984 and 1986, gave US small businesses, universities, and nonprofit organizations intellectual property rights to any discoveries and inventions made using federal funds. The idea was to give academic researchers an incentive to commercialize and profit from their inventions and discoveries. The Act effectively transferred ownership of discoveries and inventions from the government that sponsored them to the firms that performed the R&D. It also insured that individual researchers who did the work benefited. Prior to Bayh–Dole, only about 5% of the patents accumulated to the government were commercialized. In December 2005, over 4,500 firms, with roots at universities and other nonprofit organizations, had been founded based on patents generated as a result of Bayh–Dole.[2] In 2004 alone, American universities and institutes received $1.39 billion in licensing-fee revenues. They also applied for over 10,000 new patents. Other developed countries, including Germany and Japan, adopted similar acts. This apparent success has had some costs to universities and the spread of knowledge. Many academics now hesitate to reveal all the results of their research while others have been accused of paying too much attention to commercial ends rather than the knowledge for knowledge's own sake that universities are supposed to be all about. Given how much money some universities now make from their research, there now are some questions as to whether such universities should still hold onto their non-commercial research tax exemption status.

Economic Environment

Economic variables such as aggregate demand and supply for key commodities such as oil, currency movements, stock market performance, disposable incomes, interest rates, money supply, inflation, and unemployment can also represent opportunities and threats for firms. For example, when housing values in a country appreciate, as was the case in the early 2000s in the USA and Europe, house owners feel richer and spend more. An appreciation in the value of shareholders' stocks also makes them feel richer and increases their willingness to pay.[3] One estimate is that an increase in housing values of $100 can increase spending by as much as $9 while an increase of $100 in stock market values increases spending by $4.[4] Increased stock market or housing wealth can also mean more money for financing new ventures. Of course, a burst in a bubble spells trouble; that is, decreases in housing values are also likely to decrease spending.

The petroleum crisis of the 1970s resulted in more demand for vehicles with higher gas mileage than US automakers could build. This opened up an opportunity for Japanese carmakers with more fuel-efficient cars than their American competitors to gain market share. Sometimes, the opportunity is created by an innovation that takes advantage of existing macroeconomic conditions. For example, Professor C.K. Prahalad of the University of Michigan has argued that although billions of people in the world earn very little money, they constitute a large market that can be tapped through innovation of new products that can meet the needs of this group of innovations in how to get the products to them.

Sociocultural and Demographic Environments

Demographic variables include shifts in populations, age distributions, ethnic mixes, educational levels, lifestyle changes, consumer activism, birthrates, life expectancies, and household patterns in cities, regions, and countries. A change in any of these variables can be an opportunity or threat to performing new game activities. For example, as many people who started using the Internet as children grow older, firms will have to deal with many consumers who do not think much about shopping online or telecommuting.

Sociocultural variables include the beliefs, norms, and values of consumers, countries, communities, or employees. Because beliefs, norms, and values are difficult to detect, opportunities and threats that come from changes in sociocultural variables are usually some of the most difficult to detect.

Natural Environment

The natural environment consists of the air that we breathe, the water that sustains all life, climate, landscapes, grasslands, forests, wildlife, animals, oceans, mineral resources, and any other living or nonliving things that occur naturally on earth and its surroundings. When firms perform business activities, the activities often have an impact on the natural environment. For example, some activities result in the pollution of air, water, or soil. Such pollution can have major effects on climate, other resources, and ultimately the quality of life or survival of living things. Other activities use up nonrenewable or scarce resources. Consequently, businesses often face pressure from environmentalist groups or laws from governments to limit the adverse effects that business activities have on the environment. Moreover, the natural environment should have an effect on how firms conduct business. While some firms might view, for example, pressure to reduce pollution as a threat, others might see it as an opportunity to use new game activities to offer products whose development, production, and use pollute less than existing ones.

Conducive Environments to Value Creation and Appropriation

In playing its role to improve the ability of its firms to create and appropriate value, it would be nice if governments knew what makes some environments more conducive to creating wealth from new games than others. That way, these governments could tailor their activities towards building such environments. In the 1990s and 2000s, many countries poured billions of dollars into so-called high technology clusters, trying to replicate the success of the USA's Silicon Valley. In 2005, for example, the French government planned to pour €500 million per year, from 2006 to 2008, into its sixteen clusters, from aerospace to biotechnology, collectively called the *poles de compétitivité*.[5] Most of the €500 million was spent on industry R&D. By the late 2000s, however, many countries were finding out that although they invested a lot in these clusters and produced lots of patents and academic papers, they were not creating as much wealth as the Silicon Valley.[6] They had no Intels, Apples, Genentechs, Ciscos, Yahoos, Googles, eBays, etc. etc. to show for their efforts. As we argued in Chapters 4 and 5, when a cluster invents or discovers something, the invention or discovery is only the first step in creating and appropriating value. The invention or discovery still has to be converted into something that customers perceive as valuable to them, and the inventor or followers (from the cluster) must also be positioned to appropriate the value. Clusters also need complementary assets and good business models to create wealth for cluster members; otherwise, their inventions would be appropriated by firms from other countries that have the right complementary assets and business models. In general, environments that are conducive not only to invention but also to the right business models, and have the right complementary assets possess the following attributes (Figure 10.2):

1 High financial rewards for successful new games.
2 Financial support for entrepreneurial activities.
3 A culture that tolerates failure.
4 The right coopetitors.
5 A procreative destruction environment.

High Financial Rewards For Successful New Games

New game activities are risky and therefore the payoff for investing in them has to be high for firms to invest. For most firms, this payoff is financial. Yes, there are some individuals and organizations that pursue new game activities for

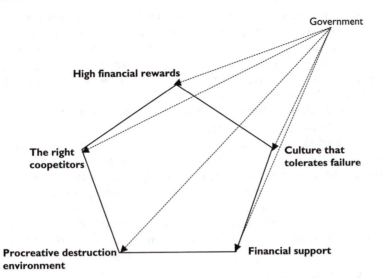

Figure 10.2 Determinants of Environments that are Conducive to Profitable New Games.

socially responsible nonfinancial reasons; but most players prefer to make money, even if in the end, they give the money that they earned to charities. Thus, an environment with good financial payoffs for new games is more likely to attract investors than one without. In the USA, the rewards for successful new game activities can be astronomical. A look at the Forbes list of 500 billionaires shows that by far the largest number of self-made billionaires is in the USA. In fact, there are more such billionaires in the USA than in all the other countries of the world combined. These payoffs come in different forms. First, there is the initial public offering (IPO) in which firms offer some of their shares to the public for the first time. The founders of Google, for example, were billionaires a few days after the company went public. A firm can also push up its net worth by spinning out an entrepreneurial unit and issuing an IPO for the unit. Expectation of such rewards can be a very good incentive for the kind of effort and dedication that it takes to pursue many innovations. Dr James H. Clark, founder of Silicon Graphics Inc (SGI) and Netscape, put it best, "Without IPOs, you would not have any startups. IPOs supply the fuel that makes these dreams go. Without it, you die."[7] Second, the rewards can also come when a venture is bought, usually by a more established firm with complementary assets. Such an acquisition can give the investors cash, shares in the established firm, or high-level positions in the established firm. In fact, many venture capitalists invest in startups largely because they expect to cash out at the IPO or when a more established company buys the venture.

Financial Support for Entrepreneurial Activities

Availability of venture capital is critical to engaging in new game activities, especially entrepreneurial ones. By making money available for projects that would normally be considered too risky by incumbent firms, venture capitalists enable entrepreneurs to be more daring in their pursuit of new games. Some entrepreneurs use personal or family savings, or loans from friends to finance their ventures, in anticipation of the potential high financial rewards. Anticipation of such rewards, coupled with readily available venture capital, allows more people to search for more ideas in more places with more combined determination. Many of those whose ventures are successful usually reinvest their earnings in new ventures. Clark reinvested some of the money that he had made at SGI in Netscape. Kleiner and Perkins reinvested some of what they made in Genentech and Tadem Computers into later ventures such as AOL, Amazon.com, Netscape, and Google.

As we saw earlier, there may be times when a government is better off sponsoring R&D activities. For example, if a project is too complex and entails too much uncertainty, and the output is knowledge with public properties, firms are likely to shy away from investing in the project and government is better off investing in it. Thus, countries in which governments invest in R&D for generating new game ideas, without too many strings attached to the results, may be more likely to be more conducive to new games than those that do not.

Culture that Tolerates Failure

Many ventures never make it to the payoff at the IPO, acquisition, or successful product. They simply fail. In some environments, such failures are fatal. In some countries, someone who is associated with a failed company may be doomed. The fear of such repercussions prevents many investors in such environments from investing in ventures. In other environments, such failures stop neither the entrepreneurs nor their financial backers. Why? First, players in such environments understand that most new games require experimentation, trial, error, and correction. Failure is therefore part of the learning that goes on. Thus, those who fail learn in the process and this can improve their chances of doing well the next time around. Second, many of the complementary players, especially venture capital firms, have seen many failures before and still come out ahead. Moreover, some of the players are serial entrepreneurs who have experienced both success and failure several times before. The culture in such environments tolerates failure. Whereas bankruptcy laws are harsh in Europe and entrepreneurs who fail are stigmatized, in the Silicon Valley, "bankruptcy is seen almost as a sign of prowess—a dueling scar if you will."[8]

Presence of Coopetitors and Factor Conditions

Recall that in performing new game activities, a firm usually needs to interact with coopetitors to obtain some of the information and other resources that it needs to create and appropriate value. Since some of the knowledge needed is tacit, having these coopetitors in close enough proximity to allow for in-person interactions can facilitate the process of knowledge identification, exchange, recombination, and transformation. Take the presence of suppliers. Being close to suppliers gives a firm the opportunity to interact with component developers and work more closely with them as both supplier and firm go through their experimentation, trial, error, and correction process. They are able to provide each other with the type of quick feedback that, in some industries, can be the difference between success and failure. Such close interaction can enable a firm to be more effective in creating and appropriating value. Having very demanding customers can also force firms into pursuing new games more diligently so as to meet the needs of these demanding customers.[9] The presence of the right inputs can also contribute to the conduciveness of an environment to new games. For example, without the availability of electrical engineering and computer science graduates in the USA, the Internet revolution may never have taken off in the USA when it did. Finally, the presence of venture capital firms can also be crucial.

A Procreative Destruction Environment

A system that encourages competition—especially between incumbents and new entrants—can be critical to creating value. Major innovations usually result in so-called creative destruction in which new firms replace some incumbents. A system that unduly protects incumbents can impede progress. For example, those developing African countries that continued to protect their fixed-line phone companies missed out on one of the biggest business success stories in Africa—the cell phone communications business. If a country's cluster invents something but cannot commercialize it because the home country is overprotective of its incumbent firms and old jobs, an entrepreneur in another country is likely to pick up the invention and commercialize it. If the idea is a success abroad, incumbents everywhere will eventually be displaced. Effectively, the home country can have one of its own startups displace its incumbents or someone else from the outside will do it. Moreover, if incumbents are overprotected, entrepreneurs and venture capitalists can take their ideas and investment to another country where they can commercialize the ideas and profit from them. Government policies that make life difficult for startups can curb entrepreneurial activity in their countries. In some countries, revenues are taxed regardless of whether or not a firm makes money. This can be difficult for startups that usually need cash early in their life cycles. In some countries, it can take as many as 23 days to start a business while in others, it takes only three days.

What Should Governments Do?

A lot of what governments can do to create environments that are conducive to new games follows directly from our discussion of what makes for conducive environments.

Foster a Culture that Encourages Financial Rewards for Successful New Games

Laws in some countries prevent a firm from issuing an IPO until it has shown several years of profits. Such laws are meant to protect investors from unscrupulous firms and their investment bankers; but they also keep out investors who can better decide the level of risk that they can handle and when they should invest in a firm. Individuals know better than their governments which companies are good investment issues. Again, investors can take their money to those countries which do not unduly restrict when a firm can go public.

In some countries, billionaires are frowned at while in others they are admired for the hard work that enabled them to earn the money, unless it was inherited. Yes, disparities in wealth can be a problem; but for every billionaire that is created during an IPO, there are thousands of employees and other stakeholders that become millionaires. If you aspire to work hard and become a billionaire (and use the money to help refugees, etc.), would you stay where billionaires are frowned upon or go where you are admired?

Encourage Financial Support for New Games

Some governments tax the revenues that startups receive, leaving cash-strapped startups even more cash-strapped. This is in contrast to other countries in which firms pay taxes only on income and get to deduct losses in their tax returns. If you were a venture capitalist, would you rather invest in a country with high tax rates on revenues and where billionaires are frowned upon, or in one where income, not revenues, is taxed at low rates and billionaires are admired as wealth creators? If you wanted to work for a startup, would you want to work for the former or the latter? Taxing revenues may be equivalent to a farmer eating most of his/her young sheep and being left with little to maintain his/her flock. Successful startups create more jobs and wealth for their employees, increasing the tax revenues for countries. With increasing globalization, venture capitalists can move their capital to the country that they believe is more hospitable to startups. Entrepreneurial employees can also move to those countries where they believe they can pursue their dreams better. It is interesting that venture capital was invented by a Frenchman while teaching in the USA, and France has little or no wealth creation by venture capitalists.

Encourage Competition and Get out of the Way

Laws that protect incumbents in the face of revolutionary new games can backfire. That is because creative destruction eventually takes hold. Thus, protecting incumbents from disruptive technologies by slowing down attackers only delays the inevitable. Moreover, if a government slows down attackers in its country, other countries may not. The more restrictive country may therefore find itself falling behind as far as the disruptive technology is concerned, and when its incumbents fall, they may be falling into the hands of foreign attackers. Thus, a country may be better off encouraging competition between incumbents and new entrants, and getting out of the way.

Build a Culture that Tolerates Failure

While it is not very clear what a government can do to build a culture that tolerates failure, a relaxation of bankruptcy laws can help. In some countries, bankruptcy laws are so strict that some failed entrepreneurs can be banned from running another company for many years. Such laws may be contributing to stigmatizing failed firms. In the USA, Chapter 11 bankruptcy proceedings allow the bankrupt firm's employees to move on to another firm, and the assets to be redeployed.[10] Relaxing these other countries' bankruptcy laws may help.

Keep Investing in Public Knowledge and Public Complementary Assets

Of course, governments need to continue to invest in R&D projects that generate knowledge with public properties, since firms are not likely to invest in such projects; but they should attach few strings to the results of the R&D, encouraging competition whenever possible. Governments are terrible at making products and therefore should not try to get too far into product-making. The job of governments is to make it easier for firms to make safe and good products. If a government stands in the way of an innovation, another government will find a way to get its firms to profit from the innovation.

Rationale for the Role of Government[11]

In describing what governments should do to create environments that are conducive to innovation, we did not explain why a government needs to play a role. In this section, we explore the rationale for why governments have a role to play in the face of new games. Because of the nature of people and the knowledge that they must turn into customer value during new games, there may be times when governments must intervene to facilitate more optimal value creation and appropriation. Whether government intervention is needed is a function of the:

1 Complementary assets needed.
2 Characteristics of the knowledge that must be transformed.
3 Amount of uncertainty and complexity involved.
4 Characteristics of the people that take the decisions and transform the knowledge.
5 Type of industry in which the firm operates.
6 Extent to which there are negative or positive externalities involved.

Public Goods as Complementary Assets

Some of the complementary assets that a firm needs to create and appropriate value are so-called public goods. A *public good* is a good that is *nonrivalrous* and nonexcludable. A good is nonrivalrous if consumption of the good by an individual does not reduce the amount of the good that is available for consumption by others. A good is *nonexcludable* if it is difficult to prevent some people from using it. An example of a public good is air. When one person breathes air, he or she does not reduce the amount of air that is available for others to breathe. Moreover, it is difficult to exclude some people from breathing air. Consequently, it is difficult for an individual to clean only the air that he or she wants to breathe. Another example of a public good is national defense. Because of their nonrivalrous and nonexcludable properties, public goods may be better provided by governments. It is difficult for each individual to defend himself or herself from a foreign bomb. A safe country, good roads, steady supply of energy, transportation systems, and a clean sustainable natural environment are public complementary assets that can be critical to the type of economy in which firms create and appropriate value. Because of the public nature of these assets, governments may need to play a major role in providing them.

Paradoxical, Public, and Leaky Nature of Knowledge

The knowledge that underpins new game ideas has certain characteristics that can make it difficult for a firm to appropriate the value from knowledge that it generates.[12] First, suppose a firm wants to sell a new game idea. A potential buyer cannot determine the value of the idea until it knows what the idea is all about; but once it knows the idea, the potential buyer may no longer have an incentive to pay for it, especially if the buyer is opportunistic. It already has the idea and can shirk. Such a situation may discourage potential suppliers of knowledge for new game ideas from investing in its generation. This situation is sometimes referred to as the knowledge paradox.[13] Second, another characteristic of knowledge is that of nonrivalry. If A sells some knowledge to B, doing so does not reduce the amount of knowledge that A has. What is more is that B, the buyer, will always have the knowledge and can keep reselling it. Unlike products or services that are used up, and the producer can sell more of them, knowledge remains in circulation no matter how many people consume it. This may also discourage potential suppliers from investing in knowledge generation, since they may end up selling only one or a few copies.

Third, if a seller of a new game idea found a buyer, the idea may leak during the process of transfer. Or, once the buyer starts to make money from it, it can be quickly copied. In either case, appropriability of the knowledge is reduced. This leakage is a function of the explicitness or tacitness of the knowledge. If it is tacit and therefore requires learning by doing, experiencing, and interacting over time with the generator of the knowledge, the risk of leakage may be reduced. In any case, this leakiness property may also reduce the incentive to invest in the production of new ideas for new games. It is important to point out that leakage of knowledge, also called spillovers, may not always be bad, from a societal point of view. It allows firms not to duplicate each other's past research efforts and waste money that could be used to extend the technology and offer society better value.

There are several things that could be done to alleviate these knowledge problems. The first is for the government to grant and protect intellectual property rights to producers of knowledge. That is what the governments of many developed countries have already done by enacting and enforcing laws that grant patents, copyrights, trade marks, trade secrets, and so on. If a firm is awarded a patent on something, it can freely discuss it with potential buyers without fear of an opportunistic buyer running away with the idea. Second, the government can engage directly in idea generation itself and give the output freely to its firms and entrepreneurs—that is, governments can generate knowledge and encourage spillover of the knowledge. By "engage" in idea generation, we mean that the government can have its own laboratories that engage in the research, or award grants to universities and other institutions to perform the research. Third, a government can provide subsidies for firms and individuals alike to encourage private production of knowledge. We will have more to say about these three remedies later in this chapter.

Uncertainty and Complexity of Value Creation and Appropriation

The uncertainty associated with the generation and application of some break-through ideas is so large that very few firms are likely to invest in the generation of such ideas. No firm could have foreseen the potential applications of the structure of the DNA before its discovery. Nobody could have forseen how far-reaching its applications would be. Thus, many profit-seeking firms are not likely to have invested in the activities that led to the discovery of the structure of the DNA. Complex projects that involve very many firms, individuals, and governments are also difficult for individual profit-seeking firms to pursue alone. Take the Internet, for example. What type of firm could have planned, discovered, and implemented the Internet?

Effectively, if the uncertainties inherent in ideas for new games are very large, firms may not be willing to take the risk of investing in their generation. One solution is to shift the risk of failure to insurers; but shifting risk to an insurer has some problems. The insured has more information about the new game than the insurer. An opportunistic insured may decide not to give the insurer all the information that is needed to write a good policy. Even if the insured were not opportunistic and honestly wanted to give the insurer all the needed information, it may not be able to articulate all of the information, given the uncertainty and complexity of the project and the fact that the insured is cognitively limited. Moreover, even if the insured could articulate all the information, the insurer may not be able to absorb and process all of the information either. This information asymmetry between the insured and insurer leads to the two potential classic problems of *adverse selection* and *moral hazard*. A large majority of firms that seek insurance for idea generation may be firms that have something to hide. Since the insurer does not have all the information that it needs to differentiate between those that are opportunistic and those that are not, it may end up getting only the opportunistic ones. This is the *adverse selection* problem. It is also possible that the insurer succeeds in selecting the right insureds. Once the contract has been signed, the insureds may become complacent and not work as hard as they would if they were not insured. Given the complexity and uncertainty associated with the innovation, it is difficult to tell when the innovator is shirking or being a bum. The problem that arises from firms behaving opportunistically once they have signed a contract is the *moral hazard* problem.

Effectively, if the uncertainty and complexity of idea generation is too high, firms may not want to invest in it; and because of the adverse selection and moral hazard problems associated with complex and uncertain projects, insurance companies may not be willing to insure the idea generation. A government can do several things to insure such idea generation. First, a government can undertake some of the risky idea generation itself. Second, a government can allow firms to cooperate in the idea generation while making sure that the firms are not colluding. Third, a government can subsidize R&D spending. Fourth, a government can extend the protection life of the intellectual property that comes from the projects. Again, we will discuss these measures below.

Heterogeneity, Self-interest, and Cognitive Limitation of People

Firms and the individuals that work for them are usually not the rational profit-maximizing players that neoclassical economics often assumes. Rather, the people who work for firms do the best they can to make sure that their firms are profitable and that their own interests are met. The satisfaction or utility that people derive from performing a particular activity varies from individual to individual and from context to context. While the Nelson Mandelas of the world derive a lot of satisfaction from working hard to give other people a chance to work hard and improve their own lives, other people work hard because they want to keep their immediate families happy. Yet others work hard to make a lot of money and then give it away to charity. Others work hard to generate ideas so that they can be recognized as the best at what they do by their professional colleagues or the Nobel committee. Thus, a government's role ought to take into consideration the fact that people are very diverse as far as their incentives to generate new game ideas are concerned.

People are also cognitively limited. Their information collection, processing, and expression abilities are limited and therefore, there is only so much that most people can learn or process at any one time. Firms are also cognitively limited. Thus, some projects may be too knowledge-intensive for such firms. Governments can facilitate cooperation between firms that want to develop such projects.

Minimum Efficient Scale Requirements of Industry

Whether or not a government should play a role in value creation and appropriation is also a function of the minimum efficient scale involved. *Minimum efficient scale* (MES) is the smallest output that minimizes unit costs.[14] In some industries or markets, the MES is equal to or larger than the market. Such an industry is said to be a *natural monopoly* because one firm can produce at lower cost than two or more firms. The natural monopoly concept was used to justify monopolies in telecommunications, railways, electricity, water services, and mail delivery. Since changes in technology usually result in reductions in MES, it may be difficult to justify the presence of natural monopolies in some of these industries today. For example, because of the nature of cell-phone technology (compared to fixed-line telephony) the introduction of competition in the telecommunications industries of many developing countries has resulted in much better customer service and profits for the providers.

Negative and Positive Network Externalities of Some Activities

In Chapter 5, we said that a product or technology exhibits network externalities if the more people that use the product or technology, the more valuable that it becomes to each user. There is another type of network externality that is defined as the cost or benefit imposed by the actions of two transacting parties on a third party.[15] It is called a *negative externality* if a cost is imposed on the third party, and a *positive externality* if a benefit is imposed on a third party. A classic example of a negative network externality is that of a power plant that burns coal to produce electricity but, in doing so, also produces sulfur dioxide that rises into the air and eventually falls as acid rain. The acid rain is a negative externality since, in calculating the cost of the electricity that it sells, the electric company does not factor in the cost of the acid to the people on whose property or bodies the acid rain falls. By regulating the amount of sulfur dioxide that a power plant can emit into the air, a government can reduce the amount of this negative externality. Pollution from cars is also a negative externality. A classic example of positive externality is that of a bee that, in searching for food, pollinates the plants that it visits. If a farmer breeds bees, it cannot tell them which crops to pollinate and which ones not to. Therefore, a government department of agriculture may be better off breeding the bees and letting them pollinate crops for everyone.

The Role of Government During New Games

In exploring the rationale for a government role in the face of new games, we hinted at some of the things that governments could do to help firms create and appropriate value better. In this section, we go into more detail of what governments could do. In particular, we explore seven government roles that can help firms in the face of new games. A government can serve as:[16]

- R&D financier
- Leader user
- Provider of public complementary assets
- Regulator/deregulator
- Facilitator of macroeconomic fundamentals
- Educator, information center, and provider of political stability.

R&D Financier

Recall that the "public good" nature of knowledge can make it difficult for firms to appropriate their inventions, thereby discouraging firms from investing in some knowledge-generation activities. Also recall that the complexity and uncertainty associated with certain knowledge-generation activities can discourage firms from investing in R&D. One solution to these two problems is to have the government perform the research and make the results available to the public. Governments spend on two kinds of R&D: basic research, and applied research. Basic research is about the search for knowledge for knowledge's own sake, with little attention given to if, whether, or how research findings could be converted into products. Applied research is research that is targeted towards a particular application. Government research is conducted largely in government laboratories, universities, within some firms, or at joint endeavors made up of some combination of the three. In 2007 alone, the US Government planned to spend over $130 billion on R&D.

Government-sponsored R&D has played a major role in the creation of new industries, or has been a key driver for many innovations within existing industries. Two examples are the Internet and the structure of the DNA. The Internet grew out of the US Defense Department's Advance Research Projects Agency

(DARPA) in which research on computer networks was sponsored by DARPA. Firms eventually joined in to help build the Internet to the phenomenon that it has become. Without the US Government's R&D funding, there would be no Internet today! The double-helix structure of genes or DNA also has its roots in government-sponsored research conducted at Cambridge University to thank for its discovery. Both these discoveries went on to become the sources of numerous new games.

Financing R&D has other benefits beyond solving the problems of the "public" properties of knowledge and of the complexity and uncertainty associated with some projects. First, in financing R&D, the government is also educating its workforce with the knowledge and skills that firms need to create and appropriate value. Once the Web took off, for example, it was easier to find employees with computer science and other information technology skills, partly because of the many students trained with DARPA and National Science Foundation (NSF) funds in the computer Science and Electrical Engineering departments of many universities. Second, government R&D spending also spurs private firms to invest in related invention or commercialization activities. Third, by focusing attention on specific areas, government R&D projects can enjoy the economies of scale that come with large R&D projects.

Although government intentions may be good, the results of their actions are not always positive. Stories of failed projects also abound and questions about just how much R&D the government should undertake haunt policy makers.

Government as Lead User

In the face of a new game or an innovation, interaction with customers can be critical to understanding the benefits that they want and to being better able to provide the benefits. Professor Eric von Hippel of the Massachusetts Institute of Technology (MIT) has argued that lead users can be critical to the process of innovation.[17] **Lead users** are customers whose needs are similar to those of other customers except that they have these needs months or years before the bulk of the marketplace does, and stand to benefit significantly by fulfilling these needs earlier than the rest of the customers. The US government was an important lead user in some critical products. For example, the US defense department saw many benefits in the transistor replacing the bulky vacuum tube when it pursued it well before most would-be users of the transistor. Since transistors were much smaller and consumed less power than vacuum tubes, electronic systems built from it would not only be lighter and provide more functionality, they would require smaller power supplies, further reducing the weight of the whole system. This made the transistor and subsequent integrated circuits particularly attractive to the Defense Department and the US National Aeronautics and Space Administration (NASA). The US government's willingness to award contracts to both incumbents and new entrants, and to work closely with them may have helped US semiconductor firms into the early industry leadership position that they occupied for a long time.[18] The US role as lead user was not isolated to semiconductors. Jet engines, airplanes, and computers have all benefited from this shepherding by governments. This role is not limited to the USA. Rothwell and Zegveld found that purchases by European and Japanese governments played a significant role in innovation.[19]

Provider of Public Complementary Assets

A country's infrastructure is critical to any new game activities that firms within the country decide to pursue. For example, without a transportation system that enables goods to be delivered to customers reliably and at reasonable costs, online firms such as eBay and Amazon would not be as successful as they have been. An information superhighway facilitates communications not only between different business units of a firm; it also facilitates interaction between coopetitors. Chip design can now take place 24 hours a day with people in Israel, Japan, and the Silicon Valley taking turns to work on the same project. Thus, by providing the infrastructure that its firms need, a country is helping its firms create and appropriate value better than countries that do not.

Government as Regulator/Deregulator

Another way to deal with the "public" nature of knowledge that can prevent firms from investing in knowledge generation is to grant inventors some monopoly privileges over their inventions. In the USA, for example, the need for such a privilege is written in Article 1, Section 8 of the constitution: Congress shall have power "To promote the progress of science and useful arts, by securing for limited times to authors and inventors the exclusive right to their respective writings and discoveries." Firms can take advantage of this privilege by seeking intellectual property protection via patents, copyrights, trademarks, and trade secrets. If a firm has patented its invention, it can reveal it to a potential buyer without being afraid of it being stolen since the patent is proof of ownership. The market power that intellectual property protection can bestow on a firm can be an incentive for firms to invest in inventions or discoveries. Patenting is not limited to technologies; business models can be patented too. For example, Netflix was awarded a patent for its Internet-based approach for renting videos to customers.

Ironically, a government is also responsible for preventing monopolies, since they can result in under-innovation. For example, antitrust legislation in the USA seeks to prevent any mergers that can unduly increase the market power of one organization, since such market power can result in the emerging organization keeping prices artificially high, or a lack of incentive to innovate. Other activities, such as collusion and predatory pricing, that can result in artificially high prices, are also illegal in some countries. In the USA, for example, the Sherman Act makes illegal any agreements among competitors that enable them to keep their prices artificially at some level by fixing the prices or coordinating their outputs. Tacit collusion is also illegal. In tacit collusion, rather than use explicit formal agreements, firms can, for example, send signals as to what their actions are going to be, inviting competitors to follow suit. In predatory pricing, a firm lowers its prices (below its cost) so as to drive out competitors and then raises them when the prey is out of the market. This is difficult to prove, especially early in the life of an innovation, because innovators can claim that they are lowering their prices to attain the kinds of volume that can take them down the learning curve (up the S-curve) rapidly, resulting in such lower cost, on average, that they can afford to sell at a loss at the beginning.

Other public goods, such as the air that we breathe and the natural environment, also have to be protected by governments. For a passenger that drives 10,000 miles a year, a 10 mpg improvement in a car's gas mileage reduces emissions to the atmosphere by 2.4 million pounds of CO_2 (for a person who drives 10,000 miles per year, every 1 mpg improvement saves 24 pounds of CO_2 each year). Governments can also deregulate. Such deregulations can radically change the nature of competition in an industry. Deregulation and privatization of the telecommunications sectors of many developing countries have resulted in competition and some profitable business with happy customers.

Facilitator of Macroeconomic Fundamentals

New games are also economic activities and therefore their health depends as much on how firms play the game as it does on the macroeconomic fundamentals of the countries in which they operate. Economic policies that spawn expectations of low inflation, low interest rates, growth, and profits encourage firms to invest more in R&D and associated complementary assets. Expectations of such profits can encourage more entrepreneurs to engage in new game activities. Expected low interest rates make it easier for projects to make firm hurdle rates. New game activities may be the engine of economic progress; but it is also true that economic processes can feed that engine.

Educator, Information Center, and Provider of Political Stability

In most countries, governments are responsible for most of the general education of its young. In the face of new games such as the Internet and biotechnology, having the trained personnel can be the difference between firms in one country performing better than those in other countries. As we stated earlier, the introduction of computer science departments in many universities in the USA and grants from the NSF may have been instrumental to the success of US firms' ability to exploit the computer revolution. The country's ability to attract smart people from all over the world may have helped not only the country's computer industry but also other industries such as biotechnology.

Alternate Explanations: Porter's Diamond

In his diamond model, Professor Michael Porter of the Harvard Business School offered an alternate explanation for why some regions or countries are more innovative than others. He argued that a firm's ability to gain a competitive advantage is a function of four factors:[20]

1 Factor conditions
2 Demand conditions
3 Related and supporting industries
4 Firm strategy, structure, and rivalry.

Factor Conditions

Factor conditions are inputs such as labor, capital, land, natural resources, and infrastructure that firms need to create and appropriate value. These factors of production can be divided into two: *key* or *specialized* factors, and non-key or generic factors. Specialized factors are inputs such as skilled labor, capital, and infrastructure that are usually created, not inherited. These specialized factors are likely to give a firm a sustainable competitive advantage, since they are more difficult to replicate. *Non-key* factors are inputs such as unskilled labor and raw materials that are easy to replicate or acquire. Non-key factors are unlikely to give a firm a sustainable competitive advantage, since they are easy to replicate or acquire. Professor Porter argued that scarcity of factors of production in a country often helps, rather than hurts, the country because scarcity generates an innovative mentality while abundance often results in waste. For example, land prices in Japan were very high and therefore factory space was very expensive. Thus, to cope better with the scarcity of space, the Japanese invented just-in-time inventory and other techniques that reduced inventory in factories.

Demand Conditions

Demand conditions in a region or country can also have an impact on the ability of local firms to have a competitive advantage. If local customers have sophisticated demands, local firms are more likely to find new ways to meet these sophisticated needs. If firms can meet the very sophisticated demands of local customers, they will find it easier to meet the relatively less sophisticated demands of other markets. If the sophisticated demand becomes global, the local firms are better positioned to exploit the demand since their competitors (from abroad) have not yet developed the skills to meet such sophisticated demand. For example, demanding French wine consumers pushed French wine suppliers to develop skills and other resources for producing some of the best wines in the world.

Related and Supporting Industries

Having suppliers, complementors, buyers, and competitors located in the same region can also help local firms to innovate better. A firm that is developing a product can have an advantage if its suppliers and buyers are located nearby, since they can all exchange critical information more easily during the experimentation, trial, and error that takes place during innovation. Suppliers can more easily find out what firms want and supply it. Firms can more easily work with buyers to find out what they want.

Firm Strategy, Structure, and Rivalry

The competitive advantage of firms in a country also depends on their domestic strategies and structure. For example, competition in domestic markets can be fierce, since firms know a lot about what their local rivals are doing. What is interesting is that such fierce rivalry can be good in the long run because competition can force firms to be more efficient or to innovate to survive. They also develop tactical skills for dealing with competitors. With the more efficient and innovative ways honed at home, such firms can have a competitive advantage when they face global markets with competitors without such capabilities.

PESTN Analysis

Recall that a firm's macroenvironment is a major source of opportunities and threats. One way to identify these threats and opportunities from a macro-environment is to use a *PESTN* (pronounced as PEST N) analysis. PESTN stands for Political, Economic, Social, Technological, and Natural environment. Most readers may be familiar with the PEST part of the analysis. In this book, however, we add the N. The factors that make up each component of the PESTN analysis are shown in Figure 10.3. Each of these components was described in detail at the beginning of this chapter. The extent to which any of these factors constitutes a threat or opportunity for a firm is a function of the industry in which the firm operates and the firm's strategy. For example, while in pharmaceuticals, "intellectual property protection" is important, it is usually not the case in retail. Thus, what a government does about intellectual property protection may not be of too much interest to many retail firms—unless, of course, they want to pursue some sort of new game in this area. Effectively, the number of factors that matter for any particular PESTN analysis will always be only a subset of those shown in Figure 10.3.[21] As can be expected, some of the factors are interrelated. For example, "physical and monetary policy" are part of the Political component as well as of the Economic component. It is not unusual for a PEST analysis of an industry to provide a laundry list of the threats and opportunities that can impact an industry. However, since we are interested in how these opportunities and threats can be exploited by a firm to create and appropriate value, we focus on how each of the factors impacts industry competitive forces, industry value drivers, and the system of activities (and associated resources) that a firm performs. Given the vast number of factors that drive each component, we will explore only one factor per component.

Political

In a PESTN analysis, one determines the extent to which the factors listed in Figure 10.3 are opportunities or threats, given the objectives of the firm in question. Take the first political factor—consumer protection laws—shown in Figure 10.3. Strict consumer protection laws are a threat to firms that do not have the capabilities to offer customers the right products. They can also be an opportunity for a firm with the right capabilities. Strict consumer protection laws can be good for local firms that want to compete globally. That is because, once a firm satisfies these strict local consumer protection laws, it can use the capabilities developed to satisfy the laws of any other country whose laws are equally strict or less. For example, once a firm meets the strict US Food and Drug Administration (FDA) requirements for approving a new drug, the firm can very easily meet the requirements for any other country. The FDA laws are meant to protect patients.

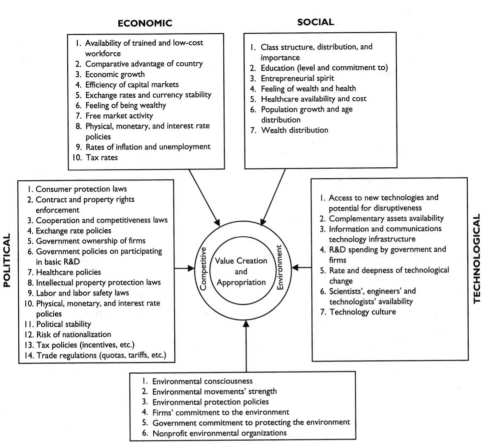

Figure 10.3 A PESTN Analysis.

Economic

Availability of a trained and low-cost workforce is an opportunity for a firm that wants to produce locally. The only caution for managers is that such opportunities do not last too long because many other firms are likely to locate there and before long, the workforce will become high-cost.

Social

If differences between classes in a country are strong, it can be difficult to get them to work together. That would make it difficult for an innovative firm that thrives on diverse inputs. Firms are also less likely to enjoy the kinds of economy of scale that can be enjoyed in environments where the lines between classes are not as strong. Customers are also less likely to enjoy fully the size benefits of network externalities. However, strong divisions between classes make it easier to segment markets into niches and to price discriminate better.

Technological

New potentially disruptive technologies can be a threat to incumbents but an opportunity for new entrants who use the new technology to attack incumbents. They can also be an opportunity for incumbents that act preemptively to adopt the technology before attackers move in.

Natural

If environmental consciousness is high, governments, firms, and consumers will see its importance better, and what it takes to act in a way that is more environmentally sustainable. Thus a high environmental consciousness is an opportunity for businesses that want to offer more environmentally sustainable products and a threat to incumbent businesses that do not want to change.

Advantages and Disadvantage of a PEST Analysis

A PESTN analysis offers one way to have a big picture of the opportunities and threats from a firm's political, economic, social, technological, and natural environments. Exploring these components together provides an opportunity to see some of the relationships among the components. It can be used to identify sources of potential new games. The PEST has several disadvantages. The list of drivers of each component can be very long. For example, the "political" component in Figure 10.3 has 14 factors, and many more could be added. Moreover, there is no way of determining which of these factors is more important than the other. The analysis says very little about the link between each of the factors and a firm's profitability.

Key Takeaways

- Firms and the industries in which they operate do not exist in a vacuum; they are surrounded by their macroenvironments of political, economic, social-demographic technological, and natural. These environments are primary sources of the threats and opportunities that firms often face.
    - The political environment includes antitrust regulation, tax laws, foreign trade regulation, and employee protection laws.
    - The economic environment includes stock performance, disposal incomes, interest rates, currency movements, economic growth, exchange rates, and inflation rate.
    - Sociocultural variables include the beliefs, norms, and values of consumers, countries, communities, and employees. Demographic variables include shifts in populations, age distributions, ethnic mixes, educational levels, lifestyle changes, consumer activism, birthrates, life expectancies, and household patterns in cities, regions, and countries.
    - The technological environments have to do with the changes in the technologies that go into products, their distribution, marketing, service, and usage.

- o The natural environment consists of the air that we breathe, the water that sustains all life, climate, landscapes, grasslands, forests, wildlife, animals, oceans, mineral resources, and any other living or nonliving things that occur naturally on earth and its surroundings.
- Environments that are conducive to profitable new games (innovation) possess the following characteristics:
  - o High financial rewards for successful new games.
  - o Financial support for entrepreneurial activities.
  - o A culture that tolerates failure.
  - o The right coopetitors.
  - o A procreative destruction environment.
- What should governments do to foster environments that are conducive to innovation? Governments can:
  - o Foster a culture that encourages financial rewards for successful new games.
  - o Encourage financial support for new games and other entrepreneurial activities.
  - o Encourage competition and get out of the way.
  - o Build a culture that tolerates failure.
  - o Keep investing in public knowledge and public complementary assets.
- For the following six reasons, governments may have to intervene in optimal value creation and appropriation:
  - o The nonrivalrous and nonexcludable properties of public complementary assets make it less likely that for-profit firms will invest in such assets without help from their governments.
  - o The paradoxical, public, and leaky nature of knowledge make it less likely that for-profit firms will invest in generating such knowledge without help from their governments.
  - o The uncertainty and complexity of some projects make it less likely that for-profit firms will invest in them without help.
  - o The heterogeneity, self-interest, and cognitive limitation of people suggests that employees may need different types of motivation; some of which can only come from the government.
  - o If an industry's MES is so large that it is inefficient to have more than one firm in the industry.
  - o If industry's activities, products, or technology exhibit negative or positive externalities.
- A government can serve as:
  - o R&D financier
  - o Leader user
  - o Provider of public complementary assets
  - o Regulator/deregulator
  - o Facilitator of macroeconomic fundamentals
  - o Educator, information center, and provider of political stability.

- Porter's Diamond model suggests that the ability of firms in a region or country to gain a competitive advantage depends on the region's or country's:

  - Factor conditions.
  - Demand conditions.
  - Related and supporting industries.
  - Firm strategy, structure, and rivalry.

- A PESTN (political, economic, social, technological, and natural environments) analysis can be used to explore the opportunities and threats of a macroenvironment.

Key Terms

Adverse selection
Minimum efficient scale
Moral hazard
Natural monopoly
Negative externality
Nonrivalrous good
PESTN
Positive externality
Public good

Chapter 11

Coopetition and Game Theory

Reading this chapter should provide you with the conceptual and analytical tools to:

- Further appreciate the significance of always taking the likely reaction of your coopetitors into consideration when deciding on whether or not to pursue a new game activity.
- Understand the differences between cooperative and noncooperative game theory that can be applied to the concepts and tools of this book.
- Appreciate the usefulness and limitations of game theory as a tool or theory for strategic management.
- Understand why one needs both cooperative and noncooperative game theory if one decides to use game theory to explore new game strategic action.

Introduction

When a firm performs a new game activity or any other activity, its competitors are likely to react to the activity. For example, if a firm introduces a new product, lowers or raises its prices, launches a new ad campaign, increases R&D or marketing spending, enters a new business, boosts manufacturing capacity, builds a new brand, or performs any other activity, its rivals are likely to respond sooner or later. Thus, how successful the firm is with the new activity is a function not only of how the firm performs the activity but also of competitors' reaction. Thus, before taking a decision, a firm may want to consider its competitors' likely actions and reactions. In particular, the firm may be better off asking itself questions such as: How are my rivals acting? How will they react to my actions? How best should I react to my rival's reaction to my actions? If the rival moves first, what should I do? A useful tool for exploring some of these questions is game theory. Game theory enables firms not only to ask what their competitors are planning to do but also to ask what is in the best interests of these competitors. In this chapter, we explore how game theory can be used to explore some of these questions. Because this book assumes no prior knowledge of game theory, most of this chapter is dedicated to reviewing some of the key concepts of both cooperative and *noncooperative game theory* that are important to understanding value creation and appropriation.

The Role of Game Theory in Strategic Innovation

Recall that to create and appropriate value, a firm often has to cooperate and compete with different members of its value system. For example, a firm can cooperate with its suppliers, complementors, or customers to create value, and compete to appropriate the value. It can also cooperate with some rivals to compete better against others, as is the case when firms enter co-marketing agreements or form strategic alliances to develop new products. Of course, firms compete against each other when they offer similar products, hire from the same pool of employees, bid for contracts, advertise, price their products, seek partners to cooperate with, or purchase components. Effectively, the fortunes of a firm and those of its coopetitors—the rivals, suppliers, customers, and complementors with which it cooperates and competes—are often interdependent. Therefore, in deciding what to do, each firm is better off taking into consideration the actions and reactions of it coopetitors. This is where game theory comes in. Game theory is a tool for formally analyzing competition and cooperation between firms as they create value and position themselves to appropriate the value.[1] Rather than be content with asking what one's coopetitor plans to do, game theory suggests that managers ask what is in one's coopetitor's best interest and how one is likely to act or react in that best interest and one's own interest.

Cooperative and Noncooperative Games

There are two major approaches to game theory: cooperative and noncooperative. Noncooperative game theory has been more commonly utilized to explore strategy questions than *cooperative game theory*. Both address different questions in strategy.[2] Noncooperative game theory is about how to better compete against rivals by taking their likely reactions into consideration when one performs activities. It has been used to analyze strategic moves whose outcomes depend on one's rivals' likely actions and reactions, such as whether to introduce a new product, increase R&D or advertising spending, retaliate against new entrants, preannounce a new product introduction, increase manufacturing capacity, raise or lower prices, or emphasize a particular brand. Noncooperative game theory is about individual rivals competing against each other. It says little about the fact that during value creation and appropriation, firms must bargain or cooperate with suppliers, compete for buyers, interact with complementors, and sometimes *explicitly* cooperate with rivals. It says nothing about the bargaining power of suppliers, complementors, and buyers, and the threat from substitutes and potential new entrants that can be critical to value creation and appropriation. Nor does it say much about how an alliance such as Wintel would compete against another coalition such as Apple. This is where cooperative game theory comes in. Cooperative game theory is useful in exploring how much value can be created by cooperating with coopetitors, how much power each coopetitor has, and how much of the value created each actor can be expected to appropriate.[3]

A *cooperative game* details the outcomes that occur when players (coopetitors) *jointly* plan their *strategies* and play as combinations of players, and not individual players.[4] The unit of analysis is a group or coalition of individual actors. The players can negotiate binding contracts that allow them to pursue these joint strategies.[5] When there is competition, it is between groups of players rather than individual players. In strategic management, these coalitions are subsets of coopetitors—suppliers, buyers, rivals, coopetitors, and complementors. In *noncooperative games*, the unit of analysis is the individual actor and there are no binding contracts between players (usually rivals) that can be enforced through outside parties. Competition is between individual competitors. If firms pursue activities that appear to be "cooperative," such as tacit collusion, it is because the self-interest of individuals (not that of a coalition) dictates that "cooperative behavior" be pursued. Note also that the terms cooperative and noncooperative may be unfortunate because cooperative games often entail not only cooperation but competition between coalitions (e.g. Wintel versus Apple).

Noncooperative Games

Consider a market in which there are two major players, each of which can impact the market by lowering or raising its prices. Coke and Pepsi in carbonated soft drinks, Boeing and Airbus in commercial aircraft, or Pfizer and Lilly in erectile dysfunction are good examples. Suppose the two major players are Boeing and Airbus and you are the manager at Airbus responsible for setting prices. Both firms are considering some price changes. The benefits to each firm of either lowering or raising prices are contingent on what its competitor does to its prices—that is, the benefits depend on whether the other firm also lowers or raises its prices. Effectively, there are several alternatives to the outcome of a firm raising its prices in such an industry with two major players. Two of these alternatives are summarized in the payoff matrix of Figure 11.1 in which each cell represents a different outcome and the *payoffs* for the particular outcome are written in the cell. In the game, Boeing and Airbus are the players. *Lower price* and *Raise price* are the two **strategies** (moves) that are available to each player. The rows represent Airbus' available strategies (lower price or raise price) while the columns are Boeing's strategies. Within each cell are two payoffs that either firm stands to make as a consequence of its move and that of its competitor. In each cell, the number to the left represents Airbus' payoff while that to the right represents Boeing's payoff. Thus, in Figure 11.1, if both Airbus

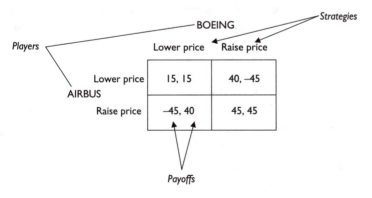

Figure 11.1 A Payoff Matrix.

and Boeing lower their prices, they each make $15 million more. However, if Airbus lowers its prices but Boeing raises its prices, Airbus' payoff is 40 while Boeing's loses sales to Airbus and ends up with a negative payoff (–45). If both firms raise their prices, each has a payoff of 45. If Boeing lowers its prices but Airbus raises its prices, Boeing's payoff is 40 while Airbus's is –45. Effectively, in noncooperative game theory, a game is made up of a set of players, a set of strategies (moves) that each player can pursue, a specification of the payoffs for each combination of strategies, and the timing of the moves. (We will return to the timing element later.) Thus, the outcome of the game depends on the payoffs that each player expects to receive. It also depends critically on what each player believes that the other will do. If Airbus believes that Boeing will raise its prices, it will raise its own prices and obtain the payoff of 45 instead of the 40 that it would receive if it lowered its prices. If it believes that Boeing will lower its prices, it will also lower its prices.

Simultaneous Games

In the game of Figure 11.1, each player takes its decision about whether to lower or raise its price without knowing which decision the other player has taken. That is, each player selects its strategy without knowing which strategy the other player has selected. Such games are called *simultaneous games*, since each player moves without knowing the other player's move. Even if the players take their decisions at different points in time, the game is still a simultaneous game so long as each player chooses its strategy without knowing the strategy that the other player has selected. The timing issue is not so much that both players took their decisions at the same time but that each one took its decision without knowing the decision that the other had taken. Each firm has its beliefs about what the other player will do but does not know what it has done before moving.

Dominant Strategy

Consider another example, where two major firms in a market can either advertise or choose not to advertise (Figure 11.2). If both firms choose not to advertise, they save on advertising costs and their market shares stay about the same, giving each the same payoff of 40. If they both advertise, their payoff is 20 each. However, if one firm advertises and its competitor does not, it takes market share from the competitor and ends up with a much higher payoff of 50 while

	Firm Y	
	Advertise	Do not advertise
Advertise	20, 20	50, 10
Do not advertise	10, 50	40, 40

Firm X (labels rows Advertise / Do not advertise)

Figure 11.2 Dominant Strategy.

the competitor receives 10. More importantly, note that if Firm X advertises, its payoff is 20 when Firm Y advertises and 50 when Firm Y does not advertise; but if Firm X does not advertise, its payoff is 10 when Firm Y advertises and 40 when Firm Y does not advertise. Thus, Firm X is better off advertising no matter whether Firm Y advertises. Effectively, no matter what Firm Y does, Firm X is better off advertising. We say that to *Advertise* is a **dominant strategy** for Firm X since, when it advertises, it is doing the best that it can, no matter the strategy that Firm Y pursues. Another examination of Figure 11.2 shows that to *Advertise* is also a dominant strategy for Firm Y since, no matter what Firm X does, Firm Y is better off advertising. Thus, the two firms end up in the upper-left cell with a payoff of (20, 20). This cell is the only noncooperative equilibrium in the game and is called the **dominant strategy equilibrium**, since it results from the fact that each player has a dominant strategy. In this cell, each firm is maximizing its payoff, given what it believes the other to be doing.

Nash Equilibrium

Two major commercial aircraft manufacturers want to introduce the next-generation commercial airplane. There is a market for a very large airplane, the so-called SuperJumbo, an aircraft that can carry up to 800 passengers compared to an existing maximum of about 500. Given the huge R&D, manufacturing and marketing investment needed, the market might not be large enough for each firm profitably to offer a SuperJumbo. There is also a market for a so-called SuperLiner, a smaller aircraft that has a longer flying range than the SuperJumbo and carries about 300 passengers, but this market might also not be large enough to support both firms. As Figure 11.3 shows, if both manufacturers (Firm A and Firm B) offer the SuperJumbo, they stand to each lose $2 billion. If they both offer the DreamLiner, they also stand to lose $2 billion each. However, if Firm A offers the SuperJumbo while Firm B offers the DreamLiner, Firm A's payoff is $5 billion while Firm B's $4 billion. If Firm A offers the SuperJumbo while Firm B offers the DreamLiner, both firms have Payoffs of $4 billion and $5 billion respectively. So long as each firm does not offer the same product that the other is offering, they will do just fine. These firms do not get together in meetings and decide who will offer what type of airplane, since to do so might be considered anticompetitive and therefore illegal in some countries. However, they can make their intentions known by the announcements that they make about future products. Suppose, for example, that Firm A announces its plans to offer the SuperJumbo. Firm B, on reading this announcement in the

Figure 11.3 Nash Equilibrium.

press, announces that it will shelve any plans that it might have had to offer a SuperJumbo and concentrate on offering a DreamLiner. Given what Firm B believes that Firm A will do (offer a SuperJumbo and not offer the DreamLiner), it has no incentive to deviate from its proposed action of offering the Dream-Liner. Similarly, given what Firm A believes Firm B will do (offer a DreamLiner and not offer the SuperJumbo), it has no incentive to deviate from its proposed action of offering the SuperJumbo (Figure 11.3).[6]

Effectively, neither firm has an incentive to deviate from its proposed action, given what it believes the other firm will do. If either firm takes the proposed action, its payoff is $5 billion. If it deviates and its opponent's proposed action remains unchanged, its payoff will be –$2 billion. Thus, the strategy set of the top-right cell of Figure 11.3 is a *Nash equilibrium*. In a Nash equilibrium, each firm is doing the best that it can, given what the other is doing. No single player can do better by *unilaterally* changing its move. In the strategy set of the top-right cell, Firm A is doing the best that it can (with a payoff of 5), given what Firm B is doing, and Firm B is doing the best that it can, given what Firm A is doing. Note that the strategy set given by the bottom-left cell is also a Nash equilibrium. A dominant strategy equilibrium is also a Nash equilibrium; but not all Nash equilibria are dominant equilibria. For example, the dominant strategy equilibrium of Figure 11.2 (top-left cell) is a Nash equilibrium; but the Nash equilibrium of Figure 11.3 (top-right cell) is not a dominant strategy equilibrium.

Prisoners' Dilemma

The example of Figure 11.2 belongs to a class of games known in game theory as **prisoner's dilemma**. In these games, the payoffs are such that each player has an incentive to pursue a strategy that will result in a worse outcome than if both players had simultaneously chosen the other strategy. In Figure 11.2, the strategy that will give both firms the highest payoff is *Don't advertise*; but because each has an incentive to advertise, they both miss out on the larger payoff. In fact, even if both players had a chance to come to some type of cooperative agreement, the incentive to deviate from the agreement may still be too strong to resist. The name prisoners' dilemma comes from a game in which two prisoners who are alleged to have jointly committed a crime are separated and told the following: if either one confesses to both of them having committed the crime, both prisoners will be convicted but the confessor will receive a light sentence while the other prisoner will receive a much heavier sentence. We have shown the light sentence in Figure 11.4 as –1 (one year in prison) and the much heavier sentence as –10 (ten years in prison). If neither prisoner confesses, both prisoners will be convicted of a lesser crime and serve about two years (–2). If both confess, they each receive a three-year sentence. As it can be seen in Figure 11.4, the incentive is to confess. The dominant strategy for both prisoners is to confess. Thus both players will end up with the top left payoff, which is lower than the payoff in the bottom right cell. Incentives could encourage players to choose the preferred outcome of the lower right cell. For example, according to the movies, the Mafia gave its members a very good incentive to *not* confess.

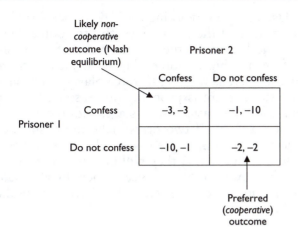

Figure 11.4 Prisoner's Dilemma.

Repeated Simultaneous Games

In many competitive arenas, firms face each other repeatedly. For example, Coke and Pepsi have repeatedly introduced new products, set product prices, and launched new product promotions in the same markets. Intel and AMD have had to negotiate prices of microprocessors with PC makers several times over each product's life cycle and each time each new product is introduced. However, the games we have explored so far have assumed that the players have no history of performing the particular activity; the games are one-shot representations with no repetition. To model interactions such as repeated new product introductions, we use repeated games in which the same game is played on many different occasions. In repeated games, a firm has a chance to establish a reputation about its behavior and learn about the behavior of its competitors. The question is, how would the outcome of a repeated game be any different from that of the standard one-shot game? It depends on whether the end of the last stage of the repeated game is specified and known or not.

By specified and known, we mean that the players, their strategies, and corresponding payoffs for each set of strategies are given, such as in the examples above. If the last stage of the game is not specified and known, and players know that they have to face each other again in the future, the fear of future retaliation may make each player behave in a more cooperative way. Effectively, if players are going to encounter each other repeatedly, one player can always punish the other player for something that he/she did in the past. Each player may cooperate with the other because he or she knows that if he or she is cheated by the other player today, he or she can punish the cheat tomorrow. Thus, the prospect of future vengeful retaliation may force players to do the right thing. Consider the *prisoner's dilemma* case of Figure 11.1. If the firms that price the products have to face each other repeatedly in the same market, they will find a way to "cooperate" and raise their prices. Tacit collusion, which we will explore later, is a good vehicle for such cooperation.

If the last stage is specified and known, then the repeated game can be analyzed by starting from the last stage and working one's way backwards to the first stage. Suppose, for example, that there is no incentive to cooperate in the last stage. Then, since it is the last stage, there is no prospect of future vengeful retaliation and therefore nothing to force players to behave more cooperatively in that final stage. If there is nothing to force players to behave more cooperatively in that last stage, there is probably no reason why they should cooperate in the last-but-one stage, last-but-two stage, and so on.

Firms can also learn from their actions. If two firms make the mistake of introducing very similar products in the same white space today when there is extra white space that they could each occupy, they will be wiser tomorrow. If firms lose a lot of money by lowering their prices when they should not (Figure 11.1), they will learn and think twice when they have to play the same game.

Sequential Games

All the games we have discussed so far are simultaneous games, since each player selects its strategy without knowing which strategy the other player has selected. These games apply in those cases where firms take their decisions without each firm knowing the decision that the other firm has taken. In many other circumstances, however, firms move sequentially, not simultaneously. In fact, in most new game strategies, firms move in turns: first movers, then followers. In sequential games, one player moves before the other. Figure 11.5 is a sequential game representation of the simultaneous game of Figure 11.3 in which Firm A moves first. The decision tree of Figure 11.5 is called the *extensive form* of the game (compared to the form of Figure 11.3 which is called the *normal form*). It captures the possibilities and sequence of events. Firm A has the first move. It must decide whether to offer the SuperJumbo or DreamLiner first. To take this decision, it must anticipate what Firm B is likely to do. Effectively, deciding what Firm A should do consists of starting from what it believes that Firm B will do and working backwards. If Firm A were to offer the Super-Jumbo, Firm B will offer the DreamLiner for the payoff of (5, 4) rather than the (−2,−2) that goes with offering the SuperJumbo; but if Firm A offers the DreamLiner, Firm B will offer the SuperJumbo for the (4,5) payoff. In this second option, Firm A's payoff is 4 rather than 5 from the first option. Thus, a

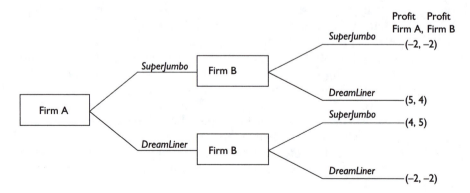

Figure 11.5 A Sequential Game.

rational Firm A will go for the first option and offer the SuperJumbo first, believing that Firm B will offer the DreamLiner. By moving first, Firm A has a chance to earn some first-mover advantages.

If a firm moves first in a sequential game, it can either try to deter entry by competitors or encourage it. If it tries to deter entry but competitors still enter, it can fight the entry, accommodate it, or change the rules of the game. We examine these cases next.

Deterrence and Sequential Games

If a player who moves first can deter entry, it is virtually a monopoly in its product-market space and stands to enjoy some monopoly benefits, including increased profitability. There are several steps that a firm can take to deter entry and therefore maintain its profitability chances.

Evoke Barriers to Entry

If an incumbent has built first-mover advantages, it can use them to deter entry. For example, an incumbent can threaten to sue any new entrants that, in entering, violate its protected intellectual property. Whether such a threat works is a function of whether the firm has a reputation for suing any firms that have violated its intellectual property protection. If an incumbent has accumulated a lot of cash, it can use it to accelerate the rate at which it preemptively acquires scarce resources to demonstrate to potential new entrants that critical resources will be more scarce and costly if they were to enter. If an incumbent has a large market share and its products enjoy economies of scale (e.g. in R&D, advertising, and manufacturing), it can use its low-cost position to threaten the new entrants with a price war if they were to enter. It can also sign agreements with suppliers, distributors, complementors, and buyers to lock up critical inputs and complements.

Limit Pricing

An incumbent can also use limit pricing to deter entry. In limit pricing, a firm keeps its prices low, hoping that the low prices will discourage profit-motivated rational new entrants who want large profits from entering. The assumption is that the prices will remain low or even drop if the potential new entrant were to enter. Limit pricing will work only if there is something about the incumbent that allows it to keep its cost lower and can therefore pass on some of its costs savings to customers in the form of low prices. That would be possible, for example, if the first mover has established a system of activities that allows it to have a low-cost structure, enjoys economies of scale, has gone up the learning curve, or enjoys any other first-mover advantage that allows it to keep its costs low relative to those of potential new entrants. One important thing about limit pricing is that, like any other deterrent measure, there should be something about the firm that makes its "threat" of limit pricing credible. For example, if a firm can demonstrate that it has a low-cost structure that is difficult to replicate, potential new entrants are more likely to take it seriously when it threatens limit pricing or starts practicing it. As we will see below, irreversible investments in assets or activities that underpin the type of first-mover advantages that can allow a firm to keep its costs low can also lend credibility to a firm's decision to practice limit pricing.

Commitment and First-mover Advantages

In sequential games, the player that moves first has the potential to earn first-mover advantages. One way to demonstrate to potential followers that one has these first-mover advantages or is in the process of earning them, is to make the right commitments. The right commitments can deter or slow down entry by followers. For example, heavy investments in R&D and intellectual property protection capabilities (including lawyers) by a first mover tells potential followers that it is committed to acquiring and protecting its intellectual property.

For a commitment to be *effective* in deterring or slowing down competitors, it must be credible, visible to competitors, and understandable.[7] A commitment is *credible* if there is something about it that makes competitors believe in it and the options that it creates or limits. The primary driver of credibility is irreversibility of the commitment. A commitment is **irreversible** if it is costly or difficult to walk away from or undo. That would be the case, for example, if the assets that underpin the commitment cannot be profitably redeployed elsewhere. The idea here is that if a player's commitment is irreversible, the player is more likely to stay and fight followers rather than accommodate them or exit. Rational followers, knowing that the player is not likely to welcome entry, are likely to refrain from entering. Wal-Mart's saturation of neighboring small towns in the Southwestern USA with retail stores and matching distribution centers and logistics are another example of commitment. Since, for example, it would be difficult or costly to use Wal-Mart's thousands of stores and distribution centers in contiguous small towns for something other than retail, rational potential new entrants are less likely to try to enter these towns. Credibility of commitments also depends on the options that are eliminated when a firm makes the commitments. If, for example, in making the commitments, a player eliminates all its options, it is more likely to stick with the commitment and fight. In choosing to operate only out of secondary airports, for example, Ryanair is giving up the option to operate out of the larger more congested primary airports. Thus, anyone that wants to fight Ryanair in one of the secondary airports that it occupies should expect the airline to fight harder than it would fight if it could just pick up and move to a larger primary airport.

Of course, for a commitment to have the right effect on competitors, they must understand the commitment and its implications. In the fluid phase of a technological change, for example, there is so much market and technological uncertainty that it is difficult to tell what commitments and their likely outcomes are all about. A firm can make parts of its plants available for tours to demonstrate that it has investment in the right equipment and personnel. Many other commitments, such as investments in intangible assets or a commitment to keep prices high, are more difficult to see and understand. This is where signaling comes in.

Signaling and Reputation

If a player conveys meaningful information about itself to other players, it is said to be **signaling**.[8] Signals from a firm are usually designed to influence the perceptions of coopetitors' and their actions or reactions. Whether the signal is successful in conveying the right message is a function of the coopetitor's perception of the signal. Thus, the reputation of the firm that sends signals plays a major role in the effectiveness of the signal. An extended warrantee, for example, can be a signal of good quality and reliability. If the warrantee comes from a firm with a reputation for reliability, coopetitors are more likely to believe that the products are reliable. Brand names, packaging, advertising, and even prices can be signals of quality. A firm might publish the number of patents that it receives in a particular area every year to signal to competitors that it has the capabilities to maintain its first-mover advantage in intellectual property. Effectively, firms can use signals to influence the actions and reactions of coopetitors. The signals can sometimes be designed to confuse or fool competitors.

Encourage Entry

Sometimes, rather than try to deter firms from entering, a first mover is better off encouraging entry. That would be the case, for example, with a new market or product that needs a certain number of firms or complementors to give the new product credibility. For example, in the late 1970s, many businesses hesitated from buying PCs because they were being offered by many startups without credibility as business customers. IBM changed all that when it entered the market in 1981. It brought in a lot of customers and grew the market for everyone. We will return to encouraging entry when we explore cooperative game theory below.

Suppose a firm's efforts to prevent entry fail and a new entrant comes into the market; what should the incumbent do? The incumbent can either fight the new entrant, accommodate it, or change the rules of the game to make the market more attractive for the incumbent despite the entry.

Fight or Change the Rules of the Game

An incumbent can fight a new entrant using predatory actions such as predatory pricing, changing the rules of the game, or taking other measures such as increasing its capacity.

Predatory Activities

An incumbent's activities are **predatory** if they eliminate or discipline a rival, or inhibit a current or potential rival's competitive conduct.[9] One of the most studied such activities is predatory pricing. In predatory pricing, a firm lowers the price of its product with the intention of driving out or punishing rivals, or scaring off potential new entrants who see the low prices as a signal that post-entry prices will be low. During the period when prices are low, the firm and its rivals lose money. If these rivals are unable to sustain the losses, they go out of business or start behaving properly. The firm is then left with fewer or no rivals, or with well-behaved rivals. The firm can then raise its prices and start making a profit again, hopefully enough for it to recover the amounts lost. Predatory pricing can also be designed to depress the market value of a competitor so that the predator can buy the competitor or parts of it at below market prices, or to establish a reputation as a firm that tolerates neither entry nor behavior that it does not consider proper.

Predatory pricing is considered to be anticompetitive and illegal in many countries, including the USA. In these countries, predatory pricing cases are usually brought by firms (presumed preys), not by governments. In any case, it is difficult to prove predatory pricing. To prove it in the USA, for example, the plaintiff has to show that the lower price was temporary; that the intention of the accused predator, in lowering the price, was to drive out the rival; that by raising its prices again the accused predator could recoup the losses that it incurred from the price cuts; and that the low price is below the accused predator's average cost.

Change the Rules of the Game

Rather than use predatory pricing to fight new entrants, an incumbent can change the rules of the game in its favor. Although, as we will see later in this book, management literature is full of good examples of new entrants who attacked an industry by changing the rules of the game, incumbents can also change the rules of the game in the face of new entrants. One of the best ways to change the rules of the game is to change the payoffs not only for new entrants but also for incumbents. The case of Sun Microsystems provides a good example. In the late 1980s, Sun was an incumbent in the computer workstation industry and its workstations, like those of incumbents in the industry at the time, used a technology called CISC. Some new entrants started entering the industry using a new technology called RISC. In response to the entrants, Sun also introduced the new technology but rather than keep its version of the technology proprietary, Sun opened it up to anyone who wanted it.[10] This contrasted with its old CISC strategy and with the RISC strategies of its competitors. By making its RISC architecture open, Sun attracted many workstation makers that would not have entered the industry or that would have adopted incompatible RISC technologies. And the more workstation makers that adopted the technology, the more software that was developed for that particular technology. The more software that was developed for a technology, the more customers that wanted workstations from the technology. Sun's RISC technology ended up winning the RISC technology standard for workstations against other RISC technologies. Sun used its complementary assets—installed base, brand, distribution channels, and relationships with software developers—to exploit its open RISC architecture and was profitable for most of the 1990s.

Accommodate, Merge, or Exit

Rather than fight new entrants, an incumbent may decide to concede some of its market share. The decision not to fight may be because the incumbent does not have what it takes to fight. It may also be because the incumbent is smart enough to realize that wars—especially price wars—produce no winner, except some customers. The incumbent may welcome the new entrant and engage in tacit collusion. **Tacit collusion** is said to take place when rivals coordinate their activities and know that they are cooperating but there is no agreement, verbal or written. When the activity in question is pricing, it is also called **price leadership** or **cooperative pricing**. In fact, when many people talk of tacit collusion, they are talking about price leadership (cooperative pricing) although firms can also collude on when to introduce products, how much to spend on R&D, etc. Tacit collusion between firms can be facilitated by so-called *meeting the competition* or *most-favored customer* clauses, which at first may appear to be good for customers. Consider two such phrases: "We will not be undersold" or "We will match our competitors' prices, no matter how low." When a firm issues such clauses, it is telling its rivals to keep their prices at the high level. If for some reason the rivals lower their prices, the firm will lower its prices too and everyone will lose money. For fear of everyone losing money when they lower their prices, rivals may decide to keep their prices high. Tacit collusion is more likely to take place in a market where (1) the number of firms in the market is small, (2) firms in the market face each other repeatedly in some sort of a "repeated game" without knowing what the end game will be, (3) profits per firm in the market are higher under collusion than when there is no collusion, (4) the discount rate is low, or (5) the incremental profits for deviating firms are high.[11]

An incumbent may also be better off merging with a new entrant rather than fighting the entrant. That would be the case, for example, if the new entrant entered using a radical technological change that renders incumbents' technological capabilities noncompetitive but an incumbent has important scarce complementary assets that are needed to profit from the new technology. New entrants, using new games, can also change the structure of an industry so much that incumbents can no longer compete. In that case, an incumbent may be better off exiting the industry when it finds out that it no longer has what it takes to compete in the industry.

Cooperative Games

Recall that in noncooperative games, the unit of analysis is a player, usually a rival that is competing against another rival. Each player seeks to maximize its payoff no matter what the other player does. Thus, noncooperative game theory can, for example, help a firm analyze its decision to raise or lower its prices, taking the likely reaction of its rivals into consideration. However, noncooperative game theory tells us little about the bargaining power of suppliers, the power of complementors, or the bargaining power of buyers and their reservation prices. Nor does it say much about the role of complements and substitutes in the pricing decision. Apart from tacit collusion, noncooperative game theory does not say much else about explicit cooperation. Cooperative game theory does all these things that noncooperative game theory does not. This is fortunate because, as we have seen throughout this book, the positioning of a firm relative to its coopetitors, cooperation between coopetitors, reservation prices, and so on all play critical roles in value creation and appropriation. In cooperative games, the unit of analysis is a coalition of players. Each coalition is made up of a subset of coopetitors. Players' strategies are coordinated so as to maximize the payoff for the coalitions in the game.

Elements of a Cooperative Game

A cooperative game has two major elements: a set (coalition) of players and a *characteristic function*. Usually, the **players** are some subset of coopetitors—a subset of suppliers, rivals, complementors, and buyers. The characteristic function specifies the value created by different coalitions of players. To illustrate these elements, consider the following example.

Example 11.1

A biotech startup (S) has discovered a new drug and has three options to get it approved by the FDA and bring it to market. It can go it alone, form an alliance with either Firm A or Firm B, or form an alliance with both. If the startup (S) goes it alone, it earns $100 million from the drug. If it forms an alliance with A, the coalition earns $150 million since A has the marketing and clinical testing assets. If S forms the alliance with B, the team earns $200 million because B not only has marketing and clinical testing capabilities, it also has a strong sales force that already sells B's drugs.

The different coalitions and the value created by each are shown in Table 11.1. If the drug is not marketed at all, no value is created. If S markets the product alone, the value created is 100. Either A or B, without S has no product to sell and therefore the value created by each is zero. The value created by the AB coalition is also zero. The value created by the SA, the coalition of S and A, is 150 while the value created by SB, the coalition of S and B is 200. Note, in particular, that SAB, the coalition of all three firms, results in the same value as the coalition of S and B. That is because SA is dominated by SB; that is, B does everything that A would be needed for. The mapping of the coalitions into value created is the **characteristic function**. Effectively, the characteristic function can also be described as the collective payoff that players can gain by forming coalitions.

Let us introduce some terminology to make things more concise. Let N be the set of players in a game, and C be any subset of the N players that can form a coalition. We say that $v(C)$ is the value created when the subset C forms a coalition. And $v(C\{p\})$ is the value created when play p is excluded from coalition (group) C. In our biotech example, $N = \{S, A, B\}$ since there is a total of three players; $v(S) = 100$ since the value of S going it alone is $100 million; $v(A) = 0$, $v(B) = 0$, and $v(AB) = 0$ since neither each of A or B working alone nor as a coalition creates value; $v(SA) = 150$ since a coalition of S and A nets $150 million; and $v(SAB) = 200$ since a coalition of all three nets $200 million.

Table 11.1 A Mapping of Coalitions into Value Created

Coalition	O	S	A	B	AB	SA	SB	AB	SAB
Value created or collective payoff (numbers in $M)	0	100	0	0	0	150	200	0	200

Also, the value created when player S is not in the coalition is 0; that is, v(C{S}) = 0; Also, v(C{A}) = 200; v(C{B}) = 150.

Marginal Contribution and Appropriation of Value Co-created

So far, we have discussed how different players come together to co-create value for their coalitions. The question remains, how do members of each coalition share in the appropriation of the value co-created? Of course, the amount that each player appropriates depends on many factors, including its bargaining power vis-à-vis the other co-creators of the value. The amount also depends, in part, on how much each player contributed to the value creation. It depends on each player's *marginal contribution* or added value. (A firm's contribution to value creation also contributes to its bargaining power.) A firm's marginal contribution or **added value** (to coalition) is the amount by which the total value created would shrink if the firm left the game.[12] Thus, to determine the added value of a firm, we calculate the total value with the firm in the game and the total value without the firm. The difference between the two numbers is the firm's added value or marginal contribution. In the biotech example:

The marginal contribution of the startup S is:

$$v(SAB) - v(C\{S\}) = v(SAB) - v(AB) = 200 - 0 = 200.$$

The marginal contribution of A is:

$$v(SAB) - v(C\{A\}) = 200 - 200 = 0.$$

That for B is:

$$v(SAB) - v(C\{B\}) = 200 - 150 = 50.$$

If we assume that the value appropriated (captured) by each actor is proportional to the value created by the actor and that no firm can appropriate more value than it has created, then we can expect A to appropriate none of the $200 million, since its contribution to the value created is zero. B, on the other hand, can appropriate up to $50 million while S can appropriate a minimum of $150 million (200–50) but not more than $200 million. Effectively, of the $200 million created, the value appropriated by S ranges from 150 to 200 while that captured by B ranges from 50 and 0. Just where in this range S and B make the split depends on those aspects of their bargaining powers that have little to do with value creation. We will return to another example a little later.

Changing the Game

Recall that a cooperative game has two major elements: a set (coalition) of players and a characteristic function that is a function of the interactions between the players. One depiction of the players that are typically involved in value creation and appropriation, and the interdependencies among these players, is shown in Figure 11.6. These players and their interdependencies

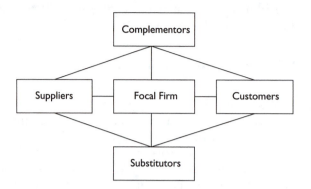

Figure 11.6 Players in a Value Creation and Appropriation Game.

constitute what Professors Brandenburger and Nalebuff called the *value net*.[13] Interactions in the value net during value creation and appropriation can be thought of as being in two dimensions. Along the horizontal dimension are the now familiar suppliers and customers with whom the firm interacts and transacts to create and appropriate value.[14] Along the vertical dimension are the complementors and substitutors with whom the firm interacts but not necessarily transacts. Complementors are the players from whom customers buy complements, or that buy complementary resources from suppliers.[15] Substitutors are players (existing rivals, potential new entrants, providers of substitutes) from whom customers may buy products or to whom suppliers can sell their resources. Note that in other strategy frameworks such as Porter's Five Forces, substitutors are all seen as competitors that must be fought and vanquished. In cooperative game theory, they are seen as potential collaborators with whom a firm can cooperate to create value and compete to appropriate it.

Changing the game entails changing one or more of its elements. Each change in any of the elements of a cooperative game that we have explored above is effectively a *new game strategy* on the part of the player that initiates the change. This has implications for value creation and appropriation.

Changing Players

A new game can arise from a firm changing one of the players, including itself. Through the right moves or set of activities, a firm can change the number of players, types of player or the roles played by players. Such changes can have a direct impact on the value created and how much of it a firm can appropriate. The more customers, suppliers, complementors, and *sometimes* substitutors that a firm has in a game, the higher the value created and the better the chances of the firm appropriating value created. Let us start with the most obvious. The more customers that a firm can bring into the value net, the more valuable the value net becomes, since it has more players who can pay for the value created. The more suppliers that are in a coalition, the better the chances of finding one with whom the firm can cooperate. The more suppliers, the better a firm's chances of having bargaining power over them. It is probably for these two reasons that most major firms insist on having second sources for their key components; that is, such firms insist on having more than one supplier of the same component. More complementors can mean more and better complements. The more complements, the more valuable a product. Effectively, a firm can change the game in its favor by changing the number of customers, suppliers, and complementors.

A firm can also change the game by changing the type of player in its value net. The classic example is that of Dell when it entered the PC market. It bypassed distributors and started selling directly to end-customers who could get computers customized *just for them*. This move had both value creation and appropriation effects for Dell. First, by dealing directly with end-customers, Dell could better co-create the type of value that customers wanted through its build-to-order capabilities. It could also offer service to some customers, making the value net more valuable to them. Second, by changing players from the more concentrated and powerful distributors to the more fragmented and less powerful end-customers, Dell increased its bargaining power vis-à-vis customers. It also lowered its sales and marketing costs.

Increasing substitutors—existing rivals, potential new entrants, and makers of substitute products—can sometimes be good for value creation. Early in the life of a product or technology that exhibits network externalities, joining forces with many competitors can increase the value of a firm's value net. That is because the more customers that use such a product/technology or compatible one, the more valuable the product/technology becomes to each customer; and the more competitors that sell the product/technology or compatible one, the more customers that will use it. Having competitors join forces to push a product can help the product win a standard. The story of the PC is now a classic example. By making it possible for new entrants and other rivals to clone its version of the PC, IBM increased the number of PC manufacturers. The more such manufacturers, the more software developers that opted to write software for PCs, thereby increasing the value of the PC value net. Increasing competition, especially in fast-paced industries, can also force a firm to become a better developer of newer and better products.

Apart from these exceptions, the goal is to eliminate substitutors or greatly to reduce their number.

Changing Value Added and Interaction Between Players

Recall that a firm's added value = total value created with the firm in the game minus the total value created without the firm in the game. Therefore, when the right player joins a game, it increases the value of the game. Thus, one way to increase added value is to add the right number of players of the right quality. The question here is, what can be done to create additional added value in a value net, without adding players? Additional value can be created by performing innovation activities that allow a firm to deliver better differentiated or lower-cost products than existing ones. Recall from Chapter 4 that value created is the difference between the benefits that customers perceive and the cost of providing these benefits. Thus the activities that a firm can perform to create additional value also include those activities that are designed to create customer benefits and influence customers' perception as well as those that are designed to keep overall costs down. (Chapter 4 was all about value creation and appropriation.)

Example 11.2

As another example, consider a market in which there are two suppliers, two firms, and one buyer.[16] The buyer is willing to pay $60 for Firm X's product but only $120 for Firm Y's product. Each supplier's cost of supplying the product is $5. We will call the suppliers S_1 and S_2, and the buyer, B.

The value created by the different groups or coalitions (submarkets) of players is shown in Table 11.2. We start our discussion of the example with suppliers. Since suppliers are identical and only one of them is needed, a market with either one or both suppliers creates the same value. Therefore the value created by S_1S_2XYB, S_1XYB, or S_2XYB is the same. Since the buyer is willing to pay $120 for Firm Y's product but only $60 for Firm X's product, the value created by a coalition of the buyer, Firm Y and any supplier nets $115 (i.e. $120 minus the $5 cost of either supplier), with or without Firm X; that is, $v(S_1S_2XYB) = v(S_1XYB) = v(S_2XYB) = v(S_1S_2YB) = 115$. Note that without the buyer, there is no value created as far as the market is concerned and therefore $v(S_1S_2XY) = v(S_1XY) = v(S_2Y) = v(S_1S_2) = 0$. Also note that with Firm X in the game, without Firm Y, the value created is only $55 ($60 – $5) since the buyer is willing to pay only $60 for Firm X's product. Thus, $v(S_1S_2XB) = v(S_1XB) = v(S_2XB) = 55$.

The value added by each player and the information for calculating these values are shown in Table 11.3. Column 2 shows the value created without the player in question. Column 3 shows the value created by a market (coalition) of all the players. The value added by any player, as we saw earlier, is the value created with the player in the market minus the value created by the market without the player; that is, value added by coalition C = $v(S_1S_2XYB) – v(C\{p\})$. Recall that $v(C\{p\})$ is the value created when play p is excluded from coalition C. Suppliers 1 and 2 do not add any value. That is because of the competitive effect that results from having two identical suppliers. When one is not in the market, the other can do the job. Firm X does not add any value when Firm Y is in the market, since the buyer values Firm Y's product more than Firm X's. When Firm Y is not in the market, then Firm X adds value to the market. Because there is only one buyer, but two firms in the market, the buyer can play the firms against each other.

If we assume that no firm can appropriate more value than it created, then the amounts in column 4 (value added column), are the maximum amounts that each firm can expect to capture. These amounts of value added by each player add up to more than the value of $115 created by the market. The question is, how are the $115 shared between the buyer and Firm Y? (The suppliers and

Table 11.2 Coalitions (submarkets) and Value Created

Coalition (submarket)	S_1S_2XYB	S_2XYB	S_1XYB	S_1S_2YB	S_1S_2XB	S_1S_2XY	S_1S_2	S_2Y	XY
Value created	115	115	115	115	55	0	0	0	0

Table 11.3 Value Added and Guaranteed Minimum

Player p	Value created without player p $v(C\{p\})$	Value created by all players $v(S_1S_2XYB)$	Value added $v(S_1S_2XYB) -$ $v(C\{p\})$	Guaranteed minimum appropriation
Supplier 1 (S_1)	$v(S_2XYB) = 115$	115	0	0
Supplier 2 (S_2)	$v(S_1XYB) = 115$	115	0	0
Firm X	$v(S_1S_2YB) = 115$	115	0	0
Firm Y	$v(S_1S_2XB) = 55$	115	60	0
Buyer	$v(S_1S_2XY) = 0$	115	115	55

Firm X cannot capture more than $0.) Since Firm X provides competition for Firm Y, the maximum that Firm Y can hope to capture is $60, the value added by Firm X. (If Firm Y were to ask for more than $60, the buyer would turn to Firm X, whose product it values at $60.) This means that the buyer is guaranteed a minimum of $55 ($115 – 60). The remaining $60 can be divided between Firm Y and the buyer, as a function of each firm's bargaining power.

Applying Game Theory to Value Creation and Appropriation

Now that we have briefly explored game theory, the question is, of what use is it in a firm's quest to create and appropriate value using new game strategies? We answer this question by first summarizing the usefulness of game theory in business in general, and then by zooming in on its usefulness to value creation and appropriation in particular.

Usefulness and Limitations of Game Theory in Business

Recall that firms create and appropriate value by performing activities of their value chain. At each stage of its value chain, a firm usually has options as to which value chain activities to perform; how, where, and when to perform them. Game theory can help firms better choose which activities to perform, when, where, and how to perform them, since it explicitly takes the likely actions and reactions of coopetitors into consideration. For example, to create value, an airplane maker has to perform R&D to develop its prototype, turn the prototype into an airplane that can be manufactured cost effectively, get it safety certified by government agencies, establish relationships with suppliers of components, build inbound logistics for components, build manufacturing capabilities, manufacture, price the planes, sell, finance, and distribute the planes. Given that the aircraft maker's competitors may be just as interested in performing these activities, game theory can help the firm to take the likely actions and reactions of coopetitors into consideration when making decisions about which of these activities to perform, how to perform them, and when. The question is, *how*?

Framing Strategic Questions

Game theory offers a language and structure for describing the interdependence between a firm and its coopetitors. By identifying the players, specifying each player's possible moves (strategies), the timing of the moves and payoffs, game theory enables firms to frame strategy questions that anticipate coopetitors' likely actions and reactions better. This enhanced framing of questions can help the decision-making that underpins value creation and appropriation. Using our aircraft maker example, simultaneous games can be used to explore what happens if the firm were to offer the same plane as its major competitor, if it raised its price, etc. Sequential games can be used to explore what happens if the aircraft maker were to offer each type of airplane first or second, etc.

Insights, Possibilities, and Consequences

Game theory can also be used to understand the structure of the interaction between a firm and its coopetitors better. It can be used to understand the options for changing the rules of the game and the consequences. It enables firms to figure out what the right moves for the particular situation are. Thus, an aircraft maker can use game theory to help it explore the consequences of offering different types of aircraft on its suppliers, complementors, customers, and rivals. It would also help in understanding what would happen if the firm were to form a coalition with one set of coopetitors rather than another.

Anticipating the Future

By using cooperative game theory questions, a firm can imagine how its relationships and industry would evolve if it were not part of it.[17] For example, a firm can ask how well-off its alliance is without it in the alliance, and how well-off it will be in the future without it. This is a powerful question because it reminds the firm not only of what it has to offer to the alliance relative to other coopetitors in the alliance but also of the self-interest of the coopetitors that might be changing. For employees, it may also be a good idea to ask themselves how much value is created without them working for their firm and with them working for the firm.[18]

Limitations of Game Theory

Game theory models, like any other model, have their limitations. To see some of these limitations, let us go back to one of the examples that we saw earlier (Figure 11.3). By taking each other's likely reaction into consideration, Firm B and Firm A can avoid building the same plane and finding themselves with too many planes and not enough sales to break even. They also avoid competing for suppliers of components and skilled employees. Thus, by helping firms to decide which planes to build, game theory helps them better to create and appropriate value. An underlying assumption in the argument of Figure 11.3 is that both firms have the resources and capabilities to develop, manufacture, certify, and perform every other activity that it takes to offer a plane that customers value, once each firm decides which plane to offer. The fact is that not every firm that decides to build a plane can build it. Game theory says little about why some firms have the resources and capabilities that it takes to create and appropriate value. Nor does it say much about the procedure for creating and appropriating value.[19] "In business, as in other games, firms can only do as well as the hand they have been dealt."[20]

Game theory also assumes that actors select those actions that maximize their payoffs, where payoffs can be any measure of performance including profits or utility. However, firms and the managers that take decisions often have nonprofit-maximizing behaviors. For example, a firm may take a decision for political reasons that has nothing to do with maximizing profits. Another assumption of game theory is that actors have no cognitive limitations and will be able to obtain and process all the information needed to take the decisions, no matter how complex the information. Most human beings are cognitively limited. Finally, game theory models usually say nothing about the focal firm's larger strategy. For example, in the case of Figure 11.3, we do not know if one of these airplane makers also offers military planes to governments and can therefore easily modify the plane that it chooses to offer to transport military gear. These shortcomings notwithstanding, game theory is still a very good tool. Like any other tool, game theory has to be used with care, paying attention to its assumptions and the context in which it is used, if one expects to get much out of it.

Game Theory and New Game Activities

With this summary of the usefulness and limitations of game theory, we return to our earlier question: how useful is game theory in a firm's quest to create and appropriate value using new game activities? One way to answer this question is to explore the extent to which game theory can be used to explain the contribution of new game activities to value creation and appropriation. To do so, we recall from Chapter 4 that there are two components to the contribution of a new game activity to value creation and appropriation: (1) the value chain factor and (2) the new game factor.

The Value Chain Factor and the Usefulness of Game Theory

As we saw in Chapter 4, new game activities, by virtue of being value chain activities, are most likely to contribute to value creation and appropriation if they:

a Contribute to lower cost, differentiation, better pricing, more customers, and better sources of revenue.
b Contribute to improving the firm's position vis-à-vis coopetitors.
c Take advantage of industry value drivers.
d Build and translate distinctive resources/capabilities.
e Are comprehensive and parsimonious.

Contribute to Lower Cost, Differentiation, Better Pricing, More Customers, and Better Sources of Revenues

A firm can use noncooperative game theory to explore which product to offer, which market segment to enter, whether to raise or lower one's prices, what brand to build, which sources of revenue to target, and which customers to target, given the likely reaction of the firm's rivals. This, however, will not say much about the bargaining that may go on between the firm and its customer (especially in business-to-business transactions). Nor does it do much for any cooperation the firm and its customers may undertake to create better customer value and possibly raise customer reservation prices. This is where cooperative game theory comes in. It can help firms to understand better how much value can be created by which coalitions (of itself and its coopetitors). Cooperative game theory helps in the analysis of the interdependencies between a firm and its coopetitors that can be critical to targeting the right customers with the right value, and pursuing the right pricing strategies and sources of revenue.

However, while game theory can say something about which brand to build, given the brands being pursued by one's rivals, it says little about cultivating the ability to build brands. While it can help with analyzing whether and when to offer a new product targeted at the right customers, it says little about the ability to build new products. An implicit assumption in many game theory models is that firms will be able to offer the new product or brand that they decide to build, given their rivals' likely reaction. Many firms that invest in new products targeted at profitable product market positions have failed because they did not have what it takes to develop and commercialize the products.

Contribute to Improving the Firm's Position vis-à-vis Coopetitors

In taking the likely actions and reactions of rivals into consideration, non-cooperative game theory can help a firm to avoid unnecessary competition. For example, in the game of Figure 11.3, both firms can avoid crashing with each other in two markets, each of which cannot support both firms: if one firm offers the SuperJumbo, the other firm should offer the DreamLiner. Thus, non-cooperative game theory can help a firm dampen or reverse the competitive force from rivalry that can impede the firm's ability to create and appropriate value. Cooperative game theory can be used to explore the bargaining and cooperation that goes on between a firm and its coopetitors. For example, by working with its customers to help them discover their latent needs in a new product, a firm can raise customer's willingness to pay. By working with suppliers to help them reduce their costs, the suppliers are more likely to accept lower prices from the firm.

Again, while game theory can help a firm to understand what activity to pursue to improve its position vis-à-vis coopetitors, given rivals' likely reaction, it says little about the ability of the firm to pursue the particular activity. For example, in Figure 11.3, while noncooperative game theory suggests that Firm A should offer the SuperJumbo, knowing that Firm B will offer the DreamLiner, it says little about how capable Firm A is at building the SuperJumbo; and while cooperative game theory can help a firm to understand which suppliers it can work with better to create value, it says little about why some firms are better at such cooperation than others. In the automobile industry, for example, Toyota has done an outstanding job working with its suppliers to innovate and keep component costs down, compared to Ford and GM. Game theory tells us little about what the superior capabilities of Toyota are in working with suppliers and how one would go about building them.

Take Advantage of Industry Value Drivers

Recall that industry value drivers are those industry factors that stand to have a substantial impact on the benefits (low-cost or differentiation) that customers want, or the quality and number of such customers. For example, in offline retailing, location is critical since it determines the types and numbers of customers who can shop there, the cost of operations, cost of real estate, and the number and types of competitor. A firm can use game theory better to take advantage of industry value drivers. For example, in choosing a retail location, a firm can use game theory to avoid head-on competition with other retailers.

Build and Translate Distinctive Resources/Capabilities

Decisions to increase or decrease R&D spending, whether or not to patent, where to build what plant, which brand to build, etc. are all decisions about building resources/capabilities and as previous examples have shown, noncooperative game theory can be used to enlighten such decisions. Cooperative game theory can also help firms to understand the extent to which a firm can cooperate with its coopetitors in building such resources and capabilities. While game theory can be used to understand whether to increase or decrease R&D spending, for example, it says little about why some firms are better at R&D than others. Sound game theoretic analysis may suggest that, given what a firm's competitors are doing, the firm should increase its R&D spending. Game theory says little about why, even with the increased spending, the firm may still not be able to effectively and efficiently carry out the experimentation, trial, error, and correction that are critical to R&D.

Are Comprehensive and Parsimonious

The idea here is to make sure that a firm performs all the activities that make a significant contribution towards value creation and appropriation while also making sure that it does not perform activities that add little or no value relative to their costs. Noncooperative game theory can help a firm to determine which activities yield the highest payoffs and keep or add them. Cooperative game theory can be used to determine which actions result in coalitions with the most value created. Effectively, game theory can be useful in determining which activities to keep or add and which ones to jettison. However, game theory says very little about why one firm may be able to perform a particular activity more effectively or efficiently than its rivals.

The New Game Factor and the Usefulness of Game Theory

As we also saw in Chapter 4, new game activities, by virtue of being *new game*, are most likely to contribute to value creation and appropriation if they:

a Generate new ways of creating and capturing new value.
b Offer opportunity to build new resources or translate existing ones in new ways into value.
c Build and take advantage of first-mover's advantages and disadvantages, and competitors' handicaps.
d Anticipate and respond to coopetitors reactions.
e Identify and take advantage of the opportunities and threats of the competitive and macroenvironment.

Generate New Ways of Creating and Capturing New Value

Cooperative game theory can help us to analyze how adding players or changing the game can create or destroy value. It can tell us which coalitions will create what value. Noncooperative game theory can tell us which moves by which players can result in what payoffs. However, game theory cannot tell us how each player actually improves its own products. It cannot help us understand the nuts and bolts of how Boeing actually designs and builds safe aircraft.

Build and Take Advantage of First-mover's Advantages and Disadvantages, and Competitors' Handicaps

Recall that sequential games are games in which some players move first. As we saw earlier, the first mover can then decide whether to yield to entry, or work hard to deter it; and if it yields to entry, whether to accommodate, fight, or exit. For example, an incumbent can decide to increase entry costs by taking advantage of economies of scale in advertising and R&D, or its accumulated scarce resources. If there is entry, the firm can decide whether to fight the new entrant or accommodate the entry. Effectively, game theory can be used to explore whether to deter entry or yield, accommodate new entrants or fight them, which first-mover advantages to pursue or take advantage of, given rivals' likely actions and reactions. However, game theory does not help much with how efficiently and effectively one can build and take advantage of first-mover advantages.

Anticipate and Respond to Coopetitors' Reactions

Recall that game theory can be used to understand the interaction between a firm and its coopetitors and to understand the options for changing the rules of the game and the consequences. Thus, one of the premier applications of game theory is to explore how best to perform new game activities, taking the likely actions and reactions of coopetitors into consideration. In some ways, the primary advantage of game theory is in taking the likely reaction of one's coopetitors into consideration when taking a decision.

Identify and Take Advantage of the Opportunities and Threats of The Competitive and Macroenvironment

When a firm identifies opportunities and threats in its environment, the chances are that its rivals also see the same opportunities and threats and would like to take advantage of them too. Game theory helps firms to take into consideration the likely actions and reactions of competitors in taking advantage of the opportunities and threats of their environments. Noncooperative game theory can help a firm to explore questions such as whether to enter a new market (say, opened up by deregulation), where to position its products in the market (identified white space), and how much money to spend on advertising or government regulations. Cooperative game theory helps firms to analyze the interaction between a firm and its coopetitors as it creates and appropriates value. However, game theory does not say much about what types of resource a firm needs so as to take best advantage of the opportunities and threats.

Summary and Conclusions

If a firm views activities as potentially profitable, the chances are that its competitors would also find the same activities or related ones as profitable. Therefore, before pursuing any activities, a firm may be better off anticipating the actions and reactions of its coopetitors—be they rivals, suppliers, complementors, buyers, or makers of substitute products. In an industry analysis tool such as Porter's Five Forces that explores the role of rivalry in profitability, emphasis is on factors such as the number of sellers in the market, whether the industry is growing or declining, differences in firms' costs, excess capacity, level of product differentiation, history of cooperative pricing, observability of prices, and whether there are strong exit barriers. Beyond these factors that impact overarching rivalry in the industry, the interactions that take place among firms can also have a huge impact on profitability. This is where game theory comes in. Game theory encourages managers to factor the likely reaction of coopetitors into their decisions; that is, it encourages managers to factor into their actions, not only what coopetitors are planning to do but also what is in the coopetitor's best interest.

Both noncooperative and cooperative game theory can be useful tools for exploring value creation and appropriation activities. The former enables firms to ask questions such as, what should my actions be, given the likely actions and reactions of my rivals who are acting in their own individual self-interests? It can be used to explore elements of both value creation and appropriation. However, noncooperative game theory leaves a firm's interaction with its coopetitors—suppliers, customers, complementors, and rivals—largely explored. Cooperative game theory is about these interactions (bargaining, cooperating, etc.) between firms and their coopetitors. The payoffs are for different coalitions and competition is between coalitions. As pointed out by Professor H. W. Stuart, cooperative game theory opens up even more interesting questions for firms, such as: if a firm were not around, from whom would its buyers buy? Would its buyers have a lower willingness to pay for the alternatives? To whom might its suppliers sell? While cooperative game theory has both cooperative and competitive elements, noncooperative game theory has largely competitive elements and limited cooperative elements. Ultimately, competitive advantage comes from a distinctive system of activities or distinctive resources. Game theory does not say much about the sources of resources or systems of activities. It does not say much about the procedure for creating or appropriating value.

Exercises

1   In the game of Figure 11.7:

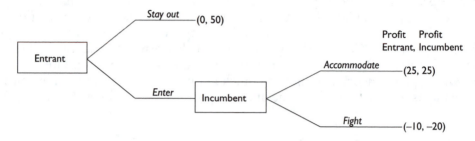

Figure 11.7 For Question 1.

    a   Would the threat of the incumbent to fight the entrant be credible?

    b   If the $20 payoff were $26, would the threat to fight the new entrant be credible?

    c   What type of new game activity could the incumbent perform to increase the payoff from $20 to $26?

2   Consider a market in which there are two suppliers, three firms, and two buyers. The buyers' willingness to pay for each firm's product is the same: $60. Each supplier's cost of supplying the product is $5.

    a   What is the value added by each player?

    b   How much value does each player appropriate?

    c   Suppose there is only one firm. What would the value added for each firm be?

3   Which one is a better tool for value appropriation: cooperative or noncooperative game theory? Why?

Key Terms

Characteristic function
Cooperative game
Cooperative game theory
Dominant strategy
Dominant strategy equilibrium
Marginal contribution
Nash equilibrium
Noncooperative game
Noncooperative game theory
Prisoner's dilemma
Simultaneous games
Strategy (in game theory)
Value net

Part IV

Applications

Chapter 12

Entering a New Business Using New Games

One of the most important decisions that a firm can take is to enter a new business. If successful, entering a new business can contribute to a firm's growth rate and profits. If unsuccessful, entering a new business can drain a firm of important resources that could have been invested elsewhere and may damage the reputation of the firm. In this chapter, we explore a framework that not only can be used to evaluate a firm's entry into a new business but also can be used to aid a firm in taking the decision to enter a new business. Our definition of a new business is very broad. Entering a new business can range anywhere from entering a new market segment using one's existing technologies, to adopting a new technology that takes one into a new market segment, to diversifying into a totally unrelated business using radically different technologies. We start off by looking at some of the reasons that managers—rightfully or wrongfully—often give for entering a new business.

Why Firms Enter New Businesses

There are several reasons why a firm would want to enter a new business: We explore seven of these reasons: growth, resources/capabilities, economies of scale and scope, internal financial markets, market power, and personal.

Growth

One of the most popular reasons offered by firms when they decide to enter a new business is the pursuit of growth. A firm's existing business may be in a mature industry that is stagnant or slowly dying and the firm wants to enter an industry with better growth perspectives to assure its long-term viability. In some cases, a firm may find itself in a situation where it grew a lot for a few years and because of that growth, its stock is now very highly valued, where the high valuation has factored in the assumption that the firm will continue to grow at the existing rate. The firm may then be tempted to move into other markets to sustain that growth rate. As we will see later on, the fact that a new business is fast-growing is neither a sufficient nor necessary condition to enter the business.

Resources/Capabilities

A firm may have distinctive resources/capabilities that can be extended profitably into different markets. Such a firm can use the resources/capabilities to enter new businesses. A popular example is that of Honda, which has used its internal combustion engine capabilities to enter different businesses that include motorcycles, automobiles, lawnmowers, marine vehicles, electric generators, and airplane engines. As another example, eBay built a brand name reputation and a large community of registered users that were originally used by members to trade in antiques and collectibles. As the community grew larger and its brand became even more popular, eBay was able to use these resources to enter other categories such as automobiles. Sometimes, firms generate lots of cash and may feel compelled to invest the cash in new businesses.

Economies of Scope and Scale

A firm enjoys economies of scope if its per unit costs of offering more than one product are less than those of offering only one product. If a firm enters a new business and can utilize some of its existing resources/capabilities to perform activities in the new as well as old business, the cost of each business may be lower than if the firm operated each business without the other. For example, the more businesses in which Honda can use its engines, the smaller the cost of some of its R&D on a per unit basis. A firm can also enjoy economies of scale by entering a new business. For example, if the new business has common inputs, a firm may be able to combine its purchasing activities, thereby reducing its costs through increased bargaining power and other cost-saving activities.

Internal Financial Market

If a firm has more than one business, some of them may generate more cash than others. The cash generated can be used to finance the activities of the businesses that are more cash-strapped. For example, a firm in a seasonal business may be out of cash during the off-season but full of cash during the on-season. Having another business that generates cash during the existing business' off-season can smoothen the cash cycle. A firm can also buy a new business that generates cash so that it can use the cash to feed fast-growing businesses that need lots of cash. By advocating the creation of a portfolio of businesses in which cash from so-called cash cows can be used to finance the activities of so-called stars that usually need lots of cash but do not generate enough, the BCG Growth/Share matrix framework epitomized this idea. The argument against entering a new business so as to promote better internal financial management is that in a world of efficient capital markets, shareholders can take the cash from the existing business and invest in any other business that they want; that is, shareholders are better able to make decisions on which business to enter than managers. Moreover, if a business needs cash, it can raise it from the financial markets. The problem with this argument is that capital markets, especially in developing economies, are not always efficient. A capital market is efficient if information about alternate investment opportunities, the firms that want to borrow, what these firms want to do with the money, their honest intentions, and so on is easily available to everyone at low cost. When capital markets are not efficient, it may make sense to enter another business so as to find cash or use existing cash to finance businesses internally. In fact, businesses often create financing units to provide financing to customers of their other business units. Some of these financing units are often very profitable.

Market Power

Consider two firms that have the potential to have a Coke and Pepsi-type coexistence that allows them to thrive. If these two firms have multiple businesses and encounter each other in more than one business, the chances of their cooperating tacitly are higher, since the benefits of cooperating are higher in more businesses than in only one business. Put differently, the losses from not cooperating can be very large when firms encounter each other in many businesses. For example, if firms engage in price wars in many businesses, they stand to lose a lot more money than if they did so in just one business. Thus, a firm may enter other businesses so as to better cooperate tacitly with a competitor that it faces in other businesses. A firm with more than one business can also use its market power in one business to give it an advantage in other businesses. This may be illegal in some countries. For example, Microsoft was accused of using its power in operating systems to have an advantage in Web browsers.

Personal Managerial Reasons

Managers' incentives for performing certain activities can sometimes diverge from their firm's interests. A manager might enter a new business not so much because he/she believes that the new business will be profitable but because he or she wants to build an empire. That would be the case, especially if the manager's compensation is tied to the growth rate of the company and to enter new businesses increases that growth rate.

Reduce Transaction Costs

If a firm's critical input or complement comes from a competitor or potential competitor and there are no reliable second sources for the input or complement, the firm may want to start producing the input or complement. Why? Because the competitor, in looking after its own interests, may decide to use the component or complement in ways that are not in the firm's interests. For example, a maker of microchips that also uses the chips to make cameras may decide to keep the latest and most critical information about upcoming chips for itself when such information can give it an advantage in cameras that more than outweigh any advantage from selling the chips to competitors. The question becomes, why not enter into agreements that specify what each party is supposed to do? In cases where there are lots of contingencies to the contract and there is a lot of uncertainty, it is too costly to draft, monitor, and enforce such a contract. Thus, many contracts are necessarily incomplete and as uncertainty unfolds, a competitor who supplies a component or complement may decide to be opportunistic. The fear of such opportunism can be enough to force a firm to enter the business of producing the component or complement for its products rather than depending on suppliers and complementors. The fear of opportunism from complementors may be one reason why Apple introduced Safari, its own Web browser.

Whatever a firm's reasons for entering a new business, in the end the firm has to be as profitable or more profitable when it enters the new business than it was before entering. Whether a firm is profitable in a new business depends on how well the firm is able to create and appropriate value, given the attractiveness of the business.

Managers may give all sorts of reasons for entering a new business. When all is said and done, the firm has to make profits either from the new business, or from the old business as a result of entering the new business. This entails creating and appropriating value in the new business or as a result of the new business.

Evaluating the New Business for Entry: The Three Tests

Since firms are in business to make money, a firm that wants to enter a new business ought to plan on being at least as profitable as it was before entering the new business. That will be the case if the firm makes money in the new business or there is something about entering the new business that increases the profitability of the firm's existing (old) business. Making money in the new business entails creating value and appropriating it. Doing so entails competing with rivals for resources and customers, cooperating and bargaining with suppliers and customers, and coping with the threat of substitutes and potential new entry. Therefore one of the first things to do in evaluating a new business for potential entry is to understand the nature of the competitive and macroenvironmental forces that firms in the new business face. This appraisal of industry forces is called the *attractiveness test* since it explores the extent to which competitive and macroenvironmental forces impact average profits in the new business.[1] The attractiveness tests tells us something about average profitability in the new business but says little about how much of these profits the firm can make, relative to its rivals, when it enters the new business. This is where the second and third tests—the better-off and *cost-of-entry tests*—come in. The **better-off test** evaluates the extent to which a firm stands to profit by entering the new industry. Finally, since building entry capabilities cost money, it is also important to evaluate the cost of entry. This is about how much it costs to enter a business relative to the profits generated by virtue of entering the business. We now explore all three tests in detail.

Attractiveness Test

The attractiveness test helps a firm that wants to enter a new business to understand better what it is getting itself into by entering the new business. The test examines the simple questions: what are the competitive and macroenvironmental forces that the firm would face if it were to enter the new business? Who are the key competitors that the firm would have to worry about if it were to enter the new business, and what is it about these competitors that the firm should worry about? Which suppliers and customers dominate? Do makers of substitutes//complements or potential new entrants pose a threat? What is the profitability of the new business?

Competitive and Macroenvironmental Forces

A business is **attractive** if it is, on average, profitable to the firms in it. Recall that a business' profitability depends, in part, on the competitive forces in the business—in particular, it depends on the rivalry in the business, the bargaining power of suppliers and buyers, the threat of potential new entry and the power of substitutes/complementors. If rivalry is high, buyers and suppliers have bargaining power, the threat of potential new entry, and of substitutes/complementors is high, then the business is not profitable and therefore termed unattractive to firms in it. This does not mean that a firm cannot make money in the business. Firms can and do make money in unattractive industries but doing so is more difficult than in an attractive one. Effectively, a firm that plans to enter an unattractive business must be ready to deal with the repressive forces that existing firms in it face. Such a firm should identify what the repressive forces are and find ways to dampen their effect or eliminate them.

If rivalry in business is low, business firms have bargaining power over buyers and suppliers, and the threat of potential new entry and of substitutes/complementors is low, the business is said to be attractive (to firms in it) since it is, on average, profitable. The fact that a business is growing does not necessarily mean that the business is attractive. High growth lowers only one of the competitive forces in an industry and little else. An attractive business is good for firms that are already in the business but not necessarily for a firm that wants to enter the business. There are four reasons why an attractive business (for firms already in it) may not be attractive to an outsider. First, one reason why the business is attractive may be because firms in the business have a history of retaliating against new entrants, thereby decreasing new entry or keeping any firms that enter in check. This may be a warning shot to any firm that is contemplating entry. Second, if one reason for the attractiveness of the business is high barriers to entry, an outsider that wants to make money in the business must overcome the barriers to entry. Doing so can be very costly. Third, incumbent firms in the business may have distinctive capabilities (including complementary assets) that are difficult for new entrants to acquire. Fourth, if the business is attractive, it is possible that many other firms want to enter and enjoy the profits. This desire to enter means that potential new entrants may end up bidding up the prices of the resources/capabilities that are required to be profitable in the business so high that whoever enters would have spent so much that any profits earned would go to pay for the high cost of entry.

A business' macroenvironment can also have a large effect on its attractiveness. For example, if a government keeps prices in a business artificially low or high, it impacts profitability directly. If a government imposes exit barriers, the business loses some of its attractiveness since firms may be forced to sell their products at very low prices so long as such prices cover their variable costs. In any case, it is important for a firm that wants to enter a new business to understand carefully the environment in which it is going to compete if it enters the business.

Frameworks of Analysis

A framework for identifying and analyzing the competitive forces that impact a business and determine average profitability for the business is Porter's Five Forces. The framework enables one to determine what underpins rivalry, potential new entry, bargaining power of buyers and suppliers, and the threat of substitutes. Another framework that can be useful in developing and understanding the profitability potential of an industry is the Structure-Conduct-Performance (SCP) framework.[2] In the SCP framework, performance (average profitability of the business) is determined by conduct. Conduct, which is determined by structure, is about the activities that firms, suppliers, and buyers in the business perform, such as R&D, advertising, strategic alliances, mergers and acquisitions, pricing, cost reductions, new product introductions, and capacity increases or decreases. Structure refers to the number of firms, suppliers, and buyers; the type of technology utilized; the degree of product differentiation; the degree of vertical integration; nature and level of competition (regional, domestic, or international), and the level of barriers to entry. By using the SCP to determine the nature and level of competition, what drives competition, critical activities, and what drives value, a firm is in a better position to perform well if or when it enters the industry. For example, if industry firms have a habit of retaliating against new entrants via activities such as pricing, R&D or new product introductions, the firm in question should better understand what it is getting into. The Five Forces are a rendition of SCP.

Key Players in the Business

A Five-Forces or SCP analysis tells one a lot about competition by providing information about the number of competitors, industry growth rate, presence or lack of product differentiation, and so on. However, it is still important for the firm that wants to enter the new business to find out as much as possible about the key players in the business. For example, if a firm wants to enter the carbonated soft drinks industry, it may be better off finding out about how dominant players Coke and Pepsi compete against each other and against new entrants to their industry. If the new business is the main source of profits or cash for a major player in the business, the player is not likely to roll over when another firm enters the business. For example, Sony's video game business was one of its biggest sources of profit in 2001 when Microsoft entered the video game business. Thus, one would expect Sony rigorously to fight back Microsoft's attempts to grab market share.

Better-off (and Alternatives) Test

The better-off tests can be thought of as consisting of three questions: what is it about the firm that will enable it to be profitable in the new business? If there is nothing, would entering the new business increase the profitability of the firm's existing (old) business? What are the firm's alternatives for making money or for growth outside of entering the new business?

What is It About the Firm That Will Enable It to be Profitable in the New Business? Old Game

One way of asking this question is: does the firm bring something to the new business that will allow it to create and appropriate value, thereby enabling it to make money in the new business? If the firm is going to enter the new business and be profitable, it has to create value for customers in the business and be in a position to appropriate the value. (It can also make money by positioning itself to appropriate value created by others.) Recall from Chapters 2 and 4 that creating and appropriating value entails performing activities that:

1 Contribute to low cost, differentiation, and other drivers of profitability.
2 Improve position vis-à-vis coopetitors.
3 Take advantage of industry value drivers.
4 Build and translate distinctive resources/capabilities in new value.
5 Are parsimonious and comprehensive.

The extent to which a firm's activities have to meet these five objectives for it to be better off is a function of how profitable its existing business is, how much competition it is likely to face in the new business, and its goal in entering the business. If a firm's existing business is not very profitable and competitors in the new business are accommodating, the firm can get away with partially meeting some of these objectives. If a firm's goal in entering a new business is to exploit a niche market that does not mean much to the key competitors in the market, the firm may be able to make some profits without attracting a lot of attention and therefore does not have to worry as much about dampening or reversing competitive forces.

In performing activities to meet these five objectives, a firm can either pursue the same *old game* in which it tries to outdo its competitors in the new business by performing the same value chain activities that are presently being performed in the business, or pursue a *new game* strategy in which it changes some of or all the rules of the game for the new business. In this section, we explore entry using old games, postponing new games for later in the chapter.

Contribute to Low Differentiation, and other Drivers of Profitability

A firm with scarce valuable resources/capabilities can use them to offer the right value (low cost, differentiation) to the right customers in the right market segments. For example, prior to entering the groceries business, Wal-Mart had developed superior logistics and information technology capabilities. It used these capabilities to its advantage when it entered the groceries business, keeping its costs lower than those of competitors so that it could pass the cost savings to customers in the form of lower prices. Virgin used its brand in transatlantic airlines activities and music records to enter other businesses. In some cases, a scarce resource such as a luxury brand can allow a firm to charge more for products in the new business.

Improve Position vis-à-vis Coopetitors

The attractiveness test lets a potential new entrant into a new business know which forces are repressive and which ones are friendly. A firm can improve its position vis-à-vis coopetitors by dampening some of the repressive forces or reinforcing existing ones using scarce capabilities from its existing business. For example, a firm can bring the power that it has over suppliers or customers in an existing business into the new business, thereby allowing it to dampen repressive industry forces. For example, Wal-Mart already had a lot of purchasing know-how and bargaining power over suppliers in its retail business when it entered the groceries business. It had also learnt how to work with suppliers to reduce costs. The firm was able to use these capabilities to have more power over suppliers than other groceries suppliers, thereby keeping its costs lower. A firm with good government relationships in a country where such relationships matter can use them to its advantage to enter a new business where competitors do not have such relationships with the government.

Take Advantage of Industry Value Drivers

Recall that an industry value driver is a factor that has the most impact on cost, differentiation, or other driver of revenues or profit. In retail, location is an industry value driver since it impacts not only the cost of operations but also the amount of customer traffic to the store as well as the image of the store, all of them key drivers of revenues and profits. By choosing to expand existing retail stores into superstores when it entered the groceries business, Wal-Mart was able to take advantage of location—a critical industry value driver in retail. Taking advantage of industry value drivers can contribute to a firm's profitability in a new business.

Build New Distinctive Resources/Capabilities or Translate Existing Ones Into Superior Value

Many of the examples above are about translating existing capabilities in the old business into value for the new business. Some of the activities can also build new resources/capabilities in the new business that the firm can use to create value and better position itself to appropriate the value. For example, in offering groceries, Wal-Mart has also built capabilities in sourcing perishable items—capabilities that it previously did not have when it offered only retail goods.

Are Parsimonious and Comprehensive

Recall that the parsimony and comprehensiveness criteria is about performing the right number of the right kinds of activities. A firm that enters a new business by buying another firm which performs many superfluous activities, can lower its costs by eliminating such activities, thereby improving its chances of being profitable in the new business. A firm can also enter a new business and perform critical activities that were not being performed before.

Would Entering the New Business Increase Profitability of Existing Business?

A firm can also be better off entering a new business, not so much because of the profits that come directly from the new business, but because of how entering the new business helps improve the profitability of the existing (old) business. We explore three cases: defending existing market position, vertical integration, and complementing a product line.

Defending an Existing Market Position

A firm can enter a new business to prevent competitors from using the new business to erode the firm's competitive advantage in its existing business. For example, when Microsoft entered the video game console business, it was speculated that the firm was doing so to prevent Sony from using the video game console business to erode Microsoft's competitive advantage in PC operating systems. The problem with this claim is that it is very difficult to prove or disprove it. This strategy is derived from warfare where by occupying an enemy in one battle, you prevent the enemy from fighting you in another battle. The problem with it is that one does not have to fight to win, and fighting often results in no true winners.

Vertical Integration

A firm can integrate vertically backwards into the business of producing its own inputs or vertically forward into disposing of its outputs so as to improve its profitability. To assure the quality of the coffee that it sells, a retailer of coffee in the USA may decide to integrate vertically backwards into growing its own coffee in South America or Africa. A firm can also integrate vertically backwards to prevent its suppliers from behaving opportunistically. As we saw earlier, for example, Apple Computers developed its own Web browser called Safari so as to avoid depending on competitor Microsoft's Internet Explorer. By integrating vertically forwards into bottling their colas in some parts of the world, Coke and Pepsi are better able to assure profitability of their concentrate.

Complement Existing Product Line

It may be the case that a firm's existing products will sell better if it were to enter a new business and in the process complement existing products, thereby making them more valuable to customers. For example, in developing countries where capital markets are not very efficient, a firm may enter the financial services business so as to better finance purchases for the many customers who may not have financing.

Alternatives Outside of Entering New Business

An obvious alternative to entering a new business is to not enter the business at all. If a firm's goal is to maximize shareholder value, the firm might be better off giving money back to shareholders in the form of dividends rather than spending the money on an unprofitable new business. Thus, a firm may be making a mistake if it entered a new business only because it had a lot of cash that it believes it has to invest. Shareholders may be better off reinvesting the money themselves. More importantly, a firm may want to conduct the three tests on many businesses before deciding which one to enter, if at all.

Cost of Entry

Entering a new business and performing the activities that enable a firm to create and appropriate value can be costly. These costs have to be weighed against the expected returns from entry. Effectively, cost-of-entry is a relative term in that costs have to be compared to the revenues that are generated as a result of entry. The idea is to keep track of the extent to which a firm's rate of profitability after entry is higher than that before. On the one hand, for example, an attractive business may hold prospects for high margins but the cost of entry may be so high that any cash flows from the business will be more than dissipated by the very high cost of entry. On the other hand, an unattractive business may have little prospect for high margins but cost very little to enter. In any case, such costs have to be carefully explored and compared to the cost of not entering prior to entry.

Drivers of Entry Costs

For several reasons, if an industry is attractive, the cost of entry is likely to be high. First, as we saw earlier, if a business is attractive (to firms in the business) barriers to entry are likely to be high. If barriers to entry are high, it is likely to cost a lot to overcome these barriers to enter the business. For example, if a barrier to entry is the brand equity of incumbents (e.g. Coke's brand), any new entrant that hopes to have a competitive advantage may have to build a comparable brand equity. This can cost a lot and takes time. Second, as we also saw earlier, if a business is attractive (profitable), other profit-seeking firms are likely to be interested in also entering. If enough such firms want to enter, they are likely to bid up the cost of the resources that it takes to create and appropriate value in the business, thereby increasing costs for whoever ends up entering the business. Third, if the business is attractive, leading firms with a competitive advantage are likely to be profitable. Such leaders are not likely to give up their profits to new entrants without a fight. In fact, if these leaders have been making a lot of money, they are likely to have war chests to fight new entrants. Thus, new entrants may find themselves in costly fights. For these three reasons, it can be so costly for a firm to enter an attractive business that even if it can create and appropriate value as a result of entering the new business, any potential profits from the entry would be dissipated by the high entry costs.

In addition to depending on the type of business, entry costs also depend on the type of firm that is entering. If a firm already has many of the resources that are needed for the new business, it may be cheaper for the firm to enter. That would be the case, for example, if the resources that the firm uses in its existing business can be profitably extended to the new business. The Honda example that we used earlier comes into play here. Since the company already had engine capabilities when it entered each new business, its cost of offering the product for the new business were lower than those of other firms that had to develop the engine from scratch. Sony already had distribution channels in place when it entered the video game console business, making its cost of entry lower than those of a startup.

Finally, entry costs can also depend on how the entry process is implemented. When a firm enters a new business, it needs people to run the business. The firm also needs to structure its organization to accommodate the new business, and establish the systems, processes, and culture that are appropriate to running the new business. The interaction of people, structure, systems, processes, and culture cost money and keeping these costs to a minimum can go a long way to keeping costs low.

Opportunity Cost of Not Entering

In addition to the cost of entry, there can also be "costs" to not entering, also called the opportunity cost of not entering. That would be the case, for example, if the new business is rooted in a disruptive technology that may later invade the existing business. In that case, if a firm in the existing business does not enter the new one, it may be too late when it finally has to do so. For example, the PC was a disruptive technology to minicomputers because it eventually did a lot of what minicomputers used to do and therefore rendered them noncompetitive in many markets. Those minicomputer makers who had not taken the PC seriously saw their minicomputer businesses eroded by the PC. Disruptive technologies were explored in great detail in Chapter 8.

Estimating Relative Cost of Entry

We consider two ways of estimating the cost of entry: breakeven and cash flow analyses.

Breakeven Analysis [3]

A breakeven analysis offers an alternative and sometimes complementary approach to cash flow analysis. Before beginning the analysis, let us quickly review some basics.

Profits = revenues − variable costs − fixed costs

$$= PQ - V_cQ - F_c = (P - V_c)Q - F_c$$

$$= \text{Contribution margin} - F_c$$

$$= (\text{Contribution margin per unit})Q - F_c \tag{1}$$

where P is the price per unit of the product, V_c is the per unit variable cost, Q is the total number of units sold, and F_c is the up-front or fixed costs. The quantity "$PQ - V_cQ$" or revenues minus variable costs, is called the **contribution margin** and represents the amount over variable costs that goes to contribute towards recovering fixed costs. The quantity "$P - V_c$," the difference between price per unit, and *per unit* variable costs, is called the **contribution margin per unit**.

We can now begin the breakeven analysis. If the contribution margin is positive, then as the quantity sold goes up, there reaches a certain quantity where all the fixed costs have been recovered. This is the quantity at which revenues equal total costs and is called the **breakeven point**. It is the point where the firm has zero profits from the investment. Below the breakeven point, the firm loses money. Above the breakeven point, the firm makes money. This point can be determined by equating equation (1) to zero since profits are zero. If we do that, we obtain:

$$\text{Profits} = PQ - V_cQ - F_c = (P - V_c)Q - F_c = 0$$

From this,

$$Q = \frac{F_c}{(P - V_c)}. \tag{2}$$

Recalling that $P - V_c$ is the contribution margin per unit, breakeven quantity can be computed as:

$$\text{Breakeven quantity} = \frac{\text{Fixed Cost}}{\text{Contribution Margin Per Unit}} \tag{3}$$

For several reasons, **breakeven time**, the time that it takes a company to break even, is also important. First, the longer it takes to break even, the longer resources may have to be tied up performing unprofitable activities, thereby forgoing potentially profitable investment opportunities. Second, the longer it takes a firm to break even, the more time competitors have to catch up or put more distance between themselves and the firm if they are ahead. Breakeven time is obtained by dividing the breakeven quantity by sales rate; that is, breakeven time (in years) is the breakeven quantity divided by sales per year. Mathematically,

$$\text{Breakeven time} = \frac{\text{Breakeven Quantity}}{\text{Sales Rate}} \tag{4}$$

$$= \frac{F_c}{(P - V_c) \times (\text{Sales Rate})}$$

Example

A software company called PrintMoneySoft spent a total of $500 million in R&D, marketing, promotion, and other upfront fixed costs to offer a software package that it sells for $100 a copy. Since the company has posted the software on the Web for customers to download, each copy that it sells only costs the company $10 dollars to produce and sell. Because of its huge installed base of customers, the company estimates that it can sell 25 million units a year. What is the breakeven quantity and how long will it take for the company to break even?

$$\text{Breakeven quantity} = \frac{F_c}{(P - V_c)} = \frac{\$500M}{\$100 - \$10} = 5.56 \text{ million}$$

Since the sales rate is $25 million per year, breakeven time (in years)

$$\frac{5.56M}{25M} \text{ years} = 0.22 \text{ years}$$

Alternatively,

$$\text{Breakeven time (years)} = \frac{\text{Breakeven Quantity}}{\text{Sales Rate}} = \frac{F_c}{(P - V_c) \times (\text{Sales Rate})}$$

$$= \frac{\$500M}{(\$100 - \$10) \times (25M)} = 0.22 \text{ years}$$

Thus, in less than three months, PrintMoneySoft has recovered the $500 million dollars that it invested and in the next five years, the billions of dollars that it collects will contribute directly to profits.

Cash Flow Method

When a firm enters a new business, it receives revenues from the business and related sources of revenue. The firm must also pay out money to cover the costs that it incurs in creating and appropriating value. Moreover, it must also cover all the costs that it incurred in entering the new business. Ideally, in evaluating a business for entry, one would determine all the future cash flows net of all expenses and discount them to the present to determine the profitability of the venture. If C_t is the difference between revenues and costs at time t, the present value of these cash flows, V_t, is given by is

$$V_t = C_0 + \frac{C_1}{(1 + r_k)} + \frac{C_2}{(1 + r_k)^2} + \frac{C_3}{(1 + r_k)^3} + \cdots \frac{C_n}{(1 + r_k)^n}$$

$$= \sum_{t=0}^{t=n} \frac{C_t}{(1 + r_k)^t} \tag{5}$$

where r_k is the firm's *discount rate*. This is the firm's opportunity cost of capital. It is the expected rate of return that could be earned by investing money in another asset instead of the company. It reflects the **systematic risk**—that is, risk that is specific to the firm's business model and therefore cannot be eliminated by diversification. This can be estimated using a model such as the capital asset pricing model (CAPM) which states that:

$$r_k = r_f + \beta_i (r_m - r_f) \tag{6}$$

That is, the discount rate consists of two parts: a risk-free rate, r_f, and a risk premium, $\beta_i(r_m = r_f)$. The risk free rate, r_f, can be proxied with the interest rate on treasury bills. The idea is that if one were to invest one's money in US Treasury bills, one would get a sure return, since the government is always going to be there and will pay its debts. This interest rate is low since it is risk free. The risk premium, $\beta_i(r_m - r_f)$ reflects the additional interest that should be expected, on top of the risk-free rate, since one is investing in a business that is more risky than treasury bills. This risk premium is equal to the systematic risk, β_i, of the firm, times the excess return over the market return r_m. The β (beta) of similar businesses (within or outside the firm's industry) is used.

A major drawback for this cash-flow valuation method is that forecasting future cash flows accurately is extremely difficult. The further out into the future, the more difficult it is to forecast cash flows. Equation (1) can be further simplified by assuming, as we did in Chapter 2, that the free cash flows generated by the firm being valued will reach a constant amount (an annuity) of C_f, after n years. If we do so, equation (6) reduces to:

$$V = \frac{C_f}{r_k \, (1 + r_k)^n} \tag{7}$$

If we further assume that the constant free cash flows start in the present year, then $n = 0$, and equation (3) reduces to:

$$V = \frac{C_f}{r_k} \tag{8}$$

Another way to simplify equation (4) is to assume that today's free cash flows, C_0, which we know, will grow at a constant rate g forever. If we do so, equation (4) reduces to:

$$V = \frac{C_0}{r_k - g} \tag{9}$$

Using New Games to Enter

The attractiveness test tells a firm if the new business is, on average, profitable for firms that are already in the business or not and why? A firm can use new game activities to make the business more attractive for itself, enabling it to be more profitable than its rivals in the new business. It can also use new game activities to lower the cost of entry, insuring that any rents that it generates in the new business are not dissipated by the cost of entry. We explore both. In either case, the type of strategy that is pursued by incumbents in the old business can also play a major role.

Using New Game Activities to Make a Business Attractive for a Firm or Lower Entry Costs

As we saw above, if a business is attractive to firms in the business, then one of several things may be happening: either barriers to entry are high, firms have power over suppliers or buyers, the threat of substitutes is low, or rivalry is low. The question is, what type of new game activities can a firm use to enter such a business and make the business more attractive for itself than the incumbents who have been in the business longer? Recall that new game activities can:

1 Generate *new* ways of creating and capturing new value.
2 Build new resources or translate existing ones in new ways into value.
3 Create the potential to build and exploit *first-mover advantages*.
4 Attract *reactions* from new and existing competitors.
5 Have their roots in the *opportunities* and *threats* of an industry or macroenvironment.

We now explore how a firm can take advantage of each of these characteristics of new game activities to make a new business attractive for itself.

Take Advantage of the New Ways of Creating and Capturing New Value

A firm can enter a new business by identifying and meeting a need in the market that is presently not being met—by occupying so-called "white space" in the market or what is considered at the time a niche.[4] A classic example is that of Wal-Mart, which located its stores in small rural towns which discount retailers at the time shunted, preferring instead to locate their stores in large towns. This unmet need can also be in providing a product with attributes that other products do not offer or it can be in providing products at a lower price point than existing products. Note that new value here does not necessarily mean that a firm has to outdo its rivals in offering products or services with more and better attributes. New value can sometimes mean stripped down attributes or even inferior product attributes. For example, when Ikea entered the US furniture industry, it did not try to outdo other furniture companies by offering better in-store service, better delivery, or more durable furniture.[5] Rather, it offered little or no in-store service compared to its high-end competitors, no delivery, and furniture that was not as durable as competing furniture from incumbents. Most of the PC's attributes were inferior to those of the minicomputer and mainframe that served the needs of most computer users when the PC was introduced.

By locating in white space and meeting the needs of customers that are not being met by firms in the business, a firm avoids immediate competition with rivals for customers and resources. This lowers the effect of rivalry on the firm. Moreover, because the firm is the first to offer the product to the market segment, these customers are less likely to have as much power over the firm as they would if it had more rivals in the market segment. In those cases where the product offered has stripped-down or inferior attributes, the cost of offering them may be lower and therefore somewhat reduces barriers to entry. If the firm rides a change such as a disruptive technological change, the cost of offering the new value can also be lower. Most important of all, since the firm is the first in the white space (market segment), it can build first-mover advantages. For example, it can build switching costs at customers, establish a brand-name reputation with these customers, or build relationships with customers and complementors. The firm can also preempt scarce important resources such as location, input factors, customer mental space, or complementary assets. The firm can go up the learning curve for providing products for the particular market segments and seek intellectual property protection for the patents or copyrights acquired in doing so. New game activities can also be geared towards increasing the number of valuable customers that the firm can reach with its products when it enters the new business.

Some new game activities can better position a firm to appropriate value without necessarily creating any in a new business. A popular example that we saw in Chapter 1 is that of Dell when it decided to bypass distributors and sell directly to end-users. This was new game in the industry at the time and enabled Dell to bypass the more concentrated and powerful distributors and sell directly to the more fragmented and less powerful users. Decreased buyer power meant a more attractive business for Dell than competitors.

Take Advantage of Opportunity to Build New Resources or Translate Existing Ones in New Ways Into Value

When a firm enters a new business, it can build some or all of the resources that it needs. If the firm occupies white space or a niche, it can preemptively build resources the way Wal-Mart did. The new business can also be a brand new industry or market that is in the fluid stage and it is not clear what resources will be needed. In that case, the firm can compete to build a competitive advantage in the new resources.

Take Advantage of the Opportunity to Build and Exploit First-mover Advantages

If in entering the new business, a firm locates in "white space" or a niche, it is effectively moving first as far as the new games are concerned. Thus, as we have seen above, such a firm has an opportunity to take advantage of first-mover advantages. Recall from Chapter 6 that first-mover advantages include:

- Preemption of total available market with associated economies of scale, size (beyond economies of scale), early collection of economic rents and equity, chance to build network externalities, and relationships with coopetitors.
- Lead in technology and innovation with associated intellectual property (patents, copyrights, trade secrets), learning, organizational culture.
- Preemption of scarce resources such as complementary assets, location, input factors, parts, and equipment.
- First-at-buyers through building buyer switching cost, making smart choices under and building a brand (preemption of consumer perceptual space).
- First to establish a difficult-to-imitate system of activities for creating and appropriating value.

A firm that enters a new business using new games and builds first-mover advantage can make the new business more attractive for itself. For example, a firm that enters a new business using new games and preemptively accumulates scarce resources in the industry can make the industry more attractive for itself.

Anticipate and Respond to the Actions and Reactions of New and Existing Competitors

If a firm enters a new business using new game activities, some of the incumbents in the business are likely to react to the entry. They can welcome the entry, fight it, or pursue some combination of both. In either case, how the new entrant behaves can be critical. It is better off taking into consideration the likely reaction of its new rivals. Finding ways to cooperate with rivals, when permitted by government regulations, may be better than engaging in destructive competition such as price wars. In markets that exhibit network externalities, a firm may be better off cooperating to build a large network, since the more customers in any particular network, the more valuable the network is to customers. If a firm has to compete, it is better off going after firms whose prior commitments, dominant managerial logics, and sunk investments prevent them from trying to replicate or leapfrog the firm. These incumbent handicaps give the firm more degrees of freedom in building first-mover advantages and translating them into superior value that the firm can appropriate.

Take Advantage of the Opportunities and Threats of the Environment

In entering a new business, a firm can take advantage of the opportunities and threats of its environment to pursue new game activities that allow it to have a competitive advantage in entering the new business. For example, eBay took advantage of the Internet, a disruptive technology, to enter the auction market. So did the numerous other firms that took advantage of the Internet to enter new businesses.

Type of New Game

The type of new game strategy that a firm uses to enter a new business as well as the type of game being played by incumbents in the new business also play a role in making the industry attractive to the new entrant or lowering its entry costs (Table 12.1).

Table 12.1 Type of New Game to Pursue when Entering a New Business

Existing game in new business	Preferred entry new game
Regular	Revolutionary, resource-building, position-building
Resource-building	Position-building, revolutionary
Position-building	Revolutionary, resource-building
Revolutionary	Revolutionary

Face Firms in Regular Game in New Business

If the dominant firms in a market pursue a regular game, trying to beat them at their game is likely to be difficult. Recall that in a *regular* new game, a firm builds on the existing resources that underpin industry competitive advantage to offer a new product that customers value but the product does not totally replace existing products in the market. A new entrant to the business is better off pursuing either a revolutionary, resource-building, or position-building new game (Table 12.1). The idea here is that it would be difficult for a new entrant to the carbonated soft drinks industry to beat Coke and Pepsi by making incremental improvements to cola drinks or to the way the drinks are marketed. One cannot beat Coke at being Coke. Rather, one has a chance if one pursues a revolutionary strategy in which the resources used and the product-market-position pursued are so different that existing resources cannot be used to offer the new product and the resulting new product renders existing ones noncompetitive. By pursuing a revolutionary strategy, a firm is in a better position to build and take advantage of first-mover advantages, making the new business more attractive for the new entrant firm. One can also take advantage of any handicaps that incumbents in the new business may have such as prior commitments from which they cannot separate themselves. If a firm has distinctive resources that it can use to pursue a resource-building strategy in the new business, the firm might be better off using such a strategy to enter a new business where the major actors play regular games. Recall that in a resource-building game, a firm uses resources that are radically different from those presently used in the market to offer products but existing products remain competitive. A firm can also pursue a position-building game in which it uses resources that build on existing resources in the new business but offers a product that renders existing products noncompetitive. That would also make the entry more attractive for the firm.

Face Resource-building New Game in New Business

If the game pursued by dominant firms in the new business is resource-building, a potential new entrant into the business may be better off pursuing either a position-building or revolutionary new game. The idea here is that if incumbents in the business have been pursuing a resource-building game, some of them are likely to have built first-mover advantages in the new resources. Thus, trying to beat these incumbents at being them is likely to be difficult. Therefore, a new entrant may be better off using a revolutionary new game that renders incumbents' existing resource advantages obsolete and their existing products noncompetitive. A new entrant could also pursue a position-building new game by identifying new needs and meeting the needs using resources that build on existing resources. This is the new game that Sony played when it entered the video console business. Its 32-bit video game technology built on existing skills, knowledge, and know-how in video games to develop consoles that addressed the needs of a new market segment: adults who wanted to play video games. The 32-bit games eventually rendered existing 16-bit machines noncompetitive.

Face Position-building New Game in New Business

If the game pursued by incumbents in the new business is predominantly position-building, these incumbents are likely to have developed competitive advantages in their PMPs. Thus a new entrant is better off pursuing a revolutionary or resource-building new game if it hopes to make the new market more attractive for itself. A revolutionary new game renders incumbent's existing products noncompetitive and the underpinning resources obsolete, and the new entrant has an opportunity to build first-mover advantages in resources and product-market positions.

Face Revolutionary New Game in New Business

If the new game pursued by incumbents in the new business is revolutionary, new entrants can also pursue the revolutionary new game. By definition, things are in a state of flux in the market if incumbents are still pursuing a revolutionary new game and no one has a competitive advantage, yet. Thus, new entrants may be better off also pursuing the same revolutionary new game until such a time as they can focus on their competitive advantages using either resource-building or position-building strategies.

When to Apply the Framework

From the title of this chapter, it is clear that when entering a new business, especially when diversifying from one's existing business, one is better off exploring the three tests. However, the tests could also be very useful when moving from one market segment to another, especially if the new segment has different coopetitors. Also, when a firm adopts a new technology, it is worthwhile to explore the three tests because new technologies often result in new ways of creating and appropriating value. Consequently, coopetitors and their interactions usually change, the industry becomes more or less attractive, and what it takes to have a competitive advantage also changes.

Key Takeaways

- A new business can be the source of profits and pride for a firm or the source of losses and regret. Thus a firm should not take entering a new business lightly.
- However, it is not usual to find firms that enter new businesses solely because their existing businesses are mature and declining while the new business is growing, or because the firms have lots of cash to invest. The growth rate of an industry is only one driver of industry profitability or attractiveness. The **attractiveness test** explores the factors that determine the extent to which the industry is profitable, on average, and helps firms to understand the competitive forces that they would face if they were to enter the new industry. This test can be performed using a Porter's Five Forces or the Structure-Conductor-Performance framework.
- Even if an industry is, on average, profitable, a firm that enters the industry may still not be profitable. Factors specific to the entering firm also play a major role in determining its profitability; that is, there should be something about the firm that will enable it to enter the new business and earn a higher

rate of return in the new business than in the old, or there should be something about entering the new business that will allow the firm to improve the profitability of its old business. Effectively, a firm also needs to explore the extent to which it is better off in the industry than other firms or than being elsewhere. This exploration is the **better-off test**.

- In any case, it usually costs money—sometimes a lot—to enter a new business. Thus, a firm that wants to enter a new business may want to make sure that it does not spend so much in entering the new business that any profits ultimately generated go to cover entry costs. If barriers to entry are high, for example, it can cost a lot to overcome them. If, for example, one reason why an industry is attractive is the ability of firms to retaliate against new entrants or noncooperators, a firm that enters the business is likely to face hostility. Thus, the cost of entry *relative* to the profits from entry is also a major factor in considering entry. This is the **cost of entry test**. Entry costs should also be carefully weighed against the opportunity cost of not entering the new business.
- Effectively, it is wise to explore the attractiveness, better-off, and cost-of-entry tests carefully before entering a new business. A firm can use these tests to evaluate different businesses before making its choice. There is always the alternative of investing in the old business or giving money back to shareholders.
- New game activities not only can enable a firm to make an industry more attractive for itself, they can also lower entry costs. Because of their new value creation property, new games can enable a firm to lower its cost or differentiate its products, thereby reducing the effect of rivalry, and substitutes on the firm. Differentiated products from new game activities also reduce the power of buyers and the negative effects of potential new entry.
- The type of new game strategy that a firm uses to enter a new business should also be a function of the type of strategy that firms in the industry are pursuing at the time of anticipated entry.
- Managers may give all sorts of reasons for entering a new business. But when it is all said and done, a firm has to make profits. This entails creating and appropriating value. The three tests can be very helpful in evaluating, ex ante, one's potential for doing well in a new business.
- The three-test framework applies not only to entering new businesses and new market segments but also to adopting new technologies. This is particularly true when the new technology generates new ways of creating and/or appropriating value, and the attractiveness of the market or industry has changed.

Key Terms

Attractive business
Attractiveness test
Better-off test
Contribution margin
Contribution margin per unit
Cost of entry test
Systematic risk

Chapter 13

Strategy Frameworks and Measures

Reading this chapter should provide you with an introduction to, or a recap of the following strategy frameworks:

- SWOT Analysis (early 1960s)[1]
- PEST (1967)
- Growth/Share matrix (late 1960s)
- GE/McKinsey matrix (late 1960s)
- Porter's Five Forces (1979/1980)
- Business systems (1980)
- Value chain (1985)
- Value configurations (1998)
- Balanced scorecard (1992)
- VRIO (1997)
- VIDE (1998)
- S^{3}PE Framework (1998)
- 4Ps (marketing, 1960s)
- AVAC (2008)

The chapter also summarizes some simple but useful accounting measures.

Introduction

When we explored the AVAC framework in Chapter 2, we noted that it had some advantages over existing strategy models for assessing the profitability potential of a strategy, product, brand, resources, business units, and so on. In this Chapter, we briefly summarize thirteen strategy frameworks and one marketing framework that have been used to explore not only the profitability potential of strategies but also strategy drivers and outputs. We also briefly summarize some useful accounting measures that can come in handy when quantifying a firm's performance. These summaries are meant to be just that—summaries. They are meant to serve three purposes: (1) act as a quick reference for the reader who has encountered them before and needs to be reminded about where they fit in the overall picture of strategy frameworks, (2) act as a motivator to the reader who has not been exposed to them before to find out more about them in the references provided, and (3) remind the reader of the advantages and shortcomings of each framework.

The question is, why would anyone need to understand thirteen strategy frameworks? After all, some of them are either too old, have too many short-comings, or apply to questions that you do not care much about. There are three reasons why students of strategic management need to understand these models. First, one of the models—and God knows which one—may be the only one that your interviewer, employer, client, potential ally, competitor, acquirer, consultant, venture capitalist, or acquisition target understands. Although fancier models exist, most people stick with the model that has worked for them, despite the push from consulting firms to change to newer and *better* models. For example, although many strategy scholars regard the SWOT analysis as antiquated, it still plays an important role in the strategic planning processes of some major firms. Second, strategic management is a very complex subject and therefore no one framework can apply to all questions. No one model fits all bills. Therefore, understanding as many models as possible gives the strategy scholar more options and flexibility in exploring different questions. Better still, it helps one understand where others may be coming from. Third, we explore the frameworks chronologically, thereby providing a sense of the history of strategic management. This history can be important in understanding different points of view, and in guessing where the field might be heading.

Advantages and Disadvantages of Using Frameworks

We start the chapter with an outline of the advantages and disadvantages of using frameworks in strategic management.

Advantages

Although each framework has some advantages that are specific to it, there are some advantages that pertain to frameworks in general.

Simplicity

Frameworks are usually simple and easy for managers to get their minds around. Some of them take the form of a 2 × 2 matrix, which is easy to visualize and understand. Such simplicity makes it easier for more people to understand and make contributions to the discussions and arguments that lead up to a manager's final decision.

Common Language and Platform

Frameworks provide a common language and platform for framing questions, proposing different scenarios, and expressing alternate solutions to a problem. They provide common starting points for discussions. A framework may not provide a final solution to a question, but can provide a starting point from where managers can work their way to a final solution.

Parsimony and Comprehensiveness

A good framework is both comprehensive and parsimonious; that is, a good framework has all that needs to be in it (comprehensive), but at the same time, avoids not throwing everything in it (parsimonious). As such, users do not have to reinvent the wheel and go through the exercise of deciding what should be included and what should not, again.

Starting Point for Collecting Data

One of the biggest problems with strategic analysis is to decide which data to collect for an analysis. The cases that students are usually asked to analyze normally have lots of tables of data and graphs attached to them, giving the students some hints as to what the solution to the case is all about. In real life, managers who face decisions usually do not have that much data and often have no idea what variables they should be collecting the data for, and where to start looking for the data. Having a framework considerably narrows down the scope and cost of data collection. One can simply collect data for the variables that are in the framework.

Disadvantages

Many of the qualities of frameworks that are advantages can also be disadvantages. Take simplicity, for example. Very simple frameworks, while easy to use, usually leave out important variables, making such frameworks less applicable to other contexts. That is one reason why strategy models should be used very carefully. When a framework constitutes a language and platform, it necessarily locks out some ideas that fall outside that language and framework. There is also the danger that some students will understand one framework well and try to apply it to any question that they are asked. These disadvantages are not a big issue if one understands the advantages and disadvantage of each framework well before applying it.

SWOT

SWOT stands for Strengths, Weaknesses, Opportunities, and Threats. The SWOT framework came out of research lead by Albert Humphrey at Stanford University in the 1960s and 1970s. It was developed as a strategic planning tool to be used to evaluate a firm's internal strengths and weakness as well as those external opportunities and threats that the firm faced and could exploit. The SWOT analysis fits in very well with Professor Alfred Chandler's 1962 popular definition of strategy as the "determination of the basic long-term goals and objectives of an enterprise, and the adoption of courses of action and the allocation of resources necessary for carrying out these goals."[2] The idea is that for a firm to meet its goals and objectives, it has to pursue certain courses of action using the appropriate resources. Depending on the goals and objectives, a firm's courses of action and resources can be strengths or weaknesses. By matching these strengths and weaknesses to the opportunities and threats of its environment, a firm could meet its goals and objectives, relative to its competitors.

Key Elements of SWOT Framework

The elements of a SWOT analysis are shown in Figure 13.1. Strengths and weaknesses are usually referred to as *internal factors,* since they are specific to a firm's activities and resources, while opportunities and threats are referred to as *external factors* because they are exterior to a firm, in its competitive and macro environments.

Strengths

In a SWOT analysis, a firm's *strengths* are those characteristics that make a positive contribution to the attainment of its goals and objectives. For example, if a firm's goals and objectives are to have a competitive advantage, then its strengths are those characteristics that make a positive contribution to its ability to earn a higher rate of profits than its competitors. Such strengths would include distinctive valuable resources and capabilities such as a brand, patents, copyrights, distribution channels, shelf space, relationships with customers, and so on. If the goal is to win a war, the strengths are those factors that make a positive contribution to winning the war.

Weaknesses

A firm's *weaknesses* are those characteristics that handicap attainment of its goals and objectives. If a firm's goals and objectives are to have a competitive advantage, then its weaknesses are those characteristics that handicap its ability to earn a higher rate of profits than its competitors. A firm's weaknesses to attaining a competitive advantage include a *lack* of distinctive resources and capabilities as well as a bad reputation or bad relationships with coopetitors. Ford and GM's weaknesses in the 2000s were that they did not have the ability to produce cars with good gas mileage that enough customers wanted to buy. Location can also be a weakness. Being born in an underdeveloped country can be a serious weakness.

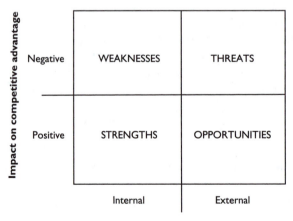

Figure 13.1 SWOT Framework.

Opportunities

Opportunities for a firm are those *external* factors that make a positive contribution to the attainment of its goals and objectives. If a firm's goals and objectives are to perform better than its competitors, then opportunities are those external factors that make a positive contribution to the ability of the firm to create and appropriate value better than its competitors. Opportunities for a firm include customer needs that the firm can satisfy, a new technology that a firm can use to attack another firm's competitive position, and so on.

Threats

Threats to a firm are those external factors that handicap its attainment of its goals and objectives. If a firm's goals and objectives are to make more money, then the threats to the firm are those external factors that handicap its ability to earn a higher rate of profits than its competitors. The threats to a firm attaining a competitive advantage would include things such as changes in customer tastes, and technological changes or hostile government regulations that reduce the firm's ability to create and appropriate value.

Context Dependence of Elements

Whether a firm's characteristic is a strength or weakness depends on the context in which the characteristic is being used. For example, a video rental firm's long-term lease contracts to video stores in good locations were a strength in a brick-and-mortar era; but in the face of the Internet, such contracts can be weaknesses if the firm cannot get out of them. An opportunity for one firm can be a threat to another. For example, a disruptive technology is an opportunity for startups that want to attack incumbents, but is a threat to the incumbents.

Application of SWOT

A SWOT analysis has been used as a tool to help formulate strategies, business plans, etc. Whatever the application, the analysis starts with an establishment of goals and objectives. Once goals and objectives have been established, the following questions can be explored.

- *Strengths*: what are the strengths for the goals and objectives in question? How can each strength be reinforced? Can each strength be utilized to achieve other goals and objectives? When might these strengths become weaknesses?
- *Weaknesses*: how can each weakness be dampened or eliminated? How can each weakness be turned into a strength?
- *Opportunities*: how can each opportunity be exploited? What might turn the opportunity into a threat?
- *Threats*: what can a firm do to dampen or eliminate the effect of threats? Can the firm turn threats into opportunities?

Advantages and Disadvantages of SWOT

Advantages

1 The framework is simple, easy to understand, and therefore many managers can use it right away. Thus a firm has an opportunity to obtain feedback from many employees.
2 It provides terminology for discussing the drivers of a firm's ability to match its internal environment to its external environment to attain its goals and objectives.

Disadvantages

The SWOT framework has several disadvantages:

1 It is difficult to narrow down the list of strengths, weaknesses, opportunities, or threats to only the important ones. Firms risk generating a long laundry list that is of little use.
2 The lists of strengths, weaknesses, opportunities, and threats generated usually says little or nothing about how these elements are going to be translated into goals and objectives. For example, a SWOT analysis that lists a pharmaceutical company's patents as its strengths says little about how patents are translated into medicines and profits.
3 The framework is static since it says little about what happens to each element of SWOT over time. Will strengths, weaknesses, opportunities, and threats today be the same tomorrow?
4 It is difficult to tell strengths from weaknesses sometimes, or distinguish opportunities from threats. Is the Internet an opportunity or threat to banks?

PEST

In a SWOT analysis, opportunities and threats usually come from the competitive or macro environment. A Political, Economic, Social, and Technological (PEST) analysis can be used to explore the threats and opportunities of the macroenvironments. The PEST analysis is usually attributed to Francis J. Aguilar who, in his 1967 book, analyzed the environment using the four components: economic, technical, political, and social (ETPS).[3] The assumption here is that the macroenvironment is limited to these five components; but as we saw in Chapter 10, other components of the macroenvironment can also be a source of the opportunities and threats that firms face. For example, the natural environment plays an important role. Thus, the version of PEST shown in Figure 13.2 is a modified version called PESTN, where N stands for natural environment. As we argued in Chapter 10, the extent to which any of the factors that determine each component constitutes a threat or opportunity for a firm is a function of the industry in which the firm operates and the firm's strategy. For example, while in pharmaceuticals, "intellectual property protection" is important in the USA, it is usually not the case in retail and elsewhere in the world. Moreover, technological factors that matter at one time may not be

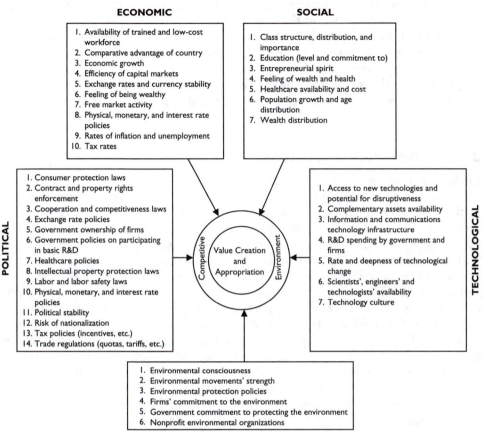

ECONOMIC

1. Availability of trained and low-cost workforce
2. Comparative advantage of country
3. Economic growth
4. Efficiency of capital markets
5. Exchange rates and currency stability
6. Feeling of being wealthy
7. Free market activity
8. Physical, monetary, and interest rate policies
9. Rates of inflation and unemployment
10. Tax rates

SOCIAL

1. Class structure, distribution, and importance
2. Education (level and commitment to)
3. Entrepreneurial spirit
4. Feeling of wealth and health
5. Healthcare availability and cost
6. Population growth and age distribution
7. Wealth distribution

POLITICAL

1. Consumer protection laws
2. Contract and property rights enforcement
3. Cooperation and competitiveness laws
4. Exchange rate policies
5. Government ownership of firms
6. Government policies on participating in basic R&D
7. Healthcare policies
8. Intellectual property protection laws
9. Labor and labor safety laws
10. Physical, monetary, and interest rate policies
11. Political stability
12. Risk of nationalization
13. Tax policies (incentives, etc.)
14. Trade regulations (quotas, tariffs, etc.)

Competitive   Value Creation and Appropriation   Environment

TECHNOLOGICAL

1. Access to new technologies and potential for disruptiveness
2. Complementary assets availability
3. Information and communications technology infrastructure
4. R&D spending by government and firms
5. Rate and deepness of technological change
6. Scientists', engineers' and technologists' availability
7. Technology culture

NATURAL

1. Environmental consciousness
2. Environmental movements' strength
3. Environmental protection policies
4. Firms' commitment to the environment
5. Government commitment to protecting the environment
6. Nonprofit environmental organizations

Figure 13.2 Elements of a PESTN Framework.

that important at other times. Thus, the number of factors that matter for any particular analysis will always be only a subset of those shown in Figure 13.2.

Advantages and Disadvantages of a PEST analysis

Advantages

- A PESTN analysis enables firms to dig deeper into the sources of the threats and opportunities that they face in their macroenvironments. For example, including the natural environment in the analysis forces firms to pay more attention to it, increasing the chances that firms will find some opportunities in it or identify threats in it before it's too late.
- It can be used as a starting point for generating new game ideas.

Disadvantages

- The framework does not provide a means to narrow down the list of factors to the few that are really important. Thus, a PEST analysis usually runs the risk of generating a laundry list with no way of determining which item on the list is more important than the other.

- The PEST analysis, unlike a Five Forces and an AVAC framework, offers no concrete way of linking the list of factors that impact each component to profitability variables.
- A PEST analysis is a static model. It is usually performed at a point in time and says very little about what happened in the past or will happen in the future.

BCG's Growth/Share Matrix

In the late 1960s and the 1970s, more and more firms increasingly added new businesses to their portfolios and therefore found themselves managing multi-businesses. With more than one business to manage, these firms faced some important questions: how much of a firm's scarce resources, such as capital, should be allocated to each unit? What businesses should a firm be in, to begin with? Which ones should be disposed of? What should the performance targets of each business be? The Growth-Share Matrix, developed by the Boston Consulting Group (BCG) in the early 1970s, could be used to explore these questions. It grew out of work on "experience curve effects" done by Bruce Henderson of BCG.[4] The idea with the experience curve was that if a firm's per unit cost fell as its cumulative output increased, the firm stood to have a cost advantage, considered by some at the time to be *the* advantage. The framework gained lots of acceptance at the time as firms used it to analyze business units, product lines, regional units, and international units of firms. It was popular not only in strategic management but also in international management, brand marketing, product management, and portfolio analysis. It would become a so-called *portfolio analysis model* since it could be used to explore different portfolios of businesses.

Elements of the Growth/Share Matrix

The key elements of the Growth/Share Matrix are shown in Figure 13.3. The vertical axis captures the market growth rate while the horizontal axis captures the relative market share. Recall that a firm's performance is driven by both industry as well as firm-specific factors. Thus, since market growth rate is a function of industry factors, and relative market share is a function of firm-specific factors, the framework could give managers some information on the performance of the different units. This was considered particularly true at the time because BCG touted experience curve effects as a key driver of firm performance and therefore strategic success. The idea was that a firm's per unit cost fell as its cumulative output increased. Thus, a business or unit with a high relative market share meant more cumulative units sold and therefore lower cost. Lower cost meant better financial performance; that is, the position of a business or unit on the matrix is a function of its performance. The matrix is divided into four quadrants: cash cows, stars, dogs, and question marks.

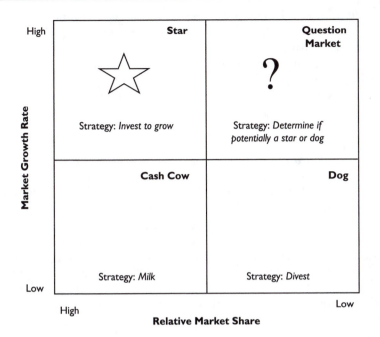

Figure 13.3 BCG's Growth/Share Matrix.

Cash Cows

Cash cows represent units that have high market shares but are in industries with low market growth rates. Their large relative market shares mean that the cumulative number of units that they sell gives them lower unit costs. Because they are in industries with low market growth rates, they do not need to spend a lot on new capital, and therefore a lot of the cash from the low-cost products is free. Hence the name cash cow. BCG suggested that one strategy for such a unit was to milk the cow by using some of the cash generated to invest in stars that needed cash. Industries with such cows were so-called mature industries that did not need the large amounts of cash needed in high growth industries.

Stars

Stars are units with high relative market shares in high growth industries. The high market share means low per unit cost. However, because the industry growth rate is high, such a unit often must invest a lot to maintain its leadership position in the growing market and therefore is not likely to have a positive cash flow. The strategy suggested by BCG was to invest the cash from the cash cow in the star and grow it into a future cash cow. If the right cash were not invested in the star, it might be relegated to a future dog.

Dogs

Dogs are units with low market shares in low growth industries. They generate little or no cash and have little potential for future growth. The strategy is to divest of such a unit and focus attention on more viable units. These units may generate enough cash to break even and sustain themselves. Although such a unit may possess some synergies with other units and provide jobs for employees, it is not very useful from an accounting point of view since it generates no cash and depresses the firm's return on assets ratio. Thus, a firm ought to get rid of dogs.

Question Marks

Question marks are units in industries with high growth rates, but that have low market shares relative to the leader in the market. The name question mark comes from the fact that it is not clear whether these units will become stars or dogs. Since they have very small market shares, their per unit costs are likely to be high relative to those of their competitors with larger market shares. Because they are in fast-growing industries, they need lots of cash to gain large market shares and become stars. The strategy is to take a deep look at the question marks and see whether they will become stars or dogs. If there is a good chance that they will become stars, the cash can be invested in them. If they lean towards dogs, they may as well be divested of.

Application of Framework

The Growth/Share matrix framework is illustrated using the four units shown in Figure 13.4.[5] The positions of the four units in 2006 and 2008 are shown by the circles. Shaded circles show the position of each unit in 2006 while blank circles show the positions of the units in 2008. The area of each circle is proportional to the revenues earned by the business. Thus, Unit 2 in 2008 had the most revenues while Unit 1 in 2006 had the least revenues. The horizontal axis of the matrix captures **relative market share** and represents a unit's market share relative to the largest competitor in the market in which the unit competes. Thus, a relative market share of 0.5, such as Unit 3's share in 2006, means that the unit has 50% of the market share of the largest competitor in the market. However, a unit such as Unit 2 with a relative market share of 4.0 in 2008, has four times the market share of its closest competitor and is clearly the leader in the market. The relative market shares of Units 1 and 2 increased from 2006 to 2008 while that of Unit 3 decreased and that of Unit 4 changed very slightly. Not only did Unit 3's relative share decrease, its revenues also went down. In general, since the vertical line that divides the matrix into two crosses the horizontal axis at 1.0, units that are located to the left of this line are market leaders while those to the right of the line are not.

The vertical axis of the matrix captures the **market growth rate** and measures the rate at which the market is growing, adjusted for inflation. It is assumed that *high*, as far as market growth is concerned, means a growth rate of 10% or higher and therefore the horizontal dividing line between high-growth and low-growth businesses is at 10%. High-growth units are above the line while low-growth units are below the line. Since a firm's profitability depends on both industry and firm-specific factors, market growth rate proxies industry factors while relative market share proxies firm-specific factors.

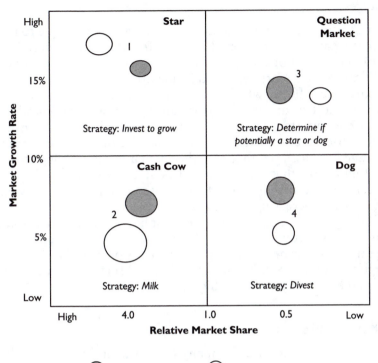

Figure 13.4 Illustration of Growth/Share Matrix.

Advantages and Disadvantages of Growth/Share Matrix Framework

The Growth/Share matrix framework has advantages and shortcomings that should be considered carefully before using it as an analysis tool.

Advantages

- The Growth/Share Matrix framework provides a common language, platform, and starting point for managers of multibusiness firms to explore the critical questions of: how much of the firm's scarce resources should be allocated to each unit? What businesses should the firm be in? Which ones should be disposed of? What should the performance targets of each business be?
- It could be used to explore not only the performance of a business unit but also to explore the performance of units in different countries or regions, different products, different technologies, brands, major customers, revenue models, and sources of revenue.
- The framework has only two simple variables: market growth rate and relative market share. This simplicity makes it easier for managers to understand and participate in a discussion of "what next" questions.

Disadvantages

- Although using only two variables makes it easier for people to understand and participate in decision-making debates, two simple variables do not capture the drivers of a unit's performance and therefore may be an over-simplification. It is worthwhile exploring other variables.
- The experience effects, which were a cornerstone of the model, turned out not to be the key driver of performance in many industries. Experience effects were important only in semiconductors and aerospace. Even in these two industries, the suspicion was that other factors were also critical.
- The framework assumes that an industry that is not growing today will not grow tomorrow; that is, the model is static. Research in technological innovation suggests that technological discontinuities can revive an industry, drastically increasing growth rates.
- Labeling a group as dogs or cows may not be a good idea. Who wants to be called a dog or a cow?
- Divesting of a business just because it is a dog may be discounting any synergies that may exist between the dog and stars or cash cows that have allowed these other units to be high performance.

GE/McKinsey Matrix

In the 1960s, General Electric Company (GE) was one of those multibusiness firms that faced the corporate level questions that we stated above, viz:

- How much of its scarce resources, such as capital, should be allocated to each business?
- What businesses should it be in?
- Which ones should be disposed of?
- What should the performance targets of each business be?

In exploring these questions, GE worked with McKinsey as a consultant. One output of the work performed by both firms in the late 1960s and early 1970s was the GE/McKinsey matrix. Like the BCG Growth/Share matrix before it, the GE/McKinsey matrix is also a portfolio analysis model. It exploits the fact that firm performance is driven by both industry and firm-specific factors. In the model, industry factors are proxied by Industry Attractiveness while firm-specific factors are proxied by Business Strength/Competitive Position (Figure 13.5).

Elements of the Framework

The vertical axis of the matrix captures industry attractiveness while the horizontal axis captures business strength/competitive position.

Industry Attractiveness

The *industry attractiveness* of the GE/McKinsey matrix replaces the *market growth rate* variable of the Growth/Share matrix. Moreover, industry attractiveness is a composite measure of the following:

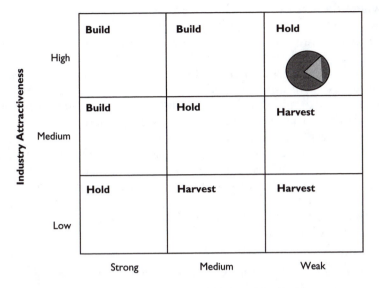

Figure 13.5 GE/McKinsey Matrix.

- Barriers to entry and exit
- Cyclicality
- Emerging opportunities and threats
- Industry profit margins
- Intensity of competition
- Macroenvironmental factors
- Market growth rate
- Market size
- Seasonality
- Technological and capital requirements.

The *Business Strength/Competitive Position* of the GE/McKinsey matrix replaces the *relative market share* variable of the Growth/Share Matrix. This was measured by a combination of the following:

- Ability to match or beat rivals on product quality and service
- Knowledge of customers and markets
- Management strength
- Possession of desirable distinctive capabilities
- Profit margins relative to competitors
- Relative cost position
- Relative market share
- Technological capability.

In the GE/McKinsey matrix, the size of each circle represents the size of the market for the unit in question while the shaded part of the circle represents the unit's share in the market (Figure 13.5). (This contrasts with the Growth-Share

Matrix where the size of the circle represents the size of revenues, and its relative market share is represented by where the circle is located.) In the 3 × 3 matrix, units that fall into the quadrant where industry attractiveness is high and a firm's business strength/competitive position is strong, are very profitable and a firm ought to invest in them and take other strategic steps to build them. A firm should also invest in and build (1) those units that are in industries whose attractiveness is medium but the firm's business strength/competitive position is strong, or (2) those that are in industries whose attractiveness is high and the firm's business strength/competitive position is median (Figure 13.5). A unit in an industry whose attractiveness is low or medium and the unit's strength/competitive position in the industry is weak, ought to be divested or harvested in some other way; so should units in industries whose attractiveness is low and the unit's business strength/competitive position is average. The units that fall into the other quadrants should be held and different strategies explored to make them more profitable.

Advantages and Disadvantages of the GE/McKinsey Matrix

The GE/McKinsey Matrix has some of the strengths and weaknesses of the BCG Growth/Share Matrix, with the important difference that the former has more complex measures.

Advantages

- Like the BCG Growth/Share matrix, the GE/McKinsey matrix framework provided a common language, platform, and starting point for managers of multibusiness firms to explore the critical questions faced by multibusiness firms.
- It could be used to explore not only the performance of a business unit but also to explore the performance of units in different countries or regions, different products, different technologies, brands, major customers, revenue models, and sources of revenue.
- The more complex measures for industry attractiveness and business strength provided a more realistic measure of the industry and firm-specific factors, two key determinants of firm performance.

Disadvantages

- By using a combination of many other variables to measure industry attractiveness, the GE/McKinsey matrix becomes very complex and difficult for managers to understand. It makes the model more difficult for managers to put their minds around. The list of variables that constitute the combination to measure either industry attractiveness or business strength can quickly become a laundry list.
- The framework is still a static model because it says nothing about how the variables change with time.
- Divesting of a unit because the industry is not attractive today and the unit's business strength is low may be discounting synergies that may exist between the unit and more profitable ones.

Porter's Five Forces

As its name suggests, Porter's Five Forces framework was developed by Professor Michael Porter of the Harvard Business School and introduced to the world in his 1979 *Harvard Business Review* paper that was followed by his 1980 book, *Competitive Strategy*.[6] It is a framework for determining the average profitability of an industry. Although the SWOT analysis had allowed analysts to produce a list of factors that posed threats to a firm and another that offered opportunities for a firm, there was no way of directly linking these factors to profitability. Porter's Five Forces enabled analysts to link the competitive threats and opportunities of an industry to the profitability of the industry. In the framework, there are five competitive forces that act on industry firms and determine the average profitability of an industry (Figure 13.6). How do these forces lower or raise industry profitability? Let's consider each force, starting with *Barriers to Entry*. If *Barriers to Entry* are high—that is, if the *Threat of Potential New Entry* is low—industry firms can afford to keep their prices high without attracting many new entrants. That tends to increase industry profits. However, if *Barriers to Entry* are low, new entrants would enter the industry if firms charge high prices for their outputs or sell lots of the output, thereby indicating to new entrants that there is a lot of money to be made in the industry. Rational industry firms, for fear of attracting many new entrants, are therefore inclined to keep their prices low, thereby tending to reduce industry profits.

If the *Bargaining Power of Suppliers* is high—that is, if suppliers have bargaining power over industry firms—the suppliers are likely to demand high prices for the inputs that industry firms need to make and deliver products. If

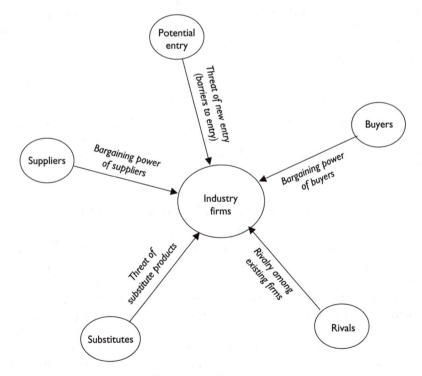

Figure 13.6 Porter's Five Competitive Forces.

suppliers have high bargaining power, they are also more likely to force industry firms to take lower quality inputs than they would ordinarily like. If industry firms are forced to pay higher prices for their inputs, their costs are going to be higher, thereby reducing their profits. If they are forced to take inferior components, industry firms are not likely to command the type of premium that they would like from their own customers. They may also have to spend more to improve the poor quality from suppliers. In either case, industry firm profitability goes down. The opposite would be true if industry firms had bargaining power over their suppliers. They (industry firms) would dictate the terms of exchange and would be more likely to extract low input prices and higher quality inputs from their suppliers. The result would be higher profitability for industry firms.

If *Bargaining Power of Buyers* is high, buyers can force industry firms to take lower prices or force them to deliver higher quality products than they would like to deliver at the prices of lower quality products. The result is that industry profitability is likely to be lower. If the *Bargaining Power of Buyers* is low, industry firms can extract higher prices out of buyers, or force them to take lower quality products at high prices. The result is higher industry profitability.

If *Rivalry Among Existing Firms* is high—for example, because industry growth is low, or firms are selling undifferentiated products—industry firms are forced to keep their prices low or end up with a lower market share. They may also be forced to spend more to differentiate themselves without the appropriate price premiums. The result is that industry profitability is lower. If rivalry is low, firms can afford to keep their prices high, thereby maintaining profitability. If the *Threat of Substitutes is high*—that is, industry products are such that customers can use substitutes—industry firms are compelled to keep their prices low, otherwise customers will switch to substitutes. The result is that industry profits are likely to be lower. If the threat of substitutes is low, industry profits are likely to be higher.

Elements of the Five Forces

The determinants of each of the forces are shown in Figure 13.7. Since space in this chapter is limited and more detailed information on the Five Forces is readily available elsewhere, we will explore only the first two determinants of each force.[7]

Determinant of Barriers to Entry (Threat of Potential New Entry)

Barriers to entry tend to be high when *Economies of scale* are high—that is, if the *Minimum efficient scale* is high relative to market share. Why? The more of a particular product that a firm produces, the lower the per unit cost of the product. However, beyond a certain volume, the decrease in unit cost stops. This volume is called the **minimum efficient scale (MES)**, the minimum volume that a firm has to produce in order to attain the minimum per unit cost possible in the market.[8] A new entrant must produce at least at this volume to have the same low per unit cost that incumbents have. If the MES is high, an entrant faces two major problems. First, it has to have enough customers that want the large volume dictated by the high MES that it has to attain. Second, if the new

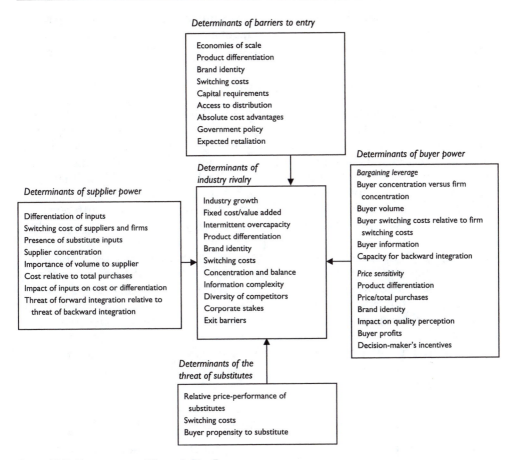

Figure 13.7 Components of Porter's Five Forces.

entrant produces that huge MES volume, it is effectively adding that much more product to the market. The larger the MES and therefore the more of the product that a new entrant would have to bring into the market, the lower the prices would be. Thus, if the minimum efficient scale is large, rational potential new entrants are less likely to enter since they can expect prices to drop considerably, given how much they have to add to the industry's capacity. Effectively, high economies of scale (MES relative to market share) can constitute a high barrier to entry.

Another barrier to entry is *product differentiation*. If a firm sells a highly differentiated product in a market, any potential new entrant that hopes to wrestle away market share from the firm has to be able to replicate the product or differentiate its own product in some other way. Doing so can be difficult. Why? It may take a lot of time and money to acquire those attributes that differentiate the product. Take Toyota's Lexus cars. First, it is difficult to put a finger on what it is that gives the car its reliability, fun and feel, and perception by customers. Second, even if one were able to identify what it takes to build all these attributes, it may still not be possible to replicate or leapfrog them. It takes time, effort and money to build such capabilities. Many potential new entrants may not have such capabilities. For these reasons, product differentiation can be a high barrier to entry. The other determinants of barriers to entry are brand identity, switching costs, capital requirements, access to distribution, absolute cost advantages, government policy, and expected retaliation (Figure 13.7).

Determinants of the Bargaining Power of Suppliers

If the products that suppliers supply to firms are highly differentiated—that is, if inputs are differentiated—firms are less likely to switch from the supplier to another supplier. That is, *differentiated inputs* give the suppliers of such inputs bargaining power. Such a supplier can extract higher prices from industry firms or force them to take inputs with inferior quality than would ordinarily be expected. Firms are not likely to find another supply with the differentiated quality of the input. For example, microprocessors are highly differentiated inputs to PCs since they have unique features that PCs need. This gives makers of microprocessors more bargaining power over PC makers than one would ordinarily expect suppliers to have over their buyers. Another determinant of the bargaining power of suppliers is the *switching cost* that firms incur if they were to switch to another supplier. The higher these switching costs, the higher the bargaining power that suppliers are likely to have. A firm's switching costs are the costs that the firm incurs when it switches from one supplier to another. For example, people who learnt to drive using a car with an automatic transmission have high switching costs if they were to switch to a car with a manual transmission. The other determinants of supplier bargaining power are shown in Figure 13.7.

Determinants of the Bargaining Power of Buyers

The bargaining power of buyers is a strong function of the *concentration of buyers* relative to that of firms. The more buyers that there are vying for firms' products, the better off firms are since they can play buyers against each other. If one buyer does not agree to their terms, firms can go to another buyer. Therefore, if buyers are in an industry that is concentrated relative to the firm's industry, buyers are likely to have bargaining power. In some cases, the buyer industry may not be concentrated but may have one or more dominant buyers who can wield a lot of power by virtue of the large quantities of products that they buy, and in that case, set the trend for prices. For example, the retail industry is not concentrated relative to industries for suppliers of items such as detergents, etc. Yet, the sheer volume of purchases that large companies such as Wal-Mart makes gives them considerable bargaining power. *Product differentiation* also plays a part in the bargaining power of buyers. If the products that buyers purchase from firms are undifferentiated, buyers are more likely to play firms against each other than would be the case when the products are differentiated. Buyers are even more likely to play firms against each other if the product has no switching costs; but if industry firms offer differentiated products, their chances of having bargaining power over buyers are increased.

The remaining determinants of the bargaining power of buyers are shown in Figure 13.7. These determinants are sometimes divided into those that have to do with *Bargaining Leverage* and those that have to do with *Price Sensitivity*. Bargaining leverage determinants are those determinants that depend more on the firms themselves while price sensitivity determinants are those that have to do with the products and their attributes rather than firms.

Determinants of Industry Rivalry

Many firms are usually under pressure from investors to increase earnings. If *industry growth* is high, firms can meet expectations of such earnings without having to steal market share from each other. However, if industry growth is slow or declining, firms may be tempted to try to steal market share from their rivals. In trying to steal market share, firms may resort to price wars, or unnecessary product promotion or introduction, which can sap industry profits. Effectively, the lower the industry growth rate, the more likely that industry rivalry will be high. Also, high *fixed costs*, relative to variable costs, can increase industry rivalry. Why? Each time a firm sells a unit of a product, the revenues from the product go to cover variable cost, fixed costs, and profit margin. In bad times, firms may be tempted to sell their products at a loss, so long as the prices cover their variable costs. The higher the fixed costs relative to variable costs, the lower that the firm can set its prices (below profitable prices) and still cover variable costs. This can reduce industry profits considerably. Effectively, the higher the fixed costs, relative to variable costs, the higher we can expect industry rivalry. The remaining determinants of industry rivalry are shown in Figure 13.7.

Determinants of the Threat of Substitutes

Substitutes are products from outside the industry or market that customers can buy instead of industry products. Customers will turn to substitutes if the substitutes perform the tasks that products usually perform for customers and do so at a good price; that is, substitutes can be a problem for industry products if the substitutes have the *right relative price-performance*. To start buying substitutes, existing customers have to switch from industry products to the substitutes. If the costs of switching from industry products to substitutes are high, substitutes are less likely to be a threat to industry firms. The remaining determinants of the threat of substitutes are shown in Figure 13.7.

Advantages: Applying Porter's Five Forces

Industry Attractiveness

One of the primary applications of Porter's Five Forces is to use it to analyze an industry's attractiveness—use it to explore the extent to which an industry is, on average, profitable. If the competitive forces acting on industry firms are low—that is, the bargaining power of suppliers, threat of new entry, the bargaining power of buyers, the threat of substitutes, and rivalry among existing firms are low—the industry is said to be attractive, since the forces suggest that industry firms are, on average, profitable. If the competitive forces that act on industry firms are high, the industry is said to be unattractive, since industry firms are, on average, unprofitable. It is important to understand that if a Five Forces analysis shows that an industry is, on average, unprofitable, it does not mean that all the firms in the industry are unprofitable. A Five Forces analysis determines only the average profitability of the firms in an industry, not the profitability of individual firms. A firm's profitability is determined by both industry and firm-specific factors. A Five Forces analysis tells us something about the *industry factors* component of performance but says very little or nothing about the *firm-specific factors* component. Firm-specific factors are those things that enable a firm to outperform its rivals in the industry in which they all compete; that is, firm-specific factors are what enable a firm to have a competitive advantage. For example, a Five Forces analysis of the PC industry would indicate that it is not a very attractive industry. Yet, Dell was extremely profitable between 1994 and 1999. Several firm-specific factors contributed to Dell's strategy, to more than compensate for the industry unattractiveness and make Dell a profit generator. One of them was the firm's new game strategy of selling directly to end-customers and focusing on those business customers that had sales of over $1 million.

Determine Opportunities and Threats

In analyzing the determinants of each force, one is effectively identifying the opportunities (friendly forces) and threats (repressive forces) of the competitive environment. A firm can then use its strengths to take advantage of the opportunities while trying to mute the threats. For example, if there is only one supplier that supplies a critical input to several firms, a firm can work with the supplier to create second sources for the component. Doing so effectively dampens the power of suppliers. Consider another example. If firms are able to differentiate their products using brand name reputations, such brands can be reinforced with the right marketing investments. For example, Coke and Pepsi spend huge amounts of money advertising to maintain their brands. Effectively, a Five Forces analysis can be seen as a framework for identifying both friendly and hostile forces so that managers can then formulate the right strategies to mute repressive forces and reinforce friendly ones. In this respect, the Five Forces model has a huge advantage over a SWOT analysis. A SWOT analysis generates a list that can quickly degenerate into a laundry list. More importantly, a SWOT analysis does not link the weaknesses and threats generated to profitability. A Five Forces analysis does.

Organizing Framework for Data

A Five Forces analysis can also be used as an organizing framework for discussions leading up to a decision. For example, in a strategic planning meeting, managers can use the framework to sketch out scenarios of what would happen if any of the determinants of each of the five forces were to change. The model provides a common language and understanding for exploring the industry context in which firms operate.

Disadvantages

Like any model, the Five Forces framework has some disadvantages.

No Mechanism for Narrowing Down

The framework has no mechanism for narrowing down the list of factors to important ones. Suppose three of the five forces are low while the other two are high. Is the industry attractive or unattractive? Now, take *rivalry among existing firms*, which has eleven determinants (Figure 13.7). Suppose five of the determinants suggest that rivalry should be high while six suggest that rivalry should be low. Should rivalry among existing firms be indicated as being low or high?

Neglects the Role of Complementors

Complementors are the firms that make complements. In many industries, the role of complements is critical. For example, PCs would not be as valuable as they are without software. Therefore neglecting the role of complementors, as the Five Forces model does, may not be a good idea.

Framework is Static

Like most strategy frameworks, the Five Forces framework is a static model. It is about the average profitability potential of an industry at a point in time. It says nothing about what the profitability potential of the industry was yesterday or what it will be tomorrow. The Five Forces takes a cross section of the average attractiveness of an industry, which is OK, so long as none of the key determinants of each of the forces changes over time. Effectively, the model neglects the dynamic nature of most industries and one should use it carefully when dealing with fast-changing industries.

No Cooperation Included

The model says little or nothing about cooperation. The Five Forces introduced the notion of extended competition—the notion that suppliers, customers, substitutes, and potential new entrants should be viewed as competitors, the way rivals are viewed. This is a great idea. But there is also a lot of cooperation that takes place between firms and their suppliers, buyers, rivals, complementors, and makers of substitutes. As we argued in Chapter 4, firms often have to cooperate and compete with coopetitors to create and appropriate value. Seeing coopetitors as competitors, the way a Five-Forces analysis does is incomplete.

Role of MacroEnvironment not Considered

The Five Forces framework does not explicitly consider the role of macroenvironmental effects. The effects of the political, macroeconomic, sociological, technological, and natural environment are not directly considered.

Business Systems

The concept of a business system was developed in work at McKinsey by Carter F. Bales, P. C. Chatterjee, Frederick W. Gluck, Donald Gogel, and Anupam

Puri.[9] It was introduced to the outside world in Frederick Gluck's and Buaron's 1980 articles in *The McKinsey Quarterly*.[10] A business system consists of the different elements of the system of activities which a firm uses to make and deliver products or services to a market. One such system is shown in Figure 13.8 for a technology-based manufacturing firm.[11] At each stage of the system, the firm has different options for performing the activities at that stage. For example, take the activities at the technology stage. As we saw briefly in Chapter 1, the firm can choose to license the technology from another firm, develop the technology internally alone, form an alliance to develop the technology, or outsource the whole product development and design process to someone. If it performs its own R&D, it can choose to patent aggressively, decide not to patent and instead depend on keeping its technology secret, or open up the technology to any one who wants. And so on. At the distribution level, a firm can choose to use all the distribution channels available to it, use only some of the channels, or bypass all of them and sell directly to end-customers. If the firm decides to use distribution channels, it can own them or outsource the distribution to someone else. It can build up inventories before and warehouse the components or build the product only after a customer has ordered it. Again, the options abound.

All these options are opportunities for new games. For example, if firms in an industry all use distributors to sell their products to end-customers, a firm can pursue a new game by selling directly to the end-customers. If firms in an industry keep their technologies proprietary, a firm can pursue the new game of opening up its technology to any firm that wants it; and so on.

Application of the Business Systems Approach

The business systems concept is about asking option-generating questions at each stage of the system.[12] These questions include:

- How is the firm performing the activities of the stage now?
- How are competitors performing the activities of the stage?
- What is better about competitors' ways of performing the activities?
- What is better about the firm's ways?
- How else might the activities be performed?
- How would the options affect the firm's competitive position?

Technology	Product design	Manufacturing	Marketing	Distribution	Service
• Patents • Product/process choices • Sophistication • Sources	• Aesthetics • Function • Physical characteristics • Quality	• Assembly • Capacity • Integration • Location • Parts production • Procurement • Raw materials	• Advertising/ promotion • Brand • Packaging • Prices • Sales force	• Channels • Integration • Inventory • Transportation • Warehousing	• Captive/ independent • Prices • Speed • Warranty

Figure 13.8 Business System for a Technology Firm.

- If the firm were to change the way it performs activities at the stage in question, how would doing so impact the other stages of the business system?

One of the primary lessons of the business systems concept is that there are many other ways, beyond product innovation, to gain a strategic advantage. One can change the conventional system for getting an existing product to the market.[13] Using the Internet to sell old books or movies is a good example.

Value Chain Analysis

The idea behind a value chain is that at each of the stages of a business system, something is done to the work-in-process to get it closer to the product that customers value. To see how, consider the business system for a firm such as an automobile maker shown in Figure 13.9. The product design unit adds value when it designs a car. After the design, a customer, C, that looks at the design has some idea about what the car will look like. The manufacturing unit adds value when it transforms the design into a car that has the features specified in the design, getting the car closer to what customers want. Marketing adds value by bringing information about the car to customers that makes customers perceive the car as being more valuable to them than they would have perceived had they not received the marketing messages. Distribution adds value by bringing the car to where customers can touch and feel, test-drive, kick the ties, or buy and drive away. The service unit adds value be servicing or repairing the car, or assuring the potential buyer that there will be service when he or she needs it.

The term value chain was coined by Professor Michael Porter of the Harvard Business School in his 1985 book, to designate the chain of activities that a firm performs to add value—as it transforms its inputs into outputs.[14] He divided the activities of a generic value chain into primary and supporting activities (Figure 13.10).

Elements of a Value Chain

Primary Activities

These consist of inbound logistics, operations, outbound logistics, marketing and sales, and service.

- Inbound logistics: these are the activities performed to receive, sort, store, retrieve, and distribute inputs to a product or service. Depending on the industry, these activities can include scheduling, inventory control,

Figure 13.9 An Automobile Maker's Business System.

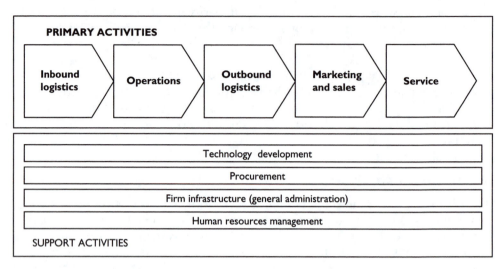

Figure 13.10 A Generic Value Chain.

allocation of inputs to different distribution centers, and handling of returns to suppliers.

- Operations: these are the activities that transform inputs into the final product. Depending on the industry, these activities can involve fabrication, machining, milling, assembly, testing, quality control, and so on.
- Outbound logistics: these are the activities that are performed to take the finished product to buyers. Depending on the industry, these activities can include gathering of the finished product, storing, distribution, and handling of returns from buyers
- Marketing and sales: these are the activities that get customers to buy the finished product at good prices. They include channel selection, promotion, pricing, advertising, responses to requests for information or quotations, merchandising, and so on.
- Service: these are activities such as installation, training, repair, spare parts supply, and disposal that enhance or maintain the value of a product.

Support Activities

Support activities for a generic value chain consist of technology development, procurement, firm infrastructure, and human resources management.

- Technology development: technology development cuts across all the primary activities. At inbound logistics, technology development can entail inventory management, transportation, materials handling, information technology, or communications. In operations, technology development can entail materials, manufacturing, packaging, building and information technology. In outbound logistics, technology development can entail transportation, materials handling, and information systems. In marketing and sales, technology development can entail communications and information systems. In services, technology development can be in testing and information systems.

- Procurement: these are the activities to purchase the inputs that are used in the primary activities. They include sending out requests for information or quotations, bargaining with suppliers, etc. The purchases include materials, equipment, buildings, land, etc.
- Firm infrastructure: these are activities such as accounting, finance, general management, planning, legal and government services, information systems, and quality management that complement the other activities.
- Human resource management: these are the activities to locate, recruit, hire, train, develop, and compensate employees.

Applying the Value Chain Analysis

The value chain analysis has several applications.

Estimating Firm-specific Effects (Estimating Value Created and Costs)

Just as Porter's Five Forces analysis can be used to estimate industry attractiveness and therefore the industry factors that can impact a firm's performance, a value chain analysis can be used to estimate the firm-specific factors that contribute to the firm's performance. By identifying the different stages of a firm's value chain, the value added at each stage, how much it costs to add the value, the capabilities needed, and the value drivers, a firm can isolate which stages of its value chain add the most value and why. Such information can help a firm decide where to invest more so as to increase its chances of attaining or maintaining a competitive advantage in the markets in which it competes.

Organizing Framework for Data

Like a Five Forces analysis, a value chain analysis can also be used as an organizing framework for managers to guide them in their scenario analysis of which activities to perform. Firms can also compare their value chains to those of their competitors.

Value System

Although we have focused our attention on a focal firm's value chain, suppliers and buyers also have value chains. The system that is made up of a supplier's value chain, the focal firm's value chain, and buyer's value chain is called a **value system** (Figure 13.11). Effectively, each value chain is part of a larger system of value chains called a value system. Unfortunately, however, most people usually just call the value system a value chain, without making any distinction between the two.

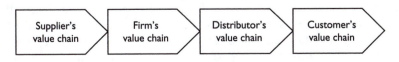

Figure 13.11 A Value System.

Shortcoming of a Generic Value Chain Analysis

The generic value chain of Figure 13.10 fairly represents the activities that are performed to add value in many manufacturing industries. However, it does not represent the value-adding activities in many other industries. Consulting, financial services, insurance, software, hospitals, search engine companies, real estate, and numerous other service organizations do not have inbound and outbound logistics. Moreover, the activities in these industries are not performed in chains as the value chain framework suggests. What is so value chain about the activities at hospital or at a Google? We explore alternate business systems.

Value Configurations

Professors Charles Stabell and Oystein Fjeldstad of the Norwegian School of Management argued that the value chain is but one of three configurations for conceptualizing the value created when firms perform value-adding activities.[15] The other two are *value network* and *value shop*. In their work, published in the *Strategic Management Journal* in 1998, Professors Stabell and Fjeldstad called the value chain, value shop, and value network *value configurations* since they are about different arrangements for adding value.[16] Recall that, in the value chain, adding value is about bringing in the right inputs, transforming them into the right outputs, and disposing of the outputs. In a value network, adding value is about building a network of customers and enabling direct and indirect exchanges among the customers. In a value shop, adding value is about resolving customer problems. Since we explored the value chain above, we now focus on value shop and value network.

Value Network

The value network is the configuration that firms, which mediate between other firms or between individuals, use to add value. Such firms include commercial banks which mediate between borrowers and savers, auctioneers who mediate between sellers and buyers, credit card companies which mediate between cardholders and merchants, and distributors which mediate between producers and end-customers. A bank adds value by building the right network of borrowers and savers and using savings to make loans. The more savers that a bank has, the better off the depositors at the bank are likely to be and vice versa. An auctioneer such as eBay adds value by creating a large network of sellers and buyers, enabling exchanges between them. The more sellers that there are, the better off the buyers, and vice versa. A credit card company adds value by building the right network of merchants and cardholders, and enabling cardholders to use their cards to make purchases from merchants. The more cardholders that use a particular card, the better off the merchants that accept the card. The more merchants that accept the card, the better off each cardholder is likely to be. For these firms that mediate between different parties, adding value is about building the network that the parties value, and performing the types of activities that enable direct or indirect exchanges between members of the network. Contrast this with a manufacturer with a value chain that must worry about incoming and outgoing logistics, transformation of physical inputs into outputs, and disposal of these outputs. *Value network* configurations get their name from the fact that value addition is about building and exploiting a network.

The elements of a value network (a bank in this case) are shown in Figure 13.12. Support activities are very similar to the support activities for a value chain that we saw earlier. Therefore we focus on primary activities.

Primary Activities

- *Network promotion and contract management*: These are the activities to invite and select potential customers to join the network. They include initialization, management, and termination of contracts.
- *Service provisioning*: These are the activities to establish, maintain, and terminate links with customers. They also include activities to bill customers.
- *Network infrastructure operation*: These are the activities to maintain firm's physical and information infrastructures.

Value Shop

Adding value in organizations such as hospitals, consulting firms, law firms, architecture firms, and engineering professional services such as petroleum exploration, has a lot more to do with solving problems than inbound and outbound logistics, and therefore requires a different configuration from the value chain.[17] It is about working with customers to identify their problems and solve them. Consider the example of a hospital. When a patient walks into a hospital or is carried there, doctors have to find out what is wrong with the patient. They examine the patient using their banks of knowledge, skills, know-how, and equipment. After the examination, they may decide that there is nothing wrong with the patient and send him or her home. They may also decide that they need to conduct some laboratory tests or more diagnostics. Depending on the result of the tests, more tests may be needed, the patient may be referred to an expert, admitted into the hospital, sent home, or sent for yet more tests. Effectively, hospitals are more about solving problems than about inbound

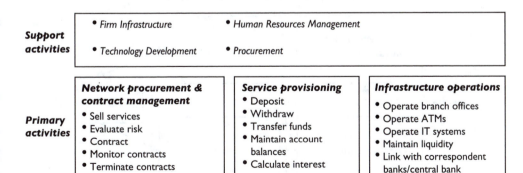

Support activities	• Firm Infrastructure	• Human Resources Management	
	• Technology Development	• Procurement	

Primary activities	**Network procurement & contract management**	**Service provisioning**	**Infrastructure operations**
	• Sell services	• Deposit	• Operate branch offices
	• Evaluate risk	• Withdraw	• Operate ATMs
	• Contract	• Transfer funds	• Operate IT systems
	• Monitor contracts	• Maintain account balances	• Maintain liquidity
	• Terminate contracts	• Calculate interest	• Link with correspondent banks/central bank

Figure 13.12 A Value Network.

logistics, transformation of physical inputs, and disposal of outputs. Hospital employees work with a patient to identify his or her illness and work to cure the illness. Patients are not input materials, all of whom are given the same treatment, and the same product expected at the end of some chain. The configurations in which problems are identified and solved are called **value shop** and are better conceptualizations for hospitals, consulting services, law firms, engineering professional firms, and architecture firms than the value chain or value network. The elements of the value shop are shown in Figure 13.13.

Primary Activities

- Problem-finding and acquisition: working with customers to determine the exact nature of their problem or need. Activities include those to record, review, and formulate the problem. Choice of general approach to solve the problem.
- Problem-solving: activities to generate and evaluate alternative solutions.
- Choice: activities to choose among alternative solutions among alternative problem solutions.
- Execution: activities to communicate, organize, and implement the chosen solution.
- Control and evaluation: activities to measure and evaluate the extent to which implementation of the solution has solved the problem targeted.

Balanced Scorecard

The balanced scorecard framework is a performance measurement system that was developed by Professor Robert Kaplan of the Harvard Business School and Dr. David Norton.[18] It takes four measurement perspectives—financial, customers, business processes, and learning and growth—that provide a snapshot of not only current operating performance but also the drivers of future performance. Traditional financial measures such as income, return on assets,

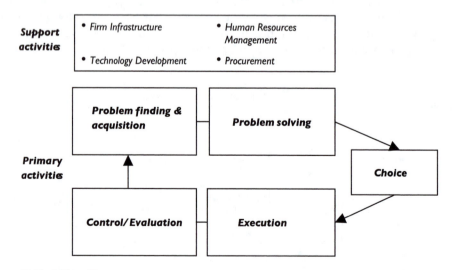

Figure 13.13 A Value Shop.

return on investments, economic value added, etc., usually reflect the results of past actions and say very little about what might drive future financial performance. They also say little about the intellectual capital embedded in relationships with customers, suppliers, and employees. By including measures from the perspective of customers, business processes, and learning and growth, the balanced scorecard captures measures of some of the drivers of future performance.

Elements of the Balanced Scorecard

The key elements of the Balanced Scorecard are shown in Figure 13.14. A firm's vision and objectives are translated into measures that take customer, business process, learning and growth, and financial perspectives. In each perspective, a firm asks a driving question and answers the question by outlining its objectives, fleshing out measures of the objective from the perspective in question, stating the targets that the firm wants to meet as far as the perspective is concerned, and detailing the initiatives that the firm would need to meet the targets (Figure 13.14).

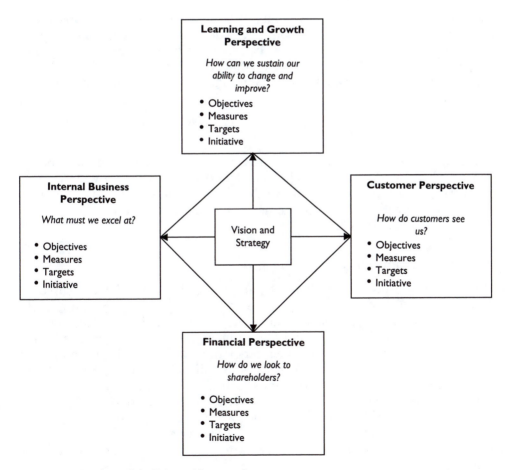

Figure 13.14 Elements of the Balanced Scorecard.

Customer Perspective

The primary question that a firm should ask itself is, how do customers see us? The idea here is for a firm to translate the customer-related aspects of its vision and objectives into measures that reflect those things that matter to customers. For example, measures such as delivery lead times, product quality, performance and service, and costs are important to most customers and therefore make good measures.

Internal Business Perspective

The primary question that a firm should ask itself as far as the internal business perspective is concerned is, at what must we excel? The idea here is to identify those things that a firm does well to meet customer needs, and then identify those measures that enable the firm to track these things that it does so well. Some of these measures include cycle time, quality, employee skills, and productivity.

Learning and Growth Perspective

Because of the rapid rate of change, especially technological change, it is important for a firm to be able to continue to do well in the face of change. Thus a firm needs to ask the question, how can we sustain our ability to change and improve? This ability can be tracked using measures such as the ability to launch new products, create more value for customers, and improve operating efficiencies.

Financial Perspective

The financial perspective measures whether a firm's strategy and implementation have been working for shareholders. Hence the question, how do we look to shareholders? How a firm looks to shareholders can be tracked using measures such as profitability, shareholder value, cash flow, operating income, return on equity, and so on.

Objectives, Measures, Targets, and Initiatives

Throughout our discussion of the balanced scorecard, we have focused on measures; but as indicated in Figure 13.14, each perspective has four parts: objectives, measures, targets, and initiatives. A firm's objectives for each perspective are where the firm would like to be as far as the perspective is concerned. For example, in the customer perspective, a firm's objective may be to increase customer satisfaction. A measure of customer satisfaction would be, for example, customer ratings of their satisfaction with the firm's products or service. A specific target for measuring customer satisfaction would be, for example, a rating of 5 out of 5. Initiatives are action programs put in place to meet the objective. Initiatives to increase customer satisfaction could include listening to customers more, training customer service representatives, and building a better product.

Advantages and Shortcoming of the Balanced Scorecard

Advantages

- Before the balanced scoreboard, one of the few ways to determine whether or not a firm's strategy was working was to use financial measures; but financial measures usually reflect the results of past actions and say very little about future performance. Moreover, it was not easy to link financial performance to firm activities. By complementing these financial measures with measures from the perspective of the customer, internal business, and learning and growth, a firm can track its progress towards meeting its objectives and future performance goals better. If the adage that "You can't manage what you don't measure" is true, these added measures of a balanced scorecard expand the scope of what managers can manage better.
- The balanced scorecard offers managers a common language, display format, and starting point for management discussions on the extent to which a firm's strategy is meeting its objectives.
- The balanced scorecard also provides a common language for benchmarking the performance of competitors, acquisition targets, and potential alliance partners.

Disadvantages

- The balanced scorecard is a set of measures, not a strategy. While it enables managers to track the performance of a strategy, it does not say what the strategy is and how it could be improved. The framework says very little about the activities that are driving a firm's performance and why the activities are indeed responsible for the performance. This is where frameworks such as the AVAC that we saw in Chapter 2 and will touch on below come in.
- If the adage that "You can't manage what you don't measure" is true, then settling on the wrong measures can mislead a firm into thinking that it is on the right track.

VRIO Framework

The VRIO (Value, Rare, Imitate, Organized) framework was developed by Professor Jay Barney of the Fisher College of Business at the Ohio State University.[19] The framework is about exploring the extent to which a firm can expect to have a sustainable competitive advantage from its resources. The central argument of the framework is that, if a firm has resources that are valuable, rare, costly to imitate, and the firm is organized to exploit these resources, then the firm can expect to have a sustained competitive advantage. It is rooted in the resource-based view of strategic management that we explored in Chapter 5.

Elements of the Framework

The framework can be understood by exploring four questions.

The Question of Value

Value in this case is about the extent to which external opportunities can be exploited or external threats neutralized. Thus the question that a firm poses is, does the resource enable the firm to exploit external opportunities or neutralize an external threat? If the answer is Yes, the firm is likely to increase its revenues, decrease its costs, or both—it is likely to increase its profits using the resource.

The Question of Rarity

If the resource is not rare, many other firms will acquire it and be able to exploit the same opportunities or neutralize the same threats, considerably reducing any profits that the firm would have made from the resource. Rarity does not necessarily mean that the firm is the only one with the resource. A few firms can have the resource, but just few enough for there still to be scarcity, enabling them to make money from the resources.

The Question of Imitability

If a resource is valuable and rare, a firm can have a competitive advantage; but such an advantage is likely to be only temporary if the resource can be imitated. Effectively, the advantage is likely to be sustainable only if competitors face a cost disadvantage in imitating the resource.

The Question of Organization

A valuable, rare, and inimitable resource still has to be exploited. Thus a firm's structure and control systems must be such that employees have the ability and incentive to exploit the firm's resources.

Advantages and Disadvantages

Advantages

- Since a firm's valuable, rare, and inimitable resources are its strengths, the VRIO framework provides the link between strengths and profitability that a SWOT analysis does not.
- It can be used to narrow down the list of a firm's resources to only the very relevant ones, allowing a manager to make better choices on where to invest. Managers can also use it to identify the areas in which they have weaknesses (in resources), allowing them to plan better on how to reduce the weaknesses.
- A VRIO analysis can also be used to determine the quality of competitors' resources.

Disadvantages

- The VRIO framework says very little about coopetitors—the suppliers, customers, complementors, rivals, and other organizations with whom a firm often has to cooperate to create value and compete to appropriate it; that is, the industry component of the determinants of a firm's profitability is largely neglected.

- The framework says very little about change. In the face of some changes, valuable, rare, and inimitable resources can become a handicap.[20]

VIDE

In 1990s, following Professors C.K. Prahalad's and Gary Hamel's seminal article on the core competence of the firm, and research by other scholars, many firms wanted to determine their core competences and nurture them.[21] Some of the firms that tried this exercise ended up with an endless list of resources and capabilities, with no way of determining which ones were really the critical ones that deserved to be nurtured. The VIDE (Value, Imitability, Differentiability, and Extendability) analysis was one attempt to narrow down the list of core competences to the ones that really matter to a firm.[22] It consists of providing answers to four questions about resources/capabilities and classifying them based on the answers. It was derived from the definition of a core competence. Recall from Chapter 5 that a core competence is a resource or capability that meets the following criteria:[23] (1) makes a significant contribution to the benefits that customers perceive in a product or service, (2) is difficult for competitors to imitate, and (3) is extendable to other products in different markets.

Elements of the VIDE Analysis

The primary questions in a VIDE analysis are summarized in Table 13.1.

Value

Since money comes from customers, a core competence must be translated into something that they perceive as valuable to them. Hence the first question that a firm may want to ask, in determining the extent to which a resource/capability is likely to amount to a core competence, is to ask whether the resource/capability makes a significant contribution towards the *Value* that its customers perceive. The skills of a plastic surgeon who performs cosmetic face surgery adds value if his/her patients can look in a mirror and say, "I like my new face." If the answer is No, then there is little chance that the resource/capability is likely to be a core competence, unless the firm finds a way to make it more valuable to customers.

Table 13.1 Elements of a VIDE Analysis

Element	Question
Value	Does the resource or capability make an unusually high contribution to the value that customers perceive in the firm's products?
Imitability	Is it difficult for other firms to duplicate or substitute the resource or capability?
Differentiation	Is the type or level of the resource or capability unique to the firm?
Extendability	Can the resource or capability be used in more than one product area?

Imitability

If a resource or capability makes a significant contribution to the value that customers perceive, the firm may not be able to make money from it for a long time if the skill can be duplicated or substituted by many competitors. Thus an important question to ask is, is it difficult for other firms to duplicate or substitute the resource or capability?

Differentiation

If a resource or capability can be imitated, the question is, can a firm set itself apart from imitators by differentiating the capability? For example, a firm can differentiate itself by having a higher level of capability. Many cosmetic surgeons can perform face surgery but some of them can do a much better job than others. Thus, an important question is determining whether a resource is a core competence is, is the type or level of the resource or capability unique to the firm?

Extendability

If a resource or capability is valuable, difficult to imitate, and a firm has found a way to differentiate the resource from copycats, the next big question is, can the resource or capability be used in more than one product area? For example, Honda's ability to design reliable high-performing engines is extendable because its engines are used not only in cars but also in boats, lawnmowers, motorcycles, electric generators, and airplanes.

Effectively, by answering Yes or No to the questions of Table 13.1, a firm can rank its resources/capabilities with the ones with the most Yesses at the top since they have the highest likelihood of being core competences.

Advantages and Disadvantages of VIDE

Advantages

- The VIDE analysis offered one of the first ways to determine the extent to which a resource or capability was likely to be a core competence and therefore presented firms with a method for narrowing down their lists of resources to a more manageable few.
- A VIDE analysis can be used to analyze the resources/capabilities of competitors and potential targets for acquisition or cooperation.

Disadvantages

The VIDE analysis has some of the same disadvantages as the VRIO analysis discussed above.

- The only mention of coopetitors in the VIDE analysis is in the Extendability component. That is because in moving to a different product area, a firm is likely to face competition; but like the VRIO, the VIDE says very little about coopetitors—the suppliers, customers, complementors, rivals, and other organizations with whom a firm often has to cooperate to create value and compete to appropriate it. The industry component of the determinants of a firm's profitability is largely neglected.

- Like the other frameworks that we have explored, the VIDE says very little about change. In the face of radical changes, core competences can become handicaps.[24]

S³PE

As we saw in Chapter 7, S³PE stands for Strategy, Structure, Systems, People, and Environment. The rationale behind the S³PE framework is that strategies are formulated and executed by people. Therefore, people are important to the success of a strategy. They are more than just a part of a profit-maximizing firm. The structure of a firm—to which people report, and who is responsible for what activities—is important, as are the systems that the firm has in place for determining how performance is measured, how people are rewarded or punished, what information goes to whom, and so on. Of course, whether a firm's strategy, structure, systems, and people enable the firm to perform well is also a function of the environment in which the firm functions.

Elements of the S³PE

The components of the S³PE are shown in Figure 13.15. These are the same components that we saw in Chapter 7 and therefore we will not spend any time on them.

Advantages and Disadvantages of the S³PE

Advantages

- The S³PE framework goes beyond the underlying economic assumption that employees' incentives are well aligned with those of their firm and are profit-maximizing. It pays attention to the incentives of employees and to the culture of organization.
- It brings in the implementation component of strategy analysis.

Disadvantages

- Like the SWOT and PEST analysis, the S³PE framework does not establish a link to profitability. As Figure 13.15 indicates, strategy, structure, systems, people and environment drive performance but it is difficult to tell the direction of the performance based on the elements of the framework.
- One of the components, environment, is too broad.

The 4Ps of Marketing (The Marketing Mix)

When a firm pursues a target market, it usually has marketing objectives for the target. To achieve these objectives, a firm needs marketing tools. The set of

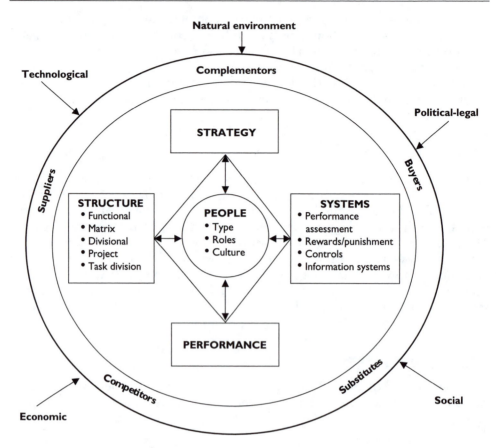

Figure 13.15 Elements of the S³PE.

marketing tools that a firm uses to pursue its marketing objectives in its chosen target market is its ***marketing mix***.[25] These marketing tools can be grouped into four groups called the 4Ps.[26] In other words, the 4Ps have come to be synonymous with the marketing mix. The 4Ps were developed in the 1960s by Professor E. Jerome McCarthy of Michigan State University. They are the marketing variables that managers can control to meet their marketing objectives in the target market.

Elements of the Model

The elements of the 4Ps are shown in Figure 13.16.

Product

These are the actual specifications of the goods or services being marketed and their relationship to customer's needs and wants. These specifications include not only the inherent characteristics of a product/service such as functionality, fit, quality, safety, packaging, and reliability, but also peripheral ones such as warrantees, brand name, guarantees, repairs/support, accessories, and service (for products). A firm must choose from all these.

Pricing

This is the process of setting a price for a product or service. The price is whatever the product/service is exchanged for, including money, time, energy, attention, or psychology. Pricing decisions include the type of pricing (fixed, auction, bundling, etc.), pricing strategy (discriminate, skim, penetration, everyday-low-prices, etc.), discounts (volume, wholesale, cash, early payment, etc.), financing, allowances, credit terms, and leasing options.

Placement

Also commonly referred to as place, placement is about distribution, how the product reaches customers. It refers to the channel through which a product is sold (retail, resellers, wholesalers, directly, online, mobile, etc.), the market

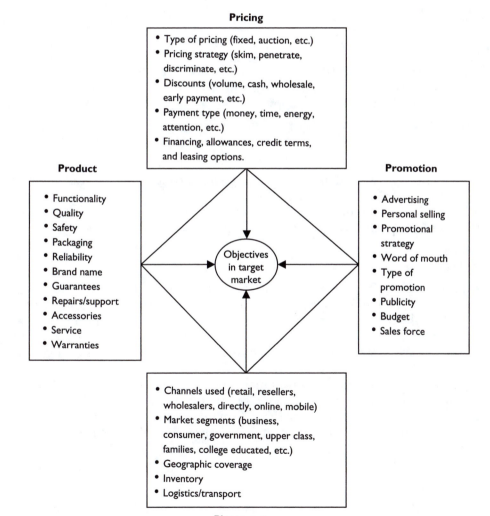

Figure 13.16 Elements of the 4Ps.

segment (business, consumer, government, upper class, families, college educated, etc.), and geographic region or national market. Decisions involved include which distribution channel to use (retail, resellers, wholesalers, directly, online, etc.), who should be within each channel, geographic location (which country) what type of inventory management to use, how to process orders, what type of market coverage (exclusive or inclusive distribution), and what type of warehousing and order processing.

Promotion

This is about the different ways that can be used to promote the product, brand, or firm. These include advertising, personal selling, promotional strategy, word of mouth, and viral. They also include the type of promotion, publicity, and budget. It is about communicating product/service, firm, and brand information to customers with the goal of improving the perception of the product, firm, or brand.

Applications of the 4Ps

As we stated above, the 4Ps are marketing tools that a firm uses to pursue its marketing objectives in the chosen target market.

Advantages and Disadvantages of 4Ps

Advantages

- It is simple, easy to remember, and a great starting point for students who are being introduced to marketing.
- It provides a common language and platform for marketing discussions about how to attain objectives in a target market.

Disadvantages

- Like the SWOT analysis, the 4Ps consist of a list of factors—close to a laundry list—with no clear link to firm profitability. There is no way of telling whether one set of 4Ps chosen by a firm will be more profitable than another.
- The 4Ps are a static framework that says little about how the Ps change with time.
- The model is primarily for consumer products, not industrial products.
- It is more oriented towards products than towards services.
- The 4Ps are not necessarily all that a firm may need to attain its objectives in a target market. For example, it has been argued that a firm also needs people to attain its objectives and therefore there should be a fifth P for people (see below).

4Ps and New Games

In using the 4Ps to pursue marketing objectives, a firm has many options from which to choose. Take pricing, for example. In formulating its pricing strategy, a firm can choose from skimming, pricing to penetrate, everyday-low-prices, and price discrimination. In choosing the type of pricing, the firm has the option of fixed pricing, Dutch auction, or reverse auction. Each of the components of the other Ps offers similar options. Therefore, the 4Ps offer plenty of opportunities for new games. For example, if industry firms practice price skimming a firm may decide to pursue penetration pricing in its new game.

5Ps and 7Ps

Since people play such a critical role in using the 4Ps to meet a firm's marketing objectives for a target market, it has been suggested that *People* should be a fifth P. In service industries, for example, it is difficult to separate the person who delivers a service from the service itself and customer experience. In fact, in some cases, customers also add to the experience that fellow customers obtain from a service. Thus, we have 5Ps (Product, Prices, Placement, Promotion, and People) where the choices that have to be made about People include training, motivation, fit, etc. Some marketers take it even further, suggesting that two more Ps ought to be added to the five, especially when services are concerned. These are the *Processes* that are involved in offering service, and *Physical evidence*. The latter is about giving potential customers physical evidence for what the service will be like, for example, using case studies, testimonials, or demonstrations.

AVAC

The AVAC framework was the subject of all of Chapter 2. Therefore we will only very briefly restate some of the points about the framework. It gets its name from the first letter of each of its four components (Activities, Value, Appropriability, and Change), and can be used to explore the profitability potential of a strategy and more. It can be used to analyze the extent to which a strategy creates value and/or positions a firm to appropriate value created in its value system, *and* what else the firm could do to improve its performance.

Elements of the Framework

The drivers of the four components of the AVAC are shown in Figure 13.17.

Activities

Recall that a firm's strategy is the set of activities that the firm performs to create value and/or position itself to capture any value created in its value system. Each activity *which* a firm performs, *when* it performs it, *where* it performs it, and *how* it performs it determine the extent to which the activity contributes to value creation and appropriation, and to the level of competitive advantage that the firm can have. Therefore the first thing to do in assessing the profitability potential of a strategy is to identify the set of activities that constitute the strategy and determine the extent to which each of the activities contributes to value creation and appropriation. This consists of determining the extent to which *each activity*:

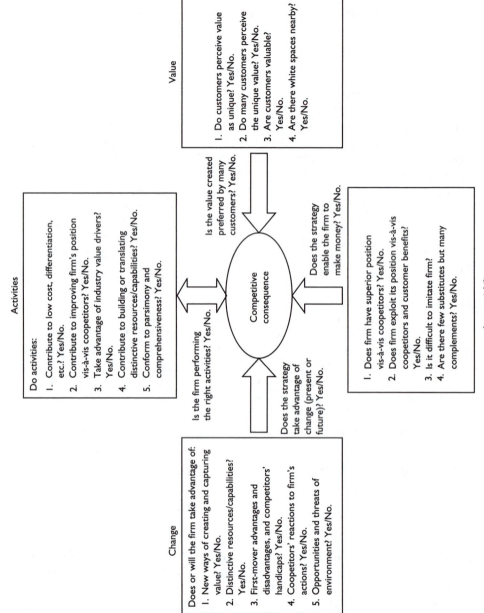

Activities

Do activities:

1. Contribute to low cost, differentiation, etc.? Yes/No.
2. Contribute to improving firm's position vis-à-vis coopetitors? Yes/No.
3. Take advantage of industry value drivers? Yes/No.
4. Contribute to building or translating distinctive resources/capabilities? Yes/No.
5. Conform to parsimony and comprehensiveness? Yes/No.

Value

1. Do customers perceive value as unique? Yes/No.
2. Do many customers perceive the unique value? Yes/No.
3. Are customers valuable? Yes/No.
4. Are there white spaces nearby? Yes/No.

Is the firm performing the right activities? Yes/No.

Is the value created preferred by many customers? Yes/No.

Competitive consequence

Does the strategy take advantage of change (present or future)? Yes/No.

Does the strategy enable the firm to make money? Yes/No.

Change

Does or will the firm take advantage of:

1. New ways of creating and capturing value? Yes/No.
2. Distinctive resources/capabilities? Yes/No.
3. First-mover advantages and disadvantages, and competitors' handicaps? Yes/No.
4. Coopetitors' reactions to firm's actions? Yes/No.
5. Opportunities and threats of environment? Yes/No.

Appropriability

1. Does firm have superior position vis-à-vis coopetitors? Yes/No.
2. Does firm exploit its position vis-à-vis coopetitors and customer benefits? Yes/No.
3. Is it difficult to imitate firm?
4. Are there few substitutes but many complements? Yes/No.

Figure 13.17 Components of an AVAC Framework.

1 Contributes to low cost, differentiation, better pricing, reaching more customers, and better sources of revenue.
2 Contributes to improving its position vis-à-vis coopetitors.
3 Takes advantage of industry value drivers.
4 Contributes to building new distinctive resources/capabilities or translating existing ones into unique positions and profits (including complementary assets).
5 Fits the comprehensiveness and parsimony criteria.

Value

Next, we determine if the contributions of all the activities, when added together, are unique enough to make customers prefer the firm's products to competitors' products. This is done by answering the following simple questions:

1 Do customers perceive the value created by the strategy as unique?
2 Do many customers perceive this value?
3 Are these customers valuable?
4 Are there any nearby white spaces?

Appropriability

The fact that a firm offers unique value to customers does not always mean that the firm will capture the value that it creates. Firms do not always make profits commensurate with the value that they have created. The *Appropriability* component tells us whether a firm has a superior position vis-à-vis coopetitors, and whether the firm translates the customer benefits created and its position vis-à-vis coopetitors into money. The analysis consists of asking whether:

1 The firm has a superior position vis-à-vis its coopetitors.
2 The firm exploits its position vis-à-vis its coopetitors and customer benefits.
3 It is difficult to imitate the firm.
4 There are few viable substitutes but many complements.

Change

Change can have a profound effect on a firm's ability to create and appropriate value. The extent to which a firm can take advantage of it is explored in two parts. First, the firm's strengths prior to the change are sorted out and a determination is made as to which of these strengths remain strengths and which ones become handicaps. Second, the extent to which a firm can take advantage of change is explored. This is done by exploring the extent to which the firm takes advantage of:

1 The new ways of creating and capturing new value generated by the change.
2 The opportunities generated by change to build new resources or translate existing ones in new ways.

3 First mover's advantages and disadvantages, and competitors' handicaps that result from change.
4 Coopetitors' potential reactions to its actions.
5 Opportunities and threats of environment. Are there no better alternatives?

Using the AVAC: Advantages

- Can be used to explore not only the profitability potential of a strategy but also that of business models, business units, products, technologies, brands, market segments, acquisitions, investment opportunities, partnerships such as alliances, functional units, corporate strategies, and ventures.
- More importantly, the framework can be used to determine which components (activities, value, appropriability, or change) have the potential to give a firm a sustainable competitive advantage. The firm can then sort out which activities and resources it needs to reinforce a sustainable advantage or build on. Within each component, a firm can determine which driver of the component constitutes a strength or weakness. Such a firm can then find ways to reinforce the strengths and reverse the weakness or dampen their effects.
- Like most frameworks, the AVAC constitutes a language and platform for strategy discussions. It can be used as the starting point for strategic planning sessions, scenario planning, new strategic move, and so on.
- Like the Five Forces, the AVAC provides a link between components and profitability.
- The AVAC is about a firm's performance, and incorporates both industry and firm-specific factors.
- The AVAC incorporates change.

Summary Statement

A comparison of the frameworks that we have explored is shown in Table 13.2. Since the ultimate goal of most firms is to have a sustainable competitive advantage, we use the drivers of sustainable competitive advantage as the basis for comparison. These are (1) industry and macroenvironmental factors (external factors), (2) firm-specific factors, which include both resource-based factors and position-based factors, (3) change, and (4) link to profitability. The rationale for choosing these variables as the basis for comparison is as follows. Since most firms are in business to make money for their owners, and strategy is about winning, a strategy framework ought to have some way of linking elements of the framework to profits. Moreover, we know that a firm's performance is a function of both industry and macroenvironmental factors as well as firm-specific factors. Firm-specific factors can be resource-based or position-based. Finally, change plays a critical role in the inability of firms to sustain competitive advantages.

A SWOT analysis is clearly about industry and macroenvironmental factors (opportunities and threats), and resource-based and position-based factors. The Growth/Share Matrix proxies industry factors with market growth rate and firm-specific factors with relative market share. Thus, it incorporates industry factors and position-based factors. Relative market share provides a link to

Table 13.2 Strategic Management Frameworks: A Comparison

Framework	For:	Industry and macro factors (external factors)	Firm-specific factors (internal factors)		Change (new games)	Link to profitability
			Resource-based	Position-based		
SWOT analysis	Evaluating the strengths and weaknesses of an entity or individual, and the opportunities and threats that it faces given its objectives.	H	H	H		
PEST	Probing deeper into the opportunities and threats that firms face in a particular environment by exploring the political, economic, social and technological factors that contribute to threats and opportunities.	H				
Growth/share matrix	Analyzing and managing portfolios of different units, businesses, projects, etc. Primary variables are *Relative Market Share* and *Market Growth Rate*.	H		H		H
GE/McKinsey matrix	Analyzing and managing portfolios of different units, businesses, projects, etc. Primary variables are *Industry Attractiveness*, and *Business Strength/Competitive Position*.	H		H		H
Porter's Five Forces	Exploring the competitive forces that act on industry firms, thereby determining the average profitability of an industry or a market.	H				H
Business Systems	Exploring different options for creating value at each stage of a business system.		H	H		
Value Chain	Exploring the value-adding activities at each stage of the chain of activities that firms perform in adding and appropriating value.		H	H		
Value Configurations	Exploring the value-adding activities of a value chain, value shop, and value network.		H	H		
Balanced scorecard	Measuring the extent to which different activities are meeting a firm's objectives, from four different perspectives. Implementing and monitoring a strategy.		H	H	H	

(continued overleaf)

Table 13.2 Continued

Framework	For:	Industry and macro factors (external factors)	Firm-specific factors (internal factors)		Change (new games)	Link to profitability
			Resource-based	Position-based		
VRIO	Exploring the extent to which a firm's resources can give the firm a sustainable competitive advantage.	H	H			H
VIDE	Narrowing down the list of potential core competences to those that are likely to give a firm an advantage.		H			H
S³PE Framework	Exploring those organizational structures, systems, and people that are critical to implementing a particular strategy in a particular environment.	H	H	H		
4Ps	Grouping, into four groups (product, pricing, placement, and promotion), the marketing tools that a firm uses to pursue marketing objectives for a target market.			H		
AVAC	Assessing the profitability potential of a strategy, business unit, brand, technology, and so on, with or without change.	H	H	H	H	H

profitability. The GE/McKinsey framework is also about industry factors and position-based factors. The Five Forces framework is about industry factors and clearly provides a link between each of the forces and industry profitability. Business systems, value chain, value network, and value shop are about firm-specific factors—both resource-based and position-based. The balanced score-card is about measures and really does not say much about the industry and firm-specific factors that impact profitability. The VRIO and VIDE analyses are grounded in the resource-based view of the firm and clearly provide links to profitability. Since a PEST analysis is about digging deeper into macroenviron-mental factors, it tells us something about the macroenvironmental opportun-ities and threats that a firm must face. An S^3PE framework is primarily about people, and the structure and systems in which they operate; but it is also about strategy and the environment in which strategy is being formulated and oper-ated. Hence the S^3PE framework is about both industry and firm-specific factors but provides no link to profitability. The 4Ps are about a firm's position in a market. The AVAC incorporates all four factors: industry and macroenviron-mental factors, firm-specific factors, which include both resource-based factors and position-based factors, change, and link to profitability.

Some Financial Measures[27]

Since strategy case analysis often involves numbers, it is worthwhile reviewing some elementary but useful financial measures (Table 13.3). A firm's **profits** are its revenues minus costs. Managers and financial analysts regularly track the profitability of firms. Sooner or later, most firms have to be profitable. What managers mean by profits often differs from what economists call profits. Economists' definition of profits uses opportunity costs rather than straight accounting costs. For economists, costs are not just straight accounting costs but the cost of what is forgone by not using the inputs some place else where they could have fetched more money. Another measure which analysts and firms track carefully is **gross profit margin**. This is a measure of the extent to which a product's revenues cover its variable costs and what is left over con-tributes towards covering fixed costs and generating a profit. The higher a product's profit margin, the more of that product the firm would want to sell, since the product covers not only its variable cost but also contributes towards covering fixed costs and generating a profit. Closely related to profit margins is the breakeven point. The *breakeven point* is the quantity at which fixed and other upfront costs have been recovered. The *breakeven time* is the time that it takes to reach the breakeven point.

When a firm makes payments for salaries, supplies inventories and other accounts payable, there should be cash available in deposits at a financial insti-tution somewhere to cover the payment made to these creditors. Thus, it is important to make sure that cash inflows exceed cash outflows. **Cash flow** is the difference between cash inflows and cash outflows. Note that although profits are highly correlated with cash flows, a firm can be profitable and still have negative cash flows. Another measure of a firm's performance is its **stock price**. This is the net present value of the firm's expected future cash flows. It is a reflection of how the market expects the firm to perform in the future. Another measure is **earnings per share**. This is the after-tax profits that are available to

Table 13.3 Summary of Some Financial Measures

Financial measure	Expression
Breakeven point (quantity): quantity at which fixed and other upfront costs are recovered.	$\dfrac{\text{Fixed cost}}{\text{Contribution margin}}$
Breakeven time: the time taken to reach the breakeven quantity.	$\dfrac{\text{Breakeven quantity}}{\text{Sales rate}}$
Cash flow: the difference between cash that a company receives and the cash that it pays out. A measure of cash that is available to fund a firm's activities or pay out to shareholders.	After-tax profits + depreciations
Earnings per share: amount that is available to owners of common shares.	$\dfrac{\text{Profits after taxes} - \text{Preferred stock dividends}}{\text{Common stock shares outstanding}}$
Economic value added (EVA): a measure of economic profit.	After-tax profits − cost of capital
Gross profit margins: a measure of the extent to which revenues cover the cost of generating the revenues and still generate a profit (after covering fixed costs).	$\dfrac{\text{Sales} - \text{cost of goods sold}}{\text{Sales}} = \dfrac{\text{Profits}}{\text{Sales}}$
Return on assets: the return on the assets that have been invested in the firm.	$\dfrac{\text{Profits after taxes}}{\text{Total assets}}$
Return on equity: the return on total shareholder equity in the firm.	$\dfrac{\text{Profits after taxes}}{\text{Total shareholder's equity}}$
Marker value (capitalization): present value of expected future cash flows.	$= \displaystyle\sum_{t=0}^{t=n} \dfrac{C_t}{(1 + r_k)^t}$ where C_t is the free cash flow at time t, and r_k is the firm's cost of capital.

holders of common shares for each share of the company that they own. A firm usually reinvests its after-tax profits in the company or pays it out as dividends to shareholders. Creating benefits for customers usually requires investment in plants, equipment, inventories and so on. **Return on investment** (ROI) measures how well the investment in capital is generating profits. Financial analysts can use ROI to compare how different firms use capital.

Another measure of performance is **Economic value added (EVA)**.[28] EVA should not be confused with the customer benefits that customers value in products or services. EVA is calculated by adjusting after-tax profits by the cost of capital. The rationale behind the popularity of the measure is as follows. It takes money (capital) to invest in all the assets (tangible and intangible) and activities that are used to create and appropriate value. This capital consists of borrowed and equity capital. Borrowed or **debt capital** is the money that firms borrow and its cost is the interest that firms have to pay on the debt. **Equity capital** is the money that shareholders provide when they buy a company's stock. By investing their money in a firm's stocks, shareholders are forgoing earning opportunities elsewhere. Thus, a firm's cost of equity capital is the price appreciation and dividends that shareholders could have earned if they had invested their money in another asset (for example, a portfolio of companies) that is as risky as the firm whose stocks they bought. Effectively, since capital costs money, this cost of capital should be taken into consideration when measuring how well a firm is performing as it uses capital to generate profits. EVA is therefore after-tax profits adjusted by the cost of capital that is used to generate the profits.

Economic value added (EVA) = Operating profits – Taxes – Cost of capital

where

Cost of capital = total capital used × weighted average of cost of debt and cost of equity.

Part V

Cases

The New World Invades France's *Terroir*

The French government official could not believe that there was talk of one more threat to his country's dominance of the global wine industry. First, it was the so-called invasion by New World wine producers. Now there was talk of transgenic wine. Scientists had unraveled the genetic secrets of the pinot noir grape that was used to produce the world's finest wines, making it possible to now produce the grape in places where cultivation had been inhospitable.[1] What would be next? Should France be worried about the New World's invasion of this ancient European industry? How about transgenic grapes? What should the country do?

The Wine Industry in 2008

In 1999, California's E&J Gallo was the world's largest producer by volume with a 1% market share.[2] The region of Bordeaux, France alone had over 12,000 producers while Italy had over a million. But in the USA, the five largest firms had a 62% share, in Australia the top four firms had an 80% share, while in Chile the top five firms had a 50% share. In the USA, 45% of wine was sold in supermarkets while in the Netherlands, the number was over 60%.[3] At the low end of the market, many producing countries drank their own, and New World producers were making inroads at large importers such as the UK. At the middle of the market, Europeans were ceding dominance to New World producers such as Australia (in Britain, for example). At the high end, Old World firms still dominated.

The Rise and Dominance of French Wine

The history of wine may go as far back as 6,500 years in Greece where researchers say wine was first produced.[4] It would become such an integral part of life in the Mediterranean and early Europe that even monasteries grew grapes, and made wine. In the nineteenth, twentieth, and early twenty-first centuries, France dominated the wine world. It had the largest market share of any country, by value, and the words fine wine had come to be associated with France. This dominance is usually attributed to several factors. First, France had the *terroir*—that unique mix of natural factors such as the soil, rainfall, temperature, humidity, altitude, slope of terrain, and orientation towards the sun—that held one of the secrets to producing the right grapes for fine wines. Second, there was a lot of local demand for wine. Whereas in the

USA, prohibition made the sale of wine illegal, in Europe, it was just another beverage that most people drank and that had become part of many liturgical services. Third, there was pasteurization of wine, invented by France's own Louis Pasteur, which enabled wine to last much longer. The Fourth factor was the series of innovations that led up to mass production of glass bottles and the introduction of the cork stopper. Wine could be pasteurized, put in bottles, and corked to last until someone wanted to drink it. The fifth factor was a series of innovations in transportation—canals, railways, steamers, horse-driven carts, and later, automobiles—which enabled wine produced in one region to be transported to other regions for consumption. Ironically, these transportation innovations gave birth to fraud.[5] Before the transportation innovations, wine was usually consumed locally and consumers had a better chance of knowing who produced what; but with the innovations, opportunists could produce wine anywhere and claim that it came from a more reputable region.

The Sixth factor was a different type of innovation. Because there were hundreds of thousands of producers, each with a different quality of wine, it was difficult for consumers to tell who was producing what, and which producers were making the right claims. In preparation for the 1855 World Exposition of Paris that he had conceived, Emperor Napoleon III ordered a group of wine producers in the Bordeaux region to classify vineyards in the area into five groups, as a function of quality.[6] They came up with the *premiers crus* (first growth), *deuxièmes crus* (second growth), *trosièmes crus* (third growth), *quatrièmes crus* (fourth growth), and *cinquièmes crus* (fifth growth). This system simplified customers' choices, and both customers and producers liked it. In 1935, the French government formalized most of it in the form of the *Appellations d'Origine Contrôlée* (AOC) laws which stipulated not only what *cru* could come from what region, but also what could be put into what wine, how it could be made and labeled, the alcohol content of different wines, what types of grapes could be grown in what region, and what type of grape varieties could go into what wine category. Growers could not use irrigation systems since that would temper with the *terroir*. Only grapes from the region specified on a bottle could be used to make the wine in the bottle. The idea was to protect the good name of each region and assure customers that they were getting what they believed they were getting. Several European countries established similar laws.

Later, other wine regions of France were officially classified as the *Vin Délimité de Qualité Superieure* (VDQS). Right below VDQS wines were the *Vin de Pays*, and *Vin de Table*. The hierarchy of wines is summarized in Exhibit 1.1.

Exhibit 1.1 Hierarchy of French Wines. (2005 market shares are shown in percentages.)

1. *Appellation d'Origine Contrôlée* (AOC, 53.4%): Wines that follow the strict AOC laws and classifications. High end wines.
2. *Vin Délimité de Qualité Superieure* (VDQS, 0.9%). Do not conform to the AOC rules. Used to classify wines from smaller areas, or as a "waiting room" for potential promotion to AOCs. Middle wines.
3. *Vin de Pays* (33.9%). Subject to very few or none of the AOC restrictions. Lower quality too. Low-end wines. Region within France is specified.
4. *Vin de Table* (11.7%). Even fewer restrictions. Only has to show the producer and the designation that it is from France. Lowest end wines.

Source: Retrieved June 21, 2008, from http://en.wikipedia.org/wiki/French_wine.

Many farmers grew and sold their grapes, by weight, to local winemakers or formed cooperatives to make the wine. Because some of the farms had been inherited by more than one sibling from one generation to the other, many farms tended to be very small. Some large growers made their own wine. A lot of the wine was then sold to middle people who then resold it to consumers or other middle people.

The Rise of the New World Winemakers

The New World winemakers came from Argentina, Australia, Canada, Chile, New Zealand, South Africa, and the USA. Many of these players were vertically integrated backwards into growing their own grapes, and because their countries had inexpensive widely available land compared to the old continent, they could own large vineyards. Many of them used drip irrigation systems, not permitted by France's AOC rules, not only to bring more land into production but also to control the variability of grape quality and yield better.[7] They also used mechanical harvesters and experimented with different kinds of fertilizer. In making wine, the New World winemakers used large steel tanks, controlled by computers, rather than the small oak barrels of the Old World. To obtain the oak taste of wine from oak barrels, they added oak chips to the steel tanks, a practice seen as repulsive by some French.[8] Effectively, these new firms could experiment with lots of things that Old World firms were not allowed to pursue. They were constantly pursuing new ways of making and marketing wine. For example, around 1999, Australia produced 20% of the world's scientific papers on viticulture and oenology.[9]

The biggest marketing innovation, pioneered in California, was putting the grape variety on the wine label.[10] This was in contrast to the labeling specified by the AOC and related laws in Europe. Customers could now worry whether they were buying a chardonnay, pinot noir, Chablis blanc, cabernet, or sauvignon rather than worry about the rather intimidating regions in France and the different categories in each region. Moreover, the European Union would later find that it was illegal for New World firms to use the names of regions in Europe, such as Champagne, to refer to wine from their own countries. New World winemakers could also brand their products. A good brand gave consumers some type of guarantee that they would get what they paid for. It was also a good starting point for beginners. Although Old World Champagne producers had some good brands, many winemakers did not have widely recognizable brands à la Coca Cola. New World winemakers were also vertically integrated into distribution, making it easier for them to experiment with new brands, products, and labels.

The pièce de résistance of the New World marketing activities came in a 1976 blind-tasting challenge set up by British wine merchant Steven Spurrier.[11] In this challenge, that would later be called "the Judgment of Paris," 15 of the most influential French wine critics were invited to a blind tasting of top wines from France and California. They used white wines made from chardonnay grapes and red wines from cabernet sauvignon. The results of the taste astonished everyone including the tasters: California wines won in both white and red wines. The French protested, arguing that the event had been rigged. In a rematch, two years later, California still won. In any case, France's worldwide market share had begun to drop. For example, from 1994 to 2003, the market share of French wine sold in the USA fell from 26% to 16% and from 37% to 23% in Britain.[12] See also, Exhibit 1.2.

Other Threats to France's Position

Beyond the threat from New World winemakers, there were others. To reduce alcohol consumption for health and public safety reasons, France had introduced a law in 1991 that forbade winemakers from sponsoring advertisements that used anything but the most basic characteristics of their products.[13] From 1999 to 2007, wine consumption in France fell from 32.2 million hectoliters to 29.9, while the share of French people drinking wine each day had fallen from 30% to 23% in the ten years to 2004.[14] In the mid-1960s, the average Frenchman had drunk 130 bottles of wine but by the mid 2000s, the number had dropped to about 75 bottles.[15]

Only 5% of the wine consumed in France was imported. This led some to speculate that other countries might want France to reciprocate and import more. Then there was always the threat posed by China and even Africa. If indeed genetically engineered grapes could bring all sorts of land into production, and all the experimentation undertaken by New World winemakers found cheaper and faster ways of making wine, then the old continent would have to compete with more than just the New World. It might also be possible to raise the levels of those ingredients in wine—such as resveratrol, quercetin, and ellagic acid—by genetically inserting the right genes in the right grapes, taking wines to a different level. These grapes may even be grown in deserts.

Was the threat to the Old World wine industry anything to worry about? What should the French government do if anything? What would happen to France's advantage from its *terroir* if, with transgenic grapes, just about any soil anywhere could be brought into cultivation? Was it time to scrap the AOC rules? France's wine sales in China had been growing fast but the question was, for how long? Would France have to move from the traditional production push to more marketing pull?

Exhibit 1.2 World Wine Exports in 1999 and 2007

Exporter	1999		2007	
	Million hectoliters	(%)	Million hectoliters	(%)
European Union (EU)	10.9	51	18.4	39
Argentina	1.0	5	3.5	8
United States	2.8	13	4.1	9
South Africa	1.3	6	5.0	11
Chile	2.5	12	6.1	13
Australia	2.6	12	7.8	17
Others	0.3	1	1.6	3
Total	21.0	100	47.0	100

Source: Kosko, S. (2008). *World Markets and Trade: Wine.* United States Department of Agriculture. Foreign Agricultural Service.

Sephora Takes on America*

David Suliteanu, CEO of Sephora USA, rubbed his temples as he contemplated the materials in front of him. All day long he had been reviewing the 2007 performance of the US beauty industry and his company's place in it because some executives from Sephora's parent company, LVMH Moët Hennessy Louis Vuitton, would be visiting the following week to discuss Sephora's competitive strategy. LVMH executives visited to discuss Sephora's performance periodically, but David felt added stress for this meeting because of rumors that had been circulating recently speculating that LVMH viewed Sephora as a noncore asset and was considering a sale.

Launched in the USA in 1998, Sephora took the US beauty industry by storm with its unique retail concept that combined a wide assortment of brands and products with distinctive store designs and knowledgeable sales consultants in a low-pressure sales environment. Sephora offered customers a choice of more than 250 brands as well as the company's own private label across a range of product categories that included skin care, make-up, fragrances, bath & body, and hair care. Most interesting, however, was the company's model which allowed customers to "try before they buy" in a hands-on, self-service shopping environment.

Company History

Sephora was founded in France in 1969. In 1993, Dominique Mandonnaud, a major shareholder in Altamir, the holding company for Shop 8, bought Sephora from the UK-based drugstore, Boots, for $61 million (360 million francs). Mandonnaud, who was also chairman and chief executive officer of the French-based Shop 8 beauty and cosmetic retailer, merged his 11 Shop 8 boutiques with the 38-store Sephora perfumery chain. The new entity was given the more recognizable Sephora name but kept the Shop 8 stores format. This format consisted of having spacious shopping areas and self-service shopping with beauty products grouped by type rather than by brand.[1] By the end of 1996, Mandonnaud had opened a 16,200 square foot Sephora superstore at the Champs-Elysees in Paris, France and given the brand major worldwide

---

* This case was written by Kathryn Morrison, Jason Paradowski, Stefan Pototschnik, Matthew Smucker, and Spiro Vamvaka, under the supervision of Professor Allan Afuah as a basis for class discussion and is not intended to illustrate either effective or ineffective handling of a business situation.

publicity. With over 100 employees and 10,000 visitors stopping by each day, Sephora aimed to create a total beauty experience featuring beauty-related advertising, online information, literature, and exhibits.[2]

The company continued to expand throughout the mid-1990s, including in the USA and in Europe. However, by 1997, Mandonnaud was ready to retire from the business and along with his partners decided to sell. Luxury retailer LVMH (Louis Vuitton, Moët, Hennessy) then entered the scene and acquired Sephora for €344 million. Under LVMH, the company quickly doubled its number of stores, and by the end of 1997, Sephora's sales had increased to FRF 2 billion.[3]

In 2000, Sephora hired David Suliteanu as the US CEO. With his experience at Home Depot where he had been Group President/Diversified Businesses, he was charged with the US market expansion. In 2008, Sephora was France's leading chain of fragrance and cosmetics stores, as well as the second largest chain in Europe with a total of 420 stores located in nine countries. It operated more than 190 stores in North America, with annual sales in the US market of over $750 million.[4] Sephora also boasted the world's "top beauty website," Sephora.com.

Overview of the Beauty Products Industry

"Personal care products" have long been a part of human civilizations with evidence of cosmetics dating back to as far as 4,000 BC in Egypt. Since that time, the industry evolved with fashion trends and new consumer demands, but it wasn't until the twentieth century that the cosmetics industry began to take off with the manufacture of lipstick in 1915.[5] The 1920s brought the launch of various dime and chain stores throughout the USA, which helped boost the distribution and appeal of cosmetics. The economic boom following World War II further stimulated growth in the cosmetics industry, which continued to evolve with a wide variety of new products. In the eleven years from 1988 to 1999, US cosmetics and fragrance stores experienced strong growth averaging approximately 5% per year.[6] In particular, the US economic boom of the late 1990s boosted the market with strong growth rates of 4.6% in 1998, 5.5% in 1999, followed by 10.2% in 2000.[7] Following this boom, growth dropped along with the slowdown in the US economy. Between 2000 and 2003, the troubles in the US economy had an adverse impact upon the industry as consumer spending declined.

Competition in the industry was based on image, price, range and quality of products, level of service, and location. Products included mass market, private label, professional and prestige brands which were sold everywhere from stand-alone boutiques and department stores to drug stores and mass retailers (i.e. WalMart).

Despite many changes in the industry, mass merchandisers remained the largest outlet for cosmetic and beauty products in the US with just under 30% of the market, followed by food stores, drug stores, and department stores. Specialty beauty, cosmetic and fragrance stores such as Sephora were estimated to account for 10% of all cosmetic and toiletry sales in the USA.[8] Within this subsegment, the top four participants held a market share of less than 40%, reflecting the generally fragmented nature of the industry.[9]

Cosmetics Retailing and Sephora's New Game

In 2008, the overall value chain for beauty products consisted of four primary activities: design and development, manufacturing, distribution, and retailing. While Sephora sold and marketed its own line of cosmetics, it primarily performed the retail portion of the value chain.

Prior to the arrival of Sephora stores in the USA, there were two primary means for consumers to purchase beauty products, and specifically cosmetics. The first was through "low-end" purchasing at self-service retailers such as pharmacies, convenience stores, and mass retailers. Mass-marketed, typically inexpensive brands were displayed on a shelf, but customers were unable to sample products before purchasing them. Little or no customer assistance was available, and selection was limited. The experience was primarily one of convenience and price.

Department stores sat on the opposite end of the retail spectrum as the other primary outlet for purchasing cosmetics in the USA. These stores, which were typically located in shopping malls, maintained brand-specific cosmetics counters staffed with sales personnel who provided individual attention to each customer. Customers were typically unable to serve themselves or sample products without the assistance of a salesperson, leading to a somewhat high-pressure sales environment. Each brand's sales counter was often staffed with the brand's own employee. While each brand's sales counter provided a wide variety of brand-specific cosmetics, there were a limited number of brands available within each department store. In addition, the customer had to go to a separate counter for each individual brand in order to purchase or try multiple brands.

Sephora's assisted self-service model fitted nicely between these two retailing models, combining the best of each extreme. Upon entering a Sephora outlet, customers would see a wide variety of more than 200 brands, openly displayed for customer sampling and a well-trained sales staff standing ready to provide assistance with any product.

Like department stores, there was a knowledgeable and helpful sales force available to provide assistance; but unlike department stores, Sephora employees did not promote one specific brand and were trained to make the sales experience welcoming and less aggressive. Perhaps most significantly, all products were openly displayed for sampling and testing, and make-up remover was available throughout the store, encouraging customers to freely try multiple products, further differentiating Sephora from other cosmetics purchasing environments.

Since cosmetics and perfumes were "experience" products, the Sephora model provided significant value to customers, and was a good fit for the products themselves. Stores even had specialized lighting meant to recreate natural daylight inside the stores, further aiding and enabling customer sampling.

Increased revenue came from multiple sources. First, customers were more likely to try multiple brands, increasing the probability that they would find and purchase a product that matched their needs. Additionally, customers might purchase more products since so many products (200+ brands) were available in one location. Notably, product-sampling allowed for ease of comparison shopping, which was unique to Sephora. The presence of a well-trained sales force that was knowledgeable of all brands and products, rather than specifically focused on one brand, provided additional value by ensuring that customers saw all options available to them.

At convenience stores, comparison-shopping was limited to price comparisons and brand advertising claims, since product sampling was not available. At department stores, a customer could not try products from multiple brands without waiting for assistance at each individual brand's counter, which typically restricted the customer's ability to compare products.

In addition to the assisted-self service brick and mortar stores, Sephora had a significant online sales business. Through its online presence, Sephora attempted to create an all-inclusive "beauty" world, with advertising, advice, and literature available to consumers. In-store customers were referred to Sephora's website, keeping them involved in the company well after leaving the store.

In 2006, it was announced that Sephora would open a "store-within-a-store" concept within J.C. Penney department stores; and by mid-2007 it had stores within 39 J.C. Penney stores. It also became the exclusive seller of beauty products for the chain, as well as for Penney's website (JCP.com). Some analysts estimated that the move might benefit J.C. Penney, a mid-tier department store that wanted to upgrade its image. In fact, "J.C. Penney's new campaign, with the slogan 'Every Day Matters,' built on the retailer's efforts to convince shoppers that it had shed its dowdy image and become a stylish retailer stocked with fashionable merchandise."[10]

Competitors

Ulta Salon, Cosmetic & Fragrance, Inc.

Ulta Salon, Cosmetic & Fragrance, Inc. (Ulta) was founded in 1990 by Dick George, using $12 million of venture capital.[11] George, a former president of Osco Drug, had studied the shopping habits of women and realized that there was a great opportunity in the beauty product market. Women, who used up to 12 different beauty products each day, had to go to as many as three different stores to buy prestige beauty products, mass-market products, and salon products. George's vision was that Ulta would make all of these products available in one store, and offer salon and spa services as well. In this way, Ulta's stores would serve as relaxing retreats for the middle- to upper-class women who were its target customers.

When Ulta opened its first location, its value consisted of offering the widest range of beauty products and fragrances possible at a discounted price. It discounted items as much as 50% from suggested retail prices, and even offered to match prices from other retailers, including low-cost competitors such as Wal-Mart.[12]

In keeping with this strategy, Ulta avoided large shopping malls and instead located its stores in strip malls with convenient parking. This strategy proved successful, and by 1995 Ulta operated 50 stores employing 800 people.[13] Sales for that year had doubled from 1994 levels, and were expected to double again the next year. Such success could not continue indefinitely, however, and by

Exhibit 2.1 Comparison of Industry Competitors in 2007

Competitor	Stores		US sales ($million)
	US	Total	
Sephora	177	756	825
Ulta	249	249	912
Bath & Body Works	1,592	1,592	2,494
Macy's	850	850	26,313

1999, increased competition in the beauty industry motivated Ulta to change its strategy.

In 2000, Ulta's new president, Lyn Kirby, started making moves to reposition Ulta in the market and move away from the discount strategy. Stores were renovated and redecorated to provide a more luxurious atmosphere, more prestigious product lines were added, and store employees were educated so that they could provide beauty expertise if a customer needed assistance. These changes proved successful and Ulta kept growing, from 129 stores and sales of $423 million in 2003 to 249 stores and sales of $912 million in 2007 (Exhibit 2.1).[14] In October of 2007, Ulta went public in a well-received IPO that raised more than $153 million and is now traded on the NASDAQ.[15]

Macy's, Inc.

Macy's marketed most of its cosmetics using the standard department store model. However, in 1999 it tried to offer an alternative sales model which caused Sephora to file a lawsuit against it. Macy's had opened a number of "Souson" cosmetics stores which utilized an "open-sell" model, and in preparation to open these stores, Macy's employees had gone so far as to visit Sephora stores with cameras and sketch pads in order to copy the store's look.

Sephora's lawsuit claimed that Macy's had infringed on their distinctive trade dress and could make shoppers think that the Souson stores were owned or operated by Sephora.[16] A judge concluded that the lawsuit had enough merit to issue a preliminary injunction freezing the further expansion of Souson stores until the lawsuit was resolved.[17] The lawsuit was eventually settled out of court and terms were not disclosed.

Bath & Body Works, Inc.

Founded in 1990 in New Albany, OH, Bath & Body Works, Inc. (BBW) expanded rapidly throughout the 1990s, and by 2008 it had become the largest competitor that operated exclusively in the beauty, cosmetics, and fragrance store industry.[18] BBW offered a wide variety of natural skin, fragrance, aromatherapy, and spa products. BBW did not offer brand-name designer products, but instead focused almost exclusively on private-label products offered under the BBW name.

In 2003, BBW acquired the rights to the C.O. Bigelow name, an apothecary that had operated in New York's Greenwich Village for over a century, and positioned stores with this name to target the high-end market.[19,20] These stores featured an open-sell sales approach and even had sinks available where customers could wash off products before they try others. In 2008, BBW operated over 1,500 stores in the USA, and planned to expand the C.O. Bigelow name to 150 stores nationwide.

Where to Go from Here?

David sat back, took a deep breath, and reflected on Sephora's position in the beauty products market. While Sephora changed the game when it created the "open-sell" approach to perfume and cosmetics, it was in danger of becoming a victim of its own success. Many other competitors had since entered the market using the same approach and selling similar products. In fact, Sephora's closest competitor, Ulta Salon, went significantly beyond the products sold by Sephora and offered salon and spa services to its customers. David was also concerned about the company's recent decision to partner with J.C. Penney. While this move could rapidly and significantly increase Sephora's potential customer base, he worried that J.C. Penney's value-based competitive position would erode the luxury-based position of Sephora and could hurt business in the long run. How could Sephora maintain its momentum in this highly competitive industry? Should it try to expand its services to match those of Ulta? Also, was the move into J.C. Penney stores a wise one or would it serve to distance Sephora from its core consumers? Then finally, and most importantly, was there a new game that Sephora could play that would change the industry again and allow the company to take control of the market?

Netflix: *Responding to Blockbuster, Again**

Reed Hastings reflected on the first half of 2008 as he drove through Los Gatos, CA on his way to Netflix headquarters. Netflix was still a growing and profitable company but several threats loomed on the horizon. Late in 2006, Blockbuster Entertainment had revamped its online movie rental site, renaming it Blockbuster Total Access. The commercials for Blockbuster Total Access were clearly aimed at stealing customers from Netflix.[1] At the same time, new technology offered the opportunity to have movies delivered to customers directly through their cable television provider or over their computer. Either Blockbuster or this new technology could make the Netflix business model obsolete. Indeed, these new technologies led *Business 2.0* to label Reed Hastings one of 2006's "10 People Who Don't Matter," citing the availability of movies through cable or Internet as the future of movie rental.[2]

Reed wanted Netflix to be more than the midpoint between brick-and-mortar rental stores and downloaded movie rentals. He knew he would be spending a lot of time in the near future reviewing and updating the Netflix strategy to deal with these threats. They had several initiatives in place, but would these be enough to overcome the competition and continue the growth of the company he founded?

Movie Rental before Netflix

In 1977, the first brick-and-mortar video rental store opened in a 600 square foot storefront on Wilshire Boulevard in Los Angeles.[3] At that time, only 50 video titles from 20th Century Fox were available on Betamax and VHS for consumers to rent. However, business was strong enough for the business owner, George Atkinson, to add 42 affiliated stores within 20 months. The business was renamed *The Video Station*, and Atkinson announced that he would start franchising the stores. The Video Station paved the way for thousands of other video rental stores, including Blockbuster Video, which opened its first store in Dallas, Texas in 1985. Within three years, Blockbuster Video captured the top video retailer spot in the USA with more than 500 stores and revenues exceeding $200 million.[4]

Video rental stores quickly discovered that rental revenues roughly followed

---

* This case was written by Christian Chock, Tania Ganguly, Chad Greeno, Julie Knakal, and Tony Knakal under the supervision of Professor Afuah as a basis for class discussion and is not intended to illustrate either effective or ineffective handling of a business situation.

Pareto's rule where 80% of the revenues were driven from 20% of the video titles. Therefore, for the 4,000–5,000 titles in stock at a typical store, most shelf space was dedicated to displaying multiple copies of new release, "hit" movies.[5]

The dynamics of the industry shifted significantly in the spring of 1997 with the introduction of the DVD-video format. The DVD player passed the 10% adoption rate milestone by late 2000 making it one of the most rapidly adopted consumer electronics products in history. By 2005, the DVD format would dominate the global recorded video sales and rental market with 91.8% market share.[6]

In 1999, while Netflix and movie rental through the Internet and snail mail were still new, Blockbuster held a 24% market share in this $18.5 billion industry.[7]

Blockbuster continued to lead the industry in market share in 2006 with approximately 35% of the market.[8]

Netflix's Entry into Rentals

The size and weight of the physical DVD facilitated shipping videos directly to customers' homes, and a new branch of the video retailing industry began with the founding of Netflix. Founded in 1997 by Marc Randolph and Reed Hastings, Netflix began offering DVD rentals requested over the Internet and delivered through the mail in 1998. The initial business model charged a fee per rental, as was typical of brick-and-mortar stores at the time. By late 1999, Netflix had changed to a subscription fee that allowed subscribers to rent as many videos as they wanted on a monthly basis.[9] It made various subscription plans available to subscribers that allowed customers to determine how many movies they wanted to have at their home at a time. This allowed Netflix to differentiate customers by how often they watched rented movies. The subscription model eliminated aggravation related to due dates and late fees. Indeed, Reed Hastings cited the unlimited-use-for-one-fee model used by his health club as one of the inspirations for Netflix's subscription model.[10] In February 2003, Netflix surpassed the one million subscriber mark, landing it firmly at the top of the online DVD rental industry.

Through Netflix's website, subscribers could create a queue of movies that they wanted to rent. These movies could be prioritized to reflect when the subscriber wanted to receive each film. Whenever a subscriber returned a movie via a prepaid mailer, the next movie in the queue was sent out. Users could create a large rental queue and not be required to visit the website while they viewed movies sent from their queue, or they could update their queue every time a movie was returned.

The Netflix subscription-based service offered several advantages over the brick-and-mortar rental store model that had been prevalent in the industry. By having a few centralized shipping centers, rather than a large number of storefronts, Netflix was able to pool resources and offer a wider range of titles than possible at a single rental store. Operating a few centralized shipping centers also offered several cost advantages over operating stores in every neighborhood. Netflix was aggressive in recruiting new customers. It increased its marketing expenses every year and its number of customers increased every year (Exhibit 3.1).

Exhibit 3.1 Summary of Netflix's Income Statements ($US millions, except where indicated)

	FY 2007	FY 2006	FY 2005	FY 2004	FY 2003	FY 2002
Total subscribers at end of period (1,000 people)	7,479	6,316	4,179	2,610	1,487	857
Gross subscriber additions during period (1,000 people)	5,340	5,250	3,729	2,716	1,571	1,140
Subscriber acquisition cost ($/customer)	40.88	42.96	38.77	37.02	32.8	32.83
Total revenue	1,205.34	996.66	682.21	500.61	270.41	152.81
Cost of revenue, total	785.74	626.06	464.55	331.71	179.01	97.5
Gross profit	419.6	370.6	217.66	168.9	91.4	55.3
Total selling, general, and admin. expenses	274.93	266.21	185.72	122.64	70.25	51.35
R&D	67.7	44.77	30.94	29.47	17.88	14.62
Depreciation/amortization						
Total operating expense	1,114.18	932.25	679.22	481.26	265.94	163.48
Operating income	91.16	64.41	2.99	19.35	4.47	−10.67
Interest Income (expense), net nonoperating	20.34	15.9	5.35	2.42	2.04	−10.28
Income before tax	111.5	80.32	8.34	21.78	6.51	−20.95
Income after tax	66.95	49.08	42.03	21.59	6.51	−20.95
Net profit margin		4.90%	6.20%	4.30%	2.40%	

Source: Netflix's annual financial statements.

Cinematch Recommendations System

To help customers identify which titles may interest them, Netflix used a recommendation engine called Cinematch. Cinematch used customer movie ratings to predict what other movies customers might be interested in. About 60% of movies requested through Netflix were identified through this recommendation system.[11] The combination of a large movie selection and a recommendation system to help customers find movies they might like appeared to increase the number of movie titles that customers rented. In June of 2006, Netflix had an inventory of 60,000 titles and on any given day 35,000 to 40,000 of these titles were rented by Netflix customers.[12]

Netflix even released some independent films that were not popular enough for a traditional distribution contract through its Red Envelope Entertainment division. When video stores only stocked 4,000–5,000 titles, these movies would not have been popular enough to justify the required shelf space. With Netflix distribution centers that served a larger number of customers and a recommendation system to help those customers find titles that may interest them, a market for these movies was created.[13]

In October 2006, it offered the "Netflix Prize" of up to one million dollars to anyone that could substantially improve its existing recommendation algorithm.[14] Netflix had also rolled out a Netflix *Friends* feature that let users see what their friends were renting and how they rated different movies. This feature enabled users to create communities of movie watchers through the Netflix Web page. The friends feature utilized past user ratings of users on Netflix, taking advantage of its longer history in the online rental business.

Watch Now Feature

In June of 2007 Netflix added a "Watch Now" section to their website. This tab allowed Netflix subscribers to have movies streamed to their computer to watch instantly. Only about 2,000 nonrecent movie titles and some current television series were available through this feature at launch, a much smaller selection than available for rental through the mail.[15]

Subscription Plans

In 2007, Netflix offered a range of subscription choices, each allowing the customer a different number of movies that could be simultaneously rented. These ranged from a basic plan allowing up to two rentals per month, rented one at a time, to a plan allowing four rentals out at one time with unlimited total monthly rentals. Each plan also included a varying amount of instant viewing hours that could be used to have movies streamed directly to the customer's computer. The 2007 prices are summarized in Exhibit 3.2.

Early Competition with Netflix

Wal-Mart

The world's largest retailer, Wal-Mart, entered the online DVD rental market in 2002, with a catalog of over 12,000 titles from which customers could choose. The system was essentially the same as that offered by Netflix, with customers creating a list of titles they wanted to see, and then ordering them online, with shipping by mail. Its subscription rates undercut Netflix by about $1, with a three movies rented at any one time DVD package costing $18.86.[16] Executives at Netflix predicted that Wal-Mart could only guarantee overnight delivery within a limited radius of its Georgia distribution center, and would have to settle for three- to five-day delivery for the rest of the country.[17] In June 2004, Wal-Mart opened three new distribution centers to support the online DVD

Exhibit 3.2 Summary of Netflix's Movie Rental Plans

Plan	Maximum rentals per month	Price per month ($)	Instant viewing hours per month
4 DVDs at-a-time	Unlimited	23.99	24
3 DVDs at-a-time	Unlimited	17.99	18
2 DVDs at-a-time	Unlimited	14.99	15
1 DVD at-a-time	Unlimited	9.99	10
1 DVD at-a-time	Limit 2 per month	4.99	5

Source: Retrieved June 10, 2007 from www.netflix.com.

rental business. Additionally, it expanded its rental catalog to 15,000 titles (at the time, Netflix offered about 22,000 titles for rent). By mid-2005, however, Wal-Mart had given up on the online DVD rental business. In leaving, Wal-Mart directed its customers to Netflix, and established a deal whereby former Wal-Mart customers could get a discounted two-DVD rental plan if they signed up for a one-year Netflix subscription (regularly priced at $14.99, and discounted to $12.97).[18] The reason for Wal-Mart's exit was thought to be a lack of sufficient subscriber sign-up, an important figure in the online rental business.

Blockbuster

On August 11, 2004, Blockbuster announced its entry into the US online movie rental business with the creation of Blockbuster Online, a move they had been discussing since that spring.[19] Like Netflix and Wal-Mart, they had a tiered monthly fee system based on the number of movies the consumer wanted to have at a time. Initial pricing was positioned between Netflix and their low-price rival, Wal-Mart. Blockbuster subscribers chose from a catalog of 25,000 titles, compared with 30,000 titles available from Netflix at that time. Part of Blockbuster's strategy was for the online service to encourage foot traffic in its physical stores, with two coupons for free rentals at the stores being sent to each online customer once a month.

Relying on its strong brand recognition among consumers and physical presence with over 5,600 company-owned and franchised brick-and-mortar stores at the time of the launch, Blockbuster hoped to reach many of the over four million estimated online renters that made up the market at the time of the launch.[20] The market for online rentals was estimated at $8 million at the time, and Blockbuster saw it as a growing area within the overall rental business. While only 8% of industry revenue came from online rentals in 2005, growth was strong, increasing from 5% in 2003, according to Adams Media Research.[21]

To accommodate the new online service, Blockbuster established a new distribution system, separate from its existing network that handled its bricks-and-mortar stores. To handle the mailing of DVDs, Blockbuster had to establish a set of distribution centers, similar to Netflix's, from which it could mail the rented DVDs. The separate distribution was also put in place to accommodate the different rental preferences of online subscribers as compared to in-store patrons.[22]

The launch of Blockbuster Online was at an estimated initial cost of $50 million, with additional losses in operating revenues for several quarters after launch. These figures, combined with the loss of revenue from late fees (usually a good source of income for Blockbuster that previously made up 13% of revenue), contributed to a difficult financial situation. Subscriber growth was thought to be a key statistic, and subscriber acquisition was expensive. By the fourth quarter of 2005, Blockbuster Online had about one million subscribers, versus four million subscribers for Netflix. This was after a 39% increase in advertising for the first three quarters of 2005.[23]

In 2005, Blockbuster's stock had dropped 50% from its 52-week high. To stem the bleeding, it announced a cost-cutting program that included advertising reductions. These cuts were to take effect from the second quarter of 2005 through the second quarter of 2006 (Exhibit 3.3). After the poor subscriber acquisition results, Blockbuster announced that it would increase advertising for its online service, despite the cost-cutting initiative.[24]

By 2005, price wars between the major online renters had broken out. Blockbuster dropped its three-out DVD rental monthly subscription by $3 to undercut Netflix (Exhibit 3.4). Also, it rolled out a trial program in Seattle where online customers had the option of returning DVDs to their local Blockbuster store,[25] foreshadowing the 2006 launch of Blockbuster Total Access.

Exhibit 3.3 Summary of Blockbuster's Income Statements ($US millions, except where indicated)

	CY 2007	CY 2006	CY 2005	CY 2004	CY 2003	CY 2002
Total subscribers (1000 people)		2,000	1,000			
Total revenue	5,542.40	5,522.20	5,721.80	6,053.20	5,911.70	5,565.90
Cost of revenue, total	2,677.80	2,479.70	2,561.00	2,441.40	2,389.80	2,358.70
Gross profit	2,804.80	2,981.30	3,088.60	3,519.80	3,425.30	3,121.40
Total selling, general, and admin. expenses	2,719.10	2,752.90	2,977.50	3,110.90	2,785.30	2,618.70
R&D						
Depreciation/amortization	185.7	210.9	224.3	249.7	268.4	233.8
Unusual expense (Income)	2.2	5.1	341.9	1,504.40	1,304.90	0
Total operating expense	5,503.30	5,448.60	6,104.70	7,306.40	6,748.40	5,211.20
Operating Income	39.1	73.6	−382.9	−1,253.20	−836.7	354.7
Interest Income (Expense), net nonoperating	−82.2	−91.7	−94.6	−34.5	−30	−45.4
Income before tax	−44.6	−12.7	−481.7	−1,286.10	−867.1	312.2
Income after tax	−74.2	63.7	−544.1	−1,248.80	−973.6	205.1

Source: Blockbuster's annual financial statements.

Exhibit 3.4 Summary of Blockbuster Total Access Movie Rental Plans

Plan		Maximum rentals per month	Price per month ($)	Additional in-store movie, or game rentals per month	Mail only price (in-store rental or return) ($)
4 DVDs at-a-time	Unlimited		23.99	1	22.99
3 DVDs at-a-time	Unlimited		17.99	1	16.99
2 DVDs at-a-time	Unlimited		14.99	1	13.99
1 DVD at-a-time	Unlimited		9.99	1	8.99
1 DVD at-a-time	Limit 3		7.99	1	6.99
1 DVD at-a-time	Limit 2		5.99	1	4.99

Source: Retrieved June 10, 2007 from, www.blockbuster.com.

Other Competitors

Many other smaller competitors sprang up once the DVD format had taken hold. Some were forced to exit the market but a few remained, existing on the fringe, trailing far behind giants Netflix and Blockbuster. These included intelliflix, DVD Overnight, DVD Barn, Rent My DVD, DVD Whiz, and Qwikfliks.

Blockbuster Total Access

In November of 2006, Blockbuster launched an updated version of Blockbuster Online, called Blockbuster Total Access. In addition to offering movie rentals requested over the Internet and delivered through the mail, as Netflix and the original Blockbuster Online had, Total Access sought to utilize Blockbuster's stores to offer additional benefits. Blockbuster Total Access' customers could return their movies rented through the mail through the mail service and have their next title shipped to them. Alternatively, customers could return movies to any Blockbuster location. When returning an online rental at a store, customers received a free in-store rental in addition to having their next online rental shipped.[26] Blockbuster promoted this advantage and the instant gratification it provided using slogans such as "Never be without a movie." Blockbuster Total Access subscriptions also gave customers a coupon for one free in-store rental each month. The coupon could be used for a movie or video game rental.[27]

On June 12, 2007 Blockbuster added Blockbuster by Mail as an option for its online service. Customers choosing this option would be permitted to return movies to blockbuster stores, but they would not receive a free rental in exchange. The return of their movie to the store would electronically stimulate the next movie in their queue to be sent from the Blockbuster distribution center. These users also would not receive a free rental coupon each month. In return for giving up these privileges, subscription fees were $1 less per month than the full Blockbuster Total Access plan. The addition of Blockbuster by Mail provided a more direct comparison with Netflix's subscription plans and drew attention to the added benefit of in-store rentals. Blockbuster promoted its plan as a way to save money for customers who did not live near a Blockbuster location.[28] While the Blockbuster by Mail service was less expensive than Netflix, it did not offer the instant viewing option available from Netflix.

Movie Downloads

In addition to threats from Blockbuster and other companies that potentially could imitate the Netflix model, there was also a rising trend in downloaded or streaming movies, similar to the Netflix *Watch Now* feature. These services allowed customers to have a movie delivered to them through their cable television connection directly to their television, or through the Internet to their computer.

Comcast and other cable companies offered a range of on-demand entertainment as part of their cable service. These services charged a fee for viewing the most popular movie titles and had a limited selection. Exclusive rights to digital distribution of many movies had already been sold for many years into the future, typically to television stations. These deals excluded DVD rentals, but applied to movies delivered over cable or Internet. Online services such as CinemaNow, iTunes, and Amazon Unbox started offering movie downloads for rental and/or purchase. These companies offered downloads to computers that must be burned to a disc or watched through the computer. Most potential customers preferred to watch movies on their television rather than their computer, and connecting one's computer to the television was still a somewhat cumbersome process. Much like the cable companies, these services also offered a very limited selection compared to the Netflix rental library. If the technology issues could be solved so that movies were easier to watch on televisions and if the selection improved, these companies could be serious competition for Netflix.[29,30] There was also ZML.com, the pirate site that had a selection of over 1,700 films to burn to DVDs, or for download to personal computers or handheld devices such as iPods.[31]

Netflix's Decision

Reed Hastings had several options for dealing with the threats posed by Blockbuster Total Access and competitors offering downloadable movies on demand. First, if customers were not willing to pay for the added convenience of returning movies to Blockbuster stores, Netflix could push an aggressive price war to try to eliminate Blockbuster from online rentals. Second, it could continue to bring out innovations such as Netflix Prize crowdsourcing idea and Netflix friends feature. Such innovations could help it fend off competitors. Third, exclusive rights agreements currently prevented many titles from being released through the Internet or by a cable provider, but as these agreements expired, movies streamed over the Internet might become the disruptive technology that displaced rental of physical DVDs. Current drawbacks to watching movies on a computer rather than on a television might be displaced by technology similar to AppleTV,[32] making streaming downloads more attractive. Netflix had started exploring this option with its *Watch Now* feature. The question was, how could it insure that it was strategically positioned to take advantage of this technology if its popularity increased?

Reed would have never thought that simply providing movie rentals would be such a complex and technology driven business, but it was becoming obvious that Netflix must be a constantly improving and evolving business if it was going to have a long future.

Threadless in Chicago

In 2000, Jake Nickell, a multimedia and design student at the Illinois Institute of Art, and Jacob DeHart, an engineering student at Purdue University, entered an online T-shirt design contest, which Jake won. However, both of them went away with the idea that having someone else compete to design T-shirts for them could lead to something interesting. They kept in touch and worked together on a few projects before starting their own T-shirt company in 2001, with $1,000.[1] Their company, Threadless, would make and sell T-shirts with colorful graphics.[2] They were venturing into the colorful T-shirt—a so-called hit-and-miss product. Traditionally, to be successful with such a product, a firm needed to have the right distribution channels and its fingers on the pulse of fast-changing trends.[3] A firm needed to have the right market research and forecasting abilities to do well. The two founders added creative director Jeff Kalmikoff later. They also took venture capital money from Insight Venture Partners, not so much because they needed the money, but because they could, well, obtain some insights from the venture capitalist firm.

The Community Designs and Markets

Threadless had a community of registered members that in 2004 was 70,000 strong and mushroomed to 700,000 by 2008. Anyone with a valid e-mail address could join free. Each week, members of the community—largely artists—uploaded hundreds of T-shirt designs to the community site. (In 2007, the firm received 150 submissions per day.) Visitors to the site then voted for their favorite designs by scoring them on a scale of 0 to 5.[4] Each design remained available for voting for seven days. From the scoring, the best six designs were chosen from the hundreds of submissions. Creators of the winning designs were awarded prizes. In 2007, these prizes were worth $2,000 per design: $1,500 in cash, $300 in a gift certificate, and subscription to T-shirts.[5] By 2008, the prize had climbed to $2,500. To many artists, there was something bigger than the cash prize. "It was how cool it was to get your shirts printed,"[6] remarked Glen Jones, a 2004 winner. The name of the designer (winner) was put on the label of the T-shirt.[7] Threadless retained the rights to the design.

To help the artists with the design process, Threadless sent digital submission kits—complete with HTML code and graphics—to each potential submitter. With these kits, artists could create advertisements for their designs that looked very professional. The artists not only spent weeks seeking advice from other community members and perfecting their designs, they posted links to their submissions to their personal websites, any online design forums that they frequented, MySpace pages, or blogs, asking their friends to vote for them and buy if and when they won.[8] Effectively, the artists not only designed the shirts for Threadless, they also premarketed them, adding to the brand. Some of the members who participated in voting for designs saw the process as one of exploring the latest in designs and learning. In effect, the firm committed financially only to T-shirt designs of which many of its customers approved.

Some Results

The company printed the winning designs and sold them to the very community that had competed to create the designs and voted to decide the winning design. By 2008, it had printed 1,000 designs[9]— all online. The T-shirts usually sold out. It had no professional designers, used no fashion photographers or modeling agencies, had no sales force, did not advertise, and except for its retail store in Chicago, it had no distributors.[10] Members of the community socialized, blogged, and chatted about designs. It even had an official fan site: http://www.lovesthreadless.com/. In 2007, its shirts cost about $4 each to make and sold for about $15.[11] The company sold 80–90,000 shirts a week.[12] Revenues were growing at 500% a year; and the company was doing all this without the help of big retailers such as Target, who had come knocking but been turned down by Threadless.

A Retail Store?

Threadless opened its first offline retail store in September of 2007, in Chicago.[13] Why would an online company build an offline store when it could keep its margins even higher by avoiding brick-and-mortar costs? Threadless offered several reasons.[14] First, the firm wanted a building that reflected the Threadless culture in which design classes could be offered, galleries with Threadless artists' work hosted, and real-world group interaction and critics facilitated. Second, the company's products changed every week and most retailers were not equipped to handle such changes. Third, there was a story behind each of their T-shirts and the person who created it, how it was created, scored and selected for print that needed to be told. Such a story would be lost in a traditional retail outlet. With the retail store, they could tell the story their own way. Of the 1,000 designs that had been created since its inception, about 300 of them were still in stock. The firm only displayed 20 designs for sale. The rest could be obtained from its website. Designs were released in the offline retail store before online.

Other Holdings

Threadless had a parent company called SkinnyCorp, also run by Nickell, DeHart and Kraikoff. In June 2008, the other units under the SkinnyCorp umbrella were Naked and Angry, Yay Hooray, and Extra Tasty.

Pixar Changes the Rules of the Game*

On June 29, 2008, on the first anniversary of the release of *Ratatouille*, a former Pixar Animation shareholder wondered if Pixar had done the right thing selling itself to Disney. *Ratatouille* had grossed more than $600 million worldwide with an undisclosed amount from merchandising. What was even more amazing than the revenues was the fact that *Ratatouille* was the eighth straight hit for Pixar, in an industry where every other movie risked crashing. Why had Pixar been so successful? Would the success continue under Disney? Should Pixar have stayed as a separate company in a continued alliance with Disney or parted ways and found another partner? Eight straight hits with most of them grossing more than half a billion dollars!

Pixar's Digital Technology Roots

University of Utah Days

Pixar's technical roots date back to 1970, when Ed Catmull joined the computer science program at the University of Utah as a doctoral student.[1] Given the program's notoriety and leadership in computer graphics, several young stars were attracted, among them John Warnock. He would later found Adobe Systems and create a revolution in the publishing world with his PostScript page description language. Jim Clark, another alumnus, would later start Silicon Graphics and then lead Netscape Communications.

During the 1970s, the program made significant headway into the development of computer graphics. Catmull himself made a significant advance in computer graphics in his 1974 doctoral thesis, which focused on texture mapping, z-buffer and rendering curved surfaces. In 1974, interest in the work of the Utah program came from an unexpected source, Alexander Schure, an eccentric millionaire and founder of the New York Institute of Technology (NYIT), who wanted to use the story from a children's record album called *Tubby the Tuba* to develop an animated film. From the ranks at Utah, Dr Catmull recruited a team of talented computer scientists and began experimenting with computer-generated animation.

---

* This case was written by Catherine Crane, Will Johnson, Kitty Neumark, and Christopher Perrigo under the supervision of Professor Allan Afuah as a basis for class discussion and is not intended to illustrate either effective or ineffective handling of a business situation.

The Lucasfilm Years: 1979–1986

While Catmull's group struggled at NYIT, Hollywood was beginning to see the benefits of computer graphics for production. One early Hollywood pioneer was George Lucas, whose *Star Wars* had been a stunning special effects achievement. With this blockbuster under his belt, Lucas became interested in using computer graphics for image editing and producing special effects for his next movie, *The Empire Strikes Back*. Lucas worked with an outside computer graphics production house, Triple I, to create effects for *Empire*, but in the end these were not used. However, the experience had proven that photorealistic computer imagery was possible, and Lucas decided to assemble his own computer graphics division within his special effects company, Lucasfilm.

In 1979, Lucas discovered Catmull's group at NYIT. George Lucas extended an offer to the team to come to Northern California to work as part of Lucasfilm; the team was more than happy to accept. Dr Catmull was named Vice President and over the next six years, the new computer graphics division of Lucasfilm would assemble one of the most talented teams of artists and programmers in the computer graphics industry.

Pixar Is Born (1984–Present): Creative Development

Enter the Story Man: John Lasseter

Like Ed Catmull, John Lasseter had long envisioned the future of computer graphics animation. Lasseter had worked on Disney's first major foray into computer-aided production—*Tron* (1981). *Tron* required nearly 30 minutes of film quality computer graphics and was a daunting task for computer graphics studios at the time. The computer-generated imagery of *Tron* was technologically dazzling, but the underlying story was an unappealing cyber-adventure. Disney sank about $20 million into the picture, but it bombed at the box office. The resultant financial loss alone served to all but kill Disney's interest in the computer graphics medium.

Despite the commercial failure of *Tron*, the film was an epiphany for Lasseter. Watching what fellow animators were doing with computer graphics imagery, he started to see the possibilities of full-scale computer animation: "the minute I saw the light-cycle sequence, which had such dimensionality and solidity," Lasseter recalls, "it was like a little door in my head opening to a whole new world."[2]

Lasseter and fellow animator Glen Keane (who went on to make *Beauty and the Beast*) tried to interest Disney in the medium by animating 30 seconds of Maurice Sendak's *Where the Wild Things Are*, using standard animation drawings in computer-generated settings. However, Disney, which was struggling to rejuvenate itself after years of lackluster box office performance, was not interested in further experimentation with untried computer animation. In 1984, a disappointed Lasseter left Disney. Ed Catmull, a friend of Lasseter, convinced him to come to Lucasfilm to experiment for just a month. John Lasseter liked what he found and never left.

Born in the "Next" Generation: Steve Jobs

While the computer graphics division of Lucasfilm was strengthened with the addition of Lasseter in 1984, George Lucas' interest in the project waned. Although Catmull saw tremendous further potential in the technologies being developed, Lucas viewed the project as complete and began looking for a buyer of the computer division. An early potential buyer of the division was a partnership between the behemoth General Motors' Electronic Data Systems (EDS) and a unit of the Dutch conglomerate Phillips NV. Much to Catmull's relief, the sale fell through.

Steve Jobs, then CEO of Apple Computer, heard about Lucas' intended sale of the computer division. Jobs thought the situation provided a strong acquisition opportunity for Apple, but unfortunately, Apple's Board disagreed. When Jobs left Apple in 1985, Pixar remained a division of Lucasfilm.

Ironically, it was the ousting of Jobs that ultimately permitted the sale of the computer division. With a personal net worth of more than $100 million resulting from his sale of Apple stock, Jobs approached Lucas and reiterated his interest in the division. In 1986, at a price of $10 million, Lucas sold the division to Jobs. Steve Jobs considered the idea of absorbing the group into his other firm, NeXT Computer, but instead decided to incorporate Pixar as an independent company, installing himself as Chief Executive Officer and Ed Catmull as Chief Technical Officer.

Along with Catmull and Lasseter, Jobs viewed the ultimate goal of the company as producing computer-animated cartoons and full-length films. However, there were still several intermediate steps required to meet this objective. One of the most important of these hurdles was developing and refining software tools that would enable the creation of the films the team envisioned.

"Innovate or Not to Innovate?"—That is NOT the Question!

Pixar developed groundbreaking software systems—Marionette, Ringmaster and RenderMan, and a laser recording system for film—Pixarvision. Marionette was an animation software system for modeling, animating, and lighting simulation capabilities (see Exhibit 5.1 for an animation value chain).[3] RingMaster was a production management software system for scheduling, coordinating, and tracking computer animation projects. Pixarvision was a

Exhibit 5.1 An Animation Movie Value Chain

		Financing, purchasing, human resources, etc.		
CREATIVE DEVELOPMENT Story and characters development	▶ PRODUCTION Modeling Layout Animation Shading Lighting Rendering Film recording	▶ POST-PRODUCTION Sound process Picture process Sound effects Musical score etc.	▶ MARKETING *and* MERCHANDISING	▶ DISTRIBUTION

laser recording system for converting digital computer data into images on motion picture film stock with unprecedented quality. These three products helped to provide a considerable competitive advantage to Pixar, as they were critical to the production of high-quality three-dimensional graphics and comparable tools were simply not available on the market.

Unlike these software systems which remained proprietary to Pixar, RenderMan software system was commercialized and quickly became a significant source of revenue, so that in 2001 approximately 10% of Pixar's total revenue came from software licensing. Released for commercial use in 1989, Render-Man, a rendering software system for photorealistic image synthesis, enabled computer graphics artists to apply textures and colors to surfaces of three-dimensional images onscreen. Pixar licensed the tool to third parties and eventually sold upwards of 100,000 copies. RenderMan quickly became an industry standard and was used extensively to augment live action films. Over a 10-year period, the software had been used to create eight out of the ten films that won Oscar for Best Visual Effects—*The Matrix, What Dreams May Come, Titanic, Forrest Gump, Jurassic Park, Death Becomes Her, Terminator 2*, and *The Abyss*. However, the true testimonial to RenderMan and people who created it was in 2001 when the Academy of Motion Picture Art & Science Board of Governors honored Ed Catmull, the President of Pixar, Loren Carpenter, Senior Scientist, and Rob Cook, Vice President of Software Engineering, with an Academy Award of Merit (Oscar) "for significant advancement to the field of motion picture rendering as exemplified in Pixar's RenderMan."

Developing the Creative Side of Pixar

In early 1990s Steve Jobs realized that sales of RenderMan and other tools alone would not be able to fund Pixar's technology research and internal projects, including film development. "The problem was, for many years, the cost of computers to make animation we could sell was tremendously high."[4] Jobs put Pixar technology to use in developing TV commercial campaigns for a variety of clients. As the company evolved into a successful animation studio producing TV ads for Listerine, Lifesavers, and others, John Lasseter, the director of the ads, became Pixar's big breadwinner. The company won a Gold Medal Clio Award for its LifeSavers "Conga" commercial in 1993, and another Gold Clio Award in 1994 for its Listerine "Arrows" commercial.

A second successful creative outlet for Pixar was short film. In 1986, Pixar's first short movie, *Luxo Jr.*, earned an Academy Award nomination for Best Short Film (Animated). In 1988, another of Pixar's short films, *Tin Toy*, became the first computer-animated film to win an Academy Award for Best Short Film (Animated). John Lasseter, who had directed both films, had established a well-deserved reputation as one of the leading animators in the industry. Indeed, his reputation set the creative foundation for Pixar. Meanwhile, Lasseter's success did not go unnoticed. Disney's Michael Eisner and Jeffrey Katzenberg tried to woo the director back, but Lasseter declined. "I was having too much fun," he said. "I felt I was on to something new—we were pioneers."[5]

A Tale of Four Animated Films

Teaming Up to Break New Frontiers: Disney and Pixar

In 1991, John Lasseter reviewed Pixar's work in short films and commercials, and was confident enough in the company's progress to propose the idea of producing an hour-long animated TV special. He pitched the idea to his previous studio, Disney, with the hope that the two companies could collaborate on the project. He was also hoping that Disney would be able to provide part of the money necessary to fund the idea.

The timing was just right. Unlike his pitch for *Toaster* in 1984, Disney in 1991 was riding high on the phenomenal success of its animation department. With smashes in *The Little Mermaid* (1989) and *Beauty and the Beast* (1991)—both had utilized computer animation to some extent—Disney was ready to invest in new technology. Although Disney CEO Michael Eisner and film chief Jeffrey Katzenberg rejected the TV project, they countered with a deal Lasseter and Pixar could hardly have hoped for: Disney proposed a full length movie, which it would fund and distribute.

In July 1991, Pixar signed a three-film deal. The deal stipulated that Disney would fund the production and promotion costs and Pixar would earn a modest percentage of box-office and video sales gross revenues. Pixar's share in the deal was estimated to amount to approximately 10–15% of the film's profits, depending on the sales levels achieved. Pixar was required to pay a portion of the costs over specified budget levels, as well as provide the funding for the development of any animation tools and technologies necessary to complete the films.

In return for taking the lower cut of box office and video profits, Pixar gained access to Disney's marketing and distribution network, as well as creative advice from Disney's veterans. However, a substantially higher share of revenues was not the only price Disney extracted from the deal. In addition, Disney retained all ownership to the characters appearing in the films. Disney also maintained sole licensing rights to the films and characters, including very lucrative ancillary merchandise such as toys and clothing. Pixar was only able to retain the rights to any direct-to-video sequels, as well as the data files and rendering technologies employed to develop the films.

When asked about the agreement signed, Steve Jobs remarked that if the first movie was

> a modest hit—say $75 million at the box office—we'll both break even. If it gets $100 million, we'll both make money. But if it's a real blockbuster and earns $200 million or so at the box office, we'll make good money, and Disney will make a lot of money.[6]

1995—Film I: Toy Story

With the deal signed, Pixar now had to prove it could deliver on its technology and creativity. In 1991 with a staff of only a few dozen people, Pixar had to quickly gear up to begin design and production of the first of the three films. By the end of 1992 all of the key ingredients were in place—screenplay was approved by Disney, character voices, led by Tom Hanks as Woody and Tim Allen as Buzz Lightyear, were signed, and the staff of animators was ready to turn a tale about the rivalry between a toy cowboy, Woody, and a plastic spaceman named Buzz Lightyear, to life.

Pixar completed *Toy Story* with a staff of 110, roughly one-sixth of the number Disney and other studios typically use to make animated productions.[7] Of the staff, 27 were animators, compared to the 75 or more animators required for previous animated Disney films. With animators earning $100,000 or more each, the total cost savings amounted to more than $15,000,000 over a three-year production for the movie.

Toy Story opened in US theaters over the Thanksgiving weekend of 1995 with great fanfare and extensive media publicity. During the five-day Thanksgiving weekend, *Toy Story* box office receipts totaled $39.1 million, a record debut for the weekend and by the end of 1995 it became the highest grossing film of the year, making over $192 million in domestic box office receipts and $358 million worldwide.

1998—A New Contract and A Bug's Life

In December 1997, riding high on the success of *Toy Story*, but making only an estimated $45 million from the release of the film, Pixar renegotiated its contract with Disney. Pixar agreed to produce five original computer-animated feature-length theatrical motion pictures for distribution by Disney. Pixar and Disney agreed to cofinance production, co-own, cobrand, and share equally the profits from each picture, including revenues from all related merchandise.

The first original picture released under the new agreement was *A Bug's Life*, which opened in theaters in November of 1998. The story, derived from the fable "The Ant and the Grasshopper" revolved around an ant colony, led by a rebel ant named Flick, and its quest to fight off the grasshoppers who stole the ants' food every winter. *A Bug's Life* broke all previous US Thanksgiving weekend box-office records, becoming the highest grossing animated release in 1998 and making over $163 million domestically in box office receipts and $362 million worldwide. After only one week of international release *A Bug's Life* captured the #1 spot in six international markets, including Thailand, Argentina, and Australia.

Computer technology had advanced to a point where the computing power used in *A Bug's Life* was ten times the power used in *Toy Story*. The results were images that were more real-life than ever before. Additionally, Pixar used Pixarvision (its laser recording system) for the first time, to convert digital computer data into images on motion picture film stock, achieving not only faster recording time, but also higher quality color reproduction and sharper images.

1999–2012: More Blockbuster Years

A Bug's Life was followed by *Toy Story 2*, which was released on November 19, 1999, and became the first film in history to be entirely mastered and exhibited digitally, and the first animated sequel to gross more than its original. It won a

Exhibit 5.2 Pixar Full-length Animation Movies

Movie Name	Released	1st Weekend ($)	US Gross ($)	Worldwide Gross ($)	Budget ($)
Toy Story	11/22/95	29,140,617	191,796,233	356,800,000	30,000,000
A Bug's Life	11/20/98	291,121	162,798,565	358,000,000	45,000,000
Toy Story 2	11/19/99	300,163	245,852,179	485,828,782	90,000,000
Monsters, Inc.	11/2/01	62,577,067	255,870,172	525,370,172	115,000,000
Finding Nemo	5/30/03	70,251,710	339,714,978	864,614,978	94,000,000
The Incredibles	11/5/04	70,467,623	261,437,578	631,437,578	92,000,000
Cars	6/9/06	60,119,509	244,082,982	461,782,982	70,000,000
Ratatouille	6/29/07	47,027,395	206,445,654	617,245,654	150,000,000
Pixar Short Film Collection—Volume 1	11/6/07				
WALL-E	6/27/08				180,000,000
Up	5/29/09				
Toy Story 3	6/18/10				
Newt	8/31/11				
The Bear and the Bow	12/31/11				
Cars 2	8/31/12				
	Totals		1,907,998,341	4,301,080,146	866,000,000
	Averages		238,499,793	537,635,018	96,222,220

Source: The Numbers. Retrieved June 21, 2008, from http://www.the numbers.com/movies/series/DigitalAnimation.php.

Golden Globe award for the Best Picture, Musical, or Comedy. This was followed by *Monsters, Inc., Finding Nemo, The Incredibles, Cars,* and *Ratatouille*—all of them blockbusters (Exhibit 5.2). Planned for release the following years were *WALL-E* (2008), *Up* (2009), *Toy Story 3* (2010), *Newt* (2011), *The Bear and the Bow* (2011), and *Cars 2* (2012).

Competitors

Pixar had competitors, chief among them, Disney, DreamWorks PDI/SKG, Fox Studio, and Lucasfilm. In fact, two of the top five spots on the all-time grossing animation movies were occupied by PDI/DreamWorks, not Pixar (Exhibits 5.3 and 5.4).

Pondering Pixar's Future—Where to Next?

In 2004, Steve Jobs and his team went to Disney for renegotiation of their agreement, confident that their strong record of six blockbusters would be enough to seal a new deal; but Ed Eisner, Disney's CEO did not see eye-to-eye with Steve Jobs and no deal was reached.[8] On October 1, 2005, however, Bob Iger was appointed CEO of Disney to replace Eisner. Iger reopened talks with Pixar. On January 24, 2006 Disney announced that it had agreed to purchase Pixar for $7.4 billion in an all-stock deal.[9] The deal was completed on May 5, 2006, after approval by Pixar shareholders.[10] However, there were still some Pixar shareholders and analysts who wondered if Pixar had done the right thing. Should the firm have remained single?

Exhibit 5.3 Top 12 Grossing Animation Movies

Animation movie	Release date	Firm	Worldwide gross ($)
Shrek 2	2004	PDI/DreamWorks	920,665,658
Finding Nemo	2003	Pixar	864,625,978
Shrek the Third	2007	PDI/DreamWorks	798,957,081
The Lion King**	1994	Walt Disney	783,841,776
Ice Age: The Meltdown	2006	Fox	647,330,621
The Incredibles	2004	Pixar	631,436,092
Ratatouille	2007	Pixar	617,245,650
Monsters Inc.	2001	Pixar	529,061,238
Madagascar	2005	PDI/DreamWorks	527,890,631
Aladdin	1992	Walt Disney	504,050,219
Toy Story 2	1999	Pixar	485,015,179
Shrek	2001	PDI	484,409,218
Cars	2006	Pixar	461,782,982

Source: The Numbers. Retrieved June 21, 2008, from *http://www.the-numbers.com/movies/series/DigitalAnimation.php.*
** *The Lion King* was also estimated to have brought in $1 billion in profits from merchandising, theme park attractions, TV rights and videos.

Exhibit 5.4 Competing Animation Movies

Digital animated movie	Date released	Firm	Worldwide gross ($)
Antz	1998	PDI	152,457,863
Shrek	2001	PDI	484,409,218
Shrek 2	2004	PDI/DreamWorks	920,665,658
Madagascar	2005	PDI/DreamWorks	527,890,631
Shrek the Third	2007	PDI/DreamWorks	798,957,081
Ice Age	2002	Blue Sky Studios/Fox	382,387,405
Robots	2005	Blue Sky Studios/Fox	260,700,012
Ice Age: The Meltdown	2006	Blue Sky Studios/Fox	647,330,621
Horton Hears a Whol	2008	Blue Sky Studios/Fox	N/A

Source: The Numbers. Retrieved June 21, 2008, from *http://www.the-numbers.com/movies/series/DigitalAnimation.php.*

Lipitor: The World's Best-selling Drug[1] (2008)

Jeff Kindler, CEO of Pfizer, pondered over sales of Lipitor. The drug had brought in $12.7 billion in revenues in 2007.[2] This blockbuster belonged to a group of drugs called statins that reduce the level of cholesterol in the body by inhibiting the process by which the body produces cholesterol. What was it about Lipitor and Pfizer that had enabled the drug to do so well? Could Pfizer or any pharmaceutical company ever repeat such a feat?

Coronary Artery Disease

In 2008, it was believed that coronary artery disease was the leading cause of death in the USA, where more than a million people suffered a heart attack every year. A leading cause of coronary artery disease is the buildup of plaque in the blood vessels, which can lead to blockage of these arteries, to heart attacks and strokes. Frequently, this plaque buildup results from excessive cholesterol levels, especially of the bad cholesterol called low-density lipoprotein (LDL). High levels of triglycerides also have the same negative effect. However, high levels of so-called good cholesterol—high-density lipoprotein (HDL)—have the opposite effect as they return LDL to the liver for elimination, thereby reducing harm to people. Cholesterol is a natural substance in the body that is used in the formation of cell membranes, gastric juices, and some hormones; but like most good things, too much of it is bad. The liver makes most of the cholesterol that the body needs but cholesterol can also be ingested directly from food.

Role of Statins

Before statins, high levels of cholesterol were treated with drugs that break down cholesterol or absorb it irrespective of whether it was naturally produced by the body or from ingested food. These therapies were somewhat effective but for many patients, the reductions in LDL levels were just not good enough. Moreover, the therapies caused many side effects, including stomach pain and nausea. All that changed when Merck introduced Mevacor, a statin, in 1987. Statins work by inhibiting a key enzyme in the body from enabling the production of cholesterol. Rather than wait for cholesterol to be produced by the body and then try to eliminate it the way earlier drugs did, statins directly intervene in the process that the body uses to produce cholesterol. Bristol Myers and Norvatis soon joined Merck in offering statin cholesterol drugs. The market shares for the statins available just prior to the launch of Lipitor are shown in Exhibit 6.1.

Exhibit 6.1 US Market Shares of Cholesterol-lowering Drugs, January 1997

Drug name	Manufacturer	Launch year	Market share (%)
Mevacor	Merck	1987	14
Pravachol	Bristol-Myers Squibb	1991	21
Zocor	Merck	1992	32
Lescol	Novartis	1994	14

Source: [1]Seiden, C. (October 8, 1997). Pfizer, Inc. JP Morgan.

Note: Market shares are based on the entire cholesterol-lowering drug market (not only on statins).

Lipitor Research and Development

The decision by Warner-Lambert to go on with the development of Lipitor was not very popular because the drug was regarded as a me-too drug since it was going to be the fifth drug in the statin family. However, a Phase I study conducted in 1992 showed that the drug reduced LDL levels much better than existing statins (see Exhibit 6.2 for the different phases through which a drug has to go before approval by the FDA). So Warner-Lambert decided to go ahead with the development of Lipitor. To reduce the time that it takes to review the data to approve or reject a new drug application (NDA) from the average of 12 months at the time, Warner-Lambert ran trials for a fatal hereditary condition called familial hypercholesterolemia that results in exceptionally high cholesterol levels. The idea was to take advantage of a law that encourages the FDA to expedite new drug applications for any new drug that treats a serious or life-threatening condition or addresses an unmet medical need. This worked as Lipitor was approved by the FDA six months after receiving Warner Lambert's application for approval.

At the request of its marketing group, Warner-Lambert took the unusual step of carrying out so-called head-to-head clinical trials in which clinical data are collected on competing drugs and compared. Fortunately, the data showed Lipitor to be superior to all the other statins. Lipitor reduced LDL levels by 40–60% and reduced triglycerides by 19–40%. Zocor, the best of the other statins, decreased LDL cholesterol by only about 40%.[3,4,5]

After arriving at Warner-Lambert in 1988, Ron Cresswell, head of R&D, had increased emphasis on biotechnology, integrated regulatory affairs, and clinical research into the R&D unit, and sought to involve marketing earlier in the new drug development process. He also sought to establish closer links to manufacturing.

Warner-Lambert was granted FDA approval for Lipitor in December of 1996, one year ahead of most analysts' expectations.

Bringing Lipitor to Market

To launch the drug, Warner-Lambert executives sought a partnership with a company that had the marketing and sales resources. Pfizer, which had a large sales force but no cholesterol drug, was considered the best candidate. Pfizer liked the idea and promptly paid $205 million up front and future payments for

Exhibit 6.2 The Drug Development Process in the USA.[6]

To insure the safety and efficacy of drugs sold in the USA, drugs have to go through Phases I, II, and III, and the results of the testing scrutinized before the drug is approved by the Food and Drug Administration (FDA) for marketing. Phase IV studies are undertaken after FDA approval to further understand the long-term effects of a drug.

Preclinical Studies
As their name indicates, these are the studies that take place before a firm can start the actual clinical trials on a drug. Preclinical studies are undertaken in vitro (that is, in test tube or laboratory), and in vivo (in animal populations) to determine the effect that the drug in question has on living organisms. In these studies, scientists monitor the drug's efficacy, toxicity, and pharmacokinetics (how well the drug is absorbed, distributed, metabolized, and excreted) to determine whether or not to proceed with the clinical testing. Preclinical trials take 3–6 years.

Phase I
This is where the first testing on human beings starts. A small group of 20–80 healthy volunteers is selected to participate in the studies. These studies are conducted to determine the basic characteristics of a potential new drug in humans—in particular, to determine its safety, safe dosage range, and to identify side effects. Emphasis here is to make sure that the drug is safe before it can be tried on patients with the target disease.

Phase II
If the safety of the drug is confirmed in Phase I, Phase II trials are performed on larger groups (100–300) of volunteers who have the target disease. The idea here is to establish that the drug is effective and to further establish its safety. Thus, the testing tries to establish that the drug has a beneficial effect on the disease that it targets, and to continue the proof of safety partially proven in Phase I. The drug fails Phase II trials if it fails to work as expected or has toxic effects; that is, the drug fails when it does not demonstrate efficacy and safety. Phase II studies take 6 months to a year to complete.

Phase III
These are multicenter, randomized controlled studies undertaken on large groups (1,000–3,000) of patients that have the disease that the drug is supposed to treat. The idea here is to establish statistically significant proof that the potential new drug is effective in treating the disease for which it is earmarked. Patients are monitored at regular time intervals for progress in treatment and side effects. At the end of Phase III trials, the pharmaceutical firm submits a New Drug Application (NDA) to the FDA for approval. If the FDA is satisfied with the application, the drug is granted approval to launch and market the drug. This approval is often referred to as conditional approval, since it can be withdrawn after Phase IV trials.

Phase IV
Also known as Post Marketing Surveillance Trial, Phase IV trials are designed to provide more data on safety and to monitor technical support of a drug after its owner receives permission (through FDA approval) to market and sell the drug. The studies offer more long-term data on the drug's effects on larger samples of patients, including the drug's risks, benefits, and optimal use. The results of Phase IV trials can result in the withdrawal of a drug from the market or its uses being restricted.

Sources: Understanding clinical trials. 2008. Retrieved July 22, 2008, from http://clinicaltrials.gov/ct2/info/understand. Clinical trials. 2008. Retrieved July 22, 2008, from http:/en.wikipedia.org/wiki/Clinical_trial.

the rights to sell Lipitor. Warner-Lambert positioned Lipitor as a therapeutically superior drug but set its price lower than that of market leaders (Exhibit 6.3).

At the launch of Lipitor, the combined sales force from Warner-Lambert and Pfizer numbered more than 2,200 sales representatives that called on about 91,000 physicians made up of cardiologists, internists, and general and family practitioners with a track record of prescribing cholesterol-lowering drugs.

Within one year of its launch in January 1997, Lipitor reached $1 billion in domestic sales, beating estimates of $900 million in worldwide sales (see Exhibit 6.4) for more estimates). On June 19, 2000, Pfizer bought Warner

Exhibit 6.3 Statin Average Prescription Pricing Structure

Drug name	1997 average prescription price ($)	1999 average prescription price ($)
Lescol	52	50
Lipitor	84	91
Pravachol	93	105
Zocor	95	125
Mevacor	125	137

Source: IMS. (January–December 1997). National Prescription Audit. Price Probe Pricing History Report, 1992–9.

Exhibit 6.4 1997 Lipitor Worldwide Sales Projections

Year	1997	1998	1999	2000	2001	2002	2003
Revenues ($B)	0.9	2.2	3.4	4.6	5.6	6.7	7.7

Source: ING Baring Furman Selz, LLC, April 12, 1999.

Lambert. Direct-to-consumer (DTC) marketing of statins by all competitors continued. In 2005 Bristol Myers Squibb conducted its own head-to-head testing to compare its Pravachol against Lipitor. The tests showed that Lipitor, not Bristol's Pravachol, was better. Poor Bristol!

CEO Kindler wondered what would become of Pfizer. Had he done the right thing in closing down the R&D facility in which Lipitor had been developed? What would he have to do to get another Lipitor? At an American Heart Association scientific meeting in New Orleans in November 2008, it was reported that Crestor, AstraZeneca's statin, cut the risk of heart attacks not only in patients with high cholesterol levels but also in those with low cholesterol levels.

Case 7

New Belgium: Brewing a New Game*

On June 11, 2008, InBev—a Belgium-based Brazilian-run, and world's second largest brewer—made a $46 billion bid for Anheuser-Busch (AB).[1] While some AB managers wondered what would happen to them if their firm were bought, many New Belgium Brewery (NBB) employees knew how they would vote if such a large brewer with an unknown environmental sustainability record wanted to buy them—No! Kim Jordan and her husband Jeff founded NBB in 1991 to turn their passion for good quality beer into a business they could work at and with which they could feel good about themselves at the end of the day. By 2008, it was not unusual for the firm to be mentioned as an example of a firm that did some socially responsible things that not only differentiated it but also kept its costs low.

The US Beer Industry

In 2008, AB alone held more than 50% of the US beer market share.[2] The next three firms held about 40%. The remaining 8% was held by many small brewers, many of them so-called microbrewers. At 59%, input materials for production and packaging, such as barley, hops, bottles, and cans, were a brewer's largest cost (Exhibit 7.1). Profit margins of 15% were not uncommon.

Exhibit 7.1 Average Cost of Goods Sold for United States Brewery

Item	Cost (%)
Purchases	59.0
Wages	7.6
Depreciation	4.5
Utilities	1.5
Rent	0.4
Others	12.0
Profit	15.0

Source: IBS World.

* This case was written by Ali Dharamsey, Lei Duran, Claudia Joseph, Steve Krichbaum, and Shama Zehra under the supervision of Professor Allan Afuah as a basis for class discussion and is not intended to illustrate either effective or ineffective handling of a business situation.

In many states in the USA, the sale of beer was restricted to certain areas, days, and hours. The legal drinking age was 21. Brewers had to sell their beer to distributors who, in turn, sold it to consumers. Distributors often maintained exclusive contracts with one of the major breweries, carrying only beer from the brewer.

Craft Beers

Craft beers were high-end premium beers that were distinguished from other beers by their quality, price, and ingredients. In the early 2000s, Craft beers were produced in small batches, allowing the brewers to produce what customers perceived as better-tasting beer, relative to the beers produced in a larger scale. Each brewer tried to market its beer as being distinct from the next, given the uniqueness of its own small batch process. For instance Pete's Brewing (Pete's Wicked Ale), one of the larger craft beer makers, sought to establish an image of hard, bold flavors for customers *"with an edge."* This image was highlighted throughout its packaging, flavors, and website.

1991: Fort Collins, Denver

Jeff Jordan became passionate about brewing beer during their bicycle trips through Europe. Back in Colorado, Jeff brewed some beer for their consumption, and his friends liked it. Kim became interested in commercializing Jeff's home-brewed beer when she noticed that nothing that she tasted from outside was as good as Jeff's. After brainstorming, they agreed that the name of their venture would be New Belgium, since Jeff's brewing process had been heavily influenced by the Belgian style of brewing. They called their first commercial beer "Fat Tire".

Kim was the CEO. She and Jeff knew that above all else, they wanted to build a company whose values and products supported their own personal core values. After more brainstorming, they decided that their firm's values would be anchored on three main tenets: philanthropy, ownership, and sustainability. She believed that these core values would attract new employees that shared their goal of creating a business that left the world a better place. They could then make products that would set them apart from other brewers in the eyes of customers. She would later be quoted as saying "The beautiful part of it is we believe in what we're doing."[3]

Sustainability

New Belgium designed its headquarters in 1995 with an emphasis on ecofriendly practices. The headquarters housed two "Steinecker" brew houses, four quality assurance labs, and a wastewater treatment facility that allowed them to cleanse their process waters and create their own energy. Additionally, their operations were also entirely wind powered, an option chosen in the wake of an employee-owner vote (see Ownership section for more information). Kim and Jeff constantly focused efforts on innovations that would help New Belgium reduce its environmental footprint. New Belgium hired a sustainability director Hillary Mizia who noted, "We're closing energy loops. That's the principal behind everything we do."[4]

New Belgium was the first brewery, among both major players and Craft, within the US to become entirely wind-powered. In 2006, it was also still the brewery with the largest wind consumption in the country.[5] This use of wind power saved 3,000 tons of coal from being burned, thus reducing CO_2 emissions by some 5,700 tons. This, however, is one of the few energy initiatives that failed to provide an economic return because of the premium of around 1 cent per kilowatt (2006) that New Belgium paid for receiving wind-powered versus standard power energy.[6] "Our efficiency projects have to make good business sense," said Hillary Mizia, New Belgium's sustainability outreach coordinator. "The social and environmental impacts are as important as the financial impact, but the financial impact is what keeps us in business."[7]

New Belgium treated its windows with low-emission glaze that reflected heat rays from sunlight to reduce heat during the summer, thereby requiring less air conditioning. The windows were retrofitted with light shelves that were made of perforated metal and painted white, similar to a window sill. The windows were retrofitted on the south-facing side to provide up to 50% additional daylight into a space, thus reducing energy needs for lighting.[8] Lastly, additional modifications were made to reduce energy costs further. This included windows that opened automatically to cool rooms, and motion-sensor lights to ensure that lights were on only when a room was in use. Through these actions, New Belgium reduced its energy consumption by 40% (compared to the average American brewer), per barrel of beer.[9] New Belgium's attempt to build a green roof to reduce energy expenditures further was not as successful; but that made Kim even more determined. "It's a gratifying way to use money, to try and push the envelope and the practice of alternative energy," she said. "It's our goal to completely close that loop, so all our energy use comes from our own waste stream."[10]

The third initiative was the purchase of a $5 million system that collected methane from brewing wastewater and used it to fire a 290-kilowatt electric generator (Exhibit 7.2). When the generator was running, for an average of 10–15 hours a day, it created up to 60% of the brewery's power. This amounted to savings of $2,500–3,000 a month. New Belgium Brewery also conserved electricity by capturing the heat created by brewing tanks and piping it back to heat water.[11] Renewable heating and cooling systems such as steam stack heat exchangers were also utilized. By treating its own wastewater, the company was able to reduce the load on the city's facilities. By recovering energy in the form of biogas and reusing water in nonbrewing processes, they were also able to create processes that support holistic sustainability. In 2006, New Belgium used 4.75 liters of water for every liter of beer brewed (there are 119 liters per barrel, which is the standard measure of beer sales).[12] These 4.75 liters were far less than the industry standard of 20 liters. New Belgium's goal was to reduce its usage down to 3 liters. The combination of reduced water consumption and the generator system created the largest savings by assisting New Belgium to avoid steep fees that would be assessed by Fort Collins to treat the brewery's nutrient rich wastewater. It would have cost the firm $4.43 million to build a system that would reprocess the used water before releasing it into the public water system, as required by local laws.

Exhibit 7.2 Cost Implications of Generator Purchase

Cost of new water treatment facility	$5,000,000
Estimated cost of discharge water treatment facility	$4,430,000
Electricity costs	
Energy use charge	$0.0164 per kWh
Fixed demand charge	$4.31 per kWh
Coincident peak demand charge	$11.62 per kWh (plus other misc.)
Estimated electricity savings per month	$2,500–3,000
Water costs	
Cost of water per gallon—Denver, CO	$0.001
Liters per gallon	3.79
Liters in a barrel of beer	119
New Belgium—liters of water per liter of beer produced	4.75
Industry average—liters of water used per barrel of beer produced	20
New Belgium—estimated barrels of beer produced per year	330,000

Ownership

New Belgium was a privately held company that allowed its employees to take shares in the company and serve as employee-owners. The company had, on average, an employee ownership of 32% and employees enjoyed equal voting rights on all company issues.[13]

The firm's books were opened to employees, consistent with "trust and mutual responsibility."[14] Private ownership also enabled New Belgium to keep its strategies, company data, performance figures, etc., from complete public disclosure. In 2006, the firm had no public debt outstanding. The collective employee culture extended beyond ownership with additional perks to increase morale. Employees were provided with generous benefits including health, dental, and retirement plans. Lunch was free to employees, every other week. Employees were also entitled to a free massage (at a salon) every year. Kim and Jeff encouraged employees to bring their children and even dogs to work. And those employees that had been with the company for over five years were given an all expenses-paid trip to Belgium to understand "Beer Culture". Employees from all departments within the organization were also given roles on the Philanthropy Committee which decided how to spend the company's social and charitable fund (see Philanthropy section for more information). Lastly, New Belgium enjoyed a fairly decentralized management structure that enabled employees to be readily involved. Employees were also encouraged to understand, guide, and take responsibility for corporate decision-making.

Philanthropy

New Belgium gaves $1 of every barrel of beer sold to local causes such as care for kids with learning and developmental disabilities.[15] From its inception to 2006, New Belgium Brewing had donated more than $1.6 million to local charitable organizations in the communities where the company did business. The donations were divided between States in proportion to their percentage of overall sales.[16]

Funding decisions were made by the Philanthropy Committee, made up of owners, employee owners, area leaders, and production workers. New Belgium targeted nonprofit organizations that demonstrated creativity, diversity, and an innovative approach to their mission and objectives. The Philanthropy committee also looked for groups that involved the community in reaching their goals. Past recipients included Volunteers for Outdoor Colorado and The Larimer County Search & Rescue team, as seen in these photos.

Marketing

Like most craft beer makers, New Belgium spent twice as much per barrel on advertising as non-craft beer makers. The primary focus was to highlight "experience" and awareness of taste and brand. With "Fat Tire" being the flagship product and with a clear idea of the core values, Kim moved forward in bringing the positioning to life with a statement that appeared on all New Belgium product packaging:

> "In this box is our labor of love. We feel incredibly lucky to be creating something fine that enhances people's lives. Know that we think about you as we're making it- enjoying Trippel by the fire, splitting Fat Tire with a friend, offering Abbey Ale as a present. Enjoy! And stop by to let us know how it was. We'd love to see you!"

Kim's success in bringing New Belgium's character to life could be seen not only through beer aficionados' avid enjoyment of the product, but more importantly through the alignment of brand champions/evangelists/ambassadors with the products and company.[17] As noted by just one set of evangelists on numerous beer aficionado targeted sites:

> Ever since we tried this beer it has been THE favorite. (We even had it kegged in for our wedding . . .) Keep bugging your local merchants to get it in their stores, it really deserves more shelf space. And thank goodness Coors lost.[18]
> (Shannon and Adam, October 10, 2005 [in reference to the Abby product])

The sentiments of these consumers highlighted their passion for New Belgium and furthermore, an understanding of the competitive environment in which their products competed. The call to action by other loyalists by rallying and demanding for higher distribution showed the alignment Kim had sought to achieve between her customers and New Belgium.

Future for New Belgium

Kim Jordan and Jeff Lebesch had grown their company into the third-largest American craft beer maker in 2006 (after Sierra Nevada and Sam Adams). They had grown their employee base to more than 260 employees.[19] Sales had grown to more than 330,000 barrels, and New Belgium was now the fastest-growing craft brewer in the U.S. Annual revenues had exceeded $70 million—with its corporate soul intact.[20] As Kim and Jeff looked to the future, they could not help but wonder what more they could do for their community and New Belgium, while still staying true to their core values.

Chapter 8

Botox: How Long Would the Smile Last?

The Allergan board member listened attentively to the words of a competitor to Botox—the popular drug used to treat facial wrinkles and a lot more. This was nothing to smile about. The drug had not had much competition in the USA since FDA approval on April 15, 2002; but there appeared to be competition on the horizon—enough to frown at. In 2008, *Reloxin*, another wrinkle remover with similar chemical composition to Botox, was rumored to be near FDA approval. Why had Botox done so well for Allergan all these years? Had it been only because of its monopoly position in the USA? Could the advantage be sustained?

Botox

Botulinum toxin A—*Botox* for short—is perhaps best known for its ability to reduce wrinkles when injected in diluted form under wrinkled skin. It works by stopping nerves from making muscles move for months at a time—it effectively paralyzes the area into which it is injected. Because of this paralyzing ability, Botox could be deadly if administered to the wrong muscles. The rise of Botox to a popular drug is a textbook case of innovation through serendipity. Botulinum toxin A was first used in humans by pioneer Doctor Alan Scott to treat twitching and crossed eyes in 1977.[1] While she was using the toxin to treat eye twitches, Dr Jean Carruthers, a Canadian ophthalmologist, noticed that those of her patients to whom she had administered the drug looked more relaxed. She and her dermatologist husband Dr Alastair Carruthers investigated this potential new application some more and published their findings on how to use the toxin to treat face wrinkles in 1989.[2] As more and more dermatologists used the drug to treat wrinkles, they found out that a large percentage of their patients who had had migraines before stopped having the migraines after injection of the toxin. Different medical specialists and Allergan would go on to find more applications for the drug.

Botox was first approved by the FDA in 1989 for use to treat eye-muscle disorders (crossed eyes) and that approval expanded in December 2000 to treat cervical dystonia, a neurological disorder that causes severe shoulder and neck contractions.[3] It received FDA approval on April 15, 2002 for use to reduce or eliminate frown lines or wrinkles between eyebrows. This approval meant that Allergan could advertise Botox's cosmetic benefits directly to consumers and doctors in the USA. (In the USA, doctors could use a drug before it was approved by the FDA, in so-called "off-label uses;" but firms could not market unapproved benefits. In fact, in 2000, two years before FDA approval, more than one million faces had been smoothened with Botox.)[4]

Used as a wrinkle fighter, Botox produced results within minutes, but wore off after about six months. The procedure required no anesthesia and the patient could return to work or other activity the same day. In some rare cases, the patient had to go back to get a few areas filled out. Contrast this with cosmetic surgery that required anesthesia, time to recover and see results, and the risks associated with surgery.

As its name—Botulinum toxin A—reminds scientists, Botox is a biological substance derived from the bacterium Clostridium botulinum, the bacterium that can produce deadly botulism. If consumed in contaminated food the bacterial toxin can paralyze and kill.[5] Botulinum toxin A is but one of seven neurotoxins produced by the bacterium, and the process of growing and isolating Botox is difficult and risky. Allergan could not patent the process but protected it by keeping it proprietary.[6] Pharmaceutical firms often patented their chemical compounds to protect them from competitors; but that also meant that when the patent protection expired, generic versions of the drug could be produced by competitors.

Marketing Botox

With FDA approval in 2002 for use in fighting frown lines, Allergan could now market it as such. It launched a $50 million marketing campaign.[7] (US pharmaceutical firms spend twice as much on marketing as on R&D, on average.) In 2002, it was estimated that a vial of Botox cost Allergan $40 to make and it sold it to doctors for $400.[8] Each vial contained 100 units, enough for 4–5 treatments. In 2002, estimates of how much a doctor could charge patients for administering the one vial ranged from $1,600 to $2,800.[9] Sales of Botox increased steadily and in 2008, it was expected to fetch $1.38 billion in revenues. Pyott, Allergan's CEO, was quoted in 2006 as saying, "To sell $830 million of this stuff, you need less than one gram [of the active ingredient]."[10] Pyott attributed some of Botox's success to the fact that vanity was "a global need."[11]

Although Botox's 2002 FDA approval was only for use in improving frown lines between eyebrows, many doctors used it to smooth horizontal lines in the forehead, shape the jaw and sides of the face, widen the eyes to produce a more rounded look, lift the brow and shape eyebrows, treat crows feet, mouth frown, dimple chins, lines on the neck, and other cosmetic areas.[12] The results of many of these applications were enhanced when the procedures were complemented by other procedures such as laser resurfacing. In addition to these cosmetic applications, Botox had other nonvanity applications.[13] It was used by physicians to treat back pain in some patients who did not respond well to traditional pain medication, treat migraine and tension headaches, excessive sweating (hyperhirosis), and bladder problems (incontinence). In Canada, it was approved for frown lines, crossed eyes, eye and facial spasm, wry neck, foot deformity, spasticity, and excessive sweating.

Competitors

Botox faced two kinds of competition. First, it was taking on established competitors in each of the different markets that Allergan hoped to invade. In the face wrinkles market, it was wrestling away market share from those surgeons that performed facelifts, eyelid surgery, and other face procedures.[14] Then there were less invasive procedures such as chemical peel and laser skin resurfacing. More menacing was the impending approval of another botulinum toxin type-A compound, with trademark name *Reloxin*. Reloxin had been developed in Canada by Ipsen, Inc., but in 2006 Medicis, a US specialist pharmaceutical firm, had entered an agreement with Ipsen to develop, distribute, and commercialize Reloxin in Canada, Japan, and the USA.[15] If and when the drug received FDA approval, Medicis would pay Ipsen $25 million. By October 2007, Reloxin had been approved in 21 countries for aesthetic use, but approval in Japan, Canada, and the USA had not yet been received. On December 6, 2007, Ipsen and Medicis announced that an application for FDA approval for aesthetic indication had been submitted.

Cosmetic Procedures Market

Cosmetic surgery used to be frowned upon but by the 2000s it had become so popular that people used to have Botox parties to discuss their latest procedures or the ones they intended to undertake soon. The average age of people who wanted to look younger was dropping. In 2008, according to WebMD, the most popular cosmetic procedures were liposuction, eyelid surgery, breast implants, nose jobs, facelifts, and Botox injections.[16] Others included breast lifts, tummy tucks, spider veins, and skin resurfacing. The fees for some of these procedures are shown in Exhibit 8.1.

Exhibit 8.1 2008 Plastic Surgery Fees

Procedure	Fees	Average fees
Breast augmentation	5,000–7,000	Surgeons fee: $3,050 Anesthesiologist: $700 Facility fee: $950 Implant fee: $1,300 Average total cost : $6,000
Breast lift	4,000–9,000	Surgeons fee: $3,500 Anesthesiologist: $700 Facility fee: $1000 Average total cost: $5,200
Breast reduction	5,000–10,000	Surgeons fee: $3,500 Anesthesiologist: $700 Facility fee: $1000 Average total cost: $5,200
Eyelid surgery	1,500–7,000	Surgeons fee: $2,500 Anesthesiologist: $700 Facility fee: $800 Average total cost: Upper and lower lids $4,000

(Continued overleaf)

Exhibit 8.1 Continued

Procedure	Fees	Average fees
Facelift	6,000–12,000	Surgeons fee: $5,000 Anesthesiologist: $1,200 Facility fee: $1,700 Hospital fee: $600 Average total cost: $8,500
Lip enhancement	300–5,000	Cost per procedure: collagen injection $333 Lip augmentation (other than injectable materials) $1,570 Surgeons fee: $1,600 Facility fee: $400 Average total cost: $2,000
Liposuction	2,000–10,000	Surgeons fee: $2,000 Anesthesiologist: $500 Facility fee: $700 Average total cost: (One Area) $3,500
Male breast reduction	6,000–9,000	Surgeons fee: $2,500 Anesthesiologist: $700 Facility fee: $1000 Average total cost: $5,200
Rhinoplasty	3,000–12,000	Surgeons fee: $3,000 Anesthesiologist: $700 Facility fee: $800 Average total cost: $4,500
Tummy tuck	5,000–9,000	Surgeons fee: $4,200 Anesthesiologist: $500 Facility fee: $700 Average total cost: $6,400

Source: Plastic surgery research information. Retrieved July 19, 2008, from: http://www.cosmeticplasticsurgery statistics.com/costs.html.

Allergan

Although with a market capitalization of $16 billion on July 17, 2008, Allergan was nothing compared to Silicon Valley's behemoths such as Intel ($128 billion), Google ($167 billion), eBay ($31.6 billion), Cisco ($128.5 billion), and Oracle ($108 billion), it was Orange County, California's largest firm and the pride of Southern California. In 2007, Allergan had net profits of $499 million on net product sales of $3.88 billion (Exhibit 8.2). Some $1.212 billion of the sales came from Botox, which grew 23% over 2006.[17] The growth was faster outside the USA where there was more competition. A third of its sales were international. Allergan claimed to have an 85% cosmetic market share in five European countries where Reloxin was being marketed under the brand name Dysport by Paris-based Ipsen.[18] As shown in Exhibit 8.2, Allergan had two divisions: Specialty Pharmaceuticals, and Medical Devices. Selected products from each of these divisions are shown in Exhibit 8.3. One of these products,

Exhibit 8.2 Allergan's Product Areas

(In $ million)	Year				
Product area	2007	2006	2005	2004	2003
Specialty pharmaceuticals					
Eye care pharmaceuticals	$1,776.5	$1,530.6	$1,321.7	$1,137.1	$999.5
Botox/neuromodulator	1,211.8	982.2	830.9	705.1	563.9
Skin care	110.7	125.7	120.2	103.4	109.3
Urologics	6.0				
Subtotal pharmaceuticals	3,105.0	2,638.5	2,272.8	1,945.6	1,672.7
Other (primary contract sales)			46.4	100.0	82.7
Total specialty pharmaceuticals	3,105.0	2,638.5	2,319.2	2,045.6	1,755.4
Medical devices					
Breast aesthetics	298.4	177.2			
Obesity intervention	270.1	142.3			
Facial aesthetics	202.8	52.1			
Core medical devices	771.3	371.6			
Other	2.7				
Total medical devices	774.0	371.6			
Total product net sales	$3,879.0	$3,010.1	$2,319.2	$2,045.6	$1,755.4

Source: Allergan Inc. 2007 Annual Financial Statement. Retrieved July 18, 2008, from http://files.shareholder.com/downloads/AGN/362148606x0x184012/BB8ED2E7-30CF-443D-A2F7-0935FE134F78/2007AnnualReport.pdf.

Exhibit 8.3 Allergan's Products in 2008

Specialty pharmaceuticals	Medical devices

1. Eye care
   a. Acular (allergic conjunctivitis)
   b. Alocril (allergic conjunctivitis)
   c. Alphagan (glaucoma)
   d. Combigan (glaucoma, ocular hypertension)
   e. Elestat (allergic conjunctivitis)
   f. Exocin (ophthalmic anti-infective)
   g. Ganfort (glaucoma)
   h. Lumigan (glaucoma)
   i. Ocuflox (ophthalmic anti-infective)
   j. Oflox (ophthalmic anti-infective)
   k. Pred Forte (opthalmic anti-inflammatory)
   l. Restatis (chronic dry eye disease)
   m. Zymar (bacterial conjunctivitis)
2. Neuromodulator
   a. Botox (neuromuscular disorder treatment)
   b. Botox cosmetic (wrinkle reduction)

1. Breast aesthetics
   a. CUI (implants)
   b. Inspira (implants)
   c. McGhan (implants)
   d. Natrelle (implants)
   e. Tissue expanders
2. Obesity intervention
   a. BIB System (stomach implant)
   b. Lap-Band (stomach implant)
3. Facial aesthetics
   a. CosmoDerm and CosmoPlast (dermal filler)
   b. Juvederm (dermal fillers)
   c. Zyderm and Zyplast (dermal fillers)

(Continued overleaf)

Exhibit 8.3 Continued

Specialty pharmaceuticals	*Medical devices*

3. Skin Care
    a. Avage (skin wrinkles or discoloration)
    b. Azelex (acne treatment)
    c. Finacea (rosacea)
    d. M.D. Forte (line of alpha hydroxy acid
        products)
    e. Prevage (skin lines or wrinkles and
        protection)
    f. Tazorac (treatment for acne and psoriasis)
    g. Vivite (anti-aging)
4. Urologics
    a. Sanctura (overactive bladder)

Source: Hoovers. Retrieved July 19, 2008, from *http://0-premium.hoovers.com.lib.bus.umich.edu:80/subscribe/col ops.xhtml?ID=ffffrffhsrccksjcsk*

dermal fillers, was of particular interest when planning for Botox. Dermal fillers were injectible products that were designed to restore the youthful firmness to tissue that had gradually broken down with age.

Looking Forward

The board member realized that he would need to do more research to understand more about Allergan's business model before the next board meeting.[19] The good old days when board members used to show up to board meetings and rubberstamp everything that management wanted were gone. He could not afford to look bad when asking questions at the next meeting. What should Allergan's next steps for Botox be?

Case 9

IKEA Lands in the New World

Who was the richest European in 2008? Ingvar Kamprad, the Swedish founder of IKEA.[1] In fact, according to the Swedish business magazine *Veckans Affarer*, Ingvar Kamprad's net worth in 2004 was $53 billion, making him the richest person in the *world*, ahead of Bill Gates ($47 billion) and Warren Buffet ($43 billion).[2] Poor Bill! Poor Warren! In any case, a look at IKEA's activities, especially in the USA, can give us some idea why the firm made its founder one of the richest people in the world.

In 2007, IKEA had revenues of €19.8 billion and 522 million customers visited an IKEA store some time during the year (Exhibit 9.1).[3] The firm had net margins of 10%, considered by analysts to be very good for a home furnishings firm. According to IKEA's CEO, Anders Dahlvig in 2005, awareness of the IKEA brand was "much bigger than the size of" IKEA.[4]

Opening of a New Store

For many customers, the IKEA experience started with the activities that lead up to the opening of an IKEA store. When the Edmonton store in north London, UK's largest IKEA store, opened its doors on February 10, 2005, the

Exhibit 9.1 IKEA Sales
By year

Year	Sales (€)
2007	19.8
2006	17.8
2005	14.8

By region in 2007

Region	Share (%)
Asia and Australia	3
North America	15
Europe	82

Source: Retrieved June 24, 2008, from http://www.ikea.com/ms/en_US/about_ikea_new/facts_figures/index.html.

discounts offered by the store and the pre-opening hype attracted 5,000–6,000 visitors. The rush to get into the store resulted in casualties and the store was forced to close temporarily after only 30 minutes.[5] Over 2,000 IKEA fanatics camped outside the new Atlanta, GA store seven days before the opening, some hoping to win one of the prizes for the first 100 people in line. The enthusiasm shown in these two cases was typical of most IKEA store openings. The local press and media picked up on the stories, arousing even more interest in IKEA.

Inside the Store

IKEA stores were located outside city centers where there was plenty of parking. In 2006, it cost $66 million, on average, to open a new store.[6] Blue-and-yellow Sweedish colors adorned the outside of each huge building—measuring an average 300,000 square feet. A daycare center allowed shoppers to drop off their kids and shop. The inside of the store was designed around a "one-way" layout to make it easy for customers to see all the products and displays. This layout contrasted with the layout of traditional US furniture stores where the inside was laid out so that a customer could go straight to what he or she was looking for. But IKEA's line of products and displays were such that many customers enjoyed the experience of going through the long one-way, picking up a bargain every so often. Of course, there were shortcuts to the displays in which one might be interested. The goal of the layout, furniture samples, displays, sample rooms, and atmosphere was to delight the customer with the shopping environment, ideas, and the IKEA experience. Located at about the center of most stores was a restaurant for shoppers to take a break from shopping and enjoy some Scandinavian or local food, before continuing with shopping. Customers who needed help with service could look for someone to help them. Those who bought furniture took it home themselves and assembled it.

Product Design, Development, Distribution, and Supply

"Designing beautiful-but-expensive products is easy. Designing beautiful products that are inexpensive and functional is a huge challenge,"[7] said Josephine Rydberg-Dumont in 2005, president of IKEA of Sweden. In 2005, IKEA had 16 in-house designers from eight different countries, and 70 freelancers from all over the world.[8] The job of these designers was not only to come up with inspiring designs—contemporary or otherwise—but to work with in-house production teams to identify the most suitable materials and lowest cost suppliers. In 2008, IKEA had 1,350 suppliers in 50 countries from which to choose (Exhibits 9.2).[9] The firm served these suppliers from its 45 trading service offices in 31 countries. It pioneered flat-pack designs so that furniture could be packed and distributed to stores, or carried home with as little inconvenience as possible. Shipping assembled furniture was regarded by IKEA as a big waste of money since one was effectively paying to ship pockets of air. Using these flat packs, supplies were transported to its 31 distribution centers in 16 countries, and distributed to its 232 stores in 24 countries.[10] Furniture was not designed to be as durable as that available in high-end furniture stores.

Exhibit 9.2 Purchasing
By region in 2007

Region	Share (%)
Asia and Australia	3
North America	33
Europe	64

By top purchasing countries in 2007

Country	Share (%)
China	22
Poland	16
Italy	8
Sweden	6
Germany	6

Source: Retrieved June 24, 2008, from http://
www.ikea.com/ms/en_US/about_ikea_new/facts_figures/
index.html.

Marketing

IKEA appeared to have made a connection with the global middle class, with low budgets who were not quite sure about what furniture to buy before going to IKEA for the first time. IKEA's layout and displays suggested what these not-so-experienced furniture buyers could buy to fit their emerging lifestyles at a manageable budget. While it had developed a cult-like following, there were still some people who were not as crazy about having to truck home furniture and assemble it—themselves. IKEA appeared to have built a global brand and following. In the USA, some of these followers could drive for as many as ten hours to get to an IKEA store. They eye-shopped online or used IKEA's catalog, of which, there were plenty. In 2007, more than 191 million copies of the catalog were printed in 56 editions and 27 languages, more than copies of the bible. About a third of IKEA's product line was replaced every year.[11] The top five sales countries were Germany (16%), USA (10%), UK (9%), France (9%), and Sweden (7%) (Exhibit 9.3).

Exhibit 9.3 Top Sales Countries in 2007

Country	Share (%)
Germany	16
USA	10
UK	9
France	9
Sweden	7

Source: http://www.ikea.com/ms/en_US/about_ikea_
new/facts_figures/index.html: Accessed: June 24, 2008.

IKEA Culture

Many of the values that underpinned the IKEA culture appeared to have come from founder Kamprad's thrifty, hard-working, value-for-the-buck mentality. No one was too important for any job. For example, during the company's Antibureaucracy Week, CEO Dahvig would be "unloading trucks, and selling beds and mattresses."[12] Wastefulness was considered a sin. Flying first class was considered unusual.

US Furniture Market

The highly fragmented US furniture market could be divided into low-end and high-end. The high-end market was exemplified by firms such as Ethan Allen that had large selections of furniture, superior in-store service, high quality furniture, classy environment, and financing, but carried a high price tag to match. These firms would customize your furniture for you, deliver your furniture to your house, install it, and even take away old unwanted furniture. Sales staff took the time to explain everything about the furniture from the fabric to the origins of the wood, and how durable the furniture was guaranteed to last— often longer than the customer's marriage or lifetime. They did not carry the many other products that IKEA carried, choosing to focus on furniture and few other furnishings. The low-end was exemplified by Wal-Mart, where the cost was lower than that at the high-end but with limited selection, quality, and service to match. The shopping atmosphere was not as flattering.

IKEA in the New World

In 2008, IKEA USA was doing very well; but things had not always been that way. IKEA opened its first US store in 1985, just outside Philadelphia. In the years that followed, it would open more stores in the USA and make some classic mistakes before correcting them. According to a former IKEA US employee, "we got our clocks cleaned in the early 1990s because we really didn't listen to the consumer,"[13] IKEA managers did not do their homework well and chose the wrong locations for many stores, their stores were too small, and their prices too high. Their beds were measured in metric units rather than the familiar American twin, queen, and king. Sofas were not deep enough, and so on. IKEA learnt its lessons and corrected its mistakes.

IKEA's Corporate Structure and Holdings: Where the Money Goes

In 2008, each IKEA store was owned by a franchisee. The largest of these franchisees was Ingka Holding, a Dutch-registered private company. In 2004, Ingka Holding operated 207 of the 235 IKEA stores (Exhibit 9.4).[14] In the year that ended in August of 2004, the Ingka Holding group had profits of €1.4 billion on sales of €12.8 billion. The remaining 28 stores were owned by a collection of other private franchisees (Exhibit 9.4). Each store paid a royalty of 3% of sales to Inter IKEA Systems, another Dutch-registered private company. Finally, Ingka Holding was itself wholly owned by Stichting Ingka Foundation, a Dutch-registered, tax-exempt, nonprofit legal entity.

Exhibit 9.4 Where the Money Goes

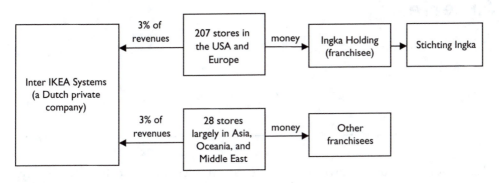

IKEA: A Global Leader?

In 2008, some academics enjoyed arguing about *whether* and *why* IKEA had become a world darling, making its founder one of the richest people in the world. Those who believed that the company was successful attributed the success to some subset of the firm's low cost offerings, designs-with-meaning, brand, store experience, its world-wide sourcing network, company culture, or growing worldwide community. Some were intrigued by what exactly Kamprad had done to become so rich selling one of the most ancient products—furniture.

Study Questions

1 Why has IKEA been so successful and what have new games to do with it?
2 What type of strategy is IKEA pursuing: global adventurer, global generic, global heavyweight, or global star?
3 What have new games had to do with Inkvar Kamprad being very rich?
4 What is new game about IKEA's structure?

Esperion: Drano for Your Arteries?*

$1.3 billion. Dr Roger Newton sat in his car after leaving the office for the day, and paused before turning the ignition and heading home. It was late November in 2003, and Esperion Therapeutics, the company Dr. Newton founded, had just received an offer from Pfizer to buy the company for $1.3 billion. He smiled a little, remembering several years earlier when he was recognized by Warner–Lambert (which was later purchased by Pfizer) for developing the world's most successful drug—Lipitor. Along with the award, Dr Newton was provided with a cash prize: $20,000. Times had certainly changed, and the award for guiding Esperion through the development of several novel cardiovascular compounds had obviously grown significantly. Dr Newton and his team invested time, money, and a great deal of thought and effort into Esperion, and while the financial offer from Pfizer was significant, he worried whether now was the right time to be acquired.

Esperion had just announced very positive clinical data for its lead candidate, and its novel method of addressing high cholesterol was generating interest in both the scientific and business communities. Was now the right time to sell, or should Esperion push on and build itself into a fully-integrated biotech company? Was Pfizer the right suitor, or was there another company which could better help continue Esperion's success? What would happen to Esperion if it was acquired—to the people who had founded and built the company, and developed the molecules so highly regarded today? Dr Newton turned his key and pulled out of Esperion's parking lot. He had several weeks to evaluate Pfizer's offer, and would need the time to think fully through his options.

Cholesterol

Cholesterol is a natural substance used in the body for a variety of purposes from cell membrane formation to the makeup of hormones. The liver makes most of the cholesterol a person needs; however, it is also found in many foods and is an inherent part of many diets. Cholesterol levels result from both genetic and dietetic influences. While genetic influences are beyond an individual's control, lifestyle choices that are marked by fatty foods and a lack of exercise serve to increase cholesterol levels for many people.

* This case was written by Brian Levy, Melissa Vasilev, Jess Rosenbloom, Scott Peterson, and Patrick Lyon under the supervision of Professor Allan Afuah as a basis for class discussion and is not intended to illustrate either effective or ineffective handling of a business situation.

Cholesterol is transported through the bloodstream when it is coupled with special carriers called lipoproteins. Low-density lipoprotein (LDL), often referred to as "bad" cholesterol, transports cholesterol from the liver to the body's cells for use. High-density lipoprotein (HDL), often referred to as "good" cholesterol, removes cholesterol and other lipids (fats) from arterial walls and other tissues, transporting them to the liver where they are eliminated from the body.

Complications from Cholesterol

Excessive levels of LDL can lead to the build-up of cholesterol and other fats in the walls of arteries, a condition known as atherosclerosis, causing a progressive narrowing of arterial walls. If unchecked, these deposits can eventually form a plaque. If a plaque ruptures and a clot forms, potentially blocking an artery, a heart attack can result. A heart attack may also result if excessive amounts of plaque form in the arteries that deliver blood to the heart, known as coronary arteries, slowly starving the heart muscle of oxygen needed to function. This set of complications is also known collectively as coronary artery disease and is the number one cause of death in the USA (Exhibit 10.1).

High LDL also increases the chances of stroke. Like dislodged plaque blocking a coronary artery of the heart, if a clot cuts blood flow to the brain, serious nervous system damage or even death may occur. Further, increased blood pressure from high LDL also poses the risk that sensitive arteries near the brain may burst, resulting in nervous system damage or death.

Treatment Options

To treat high LDL levels and reduce the likelihood of the associated health risks doctors had several options at their disposal. Base recommendations always included diets that were low in saturated fat and an increase in physical exercise. However, lifestyle changes alone were rarely enough to reduce more elevated patient LDL levels. Physicians often chose from the following options to reduce further the risks posed by cholesterol:

Pharmaceuticals (statins)—If LDL levels had not dropped enough after 6–12 months of lifestyle changes, physicians recommended a drug called a

Exhibit 10.1 Selected Disease Statistics—USA 2003

People who have one or more forms of cardiovascular disease (CVD)	71,300,000
High blood pressure	65,000,000
Coronary artery disease	13,200,000
Myocardial infarction (heart attack)	7,200,000
Angina pectoris (chest pain)	6,500,000
Stroke	5,500,000
Deaths from cardiovascular disease	910,614
Deaths from coronary artery disease	479,305
Deaths from cancer (all types)	554,642
Deaths from accidents	105,695

Source: Cardiovascular Disease Statistics, 2003—American Heart Association.

statin that works to reduce LDL levels. Statins interfere with the liver's ability to produce cholesterol and, depending on the particular patient, some statins may actually serve to increase HDL production slightly.

Angioplasty—For patients with more advanced and potentially acute atherosclerosis, a doctor may have elected for an invasive solution to counter the effects of plaque in arteries. An angioplasty is a surgical procedure in which a surgeon inserts a small tube or balloon at the spot of arterial blockage. The balloon is inflated, expanding the artery allowing for greater blood flow.

Stents—If an angioplasty was carried out on coronary arteries, standard procedure included the placing of a stent. A stent is a small metal scaffold that expands and supports the arterial wall to allow for greater blood flow. Stents are left in the patient after the angioplasty procedure to ensure greater long-term blood flow. Some stents, called drug-eluting stents, are coated with specialized pharmaceutical compounds to prevent future blockages, a condition known as restenosis.

The Cardiovascular Drug Market

The cholesterol drug market in 2003 was the world's largest pharmaceutical market, generating $17 billion annually and expected to grow at a 5% compound annual growth rate (CAGR) through 2010.[1] While the market was comprised of three therapeutic classes—statins, resins, and fibrates—the statin class dominated treatment, comprising 90% of dollar volume. Within the statin market, an oligopoly competed fiercely: Pfizer, Bristol-Meyers Squibb, and Merck promoted Lipitor, Pravachol, and Zocor against each other, generating $8 billion, $2.2 billion, and $5.5 billion, respectively.[2] With each drug having a similar efficacy and safety profile, companies utilized their significant cardiovascular experience to apply large sales forces, high marketing spend, and exhaustive post-approval clinical trial strategies to differentiate drugs to cardiologists.

While heavy market development was helping to expand the hypolipemic market, several additional characteristics were expected to contribute to the market's growth. Recent updates to treatment guidelines encouraged physicians to pursue lower target lipid levels in their patients, causing upward titration in statin dosage. Additionally, the first combination product—Zetia—had recently been launched, offering a complementary treatment to be added to ongoing statin use to increase efficacy (raising the overall cost of treatment), and additional combination treatments were expected. Lastly, patient demographics were expected to contribute to growing the incidence of cardiovascular diseases worldwide: aging populations, and increasingly unhealthy eating habits, in the USA and Europe were driving the overall number of possible patients significantly.[3]

While patient populations and new therapeutic guidelines were expanding the hypolipemic market, two issues did threaten the market's growth. Zocor, Pravachol, and Lipitor all faced patent expiry by 2010, and the entrance of generic forms of these drugs (typically at 10–20% of branded patent prices) would erode branded sales of these drugs significantly. Additionally, patient compliance with statin regimens was a continuing issue. Because statins were prescribed as a preventative measure (prior to a heart attack or other major health event), patients often did not recognize the importance these drugs played in continuing their health—they often did not adhere to the recommended treatment frequency that physicians recommended, adversely affecting sales.

The Pharmaceutical Development Process

With several well-entrenched, well-performing statins already on the market in 2003, few statins were in trials or expected to be developed in the future.[4] Instead, new classes of drug were being developed either to complement or improve upon the treatment success of the statins. New molecules in development faced tremendous difficulty reaching the market, however, due to significant regulatory and financial requirements (Exhibit 10.2).

Financial requirements for pharmaceutical research and development are extremely high, with research costs for each new approved drug compound reaching as high as $850 billion. Additionally, once the decision to pursue a

Exhibit 10.2 Drug Development Process

The Food and Drug Administration (FDA) regulates drug development and requires progression through testing stages to ensure the safety and efficacy of potential drugs.

- *Drug Discovery* is the first step in development, and is conducted in order to test a potential molecule's effect on a disease target *ex vivo* (not in a live subject). Once a basic understanding of a disease is established, scientists will screen thousands of compounds in order to determine one or several "lead" compounds which seem to have an effect on the disease mechanism and which warrant testing in vivo (in a live subject).

- *Preclinical Studies* are done in animals, to determine the effect of a new molecule on a living organism. Scientists monitor the drug's safety in the animal and also monitor its effect on the target disease, attempting to understand whether the molecule has potential benefit in humans. Preclinical studies typically take 3–6 years.

- *Phase I Studies* typically involve 20–100 healthy volunteers, and are conducted in order to gauge basic characteristics of a potential new drug in humans: how the drug is absorbed, distributed, metabolized and excreted, as well as its pharmacokinetics (how long the drug is active in the body). Phase I studies typically take six months to one year to complete.

- *Phase II Studies* typically involve 100–500 volunteers who have the target disease. In this phase, companies attempt to establish "proof of concept:" that the potential new drug actually has a beneficial effect on its target disease. Scientists monitor the drug's effect on the disease as well as potential side effects, and attempt to determine the appropriate dose for the new drug. Phase II studies typically take six months to one year to complete.

- *Phase III Studies* typically involve 1,000–5,000 sick patients, and are conducted in order to provide statistically significant proof that the potential new drug is effective against its target disease. Physicians monitor patients at regular intervals and test for side effects. Phase III trials can take from one to four years to complete. At the end of Phase III trials, companies will submit a NDA (New Drug Application) to the FDA in order to gain approval to launch and market the drug commercially.

- *Phase IV Studies* are clinical trials required after the drug has been approved (in this case, drugs are often said to have received "conditional approval") in order to provide the FDA with further data regarding the drug or more long-term evidence of its use. Companies are required to fulfill these data requirements, but may do so after launching the drug commercially. Studies can range in both years and expense.

Source: Clinical trials. Retrieved July 22, 2008, from http://en.wikipedia.org/wiki/Clinical_trial.

drug target is made, the probability of passing through each trial and success-fully reaching the market is very small. Of the compounds that are chosen to exit preclinical trials, only 8% will be approved by the FDA (Exhibit 10.3).

The large expenses of drug development, and large risk associated at each trial stage, represent significant decision points for companies engaging in drug development. Because of these factors, alliances between healthcare companies are frequent: small companies with novel compounds often partnered with larger sales and marketing-focused "big pharma" companies to help defray development costs and provide a commercial outlet for drugs. In fact, in the post-bubble year of 2002, biotech companies raised $10.5 billion in financing from venture capital, IPOs, and other financing mechanisms. However, the bio-tech sector pulled an additional $7.5 billion through 411 partnering revenues—representing 42% of all funding for the year and yielding an average of about $18 million per agreement.

Competition

In 2003, there were three major cholesterol drug makers: Merck which pion-eered the statin drug category, Pfizer, and Bristol-Myers Squibb. Pfizer's Lipitor had a 46% share of the market, Merck's Zocor had 32%, Bristol Myers Squibb's Pravachol had 13% and the remaining 9% was split among other statin and nonstatin drugs.[5] The project market for cholesterol drugs for which these firms were vying, a summary of their financials, and their costs of capital are shown in Exhibits 10.4, 10.5, and 10.6, respectively.

Pfizer

Founded in 1849, Pfizer grew to become the world's largest pharmaceutical company. The firm, based in New York, focused on discovering, developing, marketing, and delivering medications for both humans and animals. Pfizer led the statin market with Lipitor, the most popular drug in the world. In addition

Exhibit 10.3 Drug Trial Expenses per Approved Compound

	R&D	Animal	Phase I	Phase II	Phase III	TOTAL
Cost ($ billion)	358.0	12.5	42.9	117.8	325.8	857.0
Time (months)			21.6	38.0	56.5	116.1
Success rate			69%	38%	15%	8% (FDA approval)

Source: Joseph Dimasi, Ronald Hansen, and Henry Grabowski, The price of innovation: new estimates of drug development costs, Journal of Health Economics, 2003. Bain and Co., 2003.

Exhibit 10.4 Total Hypolipemic Market Sales and Expectations

Year	2000	2001	2002	2003E	2004E	2005E	2006E	2007E	2008E	20009E
Revenues ($ million)	13,937	15,830	17,210	19,845	21,990	24,232	25,390	26,725	27,680	29,115

Source: CDC IXIS Securities, Cholesterol: the battle rages on, February 24, 2003

Exhibit 10.5 2002 Select Pharmaceutical Company Financial Information ($000s)

Sales ($)	BMS 18,119	Merck 51,790	Pfizer 32,373
Cogs ($)	6,388	33,054	4,045
Marketing, sales, and admin. ($)	5,218	6,187	10,846
R&D ($)	2,218	2,667	5,176
Other costs ($)	1,648	(331)	510
Total costs($)	15,472	41,577	20,577
Pre-tax income ($)	2,647	10,213	11,796
Taxes ($)	613	3,064	2,609
Net income ($)	2,034	7,149	9,187

Source: Firm 10-Ks.

Exhibit 10.6 Nominal and Real Cost-of-Capital (COC) for the Pharmaceutical Industry, 1985–2000

	1985	1990	1994	2000
Nominal COC (%)	16.1	15.1	14.2	15.0
Inflation Rate (%)	5.4	4.5	3.1	3.1
Real COC (%)	10.8	10.6	11.1	11.9

Source: Dimasi, 2003, Tufts Center for the Study of Drug Development.

to Lipitor, Pfizer's internal development of a cholesterylester transfer protein (CETP) inhibitor called Torcetrapib stood to strengthen the company's hold on the cardiology market. Pfizer focused Phase III studies on the combination of Lipitor and the new Torcetrapib, based on promising Phase II studies. The planned Phase III trials would be the largest for any drug of any type. Torcetrapib was not only one of the most promising drugs in Pfizer's pipeline, but also within the entire spectrum of CETP-inhibitors.[6] Pfizer backed Lipitor and other drugs with the strongest sales and marketing spending in the industry.

Merck

Merck & Co., Inc. (Merck) was a global pharmaceutical company based in New Jersey and founded in 1901. It had two statins on the market: Mevacor and Zocor. Mevacor, launched in 1987, was one of the first statins to be launched. Mevacor experienced tremendous success, which built high expectations for Merck's second-generation statin, Zocor and by 2002, Zocor had replaced sales of Mevacor.[7] Zocor's popularity made it the top-selling drug for Merck and the number two cholesterol medication in the world.[8] Historically, Merck's drug pipeline created numerous successes for the company across several treatment categories, but by 2002, several Phase III setbacks called its pipeline into question. Merck continued to develop promising arthritis and diabetes drugs in its pipeline, but its cardiovascular pipeline was relatively weak.[9] The most promising cardiovascular drug was based on a joint venture between Merck and Schering Plough. They co-developed a combination Zocor–

Zetia drug that they thought might be more effective than Zocor alone through attacking cholesterol from different approaches.[10]

Bristol-Myers Squibb

Bristol-Myers Squibb (BMS), based in New York, was founded in 1914. In 2002, BMS generated $18.1 billion in revenue, 81% of which came from pharmaceuticals.[11] BMS is responsible for the third most successful statin in the world, Pravachol. Pravachol was expected to lose share over the next few years as its patent expired in 2006.[12] Pravachol was expected to be BMS's only cholesterol drug success, given the company's poor drug development track record in recent years. Two new products, Questran and Pravigard Pac, were launched in 2003, although neither was projected to generate significant revenue. A cholestyramine, Questran targeted a nonstatin method of cholesterol reduction, but its market was much smaller than the statins. Pravigard Pac was simply a combination package of Pravachol and aspirin for patients requiring both medications.[13]

Other Competitors

London-based AstraZeneca launched a new statin in 2003, Crestor. On the surface, Crestor appeared to face an already saturated market; however, Crestor also demonstrated that it could be "unquestionably"[14] the most effective statin on the market, including the wildly successful Lipitor. One analyst projected that Crestor could own 30% of the cholesterol drug market within seven years.[15] Such promising potential for Crestor could undermine the current statin oligopoly and drive current players to seek out new cholesterol treatment solutions.

In addition to large pharmaceutical companies, over 35 companies were marketing or developing lipid therapeutics that were in some stage of clinical trials. It is unknown how many additional companies were researching solutions.[16] Most of the new drug development was centered on increasing the amount of HDL through a variety of new avenues, rather than lowering LDL with traditional statins.

Esperion Therapeutics

Company History

Esperion Therapeutics was founded in July 1998 with $16 million in capital provided by four venture capital firms and several undisclosed investors.[17] Based in Ann Arbor, Michigan, the firm focused on conducting large molecule research on cardiovascular drugs with a specific emphasis on cholesterol medication.

The driving force behind Esperion was its President and CEO, Dr. Roger Newton. At the time of Esperion's founding, Newton was already a well-established name in the cardiovascular pharmaceutical industry. Newton was most famous for his work as a lead scientist at Warner-Lambert, where he was instrumental in the development of Lipitor.[18] After his experience developing

Lipitor, Newton spurred the founding of Esperion to drive development further in cholesterol drugs. He was considered one of the leading thinkers in cholesterol therapy.

Esperion made its first significant move only a month after its founding by licensing an HDL-raising drug from Pharmacia called ETC-216.[19] The research behind ETC-216 first appeared in a 30-year old study of a group of rural Italian villagers with surprisingly long life spans. The research uncovered a genetic anomaly in the villagers, forming the basis for ETC-216's development.[20] Once licensed from Pharmacia, the drug provided the cornerstone for Esperion's cholesterol research. The HDL-raising potential of ETC-216 offered a dramatic departure from the statins that target lowering LDL. Backed by the promise of ETC-216 and research on similar HDL-raising drugs (e.g. ETC-588 also showed significant promise), Esperion made an initial public offering in August of 2000. The company raised $58 million despite never having generated a single dollar of revenue.[21] Since its founding, Esperion managed to raise $200 million through venture capital and stock offerings.[22]

Esperion used the money raised in its IPO to drive forward clinical trials of its HDL drugs over the next several years. In June 2003, Esperion announced significant progress in the development of ETC-216. A Phase II clinical study revealed that ETC-216 successfully reduced the heart plaque in study participants. Although the study contained only 47 patients, too few for a statistically meaningful sample, the effectiveness and rapidity of the treatment created a buzz across the pharmaceutical industry.[23] Furthermore, the reputation of Newton in the cholesterol industry continued to grow with ETC-216's success. Esperion's stock price reached a 52-week high after the June announcement.[24]

Challenges

Despite excitement over ETC-216's Phase II clinical trials, Esperion faced a steep uphill battle. Many biopharmaceutical companies with promising early stage clinical trials had faced serious setbacks in later stages.[25] Esperion would not be immune to this statistic.

In addition, Esperion was a new biopharmaceutical firm and did not have the capabilities of its larger competitors. It currently had no way of commercializing its therapies, and therefore, had to rely heavily on the money earned from its IPO as well as venture capital funding to support its clinical trial efforts. If any of Esperion's drugs were capable of making it through clinical trials and earned FDA approval, Esperion did not have the infrastructure to commercialize its product candidates. Esperion would again have to rely on third parties to successfully bring its new drug to market.

Current Pipeline Portfolio

Esperion's pipeline of products looked to replace both statin treatments as well as surgical procedures. According to preliminary results for clinical trials, Esperion's product candidates were able to raise levels of HDL. This fostered the removal of plaque from the artery walls as well as its movement to the liver for expulsion from the body. In addition, there were also signs that the damaged arteries were able to repair themselves. If Esperion could get one of the four products in its pipeline through clinical trials, it could revolutionize the way doctors treated cardiovascular disease.

- *ETC-216 (AIM)*: ETC-216 was being developed as an infused treatment for patients with acute coronary syndrome.[26] The properties of ETC-216 allowed it to mimic naturally-occurring HDL as well as improve HDL's function. Initial preclinical studies as well as Phase I and II clinical trials illustrated positive results for ETC-216 and proved its capabilities. ETC-216 was now poised for Phase III trials. Esperion hoped ETC-216 would be a major success in the industry. As of 1999, there were already 47 drugs in the market with greater than $500 million in US sales.[27]
- *ETC-588 (LUV)*: ETC-588 was also being developed as an infused treatment for acute coronary syndromes.[28] When introduced in the human bloodstream, the biopharmaceutical served as a "sponge" for cholesterol. Preclinical animal studies showed that ETC-588 did remove cholesterol from the arteries and helped arteries regain their flexibility and function. ETC-588 was beginning Phase II trials.
- *ETC-642 (RLT Peptide)*: Esperion continued to develop RLT Peptide for the treatment of acute coronary syndromes.[29] ETC-642 had similar biological properties to ETC-216 and ETC-588 in mimicking HDL, preventing the accumulation of cholesterol on the artery walls. The completion of Phase I trials in the first half of 2002 indicated that RLT Peptide was safe and well-tolerated and several different dose levels. The trials also illustrated evidence of rapid cholesterol mobilization and increased HDL-cholesterol levels.
- *ETC-1001 (HDL Elevating/Lipid Regulating Agents)*: Esperion was "pursuing the discovery and development of oral small organic molecules that could increase HDL-C levels and/or enhance the RLT pathway."[30] Preclinical studies not only showed an increase in HDL-C molecules in animals, but also suggested that these molecules might also have "anti-diabetic and anti-obesity properties." Esperion hoped to file an NDA for ETC-1001 and begin Phase I clinical trials in 2003.

Pfizer Inc. Company Background

Strategic Overview

Pfizer fueled its growth in research and products in three primary ways: internal R&D, mergers and acquisitions, and agreements and alliances. Given this structure, Pfizer had hundreds of subsidiaries throughout the world. Despite pressures to develop drugs at a faster rate than witnessed in recent years, the industry had experienced a significant reduction in M&A activity, from $23 billion in the first half of 2001 to just $3 billion in the second half of 2002. When considering transactions, buyers were becoming more cautious, and started relying more heavily on licensing deals.[31] The actions of Pfizer proved to be exceptions to this rule, as the firm undertook two significant mergers: Warner–Lambert in 2000 (the largest hostile takeover ever) and Pharmacia in 2003. Placing pressure on competitive firms to consolidate, Pfizer boasted the industry's largest pharmaceutical R&D organization with a library of more than 700 major active collaborations and a 2003 R&D budget of $7.1 billion.[32] Pfizer's pipeline acceleration strategy was expressed through the comments of Dr LaMattina, president of Pfizer Global Research and Development:

> Pfizer's strength is its ability to maximize opportunities from our internal programs and through partnerships. Our scale and R&D breadth are obvious advantages that we secure with very strict attention to our goals. Some of our competitors believe the term 'research management' is an oxymoron, but we don't think so at Pfizer. True, it's hard to predict when discoveries will occur. The process can be managed to maximize the chances of discoveries happening . . . Before we closed the acquisition of Pharmacia, we conducted extensive due diligence and understood the value of the pipeline, and the way it complemented the R&D efforts under way at Pfizer. There were very few surprises and we have retained the great majority of projects.[33]

Proper management of acquisitions, combined with links to more than 250 partners in academia and industry, strengthened Pfizer's position on the cutting edge of science by providing access to novel R&D tools and key data on emerging trends.

Marketing

Capitalizing on the US Food and Drug Administration's 1997 decision to loosen restrictions on consumer advertising of prescription medications, Pfizer recruited a new senior media director in 1999 to establish Pfizer's first consumer media unit and form a company approach on how to use the fledgling direct-to-consumer (DTC) medium.[34] Two years later, Pfizer was regarded as being in the front tier in DTC brand building with hits such as Zyrtec and Viagra. By using consumer ads to drive sales of prescription drugs, Pfizer became a major player in the annual TV upfront season. Over the first six months of 2001, Pfizer became the second largest DTC spender with about $76 million.[35]

Manufacturing and Distribution

For decades, the manufacturing component of the pharmaceutical industry had been highly inefficient with manufacturing expenses accounting for 36% of the industry's costs. The top 16 drug companies spent $90 billion on manufacturing in 2001.[36] With inefficiencies resulting in lower quality and product recalls, the FDA updated its manufacturing regulations for the first time in 25 years in 2003. In response, Pfizer applied funding towards manufacturing research and developed a fast and accurate new way to test drugs. This technology was being tested in few of Pfizer's plants around the world.

Pfizer had the distribution capability to launch a product simultaneously in dozens of markets around the world. As of 2000, Pfizer's US sales force consisted of 5,400 representatives in nine divisions. Pfizer's rigorous training and ongoing education programs were unmatched in the industry, yielding best-in-class sales representatives who consistently communicated advances in the understanding and treatment of diseases to millions of health-care providers.[37]

In 2002, Pfizer's pharmaceutical sales organization was placed first overall in a survey of US physicians in nine core specialty groups for the seventh consecutive year.[38]

Pfizer and the Cholesterol Drug Market

Pfizer obtained the rights to the blockbuster drug atorvastatin (Lipitor) after the acquisition of Warner–Lambert in 2000. Prior to the acquisition, Pfizer had entered into a marketing agreement with Warner–Lambert to help successfully launch the drug in 1996.

Warner–Lambert faced a number of setbacks in bringing Lipitor to market. The firm had recently dealt with a series of drug recalls of some of its major products. Furthermore, Warner-Lambert's sales force was much smaller in size relative to its competitors with established cholesterol drugs already in the market. Given these circumstances, the firm signed a comarketing alliance with Pfizer. Pfizer agreed to cover a significant portion of the upfront expenses of launching Lipitor as well as use its extensive networks of sales representatives to bring the drug to market.[39] In exchange, Pfizer would receive payments based on Lipitor's sales targets.

On November 5, 1999, American Home Products Corporation announced a $70 billion dollar merger agreement with Warner-Lambert. Such a deal left a great amount of uncertainty regarding the future status of marketing rights to Lipitor and the alliance between Pfizer and Warner-Lambert. Lipitor's billions in sales represented a large portion of Pfizer's drug sales portfolio. Therefore, before the comarketing alliance came to an end, Pfizer placed its own hostile bid of $82.4 billion for Warner-Lambert. The two companies eventually merged in 2000, giving Pfizer full rights to Lipitor.[40] With Lipitor secured as a Pfizer product and Torcetrapib entering Phase III trials, Pfizer was poised to strengthen its hold on the cholesterol drug market.

Pfizer's Offer

In November 2003, Esperion published the official results of its ETC-216 study in the *Journal of the American Medical Association*. The article indicated that its drug reduced build-up of fatty plaque in arteries by over 4% in patients who were given weekly injections of the experimental medicine over a course of only five weeks during the Phase II trial.[41] According to John LaMattina, director of research at Pfizer, ETC-216 would have to be tested on "hundreds, possibly thousands (of people), and would have to be shown to significantly reduce the risk of a second heart attack" before the Food and Drug Administration would approve it. This type of clinical trial would require a significant investment.[42]

After the trial results appeared in the *Journal of the American Medical Association*, Newton publicly announced that the company would be looking for a partner to develop and market the drug. Pfizer acquired first bidding rights to co-develop and commercialize ETC-216 through its acquisition of Pharmacia.[43]

On December 21, 2003, Pfizer announced its intent to purchase Esperion Therapeutics for $1.3 billion. Pfizer made an all-cash tender offer to acquire shares of Esperion's common stock at $35 per share.[44] This price represented a

54% premium over Esperion's average closing share price over the 20 trading days prior to the acquisition.[45] At the time of the offer, Newton owned 890,000 shares of Esperion stock.

The Decision

Newton had to decide if Esperion would benefit from a buyout by a major pharmaceutical company. Dr Newton knew that his company faced an uphill battle with the continued development of ETC-216. Phase III trials would prove incredibly expensive for Esperion and they would again have to look to venture capital funding and potential stock offerings for additional cash. Dr Newton knew that despite positive Phase II results, Phase III results could always be negative and ETC-216 might never make it to FDA approval. If, however, the ETC-216 Phase III trials proved successful, Esperion would have to look for a partner to help launch and commercialize the product.

Dr Newton had a lot to consider. He had started Esperion so that he could create an entrepreneurial environment for drug discovery, in which the scientists received the rewards for their research. If he sold out to Pfizer, would he be giving up everything he had worked so hard to create? Would Esperion be able to maintain the entrepreneurial identity that had brought about the discovery of a new line of cardiovascular pharmaceuticals? Would Newton be giving up control over the development of ETC-216 and the other promising drugs in Esperion's pipeline? In addition, how would his employees react to working for a major pharmaceutical company?

Dr Newton had to decide whether Esperion's future laid as an independent biotech company, a wholly-owned subsidiary, or an integrated part of "big pharma."

Xbox 360: Will the Second Time be Better?*

In early 2006, Sony, Microsoft, and Nintendo were battling for supremacy in the $30 billion videogames industry, with each firm claiming victory. Who was right? Why?

Creation and Growth of the Home Video Game Console Market (1968–1995)[1]

Ralph Baer, the man who would come to be known as the father of the video game, created a prototype home video game unit capable of playing 12 games in 1968. This prototype was inspired by a project Baer was working on for the US military to design a system that could help improve soldier reflexes. The military project eventually fizzled but Baer continued development with an eye towards the US consumer market. It wasn't until 1972 that Magnavox introduced Baer's "Brown Box" as the first home video game system—commercially titled Magnavox Odyssey. Odyssey enjoyed mild commercial success, selling 200,000 units between 1972 and 1975.

Video game mania truly swept the USA in 1975 when an agreement between Sears Roebuck & Co. and Atari led to production of a home version of Atari's wildly successful coin-operated arcade game "*Pong*." This helped bring Atari to the forefront of the newly-emerging home video game console industry. In 1977, Atari released Atari 2600, the first programmable home console. Incorporating an 8-bit Motorola 6507 microprocessor and 256 bytes of RAM, the 2600 was on the market through 1990 and sold more than 25 million units. Over 40 different manufacturers produced 200-plus game titles for the system, and total sales volume reached 120 million cartridges.

In the mid-1980s, Nintendo quickly displaced Atari as the market leader following the 1985 launch of its 8-bit Nintendo Entertainment System (NES). The smash hit *Super Mario Brothers* and other game titles helped catapult Nintendo to the top of the console industry by the end of the 1980s. In 1989 Sega introduced the first 16-bit console, Sega Genesis. This was Nintendo's first serious threat. The Genesis had improved graphics, faster processing speeds, and the popular *Sonic the Hedgehog* video game was released on it in 1992. To

---

* This case was prepared by Katy Chai, Victor Colombo, Elizabeth Huntley, Ian Mackenzie, Justin Manly, and Tatsuyoshi Matsuura under the supervision of Professor Allan Afuah as a basis for class discussion and is not intended to illustrate either effective or ineffective handling of a business situation.

compete with Genesis, Nintendo launched its own 16-bit console, Super NES, in 1992. Super NES was a huge success; over the course of its product life, upwards of 46 million units were sold worldwide, re-establishing Nintendo as the console market leader. Sega, following two failed attempts to introduce new consoles (Saturn in 1995 and Dreamcast in 1999), exited the console industry in 2001 to focus strictly on video game development.

In June 1996, Nintendo released the Nintendo 64 (N64) in Japan to compete with Sega's Saturn and Sony's PlayStation, both of which had been launched in 1995. However, N64 continued to use cartridge media, while its competitors had moved to CD-based consoles. The largest N64 titles consisted of approximately 32 megabytes while PlayStation and Saturn games used 650–700 MB CDs. This discrepancy put N64 at a significant disadvantage because its games were limited in terms of complexity and graphics, especially for role-playing games which were becoming increasingly popular with consumers. Nintendo attempted to attract users with extraordinary titles such as the *Super Mario Brothers* series, but in 1997 Nintendo's major software developer, Square Enix, moved its legendary Final Fantasy franchise to PlayStation. The success of the new *Final Fantasy VII* elevated PlayStation's market position and helped pave the way for Sony's dominance of the video game industry.

A New Competitor Emerges—Sony's PlayStation

During the 1970s and 1980s, Sony grew into one of the world's most successful and innovative consumer electronics companies. In the 1980s, Sony focused its resources on developing game software for Nintendo but faced sluggish growth in this area. Seeking additional opportunities in the video game business, Sony entered into a development partnership with the then-market-leader Nintendo to supply sound chips for Nintendo's home video game console. However, this represented a very limited opportunity for Sony in the rapidly-growing video game industry.

In 1986, Nintendo and Sony worked together to develop a CD-ROM add-on for Nintendo's console to take advantage of the substantial data capacity of CD media. The game cartridge had been the primary media for Nintendo's game systems, but the increasingly complex game content was beginning to drive up cartridge manufacturing costs. In addition, NEC and Sega had both introduced CD-ROM-based consoles to the market. Sony and Nintendo ultimately abandoned their joint CD peripheral which Sony had reportedly completed in prototype form.[2] Nintendo then announced a new partnership with Philips to develop improved CD-ROM technology in June 1991. In response to this new relationship with a Sony competitor, Sony discontinued supplying sound chips to Nintendo and in 1993 began development of its own CD-ROM-based video game console. Code named "PS-X," the project was the origin of the first generation Sony PlayStation. In the fall of 1993, the ownership of the project was transferred to the Sony Computer Entertainment, Inc., a newly-formed division within Sony comprised of approximately 60 members from Sony, Inc. and Sony Music Entertainment, Inc.

PlayStation (PS1) Launch

PlayStation was released in Japan at the suggested retail price of JPY39,800 (approximately $395) on December 3, 1994. This launch date (12/3) was advertised extensively with the "1! 2! 3!" countdown promotional campaign. Unique ads such as this helped Sony quickly sell out of the 100,000 consoles that were initially shipped to stores. Sega had launched its Saturn a month earlier, in November, but critics heralded PlayStation as the superior machine.[3] PlayStation was introduced in North America on September 5, 1995 at the suggested retail price of $299, a full $100 less than analysts had expected.[4] Over 100,000 units were sold in the first weekend and over a million units sold over the first six months. Sony released game titles in nearly every genre, including *Battle Arena Toshinden, Twisted Metal, Warhawk, Philosoma, Wipeout* and *Ridge Racer*. PlayStation quickly became the bestselling home video game console to-date, only to be surpassed by its successor, PlayStation 2.

PlayStation 2 (PS2) Launch

In September 1999, Sony announced the introduction of its PlayStation 2 and associated pricing to the public. Most major software manufacturers decided early on to develop games for PS2, resulting in mass media predictions of a Sony-dominated game market. In February 2000, Sony began accepting preorders for PS2 on PlayStation.com. Initial orders via the website set sales records for the game industry and the site was quickly overwhelmed by heavy traffic. PS2 was released for sale on March 4, 2000 in Japan and on October 26, 2000 in North America. It sold well from the beginning (over 900,000 in Japan in the first weekend alone), partly due to the strength of the PlayStation brand and its backwards compatibility with PS1. This allowed Sony to tap in to the large installed base of PS1 customers, games, and developers. In 2001, the launches of Microsoft's Xbox and Nintendo's Game Cube increased competition in the industry, but Sony's release of several best-selling and critically-acclaimed game titles helped PS2 to continue its market dominance. These titles included the ever-popular *Final Fantasy* and *Grand Theft Auto* series. In several cases, Sony struck exclusive deals with publishers to further strengthen its position.

Competition Heats Up

Microsoft officially announced the introduction of its Xbox on March 10, 2000 and released the console to consumers on November 15, 2001.[5] By late 2001, the video game console industry had become highly competitive as Sony, Nintendo, and Microsoft all offered extremely popular and attractive units.

Price Wars

One of the ways this competition manifested itself was through pricing. The PS2 was launched in October 2000 at a retail price of $299. When the Xbox was launched 13 months later, in November 2001, Microsoft matched the PS2's price despite the fact that this meant that the Xbox was estimated to be losing $150 per unit. But Microsoft priced the Xbox below its production cost to gain market share quickly. Sony responded by slashing PS2 prices by $100 six months later, a move which Microsoft immediately followed for the Xbox. Thus, Sony enjoyed 19 total months of selling PS2 at the original $299 retail price while Microsoft was able to sell Xbox at this same price for only 6 months.[6]

Price cuts in May became an annual event. In May 2003, both Sony and Microsoft again cut their prices, this time by only $20 to bring their suggested retail prices to $179. In May 2004, prices fell again, this time to $149. In November of that year, Sony launched a thinner version of PS2 known as Slim, then dropped the price one last time to $129 in May 2006, six months after the release of Xbox 360, and six months prior to the release of PS2's successor, PlayStation 3. Xbox's price remained at $149.

Game Franchises and Online Play

The wildly popular *Halo* franchise was launched simultaneously with the Xbox, and was followed by such hits as *Project Gotham Racing* and *Dead or Alive*. However, PS2, by virtue of its earlier launch date and preexisting franchises from PS1, controlled a number of key game series, including premier sporting titles from Electronic Arts such as *Madden* and *NBA Live*, as well as *Metal Gear Solid* and *Grand Theft Auto*.

A defensive tactic that Sony employed just prior to the Xbox's launch was to negotiate a period of exclusivity with game developers, usually lasting 6–12 months, during which a new title would only be available on PS2. This, combined with disappointing reviews of a few early Xbox-specific titles, served to dampen the initial demand for Xbox.

Further complicating matters was the fact that, despite Xbox offering significantly more processing power than PS2, many of the initial games developed for Xbox did not take advantage of this capability. Thus, while Microsoft touted the superior performance offered by their machine, this power was not readily apparent to gamers.

The release of Xbox Live in late 2002 gave Microsoft a head start in the realm of online gaming. This broadband service initially allowed gamers around the world to compete head-to-head over the Internet just as if they were sitting together playing on the same console. Xbox Live also included the ability to download new games, hardware updates, and other content. Although the service initially grew relatively slowly, within two years of launch Microsoft reported having enrolled over one million subscribers. The service was seen as especially compelling for many of Xbox's hardcore gamers, and would become a standard offering among the next generation of consoles. An Xbox Live Gold subscription costs $50 a year.[7]

The year 2004 saw Xbox hit a home run with the release of *Halo 2*, which set a record by exceeding $125 million in sales on its first day. The launch received heavy national news coverage with stories of the thousands of loyal Xbox users calling in sick on the release date to wait in line, purchase the game, and then devote the entire day to mastering it.[8]

Xbox 360

Microsoft's next-generation console, the Xbox 360, was released in November 2005, a year ahead of rivals. In that first holiday season, significant shortages of the unit occurred. By its second holiday season in 2006, units were readily available and the release of the new flagship game *Gears of War* rejuvenated demand. The company had yet to make money from video games since entering the market in 2001 (Exhibit 11.1); but there was a lot of optimism about sales of Xbox 360 (Exhibit 11.2).

The graphics of the Xbox 360 were significantly better than that of second-generation consoles and, at launch time, was touted as the most graphically-advanced system on the market. Xbox 360 featured cutting-edge hardware, including a 733 MHz Intel processor and a 233 MHz nVidia graphics processor

Exhibit 11.1 Microsoft's Financials ($US millions, except where indicated)

Financial highlights (In millions) Fiscal year ended June 30	2006	2005	2004	2003	2002
Revenue ($)	44,282	39,788	36,835	32,187	28,365
Operating income ($)	16,472	14,561	19,034	19,545	8,272
Net income ($)	12,599	12,254	18,168	17,531	5,355
Cash and short-term investments ($)	34,161	37,751	60,592	49,048	38,652
Total assets ($)	69,597	70,815	94,368	81,732	69,910
Long-term obligations ($)	7,051	5,823	4,574	2,846	2,722
Stockholders' equity ($)	40,104	48,115	74,825	64,912	54,842

Home and entertainment division (In millions, except percentages)	2006	2005	2004	% Change 2006 versus 2005	% Change 2005 versus 2004
Revenue	$4,256	$3,140	$2,737	36%	15%
Operating loss	$(1,262)	$(3,485)	$(1,337)	−160%	64%

Exhibit 11.2 Xbox 360 Sales Projections

	2006	2007	2008	2009	2010
Console sales (millions)	1.5	8.5	10.0	10.0	5.0
Cumulative console sales (millions)	1.5	10.0	20.0	30.0	35.0
Console production cost ($)	525	323	323	323	323
Console MSRP ($)	399	399	399	399	399
Estimated wholesale price	279.3	279.3	279.3	279.3	279.3

Notes:
1 $4 million development costs, estimated at double that of previous generation system.
2 Console sale projections through 2007 are based on Microsoft projections. Sales growth beyond 2007 is estimated using previous generation sales figures.
3 Second-year cost reductions estimated at 38%—the same level realized by Microsoft with the Xbox 360.
4 Changes in MSRP based on price change history of previous generation console.
5 Estimated at 70% of MSRP.

capable of producing even more realistic graphics than previous machines. Not surprisingly, the system also incorporated a Windows-based operating system which Microsoft claimed simplified game development for developers.

Xbox 360 users (as well as users of the original Xbox) also had access to the Xbox Live online gaming community. Over four million subscribers could download games, compete and chat with friends, and buy maps and weapons. In addition to subscriptions, the service generated revenues through advertising and additional content sales. Microsoft expected Xbox Live members to exceed six million worldwide by June 2007.

Microsoft planned to release a game development kit for amateur game developers. The kit was expected to cost about $100 and allow developers to create shorter, less graphically advanced games. These games would then be made available on Xbox Live.

On the one-year anniversary of Xbox 360's initial release, Microsoft announced the additional capability of downloading movies and television shows. Microsoft also added an HD-DVD unit to the list of accessories available for Xbox 360. The average consumer could not yet take advantage of Blu-Ray capabilities and was unable to discern differences in quality between Blu-Ray and HD-DVD technologies. The HD-DVD addition was cheaper than Blu-Ray. Xbox 360 could play music stored on an iPod or a Zune while PS3 could only play music stored on the PlayStation Portable that was not widely used in 2006.

Sony PlayStation 3 (PS3)

Sony launched its Play Station 3 (PS3) on Friday, November 17, 2006 in the USA. With only 400,000 units available in the US and two million worldwide, demand far exceeded supply. On opening day, it was reported that long lines of customers got rowdy, with police having to disperse some crowds, a stampede occurring at one store, and a shooting at another. Retail analysts suggested that the actual number of units available to US consumers was only 150,000 on launch day. Limited supply prompted many profiteers to sell their units on eBay. Analysts were optimistic about PS3 sales (Exhibit 11.3).

The PS3's technology was proprietary. It was generally viewed as the most advanced video game console on the market in terms of processing power as well as graphics. PS3 came standard with the "Cell" processor, Blu-Ray DVD player, and high-capacity hard drive. While the Blu-Ray DVD format could store more data than Xbox 360's HDD DVD, as of 2006, HDD DVD manufacturing costs were significantly lower for both prerecorded as well as blank

Exhibit 11.3 Playstation 3 Sales Projections

	2006	2007	2008	2009	2010
Console sales (millions)	2.0	11.3	13.3	13.3	6.7
Cumulative console sales (millions)	2.0	13.3	26.6	39.9	46.6
Console production cost ($)	806	496	496	496	496
Console MSRP ($)	499	399	399	399	299
Estimated wholesale price ($)	349.3	279.3	279.3	279.3	209.3

recordable media. Blu-Ray was the format championed by Dell, while Toshiba, NEC, and Intel all favored HDD DVD. Movie studios were also divided in their support of the two technologies.

Like the Xbox 360, the PS3 could also serve as an entertainment delivery system since users could watch HD movies, listen to music, view HD photos, and search the Internet in addition to playing video games. PS3 allowed up to seven wireless controllers and included a browser, built-in Wi-Fi, and supported Bluetooth wireless earpieces. It also permitted additional operating systems to be added, including Linux.

All of these advancements, however, delayed PS3's launch by several months, and resulted in a high price for consumers. Furthermore, the Blu-Ray DVD player only benefited users with advanced television sets. These advancements also increased the PS3's complexity. Sony also added motion-sensitivity to the PS3 controller in an effort to heighten the level of realism in play. Some observers wondered if Sony's gaming division, once a cash cow for the company, would start delivering again (Exhibit 11.4).

Nintendo Wii

Nintendo launched its latest game console, Wii, in November 2006. Retail analysts predicted that 450,000 of those units would be available to US shoppers, more than double the quantity of PS3s available. Still, on November 19 when Wii debuted in US stores, it quickly sold out. Some customers camped overnight to await the arrival of Wii.

Nintendo took a radically different approach to gaming than the visually advanced, high-definition graphics of Xbox 360 and PS3. Nintendo was betting that many consumers were not technologically savvy and therefore did not care for the newest, fastest technology that PS3 offered. Additionally, with advances in technology, games had become increasingly complex and time-consuming, resulting in a small, albeit dedicated, customer base of avid gamers. Nintendo

Exhibit 11.4 Sony's Summary Financials ($US millions, except where indicated)

Financial highlights Fiscal year ended March 31	2006	2005	2004		
Revenue ($)	163,541	66,584	71,216		
Operating income ($)	1,626	1,059	940		
Net income	1,051	1,524	841		
Cash and short-term investments	10,541	11,539	10,722		
Total assets	90,166	188,342	86,361		
Long-term obligations $	35,731	35,520	35,439		
Stockholders' equity $	27,233	26,694	22,591		
Gaming division (In millions, except percentages)	2006	2005	2004	% Change 2006 versus 2005	% Change 2005 versus 2004
Revenue ($)	8,125	6,185	6,569	31%	-6%
Operating income ($)	74	365	572	-80%	-36%

believed that focusing only on these existing avid gamers limited growth opportunities. Instead, with the Wii, Nintendo hoped to attract "gamers and nongamers alike with intuitive game play."[9] Additionally, games were simpler and could be completed in less time. Nintendo expected this strategy to attract new customers to the gaming market.

A key aspect of the Wii was its controller. Rather than the traditional complicated controllers that required knowledge of each buttons' purpose, Wii used a wand-like controller that translated the movement of the player to the screen. Gamers could, depending on the game, wave the controller around in the air, using it as a tennis racket, golf club, steering wheel, gun, or sword.

The Wii lacked high-definition graphics and a DVD player. "Nintendo's stated goal is to hook people with the lure of the wireless controllers, low price and a small, cute main unit that will fit easily in most entertainment centers."[10] The Wii could also display news and weather information from the Internet. "Old games from Nintendo's back catalogue could be downloaded to draw in lapsed gamers."[11]

Officials of all three firms were optimistic about their chances. Who was right to be optimistic and why? Exhibit 11.5 provides more information about games.

Exhibit 11.5 Game Sales Information

Game sales	
Percent of inhouse titles	50%
Inhouse title profit margin	70%
Third-party title profit margin	13%
Game attach rates	
Playstation 3—launch	1.5
Xbox 360—launch	4.0
Xbox 360—one year	5.2
Wii—launch	3.0

Note: ongoing attach rates are typically one game per year after first year.

Source: GameStop Report, 11/2006. Deutsche Bank Game Sector Update, August 18, 2005.

Nintendo Wii: A Game-changing Move

The Microsoft investor could not believe the news. Seven years after entering the video game console business, Microsoft was still losing money in its video game business. Its Xbox, launched in 2001, had lost billions, and the sophisticated Xbox 360 did not appear to be making much money. Sony's even more sophisticated PS3 was also losing money. In contrast, demand for the Nintendo Wii had been so strong during the 2007 Christmas season that Nintendo had been forced to issue rain checks to customers. In fact, it was not unusual for eager Wii customers to pay prices well above Nintendo's suggested retail price of $249 in live online auctions. Why had the Nintendo Wii performed so well? Why had Microsoft done so poorly in video games? Why had Sony started doing so poorly following its initial success in video games? The Microsoft investor wondered if Microsoft had learned from the Nintendo Wii.

Competing for Gamers: The Early Years

Although the invention of the video game may date to as far back as 1947 with the patenting of a "Cathode Ray Tube Amusement Device"[1] by Thomas T. Goldsmith Jr and Estle Ray Mann, Atari is usually credited with introducing the first successful video game to the home. In 1975 it offered a dedicated home version of its popular arcade *Pong* called the Sears Tele-Game System and 150,000 units of it sold that Christmas.[2] Many other firms entered the home video game console business but Atari reigned until Nintendo introduced its Nintendo Entertainment System—a so-called third generation system—in 1985. Nintendo's leadership position would be challenged by Sega when it introduced its Sega Mega Drive (called the Sega Genesis in the USA) in 1989. The Sega Genesis was a so-called fourth-generation console. Although Nintendo fought back, Sega would emerge as the new leader until Sony's entry.

The Market that Wii Would Face

The Products

Sony entered the home video game business by introducing the Playstation in Japan in 1994 and in the USA in 1995. Sega and Nintendo fought back but Sony emerged as the winner. Sony's success would attract Microsoft, which introduced the Xbox in 2001, one year after Sony introduced the Playstation 2. The world's number one software company was rumored to have spent $2 billion to develop the Xbox and another $500 million to market it. In 2001 when the Xbox was introduced, Microsoft officials knew that they were going to lose money on each console but hoped to make up for the losses with software (game) sales. It was expected that each Xbox customer would buy three games in his/her first year of owning an Xbox console, and buy one game per year thereafter. Exhibit 12.1 shows Xbox forecasted sales, costs, and prices when it was launched. In November 2005, barely four years after introducing the Xbox, Microsoft introduced the Xbox 360 in the US market. One year later, Sony introduced the Playstation 3.

Riding the Technological Progress Envelope

The microchip technological revolution that put a cell phone in most hands, a computer on many laps and desks, an ATM at most corners, etc., and that gave us the iPod, iPhone, Blackberry, etc., was the same technology that drove the video game industry. Microchip technology pushed the technology envelope and video console makers exploited the frontier. Each new generation of consoles was driven by a new generation of faster microprocessors and graphic processors with even more graphical detail. For example, the Xbox was powered by an Intel microprocessor that ran at 733 megahertz and graphics processor that delivered about 300 million polygons per second, more than three times the graphics performance of the Playstation 2, the previous generation console that Microsoft hoped to displaced.[3] The Xbox 360, which Microsoft introduced four years after the Xbox, used a 3.2-gigahertz processor, an order of magnitude faster than the Xbox while delivering 500 million polygons. The PS3 also used a 3.2-gigahertz processor and the firm's new much-touted Blu-Ray DVD technology.

These advances in technological innovation also created more options for software (game) developers to design games for each generation of consoles that were even more lifelike and appealing to core gamers than those designed for previous generations. However, in tracking the technology frontier, console makers incurred very high console costs. Console makers had to develop custom chips dedicated to their consoles or use the fastest and best chips available in the market. The result was that each console cost so much that its maker sold it at a loss, and hoped to make money from the royalties collected on software sales and from selling accessories.

Exhibit 12.1 Xbox 2001 Forecast Sales, Costs, and Prices

	FY2002	FY2003	FY2004	FY2005	FY2006
Console forecasted sales (# of Xbox units)	4	10	11	12	13
Retail price per console ($)	299	249	249	249	199
Wholesale price ($)	209	174	174	174	139
Production cost	350	300	250	250	250
Retail price per game unit sold ($)	49	49	49	49	49
Production cost of each game unit ($)	36	36	36	36	36

Source: Microsoft forecasts and analysts estimates.

Effectively, each new generation of consoles delivered outstanding techno-logical performance, images that were more lifelike than those from previous generations, and appealed to core gamers. Each new generation was also more complex than previous generations and many games took hours, if not days, to play. Virtual violence also became more common with each generation. More-over, playing many of these games required players to master complicated com-binations of buttons on each console's complex controls, and lots of gaming know-how and expertise.[4] Each new generation of consoles rendered the previ-ous generation technologically obsolete and out of style as far as core gamers were concerned. Additionally, most games developed for new consoles often rendered previous games obsolete. The product cycle time—the time from when the first product in a new generation was introduced to the time when the first product in the next generation was introduced—was also decreasing.

The Wii

Nintendo introduced its Wii video console in the Americas on November 19, 2006, only about a week after Sony had introduced its PS3 console on Novem-ber 11, but one year after Microsoft had introduced its Xbox 360. The Wii had a simpler design than the Xbox 360 and PS3 to appeal to the casual or lapsed gamer, or noncore gamers who had neither the time (hours or days) to dedicate to a game, nor the expertise to handle the complexity of existing console con-trols and games.[5] It had easy-to-use controls and its games sought to offer real-life, rather than escapist scenarios. According to Jeffrey M. O'Brien of Fortune, the Wii differed from the Xbox 360 and PS3 in other ways:

> Nintendo used off-the-shelf parts from numerous suppliers. Sony co-developed the PS3's screaming-fast 3.2-gigahertz "cell" chip and does the manufacturing in its own facilities. Nintendo bought its 729-megahertz chip at Kmart. (Not really. But it might as well have.) Its graphics are marginally better than the PS2 and the original Xbox, but they pale next to the PS3 and Xbox 360. Taking this route enabled the company to introduce the Wii at $250 in the U.S. (vs. $599 for the PS3 and as much as $399 for the 360) and still turn a profit on every unit.[6]

The Wii also had no hard disk, no DVD, and no Dolby 5.1. Its video RAM was 24 MB compared to 256 MB for the PS3 and up to 512 MB for the Xbox 360.

However, the Wii had some innovative features that its high-tech competitors did not.[7] It had a remote (motion) wand-like control that resembled a TV remote control compared to the complex button-strewn controller carried by the PS3 and Xbox 360.[8] The wand-like control enabled a gamer's movements and actions to be directly mapped into the video game. For example, to swing a tennis racket or golf club, the player literally swung the remote controller as if it were a racket or club. The swing would be remotely detected by the Wii proces-sor and the player would get some exercise and more of a sense of playing tennis or golf from the swing. Contrast this with having to be adept and knowledge-able enough to hit the right complicated combination of buttons on the PS3 or Xbox 360's control at the right time. The other distinguishing feature was the Mii. A Mii was a digital character that a player could create on the Wii. Once a character had been so created, it could be used as participating characters in subsequent games. It allowed players to capture different personalities and caricatures including their own. According to Saturo Iwata, president of Nintendo when the Wii was introduced, the idea for the control and shorter simpler games had been developed and tested on Nintendo's handheld device called the Nintendo DS. The Wii was also connectible to the DS so that the latter could be used as the input to the former.

Beyond the remote control stick and the Mii, the Wii had other features such as backward compatibility with all official GameCube software, and the Wii-Connect24 which enabled the Wii to receive information such as news and weather over the Internet while in standby mode.

Despite the initial success of the Wii, some incumbents did not see it as much of a threat to Sony and Microsoft. Remarks such as the following from Sony Computer Entertainment of America's Jack Tretton, were not uncommon:[9]

> You have to give Nintendo credit for what they've accomplished . . . But if you look at the industry, any industry, it doesn't typically go backwards technologically. The controller is innovative, but the Wii is basically a repurposed GameCube. If you've built your console on an innovative controller, you have to ask yourself, Is that long term?[10]

The Microsoft investor wondered how long the Wii would continue to do well. Should he have invested in Nintendo instead of Microsoft? Why hadn't Microsoft followed a Nintendo-type strategy when it entered the video game console market in 2001? Was it too late to follow a Wii-type strategy?

The estimated costs, wholesale prices, and suggested retail prices for the Wii, Xbox 360, and PS3 are shown in Exhibit 12.2, while the forecasted number of units are shown in Exhibit 12.3. The exhibit is reproduced from Chapter 1.

Exhibit 12.2 Costs, Retail, and Wholesale Prices

Product	Year introduced	First year			After first year		
		Cost ($)	Suggested retail price ($)	Wholesale price ($)	Cost	Suggested retail price ($)	Wholesale price ($)
Xbox 360	2005	525	399	280	323	399	280
Sony PS3	2006	806	499	349	496	399	280
Nintendo Wii	Late 2006	158.30	249	199	126	200	150

Sources: Company reports. Various sources including: Ehrenberg, R. (2007). Game console Wars II: Nintendo shaves off profits, leaving competition scruffy. Retrieved September 8, 2007, from http://seekingalpha.com/article/34357-game-console-wars-ii-nintendo-shaves-off-profits-leaving-competition-scruff.

Exhibit 12.3 Forecasted Console and Games Sales

	2005	2006	2007	2008	2009	2010
Console						
Xbox 360	1.5	8.5	10	10	5	
Sony PS3		2	11	13	13	7
Nintendo Wii			5.8	14.5	17.4	18.3
Games						
Xbox 360	4.5	25.5	30	30	15	
Sony PS3		6	33	39	39	21
Nintendo Wii			28.8	66.5	114.3	128.8

Sources: Company and analysts reports. HSBC Global Research. 2007. Nintendo Co., (7974). Telecom, Media & Technology Software. Equity-Japan. July 5, 2007.

Notes

1 Introduction and Overview

1. Chafkin, M. (2008). The customer is the company. *Inc. Magazine*, June 2008. *http://www.inc.com/magazine/20080601/the-customer-is-the-company.html*: Accessed July 15, 2008.
2. Tischler, L. (2007). He struck gold on the net (really). *Fast Company.com*. December 19, 2007. *http://www.fastcompany.com/magazine/59/mcewen.html*: Accessed July 15, 2008.
3. Tapscott, D. & Williams, A.D. (2006). *Wikinomics: How Mass Collaboration Changes Everything*. New York: Penguin Books.
4. Rivkin, J.W., & Porter, M.E. (1999). *Matching Dell* (Condensed). Harvard Business School Case 704–440.
5. To the best of my knowledge, the phrase "New game strategies" was first used from Buaron, R. (1981). New-game strategies. *McKinsey Quarterly*, 17(1), 24–40. He defined new game strategies as "innovative competitive moves" (p. 29); but my definition is different from Buaron's. For one thing, my definition sees new game strategies as also involving cooperative moves and more. For the other, my approach builds on and extends both the resource-based view (RBV) and the product-market-position (PMP) view of strategic management as it pertains to change. Throughout this book the words "appropriate" and "capture" are used interchangeably.
6. I use the phrase "value chain" when I really mean "value chain, value network, and value shop" only to make the definition of new game activity more precise and easier to remember. For the relationship between value chain, value network, and value shop, please see Stabell, C.B. & Fjeldstad, O.D. (1998). Configuring value for competitive advantage: On chains, shops, and networks. *Strategic Management Journal*, 19(5), 413–37.
7. Ghemawat, P. (1991). *Commitment: The Dynamics of Strategy*. New York: Free Press.
8. Porter, M.E. (1996). What is strategy? *Harvard Business Review*, 74(6), 61–78.
9. We will have a lot more to say about value creation and appropriation below and in Chapter 4 of this book. Throughout the book, we will use products to mean products and services. We will also use the words *capture* and *appropriate* interchangeably.
10. See n.6.
11. Buaron, R. (1981). New-game strategies. *McKinsey Quarterly*, 17(1), 24–40. See also, Bales, C.F., Chatterjee, P.C., Gluck, F.W., Gogel, D., & Puri, A. (2000). The business system: A new tool for strategy formulation and cost analysis. Retrieved November 13, 2007, from *http://www*.kellogg.northwestern.edu/faculty/vohra/ftp/miin00.pdf

12. Porter, M.E. (1985). *Competitive Advantage: Creating and Sustaining Superior Performance*. New York: Free Press.
13. Moon, Y. (2004). *Ikea Invades America*. HBS case #504-094. Boston, MA: Harvard Business School Press.
14. Rivkin, J.W., & Siggelkow, N. (2003). Balancing search and stability: Inter-dependencies among elements of organizational design. *Management Science, 49*(3), 290–311.
15. Given the critical role that intangible resources play in market value, many firms are taking another look at their financial statement reporting. See, for example, Stewart, T.A. (1997). *Intellectual Capital: The New Wealth of Organizations*. New York: Currency/Doubleday.
16. Barney, J., & Arikan, A.M. (2001). The resource-based view: Origins and implications. In M.A. Hitt, R.E. Freeman, & J.S. Harrison (eds), *The Blackwell Handbook of Strategic Management* (124–88). Oxford: Blackwell.
17. We will have a lot more to say about first-mover advantages and disadvantages in Chapter 6 of this book. See also, Lieberman, M.B., & Montgomery, D.B. (1988). First-mover (dis)advantages: Retrospective and link with the resource-based view. *Strategic Management Journal, 19*(12), 1111–25.
18. This definition is closest to the one offered by *The Economist*. See *Economics A–Z*. (2007). Retrieved July 26, 2007, from http://www.economist.com/research/Economics/alphabetic.cfm?letter=G#globalisation
19. Deutsche Bank Game Sector update. August, 18, 2005.
20. Are big budget console games sustainable? (March 10, 2006). Retrieved April 20, 2006, from http://Biz.gamedaily.com/industry/advertorial/?id=12089
21. Playing a different game: Does Nintendo's radical new strategy represent the future of gaming? (2006, October 26). *The Economist*.
22. Ibid.
23. Porter, M.E. (1996). What is strategy? *Harvard Business Review, 74*(6), 61–78.
24. Barney, J., & Arikan, A.M. (2001). The resource-based view: Origins and implications. In M.A. Hitt, R.E. Freeman, & J.S. Harrison (eds), *The Blackwell Handbook of Strategic Management* (124–188). Oxford: Blackwell. Peteraf, M.A. (1993). The cornerstones of competitive advantage: A resource-based view. *Strategic Management Journal, 14*(3), 179–91.
25. Professors Abernathy and Clark's seminal paper also explored a similar classification. However, their classification was only about resources—technology and market resources—and not about the resources and PMP of this book. See Abernathy, W.J., & Clark, K.B. (1985). Mapping the winds of creative destruction. *Research Policy, 14*(1), 3–22.
26. *Global Gillette*. (n.d.). Retrieved March 12, 2007, from http://en.wikipedia.org/wiki/The_Gillette_Company.
27. Chandler, A. (1962). *Strategy and Structure: Chapters in the History of the American Industrial Enterprise*. Cambridge, MA: MIT Press.
28. Andrews, K. (1971). *The Concept of Corporate Strategy*. Homewood, IL: Irwin.
29. Porter, M.E. (1980). *Competitive Strategy: Techniques for Analyzing Industries and Competitors*. New York: Free Press.
30. See, for example: Prahalad, C.K., & Hamel, G. (1990). The core competence of the corporation. *Harvard Business Review, 68*(3), 79–91. For a comprehensive review of the resource-based view of the firm, please see: Barney, J., & Arikan, A.M. (2001). The resource-based view: Origins and implications. In M.A. Hitt, R.E. Freeman, & J.S. Harrison (eds), *The Blackwell Handbook of Strategic Management* (124–88). Oxford: Blackwell.
31. Porter, M.E. (1996). What is strategy? *Harvard Business Review, 74*(6), 61–78.
32. Oster, S. (1999). *Modern Competitive Analysis*. Oxford: Oxford University Press.

33. Grant, R.M. (2002). *Contemporary Strategy Analysis: Concepts, Techniques, Applications*. (4th edn). Oxford: Blackwell.
34. Hitt, M.A., Ireland, R.D., & Hoskisson, R.E. (2007). *Strategic Management: Competitiveness and Globalization*. Mason, OH: Thompson/Southwestern.
35. Mintzberg, H., Lampel, J., Quinn, J.B., & Ghoshal, S. (2003:4). *The Strategy Process: Concepts Contexts Cases*. Upper Saddle River, NJ: Printice Hall.
36. Ibid.
37. Ibid.
38. Mintzberg, H. (2007). Are strategies real things? Retrieved June 10, 2007, from http://www.phptr.com/articles/article.asp?p=378964&seqNum=5&rl=1.
39. Mintzberg, H., Lampel, J., Quinn, J.B., & Ghoshal, S. (2003: 9). *The Strategy Process: Concepts Contexts Cases*. Upper Saddle River, NJ: Prentice Hall.
40. Hambrick, D.C., & Frederickson, J.W. (2005). Are you sure you have a strategy? *Academy of Management Executive, 19*(4), 51–62.

2 Assessing the Profitability Potential of a Strategy

1. Afuah, A.N. (2003). *Business Models: A Strategic Management Approach*. New York: McGraw-Hill/Irwin.
2. See, for example, Brealey, R.A., & Myers, S.C. (1995). *Principles of Corporate Finance*. New York: McGraw-Hill.
3. This example is from: Afuah, A.N. (2003). *Business Models: A Strategic Management Approach*. New York: McGraw-Hill/Irwin. Chapter 11.
4. Kaplan, R.S., & Norton, D.P. (1992). The balanced scorecard: Measures that drive performance. *Harvard Business Review, 70*(1), 71–80.
5. Afuah, A.N. (2003). *Business Models: A Strategic Management Approach*. New York: McGraw-Hill/Irwin.
6. Note that although no arrows are shown from Activities to Values, Appropriability and Change, activities underpin the first two and the ability of a firm to exploit or cope with the last one. The arrows have been left out to make the diagram more presentable. These relationships are explained in the text.
7. Afuah, A.N. (2003). *Business Models: A Strategic Management Approach*. New York: McGraw-Hill/Irwin.
8. See Ryanair's website: Ryanair.com Home. (n.d.). Retrieved August 27, 2007, from http://www.ryanair.com/site/EN/.
9. Aviation: Snarling all the way to the bank. (2007, August 23). *The Economist*.
10. *Investor Relations: Passenger Traffic 20023/2007*. http://www.ryanair.com/site/EN/about. php?page=Invest&sec=traffic *Roadshow Presentation*. (2007). Retrieved August 27, 2007, from http://www.ryanair.com/site/about/invest/docs/present/quarter4_2007.pdf.
11. Rivkin, J.W. (1999). *Dogfight over Europe: Ryanair (version C)* (Harvard Business School Case No. 9–700–117). Harvard Business School Press. See Ryanair's financial statements, including the presentation on: http://www.ryanair.com/site/about/invest/docs/present/quarter4_05.pdf, and Ryanair's history on its website: www.Ryanair.com. http://www.ryanair.com/site/about/invest/docs/Strategy.pdf
12. Capell, K. (June 2, 2003). Ryanair Rising: Ireland's discount carrier is defying gravity as the industry struggles. *Business Week, 3835*, 30.
13. Capell, K. (June 2, 2003). Ryanair Rising: Ireland's discount carrier is defying gravity as the industry struggles. *Business Week, 3835*, 30.
14. http://www.ryanair.com/site/about/invest/docs/Strategy.pdf

3 The Long Tail and New Games

1. Anderson, C. (2006). *The Long Tail: Why the Future of Business is Selling the Less of More*. New York: Random House Business Books.
2. See similar arguments by Shirky, C. (February 8, 2003). Power laws, weblogs and inequality. Retrieved July 9, 2008, from http://www.shirky.com/writings/powerlaw_weblog.html.
3. Brynjolfsson, E., Hu, Y., & Simester, D. (2006). Goodbye pareto principle, hello long tail: the effect of search costs on the concentration of product sales. Retrieved July 9, 2008, from http://papers.ssrn.com/sol3/papers.cfm?abstract_id=953587 See also, Brynjolfsson, E., Hu, Y., & Smith, M.D. (2003). Consumer surplus in the digital economy: estimating the value of increased product variety at online booksellers. *Management Science, 49*(11), 1580–96.
4. Freeberg, D. (2005). Netflix presents at Lehman Brothers Small Cap Conference. Retrieved October 15, 2007, from http://thomashawk.com/2005/11/Rnetflix-presents-at-lehman-brothers.html.
5. Anderson, C. (2006). *The Long Tail: Why the Future of Business is Selling the Less of More*. New York: Random House Business Books.
6. Agarwal A., Johnson M., Link T., Patel S., Stone, J., & Tsuchida, K. (2006). *Botox's Makeover*. Ann Arbor, MI: University of Michigan, Ross School of Business.
7. Film history of the 1970s. (n.d.). Retrieved December 10, 2007, from http://www.filmsite.org/70sintro.html.
8. One million copies of iTunes for Windows software downloaded in three and a half days. (2003). Retrieved September 15, 2007, from htt://www.apple.com/pr/library/2003/oct/20itunes.html.
9. Taylor, C. (2003). The 99 cent solution. Retrieved December 7, 2007, from http://www.time.com/time/2003/inventions/invmusic.html.
10. iTunes. Retrieved September 8, 2007, from *http://en.wikipedia.org/wiki/Itunes*.
11. Taylor, C. (2003). The 99 cent solution. Retrieved December 7, 2007, from http://www.time.com/time/2003/inventions/invmusic.html.

4 Creating and Appropriating Value Using New Game Strategies

1. Apple iPhone to generate 50 percent margin, According to iSuppli's Preliminary Analysis. (January 18, 2007). Retrieved July 9, 2007 from http://www.isuppli.com/news/default.asp?id=7308.
2. See similar definitions in Besanko, D., Dranove, D., & Shanley, M. (2000). *Economics of Strategy*. (2nd edn). New York: John Wiley & Sons, Inc. Ghemawat, P. (1991). *Commitment: The Dynamics of Strategy*. New York: Free Press. Saloner, G., Shepard, A., & Podolny, J. (2001). *Strategic Management*. New York: John Wiley.
3. Brandenburger, A. M., & Stuart, H. W. (2007). Biform games. *Management Science, 53*(4), 537–49. MacDonald, G., & Ryall, M. (2004). How do value creation and competition determine whether a firm appropriates value. *Management Science, 50*(10), 1319–33. Lipman, S., & Rumelt, R. (2003). A bargaining perspective on resource advantage. *Strategic Management Journal, 24*(11), 1069–86.
4. Laseter, T. M., Houston, P. W., Wright, J. L., & Park, J. Y. (2000). Amazon your industry: Extracting value from the value chain. *Strategy & Business, 18*(1), 94–105. Digman, L. A. (2006). *Strategic Management: Competing in the Global Information Age*. New York: Thomson.
5. Ibid.
6. Laseter, T. M., Houston, P. W., Wright, J. L., & Park, J. Y. (2000). Amazon your industry: Extracting value from the value chain. *Strategy & Business, 18*(1), 94–

105. Apple iPhone to generate 50 percent margin, according to iSuppli's preliminary analysis. (January 18, 2007). Retrieved July 9, 2007 from http://www.isuppli.com/news/default.asp?id=7308

7. Kanoh, Y. (July 6, 2007). Samsung Electronics Supplies Largest Share of iPhone Components: iSuppli. Retrieved July 9, 2007, from http://techon.nikkeibp.co.jp/english/NEWS_EN/20070706/135572/.

8. Wallace, J. (June 27, 2006). Boeing Dreamliner 'coming to life.' Retrieved July 8, 2007, from http://seattlepi.nwsource.com/business/275465_japan27.html.

9. Gates, D. (September 11, 2005). Boeing 787: Parts from around world will be swiftly integrated. *The Seattle Times*.

10. Moon, Y. (2004). Ikea invades America. HBS case # 504–094. Harvard Business School Press. Boston, MA.

11. Creager, E. (2002). Move over, Tupperware: Botox injections are the latest thing at home parties. Retrieved September 14, 2007, from http://www.woai.com/guides/beauty/story.aspx?content_id=16358daf-d7db-4ade-a757-9e8d7cf30212.

12. Dyer, J.H., & Singh, H. (1998). The relational view: Cooperative strategy and sources of interorganizational competitive advantage. *Academy of Management Review*, 23(4), 660–79.

13. Dyer, J.H., & Singh, H. (1998). The relational view: Cooperative strategy and sources of interorganizational competitive advantage. *Academy of Management Review*, 23(4), 660–79.

14. My thanks to Scott Peterson from whom I obtained the "grape versus watermelon" comparison in a STRAT 675 MBA class at the Ross School in the Fall of 2007.

15. Tapscott, D. & Williams, A. D. (2006). *Wikinomics: How Mass Collaboration Changes Everything*. New York: Penguin Books.

16. Tischler, L. (2007). He struck gold on the net (really). Fast Company.com. December 19, 2007. Retrieved June 19, 2008, from *http://www.fastcompany.com/magazine/59/mcewen.html*.

17. Ibid.

18. Tapscott, D. & Williams, A. D. (2006:9). *Wikinomics: How Mass Collaboration Changes Everything*. New York: Penguin Books, (p. 9).

19. Ibid.

20. Tischler, L. (2007). He struck gold on the net (really). Fast Company.com. December 19, 2007. Retrieved June 19, 2008, from *http://www.fastcompany.com/magazine/59/mcewen.html*.

21. Ibid.

22. Howe, J. (2006). The rise of crowdsourcing. *Wired*, 14(6). Retrieved June 19, 2008, from http://www.wired.com/wired/archive/14.06/crowds.html.

23. Tripsas, M. (1997). Unraveling the process of creative destruction: Complementary assets and incumbent survival in the typesetter industry. *Strategic Management Journal*, 18(6), 119–42.

24. Airbus A380: The giant on the runway. (2007, October 11). *The Economist*. Airbus: Gathering clouds. (2008, June 19). *The Economist*.

25. *The Economist*. 2008. Airbus: Gathering clouds. *The Economist*, June 19, 2008.

26. Linden, G., Kraemer, K.L., & Dedrick, J. (2007). Who captures value in a global innovation system? The case of Apple's iPod. Retrieved July 10, 2007, from http://www.teardown.com/AllReports/product.aspx?reportid=8.

5 Resources and Capabilities in the Face of New Games

1. Grant, R.M. (2002). *Contemporary Strategy Analysis: Concepts, Techniques, Applications*. Oxford, UK: Blackwell.

2. Given the critical role that intangible resources play in market value, many firms are taking another look at their financial statement reporting. See, for example, Stewart, T.A. (1997). *Intellectual Capital: The New Wealth of Organizations*. New York: Currency/Doubleday.

3. Hamel, G., & Prahalad, C.K. (1990). The core competence of the corporation. *Harvard Business Review, 68*(3), 79–91.

4. Barney, J., & Arikan, A.M. (2001). The resource-based view: Origins and implications. In Hitt, M.A., Freeman, R.E., & Harrison, J.S. (eds), *The Blackwell Handbook of Strategic Management* (124–88). Oxford: Blackwell.

5. Hamel, G., & Prahalad, C.K. (1990). The core competence of the corporation. *Harvard Business Review, 68*(3), 79–91.

6. Katz, M.L., & Shapiro, C. (1992). Product introduction with network externalities. *Journal of Industrial Economics, 40*(1), 55–84.

7. Katz, M.L., & Shapiro, C. (1985). Technology adoption in the presence of network externalities. *Journal of Political Economy, 94*(4), 822–41.

8. See, for example, L. Downes & C. Mui, (1998). *Unleashing the Killer App: Digital Strategies for Market Dominance*. Cambridge, MA: Harvard Business School Press.

9. Afuah, A. N. (2007). How much does size matter? Working Paper, Stephen M. Ross School of Business, University of Michigan.

10. Parker, G., & Van Alstyne, M. (2005). Two-sided network effects: A theory of information product design. *Management Science, 51*(10), 1494–504. Rochet, J., & Tirole, J. (2003). Platform competition in two-sided markets. *Journal of the European Economic Association, 1*(4), 990–1029.

11. Cusumano, M.A., Mylonadis, Y., & Rosenbloom, R.S. (1992). Strategic maneuvering and mass-market dynamics: the triumph of VHS over Beta. *Business History Review, 66*(1), 51–94.

12. Parker, G., & Van Alstyne, M. (2005). Two-sided network effects: A theory of information product design. *Management Science, 51*(10), 1494–504.

13. Nair, H., Manchanda, P., & Bhatia, T. (2007). Social networks impact the drugs physicians prescribe. Retrieved November 5, 2007, from http://www.gsb.stanford.edu/news/research/mktg_nair_drugs.shtml.

14. Teece, D.J. (1986). Profiting from technological innovation: Implications for integration, collaboration, licensing and public policy. *Research Policy, 15*(6), 285–306.

15. This model is derived from Professor David Teece's seminal paper: Teece, D.J. (1986). Profiting from technological innovation: Implications for integration, collaboration, licensing and public policy. *Research Policy, 15*(6), 285–306.

16. Afuah, A.N. (2003). *Innovation Management: Strategies, Implementation and Profits*. (2nd edn). New York: Oxford University Press.

17. Burns, E. (March 23, 2007). U.S. search engine rankings, February 2007. Retrieved May 28, 2007, from http://searchenginewatch.com/showPage.html?page=3625336.

18. Know your subject: Topic-specific search-engines hope to challenge Google, at least in some areas. (July 12, 2007). *The Economist*.

19. Bartlett, C.A., Cornebise, J., & McLean, A.N. (2002). Global wine wars: New world challenges old. Harvard Business School Press, case # 9-303-056.

20. Yoffie, D. B., & Wang, Y. (2002). Apple Computer 2002. Harvard Business School Press, case # 9-702-469.

21. Quittner, J. (2002). Apple's latest fruit: exclusive: How Steve Jobs made a sleek machine that could be the home-digital hub of the future. Retrieved August 23, 2007, from http://www.time.com/time/covers/1101020114/cover2.html.

22. Kanellos, M. (June 11, 2002). IDC ups 2001 PC-shipment estimate. Retrieved July

16, 2008, from http://news.cnet.com/IDC-ups-2001-PC-shipment-estimate/2100-1001_3-935176.htm l.

23. Market share vs installed base: iPod vs Zune, Mac vs PC. (March 18, 2007). Retrieved August 23, 2007, from http://www.roughlydrafted.com/RD/RDM.Tech.Q1.07/9E601E8E-2ACC-4866-A91B-3371D1688E00.html.

24. One million copies of iTunes for windows software downloaded in three and a half days. (October 20, 2003). Retrieved September 15, 2007, from http://www.apple.com/pr/library/2003/oct/20itunes.html.

6 First-mover Advantages/Disadvantages and Competitors' Handicaps

1. Many of the first-mover advantages and disadvantages outlined here were laid out in an award-winning paper by Professor Lieberman of UCLA and Professor Montgomery of Northwestern University. Please see Lieberman, M.B., & Montgomery, D.B. (1988). First-mover advantages. *Strategic Management Journal, 9*, 41–58. Lieberman, M.B., & Montgomery, D.B. (1988). First-mover (dis)advantages: Retrospective and link with the resource-based view. *Strategic Management Journal, 19*(12), 1111–25.

2. See, for example: Fishman, C. (2006). The Wal-Mart effect and a decent society: Who knew shopping was so important? *Academy of Management Perspectives, 20*(3), 6–25.

3. Sheremata, W.A. (2004). Competing through innovation in network markets: Strategies for challengers. *Academy of Management Review, 29*(3), 359–77.

4. Latif, U. (May 31, 2005). Google's bid-for-placement patent settlement cover-up. Retrieved July 16, 2008, from *http://www.techuser.net/gcoverup.html*. Olsen, S. (July 18, 2003). Overture to a patent war? Retrieved July 16, 2008, from http://news.com.com/Overture+to+a+ patent+war/2100-1024_3-1027084.html.

5. The settlement included another charge against Google that Yahoo had made in connection with a warrant that Yahoo held in connection with a June 2000 services agreement between the two firms.

6. Besanko, D., Dranove, D., & Shanley, M. (2000). *Economics of Strategy*. New York: John Wiley.

7. Barney, J. (1986). Organizational culture: Can it be a source of sustained competitive advantage? *Academy of Management Review, 11*(3), 656–65.

8. Teece, D.J. (1986). Profiting from technological innovation: Implications for integration, collaboration, licensing and public policy. *Research Policy, 15*(6), 285–306.

9. Ghemawat, P. (1986). Wal-Mart Stores' Discount Operations. Case 0-387-018. Boston, MA: Harvard Business School Press.

10. Schmalensee, R. (1978). Entry deterrence in the ready-to-eat breakfast cereal industry. *Bell Journal of Economics, 9*(2), 305–27.

11. Schmalensee, R. (1982). Product differentiation advantages of pioneering brands. *American Economic Review, 72*(3), 349–65.

12. Carpenter, G.S., & Nakamoto, K. (1989). Consumer preference formation and pioneering advantage. *Journal of Marketing Research, 26*(3), 285–98.

13. Fishburne, F. (1999, April 5). Hardware winner. *Forbes* (p. 59). Rivkin, J.W., & Porter, M.E. (1999). Matching Dell. HBS Case 799–158.

14. Ghemawat, P. (1991). *Commitment: The Dynamics of Strategy*. New York: Free Press.

15. Afuah, A.N. (2003). *Innovation Management: Strategies, Implementation and Profits*. (2nd edn). New York: Oxford University Press.

16. Porter, M.E. (1996). What is strategy? *Harvard Business Review, 74*(6), 61–78.

17. Lieberman, M.B., & Montgomery, D.B. (1988). First-mover advantages. *Strategic*

Management Journal, 9, 41–58. Lieberman, M.B., & Montgomery, D.B. (1988). First-mover (dis)advantages: Retrospective and link with the resource-based view. *Strategic Management Journal, 19*(12), 1111–25.

18. Teece, D.J. (1986). Profiting from technological innovation: Implications for integration, collaboration, licensing and public policy. *Research Policy, 15*(6), 285–306.
19. Hamel, G.M., & Prahalad, C.K. (1994). *Competing for the Future.* Boston, MA: Harvard Business School Press (p. 49).
20. Bettis, R.A., & Prahalad, C.K. (1995). The dominant logic: Retrospective and extension. *Strategic Management Journal, 16*(1), 5–14.
21. Besanko, D., Dranove, D., & Shanley, M. (2000). *Economics of Strategy.* New York: John Wiley.

7 Implementing New Game Strategies

1. This section draws on Chapter 5 of A.N. Afuah, *Innovation Management: Strategies, Implementation, and Profits* (New York: Oxford University Press, 2003).
2. Galbraith, J.R. (1982). Designing the innovating organization. *Organizational Dynamics, 10*(3), 5–25.
3. This section draws heavily on, A.N. Afuah (2003). *Business Models: A Strategic Management Approach.* New York: McGraw Hill/Irvin.
4. Lawrence, P.R., & Lorsch, J.W. (1967). *Organization and Environments: Managing Differentiation and Integration.* Homewood, IL: Irwin.
5. Chandler, A.D. (1962). *Strategy and Structure: Chapters in the History of the Industrial Enterprise.* Cambridge, MA: MIT Press.
6. Miles, R.E., Snow, C.C., Mathews, J.A., Miles, G., & Coleman, H. J., Jr (1997). Organizing the knowledge age: Anticipating the cellular form. *Academy of Management Executive, 11*(4), 7–24. Byrne, J.A., & Brandt, R. (February 8, 1993). The virtual corporation. *Business Week.* Davidow, W.H., & Malone, M.S. (1992). *The Virtual Corporation.* New York: Harper Collins.
7. Afuah, A.N. (2001). Dynamic boundaries of the firm: Are firms better off being vertically integrated in the face of a technological change? *Academy of Management Journal, 44*(6), 1211–28.
8. Hill, C.W.L., & Jones, G.R. (1995). *Strategic Management: An Integrated Approach.* Boston, MA: Houghton Mifflin.
9. Christensen, C.M., & Overdorf, M. (2000). Meeting the challenge of disruptive change. *Harvard Business Review, 78*(2), 66–77.
10. Afuah, A.N., & Tucci, C.L. (2003). *Internet Business Models and Strategies: Text and Cases.* New York: McGraw-Hill. Afuah, A.N. (2003). Redefining firm boundaries in the face of the Internet: Are firms really shrinking? *Academy of Management Review, 28*(1), 34–53.
11. Allen, T. (1984). *Managing the flow of technology.* Cambridge, MA: MIT Press.
12. Uttal, B., & Fierman, J. (October 17, 1983). The corporate culture vultures. *Fortune,* (pp. 66–73).
13. Schein, E. (1985). *Organizational Culture and Leadership.* San Francisco, CA: Jossey-Bass.
14. Barney, J. (1986). Organizational culture: Can it be a source of sustained competitive advantage? *Academy of Management Review, 11*(3), 656–65.
15. Fuzzy maths: In a few short years, Google has turned from a simple and popular company into a complicated and controversial one. (May 11, 2006). *The Economist.*
16. Bettis, R.A., & Prahalad, C.K. (1995). The dominant logic: Retrospective and extension. *Strategic Management Journal, 16*(1), 5–14.

17. Walsh, J.P. (1995). Managerial and organizational cognition: Notes from a trip down memory lane. *Organizational Science, 6*(3), 280–321.
18. Hamel, G.M., & Prahalad, C.K. (1994). *Competing for the Future*. Boston, MA: Harvard Business School Press.
19. The concept of champions was first developed by Schön in his seminal article, Schön, D.A. (1963). Champions for radical new inventions. *Harvard Business Review, 41*(2), 77–86. See also, Howell, J.M., & Higgins, C.A. (1990). Champions of technological innovation. *Administrative Sciences Quarterly, 35*(2), 317–41.
20. Roberts, E.B., & Fusfeld, A.R. (1981). Staffing the innovative technology-based organization. *Sloan Management Review, 22*(3), 19–34.
21. Allen, T. (1984). *Managing the flow of technology*. Cambridge, MA: MIT Press.
22. Clark, K.B., & Fujimoto, T. (1991). *Product Development Performance: Strategy, Organization, and Management in the World Automobile Industry*. Boston, MA: Harvard Business School Press.
23. Ibid.
24. Ibid.
25. Uttal, B., & Fierman, J. (October 17, 1983). The corporate culture vultures. *Fortune*, (pp. 66–73).

8 Disruptive Technologies as New Games

1. Foster, R. *Innovation: The Attacker's Advantage*. (1986). New York: Summit Books.
2. Foster, R. *Innovation: The Attacker's Advantage*. (1986). New York: Summit Books. Afuah, A.N., & Utterback, J.M. (1991). The emergence of a new supercomputer architecture. *Technology Forecasting and Social Change, 40*(4), 315–28. See also, Constant, E.W. (1980). *The Origins of the Turbojet Revolution*. Baltimore, MD: The Johns Hopkins University Press. Sahal, D. (1985). Technological guideposts and innovation avenues. *Research Policy, 14*(2), 61–82. Foster, R.D. (1985). Description of the S-Curve. Retrieved May 27, 2007, from http://www.12manage.com/description_s-curve.html.
3. Christensen, C.M., & Bower, J.L. (1996). Customer power, strategic investment and failure of leading firms. *Strategic Management Journal, 17*(3), 197–218. Christensen, C.M. (1997). *The Innovator's Dilemma*. Boston, MA: Harvard Business School Press. See also, Christensen, C.M., & Overdorf, M. (2000). Meeting the challenge of disruptive change. *Harvard Business Review, 78*(2), 66–76. Christensen, C.M., & Raynor, M.E. (2003). *The Innovator's Solution*. Boston, MA: Harvard Business School Press. Christensen, C.M., Anthony, S.D., & Roth, E.A. (2004). *Seeing What's Next*. Boston, MA: Harvard Business School Press.
4. Christensen, C.M., & Overdorf, M. (2000). Meeting the challenge of disruptive change. *Harvard Business Review, 78*(2), 68.
5. Christensen, C.M., & Overdorf, M. (2000). Meeting the challenge of disruptive change. *Harvard Business Review, 78*(2), 69.
6. Bettis R.A., & Prahalad, C.K. (1995). The dominant logic: Retrospective and extension. *Strategic Management Journal, 16*(1), 5–14.
7. Christensen, C.M., & Raynor, M.E. (2003). *The Innovator's Solution*. Boston, MA: Harvard Business School Press.
8. Von Hippel, E. (2005). *Democratizing Innovation*. Cambridge, MA: MIT Press. Lilien, G.L., Morrison, P.D., Searls, K., Sonnack, M., & Von Hippel, E. (2002). Performance assessment of the lead user idea-generation process for new product development. *Management Science, 48*(8), 1042–59.
9. Professors Abernathy and Clark's seminal paper also explored a similar classification. However their classification was only about resources—technological and

marketing resources—and not about product-market position and resources as explored in this book. See Abernathy, W.J., & Clark, K.B. (1985). Mapping the winds of creative destruction. *Research Policy, 14*(1), 3–22.
10. See n.9.

9 Globalization and New Games

1. Nigerian Bonny Light (Bonny Light crude oil spot prices in Europe went as high as $80 in July. In France there was a tax of €0.5892 per liter of unleaded and a TVA of 19.6%.)
2. Energy Information Administration of the US Department of Energy. (2007). *Nigeria: Oil.* Retrieved July 16, 2008, from http://www.eia.doe.gov/emeu/cabs/Nigeria/Oil.html.
3. Energy Information Administration of the US Department of Energy (2006). Performance profiles of major energy producers 2006 (Form EIA-28). Retrieved July 31, 2007, from http://www.eia.doe.gov/emeu/perfpro/tab11.htm.
4. International Energy Agency (Agence Internationale de l'Energie). OECD/IEA. (2007). End-user petroleum product prices and average crude oil import costs. Retrieved August 9, 2007, from http://www.iea.org/Textbase/stats/surveys/mps.pdf.
5. Energy information administration of the US Department of Energy. (2003). *Nigeria.* Retrieved July 30, 2007, from http://www.eia.doe.gov/emeu/cabs/ngia-_jv.html. Vernon, C. (2006). *UK Petrol Prices.* Retrieved July 30, 2007, from http://europe.theoildrum.com/story/2006/5/3/17236/14255.
6. Pindyck, R.S., & Rubinfeld, D.L. (1992). *Microeconomics* (4th edn). Upper Saddle River, NY: Prentice Hall.
7. Ibid.
8. Baxter, J. (May 19, 2003). Cotton subsidies squeeze Mali. Retrieved September 10, 2007, from http://news.bbc.co.uk/1/hi/world/africa/3027079.stm.
9. This definition is closest to the one offered by *The Economist.* See *The Economist*'s definition as retrieved July 26, 2007, from http://economist.com/research/Economics/alphabetic.cfm?letter=G#globalisation.
10. *IKEA.* (2007). Retrieved August 10, 2007, from http://en.wikipedia.org/wiki/Ikea.
11. Happy meal: How a Frenchman is reviving McDonald's in Europe. (January 25, 2007). *The Economist.*
12. Bove appeals over McDonalds rampage (February 15, 2001). Retrieved September 10, 2007, from http://news.bbc.co.uk/1/hi/world/europe/1171329.stm.
13. How not to block a takeover: Spain's meddling government is the big loser in the battle over Endesa. (2007, April 4). *The Economist.*
14. Vernon, C. (2006). UK petrol prices. Retrieved July 30, 2007, from http://europe.theoildrum.com/story/2006/5/3/17236/14255.
15. AA fuel price report: Price rises hit plateau after overtaking 2006 levels (June 20, 2007). Retrieved July 31, 2007, from http://www.theaa.com/motoring_advice/news/fuel-prices-june-2007.html.
16. Energy Information Administration of the US Department of Energy (2006). A primer on gasoline prices (DOE/EIA-04). Retrieved July 31, 2007, from http://www.eia.doe.gov/bookshelf/brochures/gasolinepricesprimer/printerversion.pdf.

10 New Game Environments and the Role of Governments

1. Innovation's golden goose. (2002, December 12). *The Economist.*
2. Bayhing for blood or Doling out cash? (2005, December 20). *The Economist.*

3. Home truths: How much does housing wealth boost consumer spending? (October 12, 2006). *The Economist*.

4. Carroll, C.D., Otsuka, M., & Slacalek, J. (2006). How large is the housing wealth effect? A new approach (NBER Working Paper No. W12746). Berlin, Germany: German Institute for Economic Research.

5. Competitiveness clusters in France. (2006). Retrieved December 4, 2007, from http://www.polesdecompetitivite.gouv.fr/IMG/pdf/poles_plaquette_en.pdf.

6. The fading lustre of clusters. (October 11, 2007). *The Economist*.

7. Farrell, C. et al. (1995). The boon in IPOs. *Business Week*, December 18, 1995, (p. 64).

8. Please dare to fail (September 28, 1996). *The Economist*.

9. Porter, M.E. (1990). *The Competitive Advantage of Nations*. New York: The Free Press.

10. The fading lustre of clusters. (October 11, 2007). *The Economist*.

11. This section draws heavily on Chapter 15 of A.N. Afuah (2003). *Innovation Management: Strategies, Implementation and Profits*. New York: Oxford University Press.

12. Arrow, K.J. (1962). Economic welfare and the allocation of resources for invention. In R. Nelson (ed.), *The Rate and Direction of Inventive Activity* (pp. 609–26). Princeton, NJ: Princeton University Press.

13. Ibid.

14. For an excellent discussion of minimum efficient scale (MES), see S. Oster (1994). *Modern Competitive Analysis*. New York: Oxford University Press.

15. Oster, S. (1994). *Modern Competitive Analysis*. New York: Oxford University Press (p. 316).

16. This section also draws heavily from Chapter 15 of A.N. Afuah (2003). *Innovation Management: Strategies, Implementation and Profits*. New York: Oxford University Press.

17. Von Hippel, E. (2005). *Democratizing Innovation*. Cambridge, MA: MIT Press.

18. Borrus, M. G. (1988). *Competing for Control: America's Stake in Microelectronics*. Cambridge, MA: Ballinger.

19. Rothwell, R. & Zegveld. W. (1981). *Industrial Innovation and Public Policy*. London: Frances Pinter.

20. Porter, M.E. (1990). *The Competitive Advantage of Nations*. New York: The Free Press.

21. Some of the data items from the figure are from *PEST Analysis*. Retrieved May 26, 2007, from http://www.valuebasedmanagement.net/methods_PEST_analysis.html, and *PEST Analysis*. (2007). Retrieved June 1, 2007, from http://www.netmba.com/strategy/pest/

11 Coopetition and Game Theory

1. Oster, S. (2002). *Modern Competitive Analysis*. Oxford: Oxford University Press. Pindyck, R.S., & Rubinfeld, D.L. (1992). *Microeconomics* (4th edn). Upper Saddle River, NY: Prentice Hall. Ghemawat, P. (1997). *Games Businesses Play: Cases and Models*. Cambridge, MA: MIT Press. Kreps, D. M. (1990). *Game Theory and Economic Modelling*. Oxford, England: Clarendon Press. Dixit, A. K., & Nalebuff, B. J. (1991). *Thinking Strategically*. New York, New York: W. W. Norton and Company.

2. Brandenburger, A. & Stuart, H. (2007). Biform games. *Management Science* 53(4), 537–49.

3. Brandenburger, A. (2002). Technical note on cooperative game theory: Characteristic function, allocations, marginal contributions. Retrieved February 5, 2007 from

http://pages.stern.nyu.edu/~abranden/teachingmaterials/coop12502.pdf. Stuart, Jr, H. W. Cooperative games and business strategy. In K. Chatterjee and W. Samuelson (eds), *Game Theory and Business Applications*, Kluwer Academic, 2001, 189–211.

4. Brandenburger, A. (2002). Technical note on cooperative game theory: Characteristic function, allocations, marginal contributions. Retrieved February 5, 2007 from http://pages.stern.nyu.edu/~abranden/teachingmaterials/coop12502.pdf.

5. Pindyck, R. S., & D. L Rubinfeld. (1992). *Microeconomics* (4th edn). Upper Saddle River, NY: Prentice Hall.

6. Note that this is still a simultaneous game because, although both firms have talked about their plans to offer planes, they have not actually made the decision to offer the planes. Neither firm has made any irreversible commitments to offer either plane.

7. Ghemawat, P. (1991). *Commitment: The Dynamics of Strategy*. New York, NY: Free Press, 1991.

8. Basdeo, D. K., Smith, K. G., Grimm, C. M., Rindova, V. P. & Derfus, P. J. (2006). The impact of market actions on firm reputation, *Strategic Management Journal*, 27(12), 1205–19. Heil, O., & Robertson, T. S, (1991). Toward a theory of competitive market signaling: A research agenda. *Strategic Management Journal*, 12(6), 403–18.

9. Huyghebaert, N., & Van de Gucht, L. M. (2004). Incumbent strategic behavior in financial markets and the exit of entrepreneurial start-ups, *Strategic Management Journal*, 25(6), 669–88.

10. Afuah, A. N. (1994). Strategic adoption of innovation: The case of RISC (reduced instruction set computer) technology. Unpublished Ph.D. dissertation. Cambridge, MA: Massachusetts Institute of Technology.

11. My thanks to Professor Valerie Suslow for these insights on tacit collusion.

12. Much of the pioneering management-oriented work in this area has been done by Professors Adam Brandenburger, Barry Nalebuff, and Harthorne Stuart. See, for example, Brandenburger, A. & Nalebuff, B. (1996). *Co-opetition*. New York, NY: Doubleday. Brandenburger, A. M., & Stuart, H. W. (1996). Value-based business strategy, *Journal of Economics & Management Strategy*, 5(1), 5–24. Brandenburger, A. M. and Nalebuff, B. J. (1995). The right game: Use game theory to shape strategy. *Harvard Business Review*. July–August, 1995.

13. See n.12.

14. The schematic that we use here is somewhat different from the Brandenburger and Nalebuff rendition in Brandenburger, A. M. and Nalebuff, B. J. (1995). The right game: Use game theory to shape strategy. *Harvard Business Review*. July–August, 1995. We chose to keep the suppliers and customers in the horizontal dimension as is customary with the strategy literature. Brandenburger and Nalebuff have substitutors and complementors in the horizontal dimension.

15. Brandenburger, A. M. and Nalebuff, B. J. (1995). The right game: Use game theory to shape strategy. *Harvard Business Review*. July–August, 1995.

16. This example closely follows on in Stuart, Jr, H. W. (2001). Cooperative games and business strategy. In K. Chatterjee, and W. Samuelson (eds), *Game Theory and Business Applications*, Kluwer Academic, 2001, 189–211.

17. Brandenburger, A. and Nalebuff, A. (1997). The added value theory of business. In *Strategy & Business*, published by Booz, Allen & Hamilton, fourth quarter, 1997.

18. Stuart, Jr, H. W. (2001). Cooperative games and business strategy. In K. Chatterjee, and W. Samuelson (eds), *Game Theory and Business Applications*, Kluwer Academic, 2001, 189–211.

19. Ibid.

20. *The Economist*, January 24, 1998 (p. 63).

12 Entering a New Business Using New Games

1. Porter, M.E. (1987). From competitive advantage to corporate advantage. *Harvard Business Review, 65*(3), 43–59.
2. Tirole, J. (1988). *Theory of Industry Organization*. Cambridge, MA: MIT Press. McWilliams, A., & Smart, D.L. (1993). Efficiency v. structure-conduct-performance: Implications for strategy research and practice. *Journal of Management, 19*(1), 63–78.
3. This subsection draws heavily from Afuah, A.N. (2003). *Business Models: A Strategic Management Approach*. New York: McGrawHill/Irvin.
4. Kim, W.C., & Mauborgne, R. (2005). *Blue Ocean Strategy: How to Create Uncontested Market Space and Make Competition Irrelevant*. Boston, MA: Harvard Business School Press.
5. Moon, Y. (2004). *Ikea Invades America* (Harvard Business School case #9-504-094).

13 Strategy Frameworks and Measures

1. Year in parenthesis indicates when the first major publication that introduced the framework was published.
2. Chandler, A. (1962). *Strategy and Structure: Chapters in the History of the American Industrial Enterprise*. Cambridge, MA: MIT Press.
3. Aguilar, F. (1967). *Scanning the Business Environment*. New York: Macmillan.
4. Allen, G.B., & Hammond. J.S. (1975). *Note on the Boston Consulting Group Concept of Competitive Analysis and Corporate Strategy* (Harvard Business School note 9-175-175). See also, Stern, C.W., & Deimler, M.S. (2006). *The Boston Consulting Group on Strategy: Classic Concepts and New Perspectives* (2nd edn). Boston, MA: BCG.
5. This example closely follows that from Afuah, A.N. (2003). *Business Models: A Strategic Management Approach*, New York: McGraw-Hill/Irvin.
6. Porter, M.E. (1979). How competitive forces shape strategy. *Harvard Business Review, 57*(2), 137–45. Porter, M.E. (1980). *Competitive Strategy*. New York: Free Press.
7. Ibid.
8. Oster, S. (1999). *Modern Competitive Analysis* (3rd edn). Oxford: Oxford University Press.
9. Bales, C.F., Chatterjee, P.C., Gluck, F.W., Gogel, D., & Puri, A. (2000). The business system: A new tool for strategy formulation and cost analysis. Retrieved November 13, 2007, from http://www.kellogg.northwestern.edu/faculty/vohra/ftp/miin00.pdf.
10. Gluck, F.W. (1980). Strategic choice and resource allocation. *The McKinsey Quarterly, 1*, 22–33.
11. Buaron, R. (1981). New-game strategies. *McKinsey Quarterly, 17*(1), 24–40.
12. Ibid. See also, Bales, C.F., Chatterjee, P.C., Gluck, F.W., Gogel, D., & Puri, A. (2000). The business system: A new tool for strategy formulation and cost analysis. Retrieved November 13, 2007, from http://www.kellogg.northwestern.edu/faculty/vohra/ftp/miin00.pdf.
13. Bales, C.F., Chatterjee, P.C., Gluck, F.W., Gogel, D., & Puri, A. (2000). The business system: A new tool for strategy formulation and cost analysis. Retrieved November 13, 2007, from http://www.kellogg.northwestern.edu/faculty/vohra/ftp/miin00.pdf.
14. Porter, M.E. (1985). *Competitive Advantage: Creating and Sustaining Superior Performance*. New York: Free Press.
15. Stabell, C.B., & Fjeldstad, O.D. (1998). Configuring value for competitive

advantage: On chains, shops, and networks. *Strategic Management Journal, 19*(5), 413–37.

16. Ibid.

17. Ibid.

18. Kaplan, R.S., & Norton, D.P. (1992). The balanced scorecard: Measures that drive performance. *Harvard Business Review, 70*(1), 71–80.

19. Barney, J.B. (1999). How a firm's capabilities affect boundary decisions. *Sloan Management Review, 40*(3), 137–45. Barney, J., & Hesterly, W. (2007). *Strategic Management and Competitive Advantage: Concepts* (2nd edn). New York: Prentice Hall.

20. Henderson, R.M., & Clark, K.B. (1990). Architectural innovation: The reconfiguration of existing product technologies and the failure of established firms. *Administrative Science Quarterly, 35*(1), 9–30.

21. Hamel, G., & Prahalad, C.K. (1990). The core competence of the corporation. *Harvard Business Review, 68*(3), 79–91.

22. Afuah, A.N. (1998). *Innovation Management: Strategies, Implementation, and Profits.* New York: Oxford University Press.

23. Hamel, G., & Prahalad, C.K. (1990). The core competence of the corporation. *Harvard Business Review, 68*(3), 79–91.

24. Henderson, R.M., & Clark, K.B. (1990). Architectural innovation: The reconfiguration of existing product technologies and the failure of established firms. *Administrative Science Quarterly, 35*(1), 9–30.

25. Kotler, P. (1998). *Marketing Management: Analysis, Planning, Implementation, and Control* (9th edn). Upper Saddle River, NJ: Prentice Hall.

26. The 4Ps (Product, Pricing, Promotion and Placement) framework is a marketing framework and does not belong to a strategy textbook. However, since students often ask questions about it, I have decided to add a very short note on it. Those readers who need details can refer to the references.

27. This section closely follows a section in the author's previous book. See Afuah, A.N. (2003). *Business Models: A Strategic Management Approach.* New York: McGraw-Hill/Irvin.

28. Tully, S. (1993). EVA, the real key to creating wealth. *Fortune 128* (September 20, 1993), 38–50. Stern, J., Stewart, B. & Chew, D. (1992). The EVA financial management system. *Journal of Applied Corporate Finance, 8*, 32–46.

Case I The New World Invades France's *Terroir*

1. Genetically modified wine: Unleash the war on terroir. (December 19, 2007). *The Economist.*

2. Terroir and technology. Survey: Wine. (December 16, 1999). *The Economist.*

3. The brand's the thing. Survey: Wine. (December 16, 1999). *The Economist.*

4. Viegas, J. (2007). *Ancient Mashed Grapes Found in Greece.* Retrieved June 16, 2008, from http://dsc.discovery.com/news.

5. Jefford, A. (July 13, 2007). Rise of the terrorists. *Financial Times.*

6. Médoc 1855 classification. (n.d.). Retrieved June 16, 2008, from http://www.thewinedoctor.com/regionalguides/bordeauxclassifications.shtml.

7. Bartlett, C.A. (2002). *Global Wine Wars: New World Challenges Old (A)* (HBS case # 9–303–056). Harvard Business School Press.

8. Terroir and technology. Survey: Wine. (December 16, 1999). *The Economist.*

9. Rachman, G. (December 16, 1999). The globe in a glass. Survey: Wine. *The Economist.*

10. The brand's the thing. Survey: Wine. (1999, December 16). *The Economist.*

11. Rachman, G. (December 16, 1999). The globe in a glass. Survey: Wine. *The Economist*.
12. France's wine industry: Those vulgar markets. (January 20, 2005). *The Economist*.
13. Wine consumption: Sour grapes in France. (December 21, 2007). *The Economist*. Johnson, J. (July 22, 2004). Europe: New World ferment crisis for French wine. *Financial Times*.
14. France's wine industry: Those vulgar markets. (January 20, 2005). *The Economist*.
15. Johnson, J. (July 22, 2004). Europe: New World ferment crisis for French wine. *Financial Times*.

Case 2 Sephora Takes on America

1. Raper, S. (1993). Business & Company Resource Center: News/Magazines, Shop 8 and Sephora to merge. *WWD, 166*(21), 6.
2. Aktar, A. (1996). Business & Company Resource Center, Ross B-School, Kresge: News/Magazines, Sephora's superstore: Setting a faster pace for French cosmetics. *WWD, 172*(94), 1.
3. Ibid.
4. Business & Company Resource Center, Ross B-School, Kresge: Source Citation: "Sephora Holdings S.A." *International Directory of Company Histories, Vol. 82.* St James Press, 2007.
5. IBISWorld Industry Report. (March, 2008). Beauty, cosmetics & fragrance stores in the US (p. 38).
6. Ibid.
7. Ibid.
8. IBISWorld Industry Report. (March, 2008). Beauty, cosmetics & fragrance stores in the US (p. 11).
9. IBISWorld Industry Report. (March 2008). Beauty, cosmetics & fragrance stores in the US (p. 9).
10. Maestri, N. (February 14, 2007). J.C. Penney kicks off brand campaign. Reuters UK.
11. Business & Company Resource Center. Ulta Salon, Cosmetic & Fragrance, Inc. Company History.
12. Ibid.
13. Ibid.
14. Annual Report. (April 2008). Ulta Salon, Cosmetic & Fragrance, Inc. 2007 (p. 26).
15. Hoover's Online. Ulta Salon, Cosmetic & Fragrance, Inc. Company Profile.
16. Sephora files suit against federated department stores. (August, 1999). *Business Wire*.
17. Injunction granted: Sephora wins round in federated battle. (February, 2000). *Women's Wear Daily*.
18. IBISWorld Industry Report. (March, 2008). Beauty, Cosmetics & Fragrance Stores in the US (p. 22).
19. Hoover's Online. Bath & Body Works, Inc. Company Profile.
20. IBISWorld Industry Report. (March, 2008). Beauty, Cosmetics & Fragrance Stores in the US (p. 24).

Case 3 Netflix: *Responding to Blockbuster, Again*

1. Spielvogel, C. (2007). Blockbuster's total access gains subs. Retrieved May 2, 2007, from http://www.videobusiness.com/article/CA6438581.html.
2. Business 2.0 Magazine Staff. (2006). 10 people who don't matter. Retrieved July

21, 2008, from http://money.cnn.com/2006/06/21/technology/10dontmatter.biz2/index.htm.

3. A history of home video. (2005). Retrieved July 21, 2008, from http://www.idealink.org/Resource.phx/vsda/pressroom/history-of-industry.htx.

4. Ibid.

5. Ault, S. (2007). Rental stores stock more niche titles. Retrieved July 21, 2008, from http://www.videobusiness.com/article/CA6446483.html?q=Rental+Stores+Stock+More+Niche+Titles.

6. Datamonitor. (June 2006). Global recorded DVD & video industry profile.

7. Blockbuster annual report, 1999.

8. IbisWorld. (May 8, 2007). IbisWorld industry report: Video tape and disc rental in the U.S.

9. O'Brien, J.M. (2002). The Netflix effect. Retrieved July 21, 2008, from http://www.wired.com/wired/archive/10.12/netflix.html.

10. Andrews, P. (2003). Videos without late fees, Reed Hastings, digital entrepreneur. Retrieved July 21, 2008, from http://www.usnews.com/usnews/culture/articles/031229/29hastings. htm.

11. Netflix consumer press kit. (2007). Retrieved July 21, 2008, from http://www.netflix.com/MediaCenter?id=5379.

12. Leohardt, D. (June 7, 2006). What Netflix could teach Hollywood. *New York Times*.

13. Dornhelm, R. (2006). Netflix expands indie film biz. Retrieved July 21, 2008, from http://marketplace.publicradio.org/shows/2006/12/08/AM200612081.html.

14. *Netflix Prize*. (2006). Retrieved June 10, 2007, from www.netflixprize.com.

15. *Netflix* website. (2007). Retrieved June 10, 2007, from www.netflix.com.

16. Netherby, J. (October 21, 2002). Three's company in online rental. *Video Business*.

17. Ibid.

18. Lieberman, D. (April 20, 2005). Movie rental battle rages. *USA Today*.

19. Kipnis, J. (September 4, 2004). On the video beat. *Billboard*.

20. Daikoku, G., & Brancheau, J. (August 12, 2004). Blockbuster moves to capture online DVD rental business. Gartner G2 Analysis.

21. Wasserman, T. (December 19, 2005). Category wars: Blockbuster to hit replay on ads for online service; Service still trails rival Netflix by 3 million subscribers. *Brandweek*.

22. Sweeting, P. (February 28, 2005). Blue turns to distributors for online product. *Video Business*.

23. Oestricher, D. (May 5, 2005). Blockbuster's new initiatives produce mixed results in 1Q. *Dow Jones Newswires*.

24. Wasserman, T. (December 19, 2005). Category wars: Blockbuster to hit replay on ads for online service; Service still trails rival Netflix by 3 million subscribers. *BrandWeek*.

25. Ibid.

26. *Blockbuster (video store)*. (2007). Retrieved June 10, 2007, from http://en.wikipedia.org/w/index.php?title=Blockbuster_%28video_store%29&oldid=137206813.
27. *Blockbuster Online*. (2007). Retrieved June 10, 2007, from www.blockbuster.com.

28. *Blockbuster announces new lower prices subscription plans for online subscribers*. (2007). Retrieved June 12, 2007, from http://www.b2i.us/profiles/investor/ResLibraryView.asp? BzID=553&ResLibraryID=20305&Category=1027.

29. Gonzalez, N. (2006). *Movie downloads: iTunes v. the rest*. Retrieved July 21, 2008, from http://www.techcrunch.com/2006/10/15/itunes-movies-v-the-rest/.

30. Leohardt, D. (June 7, 2006). What Netflix could teach Hollywood. *New York Times*.

31. Hollywood and the Internet: Coming soon. (February 21, 2008). *The Economist.*
32. *Apple TV.* (2007). Retrieved June 10, 2007, from www.apple.com/appletv.

Case 4 Threadless in Chicago

1. Brabham, D.C. (2008). Outsourcing as a model for problem solving: An introduction and cases. *Convergence: The International Journal of Research Into New Media Technologies, 14*(1), 75–90. Gilmour, M. (November 26, 2007). Threadless: From clicks to bricks. *Business Week.*
2. Ogawa, S., & Piller, F.T. (2006). Reducing the risk of new product development. *MIT Sloan Management Review, 47*(2), 65–71.
3. Ibid.
4. Weingarten, M. (June 18, 2007). "Project runway" for the T-shirt crowd. *Business 2.0 Magazine.*
5. Kawasaki, G. (2007). Ten questions with Jeffrey Kalmikoff, Chief Creative Officer of skinnyCorp/Threadless. Retrieved June 17, 2008, from blog.guykawasaki.com/2007/06/ten_ questions_w.html.
6. Chafkin, M. (2008, June). The customer is the company. *Inc. Magazine.* Retrieved July 21, 2008, from http://www.inc.com/magazine/20080601/the-customer-is-the-company.html.
7. Boutin, P. (2006). *Crowdsourcing: Consumers as creators.* Retrieved June 26, 2008, from http://www.businessweek.com/innovate/content/jul2006/id20060713_755844.htm.
8. Chafkin, M. (June, 2008). The customer is the company. *Inc. Magazine.* Retrieved July 21, 2008, from http://www.inc.com/magazine/20080601/the-customer-is-the-company.html.
9. *Threadless Chicago.* (2008). Retrieved June 17, 2008, from http://www.threadless.com/retail.
10. Chafkin, M. (2008, June). The customer is the company. *Inc. Magazine.* Retrieved July 21, 2008, from http://www.inc.com/magazine/20080601/the-customer-is-the-company.html.
11. Weingarten, M. (June 18, 2007). "Project runway" for the T-shirt crowd. *Business 2.0 Magazine.*
12. Kawasaki, G. (2007). Ten questions with Jeffrey Kalmikoff, Chief Creative Officer of skinnyCorp/Threadless. Retrieved June 17, 2008, from blog.guykawasaki.com/2007/06/ten_ questions_w.html.
13. *Threadless Chicago.* (2008). Retrieved June 17, 2008, from http://www.threadless.com/retail.
14. Ibid.

Case 5 Pixar Changes the Rules of the Game

1. Hormby, T. (2007). The Pixar Story: Dick Shoup, Alex Schure, George Lucas, Steve Jobs, and Disney. Retrieved June 21, 2008, from http://www.the-numbers.com/movies/series/Pixar.php.
2. Toy' wonder. (1995). Retrieved June 29, 2008, from www.ew.com/ew/article/0,,299897,00.html.
3. From "Toy Story" to "Chicken Little." (2005, December 8). *The Economist.*
4. Schlender, B., & Furth, J. (1995). Steve Jobs' amazing movie adventure. Disney is betting on Computerdom's ex-boy wonder to deliver this year's animated Christmas blockbuster. Can he do for Hollywood what he did for Silicon Valley? Retrieved June 21, 2008, from http://money.cnn.com/magazines/fortune/fortune_archive/1995/09/18/206099/index.htm.

5. Toy' Wonder. (1995). Retrieved June 29, 2008, from www.ew.com/ew/article/0,,299897,00.html.
6. Schlender, B., & Furth, J. (1995). Steve Jobs' amazing movie adventure. Disney is betting on Computerdom's ex-boy wonder to deliver this year's animated Christmas blockbuster. Can he do for Hollywood what he did for Silicon Valley? Retrieved June 21, 2008, from http://money.cnn.com/magazines/fortune/fortune_archive/1995/09/18/206099/index.htm.
7. Hormby, T. (2007). The Pixar Story: Dick Shoup, Alex Schure, George Lucas, Steve Jobs, and Disney. Retrieved June 21, 2008, from http://www.the-numbers.com/movies/series/Pixar.php.
8. Face value: Finding another Nemo. (February 5, 2004). *The Economist*.
9. Disney: Magic restored. (April 17, 2008). *The Economist*.
10. Kafka, P. (January 23, 2006). Mickey's big move. *Forbes*.

Case 6 Lipitor: World's Best-selling Drug (2008)

1. This minicase draws heavily on the case of Leafstedt, M., Marta, A., Marwaha, J., Schallwig, P., & Shinkle, R. (2003) Lipitor: At the heart of Warner-Lambert. In A. Afuah, *Business Models: A Strategic Management Approach* (356–70).
2. Loftus, P. (2008). Pfizer to protect Lipitor sales until November 2011, Retrieved June 20, 2008, from http://www.smartmoney.com/news/ON/index.cfm?story=ON-20080618-000684-1151.
3. Grom, T. (May, 1999). Reaching the goal. *PharmaBusiness*.
4. Mincieli, G. (June, 1997). Make room for Lipitor. *Med Ad News*.
5. Lipitor. (March, 1997). *R&D Directions*.
6. Understanding clinical trials. (2008). Retrieved July 22, 2008, from http://clinical-trials.gov/ct2/info/understand.

Case 7 New Belgium: Brewing a New Game

1. A bid for Bud. (June 19, 2008). *The Economist*.
2. Ibid.
3. Inc. staff. (2006). *Bringing fundamental change to everyday life. And, for that matter, death.* Retrieved July 22, 2008, from http://www.inc.com/magazine/20061101/green 50_integrators.html.
4. Kessenides, D. (June 2005). Green is the new black. *Inc Magazine, 27*(6), 65–6.
5. The brewery with the big green footprint. (2003). *In Business, 25*(1), 16.
6. Raabe, S. (2005, June 1). Brewery supplements profits with energy savings. *Knight Ridder Tribune Business News*, (p. 1).
7. http://fcgov.com/utilities/wind-power.php.
8. Kessenides, D. (June, 2005). Green is the new black. *Inc Magazine, 27*(6), 65–6.
9. Raabe, S. (June 1, 2005). Brewery supplements profits with energy savings. *Knight Ridder Tribune Business News*, (p. 1).
10. Cohn, D. (2006). *This green beer's the real deal.* Retrieved July 22, 2008, from http://www.wired.com/news/technology/0,70361-0.html.
11. Kessenides, D. (June 2005). Green is the new black. *Inc Magazine, 27*(6), 65–6.
12. http://www.paulnoll.com/Oregon/Canning/number-liters.html.
13. "*Liquid—metric to non-metric.* (n.d.). Retrieved July 22, 2008, from http://www.paulnoll.com/Oregon/Canning/number-liters.html.
14. *Brewing up fun in the workplace.* (n.d.). Retrieved July 22, 2008, from http://www.e-businessethics.com/NewBelgiumCases/NBB-BreweryFun.pdf.
15. Armstrong, D. (November 28, 2006). Philanthropy gets serious for some com-

panies: Growing number are making donations from revenue, not from profit. *Inc.com*.

16. www.newbelgiumbrewery.com/philanthropy.
17. Brand evangelists/ambassadors/champions are consumers that feel so strongly connected with the brand that they spread the word of the brand and attempt to help the brand succeed.
18. http://www.mylifeisbeer.com/beer/bottles/bottledetail/293/.
19. Inc. staff. (2006). Bringing fundamental change to everyday life. And, for that matter, death. Retrieved July 23, 2008, from http://www.inc.com/magazine/20061101/ green50_ integrators.html.
20. Ibid.

Case 8 Botox: How Long Would the Smile Last?

1. Weise, E. (2003). The little neurotoxin that could. Retrieved February 16, 2008, from http:/www.usatoday.com/news/health/2003-04-20-botox_x.htm.
2. Ibid.
3. Fletcher, A. (2002). Boon for Botox injections expected with FDA's approval. Retrieved July 18, 2008, from http://www.bizjournals.com/denver/stories/2002/04/22/newscolumn2.html.
4. Smooth face, big Botox: A poison turned cosmetic treatment that might be the next blockbuster. (2002, February 14). *The Economist*.
5. Vangelova, L. (1995). Botulinum Toxin: A poison that can heal. Retrieved July 17, 2008, from http://www.fda.gov/fdac/features/095_bot.html.
6. Brush, M. (2003). Company Focus: 3 body-beautiful stocks for bountiful returns. Retrieved July 17, 2008, from http://moneycentral.msn.com/content/P65606.asp.
7. Weisul, K. (2002, May 6). Botox: Now it's a guy thing. *Business Week Online*.
8. Creager, E. (2002). Move over, Tupperware: Botox injections are the latest thing at home parties. Retrieved February 16, 2008, from http://www.woai.com/guides/beauty/story.aspx?content_id=16358daf-d7db-4ade-a757-9e8d7cf30212.
9. Smooth face, big Botox: A poison turned cosmetic treatment that might be the next blockbuster. (2002, February 14). *The Economist*. Creager, E. (2002). *Move over, Tupperware: Botox injections are the latest thing at home parties*. Retrieved February 16, 2008, from http://www.woai.com/guides/beauty/story.aspx?content_id=16358daf-d7db-4ade-a757-9e8 d7cf30212.
10. Smith, A. (2006). Plenty of smooth sailing ahead for Botox. Retrieved July 17, 2008, from http://money.cnn.com/2006/04/03/news/companies/allergan_botox/index.htm.
11. Ibid.
12. Emerging uses of Botox. (2005). Retrieved July 18, 2008, from http://www.botoxfacts.ca/uses.html.
13. Ibid.
14. Facelift information. (2008). Retrieved February 17, 2008, from http://www.cosmeticplasticsurgerystatistics.com/facelifts.html#INFO.
15. Reloxin, botulinum toxin type A: Treatment for Aesthetics. (2007). Retrieved July 17, 2008, from http://www.drugs.com/nda/reloxin_071206.html.
16. The most popular cosmetic procedures: popular cosmetic surgery. (n.d.). Retrieved July 17, 2008, from http://women.webmd.com/features/most-popular-cosmetic-procedures.
17. Realizing opportunities: Annual Report 2007. (2008). Retrieved July 18, 2008, from http://files.shareholder.com/downloads/AGN/362148606x0x184012/BB8ED2E7-30CF-443D-A2F7-0935FE134F78/2007AnnualReport.pdf.
18. Rundle, R.L. (2007). Botox faces worry lines in smooth skin game. Retrieved July

18, 2008, from http://medicalnewstouse.blogspot.com/2007/12/botox-may-face-competition.html.

19. I would like to thank Adeesh Agarwal, Michael Johnson, Tyler Link, Samir Patel, Jonathan Stone, and Kevin Tsuchida for drawing my attention to Botox when they wrote a case on Botox in the class *New Game Business Model* at the Stephen M. Ross School of Business at the University of Michigan.

Case 9 IKEA Lands in the New World

1. List of the 100 wealthiest people. (2008). Retrieved June 24, 2008, from http://en.wikipedia. org/wiki/List_of_billionaires.
2. Tycoons: Bill v Ingvar. (April 7, 2004). *The Economist*.
3. Facts & figures. (2008). Retrieved June 24, 2008, from http://www.ikea.com/ms/en_US/about_ikea_new/facts_figures/index.html.
4. Ibid.
5. Crush chaos at Ikea store opening. (2005). Retrieved June 27, 2008, from http://news.bbc.co.uk/2/hi/uk_news/england/london/4252421.stm.
6. Capell, K., Sains, A., Lindblad, C., Palmer, A.T., Bush, J., Roberts, D., & Hall, K. (2005). Ikea: How the Swedish retailer became a global cult brand. Retrieved June 27, 2008, from http://www.businessweek.com/magazine/content/05_46/b3959001.htm.
7. Ibid.
8. Chang, J. (2005). How IKEA, MoMA connect with design talent. Retrieved June 27, 2008, from http://www.metropolismag.com/cda/story.php?artid=1391.
9. Facts & figures. (2008). Retrieved June 24, 2008, from http://www.ikea.com/ms/en_US/about_ikea_new/facts_figures/index.html.
10. Ibid.
11. Capell, K., Sains, A., Lindblad, C., Palmer, A.T., Bush, J., Roberts, D., & Hall, K. (2005). Ikea: How the Swedish retailer became a global cult brand. Retrieved June 27, 2008, from http://www.businessweek.com/magazine/content/05_46/b3959001.htm.
12. Ibid.
13. Ibid.
14. IKEA: Flat-pack accounting. (2006, May 11). *The Economist*.

Case 10 Esperion: Drano for Your Arteries?

1. CDC IXIS Securities. (February 24, 2003). *Cholesterol: The Battle Rages On*.
2. Ibid.
3. Ibid.
4. Two drugs are notable exceptions. Crestor (AstraZeneca) was expected to be launched in 2003 with a better safety and efficacy profile than any currently marketed statin. Additionally, Novartis/Sankyo's Pitavastin was a statin currently in Phase IIb trials in Europe expected to be launched in 2007.
5. CDC IXIS Securities. (February 24, 2003). *Cholesterol: The Battle Rages On*.
6. Deutsche Bank Securities. (December 22, 2003). *Pfizer Inc.: Building Cardio Dominance*.
7. How far we've come. (August 1, 2006). *Pharmaceutical Executive*.
8. CDC IXIS Securities. (February 24, 2003). *Cholesterol: The Battle Rages On*.
9. UBS Investment Research. (November 21, 2003). *Merck & Co*.
10. Harper, M. (2003). Merck's troubles, Schering's solution. Retrieved December 6, 2006, from http://www.forbes.com/2003/11/21/cx_mh_1121mrk.html.
11. Bristol-Myers Squibb Co. (2002). *10-K*.

12. Bristol-Myers Squibb Co. (November 19, 2003). Where's the Growth? Oppenheimer Equity Research
13. Ibid.
14. CDC IXIS Securities. (February 24, 2003). *Cholesterol: The Battle Rages On.*
15. Ibid.
16. Frost & Sullivan. (November 10, 2005). *U.S. Lipid Therapeutics Market.* (Section 2.6.1).
17. Thomson Financial Venture Economics. (September 27, 2006). Esperion Therapeutics, Inc Company Report (VentureXpert).
18. Rozhon, T. (December 22, 2003). Pfizer to buy maker of promising cholesterol drug. *New York Times.*
19. Datamonitor Company Profiles. (January 24, 2004). Esperion Therapeutics—history.
20. Winslow, R. (November 5, 2003). New HDL drug shows promise in heart study. *The Wall Street Journal.*
21. PR Newswire. (October 31, 2000). Esperion Therapeutics, Inc. announce results for third quarter 2000.
22. Rozhon, T. (December 22, 2003). Pfizer to buy maker of promising cholesterol Drug. *New York Times.*
23. Winslow, R. (November 5, 2003). New HDL drug shows promise in heart study. *The Wall Street Journal.*
24. Braunschweiger, A. (June 26, 2003). Esperion shares surge on study of heart-plaque treatment. *Dow Jones Business News.*
25. Esperion. (2002). *10-K.*
26. Ibid.
27. Dimasi, J., Hansen, R., & Grabowski, H. (2003). The price of innovation: New estimates of drug development costs. *Journal of Health Economics, 22*(2), 151–85.
28. Esperion. (2002). *10-K.*
29. Ibid.
30. Ibid.
31. Young, P. (September 18, 2002). Troubling times for Pharma. *Chemical Week.*
32. Pfizer.com. (March 2004). *Press Release.*
33. Ibid.
34. Goetzl, D. (October 1, 2001). Media mavens: Donna Campanella. *Advertising Age.*
35. Ibid.
36. Abboud, L., & Hensley, S. (September 3, 2003). Factory shift: New prescriptions for drug makers; update the plants—after years of neglect, industry focuses on manufacturing; FDA acts as a catalyst; The three story blender. *Wall Street Journal.*
37. Physician survey ranks Pfizer sales force first in industry for fifth consecutive year. (January 20, 2000). *PR Newswire.*
38. Pfizer sales force most esteemed by US doctors. (February 18, 2002). *Marketletter.*
39. Mintz, S.L. (2000). *What is a merger worth?* Retrieved October 12, 2006, from http://www.cfo.com/article.cfm/2988576
40. Morrow, D.J., & Holson, L.M. (November 5, 1999). Warner—Lambert gets Pfizer offer for $82.4 billion. *New York Times.*
41. Pfizer to buy maker of promising cholesterol drug. (December 22, 2003). *New York Times.*
42. Ibid.
43. Ibid.
44. Pfizer to acquire Esperion Therapeutics to extend its research commitment in cardiovascular disease. (December 21, 2003). *Pfizer press release.*
45. *Pfizer to buy Esperion for $1.3bn.* (2003). Retrieved October 10, 2006, from http://www. cnn.com/2003/BUSINESS/12/21/us.pfizer.reut/.

Case 11 Xbox 360: Will the Second Time be Better?

1. PONG-story: Introduction. (2008). Retrieved July 15, 2008, from http://www.pong-story.com/intro.htm. Atari Museum home page. (n.d.). Retrieved July 15, 2008, from http://www.atarimuseum.com/mainmenu/mainmenu.html.
2. Herman, L., Horwitz, J., Kent, S., & Miller, S. (2002). The history of video games. Retrieved July 15, 2008, from http://www.gamespot.com/gamespot/features/video/hov/index.html.
3. Ibid.
4. Ibid.
5. Vogelstein, F. (n.d.). Rebuilding Microsoft. Retrieved December 20, 2006, from http://www.wired.com/wired/archive/14.10/microsoft_pr.html.
6. Wii price is high by historical standards. (2006). Retrieved July 15, 2008, from http://diggy.wordpress.com/2006/10/17/wii-price-is-high-by-historical-standards/.
7. Xbox live. (n.d.). Retrieved July 15, 2008, from http://en.wikipedia.org/wiki/Xbox_Live.
8. Becker, D. (2004). "Halo 2" clears record $125 million in first day. Retrieved July 15, 2008, from http://news.com.com/Halo+2+clears+record+125+million+in+first+day/2100–1043_3–5447379.html.
9. Gamers wipe out supply of Nintendo's new Wii. (2006). Retrieved July 15, 2008, from http://www.pcmaczone.co.uk/modules.php?name=News&file=article&sid=386.
10. Ibid.
11. Playing a different game. (October 26, 2006). *The Economist.*

Case 12 Nintendo Wii: A Game-changing Move

1. Video game. (2007). Retrieved December 25, 2007, from http://en.wikipedia.org/wiki/Video_games.
2. Afuah, A.N., & Grimaldi, R. (2003). Architectural innovation and the attacker's advantage from complementary assets: The case of the video game console industry. Working Paper, Stephen M. Ross School of Business at the University of Michigan, Ann Arbor, MI.
3. Megahertz is a crude measure of the speed or power of a processor. The higher the Megahertz, the faster the processor is supposed to be. The "number of polygons" is a measure of the graphical detail in the resulting images.
4. Playing a different game: Does Nintendo's radical new strategy represent the future of gaming? (October 26, 2006). *The Economist.* Gapper, J. (July 13, 2007). Video games have rediscovered fun. *Financial Times.*
5. Ibid.
6. O'Brien, J.M. (2007). Wii will rock you. Retrieved December 27, 2007, from http://www.mutualofamerica.com/articles/Fortune/June%202007/fortune2.asp.
7. Turott, P. (2007). Xbox 360 vs. PlayStation 3 vs. Wii: A technical comparison. Retrieved December 27, 2007, from http://www.winsupersite.com/showcase/Xbox360_ps3_wii.asp.
8. Gapper, J. (July 13, 2007). Video games have rediscovered fun. *Financial Times.*
9. Bird D., Bosco N., Nainwal S., & Park E. (2007). The Nintendo Wii. Working Case, Stephen M. Ross School of Business at the University of Michigan, Ann Arbor, MI.
10. O'Brien, J.M. (2007). Wii will rock you. Retrieved January 2, 2008, from http://money.cnn.com/magazines/fortune/fortune_archive/2007/06/11/100083454/index.htm.

Author Index

Subject Index